RUSSIA
1917

*

The February Revolution

RUSSIA
1917

❧

The February Revolution

GEORGE KATKOV

GREENWOOD PRESS, PUBLISHERS
WESTPORT, CONNECTICUT

Library of Congress Cataloging in Publication Data

Katkov, George.
  Russia, 1917.

   Reprint of the 1st ed. published by Harper, New York.
   Bibliography: p.
   Includes index.
   1. Russia--History--February Revolution, 1917.
I. Title.
[DK265.19.K3 1979]   947.084'1   78-31187
ISBN 0-313-20932-4

First U.S. edition published in 1967 by Harper & Row,
Publishers, New York

Reprinted with the permission of Harper & Row,
Publishers, Inc.

Reprinted in 1979 by Greenwood Press, Inc.
51 Riverside Avenue, Westport, CT 06880

Printed in the United States of America

10 9 8 7 6 5 4 3 2 1

TO THE SACRED MEMORY
OF THE AUTHOR OF
Doctor Zhivago

Errata

Page 192, line 23: For September read October

Page 192, line 33: For September read October

Page 193, line 15: For September read October

Contents

Illustrations

Maps

Acknowledgements

This book would never have been completed had it not been for help and encouragement from so many quarters that it is impossible to mention them all in a short note of acknowledgement. My first and foremost debt of gratitude is to the Warden and Fellows of St Antony's College, Oxford, who for many years made it possible for me to work in a field of scholarship with which I was not particularly familiar. It is thanks to their generous material support, to the interest they showed in my work in the various seminars and study groups of the College, and to their limitless solicitude in private contacts with me that I was able to sustain over a number of years the effort of completing this book. I am also particularly grateful to the Astor Foundation for having facilitated a study trip to the United States in 1963, for work on the various archives there. Without this research, indeed, I should never have had the courage to put forward the views expressed in this book. In this connection I would like to thank the director and staff of the University Library of Helsinki and of the Finnish State Archives in Helsinki; Dr Witold Sworakowski and his assistants at the Hoover Institution in Stanford, California; and especially the late Boris Nicolaevsky, for his advice and permission to use the many rare and precious sources in his possession. My special thanks go also to Professor Philip Mosely, the Director of the Columbia University archives on contemporary Russian history, and to the curator, Mr Lev Magerovsky. Dr Alexis Rannit and Mrs Fedorova, of the archives of Yale University, have also been helpful, as will be clear from the text. I remember with sadness and gratitude the late Director of the Houghton Library at Harvard University, William A. Jackson, whose kindness enabled me to draw on a number of sources as yet untapped by historians. More personal but no less heartfelt are my thanks to the many friends who helped me to overcome the frequent attacks of despair and despondency caused by the enormity of my task and my own limitations. Over the years David Footman has closely followed the making of this book, from its first unsteady draft to the present version, and discussed practically every detail of it. So also, from another angle, has Professor

L. Schapiro. Dr Michael Futrell came to my rescue at a moment when I was about to give up the work, which was largely completed, and assisted me particularly with the final chapters. Max Hayward took endless trouble to help me find adequate and forceful expression in English for ideas which would otherwise have been lost through linguistic shortcomings. Harry Willetts and Professor D. Obolensky helped with the difficult task of proof-reading. Of the many ladies who, with infinite patience, copied and recopied the various earlier versions and helped with the final draft, I can mention here with thanks only Mrs Valerie Jensen and Mrs Ann Shukman, as well as the clerical staff of St Antony's College. I can only hope that the future of this book, for which of course I bear sole responsibility, will not make all these and many other friends regret the selfless efforts they made to assist its writing.

I am indebted to the following for permission to reproduce copyright material: Mrs S. Bocharskaya for an extract from *Na putyakh k svobode* by her mother, Mrs A. Tyrkova-Williams; Jonathan Cape Ltd. for an extract from *Lost Splendour* by Prince Felix Youssoupoff (translated by myself from the French edition, *Avant l'exil 1887–1919*); Mr Boris Elkin for an extract from *Vospominaniya* by P. N. Milyukov; the author's agents for extracts from the letters of P. B. Struve quoted in *The Fourth Seal* by Sir Samuel Hoare; and the Yale University Library for extracts from the papers of A. I. Spiridovich.

Preface

Truth has many enemies. Of these the lie is the most conspicuous, but the least pernicious and insidious. The blatant and conscious lie has, as the Russians say, 'short legs' and does not go far. Much greater obstacles to the establishment of truth are wishful thinking, mythomania and the semi-conscious fear that beliefs which have become dear to us might be exposed as errors in the glare of newly-discovered facts.

This is a difficulty which all students of contemporary history have to face. They have to decide whether an account of a given event is intended to establish the factual truth or is made in an effort to spare the susceptibilities or bolster up the ambitions of individuals, classes and nations. This is by no means easy when the historian is dealing with such matters as, e.g., 'war guilt', or class exploitation. The distortion of factual truth in such cases usually centres around details for which there is no decisive evidence.

The history of the Russian revolution in 1917 has been bedevilled by unconscious distortion and deliberate falsification more than any event in modern history. From widely varying motives, different parties to the event, on whom we depend for our information about it, have systematically applied themselves to withhold or distort evidence in their possession in order to blur the picture of the revolution or to give rise to completely unfounded legends.

The major factor in this suppression of truth has been the dependence of the Soviet government and Soviet Communist Party on a conception of the revolution without which its claim to political and national leadership would collapse. Any attempt to give an account of Russia in 1917 at variance with the official 'Marxist–Leninist' version is considered by the Soviet authorities to be seditious and treasonable. This was clearly shown at the height of the Pasternak affair, when the author of *Doctor Zhivago* was accused of an 'anti-revolutionary attitude' just for having described in a matter-of-fact way conditions which had existed within living memory. In the earlier years of the Soviet régime, when this memory was still vivid, the task assigned to the historians by the Party was to make the best of a bad job by somehow fitting widely

known facts into the 'Leninist' pattern. The process of falsifying history
has since become more refined. It now begins with the publication of
carefully selected archive material considered appropriate for the
purpose.[1] At the same time, however, much archive material which
was accessible to Soviet researchers in the twenties has not been published and some of it may well have been destroyed. Occasionally we
get a public admission that important documents have been tampered
with by the editors of various collections.

The publication of documents by and about Lenin himself is con-
sidered too serious a matter to be left to the historians. At a meeting of
Soviet historians in 1962 the Party ideologist Academician P. N.
Pospelov stated:

> 'Some Comrades . . . have raised the question as to whether or not one
> should give researchers free access to all unpublished Party documents
> and archives. It is impossible to support such a move. The Party archives
> are not the patrimony of one or another researcher, nor even of the
> Institute of Marxism-Leninism . . . but of our Party, and only the
> Central Committee has authority over it. Some documents of great
> Party importance, [such as] Lenin's papers, can be published only by
> decision of the C.C.'[2]

Work on the Russian revolution by historians not under the control
of the Soviet government and the Communist Party is denounced as
the product of a vast conspiracy of 'falsifiers of history'. This will
certainly be the fate of the present book, provided of course it is not
passed over in silence as an unmentionable obscenity.

In the absence of Soviet sources on important aspects of the revolution of 1917 we turn to the writings of Russian émigrés and Western
observers. But here again we find that facts have been deliberately
withheld. It is not only that these writers find it painful to relive
events, particularly if their part in them is something of which they are

---

1. See my article on Soviet historical sources in *Contemporary History in the Soviet
Mirror* (London, 1964), where I quote from the 'Rules for the publication of documents of the Soviet period' issued by the Main Archive Administration. A. F.
Kerensky's latest publication 'Russia and History's Turning Point' (1965) could not
be taken into account at the advanced stage of production of this book.
2. *Vsesoyuznoe soveshchanie istorikov, 18–21 dekabrya 1962 g.* (Moscow, 1964), p. 296.

not necessarily proud. This is only human. The historian's task is rendered more difficult when the truth is suppressed out of a sense of duty, in fulfilment of moral obligations which are still honoured in circumstances entirely different from those in which they were undertaken. There is for example no doubt, as we shall show, that a widespread net of conspiratorial organisations modelled on freemasons' lodges worked for revolution in Russia and played a decisive role in the formation of the first Provisional Government. It is, however, impossible to assess the political aims and actual impact of these organisations without documentary evidence. Two members of the Provisional Government — Tereshchenko and Konovalov — who were prominent in this movement and who subsequently lived in emigration for many years, died without leaving any published account of their doings before and during the revolution. The most important surviving member of the group, A. F. Kerensky, has not yet found it possible to clarify this crucial point. Whatever his reasons, which are no doubt weighty, he is fully aware of the importance of this factor and has taken measures to release evidence on it — 'in thirty years' time'.[1]

This obfuscation of what happened in 1917 by Soviet and non-Soviet witnesses alike is compounded by the evasiveness of German sources. The Russian revolution occurred at a moment when World War I was rapidly moving to a climax. Its impact on the course of military events was enormous, and yet for decades the question of the part played by Germany in fomenting revolutionary unrest in Russia seems to have been taboo on all sides. In 1921 an attempt by Eduard Bernstein, the leading German Social-Democrat, to lift the curtain was countered by an official *démenti*, and pressure was put on him by his Party friends not to persist. This *démenti* was entirely misleading. We now know from the files of the German Ministry of Foreign Affairs that '*Revolutionierungspolitik*' was an essential part of Germany's grand strategy in World War I. Unfortunately these files do not throw light on all the activities of the numerous German agencies involved. Here again, many material witnesses remain silent, as though the state which once pledged them to secrecy still existed.

The memoirs of German officials like Kühlmann and Nadolny, who played a large part in determining the policy of their country towards

1. See below, p. 168.

Russia during World War I, are disappointing, particularly since we know from the Archives of the Ministry of Foreign Affairs how deeply implicated in it they were. The extent to which *suppressio veri* can go is further illustrated by the following story, which has recently come to light. It appears that Kurt Riezler, a key figure in Russo-German relations, wrote detailed diaries covering the period 1914–17. From a recent article in the German illustrated magazine *Der Spiegel*[1] we learn that Kurt Riezler intended to publish his diaries after World War II, but was dissuaded from doing so by an eminent German historian, Professor H. Rothfels, who felt he had good reason to consider their publication at that time inopportune. The diaries narrowly escaped destruction after Kurt Riezler's death, and have now been shown to a German historian who so far has not revealed any references in them to the *Revolutionierungspolitik* with which Riezler was so intimately connected.

It is this conspiracy of silence which prompted the author of the present work to undertake a close scrutiny of hitherto unconsidered aspects of the Russian revolution, in the hope of throwing a little light on some dark corners, and with the avowed aim of showing how wary we should be of the many well-established and plausibly-documented myths which unfortunately pass for 'objective' writing of history.

The book is divided into three parts. The five chapters in Part One discuss some features of the Russian political scene before the revolution, and provide a background for an understanding of the chronological account of events in the second and third parts. The first chapter is about the 'liberals', their policies and organisations during World War I. The second chapter gives a short sketch of the socialist and revolutionary parties inside Russia in the same period. The third deals mainly with the army.

The last two chapters of Part One are of a somewhat different kind. Chapter 4 is devoted to the Jewish question, which is more bound up with the February Revolution than that of any other minority in the empire. I have dwelt on this matter not because the Jews played an outstanding part in bringing the revolution about but because the fall of Tsarism in Russia was believed to inaugurate a new and happy era in the life of the Jews in Russia. The prestige of the revolution as a great

1. November 1964.

liberating feat lived on in the hearts of many Jews in Russia and outside even when the hopes and expectations to which the revolution gave rise remained sadly unfulfilled.

Chapter 5, on German intervention, is one to which the author attaches great importance, since he feels that he is here breaking new ground. Because the activities of the various German agencies involved can be understood only in the light of the final fruition of their efforts, with the coming to power of the Bolsheviks, the author has overstepped his chronological limits in this instance and taken the story beyond February almost to October 1917.

The four chapters in Part Two deal with certain aspects of Russian history during World War I, which seem to the author to be of exceptional importance for an understanding of the February Revolution. This part does not pretend to be a history of World War I in Russia, and highlights certain episodes only in so far as they reflect the profound malaise of Russian society on the eve of the revolution. The brutal judicial murder of a colonel of the Gendarmerie chosen as a scapegoat for the shortcomings of the military leadership, the emergence of caucuses within the Tsarist government, the extraordinary campaign of rumour-mongering, the instigators of which may well themselves have fallen victim to deliberate deception, the belief in conspiracy and assassination as instruments of political and social progress—all this helped to undermine the Russian state and the national war effort, thus making the country an easy prey for the forces bent on its destruction.

Part Three is an attempt at a straightforward account of what occurred between 23 February and 4 March (Old Style)[1] in Russia. Stripped of its legendary embellishments, we find it to be a sorry tale of mutual misunderstandings, breaches of trust, loss of confidence at the seat of power and a stampede on the part of the long-suffering and baffled population of Petrograd and Moscow.

The author ends his narrative with the formation of the Provisional Government on 3 March 1917. He merely notes without comment the ensuing wave of revolutionary enthusiasm and popular jubilation; this will not, it is hoped, be attributed to callous indifference to the fate of a great nation.

1. All dates referring to events in Russia are given according to the Julian Calendar or so-called Old Style, which in the twentieth century is thirteen days behind the Gregorian Calendar used in the West.

Introduction

Russia, both in its Muscovite period and in its imperial St. Peters-burg period, underwent in the course of centuries many dramatic changes without any breach of its autocratic structure permanent enough to deserve the name of revolution. Even in the dynastic crisis during the 'Time of Troubles' at the beginning of the seventeenth century auto-cratic power was maintained and indeed strengthened by the support of a traditional representative institution, the Zemsky Sobor. In the seventeenth and eighteenth centuries, throughout the series of violent palace coups, political power always remained in the hands of an autocrat. When, by some accident of succession, the autocrat was weak, political decisions were determined by the balance of rival influences of which he was the pivot. But when the monarch had a mind of his own and the skill to achieve his aims he, or she, as in the case of Catherine the Great, would organise the political administration and mould the social order on which autocratic power rested according to his own ideas and preferences. Political initiative or opposition could make itself felt only by humble advice, petition and supplication to the supreme ruler or by open rebellion.

In the course of centuries rebellions recurred in two distinct forms which had little in common. One was by social groups nearest the throne for the establishment of their privileges or in defence of them, if they were threatened by the policy of the monarch: such were the struggles of the various aristocratic clans during the minorities of Ivan IV and Peter the Great; such were the palace coups of the eighteenth century; such also were the bloodily suppressed risings of the *streltsy* at the beginning of Peter the Great's reign. All these disturbances were centred on, and mostly confined to, the capital, or even the palace; and whatever their immediate outcome they were closely followed by the restoration of the *status quo* in which all political decisions remained the exclusive prerogative of the monarch.

Rebellions of the other type were not in defence of any privilege; they were started by people who, having abandoned what little vested interest they might once have had in the existing social order, had fled

xxi

to one of the free associations of the dispossessed – the Cossack democracies – which grew up on the confines of the realm beyond the reach of the central administration. At various times throughout the seventeenth and eighteenth centuries these elements broke into the area policed by the central government and appealed to social strata akin to them to rise and overthrow the social and political order. Such intrusions became major upheavals when led by determined and gifted men like Razin, Bolotnikov or Pugachev. Had any of these movements succeeded, they would doubtless have led to what could be termed a social revolution. They were, however, peripheral, and their snowball advance on the capital, collecting disaffected elements as they progressed, always broke against a determined and organised counteraction by the central government. The ultimate reason for the failure of such insurrections was, however, social, and lay in the fact that the population living under the protection of the Tsar-Emperor on the whole preferred the security of the little they had to the uncertain prospects of bandit rule.

Towards the beginning of the nineteenth century a new factor emerged which, after many abortive attempts, made possible a link-up between the sedition of the privileged and the rebellion of the dispossessed: this was the awakened social conscience of the upper classes. Its first unmistakable manifestation was Radishchev's famous book *Journey from St. Petersburg to Moscow*, which appeared, and was condemned, in 1790. From this time on, the political disaffection of the upper classes was no longer determined merely by their own group interests, but also by what they believed to be the interests of the people. The contrast between the conspiracy which led to the murder of Paul I in 1801 and the one which resulted in the Decembrist uprising of 1825 illustrates the fundamental change in the character of upper-class sedition. The first was a political plot by Guards officers in defence of the privileges granted to the gentry by Catherine and threatened by Paul. The second was a movement by members of the same social group who were now spurred to action by the idea of service to the people, even to the point of self-immolation. From then on began the tragic quest of the upper-class radicals and revolutionaries for a link with the potentially unlimited explosive force of popular discontent which they were ready to guide and whence they hoped to draw their revolutionary strength. This quest is the main theme of the history of the Russian revolutionary movement in the nineteenth century. The Russian Fourierists (the Petrashevsky group, 1846–49), the Nihilists, the Populists (Narodniks) and their extreme terroristic offshoots, the fantastic aristocratic revolutionary Bakunin, were all engaged in the search for an effective political understanding with those whose vital material appetite the revolution was to satisfy. Such an understanding was, however, difficult to achieve, and its absence was one of the main reasons for the failure of the revolutionary movement in Russia in the nineteenth century. There was certainly no lack of agrarian unrest and military mutinies in that period, but the government's improved control and more efficient policing of outlying regions prevented these movements from assuming the dimensions of a Pugachev rising. Such spontaneous uprisings of the dispossessed remained, however, still unaffected by the political theories and the political organisations of the revolutionary intelligentsia. This consisted of representatives of the upper classes who had gone over to the revolution, and of *raznochintsy* from the lower ranks of society who had risen through education and public service to a level where their political aspirations were dictated by ideology rather than social appetite. The revolution seemed to await the appearance of 'a Pugachev with a university education'; but when the Pugachevs got their university education this either weakened their revolutionary fervour or estranged them from the crude aspirations of the 'dark people' who were hoping for an improvement of their own material lot rather than for universal justice. And so it happened that when the revolution finally broke out, it was led not by a man of the people but by a member of the petty gentry, who professed revolutionary ideology of a Marxist brand but also knew how to make use of the latent passions of popular rebellion without ever espousing them. By that time, however, certain contacts between both poles of the revolutionary movement had been firmly established: organised industrial labour, the technical units of the armed forces (in particular, the navy), and the intelligentsia of the peripheral national minorities, such as the Jews and the Georgians, who were less alienated from their own people than the Russian intelligentsia, had become the main links between the ideologists of revolution and the disaffected masses.

The scope of these contacts was first revealed during the revolution of 1905. The Petersburg Soviet of Workers' Deputies, led by a lawyer, Khrustalev-Nosar, and an intellectual, Trotsky, was able to establish something like a revolutionary administration which for a time competed with the government bureaucracy. And this pattern was repeated all over Russia in the provinces and in the armed forces: the mutiny on the battleship *Ochakov*, for instance, was headed by an enthusiastic young naval officer, Lieutenant Schmidt. In all such cases the revolutionary intelligentsia proved itself for the first time able to release and channel popular anger and aggressiveness, while for their part the masses began to look to the revolutionary intelligentsia for leadership, and to see in revolutionary ideology an expression of their own inarticulate social and economic grievances and aspirations. For the first time, also, provincial risings were somehow coordinated with events in the capital, and the railway strikes, which disrupted the established order in the country, helped to consolidate still further the unity of the revolutionary forces. This new cohesion between the two elements of the revolutionary movement brought the ultimate aim of a social revolution within practical reach.

To the sensitive observer of the Russian scene the events of 1905 revealed for the first time the extreme brittleness of the existing system. Russian literature, especially poetry, always foremost in reflecting the mood of the country, reacted to events by voicing vague eschatological forebodings and creating the symbolism of revolutionary thinking.

The tremors that shook the autocratic régime in those revolutionary months were so severe, and the general mood of expectancy was so tense, that it is surprising how rapidly life returned to normal; even more surprising was the decrease in revolutionary pressure on public affairs in the following decade. Revolutionary trends were in fact overshadowed by the emergence into the political arena of the Russian liberal tradition, which until then had been developing as an ideology with little or no direct political application.

The awakening social conscience which had driven a part of the upper-class dissidents to look for an alliance with popular disaffection had prompted others to seek reform within the framework of the existing social order. This liberal tradition, which had its heyday in the social reforms of 1861–64, was represented both in the high bureaucracy, among personal advisers to successive autocrats, and in the intelligentsia. The liberal intellectuals generally avoided service in the government administration, and were often frowned upon and even persecuted by the authorities as allies of the revolutionaries. The presence of liberals in the two opposing camps still blurs the picture of Russian political development in the nineteenth and twentieth centuries. The liberals, when not directly serving the régime, were grouped together with the radicals as 'intelligentsia' and wrongly believed to have been moving towards a revolutionary attitude through the various stages of political radicalism. Conversely, the government's sporadic efforts to introduce politically and socially progressive measures are still often considered to have been purely reactionary and retrograde in intention. It needed the subtle analysis of a historian and lawyer like V. Leontovitsch[1] both to point out the persistence of liberal tendencies in the development of the Russian state itself and to distinguish clearly between 'liberal' and 'radical' trends within the intelligentsia.

The scope and near-success of the revolutionary movement in 1905 was a greater stimulus to the liberal forces in Russia than to the revolutionaries. The constitution granted, however grudgingly, by the Tsar in 1905 made certain party activities in Russia legal. Moreover, the violence of the revolutionary events aroused the apprehension of the liberals, and made them more conscious of the differences between themselves and the revolutionary radicals. A number of prominent intellectuals who had been closely connected with the revolutionaries at the turn of the century defected, and came into the open with an ideological manifesto.[2] Although no rapprochement took place between such liberal intellectuals and the state authorities, the danger revealed by the events of 1905 gave strength – even in the eyes of diehard supporters of autocracy – to liberal arguments. The government awoke to the necessity of planning and regulating social development. Since the intellectual revolutionaries had succeeded in making contact with the forces of social disruption in the country, the liberals and even the conservatives began in their turn to look for the support of the masses against the revolutionary movement. These tendencies explain a number of features in Russian politics at the beginning of this century. At the lowest level of political activity, the newly-discovered need for popular support induced the government to organise 'reaction from below' in the shape of the so-called patriotic unions, such as the Union of the Russian People and their terrorist excrescences, such as the Black Hundreds. On a somewhat higher level, the hope that the

1. *Geschichte des Liberalismus in Russland* (Frankfurt-am-Main, 1955).
2. *Vekhi.* See Leonard Schapiro, article in *Slavonic and East European Review* (1955).

peasantry would support the existing régime out of devotion to the Tsar caused the government to extend indirect franchise to the peasantry. This, however, had to be curtailed when the election returns for the First and Second Dumas fell short of the government's expectations. Finally, at the highest level – that of political planning – the need to base the régime on a broad social foundation led to the reform connected with the name of Stolypin.

The great mass of Russian peasants, who tilled land allotted to them by the village commune (*mir*) which owned it, were at last to be made hereditary proprietors of self-supporting holdings. This reform aroused the opposition both of the reactionaries and of the left, the latter bewailing the threatened disappearance of the medieval Russian land commune as a blow to an allegedly native Russian type of socialism.

The Stolypin peasant reform coincided with an accelerated economic and industrial development which bore all the marks of the initial stages of an industrial revolution. Thus it happened that both the planned policy of the government and the spontaneous development of the country created conditions unfavourable to the further development of the revolutionary movement in Russia. What remained of this movement was more easily controlled by the state security police, and by the ferocious measures of suppression which Stolypin and his followers had no hesitation in resorting to whenever open rebellion broke out. The right wing of the Social-Democrats tended to give up revolutionary activities and to concentrate on organising labour, conducting propaganda and educational work among the masses and exerting political pressure through its representatives in the Duma. The Socialist Revolutionary Party did not give up its terrorist activities until the double agent, Azef, who directed them, was unmasked in 1908. Terrorism, however, had sapped the organisational capacity of the party and alienated it from the masses, who never understood the purpose of political terror. The Bolshevik branch of the Russian Social-Democratic Party, whose principal leaders were in emigration, lost much of their following among the workers to the 'liquidators' (right-wing Mensheviks and similar groups) and were discredited in the eyes of other revolutionaries by their connection with bank robberies (the so-called 'expropriations'). In the fourth Duma their representatives were led – and betrayed – by the police agent Roman Malinovsky.

And so it came about that in the decade 1905–15, so sadly neglected by historians, even the profoundly disturbed social conscience of the intelligentsia could find outlets other than revolutionary action. At the same time the inarticulate discontent of the lower classes which had had no natural outlet in the nineteenth century became less intense through increasing social mobility and new hopes of betterment for the peasant and industrial worker.

The loss of revolutionary momentum was clearly understood by Lenin at the beginning of the war, although this did not discourage him. Not even the strains of the war and the incidents of disruption, mutiny and disaffection unavoidably accompanying it could persuade Lenin of the imminence of a revolution in Russia in 1917. In a lecture delivered in Zurich in January of that year, he said that the revolution might well come when those of his generation were no longer among the living. This, and Lenin's first reaction to the early reports of the revolution in March, shows that both its form and timing took him completely by surprise.

But Lenin was not the only one to be caught unawares by the events of February 1917 in Petrograd. One of the principal participants[1] wrote five years later:

> The Revolution surprised us — the party men of those days — sound asleep like the foolish virgins of the Gospel. Now, five years later, it seems incredible that we could have failed to realise that the February wave was rising (not to speak of the oncoming storm). So many of us had spent years under the Tsarist régime preparing underground for those days with tense and eager faith, and when at last it came — the long-awaited and ardently-desired revolution — we had nowhere to go.

The same inability to grasp the implications of the new situation was also to be found in official circles. The official chronicler of the court, General Dubensky, who had just arrived in Mogilev with the Tsar from Tsarskoe Selo, wrote under the dateline 24 February:

> A quiet life has begun here. Everything will remain as it was. There will be no move on the part of the Tsar. Only incidental, outside reasons

1. S. Mstislavsky-Maslovsky, *Pyat dney* (Moscow, 1922). Mstislavsky was a member of the SR Party who took part in the street combats of 1905 and composed a manual on street fighting. During the war he served as a librarian in the Library of the Military Academy of the General Staff in Petrograd. During the February days he became head of the Military Commission of the Executive Committee of the Petrograd Soviet.

could force any kind of change. There have been 'food riots' in Petrograd, workers of the cartridge factory came out onto the Liteyny Prospekt and moved towards the Nevsky Prospekt, where they were dispersed by the Cossacks.[1]

The memoirists of the period are almost unanimous in admitting that they only realised the revolution had begun long after it was actually in full swing. Perhaps the officers of the secret police in Petrograd came nearest to a realistic assessment of what was going to happen: throughout February General Globachev, the chief of the secret police, repeatedly mentioned in his reports the imminence of large-scale disturbances in the capital. But he agreed that this discontent was more likely to lead to a monarchist patriotic pogrom of the Jews or Germans than to a social revolution.

One of the reasons why the revolution came as a surprise was the fact that no report of any major disturbance was received from anywhere in the vast empire other than the capital. As we shall see, the position at the front also seemed fairly stable and, in contrast to the anxious days of the retreats of 1915, did not affect the confidence of the military leaders. In the capitals, nervousness had increased — but chiefly among the newspaper-reading public, a very small part of the population; so had industrial unrest, exacerbated by the police's ham-handed treatment of the accredited working-class representatives in the War Industry Committees.[2] But nothing seemed to indicate that the ferment originating in the nervous and unstable atmosphere of the capitals would spread to other parts of the country, still less to the army in the field.[3] Yet this is exactly what happened, and the reaction of the country to the February events in Petrograd could not have been more uniform if it had been organised and rehearsed. This uniformity, the total absence of resistance, the unquestioning acceptance of a change which a few days before nobody dared forecast, seemed miraculous to its contemporaries and earned the revolution the title, not fully deserved, of the 'Great Bloodless Russian Revolution'. This uniformity was not to be repeated in the subsequent revolutionary developments in Russia.

1. Quoted by A. Blok, *Poslednie dni starogo rezhima*, in *Arkhiv Russkoy Revolyutsii*, (Berlin, 1921-37—hereinafter abbreviated as ARR), IV, p. 27.
2. See below, p. 231 ff.
3. With the one exception of the Baltic Fleet, where political tension was felt before the outbreak of the revolution.

Part One

I

The Duma and the Voluntary Organisations

The origin of the Voluntary Organisations; The Voluntary Organisations and the political parties; Patriotism and revolution; The Labour Groups of the War Industry Committees

1. THE ORIGIN OF THE VOLUNTARY ORGANISATIONS [1]

When World War I broke out, the protracted constitutional crisis — the outcome of concessions made by the autocracy in the autumn of 1905 and of the attempt to withdraw some of them in 1907[2] — had not yet been resolved. The Fourth Duma, elected in September–October 1912, had a majority which was willing to co-operate with the government in carrying out a legislative programme. The liberal opposition, however, would not reconcile itself to a parliament which could control and initiate legislation but had no power to interfere with the administration of the country. The Duma had no effective control over the actions of the government and no say in the appointment of ministers.

The Council of Ministers itself was not a cabinet in the sense in which the term is used in a parliamentary system. Individual ministers, appointed directly by the monarch and responsible exclusively to him, were independent heads of their respective departments. They were answerable neither to the Chairman of the Council of Ministers nor to the Council itself. The latter was merely a co-ordinating committee —

1. The Voluntary Organisations were those bodies, known in Russian as *obshchestvennye* or 'public' organisations, which were formed initially to assist the government in the care of wounded and sick soldiers and of civilian refugees, and which later took on all sorts of duties connected with supplying the armed forces. They were the Union of the Zemstvos (rural local government), the Union of the Municipalities, and — from the summer of 1915 onwards — the local and the Central War Industry Committees (referred to hereinafter as WICs).
2. This was carried out by Stolypin in June 1907, when the Second Duma was dissolved and a new electoral law promulgated. It restricted the franchise in violation of the basic laws of the Empire.

not a body which implemented a political programme on which the ministers had reached agreement. At any meeting the ministers might and often did find that one of their colleagues had been removed by the monarch and replaced by someone else.

From the convocation of the First Duma the liberal parties had unremittingly opposed this order of things and grasped every opportunity to press for an executive responsible to Parliament. These demands were voiced primarily by the Constitutional Democratic Party, the so-called Kadets, whose undisputed leader by 1914 was P. N. Milyukov. But in the Fourth Duma the Kadets were in opposition to a right-wing majority formed of the moderate right and the Octobrist Party. The Octobrists, led by A. I. Guchkov, member of the State Council (i.e. the Upper Chamber), mainly represented the property-owning classes; they were not against progressive constitutional changes in the long run, but were willing, in the meantime, to give the curtailed constitution a fair trial. They were ready to co-operate with the government on legislation and to make the best of their right to put questions and interpellations to the ministers concerning current administration. The latter could answer or ignore such questions at their discretion.

The outbreak of war brought considerable changes in the political weight of the persons and institutions involved without bringing the conflict any nearer to a solution. The support given by the Duma on 26 July, 1914 to the government in its decision to proceed with the war created a false impression of national unity. Large-scale, spontaneous, pro-Tsar popular demonstrations in both capitals and in the provinces seemed to inaugurate a truce to internal strife. Having voted quasi-unanimously[1] the necessary war credits, the Duma was prorogued, and did not meet, except for a few days in January 1915, until the important session of the summer of 1915.

As a purely legislative body, the Duma had indeed little to do at that time. Long-term legislative programmes were shelved for the duration of the war, and necessary wartime regulations were issued by the government departments under the 'State of Emergency Law'. One might have expected the government to profit from the political truce to strengthen its authority, but this was not to be the case. For what the Duma liberals had offered the government on 26 July was not freedom

1. The Social-Democrat deputies did not vote for the credits, but as they walked out of the Chamber they were not considered to have voted.

from parliamentary control but their loyal and active collaboration in the war effort. The Duma itself had no apparatus for such collaboration, but there were the local government institutions — the Zemstvos and Municipalities — through which the liberals could work, in support of, and frequently in competition with, the bureaucratic machinery.

The Zemstvos were a form of local government introduced in 1864 at the same time as the structure of the Municipalities was put on a more representative basis. Since then the liberals had come to consider these institutions as the seed out of which a representative government on a national scale should grow. The demand for a parliamentary régime was often, in the second half of the nineteenth century, couched in such terms as 'the completion of the reforms which gave Russia the Zemstvo institutions', or, 'the crowning of the reforms of the reign of Alexander II'. It was around and inside the Zemstvos that the legal political parties, such as the Kadets and Octobrists, were formed in the period immediately preceding the establishment of the Duma in 1906. The influence of the Zemstvos in Russian political life had been strengthened during the Russo-Japanese War of 1904-5 by the assistance they gave the Red Cross in the relief work for the wounded and sick soldiers evacuated from the front area. The experience of the Russo-Japanese War served as a pattern for renewed attempts by the Zemstvos and Municipalities in World War I to achieve political hegemony. And as this time the scope of their work, the means at their disposal and the importance of their efforts grew far beyond what they had been in 1904-5, so also did their political aspirations.

The memories of co-operation in 1904-5 between the local government institutions and the Petrograd bureaucracy were not happy for either side. Yet when the world war broke out it was inevitable that the government should call upon their goodwill and that the Zemstvos and Municipalities should offer it enthusiastically. Russia, although a strictly policed country, was very loosely administered, and the government simply had no means at its disposal to mobilise at short notice the vast resources of the country, whose potentialities they were not always even able to assess.

The mobilisation of enormous masses of recruits and reservists and the considerable casualties sustained in the first few weeks of the war put a greater strain on the medical and welfare services of the army than its administration could bear. Thus the organisation of hospitals and the distribution of comforts to the troops were the first tasks undertaken by the Municipalities and Zemstvos.

In these activities they competed not only with the State administration and the Red Cross Society, but also with private benefactors. The government would certainly have preferred them to have accepted the status of these private patrons, but this was not at all how the organs of local government saw their function in the war effort. Nor was such a status compatible with their activities as these increased in scope and grew to a national scale.

In addition to welfare and medical work of every description, the Voluntary Organisations — as we shall henceforth refer to the Zemstvos and Municipalities — were soon faced with unforeseen problems created by the influx of refugees and evacuees from enemy-occupied territory and the front line. Housing and feeding them were not the only jobs on hand. The Voluntary Organisations soon extended their activities to legal assistance, both for the refugees and the families of servicemen: they helped them to obtain relief, pensions and restitution for losses they had incurred. They co-operated with private organisations, especially with the various committees for aid to the Jewish population forcibly deported from the 'pale of settlement'.

Very soon it became apparent that the two Voluntary Organisations were the main buyers of a number of articles necessary for the supply of the army. This led them to the further step of organising themselves the production of a great number of commodities, and by 1916 the number of factories and workshops controlled by the joint committee of the Union of Zemstvos and the Union of Municipalities for the supply of the army exceeded two thousand.

To cope with these tasks on a national scale, the Zemstvos and the Municipalities, reverting to a practice which had already been tried out in the Russo-Japanese War of 1904–5, had, early in the war, formed All-Russian Unions. These were strictly voluntary associations of the Zemstvos and Municipalities of individual provinces and towns, which joined hands to work, under the direction of head offices in Moscow, according to a uniform plan. The formation of these unions was spontaneous: they were neither ordered nor authorised by the government. Gradually, however, they came to be officially recognised. When Special Councils (*osobye soveshchaniya*) were established by an imperial *ukaz* in August 1915, the Voluntary Organisations were represented on them.[1]

Thus the All-Russian Unions of the Zemstvos and Municipalities had become powerful factors in Russian public life, employing thousands of people, spending enormous sums and dealing with the private affairs of millions of Russian subjects. Yet neither the Zemstvos nor the Municipalities possessed the necessary financial means to work on this scale, and from the very outset they were largely dependent on State grants. Originally, the control of this expenditure by means of their own accounting and auditing systems was left to the Voluntary Organisations themselves. Later, when relations with the government had thoroughly deteriorated and a mud-slinging campaign had begun on both sides, the government and the Voluntary Organisations accused each other of bribery and embezzlement. Special committees for the control of state funds issued to these organisations were established and this, as we shall see, led to further friction.

In May 1915, a third national Voluntary Organisation was formed, which became a no less powerful political factor than the two original ones. As the news of the arms and ammunition shortage at the front reached the country in April–May 1915, allegations were made that the government had not done enough to tap Russia's resources for war-time production. A conference of various associations of industrialists was called in Petrograd for 26 May 1915, at which the Moscow industrialist P. P. Ryabushinsky made a thundering speech relating the impressions he had just gained from a visit to the army in the field and demanding that industry itself should spontaneously organise arms and ammunition production. A resolution was passed to establish 'War Industry Committees' in every province and to form a 'Central War Industry Committee' to co-ordinate the activities of the provincial branches.

The Central War Industry Committee (Central WIC in the following pages) had to ascertain the needs of the armed forces, to establish priorities, and to distribute orders to the provincial WICs. The provincial committees would, in their turn, distribute them to the factories and take measures to procure raw materials and labour. As soon as the

1. The legal argument in favour of constitutional status for the two Unions was put forward both in the liberal press and in the special publication of their joint committee for supplies to the army.

WICs were formed, a conference was called in Petrograd, which elected A. I. Guchkov Chairman of the Central WIC and A. I. Konovalov, the Moscow industrialist, as his deputy.

Guchkov took extraordinary measures to obtain official recognition for the newly-formed WIC. With the help of his personal friend, General A. A. Polivanov, who became Minister of War in June 1915, he obtained the government's approval of the statutes of the new organisation. He even took part in one of the relevant meetings of the Council of Ministers. The new Voluntary Organisation, like the others, also secured representation on the boards of the various Special Councils for Defence.

2. THE VOLUNTARY ORGANISATIONS AND THE POLITICAL PARTIES

The three Voluntary Organisations — the Union of Zemstvos, the Union of Municipalities and the Central War Industry Committee — never fused into one body, although in 1917 the Union of Zemstvos and the Union of Municipalities were united in the so-called *Zemgor*. Until that time, all three preserved their individuality: they met at separate congresses, their resolutions on questions of general policy differed to a certain extent, and their attitudes towards the government and the Duma varied. Yet they shared the same political aim: claiming that the government was incapable of winning the war, and that the Voluntary Organisations alone could improve the situation, they called for a 'government of public confidence', that is, a government which would fully co-operate with them and which would in a more or less formal way be responsible to 'the people', that is to the State Duma.

Their unity of political purpose was reinforced by a geographical and a personal factor. The administration of all three organisations centred on Moscow.[1] Ever since the ancient Russian capital had had, in the words of Pushkin, 'to bow like a dowager empress' to her northern rival, Moscow had become a centre of oppositionist feeling against the Petersburg bureaucracy. In the nineteenth century this opposition took

1. The Central WIC was in Petrograd, but its leaders lived in Moscow and maintained close contacts with the heads of the other two organisations.

the form either of Slavophil liberalism, based on a romantic conception of specifically Russian social justice (*pravda*), or of a radicalism of the Westerners' type, linked with the liberal and radical traditions of the West. In the decade preceding the revolution, Moscow had become the centre of activity of the Constitutional Democrats – the Kadets. Conferences, meetings and seminars took place in the homes of the nobility (such as the Princes Peter and Paul Dolgorukov) and of the industrial tycoons of the merchant class (e.g. Ryabushinsky and Konovalov), who preferred Moscow to Petersburg. With the help of professors from Moscow University, the programmes of the Russian liberal parties were hammered out and political tactics evolved. These Moscow intellectual, industrial, commercial and artistic circles always prided themselves on their independence from the Petersburg spirit of bureaucratic formalism and court sycophancy.

Even the church life of Moscow contrasted sharply with that of the Petrine capital. Moscow had its own style of piety, influenced by the Old Believer tradition of the great merchant families and very different from the ornate baroque and empire styles of the Petersburg cathedrals. On Moscow centred the hopes for a regeneration of Russian religious life, which were linked with a longing for the restoration of the Patriarchate and a vague, dreamlike vision of a people's theocracy. Similarly patriotism and devotion to monarchy bore different aspects in Moscow and Petersburg. The differences in style and tradition of the capitals contributed to the progressive alienation of Tsar Nicholas II from his subjects during the last reign. On state occasions in Moscow the Empress Alexandra found it difficult to comply with local traditions and did not feel at ease. She often gave involuntary offence, and gradually developed a dislike for the Moscow style of life. Indeed, after the tragedy of the Khodynka during the coronation, when hundreds were crushed in a crowd stampede, hardly a visit passed without some awkwardness, some unpleasant incident arising from the Empress's lack of sympathy and understanding for the susceptibilities of the Muscovites. In Moscow, therefore, the leaders of the Voluntary Organisations had chosen terrain particularly favourable for opposing bureaucratic control and challenging the authority of Petrograd.

The heads of the three organisations were not only in close personal contact with one another, but had been working in the same organisations and unions for the previous two decades. Prince G. E. Lvov, later head of the Provisional Government, was simultaneously High Commissioner of the All-Russian Union of Zemstvos, a member of the Central WIC and Deputy Chairman of the Moscow WIC. The Mayor of Moscow, M. V. Chelnokov, head of the Union of Municipalities, was a member of the Central Committee of the All-Russian Union of Zemstvos and Deputy Chairman of the Moscow WIC. The Chairman of the Central WIC, A. I. Guchkov, had worked at the beginning of the war as Red Cross commissioner for the Union of Zemstvos. His deputy, Konovalov, was himself closely connected with the work of the Union of Municipalities. The collaboration between all three Voluntary Organisations became so intimate by the middle of 1915 that Prince Lvov could in all truth declare:

> The Central Committees of the All-Russian Union of Zemstvos and of the All-Russian Union of Municipalities have now become one organisation, and the Moscow War Industry Committee is working hand in hand with them, so that we not only co-ordinate our labours but work together on a principle of parity and mutual confidence.[1]

The leaders of the Voluntary Organisations did not all belong to the same political party. Prince Lvov was a Kadet; so was Chelnokov, while Guchkov was one of the founders of the Octobrist Party. Konovalov belonged to the 'Progressive Party' situated somewhere between the Octobrists and the Kadets. However, such party differences, which still retained significance on the Duma floor even after the formation of the coalition of opposition parties known as the 'Progressive Bloc' in August 1915, meant little to the work of the Voluntary Organisations.

The Voluntary Organisations did not ostensibly pursue political aims, and they insisted that in demanding a government responsible to or enjoying the confidence of the legislative assemblies they were not playing politics but were asking for something which had long been recognised as a national and historical necessity. According to their professed view, they could not successfully discharge the tasks entrusted to them without such constitutional reforms. The Voluntary Organisations, at their meetings and congresses, therefore gave their full support to the demands for constitutional reform put forward by the Progressive Bloc, insisting that this was their patriotic duty.

1. *Tsentrarkhiv. 1917 god v dokumentakh i materialakh. Burzhuaziya nakanune fevralskoy revolyutsii* ed. by B. B. Grave (Moscow and Leningrad, 1927), p. VII f.

This was a particularly important point, because it emphasised the special relations of the Voluntary Organisations with the army. Any appeal by the Duma majority to the army for political support would have been contrary to the principle that the army should remain outside politics. The infringement of this principle would have lost the Duma politicians the sympathy of the military. But the Voluntary Organisations were in a different position. The army's efficiency and its fighting capacity were largely dependent on their work. This was understood not only by the generals at the front but by the government itself, even when relations between the Voluntary Organisations and the Petrograd administration were at their worst.[1]

The Duma parties which formed the Progressive Bloc in the summer of 1915 in order to demand constitutional reform saw all the advantages of the support which the Voluntary Organisations could give them in achieving their political target. And yet it would be a mistake to think that the Voluntary Organisations, or at least their leaders, regarded themselves as mere instruments in the hands of the Duma. In a sense their position was much stronger than that of the Duma. The Duma was bound by its standing orders; its proceedings were public, while the Voluntary Organisations were free from such restraints. They sometimes met in private and could go further in their criticism of the government than the Duma opposition parties. It was in the Moscow committees of the Voluntary Organisations – not among the Duma parties – that in the course of 1916 the plots and plans for a palace *coup* were worked out.

3. PATRIOTISM AND REVOLUTION

The Duma leaders, with the exception of those belonging to the revolutionary parties (i.e. to the Socialist Left: the Social-Democrats and the

1. In a letter of 1 September 1916 to the provincial governors informing them of the government's decision not to authorise congresses of the Unions of the Zemstvos and Municipalities, the last Tsarist Minister of the Interior, Protopopov, wrote that the measures to prevent such congresses should be taken with tact and without causing undue irritation to these Voluntary Organisations, 'because of the important and necessary work which they are doing at present for our gallant army.' See Grave, op. cit., p. 154.

'Trudoviks'[1]), were never completely won over to the cause of the revolution. They frequently acted as a brake on the political activities of the Moscow committees of the Voluntary Organisations. Thus V. I. Gurko, a member of the State Council, reports in his memoirs that Prince Lvov and Chelnokov attended a session of the Progressive Bloc in Petrograd in January 1917, and expressed their opinion that Russia could not achieve victory under the existing régime, and that her only salvation lay in revolution. They were met with marked hostility: Petrograd members of the Progressive Bloc 'pointed out frankly that to agree to a revolution during the war was to be guilty of treason against one's own country'.[2]

The leader of the Duma Kadets, P. N. Milyukov, was the main restraining influence on the revolutionary tendencies among the liberals. Throughout the war and until the February revolution, Milyukov steadfastly opposed any suggestion, whether inside or outside the Duma, of revolutionary and unconstitutional action to bring about the change of régime he himself so ardently desired. He did so for fear that a revolution under war conditions might lead to anarchy and engulf the parliamentary institutions on which he had built all his hopes for his own career, for his party, and for the liberal cause. For this attitude he was frequently attacked both in the Kadet parliamentary party and at meetings and conferences outside the Duma at which Kadet Party tactics were discussed. Milyukov's attitude can be traced to his memories of the abortive revolutionary demonstration – the so-called Vyborg Appeal[3] – initiated by the Kadets in 1906 after the dissolution of the First Duma. Even greater was his fear of Russian anarchy, of the terrible 'Russian revolt with neither sense nor mercy', in the words of Pushkin, which Milyukov quoted as a warning to his party colleagues as late as June 1916.[4]

But the motives for Milyukov's attitude were not only negative. The

1. A labour party made up of all sorts of non-Marxist socialists, including crypto-Socialist Revolutionaries.
2. V. I. Gurko, Features and Figures of the Past, ed. by Sterling, Eudin and Fisher (Stanford University Press, 1939), p. 582.
3. Members of the First Duma assembled in Vyborg after the dissolution in July 1906 and issued a proclamation urging the Russian people to refuse to pay taxes and provide recruits for the army. The appeal misfired, and most of the signatories were tried and sentenced to short terms of imprisonment.
4. At a Kadet meeting; see Grave, op. cit., pp. 61 ff.

short period of 'national unity' which was inaugurated at the Duma session of 26 July 1914 had given Milyukov the opportunity to get together with the Duma parties to the right of the Kadets and to work out a common programme on which all these parties could agree and for which, it was then hoped, the support of the liberal members of the Council of Ministers might be won. Negotiations for the formation of such a new parliamentary majority coalition went on through 1914–15 and culminated in an agreement signed on 25 August 1915 by a number of parties of the Duma and of the State Council. This coalition of parties was known as the Progressive Bloc, and its creation was the highlight of Milyukov's parliamentary activity.

The programme of the Progressive Bloc was rather eclectic and the agreement reached among the parties was never expected to be very stable.[1] None of the parties who signed it believed that the programme could be fully implemented immediately, particularly under wartime conditions. More important was the organisational side of the Progressive Bloc: for the first time in the Fourth Duma, a Duma majority was formed which had powerful support from the liberal members of the State Council. It intended to negotiate with the government for the formation of a 'government of public confidence'.

As long as a certain liberalisation of government could be expected, Milyukov firmly believed that collaboration with the government in wartime would strengthen the position of the Kadets in their struggle for constitutional reform. Later, after an attempt by the liberal ministers to come to an agreement with the Progressive Bloc had been frustrated by the Premier, Goremykin, in August–September 1915, Milyukov gave up the idea of loyal collaboration with the subsequent governments of Goremykin, Stuermer and Trepov. But he never stopped warning his party colleagues and the leaders of the Voluntary Organisations against setting their sights too high and embarking on an overtly revolutionary course. In Milyukov's view, this would only lay the Progressive Bloc open to a charge of intransigence and provoke the government to strong reactionary measures. Milyukov also supported the decision of the Duma Kadets to reduce their demand for a government responsible to parliament to a milder one for a 'government

1. For the text of the agreement and the programme in English translation see Sir Bernard Pares, *The Fall of the Russian Monarchy* (London, 1939), p. 171. See also our comment on this document below, p. 142 f.

enjoying the confidence of the people'. At a political banquet in Moscow on 13 March 1916, Milyukov was asked how he reconciled this formula with the Kadet Party programme, which required the establishment of a parliamentary régime. Milyukov answered:

> A Kadet in general is one thing; a Kadet in the Progressive Bloc is another. As a Kadet I stand for a ministry responsible to parliament, but as a first step, for tactical reasons, we are advancing now the formula of a 'ministry responsible to the people'. Let us obtain such a ministry, and then by force of circumstances it will very soon be transformed into a really responsible parliamentary government. *You* and *we* shall see to it that the proper meaning is given to this demand.[1]

Milyukov was certain that at the final settling of accounts at the end of the war, the position of the Tsarist government would be hopeless, and the victory of Russian liberalism, that is of the Kadet Party, would be complete and absolute. 'The government', he said at a meeting of the Duma Kadets in February 1916, 'is heading for the abyss, and it would be quite senseless for us to open its eyes prematurely to the complete foolishness of its game'. According to a summary of the Moscow Department of the Security Police, reporting on the psychological situation in Moscow in February 1916,[2] Milyukov believed that the end of the war would require tremendous financial efforts of the government, the means for which could be obtained only through foreign loans. In this situation the Duma would become all-important, and would be able to deliver a decisive blow to the autocratic government. Without the support of the Duma the government would be unable to get a penny from abroad!

Milyukov's utterances in the Duma should be judged against the background of his counsels for moderation urged in private. Even his speech of 1 November 1916 could not be considered as a call for a rising of the masses. His violent denunciation of the government and aspersions on the authority of the absolute monarchy were not meant as a signal for a *levée en masse*, but as the last count in a long indictment of the autocratic régime. By discrediting the existing régime Milyukov hoped to speed up the historical development which he believed would

1. See Grave, op. cit., p. 94.
2. See Grave, op. cit., p. 75.

inevitably lead to the establishment of a constitutional monarchy in Russia.[1]

Milyukov's views were not shared by all members of his own party, or by the leaders of the Voluntary Organisations.[2] A forceful, stubborn personality and a strong party disciplinarian, Milyukov managed to keep control of the Kadet parliamentary faction, but at numerous party congresses, particularly in Moscow, he faced strong opposition led by N. V. Nekrasov and Prince Lvov, supported by the lawyers Mandelstam and Margulies. They argued openly in favour of a revolutionary course for the Kadet Party, which, they said, should seek direct contact with politicians of the left and with the common people. The left Kadets — mostly those from Moscow and the provinces who worked in the Voluntary Organisations and knew the mood of the electorate — feared that Milyukov's constitutionalist attitude would not appeal to

---

1. See below, p. 189.

2. The 'defensist' slant of Milyukov's attacks on the régime does not fully reflect Kadet ideology even in 1915–16. There is some evidence that alongside, and in spite of, the feeling that they were called upon to bring about a constitutional change in Russia in order to secure victory over the external enemy, there was also a trend of thought among them which cannot be characterised otherwise than as 'patriotic defeatism', as distinct from the 'revolutionary defeatism' of the Bolsheviks and some other Socialists. The feeling that defeat in the war would bring about a catharsis in the stagnating political atmosphere in Russia was very strong. How else can we explain that in 1915, in a volume of essays by the Professor of History at Moscow University, a prominent member of the Kadet Party, A. A. Kizevetter, the internal situation in Russia at the beginning of the Crimean War in 1855 was described in the following terms:

'The war began, and as it developed the hypnotic power of the colossus with feet of clay rapidly waned. It was as if an electric shock had hit the whole of thinking Russia. That real patriotism which is so dreaded by rulers who are alienated from the people spoke loudly in the souls of the best representatives of the nation. The Sevastopol tragedy appeared to them as a redeeming sacrifice for the sins of the past and an appeal for regeneration. The sincerest patriots put their hopes in the defeat of Russia by the external enemy. In August 1855, Granovsky wrote: "The news of the fall of Sevastopol made me weep. . . . Had I been well enough I would have joined the militia, not because I desired the victory of Russia but because I longed to die for her." '

The parallel between the mood prevailing in Russia during the Crimean War and the intelligentsia's feelings at the time when Kizevetter's essays were published could not escape any reader in 1915–16. See A. Kizevetter, *Istoricheskie otkliki* (Moscow, 1915), pp. 191 ff.

the voters, and that the leadership of the opposition in the next Duma would pass from the Kadets to the Socialist parties.

The conflict inside the Kadet Party remained unresolved until February 1917 and even later. Milyukov had the better of his opponents in the party before the revolution, but immediately after it his grip on his followers weakened, and he was forced to resign from the Provisional Government without protest from his own party. We shall see later that the strength of the Kadet Party opposition to him and its final victory were partly due to the influence of secret societies — the Russian political freemasons — which had infiltrated the Kadet Party and competed with its leaders for the allegiance of many of its members.

4. THE LABOUR GROUPS OF THE WAR INDUSTRY COMMITTEES

An original and particularly important feature of the WICs was the so-called 'Labour Groups' attached to them. Workers employed in the war industries were asked to send delegates to provincial WICs as well as to the Central WIC. This was a new departure in labour relations in Russia and one of considerable political complexity. In fact, Labour Groups functioned consistently only in the Petrograd, Moscow and Kiev provincial WICs and in the Central WIC. Nevertheless, the part they played in the political turmoil preceding the February revolution was of the greatest importance, and we shall revert to it in due course.

The creation of the Labour Groups of the WICs was planned and carried out in 1915–16 by Guchkov and Konovalov in Petrograd and Moscow, and by M. I. Tereshchenko in Kiev. Even before the outbreak of the war, the textile magnate A. I. Konovalov had made contact, through the Bolshevik I. I. Skvortsov-Stepanov,[1] with revolutionary circles and had tried to form a committee for the exchange of political information on which all parties and opposition groups from the Octobrists to the Social-Democrats would be represented, and which would co-ordinate their activities.[2]

A further attempt at co-ordination — this time among Social-Demo-

1. See below, p. 172 f.n.
2. See the report of the Director of the Department of Police, Brune de Saint-Hippolyte, of 13 May 1914, published in Iv. Menitsky, *Revolyutsionnoe dvizhenie voennykh godov, 1914–17* (Moscow, 1925), vol. I, pp. 408 ff., as well as below, p. 172.

crats of all shades — was made on 6 January 1915, when a meeting was called in Moscow. It was attended by Bolsheviks, including Skvortsov-Stepanov, as well as by moderate and patriotic Social-Democrat intellectuals such as the economist S. N. Prokopovich and his wife, E. D. Kuskova, and Maxim Gorky. No general line acceptable to all participants could be found at this meeting. Even on such questions as the approval of war credits in the Duma, unanimity was not achieved. The split inside the Social-Democratic movement did not, however, involve any difference in attitude to the Tsarist government. All Social-Democrats, like the Social Revolutionaries, considered a final and decisive battle against Tsarism inevitable. Their disagreements were mainly about tactics and timing.

The moderates insisted that the victory of Prussian militarism would be detrimental to the proletariat's struggle for political control. They urged the workers to take advantage of wartime conditions to organise themselves politically. The moderates condemned agitation for immediate revolutionary action in wartime as senseless revolutionary pyrotechnics (vspyshkopuskatelstvo). Such a reckless course would only lead to unnecessary sacrifices, and would jeopardise the chances of a successful rising after the end of hostilities, during the demobilisation period. Such views found support even with some of the Bolsheviks.

There was, however, always a hard core of Social-Democrats (both Bolshevik and Menshevik) who, following instructions from abroad from Lenin and Martov,[1] continued to adopt an irreconcilable attitude towards the war, to denounce work in munitions factories as 'treason to the cause of the proletariat', and to insist on immediate revolutionary action, regardless of its chances of success and possible repercussions on the fighting at the front.

When, therefore, in the summer of 1915, the industrialist organisers of the WICs proposed that the workers form special Labour Groups in the WICs, this suggestion met with diametrically opposed reactions from the two camps of organised labour. The Bolsheviks and other defeatist socialist groups (the Maximalist Socialist Revolutionaries, the Internationalist Mensheviks, the Mezhrayonka group in Petrograd and

---

1. Lenin's standpoint is well known from his articles in *Sotsial-Demokrat* and other material which appears in his collected works. Martov's letter on the war has been published by I. Menitsky, op. cit., pp. 174–179. Note the ambiguous comment by Menitsky on p. 179.

others) determinedly opposed the elections to these Labour Groups. They accused the moderates, who were in favour of the Labour Groups, of having become lackeys of imperialism and of helping war profiteers to exploit workers in the war industries. On the other hand, most of the moderates — or 'liquidators' (that is, those Social-Democrats who insisted on legal rather than underground methods of struggle) — were tempted by the opportunities of organising trade-unionism on a large scale with the connivance and support of the industrialists. Guchkov and the other politically-minded industrialists held out dazzling prospects for the future of organised labour in Russia. They spoke of convening an All-Russian Congress of Workers representative of the working classes as a whole; this body would elect an All-Russian Workers' Union, which, in conjunction with the other Voluntary Organisations, would be capable of taking over the administration of the country from the discredited autocratic bureaucracy. The assistance offered by Guchkov, Konovalov and Tereshchenko was welcome to the Labour Groups, although they realised its potential dangers. Trade-unionism could provide a legal basis for the non-violent struggle to achieve purely economic aims, that is, better living and working conditions. Trade-unionism, however, as the main form of political organisation of the working class was anathema to the Bolsheviks and in particular to Lenin, who had always denounced it as a betrayal of the cause of the revolution, which alone could provide an answer to social problems. In the eyes of the Bolsheviks and other extremist revolutionaries, trade-unionism, especially in the form envisaged by 'Messrs Guchkov, Konovalov and Company' was comparable to the police-sponsored labour organisations set up by the notorious Zubatov in the years preceding the 1905 revolution.

The extremists attacked the idea of the formation of the Labour Groups even before they came into being. The first meeting, convened in Petrograd on 29 September 1915 to elect representatives to the Labour Groups, proved abortive; it was decided not to proceed with the elections to the central or to the provincial WICs. K. A. Gvozdev, a Menshevik delegate of the Erikson works who was present, protested in the left-wing papers about alleged irregularities at the meeting, and his protest was supported by the Central WIC. On 29 November another meeting was held, and this time some Mensheviks and Socialist Revolutionaries were elected to the Central WIC (ten persons in all, among them Gvozdev and the secret police agent V. M. Abrosimov). At the same meeting six representatives, equally divided between Mensheviks and Socialist Revolutionaries, were elected to the Petrograd provincial WIC.

Two days after the committee was elected, the Petersburg Committee of the Bolsheviks issued a leaflet addressed to 'all Petersburg proletarians', which began with the words:

> Comrades, treachery has been committed. On 29 November, under the leadership of Guchkov, Mr Gvozdev and Co. enacted a comedy of electing representatives of the Petersburg proletariat to the Central and Petersburg War Industry Committees. A handful of traitors and renegades, acting behind the backs of the working class, has entered into a shady deal with the bourgeoisie and has sold class intransigence and international solidarity of the proletariat for the honour of lounging in the soft easy chairs of the War Industry Committees, under the chairmanship of Guchkov, that henchman of Stolypin who defended the courtmartialling of revolutionaries in 1906. . . .[1]

Kuzma Gvozdev, the leader of the Labour Group on the Central WIC in Petrograd, had to fight on two fronts. On the one hand he had to put pressure on the employers in order to defend the interests of the workers both in the Committee itself and in the Special Councils for Defence on which the Committee was represented. On the other hand, he had to ward off the attacks of the Bolsheviks and placate the wavering workers who had elected him to the Labour Group.

In order to ward off the attacks of the extremists, Gvozdev and his friends drew up a general instruction stating the political principles according to which the representatives of the Labour Group on the Central WIC were to act. This instruction, together with a number of other resolutions passed at the electoral meeting of 29 November, reflected the ambivalence of Gvozdev's position, and was regarded by the Police Department as proof of crypto-defeatism and camouflaged

1. This leaflet was reprinted in No. I of the magazine *Sbornik Sotsial-Demokrata* published by Lenin and Zinovyev in Switzerland. It was sent there by Aleksandr Shlyapnikov, who published in the same issue under the pen name of Belenin an account of Bolshevik activities during the first twenty months of the war. Note that the Bolsheviks refused to accept the new name of 'Petrograd' given to St. Petersburg, denouncing it as jingoistic.

political subversion. The police report[1] quotes the instruction as saying:

> The irresponsible Russian government, having decided to take part in this war, continues at the same time to wage merciless war on its own people, thus bringing the country to the brink of defeat. We declare that this irresponsible government is guilty of all war disasters, but we also think it necessary to declare that part of the responsibility falls on the State Duma and the political parties constituting its majority, which for a whole year have given their support to a régime of military dictatorship and concealed the true facts from the people. . . .
>
> We therefore believe that the immediate task . . . is the convocation of a constituent assembly on the basis of universal . . . suffrage; the immediate introduction of all the civil freedoms (speech, assembly, press and association); as well as the abolition of all national discrimination; the . . . self-determination of all the nationalities inhabiting Russia; immediate new elections to all municipal and zemstvo institutions on the basis of the four-point formula, [i.e. universal and equal suffrage, direct and secret ballot]; comprehensive social legislation, an eight-hour working day, land for the peasants, and immediate amnesty for all those persecuted on political or religious grounds.
>
> While fighting for these demands, the working class will, as always, back every genuine effort by bourgeois circles towards a gradual liberation of the country, but will relentlessly criticise all half-heartedness, lack of determination, and conciliatory tendencies on the part of the liberals and will spur them on to fight the régime with more determination.

In accordance with this resolution, the newly elected labour members of the Central WIC issued on 3 December 1915 a declaration quoted in the same police report as follows:

> Having regard to the present situation in the country and to what is necessary for its defence . . . and believing that the only way out . . . consists in the complete disruption of the existing régime, the working class cannot at present, without deceiving both itself and the people, shoulder responsibility for the defence of the country. Nor can the workers assume reponsibility for the work of the Central WIC, which

1. See *Rabochee dvizhenie v gody voyny*, published by Tsentrarkhiv in the series *Materialy po istorii rabochego dvizheniya*, under the general editorship of Lozovsky, prepared for publication by M. G. Fleer and published by *Voprosy Truda* (Moscow, 1925 or 1926), hereinafter referred to as 'Fleer'. The report of the Police Department is on pp. 269–291.

is essentially an organisation of bourgeois industrialists. If, nevertheless, we decided to take part in the WIC, we did so solely because we considered it our duty to use these institutions to set forth our views on the needs of the country and the means of saving it from destruction; and also to defend the interests of the workers by parrying all attempts to deprive them of their gains, and to help to organise the workers in every possible way.[1]

The police report attached considerable importance to the last point, namely the organisation of labour by the Labour Groups of the Central WIC. It pointed out that the WIC provided the workers' groups with facilities to organise themselves. They were allocated two rooms and a telephone line of their own on the premises of the committee. The Menshevik Bogdanov was appointed secretary to the group, with a salary of 250 roubles a month, and a further allowance was made for an assistant secretary, two clerks, a fund for travel expenses, a fund for the compensation of loss of earnings by members of the group, and petty cash for the office.

The Labour Group thus constituted at once started campaigning for the convocation of an All-Russian Workers' Congress, an object which, as we know, had the support of the Central WIC. The members of the group do not seem to have expressed particular gratitude for the munificence of the WIC leaders. One of them is reported to have said at a meeting of the Central WIC:

> It is perfectly clear that, having created the Central WIC, the representatives of industry are now pursuing three aims: to contribute to the defence of the country, gradually to seize all power, and lastly to line their pockets; all this is alien to the interests of the working class. We therefore ask to be allowed, as representatives of the working class, to attend to the organisation of the workers and the satisfaction of their needs.[2]

The leaders of the WIC continued nevertheless to support the organisational and propaganda work of the Labour Group under Gvozdev, and on 4 January 1916 the Deputy Chairman of the Central WIC, Konovalov, asked the Minister of the Interior to allow the Labour Group to organise workers' meetings—a request which was refused by the Minister.

1. Fleer, p. 278.   2. *Ibid.*

The Police Department was suspicious of the Labour Groups and considered their attempts to organise the labour movement and to act in defence of class interests to be inconsistent with the original charter of the WIC approved by the Council of Ministers in August 1915. Certain industrialists (e.g. the Deputy Chairman of the Moscow provincial WIC, Tretyakov) were also opposed to the formation of Labour Groups and to their claim to cater for working-class interests. However, the energetic intervention of the leader of the Moscow Labour Group, Cheregorodtsev, who was supported by Konovalov, secured the formation of a Moscow Labour Group on the same lines as the Petrograd body. In other towns in the country (Kiev excepted), attempts to hold elections of workers' representatives to the WIC failed, mainly because resolutions of an openly revolutionary character were passed at the electoral meetings. Thus the police reports quote a resolution dated 26 February 1916 passed at the electoral meeting in Samara, which states:

> We are not entering the WIC in order to produce guns to kill our German comrades — we regard this as harmful to ourselves and our brothers-in-arms at war with us, and this is why the war should cease without annexations or reparations, and we list our demands: (1) state insurance for the workers; (2) confiscation and distribution among the peasants of all lands belonging to the crown and the landowners; (3) separation of Church and State; (4) an eight-hour working day; (5) the freedom to strike and to form unions; freedom of the press and inviolability of the person; (6) a general amnesty; (7) a democratic republic.[1]

As we have seen, the police were fully aware of the defeatist and subversive tendencies in the labour circles whose participation in the WIC Guchkov had managed to secure. We shall show later that the police, through its agent inside the Labour Group of the Central WIC, Abrosimov, fostered and encouraged the spread of defeatism and subversion among the workers.[2] They tolerated this propaganda, possibly in accordance with a plan of the Ministry of the Interior to compromise and later indict not only the Labour Groups of the WIC but also those who had insisted on their formation. The final attack on the WIC had to be postponed, however, until, with the imminent end of the war, the WICs would have outlived their usefulness.

1. Fleer, op. cit., p. 284 f.   2. See below, p. 232 f.

2

Labour and the Revolutionary Movement

The Defensists; The Defeatists

I. THE DEFENSISTS

The close co-operation between the 'bourgeois', patriotic leadership of the Voluntary Organisations and the Menshevik and Socialist Revolutionary workers on the WIC was made possible by their common purpose of shaking the foundations of the imperial régime. This was a tactical alliance which could hardly conceal the differences in their ultimate aims. Men such as Guchkov and Konovalov hoped that by weakening the government and discrediting the Tsar they would obtain constitutional concessions; the workers, on the other hand, hoped to open the floodgates of revolution. The co-operation of defensist revolutionaries and liberal reformists was overt and avowed; but a tacit and clandestine understanding between defeatist or 'crypto-defeatist' revolutionaries and the Voluntary Organisations can also be detected. Despite the ferocity of Bolshevik attacks on the Labour Groups and the workers in the war industries, comradely links still existed in the shape of mixed Bolshevik-Menshevik workers' committees in a number of industrial centres. Through such channels arrangements were made for revolutionary workers to evade military service. These workers entered the Voluntary Organisations in 'reserved occupations', which made them immune to conscription. Later the apologists of the Voluntary Organisations tended to deny this practice. But the early memoirs of revolutionaries frequently admit the use of this method of avoiding service at the front.[1] Even Molotov himself (under his real name of V. M. Skryabin) served for a time in the Union of Municipalities in Moscow, before his arrest in June 1915.[2] Other Bolsheviks adopted an ostensibly defensist attitude and gave their services to the

1. See Menitsky, op. cit., and some of the biographies of revolutionaries of that time in the encyclopedia *Granat* (Moscow, 1910–38), vol. XII.
2. Menitsky, op. cit., vol. II, p. 265.

Voluntary Organisations. In fact, they could later claim that they had been much more deeply engaged in the onslaught on autocracy than in the organisation of the war effort. This was true, for instance, of N. I. Iordansky, the regular commentator on topical subjects in the confidential journal published by the Unions' joint committee for the supply of the army.

The activities of the small groups of Bolshevik and other revolutionary defeatists among the working masses in Russia must be viewed against the background of the new industrial situation created by the disruption of the peacetime order, and by the formation of the Voluntary Organisations, especially of the WICs. In comparison with the possibilities for effective action which this new situation presented, the traditional methods of mass agitation used by the revolutionaries — the issue of proclamations on questions of principle, such as the famous resolution on the war published in Switzerland in No. 33 of Lenin's newspaper, *Sotsial-Demokrat* — appeared futile.

The Socialist Revolutionaries were the first to realise that the best hope for furthering the cause of revolution in wartime did not lie in the exploitation of the supposed anti-war feelings of the popular masses — feelings which existed mainly in the imagination of a few revolutionary dogmatists and were given the lie by the spontaneous, patriotic and monarchist demonstrations on the outbreak of war — but in infiltrating the wartime administration, strengthening it and then using it as a shadow government on the day of reckoning, before the demobilisation of the armed forces.

Typical of this attitude was, for instance, a resolution of the Samara group of the Socialist Revolutionary Party.[1] They wrote:

> Taking into account the present war — to which our general attitude can only be negative — and considering that the policy of militarism and imperialism, which is basically opposed to the interests of democracy and was pursued by Germany for many years until it led to the outbreak of the present war, would only become firmer and stronger if Germany emerged victorious in this war; strongly desiring the victory of the coalition over Germany, we are at the present time refraining from all action which might result in the weakening of Russia's power of resistance.
>
> Being firmly convinced that in the event of victory our government

1. Published in Menitsky, op. cit., vol. I, p. 145.

will use every opportunity to strengthen its position, and that the popular enthusiasm aroused by recent events — if it does not assume a revolutionary form — will at best force the government to insignificant concessions which will not lead to democracy; we should, considering the mood of the country, concentrate all our efforts on bringing about — after the end of the war and even earlier if conditions are favourable — a revolutionary movement of the type of an armed rising and a general strike. Our present task, which determines our tactics, is to prepare the popular masses and the army for such action.

The same ideas found far more literate expression in the manifesto[1] issued in September 1915 by a conference of defensist Socialists abroad (including Social-Democrats, followers of Plekhanov, and Socialist Revolutionaries) which claimed that the victory of Germany would result in the degeneration and corruption of a considerable part of the Russian workers. The appeal stresses the danger of a lack of interest on the part of the working class in the outcome of the war, which would be tantamount to political suicide. Those who desired the defeat of Russia out of hatred for the Tsarist government were confusing the government with the fatherland. 'Russia does not belong to the Tsar but to the Russian working people. In defending Russia the working people defend themselves and the cause of their liberation.'

The manifesto goes on to accuse Russian reactionaries of adopting a conciliatory attitude towards Germany, and mentions the rumour that the 'recently retired ministers, Maklakov and Shcheglovitov, handed a memorandum to the Tsar in November of last year in which they explained the advantages of making peace with Germany'.[2]

Adopting a biblical style, the manifesto enjoins the working class to be

as wise as serpents in manipulating the slogan of victory over the external enemy. Every display of revolutionary pyrotechnics (*vspyshkopuskatelstvo*) at the rear of an army in the field would amount to treason; it would help the external enemy and also assist the internal enemy by creating a

1. We quote from the text reprinted in the official report of the Ministry of the Interior 'Review of the Activities of the Russian Social-Democratic Labour Party for the Period from the Start of the War of Russia against Austro-Hungary and Germany up to July 1916', pp. 60 ff. It was originally published in No. III of *Rossiya i svoboda* by G. Aleksinsky in Paris.

2. Those who drafted the manifesto — probably Plekhanov and Chernov — were careful not to insist too much on the correctness of this rumour.

misunderstanding and a rift between the Russian Army and the progressive part of the Russian people. . . . If these elements in our population refuse to take part in the defence of Russia until our present government has fallen, they will only delay this fall.

The manifesto also warns against the revolutionary slogan of 'all or nothing', and claims that the German General Staff would like to see the revolutionaries accept it and would give their support to the preachers of this slogan in Russia. The German General Staff 'needs riots in Russia, strikes in England — anything to facilitate its plans for conquest. But the Russian working people will not come to their assistance.' Finally, the manifesto stresses the importance of penetrating the institutions

> which, under the pressure of public opinion, are now being established for the struggle with the external enemy.[1] . . . The more solid a foothold [representatives of the working people] get in such institutions, the easier it will be for them to fight for the liberation of Russia from its internal enemy. Your representatives should take part in the work not only of special technical organisations (such as the WICs) which have been established to meet the needs of the Army, but also of all other organisations of a public and political character (organs of rural self-government, village co-operatives, workers' unions and workmen's sick funds, zemstvo and municipality institutions and the State Duma).
>
> Freedom cannot be achieved except in the course of national self-defence.
>
> Note, however, that we are far from saying: 'First a victory over the external enemy and only then the overthrow of the internal one.'
>
> It is quite possible that the overthrow of the latter could become a pre-condition and a guarantee of the salvation of Russia from the German threat.[2]

The defensist manifesto can be considered as the basic creed of all the workers' organisations which co-operated in the war effort.

1. i.e. the wartime Voluntary Organisations.
2. The defensist manifesto was signed on 10 September 1915 in Geneva. Note the parallel between the idea of a constitutional change as an essential condition for victory over Germany and similar slogans formulated at this very time, on the eve of the Congresses of the Unions of Zemstvos and Municipalities, in Moscow. Note also the expression 'internal' and 'external' enemy in the manifesto and in Disposition No. 1 of the mysterious Committee of Public Safety, composed presumably also at the beginning of September 1915; see pp. 165 ff.

But in its verbose way it also reflects the essential fallacy of conditional defensism. After all, it was the government machinery which carried the main weight of the war effort. The workers were told to assist this machinery in co-ordinating and directing the war industries, and at the same time they were told to undermine and disrupt its internal structure. Such subtle distinctions were typical of an intellect like Plekhanov's; they could not inspire either a revolutionary man of action or a discontented worker in Russia. On the whole, the defensist workers' organisations interpreted such ambiguous instructions as a call to moderate their demands and renounce the strike weapon in wartime. This is how they were advised by their leaders, Potresov and Maevsky, and by Duma politicians like Kerensky, in whom the workers had some confidence.

2. THE DEFEATISTS

The dividing line between defensists and defeatists was not identical with that between Bolsheviks and Mensheviks, or right and left Socialist Revolutionaries. Some Mensheviks followed Martov in his internationalist, non-defensist attitude; some of the SRs in Russia tried to organise themselves on an anti-war basis. On the other hand, some Bolsheviks abroad (e.g. Aleksinsky) and in Russia (e.g. N.D. Sokolov) joined the defensist ranks. As far as isolated revolutionary outbursts were concerned the attitude of the Bolshevik leadership in Russia underwent a change. If, in 1916, the Petersburg Bolshevik Committee urged the workers to demonstrate and supplied them with arms, we find convincing evidence that on the eve of February 1917, the Bolshevik leaders in Petrograd were far more cautious. They appear to have become the dupes of their own and the liberals' propaganda. They expected that the Minister of the Interior, Protopopov, would emulate his predecessor in 1905–6, Durnovo, and bring the revolution into the street in order to have it shot down by the army. They might also have felt that, with the war nearing its end, the final onslaught on the Tsarist régime should be postponed till the beginning of demobilisation. This is why the Bolsheviks were almost twenty-four hours behind the Mezhrayonka (a mixed organisation of Bolsheviks and Mensheviks in the capital) in issuing their manifesto on 27 February, when the victory of the Petrograd revolutionary crowd and garrison had become obvious.

The influence of the few Bolsheviks who remained active after the outbreak of war in Russia was far less important than official Soviet historiography would have us believe. The number of those who shared Lenin's defeatist attitude was reduced by arrests and deportations, by the call-up, and, to a lesser degree, by defection to the defensists. The remaining active groups were almost without exception closely watched by the secret police, penetrated by their agents, and liable to arrest at any moment. Of some two hundred and forty biographies and auto-biographies of 'Personalities of the U.S.S.R. and of the October Revolution' published in the encyclopedia *Granat*, some forty-five subjects were in emigration and took no direct part in events in Russia; some seventy-three were inactive either because they had lost their faith in the effectiveness of revolutionary struggle (like Krasin) or because they had been deported to Siberia before the war (like Stalin) or in the early months of the war (like the Bolshevik members of the Duma and Kamenev). Of those who were active in the underground during the war (about ninety in all), approximately half were at one time or another betrayed to the police and rendered harmless. Many of those who evaded arrest were merely contributors of moderate Marxist articles to the periodical press; others were working in the revolutionary underground in their place of exile, without making much impact on the situation in the industrial centres.

A few determined and courageous men, like Molotov and Zalutsky, did not give up the struggle even after their arrest and deportation. They escaped, returned to the capitals, and – constantly changing their aliases and living quarters – sometimes succeeded in organising Bolshevik sympathisers among the workers.

In this respect, the career of Aleksandr Shlyapnikov as an active Bol-shevik in Russia is certainly exceptional. One of the few leading Bolshe-viks who qualified as a genuine proletarian, Shlyapnikov had spent some six years as an industrial worker in western Europe, returning to Russia in the spring of 1914 under the alias of a French citizen named Noët. He worked as a metal worker in various factories and took part in the mass strikes in Petrograd both before and immediately after the outbreak of war. He was again abroad when the leaders of the party who were still at large were arrested in the village of Ozerki

(Finland) on 4 November 1914. The Petersburg Committee made desperate attempts to arrange strikes and demonstrations in defence of the arrested Bolshevik Duma deputies and later in protest against their trial and deportation in February 1915. The lack of response from the working masses gives us the measure of the influence the Bolsheviks could exert at that moment. Shlyapnikov blamed the arrested leaders themselves for this lack of sympathy on the part of the workers:

> The deputies' trial went on in an atmosphere of indecision and wavering. The attitude adopted by the deputies in court was perplexing. One got the impression that the deputies did not comport themselves as would befit the supreme responsible centre of the proletariat, but rather as provincial party committees sometimes behave. Many regretted that the comrades' deputies showed so little firmness, but saw the reason for it in the atmosphere of terror. . . .[1]

Shlyapnikov left in September 1914 for Scandinavia on the instructions of the Petersburg Committee in order to establish contacts with the Central Committee of the party. There he met Alexandra Kollontay, the Egeria of the Bolshevik élite, who was then in close contact with Lenin and Krupskaya. Shlyapnikov became her acknowledged consort, and thus enhanced his position in the party considerably. It did not prevent him from returning to Petrograd in November 1915 to carry on underground work. In 1915, he was co-opted member of the Central Committee of the party. He managed in 1916 to go abroad for the second time during the war on a fund-raising expedition to America. On his return he found the Russian Bureau of the Central Committee 'partly arrested and partly disorganised, so that I had to set up a new bureau of the Central Committee'.[2]

Later, in his memoirs of the Russian revolution, Shlyapnikov, despite his party bias, showed himself an honest and intelligent observer of the revolutionary scene. His personal success, however, in those days of underground work and clandestine contacts with the party leadership in exile, must have gone to his head and made him overstate the importance of the Bolshevik underground. In his report on the situation in Russia in the first twenty months of the war, he claims that in spite of lack of assistance from the revolutionary intelligentsia, the

1. From a report by Belenin (Shlyapnikov's *nom de plume*) in No. I of the magazine *Sbornik Sotsial-Demokrata*, published by Lenin and Zinovyev in Switzerland, p. 57.
2. *Granat* autobiography of Shlyapnikov, vol. XLI, part 3, p. 249.

underground activities of the working class never came to a standstill. Shlyapnikov wrote:

> The workers' organisations have put forward their own full-blooded proletarian leaders. . . . As in peacetime, the organisational basis of the underground workers' organisation is the factory, the workshop, the plant. . . . Apart from the permanent organisations of our party, in certain factories, where there are other —not our own— illegal groups (Socialist Revolutionaries, 'united socialists', anarchist-communists), informal conferences of such groups are called to deal with problems of a local nature, mainly arising from clashes among themselves. The attitude towards the war and the struggle against chauvinism and 'patriotic' exploitation is at the centre of all ideological work in industrial centres all over Russia. This wartime work of our organisation demands its own historian. Its grandiose dimensions can be judged by the waves of strikes which never cease to shake the rotten framework of the Tsarist monarchy.

Shlyapnikov admits, however, that the underground printing works could not meet the widespread demand for Bolshevik literature. But he claims that Lenin and Zinovyev's pamphlet 'War and Socialism' of over a hundred pages was distributed in Moscow in typewritten copies, and that photographs of the Bolshevik Duma deputies deported to Siberia (the very same whose undignified behaviour Shlyapnikov deplored in the same article) had been sold in no less than 5,000 copies.

Shlyapnikov's enthusiasm for the new proletarian leadership of the Bolshevik underground groups would have been less pronounced in his report of March 1916 had he known what was fully revealed after February 1917, namely the enormous part played by police agents, both spies and *agents provocateurs*, working in the revolutionary underground. Doubtless leaflets were published in considerable quantities, as Shlyapnikov says, by various ephemeral committees in Petrograd, Moscow and elsewhere; but we now know that this happened with the knowledge of the Okhranka. The Okhranka would usually allow such organisations a certain period of undisturbed activity. As soon as a committee was duly constituted and had acquired the necessary *tekhnika* (that is, the equipment for an underground press) and started publication, the police would descend on it, arrest those concerned, and seize both the printing equipment and the stocks of leaflets. Sometimes they would hand over the evidence of subversive activities to the State Prosecutor's Office for legal action. The suspects would be accused

either of open sedition by issuing appeals for violence or else of belonging to a criminal organisation, the Russian Social-Democratic Party. In
wartime such trials took place in district military courts. These, however, were properly constituted courts with counsel for the defence,
very different from the military courts in zones under the immediate
control of the military authorities. On the whole it is surprising how
lenient these courts were to the accused, whose participation in subversive activities seemed beyond doubt and was later, after the revolution, triumphantly avowed and boasted of by the 'delinquents' themselves.[1] One gets the feeling that certain acquittals were meant by the
courts as a kind of challenge to the authority of the Tsarist government,
and that they were inspired by the anti-government campaign of the
liberal circles and the wartime Voluntary Organisations. In any case,
they betrayed a profound and on the whole justified mistrust of
evidence emanating from the security police, whose practice of provoking revolutionary activities was widely talked of, probably even in
exaggerated terms.

The names of the police agents who had joined underground groups
were indeed legion. Menitsky mentions some fifty of them working in
Moscow alone in the years 1914–16, and other revolutionaries referred
to Moscow as the 'city of provocateurs'.[2] The situation in Petrograd
was not very different from that in Moscow. Perhaps many police
agents were spared exposure because of the sacking and burning of the
secret police headquarters there on 27 February 1917.

It seems, however, that the secret police department in Moscow was
headed by a particularly able and determined officer, Colonel Martynov. Even revolutionaries so well-trained in conspiratorial technique as
Krylenko and Mme Rozmirovich, who arrived in Moscow under
aliases from Switzerland in the summer of 1915, soon fell victim to
Martynov's agents. By November they were under lock and key. Both
had come to Russia as emissaries of Lenin, with whom they had close, if
not always cordial, contacts in Switzerland.[3] Their assignment was to

1. See, for instance, the proceedings against the so-called 'Presnya' group of the
R.S.D.R.P., published in the appendix to Menitsky, op. cit., vol. II, pp. 274–304.
2. See the lists of Moscow Okhranka agents in the appendices to Menitsky, op. cit.,
vols. I and II.
3. They spent some time there in 1915, and Krupskaya had some complaints about
their undisciplined behaviour. See *Leninsky Sbornik*, vol. XI (Moscow, 1931).

help revive the Moscow Bolshevik underground. The police used their discretion in not bringing them to trial; they were deported instead by 'administrative order' – Rozmirovich to Siberia for five years and Krylenko to Kharkov, where he was forced to join the army.

This, incidentally, put an end to the only serious attempt ever made by Lenin to send emissaries to Russia in wartime. He kept in close touch with events in the country by correspondence, in particular with his sisters Maria and Anna, who were themselves under observation by the Okhranka. He seems to have been fully conscious of the difficulties encountered by the Bolsheviks in Russia at that time. His advice and instructions to Shlyapnikov mostly concerned the improvement of conspiratorial technique and the creation of a thin network of underground organisations with very little or no appeal for direct mass action. Lenin was also obsessed by the need to combat contamination by defensists, semi-defensists and 'conciliators', whose chief representative Lenin saw at this time in the person of the head of the Menshevik faction of the Duma, Chkheidze.

Lenin fervently hoped that the upheaval of the war would at some point crack the existing social system. Hence his appeal to the armed forces of the belligerent countries to transform the international war into civil war and to turn their bayonets against their own rulers. But although he warned them not to be deceived by 'the tomb-like silence in Europe at present' (this was written in January 1917!) and claimed that 'Europe is pregnant with revolution', he seemed in those days to expect at best a rising similar to the Russian 1905 revolution in some other country:

> We, the elder generation, will possibly not live to see the decisive battles of this approaching revolution. But I think I can express with great confidence the hope that the younger generation, which is working so wonderfully in the socialist movement in Switzerland and in the whole world, will have the happiness not only to fight but to conquer in the future proletarian revolution.[1]

The later attempts of Bolshevik historians to recreate a heroic past for the party, and to make out that it systematically prepared for the leader-

1. From a lecture to young workers delivered by Lenin on 22 January 1917. See Lenin, *Sochineniya* (2nd and 3rd editions, 30 vols, Moscow and Leningrad, 1926–32 and 1928–37), vol. XIX, p. 357.

ship of the revolutionary movement in February 1917, are a mixture of bombast and falsehood. Not that such people as Shlyapnikov or Molotov did not carry on a courageous and desperate struggle in the face of determined counter-action by the security police. But to claim, as the *Large Soviet Encyclopedia* (first edition) does, that 'Molotov in 1916 succeeded in evading arrest and in taking part directly in the Bolshevik leadership of the revolutionary movement which had prepared the February bourgeois–democratic revolution of 1917' is a travesty of the facts. Molotov had made a determined attempt to re-organise the Bolshevik underground in Moscow in 1915, when he took a job with the Union of Municipalities and was active as a propagandist and Bolshevik organiser among the workers of the Lefortovo district. In June 1915 he was betrayed, arrested and deported to Siberia. On the way he met a number of other Bolsheviks, with whom he escaped back to European Russia. In the spring of 1916, we again find him active, and living on an illegal footing in Petrograd. There he, Shlyapnikov and Zalutsky formed the so-called 'Russian Bureau of the Central Committee of the Bolshevik Party'. This body did not expose itself by maintaining contacts with workers, and thus evaded capture even when the newly-reconstituted Petersburg Bolshevik Committee was arrested on the very eve of the revolution, having been betrayed by the *agent provocateur* Chernomazov. This is why the members of the 'Russian Bureau' were able to take part in the demonstrations of the 27th and 28th, and in the formation of the Petrograd Soviet.

All this does not prove, however, that the February demonstrations, and especially the soldiers' rising, were planned or organised by the Bolshevik leadership. On the contrary, all the evidence goes to show that the Bolsheviks had not managed to set up an organisation capable of provoking mass demonstrations at that time, that they did not expect the revolution to break out before the end of the war, and that in the spring of 1917 in particular they did not believe mass action at all desirable and feared police provocation. The Bolshevik leadership seems to have been taken by surprise by the course of events. As soon as they realised the magnitude of the popular movement and its possible political implications, they decided to jump on the bandwagon. But so after all did everyone who believed that the hour of the old régime had struck, even – after some wavering – the President of the Duma, Rodzyanko.

3

Army and Revolution

*The army at peace and at war; The army and the government;
The army and the Voluntary Organisations; Rodzyanko and the
army; The condition of the army by the end of 1916*

I. THE ARMY AT PEACE AND AT WAR

The overwhelming majority of observers of the Russian revolution
agree on one point: it was brought about and shaped by the war and
war conditions. This, however, is as far as the consensus goes, for
opinions differ widely over the ways in which the war determined the
origins and course of the revolution. In the past it was widely believed
that lack of success at the front and the failure of the government in
the war effort in the rear was, by and large, the primary cause of the
revolution. This interpretation originated in the violent polemics of
liberal and radical circles against the Tsarist government in 1915–17,
and may be suspected of bias. However true this indictment by the
wartime opposition might appear, we must dispute the underlying
contention that a war waged inefficiently and unsuccessfully must
bring about the downfall of the government and of the régime which
carry it on. Defeat in war is not necessarily a prelude to revolution. The
Decembrist uprising of 1825 followed a victorious war. The humiliating
defeat suffered by Russia in the Crimean campaign did not lead to
revolution. But whenever the government and its agencies prove
incapable of channelling and inspiring the energies which emerge
within a nation at war, a revolutionary situation inevitably arises. For
whatever reasons, Nicholas II and his government showed themselves
utterly unable to master these forces, and lost control of them long
before they had become overtly seditious.

This generalisation applies in the first place to the Russian army
itself. The Russian army, after the introduction of general conscription
in 1874, remained a pliant and reliable tool in the hands of the
government. During the 1905 revolution, despite sporadic defections

and mutinies, it was mainly the army and the Cossack units who ensured the victory of the government over the revolutionaries and the masses controlled by them. The armed forces owed special allegiance to the person of the Tsar, and it was no mere formality either for the predominantly peasant other ranks or for the officer corps. This allegiance was maintained both by the mystique of a monarchy ordained by God and the social alienation of the military, who, in their seclusion, were little affected by the political ferment of the time.

The large-scale intake of new conscripts and reservists on the outbreak of World War I changed the situation completely. Young Russian peasants made excellent soldiers, and were rightly considered to be outstandingly hardy and pliable: not so the great mass of bearded family men, their interests deeply rooted in the life of their villages and homesteads, who, after a brief period of re-training, were despatched to the front as reinforcements, ill-armed and often poorly clad and shod.

In the course of the three years preceding the revolution the officer corps underwent an even greater change. The percentage of casualties among officers in the field was even higher than among the soldiers. The mushroom growth of all sorts of headquarters demanding personnel with experience in the field led to rapid promotions and drained the front lines of officers commissioned in peacetime. They were replaced by large numbers of second lieutenants and ensigns who had undergone short-term training at officer-cadet training schools. A course lasting over two years in peacetime was compressed, by 1916, into six months. The social composition of these new officer contingents also changed. An officer's career – with the exception of the Guards – had long since ceased to be the preserve of the upper classes. On the contrary, an army commission was open to people who could by no means be considered privileged, and was in fact one of the main ladders of social mobility. Many high-ranking officers in the war were of far more modest origins and means than some of the leaders of the revolution.[1] An officer's career, however, bound him to a fraternity which was very real, and imposed upon him the demands of an exacting *esprit de corps*. A basic change in the social structure of the officer corps was caused by the tidal wave of newcomers from the wartime emergency officer-training courses. Most of these young men had

1. Compare the lives and backgrounds of Kornilov or Denikin with those of Lenin or Trotsky.

never envisaged the army as the career of their choice; many of them came from the universities and belonged, in their whole outlook, to the Russian radical intelligentsia. Many were involved in the activities of the so-called 'third element', that is, the employees of the Municipalities and Zemstvos, through which the revolutionary parties – predominantly Socialist Revolutionaries – tried to enter the administrative machinery of Russia. Others were in sympathy with the revolutionary parties as such. For the wartime commissioned officers, service in the army had ceased to be a matter of professional pride and emotional involvement, even though most of them had enlisted from patriotic motives. But patriotism as they understood it meant allegiance to their country rather than to the person of the Tsar, even when a conflict between the two was not consciously felt.

2. THE ARMY AND THE GOVERNMENT

The changes in the army affected its relation to the government: it ceased to be a reliable instrument for use against an incipient revolution. When the unrest broke out in Petrograd in 1917 and the question of suppressing the garrison mutiny by force of arms was raised, it was argued on many sides that the army would be both unable and unwilling to do so: it was no longer a select body largely secluded from the prevailing political climate, but had become merely part of the populace clothed in soldiers' greatcoats. There was some strength in this argument, but it must be qualified. In 1917, the assumption that any man in uniform would take orders unquestioningly from the government in an internal conflict was certainly without foundation. And yet it has never been proved that there were *no* units either at the front or even in Petrograd itself ready to answer the call of the government unswervingly. In particular the regular cavalry, where the turnover of men was much slower than in the infantry and where fifty per cent of the men had served under the colours before the outbreak of war, could still be considered reliable.

Relations between the government and the armed forces were further bedevilled by the organisation and the pretensions of the Stavka (GHQ). The constitutional head of the army was, by definition, the Emperor himself. And it was touch and go at the beginning of the war whether or not he might, in view of the magnitude of the conflict, feel it his duty to assume forthwith the command of the armies in the field. For reasons which emerged in later months this did not happen straight away, and the Emperor's ministers and advisers succeeded in persuading him to appoint a commander-in-chief in his stead. For a brief moment the choice wavered between the War Minister, Sukhomlinov, and the Emperor's uncle, the Grand Duke Nikolay Nikolaevich. The eventual appointment of the latter was not conducive to smooth relations between the Stavka and the Ministry of War. In fact, the Grand Duke never missed an opportunity to snub or humiliate the War Minister, although Sukhomlinov enjoyed the full confidence and even esteem of the Emperor. The Grand Duke was an authoritarian, a mystic and a fatalist. He was somewhat handicapped by a singular lack of physical courage, and was conscious of it, although he would not admit to it.[1] Nonetheless, he had a reputation for ruthlessness and the soldierly straightforwardness of one who is harsh with the generals and mindful of the needs and difficulties of the rank and file. His well-known extremely anti-German feelings made him acceptable to the 'hurrah-patriots', and a story that he had persuaded his nephew to sign the manifesto of 17 October 1905 laid a basis for an understanding with the liberal opposition.

The formation of a strong centre of military administration at GHQ led to an encroachment by the military over the civil authorities both at the front and in the area adjoining it. Pronouncements which one would have expected to come from the government, such as the declaration of August 1914 promising autonomy to the Poles, were issued with the authority and over the signature of the Grand Duke. There was persistent and increasing interference from the military in all branches of administration; this affected the whole bureaucratic machinery of the country, especially in transport and supplies.[2] These conflicts between the government and the Stavka opened the way to political manoeuvring and intrigue, which, as we shall see, resulted in a reshuffle of the government in June 1915. In itself the reshuffle could not resolve the basic conflict. The new Council of Ministers seemed inclined to

1. See the rather malicious character sketch of the Grand Duke in the gossipy memoirs of the Chaplain-in-Chief to the Russian Forces, Father G. Shavelsky: *Vospominaniya poslednego protopresvitera russkoy armii i flota*, 2 vols. (New York, 1954).
2. See below, chapters 4 and 7 on the Jews and the 1915 crisis.

accept the situation as permanent, vaguely hoping to fight out their battle with the Stavka at a proposed war council which they hoped would meet under the chairmanship of the Emperor. These and possibly other plans and political intrigues went by the board with the unexpected decision of the Emperor in August 1915 to take over the supreme command of the armed forces.

Henceforth there was much less friction between GHQ and the Council of Ministers, and the centre of gravity in wartime politics shifted to the ever-worsening relations between the Duma and the Voluntary Organisations on the one hand, and the government and Tsar on the other. The considerable recovery of the army's fighting capacity, of which the 1916 summer offensive was a spectacular manifestation, did little or nothing to ease tension. In fact, the opposition's campaign denouncing the government for its allegedly half-hearted war effort and its suspected desire to defect from the Entente was stepped up until accusations of treason were openly voiced both in private and in the Duma. Originating with the upper strata of Russian society, this campaign spread to the popular masses of the capitals and the officers at the front. Wild rumours of Rasputin's influence at court and on policy-making also played a large part in undermining the prestige of the imperial couple and of the government in the whole country.

The decision of Nicholas II to assume supreme command appeared to be his last attempt to preserve the monarchy and forestall the gathering storm by positive action. We have seen how profound were the changes in the composition and organisation of the armed forces after the first year of war. Only the spectacular step chosen by the Emperor gave any hope of re-establishing the traditional link between the monarchy and the army. Nicholas II felt, and rightly so, that only by becoming supreme commander could he renew and strengthen the personal allegiance to himself of the commanders-in-chief, the officer corps and the rank and file. The events of 1916 — the recovery on the front and the regaining of the army's self-confidence — seemed to confirm his expectations. There was, however, one factor which he obviously underestimated: the determination of the leaders of the Voluntary Organisations and of the Duma opposition to win the *élite* of the officer corps to their political ideas and enlist their support for a constitutional reform. In fact what they achieved was to deprive the monarchy of its sole defence against the threat of revolution — the armed forces.

3. THE ARMY AND THE VOLUNTARY ORGANISATIONS

Little has been divulged of the clandestine contacts maintained between the commanders-in-chief of the fronts and the leaders of the political groups dominating the Voluntary Organisations. But the little we know gains enormously in significance if we consider the decisive part played by the commanders-in-chief on the eve of the abdication — a part which made it possible to speak of 'an aide-de-camp generals' revolution'.

It was unavoidable that the generals who were appointed commanders-in-chief of the various fronts should come into official contact with the leaders of the Voluntary Organisations, whose function was to assist the army in the care of the wounded and sick and to organise on an increasing scale the supply of food, clothing, fodder and even ammunition and arms. The leaders of the Voluntary Organisations, as we shall see, were not slow to use these official contacts to complain about the inertia of the government departments and to raise any matter which could exacerbate the relations between the commanders-in-chief and the ministries. Guchkov himself and his deputy, Konovalov, worked on Alekseev at GHQ, while Tereshchenko, the head of the Kiev WIC, busily influenced Brusilov, C.-in-C. of the South-western front, in the same spirit.

Yanushkevich, who had been Chief of Staff under the Grand Duke, was succeeded in August 1915 by General Alekseev, whose excellent work in the extremely difficult retreat operations of 1915 recommended him for this post. He was a modest and retiring man – a scholarly general who was treated by the Emperor with extreme consideration: he used to lunch and dine every second weekday and every Sunday and holiday at the Emperor's table, where he was always treated as the guest of honour. Every morning the two men spent a few hours together discussing the military situation. The harmony between them seemed complete, and there is no indication that the Emperor tried to press any strategic or tactical ideas on his Chief of Staff. In fact, Alekseev was his own commander-in-chief, and every initiative of his was supported by the Emperor. Alekseev was an indefatigable worker, and did not like to delegate much of his power at GHQ to his subordinates. His strategic ideas were influenced by the theories of a most unconventional personality, a certain General Borisov, who had been Alekseev's Quartermaster-General of the Western Front and remained his adviser in a semi-retired capacity.

Alekseev was no courtier, and did not seek any outward sign of recognition of his services. Yet half a year after his appointment as Chief of Staff he was made aide-de-camp general, the highest personal favour the Emperor could bestow on military commanders. On the crucial question of Rasputin's influence on state affairs Alekseev took a passive line. We do not know whether he attacked Rasputin in his reports to the Emperor, but when the Empress, during one of her visits to GHQ, took Alekseev aside and sounded him out on a possible visit by Rasputin to the army in the field, he firmly spoke against it, thus incurring Her Majesty's grave displeasure.

Alekseev's relations with the Tsar remained cordial until his contacts with Guchkov, the chairman of the Central WIC, came to the Tsar's knowledge. The origin and character of these contacts are best illustrated by the telegram sent by Guchkov from his sickbed to the Chief of Staff on 14 February 1916:[1]

> There is an urgent need to talk to you, to give you a report on all the aspects of the WIC's activity, and to obtain your instructions, which are of great importance to the Committee.

As Guchkov was not in a state to come to GHQ, he asked Alekseev to receive his assistant, A. I. Konovalov.

As the political aspirations of the leaders of the Voluntary Organisations became more widely known, Alekseev's contacts with them became less and less innocent. On 14 February 1916, the same day that the above-quoted telegram from Guchkov was received, Lemke noted in his diary that according to certain remarks dropped by General Pustovoytenko (Quartermaster-General) it appeared that there was a kind of conspiracy afoot between Guchkov, Konovalov, General Krymov and Alekseev. It may well be that Lemke, who in spite of his near-Bolshevik

1. The Voluntary Organisations were spreading the rumour that Guchkov was dying, 'having been poisoned by the Rasputin gang'. See M. K. Lemke, 250 *dney v tsarskoy stavke* (Petrograd, 1920), p. 341.

convictions was an accredited war correspondent at GHQ, interpolated this passage in his diary, published in 1920, and antedated the plot. But there can be no doubt about the systematic campaign on the part of the leaders of the WICs, Guchkov, Konovalov and Tereshchenko, to denounce to the Chief of Staff the extent to which the Stuermer government was sabotaging, as they put it, their efforts to secure a steady flow of supplies to the front. The famous letter which Guchkov wrote to Alekseev in August 1916 was only the culmination of this campaign.[1] Alekseev's reaction to these complaints and accusations was to try to get the best he could for the army out of the Voluntary Organisations, without encouraging their political appetites or exacerbating their relations with the government. Still, the plotters from the Voluntary Organisations did not desist and, to judge from the generally accurate factual reports of General Denikin, they continued importuning Alekseev with plans for an immediate constitutional change even when he was recuperating from his illness in the Crimea in the winter of 1916–17.

During Alekseev's absence General Gurko acted as Chief of Staff. The clandestine relations with Guchkov, however, continued under him. The security police, who kept a secret watch on Guchkov's visitors, reported General Gurko among them. This is not surprising: Guchkov and Gurko had known each other ever since the time when Guchkov had served as a volunteer on the Boer side in 1898 and Gurko was Russian Military Agent attached to the Orange Republic. Later, when Guchkov took a great interest in army reform, Gurko belonged to the group of officers who discussed with him the legislative measures which he was piloting through the Duma committees. Early in 1917, Gurko sided openly with the political demands of the opposition: before relinquishing his post as acting Chief of Staff, he impressed on the bored and unwilling Nicholas II the urgent need for 'a government of public confidence'.

The pressure applied by the Voluntary Organisations on the high officers of the army did not seem to have the immediate effect desired. Guchkov at least, in his rather vague testimony to the Muravyev Commission, does not confirm the participation in his plot of the commanders-in-chief.[2] And yet the relentless attacks on the government

1. See below, p. 183 ff.
2. See *Padenie tsarskogo rezhima* (7 vols, Leningrad, 1924–27; the proceedings of the

and the repeated claims that the Voluntary Organisations would have been able to do much more and better for the army, had they not been impeded in their efforts by the ministers, must have caused some heart-searching among the generals. Would not indeed a liberal government — that is, a 'government of public confidence' — working in harmony with the Voluntary Organisations have done better for the army than the existing one? It seems that the generals, or at least Alekseev, had no particularly high opinion of the administrative abilities of those who tried to involve them in the political struggle. But even so, both he and Gurko, as well as the commanders-in-chief of the fronts, were aware of the pressure of public opinion in favour of constitutional change, and they must have felt that this opinion could not be completely ignored lest the nation's morale should drop and the whole war effort collapse.

4. RODZYANKO AND THE ARMY

After September 1915 the Voluntary Organisations, which had criticised Russian military leadership in the dark days of 1915, showed more reticence in this respect, for they did not want to alienate the generals whose support for their political aspirations they hoped to secure. The same cannot be said of the President of the Duma, Rodzyanko. He continued to meddle both in questions of army supplies and of strategy and tactics. This irritated not only the Emperor but obviously the Chief of Staff, Alekseev, himself. On one occasion, when Rodzyanko criticised the purchase of aeroplanes for the army, Alekseev had to warn him, on the Emperor's orders, not to overstep the limits of his office. During a visit to the front in the summer of 1916, where he went in the company of the Duma member V. Maklakov and the chairman of the Kiev WIC, M. Tereshchenko, he visited Brusilov and other generals. There he collected some data for his armchair strategy. As so often happens, generals complained to him that they could have achieved much more in the summer offensive had they been given better troops to command; representatives of the Red Cross petitioned for improvements in their equipment, and complained of the difficult conditions

Extraordinary Investigation (Muravyev) Commission of the Provisional Government, edited by P. E. Shchegolev and referred to as *Padenie*), vol. VI, pp. 278–280, and below, pp. 174 ff.

in which they had to cope with ever-increasing casualties. Rodzyanko also met his son, a young officer at the front, who told him that he should protest to the Emperor about the heavy casualties sustained in the June 1916 offensive. 'The commanding officers are no good at all', the young man is reported to have said:

> Everyone in the army feels that, for no reason, things are getting worse. the men are splendid, there are plenty of guns and ammunition, but there is a lack of grey matter in the generals' heads.... Nobody trusts GHQ. Nobody trusts his immediate superiors.... We are ready to die for Russia, but not for the whim of a general.... Our soldiers and officers all think the same—that if things do not change we cannot achieve victory. You must open the eyes of the Emperor to all this.[1]

As a result of all these impressions, the zealous President of the Duma sent Brusilov a sort of memorandum which the latter forwarded to GHQ. In it Rodzyanko said:

1. The Russian Supreme Command either does not plan its operations in advance, or if it does, fails to carry them out (e.g. the Kovel operation).
2. The Supreme Command does not know how to, or cannot organise a major operation on a new front, partly because it lacks the necessary information, partly because of the total incompetence of military authorities in husbanding their resources (e.g. the Rumanian operation).
3. The Supreme Command has no unified methods of defence and attack, and does not know how to prepare an offensive.
4. There is no system in the appointment and replacement of commanding officers; the appointments to the highest posts are often haphazard and therefore they are filled by people who are quite out of place in them.
5. The Supreme Command ignores the heavy losses, and does not care as it should for the welfare of the soldiers.

Rodzyanko followed this indictment with a long lament on the mismanagement of the 1916 operations, and concluded: 'If things continue in the same way until next spring, when everyone expects that we

1. M. V. Rodzyanko. *Krushenie Imperii*, in *ARR*, XVII, pp. 134 ff.

or the Germans will start an offensive, we cannot expect any better results in the summer of 1917 than in the summer of 1916.'[1]

Doubtless the Brusilov offensive in 1916 had been extremely costly in human lives. Rumours about it spread all over Russia, and Rodzyanko was not the only one to protest against the heavy losses and to doubt their military necessity. Another critic was Rasputin, but whereas Rodzyanko's patriotism was never questioned, Rasputin was later accused of acting in the interests of the Germans, using the losses as a pretext to stop the Brusilov offensive. No such criticism was made of Rodzyanko at the time, but many years later the military historian Golovin remarked, having quoted the above passages from Rodzyanko's memorandum to Brusilov: 'Reading these lines now one can hardly imagine that they were written after a great victory, unequalled in the years 1914, '15, '16 by any of the Entente powers.'[2] Needless to say, these pronouncements of the President of the Duma did not greatly endear him to Alekseev. After the formation of the Provisional Government, Rodzyanko warned it against appointing General Alekseev Supreme Commander of the armed forces.[3]

5. THE CONDITION OF THE ARMY BY THE END OF 1916

As regards Rodzyanko's estimate of army morale, supplies and leadership, it was certainly influenced by the atmosphere at the rear, by the commentaries of his fellow-travellers on the journey to the front, Maklakov and Tereshchenko, and by the tendency of an authoritarian but ill-informed mind to pronounce judgement on every subject under the sun with complete self-assurance. It is in striking contrast to the opinion of General Knox, a competent British soldier who had been attached to the Russian army throughout the war. According to him

> ... the prospects for the campaign of 1917 were brighter than they had been in March 1916 for the campaign of that year.... The Russian infantry was tired, but less tired than it had been twelve months earlier.

1. General N. N. Golovin, *Voennye usiliya Rossii v mirovoy voyne* (Paris, 1939), vol. II, pp. 165 ff.
2. Golovin, op. cit., vol. I, p. 166.
3. *Krasny Arkhiv* 1922, vol. II, pp. 284–286.

... The stocks of arms, ammunition and technical equipment were, almost under every heading, larger than they had been even on mobilization—much larger than they were in the spring of 1915 or of 1916, and for the first time supplies from overseas were arriving in appreciable quantities.... The leading was improving every day. The army was sound at heart.... There can be no doubt that if the national fabric in the rear had held together ... the Russian Army would have gained fresh laurels in the campaign of 1917, and in all human probability would have exercised a pressure which would have made possible an Allied victory by the end of the year.[1]

Notwithstanding General Knox's optimistic estimate of the state of the Russian army on the eve of the revolution, a grave situation was threatening: Russia's resources were almost exhausted. Surprisingly, this applied first of all to manpower reserves. Russia had over-mobilised her manpower, and any further drain on it for the armed forces threatened to weaken the depleted labour force to a degree which would make the work of war industry and transport impossible. The legislative assemblies issued a warning against complying with renewed demands from GHQ for men. Members of the State Council and the Duma who also sat on the Special Council of Defence presented a well-argued memorandum against further mobilisation and suggested alternative measures for increasing the fighting capacity of the armed forces. Although GHQ rejected these arguments, at heart they knew that by the end of 1916 the call-up of further age-groups would meet with ever-increasing opposition.

General Gurko, after he replaced Alekseev as acting Chief of Staff, in November 1916, initiated a reform in the structure of the army to reduce the number of battalions in a regiment from four to three. The battalions thus made available were to form, with the addition of some rearguard troops, the so-called 'third divisions', so that with one new division for every two former ones the total number of divisions would be increased by fifty per cent. This would, according to Gurko, provide the additional operational units required by GHQ for their planned spring offensive of 1917. Gurko's initiative proved to be an unhappy one. The reform was launched too late, seriously affected the

1. Sir Alfred Knox, *With the Russian Army, 1914–1917* (London, 1921), pp. 551–552. Winston Churchill's estimate of the military situation was substantially the same. See Winston S. Churchill, *The World Crisis 1916–1919* (London, 1927), vol. I, p. 223.

cohesion of the front, and threatened to delay the start of the spring campaign. The men released by the front-line divisions were usually inferior from the physical and moral point of view. The front-line divisions refused to share technical equipment and ammunition with these new units, and so they remained in the rear, unarmed and ill-equipped, forming a kind of third-class reserve rather than units inter-changeable with the original divisions. After the outbreak of the revolution, these grey-coated 'third divisions' disintegrated into the idle, emotionally unstable and politically confused mob which attended the endless meetings so typical of the street scenes of those days.[1]

The threat of a breakdown in railroad transport and supplies of food and fodder for the army also began to be felt in the winter of 1916–17. The first signs of strain were probably the slowing down of the turnover of rolling-stock on the railways and a shortage of serviceable loco-motives. This affected, in the first instance, bulky consignments such as fodder. Alarming as the situation might have appeared in February 1917, one could confidently expect that a seasonal improvement would take place by the time the spring offensive operations agreed on by the Allies were due to begin.

In addition to the strain on manpower and transport, a grave crisis in Russian agriculture began to loom late in 1916. Throughout the war Russia had had good harvests, but the depletion of the labour force through over-mobilisation made harvesting increasingly difficult, es-pecially on the larger estates. Then there was steady depreciation of agricultural implements, which were difficult to replace now that industry had switched over to wartime production. Very much the same factors as in agriculture affected the situation in the fuel industry, especially in the mines of the Donets coal basin, where production was falling alarmingly.

How far all these difficulties were due to the incapacity and negligence of the government it is difficult to say. Sooner or later they would have arisen as a result of the exigencies of the war effort, whatever the administration might have done, as they had arisen in the other belli-gerent countries of Europe. But in Russia they were used as evidence that the government was leading the country 'to the verge of ruin', and that the only means of salvation lay in a constitutional change and in the formation of a 'government of public confidence'. Just as

1. Golovin, op. cit., vol. I, pp. 97 ff.

Rodzyanko put the blame on GHQ for the enormous losses suffered in the Brusilov offensive of 1916, so the Voluntary Organisations used every crisis which emerged as the war developed to discredit the government and bring nearer the radical change they desired.

For a few weeks at the beginning of 1917, the lobbies of the Inter-Allied Conference in Petrograd became a focal point in Russia's internal political battles. Pressure was brought to bear on the Allies, and in particular on Lord Milner, to intercede with the Emperor in favour of constitutional reform. General Gurko, who had been won over to the point of view of the Voluntary Organisations, even ventured to approach the Emperor himself.[1] Lord Milner, as we shall see, was more diplomatic and cautious than Gurko or the British Ambassador in Petrograd, Sir George Buchanan. Was it perhaps because he was not entirely convinced that the people vested with 'public confidence' would do a better job than the ministers appointed by the Tsar? His pronouncements before leaving Russia, on the very eve of the revolution, seem somewhat ambiguous and bent on pleasing all sides. They reflect, however, the peculiar atmosphere at that critical moment. Reporting on Lord Milner's last statement before he left Russia, *The Times* correspondent noted in a dispatch (25 February/9 March), which happened to be the last he sent before the revolution, that Lord Milner's statement was 'received here with satisfaction'. The correspondent added the obviously Russian-inspired commentary:

> The best answer to any misapprehension or misgivings that may have been engendered by the failure of the administrative machine to cope with the enormous difficulties of the present war will be forthcoming when the great armies assembled on the eastern front enter upon the spring campaign.

This was not to be, for as *The Times* correspondent pronounced his '*les jeux sont faits*' for the great gamble at the front, the red ball of revolution started spinning through the blizzard-swept streets of Petrograd.

1. See below, p. 238, and General N. N. Golovin, *Rossiiskaya kontr-revolyutsiya v 1917–18*, part I (Paris, 1937; copyright Hoover Library), Gurko's statement on p. 109.

4

The Jews and Revolution

The historical background: The Jews and the war

Much has been said about the part played by the Jews in the Russian revolutionary movement and in the revolution of 1917. There is, we believe, no case for treating the part of Russian Jewry in the latter as a uniformly revolutionising factor. If in this chapter we deal expressly with the crisis which the so-called Jewish problem in Russia had reached in the third year of the war, this is because we think that it may explain a widespread tendency among Russian and non-Russian Jews alike to consider the fall of the Tsarist régime as a twelfth-hour solution to an otherwise insoluble situation. The full significance of this attitude became clear only in the phases of the revolution which followed the period under investigation in this book. We felt, however, that we should deal with the problem of the Jews in Russia on the eve of the February days, if only because it represents an important aspect of the background to the break-up of Imperial Russia.

I. THE HISTORICAL BACKGROUND

The presence of 'second-rate citizens' who by law are denied certain essential rights always tends to become a festering sore on the body politic. This condition is usually malignant, for it shows a tendency to persist despite the increasing strains it causes in national life. Even where the original disparity in the legal position of citizens does not derive from violent oppression as the result of conquest or colonisation, the prolonged underprivileged status of disinherited groups leads to the building up of vested interests. On the other hand, the manifest injustice of such a system undermines national solidarity and the civic loyalty of its victims, and this in turn is then used as an argument for the mainten-ance of the very evil which was the cause of their disaffection in the first place.

48

The history of the sporadic attempts by the Russian state to solve the so-called Jewish problem is a vivid illustration of these truisms. The Jews found themselves subject to Russian rule in the eighteenth and nineteenth centuries by no choice of their own; they did not come as refugees or settlers to the Russian realm. Nor was it ever the explicit intention of the Russian government to incorporate or accept a large number of Jews as the Tsar's subjects. The great majority of the Jewish population was incorporated as a result of the westward expansion of the realm and the inclusion in it of the Ukrainian and Lithuanian provinces, as well as through the successive partitions of Poland. The Jewish communities were taken over by the Russian administration in the form in which they had existed for centuries in these western provinces. Their co-existence with the local population and their relations with the state authority were based on an official recognition of the Jewish communities' autonomy in their internal affairs. Nor were the Jews originally expected — or willing — to assume the same duties, profess the same allegiance, or claim the same privileges and rights as other citizens. They were in this sense foreigners whose presence was tolerated and sanctioned by long-term agreements considered profitable both for the state and the Jewish communities. This sort of relationship was not altogether unfamiliar to the Russian authorities. Similar relations were maintained in some eastern and southeastern provinces with small groups of ethnic minorities (*inorodtsy*), mostly of Muslim culture. In the course of time, these minorities tended to break up and become Russified, but there always remained a traditionalist hard core which was content to vegetate quietly, surrendering most of its autonomy to administrators appointed from Moscow or Petersburg. Progressive revivalism in such communities did occur in the nineteenth century, but was mostly confined to small intellectual groups without any appreciable following in the masses.

The Jewish minority which the Russian state unintentionally incorporated in the western provinces was of a very different character. Here a deep-rooted devotion to the preservation of a national religious tradition was always combined with an expectation of future developments which would radically change the destiny of the nation for the better, and vindicate the suffering and sacrifices sustained in the maintenance of the ancient heritage.

This expectation of a redemption which, unlike that of the Christians, would not be personal but would affect the whole Jewish nation and, through it, the destiny of mankind, provided the moral and ideological justification for the adventurous and the enterprising to break with the stuffy, inbred and decayed atmosphere of the ghetto communities. During the eighteenth and nineteenth centuries, Russian governments, themselves traditionalist and harbouring vague expectations of an historical apotheosis (e.g. Dostoyevsky's cross on the Hagia-Sophia and similar historiosophic visions), were naturally prone to view such escapees from the Jewish communities with extreme suspicion. They were always determined not to admit Jewish settlers into the Russian provinces proper, and in the eighteenth century set up a barrier known as the 'pale of settlement' beyond which Jews were not allowed to establish legal domicile.

The area of the pale and the conditions of settlement varied throughout that period, as did all regulations concerning the Jews' legal disabilities, in a kind of pendulum swing of limited amplitude. There were areas where Jews were allowed to live in towns but not in the country; areas where they could lease land but not own it; they could at times operate taverns, even in villages, only to be unexpectedly deprived of their licences and livelihoods; Jewish artisans could at one time practise their crafts outside the pale, but this privilege was withdrawn when it was discovered that some so-called artisans were using their permits for small trading or other middleman activities. On the whole, the policy of the Russian government was to give to those who had and to dispossess the have-nots. Thus Jewish businessmen who had qualified as merchants 'of the first guild' – that is, had achieved a considerable turnover – were allowed to reside anywhere in the empire. Some of them amassed enormous fortunes and became important factors in the economic life of the country (for example, the Polyakov, Ginzburg, Brodsky, Zaitsev and other families). The same freedom to settle extended to bearers of recognised scholarly degrees, qualified lawyers, doctors, veterinary surgeons and the like. Prominent artists were also in this category.

The Jewish contribution to Russian cultural life had become appreciable towards the end of the nineteenth century, and yet important limitations remained in force, even for those to whom the law of the pale of settlement did not apply. No Jews were allowed to become civil servants in the strict sense of the word, although many were in one way or another employed by the state. No Jew could become an officer in the Russian army, although all were subject to military duty on the same basis as the other subjects of the Tsar. Admission to state secondary schools, universities and other institutions of higher education was limited to a certain percentage of the total number of students, the so-called *numerus clausus*. No legal marital bond could be entered into by an Orthodox Christian with a person of Judaic (or any other non-Christian) confession. While a Jew was allowed to practise as a solicitor he was debarred from being a public notary. None of these regulations was absolutely watertight: Jewish doctors were at times allowed to serve in the army; Jews were sometimes allowed to teach in art schools, and so on.

But the very application of restrictive legislation, however lenient, led to further abuses. These limitations channelled the activities and aspirations of enterprising and energetic men towards those occupations still open to them, especially in trade. This resulted in what were considered to be Jewish monopolies in certain branches of trade (timber, wheat export, stockbroking), which in turn caused irritation among the Russian population and led to a clamour for further legal restrictions or restrictive police practices. In other words, the very existence of citizens of different legal status inevitably brought in its train an increase of gross administrative malpractices.

It is remarkable that the one step which could have brought a solution in any individual case, namely the adoption of Christianity, if not Orthodoxy, was very rarely resorted to. We must not forget that the legal definition of 'Jew' in all the laws and regulations establishing legal disabilities was that of a person of 'Judaic confession'. Conversion automatically removed these limitations. Why, then, was it such a rare occurrence? Through centuries of life in the *diaspora* Judaism had developed its own methods of defence against possible defection. Every religious Jew was brought up to believe that by 'betraying the faith of his fathers', he would not only lose his soul but inflict irreparable damage on the family and community he was leaving. He and his posterity would be cursed, and any link between him and his family, friends or community would have to be broken forever. A father who refused to break off personal contacts with a daughter who had been converted to Christianity could not normally continue to reside among his co-religionists, however respected and influential a person he might be.

Under these circumstances it is understandable that, however strong the desire for assimilation among the educated Jews in Russia proper, and however tenuous their links with their family and community of origin, a barrier remained which prevented them from breaking with their religion. This barrier could only be overcome either by a cynical disregard of any pietistic values, or by a genuine change of religious conviction powerful enough to outweigh awe-inspiring taboos and to replace the spiritual links maintained from childhood with those provided by the new faith. Outside these two groups, conversion was psychologically impossible, even for those Jews who had thoroughly assimilated all the elements of Russian culture and especially its literature and poetry, which were themselves deeply rooted in the Christian tradition of the country.

Their tacit hostility to the Christian elements in Russian civilization, and especially to its Orthodox expression, did not make the attitude of the assimilated Jews to the Russian state any easier. Having freed themselves from all but a formal tie with the obscurantism of the theologically-controlled Jewish community, such Jews could hardly be expected to accept the official concept of a theocratic monarchy; the more so since the liberal and radical movements in the Russian intelligentsia gave grounds for hope that this concept would be replaced by the idea of the common will or representative government, with no theological strings attached. Liberal and radical circles were only too glad to accept reinforcements from the Jewish camp in their struggle against autocracy, and did not expect them to make the difficult decision on conversion. In the Kadet Party, in the legal profession, among fellow doctors, the Jews in Russia could feel themselves part of a movement to which they could give their unrestricted allegiance. And yet this path was open only to the relatively few, who had, by force of exceptional personal gifts or family wealth and influence, squeezed through the bottleneck of the *numerus clausus*. Most of them were enlightened and courageous men whose moderation in the face of continual provocation, childhood memories of persecution, and pressure on the part of their less-fortunate brethren appears both admirable and moving. Many of them, such as Pasmanik, Sliozberg, Vinaver and others, have left us detached and illuminating memoirs of their lives and of the crises through which they lived. The collapse of Russian liberalism did not shake their allegiance to the ideals of the Russian intelligentsia, and there were hardly any among them who would have preferred life and service under the Soviet régime to the existence of so-called 'White Russian' political émigrés. A few of them even took part in the struggle of the White armies against the Bolsheviks, despite the anti-Semitic excesses which were not infrequent in the areas controlled by the White armies.

But, as we have said, assimilation and indeed incorporation into the Russian radical intelligentsia were open only to the select few. The rebel who had broken out of the ghetto was naturally drawn to the revolutionary movement. It is remarkable, however, that relatively few of the Jewish revolutionaries who swelled the ranks of the underground parties at the beginning of the century joined the terrorist group of the Socialist Revolutionaries. The majority of them became Social-Democrats, Marxists and predominantly Mensheviks. For this there are probably many reasons, of which at least two — an ideological and a social one — are obvious. Marxism provided a theory of radical social transformation which was not unlike traditional Jewish Messianism but claimed to be based on common sense and scholarly theory. It promised also a society which would break with Christianity, and to which the Jews could therefore assimilate more completely than to the existing social and political order whose very language was steeped in the Christian tradition. Apart from this ideological attraction the practical side of Social-Democracy also attracted the Jewish social rebel. The organisation of workers and the use of the strike weapon for the improvement of their condition was first tried out systematically in the Russian Empire in the pale of settlement in Jewish-owned factories employing Jewish labour. The experience and tradition of the Jewish Social-Democrats, as organised in the 'Bund', were taken over more often than not, together with their propagandists and organisers, by the Russian Social-Democratic movement.[1] The 'Bund' soon clashed with the Bolshevik wing of the Russian party over the former's claim to the exclusive right to organise all Jewish workers in Russia. The Menshevik wing, however, later maintained close relations with the 'Bund', and it was from the 'Bund' that they learned the tactics which were to replace terror and insurrection as the main weapons in the social struggle. On this point the Mensheviks again came into sharp conflict with the Leninists, who denounced them as 'liquidators' and accused

1. See H. Shukman, *Relations between the Jewish Bund and the RSDRP, 1897–1903.* D.Phil. thesis, Oxford, 1961 (unpublished).

them of class treason and of the betrayal of the great principle of social progress through revolution.

The attraction of revolutionary theories for the emancipated Jew was quite natural, and yet it was considered by the government to indicate seditious tendencies deeply rooted in the mentality of the Jews as such. After 1905, when the part played by Jews as propagandists and organisers of the revolutionary parties became manifest, the government began to realise that something must be done to counteract their increasing support of these revolutionary parties. Stolypin attempted a statesmanlike approach to this problem. He planned to abolish restrictive anti-Jewish legislation, but met with the opposition of the Tsar. It was clear that Nicholas II would not think of the Jewish question in terms of social dynamics, but rather of police methods. If the Jews were seditious they must be rendered harmless by limiting their activities. That this limitation was itself a cause of sedition was an intellectual subtlety which a responsible administrator could not even discuss. Moreover, the so-called patriotic organisations, such as the Union of the Russian People, the Union of the Archangel Michael and the Union of the Double-Headed Eagle, proclaimed themselves leaders of the popular masses in a crusade against the revolution and especially against Jewish subversion. This 'crusade' soon took on the traditional form of pogroms. The connivance of the central government and of the local authorities in the pogroms may have been exaggerated both by the Jews and the radical Russian intelligentsia, who were eager to grasp every opportunity to expose the lawlessness and arbitrariness of the Russian administration. One cannot, however, argue in defence of the Tsarist government on this count. The government actively supported the so-called 'spontaneous patriotic organisations' and was hence responsible for the excesses they committed.

Their conviction that anti-Semitism in its most objectionable form was predominantly government-inspired led the liberal and radical intelligentsia to assume that by abolishing government restrictions and introducing 'equality of rights for Jews', the Jewish problem would be solved and anti-Semitism would wither away. It needed the experience of Hitlerism and even more the recently documented manifestations of anti-Semitism in the Soviet Union itself to show that formal legal equality would not, even in the long run, remove the most insidious and socially dangerous forms of anti-Semitism. But at the beginning of this century, the radical and liberal intelligentsia believed that the problem could be solved simply by the abolition of restrictions on the Jews, and it lost no opportunity of putting the responsibility for all anti-Semitic excesses on the government and administration.

2. THE JEWS AND THE WAR

And yet there is no reason to assume that the 'Jewish problem' in Russia had reached an impasse by the time World War I broke out, or that a solution to it could be found only in social revolution. The growth of legal guarantees for the freedom of the individual seemed to hold out a promise for the gradual disappearance of bureaucratic arbitrariness and abuses. The cultural assimilation of educated Jews to the Russian intelligentsia was making rapid progress despite the countervailing influence of Zionist nationalism. The strongholds of anti-Semitism, the so-called patriotic organisations, had by then been discredited both in the eyes of the government and of the public, although for different reasons. The liberal intelligentsia had become conscious of the need to fight anti-Semitism with enlightened propaganda such as that undertaken, for instance, by the writer Korolenko. All these factors favouring a peaceful solution of the Jewish problem were destroyed at one blow soon after the outbreak of war by the wicked and inane policy of the military administrations toward the Jews in the areas adjoining the front.

Declarations and protestations of loyalty by Jewish representatives at the beginning of the war were in full harmony with the general upsurge of patriotic feelings and clamour for national unity throughout the empire. There was no indication of any seditious movements among the Jews during the mobilisation; representatives of Jewish communities insisted on being received everywhere the Emperor went, and munificent donations by Jewish committees to hospitals and the Red Cross were widely advertised. However, the sincerity of these manifestations was naturally questioned by all those who knew the degree of the Jews' alienation from a state which recognised them only as second-class citizens.

Certain moves by German Jewry at the time were bound to heighten suspicion against the Jews in the western provinces. Not only did the

German Zionists proclaim their full support for the cause of the Central Powers, but one of them, the financier Bodenheimer, created, with the collaboration of both Zionist and non-Zionist Jews in Germany and with the support of the German Ministry of Foreign Affairs, a 'Committee for the Liberation of Russian Jews' whose task it was to undermine any allegiance to the Russian cause subsisting among the Jews of the pale of settlement and to win them over to the idea of a German victory. Unfortunately Bodenheimer got in close touch with the Political Section of the German General Staff, at the time organised by Count von Hutten-Czapski. But the idea of German-Jewish co-operation was short-lived. When hopes for a *Blitzkrieg* victory vanished after the battle of the Marne, the German Jews became less eager to enlist the support of Russian Jews in the German cause. The international Zionist conference in Copenhagen in December 1914 called upon all Zionists in the belligerent countries not to compromise the movement by identifying it with either of the warring camps. But the damage of the first weeks of the war had been done. A flood of propaganda from the 'liberation committee' had been directed towards the Jewish population in Russia. Not much of this propaganda can have reached its target in war conditions, although among the Jews of Galicia, to whom it was easier to distribute the tracts of Bodenheimer's committee, it may have had some effect. The Political Section of the German General Staff had gone so far as to plan an appeal to the Jews in Russia to rise in arms and strike at the rear of the Russian army. Even Bodenheimer recognised the terrible implications for Russian Jewry of such an appeal, and the appeal which was actually issued by the German and Austrian High Commands was on more moderate lines. Nevertheless, it was still more than enough to alarm the Russian military authorities. Warnings were issued to the Russian troops about the dangers of the Jewish population collecting information on troop movements in their towns and villages. Such instructions, when they were received by anti-Semitic officers or traditionally Jew-baiting Cossack troops, led to the discovery of large numbers of Jewish 'spies' who had observed the passing of a battery or a cavalry unit and were therefore seized, summarily court-martialled, and hanged.

The frequent reports of such incidents confirmed the Chief of Staff, Yanushkevich, in his pathological suspicions concerning the wholesale disloyalty of the Jewish population of Poland, Galicia and the

Bukovina.[1] These suspicions in their turn led to the mass deportations of Jews from large areas adjoining the front in the spring and summer of 1915. Later, when such deportation orders were sometimes revoked, a system of taking hostages was instituted. These hostages were to answer for any denunciations by Jews of Russian citizens in areas which had fallen to the German armies. This measure was less troublesome to the local authorities inside Russia than mass deportations, but if possible only increased the bitterness of Jewish feelings.[2]

The mass deportations were the most tragic consequence of the campaign of 1915, which the then Minister of War, Polivanov, described with bitter irony as 'the stage of refugee evacuation in military operations'. In a summary of the discussion in the Council of Ministers dealing with the refugee problem, A. M. Yakhontov noted the following points made by various ministers.[3] The scorched earth policy carried out over a wide area by GHQ in the face of powerless opposition by the government had led to a further disruption of life inside Russia after the defeats at the front. In the flood of refugees the Ministers distinguished three main categories:

First of all the Jews, who despite repeated warnings by the Council of

1. See a short collection of documents on the persecution of the Jews during the war in *ARR*, XIX, in particular Document 9, p. 250.
2. In a pathetic protest against the taking of hostages, the Jews in the town of Vilkomir wrote to the Commander-in-Chief of the armies of the north-western front: 'We are extremely grieved by the demand for hostages, implying an admission of the wholesale accusations of Jewish treachery spread maliciously despite the fact that such accusations have almost always been proved false when examined by duly-constituted judicial authority. The firm conviction of the non-existence of Jewish treachery does not lessen our fear of malicious provocation or false denunciations by perjurers, which could easily influence a hastily-convened court-martial whose decision might spell doom for hostages. . . . Please punish with the full severity of wartime legislation any of us whose guilt is proved, but do not force us to jeopardise the lives of innocent co-religionists by delivering them as hostages to the tender mercies of the enemies of Jewry.' *ARR*, XIX, p. 257.
The Jews of Vilkomir, when referring to judicial investigations of Jewish treachery, obviously had in mind such cases as the Mariampol affair. Jews in that town were accused of assistance to the Germans after the town had been abandoned by Russian troops in 1914. Owing to the intercession of the writer Korolenko and Gruzenberg' defence, the case was retried and all the accused were acquitted. See O. Gruzenberg, *Vchera* (Paris, 1936), pp. 89–95.
3. See *ARR*, XVIII, pp. 32 ff. On Yakhontov and his notes, see below, p. 134 n.

Ministers are being driven with *nagaykas* [cossack whips] from the area adjoining the front, and who are all indiscriminately accused of espionage, signalling and other acts of assistance to the enemy. Of course all this Jewish crowd is extremely embittered and comes to its place of banishment in a highly revolutionary mood. The situation is rendered even more difficult by the fact that local people, who are increasingly feeling the burden of war, give the hungry and homeless Jews a rather unfriendly reception. Secondly, there is the personnel of the civil administration and military organisations in the rear, with scores of wagonloads of personal property. As thousands of people tramp along the railway tracks they are passed by trains loaded with upholstered furniture from Army Officers' Clubs and all sorts of rubbish, including canary cages belonging to bird-loving supply officers. Then, thirdly, there are the voluntary refugees, most of them terrified by rumours of extraordinary German atrocities and violence....

People have been thrown out of their homesteads with only a few hours to prepare for their departure, and have been chased into the unknown. Whatever supplies they had, and sometimes even their homes, were set ablaze before their eyes. It is not difficult to understand their feelings.... All this confused, exasperated, exhausted crowd fills all the roads in a continuous stream, impeding troop movements and throwing life at the rear of the army into utter chaos. Everywhere slow-moving carts with household goods and cattle dragging their feet... people dying in hundreds from cold, hunger and disease... child mortality reaching terrific dimensions... unburied corpses by the roadside, and so on and so on.

A few days later, on 4 August 1915, the refugee situation was again bemoaned at the meeting of the Council of Ministers, this time with particular reference to the Jews. Enlarging on the conditions in which compulsory evacuation was carried out, Yakhontov gives the following picture pieced together from the reports given by various ministers at this meeting:

Since the beginning of our retreat at the front, the Council of Ministers has more than once had to deal with questions concerning the Jews. At GHQ they have formed the opinion that the Jewish population in the war theatre is a hotbed of espionage and assistance to the enemy. Thus the idea was put forward that it was necessary to evacuate the Jews from the areas adjoining the front. This measure was first applied in Galicia. Authorities at the rear of the army began to deport thousands upon thousands of Jews into the interior of Russia. This of course was done on a compulsory, not a voluntary basis. Jews were expelled wholesale regardless of age or sex. The deportees included the sick, the invalid, and even pregnant women. Rumours concerning this measure and the accompanying violence have spread both inside Russia and abroad. Influential Jewry has sounded the alarm. Allied governments have begun to protest against this kind of policy and have pointed out its dangerous consequences. The Ministry of Finance has experienced various difficulties in carrying out its financial operations. The Council of Ministers has repeatedly drawn the attention of the Supreme Commander and of General Yanushkevich, both in writing and in personal representations by the Premier and individual ministers, to the necessity of dropping the persecution of Jews and the wholesale accusations of treason against them, explaining that this was required by considerations of both internal and foreign policy. Yet G.H.Q. has remained deaf to all arguments and persuasion. On the contrary, when in the course of our retreat the evacuation of Russian provinces began, compulsory migration of Jews on a large scale was carried out by specially assigned military detachments, first in Courland and then elsewhere. What went on in the execution of these operations defies description. Even inveterate anti-Semites came to members of the government with protests and complaints concerning the revolting treatment of Jews at the front. As a result, life in those provinces of the pale of settlement to which the involuntary refugees have been driven by the military authorities has become intolerable not only for the motley crowd of destitute newcomers but also for the indigenous population. All sorts of crises — of food supplies, housing and so on — have become even more acute. Epidemics have broken out. The mood on the spot has assumed an increasingly alarming character: the Jews have a grudge against all and sundry, and the local people resent both the uninvited guests, who in any case are branded as traitors and spies, and also the intolerable deterioration in their own living conditions.

The Jewish intelligentsia and Russian public opinion, which is at one with them, are indignant to the highest degree; the press, the Duma parties, various organisations, individual prominent representatives of Russian Jewry are demanding from the government decisive action to stop this mass persecution. In allied countries, and especially in America, fervent appeals are being issued to aid the suffering Jews in Russia; protest meetings are taking place against ethnic persecution, and so on. As a result of this movement, we are experiencing increasing difficulty in obtaining loans both on the internal and foreign markets.

In this threatening atmosphere the Minister of the Interior, Prince Shcherbatov, urged the Council of Ministers to take immediate steps to remedy the situation:

> Our efforts to talk reason to GHQ [he said] have all been in vain. We have tried all possible means of combating their prejudiced attitude. All of us, both together and individually, have spoken, written, begged, complained. But the almighty Yanushkevich does not feel bound to consider the interest of the state as a whole. Part of his plan is to nurture the army's bias against all Jews indiscriminately and to make them responsible for the setbacks at the front. This policy has already borne fruit, and a pogrom mood is ripening in the army. However unpleasant it is to mention it, I will not conceal my suspicion from you in this private meeting that Yanushkevich is using the Jews as a scapegoat ... [for his own failures].

Having dwelt once more on the horrors of the compulsory deportations, Shcherbatov pointed out that they threatened to increase revolutionary feelings among the Jews. But the main argument in favour of practical measures to alleviate the sufferings of the refugees was the difficulty encountered by the government in obtaining credit both at home and abroad. Shcherbatov proposed to lift the ban on the settlement of Jews in all the cities and towns of the empire. This proposal to extend the Jews' freedom of movement was limited to urban districts because of endemic anti-Semitism among the rural population, which the government had no means of controlling. But even that seemed too radical for the Minister of War, Polivanov, who claimed it would be too dangerous to settle Jews in towns with a Cossack population: this could easily lead to a wave of pogroms. Finally, Shcherbatov's reasonable proposal was accepted by the Council, with one dissentient (the Minister of Railways, Rukhlov). Krivoshein tried to bring a note of solemnity to the acceptance of Shcherbatov's proposal: he referred to an earlier conversation he had once had with the late Count Witte. Witte had told Krivoshein that 'allowing the Jews to settle in all the towns of the empire was tantamount to the solution of the Jewish problem'. The effect of Krivoshein's intervention was somewhat spoiled by a cynical joke from the State Comptroller, Kharitonov. He asked the Ministers whether they did not expect difficulties with the police: the new pro-Jewish measure would deprive constables and inspectors of a nice little income. They might go on protest strike against the government's encroachment on their rights and 'even organise a couple of little pogroms to prove that the measure is not in accordance with the wishes of the truly Russian people'.

The decision of the Council of Ministers may have relieved the strain on the local administration in the refugee reception areas by spreading the burden among all Russian towns and cities instead of concentrating it on the few towns in the pale of settlement. It may also have resulted in some alleviation of the sufferings of the evacuees themselves. What it could not do was to abate the general feeling of intense bitterness among the Jews against the régime which had inflicted this treatment upon them. It was widely known that even this partial remedy was being extorted from the government by the threat of financial boycott. The Jews' bitterness and resentment led — as the government clearly realised — to an increase of revolutionary feeling. But it is quite certain that, however strong these feelings, they could not have had a direct bearing on the course of revolutionary events in 1917. The Jewish refugees were far too depressed and alienated a body to exert any political influence. And yet these feelings are of the greatest consequence for the further course of the revolution in Russia. For millions of Russian Jews, the revolution, with its proclaimed slogan of 'equality of all Russian citizens before the law', came as a liberation at the moment of the greatest danger for the physical and moral existence of the Jewish nation — a last-minute salvation from a deadly peril similar to that of the Exodus. Like any miraculous event, it was hard to believe even when actually experienced. The fear that it might not be true, that next day they might wake to see the old order restored, was naturally an obsession of many of these ex-refugees. This fear was vaguely but firmly connected with a feeling that a counter-revolutionary movement might come from the army as long as any of the old traditions were still alive in it, and the old personnel which had carried out the inhuman decisions of the semi-demented Yanushkevich were still in command. This attitude explains the enthusiasm and elation with which the Jewish intelligentsia and semi-intelligentsia greeted the revolution and adhered to left-wing movements in defence of 'the conquests of the revolution'. This is why a large number of Jews offered their loyal services as 'Soviet employees' to the Soviet régime in the years of civil war and reconstruction. The same complex psychological foundation of Jewish-Bolshevik co-operation explains its dissolution and the return under later Communist rule to anti-Semitic practices, which persist in spite of official protestations to the contrary. 'The Party and the government', or rather the successive autocratic rulers in whom the combined functions of Party and government have been vested, have never shown much confidence in the political allegiance of the Jews, which originated not in any innate affinity with Bolshevism but in an instinct of national self-preservation for which Communist ideology shows neither interest nor sympathy.

5

German Political Intervention

Introduction; Separate peace feelers and their repercussions in Russia; The beginnings of the Revolutionierungspolitik; *Lenin, Helphand and Keskülä; Helphand in Copenhagen; Helphand and labour unrest in Russia; Keskülä; German policy after February 1917; The return of Lenin; 'Channels and labels'; 'The great slander' and the greater denials; Conclusions*

I. INTRODUCTION

The story of the political intervention of Germany (and Austria-Hungary) in the internal affairs of Russia during World War I, and in particular during the events of 1917, has never been told in full. Indeed, many of those concerned had a vital interest in concealing the scope and tactics of this intervention. In the absence of documentary evidence, rumours and conjectures were put forward accusing Russian revolutionary circles, mainly the Bolsheviks, of having acted in agreement with and in support of the German government. Such accusations were also directed before the revolution against the Tsar's court and administration, and did much to discredit them. This made the Bolsheviks particularly sensitive to such allegations, which were angrily dismissed by them as reactionary slanders.

During the civil war in Russia (1918–20), the controversy about the Bolshevik involvement with the Germans was of considerable political importance. At that time a series of documents known as the Sisson Papers was produced as evidence that Lenin and his supporters had been working under German instructions and with German money.[1] The documents themselves were dubious and proved later to be fakes (with the exception of a few irrelevant ones introduced into the collection to make it appear authentic). The genuineness of the whole

1. The Sisson Papers, with facsimiles, appeared in Edgar Sisson, *100 Red Days* (Yale/London, 1931). See also S. P. Melgunov, *Zolotoy nemetsky klyuch k bolshevistskoy revolyutsii* (Paris, 1940), and George Kennan in *The Journal of Modern History* (1956), where the whole story is circumstantially analysed.

collection was questioned at the time, and the exposure of the forgeries was of great help to all those who considered the original allegations against the Bolsheviks to be slanderous.

There the matter rested until the mid-fifties, when some authentic documentary evidence came to light on this vexed question. This was found in the files of the German Ministry of Foreign Affairs, which fell into the hands of the Allies at the end of World War II. Some of the documents have been published, but little has been done in the way of interpretation or reassessment of the events of 1917 in the light of this new evidence.[1] It is therefore imperative to attempt a survey of the whole field in a separate chapter, even though much more evidence may be forthcoming in the next few years, when the fifty-year embargo on many official archives is lifted.

When, in 1914, Germany found herself engaged in a major war on two fronts, she immediately realised the importance of breaking up the alliance of her adversaries and, if possible, of getting one or other of her major opponents out of the way by concluding a separate peace, even at the cost of forgoing certain war aims. There were two ways in which the German government tried to achieve this. One was to appeal to influential people in the enemy camp who were believed to be in sympathy with the general political aspirations of Germany and who might consider the war with Germany a disaster for their own country; such people, it was hoped, might be willing to work for a separate peace and to use their influence on their respective governments and on public opinion. The other way was to seek out disruptive forces in the enemy camp and to support every type of seditious movement, whether pro-German or not.

2. SEPARATE PEACE FEELERS AND THEIR REPERCUSSIONS IN RUSSIA

In pursuit of the first course, the German government made use of dynastic connections in order to persuade the sovereigns of enemy countries to drop out of the war or even to join with Germany against their former allies. As far as Russia was concerned such approaches to the court were made on numerous occasions, mainly through the inter-

1. See Bibliographical Notes.

mediary of Etat Councillor Andersen of the Copenhagen court and through various German relatives of the Empress Alexandra and connections of the Dowager Empress Maria. We now know with absolute certainty that none of these approaches yielded any returns for the German government; the last attempt was abandoned in the summer of 1916 after Nicholas II had intimated to King Christian of Denmark that only a general peace could be discussed and that separate peace talks were neither desirable nor possible. But general peace negotiations were unacceptable to the German government. When the Japanese middleman Baron Ushida advised general negotiations with all the Entente powers, the Kaiser burst into a rage and noted on Lucius's report of 17 May 1916:

> Since a separate peace cannot be made, the whole swindle is of no interest whatever. More is achieved by thrashing. We do not need them [i.e., the Japanese] as *mediators* for a general peace.[1]

Nicholas II probably never learned that the originator of the diplomatic moves to the Russian court was his former Prime Minister, Count Witte. Early in the war Witte had written to the head of the German Mendelssohn-Bartholdy Bank, in which he had considerable holdings, blaming the war on the British and asserting that, had he been in power, 'this hell would never have been let loose'. He proposed 'frank discussions between the Emperors' which should be initiated through their family connections. Robert Mendelssohn passed on these proposals to the German Foreign Minister, von Jagow.[2]

1. *L'Allemagne et les problèmes de la paix. Documents . . . publiés et annotés par A. Scherer et J. Grunewald* (Paris, 1962), pp. 343 ff.; and Fritz Fischer's comment in *Griff nach der Weltmacht* (Düsseldorf, 1962), pp. 281 ff. Baron Lucius von Stoedten was German Minister in Stockholm at the time.

2. Scherer and Grunewald, op. cit., p. 64. Whatever Witte's motives, his behaviour was both injudicious and mischievous. The origins of his fortune are worth investigation. In 1912, Witte had approached the Emperor for a gift of 200,000 roubles as he claimed to be in straitened circumstances. Kokovtsov supported the application and Nicholas II grudgingly agreed to it. (See Count V. N. Kokovtsov's memoirs, *Out of My Past* (Oxford University Press, 1935), pp. 329 ff.) On the outbreak of war Witte's holdings in Germany were sequestrated, and this obviously worried him. On 25 January (7 February) 1915, Witte wrote to Mendelssohn telling him that as it had been intimated to him that he would be appointed negotiator for Russia at the peace conference after the war, he would have to clear his contacts with the German bank. He therefore asked Mendelssohn, if he considered his appointment desirable

An important advocate of the German cause in Russia was Witte's one-time secretary, a certain Kolyshko, who had become an established journalist.[1] He had married a German and had a pro-German outlook, although outwardly he kept up appearances as a Russian patriot. Through his wife, who had settled permanently in Stockholm, he maintained close contacts with a Swedish banker who was working for the Wilhelmstrasse (the German Foreign Ministry documents call him 'Director Bockelmann') as well as with the German industrial tycoon, Hugo Stinnes.

Kolyshko discussed various projects with the Germans, such as the purchase of a Russian newspaper in order ultimately to spread the idea of a separate peace and to foster anti-British and anti-French feeling. He received some German financial support and hoped for a greater reward after the war, when he intended to settle in Germany. But the Germans allowed him to keep up an appearance of patriotism and independence of action: in the summer of 1916, for instance, he suggested to his German friends that the success of the Brusilov offensive in Galicia was actually favourable to Germany, because in the event of a separate peace it would make it easier for Germany to surrender Eastern Galicia in exchange for territories in the Baltic.[2]

---

from a German point of view, to transfer all his funds to a bank in Copenhagen or Stockholm in his wife's name. Even Mendelssohn thought that such an operation would compromise Witte completely, and therefore advised that the funds be put in the name of a trustworthy neutral. Nothing came of all this because Witte died a few weeks later, a lonely and disillusioned man.

1. Iosif Kolyshko wrote in the papers *Grazhdanin* and *Russkoe Slovo* under the pen-names of Serenky and Bayan.

2. In his negotiations with the Germans, Kolyshko was joined, in 1916, by Prince Bebutov, a former member of the First Duma who was well known in Kadet and Masonic circles and who in the last years before the war and until 1916 had lived in Germany, where he was certainly in contact with the Intelligence Department of the German General Staff.

In 1916 Bebutov turned up in Stockholm and was received and dined at the Russian Embassy. At the same time, through his contacts with German military intelligence agents, he tried to approach German diplomats in Scandinavia. The German Foreign Ministry was, however, suspicious of Bebutov and allowed him to deal only with the middleman 'Director Bockelmann', who was also dealing with Kolyshko. After the revolution Bebutov returned to Russia, where at one time he was put under house arrest by the Provisional Government. For more of Bebutov's many-sided and dubious activities, see below, pp. 163 ff.

Purchasing a newspaper for government purposes was also one of the favourite ideas of the Russian Prime Minister Stuermer and his one-time Minister of the Interior, A. N. Khvostov. It is in connection with such journalistic plans that Kolyshko managed to obtain an audience with Stuermer in the summer of 1916. But although the interview lasted for hours and questions of general policy were discussed, it appears from Kolyshko's report to the Germans through Director Bockelmann that he was very cautious in his approach to Stuermer and that the latter, as usual, remained non-committal. But Kolyshko later made some extravagant and unfounded claims. He boasted to Stinnes[1] that he had discussed peace conditions with Stuermer and that he had received Stuermer's blessing for a further sounding of German attitudes towards a separate peace. There is no reason to doubt Kolyshko's acquaintance with Stuermer or even the fact that he had a conversation with him. But his boast that he had discussed the possibility of separate peace negotiations is in no way substantiated. The same document in which the conversation between Stinnes and Kolyshko is reported creates the impression that Kolyshko lied as far as his mandate to make contact with the Germans on Stuermer's behalf is concerned: when Stinnes offered to write a joint letter with Kolyshko to Stuermer, Kolyshko first agreed, then backed out and tried to get Stinnes to address the letter instead to Stuermer's Head of Chancellery, Manasevich-Manuilov,[2] who was to come to Stockholm as an unofficial first contact for separate peace negotiations. We know that nothing came of these plans of Kolyshko's because of Manasevich's arrest on 16 August.[3]

1. Scherer and Grunewald, op. cit., p. 371 ff.
2. Manasevich-Manuilov, a former secret police agent and a shady figure who intrigued in the entourage of Rasputin, was soon to be arrested. To describe him as Stuermer's Head of Chancellery or secretary was certainly an exaggeration of Kolyshko's. He was Stuermer's adviser on confidential affairs relating to the counter-espionage service. He was arrested for alleged blackmail in connection with these activities. His trial let loose a cataract of scandal in Russian public life. It started in December 1916 and was adjourned on the orders of the Emperor, who yielded to the pressure of Manasevich's chiefs in the counter-espionage service, Generals Batyushin and M. D. Bonch-Bruevich, as well as to the interference of the Empress. However, the trial revealed the unsavoury methods employed by the counter-espionage service under Batyushin. It was resumed in February and ended a few days before the outbreak of the revolution with a verdict against Manasevich and the opening of an investigation of Batyushin himself.
3. Scherer and Grunewald, op. cit., pp. 371 passim.

Two months later, the hope of separate peace negotiations with Russia seemed even more remote to Bethmann-Hollweg than in the spring of the same year. At a meeting of the Prussian Council of Ministers on 28 August 1916, he stated that:

> In March our military situation was more favourable than now after the collapse of Austria [meaning the Austrian defeat in Galicia in the summer of 1916 during the so-called Brusilov offensive]. At that time we might still have hoped that after taking Verdun we could make peace in the autumn. At present the military prospects have much worsened and the already shaken hopes of His Majesty that Russia would be ready for a separate peace after we had restored our position in the East have now become even less well-founded.[1]

Nothing came of Kolyshko's projects, but his irresponsible talk had important indirect consequences. Rumours of peace negotiations between Russia and Germany were reported as reliable information in the Swiss Social-Democratic newspaper, *Berner Tagwacht*, which was edited by Robert Grimm in close collaboration with Karl Radek. As we shall see, Milyukov's famous speech in the Duma on 1 November 1916, in which he accused Stuermer's government and court circles of working for a separate peace with Germany, was inspired by these rumours and by the reports in the *Berner Tagwacht*.[2]

By the summer of 1916, the Kaiser had grown impatient with his government's efforts, and he urged Chancellor Bethmann-Hollweg in one of his letters to make a greater effort to penetrate Russia by means of 'bankers, Jews, etc.' (*sic*). In his reply[3] Bethmann-Hollweg assured the Kaiser that the Foreign Ministry had acted on his suggestion but that unfortunately the most 'promising personality' in this respect, the banker Dmitri Rubinstein, had been arrested in Petrograd during an 'anti-Jewish razzia'. Bethmann-Hollweg did not reveal what made him believe Rubinstein to be a 'promising personality'. In fact, Rubinstein was in personal and business relations both with the Empress's *confidante*, Vyrubova, with Manasevich-Manuilov, and with Rasputin himself, whom, according to police records, he supplied with the holy man's favourite drink, madeira.[4]

1. Scherer and Grunewald, op. cit., p. 464.   2. See below, pp. 191 ff.
3. See Scherer and Grunewald, op. cit., p. 435.
4. A. Spiridovich, in his *Les dernières années de la cour de Tzarskoïe Selo* (Paris, 1928–1929), vol. II, pp. 419 ff., says: 'Dmitri Lvovich Rubinstein was educated at the

After Rubinstein's arrest on suspicion of illicit financial dealings, a further approach to influential persons was made in the summer of 1916, when the Russian parliamentary delegation was on its return journey from the allied countries to Petrograd. The head of the delegation, then Vice-President of the Duma, was A. D. Protopopov, who was soon to be appointed Minister of the Interior. A fellow-passenger on the boat approached him with a proposal to meet a German industrialist belonging to the influential banking family of Warburg for an off-the-record talk. Protopopov consulted the Russian *Charge' d'Affaires* in Stockholm, who thought the meeting might be interesting, and asked another member of the delegation, Count Olsufyev, to join him at this interview. A record of what happened was made by both Olsufyev and Protopopov on the Russian side, while the German Foreign Ministry files contain Fritz Warburg's account.[1] All the accounts agree that the question of a separate peace was not discussed, and that as far as the Germans were concerned the approach was abortive. This was, however, not the end of the story. In spite of the fact that Protopopov — acting for once with circumspection — gave a full account of his conversations in Stockholm both to his Duma colleagues and to the Ministry of Foreign Affairs on his return to

Demidov Lyceum [a Faculty of Law in Yaroslavl], was director of a bank in Kharkov, and had become financial manager of the estate of the Grand Duke Andrey Vladimirovich. This helped him to become managing director of the Private Commercial Bank in Petrograd. Rubinstein donated large sums to various charities, and was decorated with the Cross of St. Vladimir and appointed Active State Counsellor [which entitled him to be addressed as 'Excellency'].'

Spiridovich suggests that Rubinstein had known Vyrubova since 1908 and believes that he started financial operations on her behalf before 1913. He gave financial help to various persons she recommended, and in April 1914 he asked her to accept the sum of 100,000 roubles for her charities. Vyrubova foolishly accepted and sent Rubinstein a detailed account of how the money had been used. Soon afterwards Rasputin summoned Rubinstein and made his acquaintance. From then on he used to pay money to Rasputin. He also paid Rasputin's rent. Spiridovich evidently knew of these dealings from his official activities as head of the palace security service and from his contacts with the Director of the Police Department, Beletsky. Spiridovich writes: 'All this financial side of Rasputin's activities was carefully concealed from Their Majesties. The august inhabitants of Tsarskoe Selo continued to see in Rasputin the man of prayer, exclusively preoccupied with questions of religion.' Rasputin secured Rubinstein's release in December 1916.

1. Scherer and Grunewald, op. cit., pp. 392 ff.

Petrograd, the mere fact that he had been 'in touch with the Germans' was held against him as soon as he was appointed Minister of the Interior. It was then widely rumoured that one of the reasons why he was selected for this post was that he had joined the Empress's alleged pro-German party and was ready to work for a separate peace.

Although Germany's attempts to weaken Russian determination to carry on with the war brought her diplomats nothing but disappointment, they had an unintended effect on the political situation in Russia. Enough information about these approaches filtered through to the general public to lend some plausibility to the rumours that a separate peace was being prepared in high quarters with the help of 'dark forces'. That 'high quarters' never countenanced such a plan is now beyond question. As far as 'dark forces' are concerned – that is, the shady characters who tried to gain influence at court through Rasputin and Madame Vyrubova – they never formed anything like a lasting alliance with a political programme, still less acted as an organised 'black bloc'. Indeed, by the end of 1916, the Germans themselves had become tired of pursuing such an unrewarding line.

The various counter-espionage services in Russia were well aware of German efforts to promote the desire for a separate peace. But from such fragmentary information as we have on the activities of these services, it is clear that there was a great deal of muddle, duplication, corruption and inefficiency, and that prejudice and lust for witch-hunting prompted many of their exploits. At the beginning of the war patriotic and chauvinistic feelings were stirred up among the people by propaganda of racial hatred and denigration of the German who replaced to a certain extent the bogey of the Jew as an 'alien bloodsucker'. German-baiting affected all manner of Russian subjects of German descent in widely varying categories: businessmen and technicians from Germany and Austria-Hungary, German landowning gentry from the Baltic provinces, German agrarian colonists (of whom the largest group had lived on the Volga since the eighteenth century), and finally those innumerable Russians of German descent who were entirely assimilated into Russian society. All these groups were to varying degrees open to accusations of 'careerism' and a lack of understanding of the Russian national spirit. The expression 'the plague of Germans' (nemetskoe zasilye) vaguely denoting economic penetration, unfair privileges and Teutonic arrogance was on all tongues. At the lowest level, agitation against the 'plague of Germans' led to anti-German pogroms, with looting of the business premises and homes of people with German names. In both capitals, and elsewhere, labour unrest took an anti-German, patriotic and chauvinistic turn.[1] The anti-German campaign hit many businessmen, who were accused of intentionally slowing down the war effort. Germans and Austro-Hungarians, even those already naturalised, lost their jobs, and many were deported to the eastern and northern provinces. The position of Guards, and army officers with German names, particularly those in high command, became increasingly difficult. The imperial court was possibly the place where the campaign had least effect. The personal protection of the Emperor guaranteed court dignitaries against chauvinistic attack. This had, however, an unfavourable effect on public opinion, which took the presence of Germans, including the Minister of the Imperial Court, Count Frederichs (who in fact was of Swedish and not of German descent), as proof that 'the German woman' (nemka, that is, the Empress) was heading a pro-German party.

One of those who was most active against the German zasilye was General M. D. Bonch-Bruevich,[2] the very same who had Colonel Myasoedov arrested and hanged as a German spy.[3] The anti-German witch-hunt, carried out by the counter-espionage service with which Bonch-Bruevich was connected, seriously disrupted industrial activities and affected even war industry. Thus Bonch-Bruevich systematically persecuted the large Singer firm, which had established a network for the sale and servicing of their sewing-machines all over the country on the then novel principle of hire-purchase. The counter-espionage service claimed that the Singer agents were in fact a camouflaged German spy ring.[4]

1. See below on the strike movement in the Putilov works, p. 89, and on the Moscow anti-German pogrom in May 1915, p. 199.
2. General M. D. Bonch-Bruevich was the brother of the Bolshevik scholar V. D. Bonch-Bruevich, who was interested in Russian sectarians, and was agitating among the Cossacks billeted in Petrograd in February 1917. See below, pp. 266 ff. This did not affect the exalted position of the General, who was received at court, and was highly thought of by the Commander-in-Chief of the Northern Front, Ruzsky. The Bonch-Bruevich brothers remained in close contact throughout the war and the revolution.
3. See below, ch. 6.
4. See M. D. Bonch-Bruevich, *Vsya vlast sovetam* (Moscow, 1957, p. 79); and

The liberals, whom one might have expected to oppose chauvinism and to denounce the hounding of innocent individuals, did not raise their voice in protest against these campaigns except in the case of the Moscow pogrom of May 1915, which provided them with a convenient stick to beat the government. Indeed the exposure of the supposed 'German party' and of the mythical 'black bloc' was part of their ammunition against the government, which was rumoured to be negotiating a separate peace behind the back of the people.

In fact the German government's efforts to promote such negotiations were, as we have seen, ineffective, and by the end of 1916 the second course of action, the *Revolutionierungspolitik*, which had all along run parallel to the feelers for a separate peace, came more into favour both with the Wilhelmstrasse and especially with the Political Section of the German General Staff.

3. THE BEGINNINGS OF THE *Revolutionierungspolitik*

Support of subversive activities in Russia, as well as in the British and French Empires, had been part of the programme of the German High Command from the very beginning of the war. Austria-Hungary had already begun to support separatist movements in Russia in the years immediately preceding the war, though the close personal contacts which Emperor Wilhelm tried to maintain with Nicholas II imposed greater caution on the German government in this respect than on the Austrians.[1] Lenin had established his headquarters on Austrian territory at Poronino near Cracow in 1912; Ryazanov, one of the most prominent theoreticians of the Social-Democratic movement, was working in Vienna. Trotsky had been living in Vienna since 1910, directing from there his various journalistic activities in Russia and abroad. At the same time the Austrians tolerated and harboured a

Ekonomicheskoe polozhenie Rossii nakanune oktyabrskoy revolyutsii (2 vols., Moscow, 1947), vol. I, pp. 460–476.

1. Yet some of the most vicious anti-Tsarist propaganda was published in Germany just before the war. For instance, the anonymous, lavishly-illustrated folio volume *Posledny russky samoderzhets* (Berlin, 1913). According to General Spiridovich (op. cit., vol. II, pp. 328 ff.) the author was the notorious Prince Bebutov, mentioned above, see p. 66 n. and below, pp. 163 ff.

number of Ukrainian separatists, possibly as a reprisal for pan-Slav propaganda in the Russian press, especially in *Novoe Vremya*.

As the war progressed, however, the various German departments dealing with political warfare took over most of the activities and agents employed originally by the Austrians. German embassies in neutral countries were constantly besieged by a crowd of Finnish nationalists, Polish counts, Ukrainian clerics, Caucasian princes and highwaymen, and revolutionary intellectuals of every description, who wanted to establish liberation committees, publish nationalist propaganda and work for some independent and free national state which they fondly hoped would result from the partition of the Russian Empire. At first, among those who volunteered to assist the Germans, there were no representatives of the established Russian revolutionary parties – the Social-Democrats of either branch, or Socialist Revolutionaries.

At the outbreak of war police treatment of enemy aliens stranded in Germany seemed to take no account of whether they were supporters or enemies of the existing régimes in their countries; there was little consistency in the arbitrary decisions to intern or expel such foreigners, or to allow them to remain under police supervision. Some Russian revolutionaries were deported to Scandinavia, whence those who could returned to Russia. Others crossed the Swiss border and joined the political émigrés there. Some of them, especially those who followed the veteran Russian Marxist Plekhanov in his defensist and pro-Entente attitude, went to Paris, where they even managed to publish a newspaper of their own – *Nashe Slovo*. Others, such as the one-time Bolshevik Duma deputy, Malinovsky, who had left Russia after resigning his mandate in 1913 (having been accused of acting as an informer for the Ministry of the Interior), seem to have been interned and then used by the Political Section of the German General Staff as propagandists among Russian prisoners of war. Malinovsky's connection with the Russian police had not yet been made public, and he maintained contact with Lenin, who was still backing him and terrorising into silence the Mensheviks and those Bolsheviks who denounced him.[1]

---

1. Lenin, with Fürstenberg-Ganetsky and Zinovyev, set up a kind of court of honour which cleared Malinovsky's name. On Malinovsky's further moves, see below, p. 101. See also B. Wolfe, *Three who made a Revolution* (New York, 1938), p. 550 f. and *Byloe* (ed. Burtsev), No. 1, new series (Paris, 1933), pp. 120 ff.

Others again, who were in one way or another connected with politically influential persons in Germany and Austria, were allowed to stay unmolested under police supervision.

Lenin himself was arrested in Poronino on the outbreak of war. But his collaborator Fürstenberg-Ganetsky made an approach to the Austrian socialist leader Victor Adler, who intervened with the Austrian authorities, arguing that Lenin's anti-Tsarist attitude might possibly be of some use in the near future. Adler obtained Lenin's release after fourteen days and Lenin, his wife Krupskaya, and his closest acolyte of the moment, Zinovyev, were allowed to leave for Switzerland in September 1914.[1]

Lenin and his group arrived in Switzerland with very little money and no regular papers, but Lenin had friends who put him in touch with a Swiss socialist of German descent, Karl Moor, a member of the Berne Great Council and a former editor of the socialist *Berner Tagwacht*. Karl Moor's name was not the only fanciful feature about him. Born in 1853, he had made an honourable name for himself in the Swiss Social-Democrat movement while at the same time working for the Austrian and German General Staffs as an informer on the socialists living in Switzerland. He was a shrewd and cautious man, and his contacts with the Germans were very carefully camouflaged. He gained entry to the world of *Under Western Eyes*[2] by helping the émigré socialists in their dealings with the police and local authorities, and by occasional loans of cash. He was on particularly friendly terms with the Bolshevik, Dr Grigory Shklovsky, and also with the veteran Menshevik leader, Paul Akselrod. Karl Moor arranged for Lenin's stay in Switzerland and seems, through Shklovsky, to have had other business with him.[3]

In Switzerland Lenin found himself surrounded by a small group of supporters, but he had lost contact with many of his followers inside and outside Russia through the disruption of the postal services at the begin-

1. Olga H. Gankin and H. H. Fisher, *The Bolsheviks and the World War* (Stanford University Press, 1940), p. 139.
2. See Joseph Conrad's novel, *Under Western Eyes*, for an evocation of the atmosphere of the émigré revolutionary underworld in Switzerland.
3. There are two letters from Lenin to remind G. Shklovsky of the necessity of asking 'that rascal Moor' to return some unidentified papers. 'Rascal' in this context seems to be an expression of familiarity rather than abuse. See *Leninsky Sbornik*, XI (1931), pp. 214, 226.

ning of the war. In time Krupskaya managed by devoted efforts to restore most of Lenin's contacts.[1] But his break with the defensists all over Europe, and the intransigent attitude Lenin adopted towards the 'centrists' such as Kautsky in Germany and the group which formed around the paper *Nashe Slovo* in Paris, all contributed to his isolation.

The German government took little notice at the outbreak of war of the friction and quarrels among the Russian political émigrés. Their first approach to these circles was in connection with propaganda among prisoners of war, whose numbers rapidly grew after the defeat of the Samsonov army in East Prussia in August 1914. Following the Austrian method, the Germans divided their propaganda for prisoners of war into propaganda for the national minorities and for Russian subjects in general. As far as the first was concerned the Ukrainians and the Finns were the most important. For the Russians it was decided to publish a newspaper (*Na Chuzhbine*) and for this the Germans sought the collaboration of revolutionary groups. Work on the paper seems to have been organised mainly by the Political Section of the German General Staff, but contacts abroad were maintained through accredited diplomatic representatives. Thus it happened that the German Legation in Berne began to show an interest in the Russian revolutionary émigrés. The Germans approached them diffidently, mindful of their political susceptibilities and sparing them the humiliation and risk of exposure as German agents. Very many of those who agreed to contribute to the newspaper, including such people as the leader of the Socialist Revolutionaries and theoretician of agrarian socialism, V. Chernov, or the distinguished bibliographer Rubakin, believed that they were acting independently and attending to the political education of the unfortunate prisoners of war, whom the Tsarist government had kept in ignorance.[2]

---

1. Some of the work which this involved is revealed by the publication of Krupskaya's address books in *Istorichesky Arkhiv* (1959), No. 3.
2. N. A. Rubakin, who is known in the German reports under the cover name of Dr Martel, had for instance written an anti-Tsarist pamphlet which he wanted to publish in Germany for the prisoners of war, stipulating that at the same time it should also appear in German for German soldiers. The German military authorities naturally opposed this. It is difficult to say who was trying to cheat whom in this peculiar deal. See the files of the German Legation in Berne.

4. LENIN, HELPHAND AND KESKÜLA

It is hard to believe that these German activities were unknown to Lenin in the first year of his stay in Switzerland, although there is nothing to indicate that he was approached personally at this time. However, as early as September 1915 one of the Estonian émigrés in Switzerland, a certain Alexander Kesküla, had taken the initiative of contacting the German Minister in Berne, Romberg, and enlightening him on the attitude of the Russian émigrés to the war. During the 1905 revolution Kesküla had been a member of the Bolshevik Party in Estonia and had shown considerable leadership ability. It seems that in emigration he gradually veered from Marxism towards a romantic conception of Estonian nationalism. For Russian revolutionaries as a body Kesküla felt profound contempt — except for Lenin, whose organisational talents and consistency of purpose he admired and considered outstanding. Kesküla admits having met Lenin only once, although he maintained indirect contact through another Estonian Bolshevik called Siefeldt.[1] It is through Kesküla that Lenin's views on the war came to the notice of the German Ministry of Foreign Affairs.[2] Romberg reported on the so-called Lenin programme for a separate peace with Germany on 30 September 1915.[3] This must have produced a considerable impression in the Wilhelmstrasse. A vague suggestion made by Romberg that the contents of the Lenin programme should be passed on to German agents in France for dissemination there was

1. From the enormous and detailed literature on Lenin's wartime activities we learn nothing about the existence of a man called Siefeldt. This in itself is a reminder of how critically such sources, however bulky and outwardly authoritative, should be approached. The existence of Siefeldt was first revealed in an interview which Dr M. Futrell had with the aged Kesküla. This led to a further investigation, in the course of which an article by Siefeldt came to light. It had appeared in the Soviet provincial paper *Bakinsky Rabochy* in 1924. The article, bearing all the internal marks of authenticity, gives a vivid account of Siefeldt's acquaintance with Lenin and of the life of the Russian émigrés in Switzerland at the time. It also incidentally provides first-hand evidence of the visit of A. Helphand (Parvus) to Switzerland in the spring of 1915 (see below, p. 80 f.). Siefeldt's presence in Switzerland at the time is confirmed by the Okhrana files in the Hoover Library. See also Michael Futrell, *Northern Underground* (London, 1963), particularly p. 173.
2. Futrell, op. cit., pp. 119–151 *passim*.
3. Z. A. B. Zeman, *Germany and the Revolution in Russia, 1915–18* (London, 1958), pp. 6 7.

immediately quashed in Berlin. The Deputy Minister for Foreign Affairs, Zimmermann, commented that the contents should not be communicated because they might fall into the hands of the Tsarist government and provoke intensified persecution of the revolutionaries. The Minister himself, von Jagow, wired Romberg to this effect.[1] Evidently Lenin's views had been taken seriously, and had he made the slightest show of wanting to contact the Germans directly, he would have been welcomed. It seems, however, that no direct contact between him and the German authorities was ever made, although one cannot rule this out with absolute certainty. Lenin was a highly accomplished conspirator, and the Germans would have behaved with maximum discretion.

According to Keskülä, through him and Siefeldt small sums were put at Lenin's disposal from a camouflaged source. In fact Keskülä obtained the money from Romberg.[2] In 1916 the German Legation started taking an interest in Lenin's journalistic activities. Lenin published at irregular intervals a newspaper called *Sotsial-Demokrat* and a magazine, *Sbornik Sotsial-Demokrata*, whose main contributors were Lenin himself and Zinovyev. Two issues of the magazine appeared during the war; the third was delayed by lack of funds. The files of the German Legation in Berne contain some correspondence showing that after some doubts the Germans decided to provide funds for it in a way which would be acceptable to Lenin. The issue never appeared, however, because of the outbreak of the February revolution.

Keskülä's report on Lenin to the German Legation in Berne in September 1915 was not the first the Germans had received on him. Their attention had been called to the 'majority faction' of Russian Social-Democracy, that is the Bolsheviks, in a memorandum[3] presented to the Auswärtiges Amt in March 1915 by a man of vital importance in the story of German subversion in Russia. This was Dr Alexander Helphand, alias Parvus, a living proof that adventurers could play as effective a part in Great Power politics in World War I as they played in the intrigues of the Italian Renaissance states.

1. And yet Inessa Armand went to France and worked there in the Zimmerwald Movement. See A. Kriegel, *Sur les rapports de Lénine avec le mouvement Zimmerwaldien français. Cahiers du Monde Russe et Soviétique* (Paris), vol. III: 2. April-June 1962, p. 299.
2. Futrell, op. cit., p. 146.
3. 'Preparations for a Political Mass Strike in Russia.' See Zeman, op. cit., pp. 140–152.

Helphand, a Russian Jew, born in Berezina (Belorussia) and educated in Odessa, had become converted to Marxist revolutionary socialism early in life. He soon understood the enormous personal advantages which a thorough knowledge of economic and social conditions in different parts of the world provides, and learned to trade in this knowledge in exchange for influence and power in international politics. In the nineties he had emigrated to Germany and established contact with German socialist circles, but returned to Russia during the famine of 1898–99, of which he published a remarkably well-documented account.[1] In the period preceding the 1905 revolution he was considered to be one of the leading Marxist theoreticians. He played an active part in the Petersburg Soviet of 1905, and collaborated closely with Trotsky, publishing articles in Trotsky's papers (occasionally under the pen name of Molotov). Arrested and deported to Siberia in 1906, he escaped at about the same time as Trotsky and established himself in Germany again, where he carried on business as a publisher and literary and theatrical agent. He continued to write for the German Social-Democratic press. He remained aloof from the internal struggles of the Russian Social-Democrats but was generally considered to be on the side of the Mensheviks. He never got on very well with Lenin, with whose theory of a revolutionary élite he did not agree; for him, a revolutionary party was necessary only as a kind of yeast to produce the fermentation which was to lead to social progress, and he believed the masses should be trained to form and promote their own leadership.

As he always thought of the socialist movement on an international scale, Helphand became interested in the increasingly unstable situation in the Balkans. In 1910 he transferred his activities to Constantinople, where he carried on Social-Democratic propaganda and simultaneously a large import-export business. He boasted of having concluded with Russia the grain deal which, he claimed, had saved the régime of the Young Turks from disaster. He is also said to have dabbled in smuggling obsolete German arms, for which there was a great demand in the Balkans, and to have made a considerable fortune out of these deals. In 1914 he worked to influence left-wing Turkish opinion in favour of Turkey's entry into the war on the side of the Central Powers,[2] and gave

1. C. Lehmann and Parvus, *Das Hungernde Russland* (Stuttgart, 1900).
2. Helphand's notebooks contain some poetical attempts at war propaganda calling on Muslims to fight a sacred war against Russia, the historic foe of Islam.

further services to the Germans by collaborating with a certain Dr Zimmer in organising a Ukrainian fifth column based on Turkey.

Soon after the outbreak of war Helphand set off for Germany via Sofia, Bucharest and Vienna. In Bulgaria he spread undisguised pro-German propaganda among the Bulgarian Social-Democrats, and in Rumania he established firm contacts, which were maintained throughout the following years, with Christian Rakovsky and other Social-Democrats. In Vienna he renewed his friendship with Ryazanov, who as a Russian subject was living there for the duration of the war under the protection of the Spanish Embassy. From Vienna Helphand proceeded to Berlin, where early in March 1915 he laid his plans for instigating a revolution in Russia before the German Foreign Ministry and asked for German financial support for them.[1] According to Wangenheim, the German Ambassador in Constantinople, who recommended Helphand to the Foreign Ministry, Helphand believed that 'Russian democrats could achieve their aim only with the total destruction of Tsarism and the division of Russia into smaller states', and that the interests of the German government were therefore identical with those of the Russian revolutionaries and separatists.[2] To bring about this aim, Helphand proposed the following plan: local economic strikes should be fomented in various parts of Russia, mainly Petrograd and the Black Sea ports, and these should gradually be transformed into strikes for political demands; the movement would culminate in a general strike which would lead to the fall of the Tsarist régime.[3]

1. See Zeman, op. cit., pp. 1 ff., pp. 140–152; W. B. Scharlau, 'Parvus-Helphand in the First World War' (Oxford doctoral thesis, 1963, unpublished). While in Berlin Helphand met the diplomat Dr Kurt Riezler who had been seconded from the Wilhelmstrasse to the General Staff, where he was working closely with Colonel von Huelsen of the Political Section.
2. Zeman, op. cit., p. 1.
3. Ibid., pp. 140–152. Particularly interesting are Helphand's remarks on agitation in the Black Sea ports. He insisted that agitation here should be started at once, simultaneously with the basic preparation for a mass strike: 'Through Bulgaria and Rumania communications can be established with Odessa, Nikolaiev, Sevastopol, Rostov (on the Don), Batum, and Baku. During the [1905] revolution, the Russian workers in these areas made local and occupational demands which were first granted, but later repudiated, and they had not abandoned these demands. Only two years ago there was a strike of sailors and dock-workers which brought these old wishes into the limelight once again. Agitation should be based on these points, and then

The Germans were impressed with this plan. The Foreign Ministry immediately made available considerable sums for 'revolutionary propaganda in Russia', and Helphand was given special facilities for travel in Germany and abroad.[1] He returned to Constantinople through the Balkans in order to liquidate his interests there and set up his underground network. On his return to Germany, in the early summer of 1915, he stayed some days in Switzerland in order to organise the Russian émigré revolutionaries.

Helphand hoped that the Russian Social-Democratic defeatists, of whom — as he told the Germans — Lenin was the chief protagonist and theoretician, would co-operate with him in his plan for immediate revolutionary action in Russia. His earlier relations with Lenin had, however, never been cordial. As we have seen, Helphand's and Lenin's conceptions of the part which professional revolutionaries should play differed both in theory and practice. Lenin knew of Helphand's support of the Social-Democratic defensist majority in Germany at the beginning of the war, and nothing could have made him more suspicious of the man.

Helphand, for his part, understood that Lenin's defeatism was basically different from his own desire for the destruction of Russia. For him the collapse of the Tsarist régime and the dismemberment of the Russian Empire were necessary in order to secure the hegemony of Germany, where, as he understood it, the ideals of socialism were about to triumph, possibly without a revolution. For Helphand's purpose the German government and the German war machine were far more promising allies than the Russian Bolsheviks, who were waiting for a revolution in Russia without having yet worked out an effective method of bringing it about. A revolution in Russia was necessary only to clear the way for the advance of the progressive principles embodied in German Socialism.

Despite all this, Lenin, in the late spring of 1915, was not averse to

---

also take a political direction. While a general strike could probably not be achieved in the Black Sea basin, it might be possible, in view of the current unemployment there, to arrange local strikes in Nikolaiev, in Rostov, and among certain trades in Odessa. Such strikes would take on symptomatic significance by disturbing the peace which descended on internal strife within the Tsarist Empire at the beginning of the war' (Zeman, p. 141).

1. Zeman, op. cit., p. 3.

meeting Helphand and hearing what he had to say. The outcome of this interview remained secret at the time, and Helphand left Switzerland without having reached agreement with any of the Russian émigré groups there. To the Germans he reported an estrangement between himself and Lenin, and he decided to proceed with his plans for revolutionising Russia on his own. The Helphand–Lenin meeting did not escape the notice of the Russian émigrés in Switzerland and elsewhere. Later, Lenin's former collaborator, who became his main detractor, Grigory Aleksinsky, claimed knowledge of a secret agreement between Lenin and Helphand for co-operation in revolutionising Russia and for German financial support of Lenin's enterprises. The allegation was the basis of the accusations made in 1917 that the Bolsheviks were German agents. Lenin himself claimed to have broken off relations with Helphand after the brief encounter at Berne, and Helphand in his pamphlet[1] issued in 1918 confirms this. Helphand wrote:

> The reader knows that although the Bolsheviks were also in favour of a military defeat of Russia, there was a difference of opinion between me and them. I took into account the effective factors, economic, political, military — the correlation of forces, the possible results; for the Bolsheviks there was one, and only one, ready answer to all and everything: REVOLUTION. They had been sufficiently warned and shown the real position and circumstances.
>
> I met Lenin in the summer of 1915 in Switzerland. I laid before him my views on the social and revolutionary consequences of the war and at the same time I warned him that as long as the war lasted there would be no revolution in Germany, that revolution was possible in this period only in Russia, and that it would be the result of German victories.

Siefeldt, in his reminiscences,[2] also describes the meeting, naturally emphasising the inimical reception which Lenin and Krupskaya gave to Helphand and the negative results of the interview. Aleksinsky's hostile attitude to Lenin and the testimony of both participants as to the negative outcome of their meeting speak strongly in favour of the failure to agree. On the other hand there was no open breach of the kind alleged by Siefeldt, who says that Lenin showed Helphand the door. Lenin refrained from attacking Helphand in print before he

---

1. *Pravda Glaza Kolet* (Stockholm, 1918).
2. See above, p. 76, n. 1.

was provoked into doing so by the appearance of the first number of Helphand's magazine, *Die Glocke*, in September 1915. Nor did Helphand bear any ill-will towards Lenin. On the contrary, when the February revolution broke out he was one of the main sponsors, if not the initiator, of the plan to transport Lenin by one means or another to Russia. Even as late as 1918 Helphand hoped to make it up with Lenin and to jump on the bandwagon of the victorious Bolshevik revolution.

Lenin's attitude to Helphand remained distant and negative throughout. He certainly advised young Bukharin not to collaborate in the 'Research Institute for the Study of the Economic Consequences of the World War' which Helphand had founded in Copenhagen. On the other hand, he must have known of the intimate relations between one of his main supporters, Fürstenberg-Ganetsky, and Helphand, and he never did anything to stop them.[1] Later he claimed that Fürstenberg was merely an employee in Helphand's trading enterprise in Denmark.

This was an understatement. Fürstenberg became a close associate in the large-scale black-marketeering and war-profiteering activities which Helphand developed in Denmark[2] with the knowledge and assistance of the German authorities. These activities were intended by Helphand to finance the *Revolutionierungspolitik* which he had outlined in his memorandum of March 1915 to the German government. Fürstenberg, as Helphand's cover-man, undertook some of the more risky business transactions, and was indeed expelled from Denmark in January 1917 for infringing wartime trade control regulations. He never revealed his contacts with Helphand, and on this occasion acted as the latter's screen.[3] Lenin could not have been unaware of this side of Fürstenberg's activities, to which he must have given his tacit approval. In fact Lenin put more trust in Fürstenberg as an underground worker than in the far more scrupulous Shlyapnikov. In 1917, before returning to Russia, Lenin suggested that 'Kuba' (as Fürstenberg-Ganetsky was called in revolutionary circles), being 'a reliable and

1. See an article on Fürstenberg-Ganetsky in *Voprosy istorii KPSS*, 3 (1964), where it is admitted that in 1916 Fürstenberg was working for Lenin in Stockholm. There is, however, no mention of his earlier activities in Copenhagen.
2. Futrell, op. cit, pp. 152–196 *passim*, and below, pp. 85 ff.
3. See Futrell, op. cit., ch. 7.

intelligent fellow', should go to Petrograd to correct the deviations of the Bolshevik leaders in Russia.[1]

In one respect allegations of a secret agreement between Lenin and Helphand are certainly unfounded: we refer to the financial support which Lenin was supposed to have received from Helphand. In spite of the occasional small sums, mentioned above, which Lenin received unwittingly from the Germans via Kesküla and Siefeldt, there can be no doubt of his penury in Switzerland, both as far as his private means and the financing of his publications are concerned. In a letter to Shlyapnikov in Copenhagen dated September/October 1916, Lenin wrote:

> As for myself, I must say I need an income. Otherwise I shall simply perish. Truly! The fiendishly high cost of living — there is nothing to live on. Money must be squeezed out forcibly (Belenin should speak about money to Katin and to Gorky himself, if this is not too awkward) from the publisher of *Letopis*, to whom two of my pamphlets have been sent (let him pay immediately and as much as possible!). The same with Bonch with regard to the translations. If this is not arranged, then I shall not to able to hold out. Of this I am sure. This is very, very serious.[2]

The German authorities did not interfere with Lenin's political activities, connected with the Zimmerwald and Kienthal conferences. They were kept informed on what was going on by their contact-man, Karl Moor, and possibly by Rakovsky. They were not unduly worried about the effect of Lenin's defeatist propaganda on wider circles of German Social-Democracy. Nor did they have much faith in Lenin's ability to bring about a revolution in Russia. Lenin's own frequent sceptical utterances about the unlikelihood of the fall of Tsarism in the near future or even in his lifetime only confirmed them in this attitude. And yet the German foreign and secret services were obviously conscious, at least after Kesküla's report in 1915, that should the windfall of a revolution in Russia really occur, Lenin would be called upon to play an important part in it. This conviction was maintained by the reports of every agent they were employing, including Helphand, Kesküla, Moor

1. Lenin, *Sochineniya*, 3rd ed., vol. XX, p. 55.
2. Ibid., vol. XIX, p. 276. *Letopis* was a left-wing magazine in which Sukhanov's barely disguised defeatist articles appeared in Petrograd. Gorky was a leading contributor. Belenin stands for Shlyapnikov, Bonch for Vladimir Bonch-Bruevich (see p. 71, n. 2).

and the unscrupulous Social Revolutionary émigré, Zivin. But as long
as the revolution was no more than a remote possibility Lenin, in
German eyes, remained ineffectual and unapproachable, and was kept
in 'cold storage' in his retreat in Switzerland.

5. HELPHAND IN COPENHAGEN

The failure of Helphand's mission to the émigrés in Switzerland and of
his interview with Lenin did not discourage him in any way. He was
not a person to shrink from difficulties or feel despondent at the lack
of sympathy and understanding. If Lenin and his followers would not
co-operate with him, he would have to 'go it alone'.

From Switzerland Helphand went in the summer of 1915 to Copenhagen, where in the course of the next two years he set up enterprises of
astonishing scope and diversity. In the first place he established a
'Research Institute for the Study of the Economic Consequences of the
World War'. The Institute collected statistical information on social and
economic questions in the belligerent and neutral countries, ostensibly
in order to draw up a plan for the economic organisation of the post-
war world. In fact it was a convenient cover for employing certain
Russian revolutionaries who were at a loose end during the war and
were only too glad to put their knowledge and personal contacts at the
disposal of such a munificent employer as Helphand.

Secondly, Helphand founded in Germany a political fortnightly
(later a weekly), *Die Glocke*, in which he propagated his ideas of socialist
support for the German war effort. Thirdly, he embarked on a feverish
business drive, directed from Copenhagen through a number of
trading companies which he financed and which greatly augmented his
already appreciable personal fortune.

Helphand left hardly any documentary trace of his wartime activities
in Denmark, but these can be reconstructed from indirect evidence.[1] The
general picture is as follows: Helphand himself came into the open only
as director of the Research Institute and as the first editor of *Die Glocke*.[2]

1. This has been done in a masterly way by M. Futrell in his book quoted above.
2. He soon handed over the editorship to one of the few German Social-Democrats
who had remained faithful to him, Haenisch, who ran it on his behalf with a couple
of other German Socialists or, to use the Leninist term — 'social patriots'. Under

His various commercial enterprises were run by cover-men, chief among them Lenin's friend Fürstenberg-Ganetsky and the brothers Georg and Heinrich Sklarz, who were themselves working on behalf of the Political Section of the German General Staff. Such many-sided activities were a method of camouflaging and financing the real purpose of Helphand's stay in Copenhagen: this was then, and remained throughout, the promotion of revolution in Russia.

Helphand had little difficulty in enlisting the support of the German Minister in Copenhagen, Count Brockdorff-Rantzau. Brockdorff-Rantzau's first attempts to put out feelers for a separate peace with Russia through the Danish court had just suffered a setback. The Count was vaguely 'progressive', and believed in some way in a 'greater participation of the masses in political life in Germany'. It needed little effort on Helphand's part to convince him that no social or political progress was possible in Germany until the reactionary giant in the east had been subverted and dismembered.

Brockdorff-Rantzau's enthusiastic reports on Helphand to the Foreign Minister were confirmed in a special report made by Helphand's old Constantinople friend, Dr Zimmer, who came to inspect his activities and finances on behalf of the Ministry of Foreign Affairs. Dr Zimmer stated that Helphand had eight agents in Copenhagen and ten travelling in Russia. None of the latter have been identified. Helphand was under no obligation to divulge their names to the Germans. Although there is ample circumstantial evidence about his relations with Christian Rakovsky in Bucharest, there is as yet none to show who 'our men in Petrograd', or elsewhere in Russia, were.

Right from the start of his relations with the German government, Helphand had put his association with them on a unique basis. Not only did he lay before the Germans his own plan for the destruction of

their leadership the paper took an even more pro-war course than under Helphand, and statements to the effect that it was Hindenburg who was actually the present-day fighter for socialism can be found on the pages of this amazing publication. After the German revolution Helphand expressed embarrassment at his paper's political stand and explained that he had had no time to check on his editorial board. In fact the patriotic articles in Die Glocke served the purpose of placating the German authorities and showing them that they were not taking undue risks in supporting the activities of an international revolutionary of Russian Jewish descent. See W. B. Scharlau and Z. A. B. Zeman, *Freibeuter der Revolution* (Cologne, 1964), p. 347, and Scharlau's Oxford doctoral thesis (see p. 79 n.).

Russia, but he offered to use his own contacts and organisation for this purpose. As we have seen, he could claim to have established lines of communication via Bulgaria, Rumania and the Ukraine. Furthermore he offered his commercial experience and talent to supply Germany with raw materials badly needed for the war. In 1916 Helphand concluded an enormous deal in Denmark which ousted British coal from the Danish market and replaced it with German coal, for which the German Treasury received welcome neutral currency. Helphand was a man of independent means who had made a fortune for himself and who was in no need of personal subsidies. Such, therefore, was his standing that he was able to extract from the Germans far larger sums than any other rival — sums which he claimed were necessary for the implementation of his plan.

Although the German Foreign Minister, von Jagow, was somewhat sceptical of Helphand's plan, and Helfferich, the head of the Economic War Department, scoffed at certain of Helphand's financial proposals,[1] Helphand received large sums of money from the Ministry of Foreign Affairs during 1915. Besides the one million marks which he received in March before returning to the Balkans, mainly for his contacts in Bucharest, he obtained a million roubles in December, and another appropriation of five million marks which Jagow requested for 'revolutionary propaganda in Russia' in July was also no doubt prompted by Helphand and his supporters in Copenhagen.[2]

But the Foreign Ministry was probably not the only German government department with which Helphand was in contact. Other departments, notably the Political Section of the General Staff, were also working to promote revolution in Russia. It may be assumed that Helphand had contacts — direct or indirect — with it. The Political Section was run by Colonel von Huelsen and maintained liaison with the Foreign Ministry through Kurt Riezler, who had met Helphand in Berlin in March 1915.[3] Dr Zimmer was also connected with the Political Section, and so were the Sklarz brothers who worked for Helphand. The Foreign Ministry was not automatically informed, except on general lines, of the enterprises run by the Political Section, and the German legations in Scandinavian countries were as a rule out of bounds to the agents of this department.

1. Zeman, op. cit., p. 10.   2. Ibid., pp. 3 and 10.   3. See above, p. 79, n. 1.

Having established himself in Copenhagen and having been assured of German support, Helphand proceeded to implement the plan outlined in his March memorandum undeterred by Jagow's scepticism or by Lenin's indignant denunciation after the first appearance of *Die Glocke*.

In December 1915, Helphand explained to Brockdorff-Rantzau that there was no time to lose, that the industrial situation in Russia was such that her economic difficulties could easily be politically exploited, and that internal developments after the adjournment of the Duma on 3 September 1915 favoured a rising.[1] Essentially Helphand did not mislead the Germans: the internal political situation in Russia had considerably deteriorated by this time, and the struggle between the Duma and the Voluntary Organisations on the one side and the government and the Tsar on the other had become acute after the Tsar decided to take over supreme command of the army in August 1915.

Helphand's wooing of the German Foreign Ministry culminated in a definite offer to bring about a revolution in Russia at the beginning of January 1916. This was to be instigated by some confidential agent, who remains unnamed, and who was to provoke a general strike on 9 January, the anniversary of 'Bloody Sunday' of 1905. Helphand claimed that his agents could bring 100,000 men into the streets, and that the strike in the capital would find support in the country at large. His confidential agent would 'immediately start on the organisation of connections between the various revolutionary centres'.[2]

Neither Helphand nor his confidential agent could promise absolute success. They said only that 'the revolution would be set in motion about 9/22 January [Old and New Styles], and that, even if it did not immediately take hold of the whole country, it would certainly prevent any return to stable conditions from taking place'. At the same time Helphand pointed out that although the working masses were as ready for revolutionary action as they had been in 1905, the bourgeois parties were at present unwilling to support the revolutionary movement financially. Helphand therefore asked 'that the sum of one million roubles should at once be put at the disposal of his confidential agent'.[3] The German Foreign Ministry immediately made this sum available,[4]

1. Zeman, op. cit., p. 8.
2. Ibid., p. 9.
3. Ibid., p. 9.   4. Ibid., p. 10.

and Helphand reported to Brockdorff-Rantzau that the money had been transferred to Petrograd.[1]

Over-confident and rash as Helphand's claims were, they were not totally without foundation. 9 January was a convenient day to start a strike movement, as it had become a kind of unofficial labour holiday, at least in Petrograd. There is, moreover, evidence that on this occasion something like a general strike was indeed being planned in Petrograd.

6. HELPHAND AND LABOUR UNREST IN RUSSIA

This is corroborated by what an active Bolshevik agitator in Petrograd, a prominent member of the Petrograd trade union of bakers, Pavel Budaev, wrote to a friend in exile in Eastern Siberia early in March 1916; this letter, intercepted by the police, was found in the police archives.[2] Budaev writes:

> On 9 January [1916] all factories went on strike, the initiative coming from the Vyborg district. The position of the liquidators [that is, the Mensheviks, in Bolshevik jargon] was interesting — most of them spoke against a strike on 9 January, arguing without success that in a fortnight all the factories would stop working anyway, because of lack of fuel. Only in the Novy Aivaz factory were the liquidators in favour of the strike. . . .
>
> There were demonstrations in which soldiers who were driven in lorries greeted the demonstrators with shouts of "Hurrah!" But the soldiers were not allowed out of their barracks; sentries in the barracks and the guards on the telephones were reinforced; the soldiers who remained in barracks enjoined those who went on patrol not to shoot. The demonstrations recurred the next day, 10 January, and in the Vyborg district at 6 p.m. there was a joint demonstration with soldiers who were

1. Zeman, op. cit., p. 14. Brockdorff-Rantzau reported on 23 January 1916 that 'the sum of a million roubles which was put at his [Helphand's] disposal was immediately sent on, and has already reached Petrograd and been devoted to the purposes for which it was intended'.

2. *Krasnaya Letopis*, VII (1923), pp. 208 ff. The Soviet archivist who published it — a certain Bystryansky — wonders why A. Shlyapnikov does not give more details of these events in his 'otherwise so valuable book', *Kanun 17-go goda* (Moscow, 1923). According to Bystryansky, the police archives, which have still not been published in the Soviet Union, contain much important information about revolutionary activities in the first months of 1916. On the Bolshevik Shlyapnikov, see ch. 2 above, pp. 28 ff.

themselves carrying a red flag. Before 9 January there had been 600 arrests in all.[1]

Budaev's report is borne out by other accounts both from the leaders of the revolutionary movements and the police. The number of demonstrators on 9 January is variously estimated at forty-two, forty-five, sixty-six and even one-hundred thousand.[2]

The next wave of industrial unrest started in February in the Putilov Works in Petrograd. In Helphand's memorandum of March 1915 he specifically mentions this works, with two others, as a target for his revolutionary activity.[3] The unhappy story of industrial relations in the Putilov Works dates back to the first days of the war. The workers, rightly or wrongly, were convinced that the management was in the hands of Germans and Jews, who were actually sabotaging, or preparing to sabotage, the war effort. The management did not improve relations by its tactless handling of the conscription exemption order.[4]

1. It was a regular police practice to arrest potential ringleaders when their secret agents reported imminent labour unrest.
2. See M. Balabanov, *Ot 1905 k 1917 godu* (Moscow and Leningrad, 1927), p. 411, who believes that the figure of 100,000 reported by Shlyapnikov may well be correct. 100,000 demonstrators was the number that Helphand in his conversations with Brockdorff-Rantzau claimed to be able to call into the streets on 9 January.
3. Zeman, op. cit., p. 140.
4. A secret police report describes the situation as follows:

After the German declaration of war on Russia many alien subjects were removed from the works. In spite of this, relations between the workers and the German management (i.e. directors of German descent) continued to deteriorate. The workers became particularly critical of all administrative arrangements at the factory, suspecting evil intent on the part of foreigners wishing to harm the interests of Russia. The workers knew all about the malpractices of the works management and were so moved by patriotic feeling that disturbances might have occurred at any time. Thus, having learnt that the strike which broke out at the Putilov dockyard at the beginning of the war had been provoked by the former director, the German Orbanovsky, the workers warned the management that should any of the directors who were German subjects, including Orbanovsky himself, turn up at the works, they would be killed. After most influential German subjects had been dismissed from the works, production was speeded up, but some time later the fulfilment of war orders was again delayed for one reason or another. In view of this, the works management was allowed to retain those workers indispensable to production. Taking advantage of this permission, however, it started exempting from conscription not those workers who were really useful in the factory, but those whom it favoured, who were not of great use. This

Up to the middle of 1915 the workers' discontent seems to have been rooted in economic demands and excessive patriotic zeal, but in August 1915 they started voicing political demands.[1] On 3 February 1916, mechanics in the electrical workshop demanded a seventy per cent wage rise. The works management refused to countenance such a demand and appealed to the Commander of the Petrograd Military District, Prince Tumanov, who posted an order in the works threatening to 'militarise' the whole enterprise, i.e. to mobilise all those of conscription age and employ them under military discipline. The management closed the works for three days on 16 February, and, as the unrest continued, for a further week on the 23rd of the same month — exactly a year before the outbreak of labour unrest in 1917.

Budaev claims that these disturbances at the Putilov Works were directed by the Petersburg Committee of the Social-Democratic Party and by the Socialist Revolutionaries, and that one of the strikers' slogans was 'Down with the war!' A contemporary police report also blames 'the Leninists' for turning the strikers' economic demands into political ones.[2] Particularly interesting in this respect is the leaflet

led to a shortage of qualified labour and further delays in the fulfilment of orders, however urgent' (Fleer, op. cit., pp. 256 ff.).

The agitation against Germans in the works management continued, and in August 1915 the workers demanded the removal of naturalised subjects of German and Austrian origin.

1. A police report quoted by Fleer op. cit. p. 259, ascribes the change of mood to the agitation of 'revolutionary parties': 'This agitation, which was strongest in the capital, led to the formation of secret cells in the local factories and works, to the holding of meetings and unauthorised gatherings, and to partial strikes. . . . At the end of August 1915, the workers of the Putilov factory presented the management with a number of economic and political demands. The political demands were: liberation of the five Bolshevik members of the Duma deported to Siberia in February 1915; universal suffrage; freedom of the press; and an extension of the session of the State Duma. These demands were backed up by a go-slow strike.'

2. Fleer, op. cit., p. 262. ' . . . It is clear that the reasons for the strike were purely economic and that they would probably have remained so, had the revolutionary element not intervened in this case.

'The leading "Leninist" group, which calls itself the "Petersburg Committee of the Social-Democratic Workers' Party" considers all economic action on the part of the working masses untimely at the present moment and opposes the workers' unorganised attempts to express their discontent with the difficult economic living conditions in individual industrial enterprises. This group remains faithful, however, to the plans and aims of its underground leaders, who are always keen to use large

calling for a political strike which was issued by the Bolshevik Petersburg Committee at this time. It attacks General Tumanov's order as
bare-faced intimidation by the military authorities, and calls for a
determined rebuff.

> The cause of the Putilov workers [says the leaflet] is the cause of the
> Petersburg proletariat as a whole. . . . The action of the Putilov workers
> must be supported actively by the whole of the Petersburg proletariat.
> Otherwise there will be no limit to the brazen mockery of the robber
> gang of the Romanov dynasty. . . . Comrades, if you do not decisively
> repulse all attempts to enslave you, you will yourselves be donning the
> shackles which await you. In declaring a political protest strike, the
> Petersburg proletariat is assuming a great responsibility. The black
> forces of Tsarism will use this action to spread slander and sow con-
> fusion in the army. The proletariat, transcending the bounds of the factory
> and works, must carry its cause into the streets to make it clear to all and
> sundry, to reach out to our brothers in the army, who might otherwise
> be used against us. . . . Down with the bullying of the Tsarist hirelings !
> . . . Down with the Romanov monarchy ! Long live proletarian soli-
> darity and the class struggle ! Long live the revolutionary proletariat
> and the Russian Social-Democratic Party !¹

But this high-flown rhetoric was to have but little effect. The police
had infiltrated the ranks of the Bolshevik organisation and, fearing that
the labour disturbances threatened 'the normal course of state affairs'
and the war effort, proceeded to arrest the members of the Petersburg
Committee. Events in the Putilov Works were the subject of a question
in the Duma on 7 March 1916. The Minister of War, Polivanov, made
a patriotic speech and the Duma adopted a resolution appealing to both
workers and industrialists to discharge their civic duties in a voluntary,
responsible and enthusiastic manner.

With the arrest of the leaders, the lock-out at the Putilov Works, and

social movements for their purposes. This organisation tried to make use of the present
strike of the Putilov workers to bring nearer the realisation of the ultimate ideals of
Social-Democracy. . . .'

The police report pointed out that the agitation of the Bolshevik and Bolshevik-
tainted Social-Democrats was directed against the Bill about to be introduced in
the Duma on the militarisation of industrial enterprises, and called for a civil war to
begin on 10 February, the anniversary of the sentencing of the Bolshevik Duma
deputies.

1. Fleer, op. cit., p. 266.

possibly the issuance of last-minute instructions by the strike organisers, the movement temporarily died down in Petrograd, only to resume and gather strength during the following months until it grew into the full-scale popular rising of February 1917.

It is pertinent to compare the strikes and demonstrations in Petrograd in January and February 1916 with what happened at approximately the same time at the Nikolaev shipyards in the estuary of the Dnieper, where two large dreadnoughts were being built for the Black Sea Fleet.[1]

In January 1916, at the same time as the strikes and demonstrations in Petrograd, a strike broke out at the naval shipyards in Nikolaev, and the disturbances continued until the works were closed on 23 February.

In a secret report by Vice-Admiral Muravyev found in the archives of the Council of Ministers and quoted by Fleer,[2] the story of the strike is given in considerable detail. The exorbitant wage claims advanced by the workers at the very beginning of the strike and the subsequent course of the unrest convinced Muravyev that this was in fact a political strike organised on the pretext of economic demands, a fact which according to him neither the police nor the labour inspectorate nor any other government department had discerned. The management had consequently started making piecemeal concessions, a blunder which only led to further unrest until the works were closed.

In support of his contention that the strike had a concealed political purpose, Muravyev points to the following:

> For one thing the nature of the workers' demands would be unacceptable in principle to any industrial concern, and for another, these unacceptable demands coincided in scope, form and timing with similar demands put forward in a number of works in Petrograd.[3] Furthermore the allegedly inadequate and even intolerable material conditions said to have forced the employees of the 'Naval' works to come out on strike seemed quite

1. The ships were the *Empress Maria* and the *Alexander III*. The former was delivered to the navy in the autumn of 1916 but was sabotaged in October in the port of Sevastopol and became a complete loss. Significantly, Helphand in his Memorandum sets much store by sabotage, which according to him should always go hand-in-hand with revolutionary propaganda.
2. Op. cit., pp. 247 ff.
3. Muravyev is of course referring to strikes such as the one at the Putilov Works described above.

tolerable to the workers of the nearby 'Russud' works, where conditions were identical in every respect to those at 'Naval' and where the management consisted of the same persons.

Admiral Muravyev's analysis echoes Helphand's Memorandum of March 1915, of which of course he had never heard. Helphand had written: 'Particular attention should be devoted to Nikolaev, as the shipyards there are working under great pressure for the launching of two large warships. Efforts should be made to start a strike among the workers there. This strike need not necessarily be political in character; it could just as well be based on the workers' economic demands.'[1]

Admiral Muravyev concluded cautiously: 'We must leave open the question whether this political strike is the work of enemies of the present régime — i.e. the leftist parties — or whether the hand of the enemy of the State (Germany) can be detected in it.'

The Russian authorities had, however, been aware for some months of the provenance of the revolutionary propaganda which was circulating among the shipyard workers. The Minister for the Navy, Grigorovich, in a letter to the Chairman of the Council of Ministers on 28 April 1915 (only eight weeks after Helphand had presented his Memorandum in Berlin) reported that 'according to the latest information to reach me the appearance of proclamations is due to the activity of emissaries of the powers who are at war with us and who do not hesitate to resort to base expedients of this kind'. Four months later, on 26 August 1915, at the memorable meeting of the Council of Ministers which discussed the prorogation of the Duma, Grigorovich further stated: 'According to my information unrest is unavoidable if the session of the Duma is adjourned. The workers' morale is very low. The Germans are carrying out intensive propaganda and are giving money freely to subversive organisations. The situation is particularly acute in the Putilov Works.'[2] Grigorovich's statement caused no sensation in the Council: apparently all the Ministers were aware that the Germans were fomenting industrial unrest in preparation for an imminent uprising.

1. Zeman, op. cit., p. 149.
2. Grigorovich's letter to Goremykin is quoted partially in Fleer, op. cit., p. 11. The statement of 26 August 1915 appears in the Minutes of the secret meetings of the Council of Ministers, published in ARR, XVIII, p. 105. Yakhontov's manuscript contains other references made by Grigorovich to German subversion. On Yakhontov, see below, p. 134 n.

The Nikolaev strike of February 1916 was broken by police and military measures, a lock-out at the 'Naval' wharf and the mobilisation of the strikers.

The failure of the movements which had started in Petrograd and Nikolaev in 1916 to develop into a revolutionary uprising must have been a heavy blow to Helphand. Yet he did not try to sustain false expectations or to gloss over the fact that the promises he had made to Brockdorff-Rantzau in December had not been fulfilled. In his report of 23 January, Brockdorff-Rantzau states that Helphand in an interview with him had explained that it had been found inadvisable to launch the revolution at that moment because of the changing situation. The reasons which Helphand gave for this decision were: (a) increased resistance from the bourgeois opposition to an immediate revolution; (b) the enlistment of some labour leaders for war work; (c) the extraordinary measures taken by the government to relieve the food shortage in Petrograd; and finally (d) the fear of the revolutionaries that they might not be able to control the masses in the streets, that the movement might turn into anarchy and thus easily be crushed by the government.[1]

Budaev confirms one of Helphand's reasons for the failure of the revolutionary attempt — the opposition of some labour leaders to the strike. He writes: 'At the beginning of February, a strike broke out at the metal works, but two workshops did not down tools. The liquidators in these workshops proposed to ask Gvozdev in the WIC for permission [to strike] and the WIC decided that the workers were wrong to strike and suggested they should liquidate the strike, but the workers went on with it.'[2]

Yet the general situation in Petrograd, as observed by a revolutionary worker like Budaev, seemed to confirm Helphand's confident belief that the revolutionary movement had great possibilities. Budaev wrote in March 1916: 'Generally speaking, life here is at boiling point. Among

1. Zeman, op. cit., pp. 14–15. Helphand's explanations were not quite clear to Brockdorff-Rantzau, who gives a somewhat garbled version of them. For instance, he says that the government of Russia has 'called several men who before the war were spokesmen of the revolutionaries to leading positions and has in this way considerably weakened the [revolutionary] movement'. This is an obvious reference to the formation of the Labour Groups of the WIC.
2. *Krasnuyu Letopis*, VII (1923), pp. 208 ff.

the printers, nine enterprises are at a standstill because of a strike. Estonian Social-Democratic organisations have contact with organisations in other towns. Leaflets are appearing here all the time. Some have been received from Narva (Social-Democratic ones).'[1] Indeed the strike movement which started early in 1916 went on in spurts, becoming particularly intense in June/July and again in October, and culminating in a full-scale revolutionary movement in February 1917.

Soviet historians have been surprisingly reticent about the development of the strike movement in these months, and few of the police archives have been published. It is important to note also that for this whole period between February 1916 and February 1917 the documents of the German Foreign Ministry contain no indication of any political action taken by Helphand, nor of any German money passed on to him for revolutionary purposes. In our opinion, however, it would be a mistake to believe that Helphand abandoned his aim of revolutionising Russia because of the failure of his first attempt on 9 January 1916. As he himself said, he was not absolutely confident that the movement would succeed at once, but he was sure that it would certainly prevent any return to stable conditions in Russia. On 23 January Brockdorff-Rantzau reported that the decision of Helphand's organisation to launch revolutionary action was still firm and unchanged. How then can we explain the absence from the Foreign Ministry archives of evidence of further negotiations and correspondence with Helphand on these all-important matters?[2]

The loss of face which Helphand suffered, especially with the sceptical and suspicious State Secretary, Jagow, must have made him worried about further direct contacts with the Auswärtiges Amt on the question of revolutionising Russia. In the meantime the trade companies he had

1. Ibid.
2. In a volume of cautiously-weighed reminiscences, Fritz M. Cahén, who served as a kind of press attaché in Copenhagen under Brockdorff-Rantzau, claims to know more than he can reveal about the Helphand scheme to promote a Russian revolution in 1916. He points out that there are 'certain things [mancherlei Dinge] which are still concealed and will remain so because not everything is to be found in the files' of the Foreign Ministry. Cahén names the German Ministers in Berne, Stockholm and Copenhagen as the protagonists of the scheme, but leaves the reader to understand that other German agencies also contributed to its success. Fritz M. Cahén, Der Weg nach Versailles (Boldt, Boppard/Rhein, 1963), pp. 197 ff.

created grew and prospered with astonishing speed. Money was pouring into the pockets of Helphand and Fürstenberg, and some of it, coming from an illicit trade with Russia in medical supplies, contraceptives, pencils and cosmetics, was kept in that country for purposes which have not been disclosed.[1] As far as Helphand was concerned his trading activities, economic research and journalism were all closely interconnected, and all served one great purpose – the downfall of the Russian empire. By the middle of 1916 there was no need for him to beg the Auswärtiges Amt for subsidies for his work, and therefore to be made to give account of what he was doing and to suffer petty criticism and disclose information which was better kept secret even from the Germans. By that time Helphand must have known that the security arrangements of the Auswärtiges Amt were not always watertight, and he might well have preferred financial independence to occasional subsidies involving official correspondence. Despite the lack of any documentary evidence in the Auswärtiges Amt archives, the continuous character of the strike movement in Russia in 1916 and at the beginning of 1917 strongly suggests that it was controlled and supported by Helphand and his agents. None of his contact men in Petrograd or Nikolaev were uncovered by the Russians, and with the increase of German clandestine imports into Russia through the agency of Fürstenberg-Ganetsky they no doubt prospered and their ventures developed.

Our belief that Helphand's trade activity was, though important in itself, also a powerful auxiliary in achieving his revolutionary aim is confirmed by the report of a German auditor who investigated the activities of one of Helphand's subsidiary companies directed by Georg Sklarz. The auditor was very surprised at the 'unbelievable transactions' carried out by Sklarz in violation of the German wartime trade regulations, but with the knowledge and consent of the German Foreign Ministry. The auditor felt himself duty bound to ask whether such transactions were not condoned in order 'perhaps to facilitate the achievement of other aims for which Sklarz was being used by the Auswärtiges Amt'.[2]

1. See Scharlau and Zeman, op. cit., p. 232 *passim*.
2. See the report of the auditor, Knatz, of 7 December 1917, WK 2 geh., quoted by Scharlau in his Oxford doctoral thesis, p. 211. See also Scharlau and Zeman, op. cit., p. 232.

7. KESKÜLA

In the meantime, the Germans never thought of putting all their reliance on Helphand. They employed a number of other agents who had no connection with him. These were supervised by liaison officers of the Political Section of the General Staff, such as Steinwachs. Some of them seem to have been ordinary crooks; others, such as Zivin (cover name Weiss) and his associate Levinstein (also known as Blau) were rather ineffectual.

The only man who can be at all compared with Helphand is Alexander Kesküla, whom we have mentioned above. Having drawn the attention of the Germans to Lenin, Kesküla went to Stockholm late in 1915 to organise contacts with revolutionaries in Russia. Unlike Helphand, he had no independent means, and his attitude to the Russian revolution was very different. His main interest was in Estonian independence and he was equally opposed to Russian or German domination of his small country. He had the lowest opinion of the organisational abilities of Russian revolutionaries, with the exception of Lenin, but thought that they could be managed by 'a little *Organisatorik*' – as he described his activities. On his arrival in Stockholm, Kesküla gained influence with the Bolshevik committee there through its secretary, Bogrovsky. He subsidised the activities of that committee, such as the printing of leaflets and pamphlets for clandestine transportation to Russia. He also arranged for a certain Alfred Kruse, a Danish Social-Democrat, to undertake, under the cover of journalistic activities, various commissions in Russia on behalf of both Kesküla and Helphand. Kruse went twice to Russia with messages from Bukharin to his wife and with other business from the Bolshevik Bureau in Stockholm for Bolshevik organisations in Moscow and Petrograd. He duly contacted the Petrograd Bolshevik organisations, and his visit is recorded in the memoirs of the worker Kondratyev, published in *Krasnaya Letopis*.[1] Kruse brought back important material from the Petersburg

---

1. No. 7 (Petrograd, 1923). Kondratyev writes: 'Approximately at the end or at the beginning of the campaign [for the strike on 9 January 1916] Krauze [Kondratyev misspells the unusual name of Kruse] arrived and stopped on the Sadovaya in the hotel "Dagmara". Having had an assignation with someone [note the discretion of Kondratyev], he had a number of interviews with me and Comrade Schmidt. He was handed over certain materials for the Central Committee of our party on the progress

Committee, some of which was later used in Lenin's paper, *Sotsial-Demokrat*.[1] Throughout the spring and summer of 1916 the Petrograd Bolsheviks were supplied through Keskülä's organisation with revolutionary literature from abroad. Copies of these pamphlets, such as 'The High Cost of Living and the War', 'Who Needs War?' and Bukharin's 'The War and the Working Class', were passed on to the Auswärtiges Amt.[2]

8. GERMAN POLICY AFTER FEBRUARY 1917

The disappointment of the Germans at the failure to provoke a revolution in Russia early in 1916 led to a temporary resurgence, in high places in Germany, of the idea of a separate peace. In the latter half of 1916 the war was not progressing to the satisfaction of the German diplomats. The Foreign Ministry documents reveal a constant concern about the possible defection of Germany's allies, and desperate efforts to ease the strategic situation by making a separate peace with any one of the Entente powers. A new attempt to appeal to Nicholas II through the Danish court was made in the summer of 1916, but failed (as has been described above, p. 65) when Nicholas told King Christian that only a general peace could be considered. The Germans put great hopes on the interview between Fritz Warburg and the members of the Russian parliamentary delegation to the Allies, Count Olsufyev and A. D.

of the campaign for [organising] the work of the Petersburg Committee. He was also given information on the latest economic strikes in Petrograd.'

Then follows an interesting passage, which might well be a later interpolation, to show that no money was received from Kruse. It might, however, be quite genuine. Keskülä had no large sums for distribution in Russia, and Helphand would not have used Kruse as a go-between in financial matters. The passage runs: 'I remember that at one of the interviews with Krauze, when I was present with Comrade Schmidt, the question of a financial contribution to the funds of the Central Committee was raised; this was needed for Krauze's return journey. At the time we had absolutely no possibility of making such a contribution to the funds of the Central Committee and we offered Krauze 25 roubles, which the latter naturally refused.'

1. For a detailed account of Kruse's life and fortunes, see Futrell, op. cit., ch. VI *passim*.
2. Zeman, op. cit., pp. 12–14. One of the documents brought out of Russia by Keskülä's organisation was the Disposition No. 1 of the Committee of Public Safety. See below, p. 166.

Protopopov.[1] Further attempts at inducing the Russian government to enter into negotiations were made through the intermediary of the Swedes (the Wallenberg operation) and the Bulgarians (the Rizoff operation).[2] How desperate the desire for a separate peace was in certain circles in Germany can be judged from the incredible plan put forward by the industrialist Fritz Thyssen through the Reichstag deputy, Erzberger, to the Ministry of Foreign Affairs. Thyssen proposed to buy Russian goodwill at the expense of Norway by offering Russia Narvik and the northern Scandinavian ore fields. This would have meant a considerable sacrifice for Germany (*sic*), Thyssen remarked, but could be made good by the annexation of the French iron ore fields in Briey.[3] In the meantime Kolyshko and his friends were being encouraged by the Germans to buy a Russian newspaper to agitate for a separate peace, and the German Foreign Ministry was closely following the penetration of defeatist ideas, in the guise of Zimmerwald propaganda, into Russia; particular interest was aroused by Sukhanov's articles in *Letopis*, published in Petrograd with the assistance of Gorky, in which Sukhanov put forward the case for defeatism in Aesopian language.

In the middle of December 1916 the Central Powers made an overt peace offer to the Entente, the motives for which have been frequently debated. There was no prospect of such a peace proposal, couched in arrogant terms, ever being accepted by the Allies, but it is quite possible that it was intended to provoke differences between the Entente powers, especially between Russia and her western allies. When this failed completely and the Duma adopted an extremely patriotic attitude, the Germans seem to have abandoned all hope of a separate peace, deciding to stake everything on the *Revolutionierungspolitik* in Russia and indiscriminate U-boat warfare in the West.

It no doubt seemed to the Germans that there was a long way to go before their various intrigues and propaganda efforts directed against Russia were transformed into political action. The fall of the Tsarist régime was hence as much a surprise to the German authorities as to anyone else (including the leaders of the Bolshevik Party), despite the fact that it was the reward of their own relentless efforts.

The February revolution brought a certain clarification into the

1. See above, p. 69.
2. Scherer and Grunewald, op. cit., pp. 488, 570, 689.
3. Ibid., p. 467.

conflicting tendencies of German policy towards Russia. Of the two main courses — the quest for a separate peace with Russia and the policy of revolutionising her — the first was soon abandoned when the Provisional Government refused to denounce its alliance with the Western powers. The policy of revolutionising now resolved itself into definite support for the only defeatist Russian party – the Bolsheviks. It was in the various emergency measures which the Germans took to support this initially weak and disorientated party that the mechanism of the *Revolutionierungspolitik* became more sharply delineated. It is for this reason that it is necessary to continue our survey of German political intervention in Russia into the first months of the new régime.

Throughout the years before February 1917, conscious German efforts to promote a revolution in Russia had been confined to the incitement and support of labour unrest in the hope that, in accordance with Helphand's theory, it would grow into an effective political movement. The Germans had made no attempt to organise revolutionary leaders among the émigrés or in Russia. Such an attempt was completely out of the question during World War I. Any suspicion of direct contact with the German authorities would have discredited anybody foolish enough to have put himself into this position. Both the Germans and the revolutionaries understood this very well.

But after the success of the February revolution and the emergence of two rival ruling bodies – the Provisional Government and the Petrograd Soviet – the Germans were faced with a new situation. They did not influence either body directly, except perhaps through such intermediaries as M. Kozlovsky, (a close associate of Fürstenberg-Ganetsky) who joined the Executive Committee of the Petrograd Soviet at the time it was formed.

The Germans feared, moreover, that the delirious enthusiasm with which the change of régime was greeted by all sections of the Russian population threatened to create a sort of *union sacrée* which might infuse new vitality into the Russian war effort. Even the Bolshevik leaders in Petrograd under Kamenev and Stalin, who had returned from Siberia, were affected by this atmosphere, and seemed inclined to accept the war with Germany as part of the struggle for securing the newly-won freedom. The slogan 'Down with the war' which had been used for agitation among the masses before the February revolution had to be temporarily dropped because it threatened to split the revolutionary movement and alienate the support of both the middle class and the military.

The German authorities were aware of the danger, of which they had been warned by their Russian advisers, that the revolution might develop into a patriotic movement. The fact that the new régime was immediately recognised and indeed welcomed by the Western Allies only increased the Germans' fears. Immediate action was necessary, lest the unique opportunities inherent in the upheaval should slip away. From both the Germans' and Lenin's point of view, anything was better than the consolidation of a régime dominated by Milyukov and Guchkov.

The importance to the Germans of such advisers as Helphand and even Zivin rose immediately. Possibly their stock soared even higher as a result of the unexpected defection of Kesküla. In a letter to Steinwachs which reveals a somewhat megalomaniac trend in Kesküla's mind, he took leave of the Germans, telling them that from now on their paths must diverge but that he, after all, had rendered them the greatest service by drawing their attention to Lenin.[1]

The German Foreign Ministry clearly understood that, in order to forestall the new spirit of national unity to which the enthusiasm of the February days might lead, they had to support any faction, however small and insignificant, which was against continuing the war. It is interesting to note that one of the first names which occurred to the Germans as a possible protagonist of defeatism was that of the former Bolshevik deputy of the Fourth Duma, Malinovsky, who has been mentioned before (see above, p. 73). But no sooner was this idea put forward than it had to be abandoned: the secret police archives were thrown open in Petrograd and the President of the Duma, Rodzyanko, announced that Malinovsky had in fact worked as an informer for the Ministry of the Interior throughout his parliamentary career. The Germans thereupon turned their attention to Lenin.

9. THE RETURN OF LENIN

The momentous news of the outbreak of the revolution in Russia was brought to Lenin by an Austrian Social-Democrat, Bronsky, on 14

1. See letter to Steinwachs in the archives of the German Legation in Berne.

March (New Style). By 16 March he had received confirmation of the event in official dispatches from Petrograd. The news was unexpected, but Lenin immediately realised its significance for his destiny. And yet he resisted the temptation to indulge in the form of delirious rejoicing with which it was greeted by Russian revolutionaries both in Russia and abroad. His first reaction to the news was full of bitterness and determination to fight on. On 16 March he wrote to Madame Kollontay:

> We have just had the second batch of government wires about the revolution in Petrograd on 1 (14) March. A week of bloody battles by the workers and then Milyukov, plus Guchkov, plus Kerensky in power! All according to the 'old' European pattern. . . .
> Can't be helped! This 'first stage of the first of the revolutions which are to be brought on by the war' will not be the last. Neither will it be a Russian stage only. Of course we shall continue to stand against the defence of the fatherland, against the imperialist slaughter conducted by Shingarev plus Kerensky and Co.
> All our slogans remain the same. . . .
> . . . The main thing now is the Press, the organisation of the workers into a revolutionary Social-Democratic party. . . . The greatest disaster would be if the Kadets were now to promise a legal workers' party and if our people were to agree to a 'union with Chkheidze and Co.'.[1] But this is not to be. In the first place the Kadets will not allow a legal workers' party to anyone except Messrs Potresov and Co.[1] In the second place even if they do allow such parties, we shall as before create our own separate party and in any event combine legal and illegal work.
> . . . We must now have a more revolutionary programme and tactics (the elements of which are to be found in K. Liebknecht, the Socialist Labour Party in America, the Dutch Marxists, etc.) and the necessary combination of legal and illegal work.

Having then proclaimed for the first time the slogan that the revolution should end with the seizure of power by 'the Soviet of Workers' Deputies' (and not Kadet groups) Lenin closes with the indignant remark: '. . . After the "great rebellion" of 1905 the "glorious revolution" of 1917! . . .' When he sketched this first draft of a revolutionary manifesto, Lenin had no idea how hard it would be to find a field of activity which would be considered illegal in Russia in the first weeks after the February revolution.

1. That is, the defensist Mensheviks.

Lenin had all along made it clear to his followers, to his friends — and through them to the German government — that he would oppose a defensive war even after the fall of the Tsarist régime. In his farewell address to the Swiss workers, written shortly before his departure for Russia, Lenin referred to the declaration published in his paper *Sotsial-Demokrat* on 13 October 1915, and added:

> In this we said that if the revolution is victorious in Russia and a republican government comes to power which wants to continue the imperialist war, a war in alliance with the imperialist bourgeoisie of England and France, a war for the conquest of Constantinople, Armenia, Galicia, and so on and so forth, then we will be decided opponents of such a government, we will be *against* 'the defence of the Fatherland' in *such* a war.
>
> Now such an eventuality has arisen. The new government of Russia which negotiated with the brother of Nicholas II with a view to restoring the monarchy in Russia, and in which the monarchists Lvov and Guchkov occupy leading positions, this government is trying ... to represent as a defensive war ... its imperialist war with Germany, to represent as a defence of the Russian republic ... the defence of the predatory imperialist bandit-like aims of Russian, English and other capital.[1]

The Germans were impressed by this declaration of policy and they began the delicate operation of conveying Lenin and his supporters to the scene of the revolutionary turmoil in Petrograd. The question of who initiated the negotiations for the return of Lenin through Germany is a minor detail: the main point is that all parties concerned were in full agreement on it.[2] The Swiss Minister of Foreign Affairs, the Social-Democrat Hoffmann, who collaborated closely with the German government, initiated the actual contacts between Robert Grimm, the editor of the *Berner Tagwacht*, and the prospective travellers. But at the beginning of January Lenin had had a violent quarrel with Grimm, whom

1. Lenin, *Sochineniya*, vol. XX, pp. 66 ff.
2. The German Chancellor claims to have instructed his Minister in Berne to organise this operation as soon as he received the news of a revolution in Petrograd. Helphand was in favour of it. The General Staff, in the person of the head of the Political Section, Colonel von Huelsen, was ready to facilitate it in every way, with the full approval of Ludendorff; indeed, had the Swedes refused to allow the political émigrés to pass through Sweden, the German army would have arranged for them to cross the front line.

he accused of Swiss 'social chauvinism'. And so Grimm was replaced as middleman in these negotiations by another Swiss Social-Democrat, Fritz Platten, who had followed Lenin's line far more faithfully and was at the same time on the best of terms with Romberg, the German Minister in Berne.

There is no need to repeat in detail the story of this journey.[1] The German government was fully aware of the real danger of the operation, which was that their conspicuous solicitude towards the returnees would compromise Lenin in Russia, thus defeating their own ends. The German authorities therefore behaved with the utmost, indeed unusual, discretion.[2] One of the ways in which they camouflaged their intentions was by including in the first train (as well as in those which followed) socialists who were not Leninists. It is interesting to note, however, that Lenin attached little importance to the effectiveness of such precautions: on arrival in Petrograd he openly admitted that the German government had let him through for the sake of their own imperialist aims, and that he had taken tactical advantage of this. On his homeward journey Lenin was careful to avoid all contacts with official representatives of the German Social-Democratic majority; Helphand he avoided even more assiduously, in spite of the latter's desperate attempt to contact him during his short stay in Stockholm. On the other hand, while in Stockholm he did see Fürstenberg-Ganetsky, who, with Radek and Vorovsky, drew up and signed a statement testifying that there had been no interview between Lenin and Helphand.[3] With Fürstenberg, whom Lenin treated as a trusted friend and member of his party, Lenin discussed party-organisational questions.

After a day's break, Lenin and his group proceeded on their long journey to Haparanda, the Swedish-Finnish frontier station. Platten went with them, intending to travel to Russia and witness Lenin's

1. A documented account will be found in Werner Hahlweg, *Lenins Rückkehr nach Russland* (Leiden, 1957), against which all other accounts should be checked.
2. The Kaiser was wisely kept out of it all. When he later learned from the papers of the desire of some Russian revolutionaries to return home through Germany, he immediately began to give instructions as to how the thing should be arranged, stressing the demands which should be put to them and the orders they should be given. Luckily for the German authorities these instructions, which might have jeopardised the whole operation, came too late, and the Kaiser was appeased with a report that all his desiderata had been anticipated. See Hahlweg, op. cit., pp. 93 ff.
3. Zeman, op. cit., p. 42, quoting Radek.

arrival in Petrograd. But this was not to be: at the frontier, so he said in his report to Romberg, he was turned back by British intelligence officers who were in charge there.[1] Platten must, however, have been made privy to the operational plans which Lenin had worked out with Fürstenberg and Radek. On his return to Berne at the end of April Platten gave Romberg a detailed account of the journey, emphasizing that 'the émigrés lack the means for the conduct of their propaganda, while the means of their enemies are unlimited'.[2] Romberg immediately instructed the assistant military attaché, Nasse, to find out in what way money could best be conveyed to the returnees; at the same time he asked the Auswärtiges Amt whether 'the revolutionaries are being supported in any other way'. The Marquis de Pourtalès of the Auswärtiges Amt gave Romberg an answer by word of mouth, and no record of it was kept.[3] Nasse's report to Romberg, is, however, available. It says that a certain 'Herr Baier' had at once made contact with the Bolshevik Grigory Shklovsky and the Menshevik leader Paul Akselrod, who were still in Switzerland, and found out that financial help would be acceptable to them, provided it was presented as a donation from 'an unobjectionable source' and that certain technical conditions were observed.[4] At this point there is a tantalising blank in the documents of the Auswärtiges Amt concerning the activities of Nasse and the mysterious Herr Baier. If one were to rely exclusively on this source it would seem that the Baier-Nasse negotiation led to nothing. Evidence to be found elsewhere, however, proves that this was not so.

10. 'CHANNELS AND LABELS'

Among the many advisers and agents with academic qualifications whom the German government used in World War I was a certain Dr Gustav Mayer, who had made a name for himself as a biographer of Engels and later as the editor of Lassalle's letters. His widespread contacts among socialists in Europe made his services valuable, particularly in Belgium, where the German government was sounding out

1. Ibid., p. 52.
2. See Hahlweg, op. cit., pp. 93 ff. Zeman, op. cit., p. 53.
3. See Zeman, p. 53.
4. Ibid., pp. 54–56.

Second International circles to find out whether they would accept the German solution to the Belgian problem. In May 1917 Mayer approached the German Foreign Ministry and offered to attend the forthcoming Socialist conference in Stockholm in order to renew his personal contacts, and the Ministry delegated him to observe and report on the proceedings. Mayer also had many acquaintances among leading officials in Berlin, and in particular he was on very friendly terms with the assistant military attaché in Berne, Nasse, whom we have mentioned above.

In his posthumously published memoirs,[1] Mayer recalls, on the basis of diaries kept at the time and letters to his wife, that shortly before leaving for Stockholm at the end of May he was seen by a high official of the German Treasury, Dr Moritz von Saemisch. Saemisch asked Mayer to help in a matter of 'extreme political importance', which must be kept absolutely secret, even from the Foreign Ministry. Mayer was to meet a certain person known to him — it proved to be Nasse — on his arrival in Stockholm, and give him whatever assistance he required. Mayer agreed to this, believing, as he says with a certain disingenuousness, that this would not involve him in anything dishonourable.

When he met Nasse in Stockholm he found that the main service he was to render was to act as a post-box for letters, papers and on occasion also money deposited by people whom Mayer says he could not identify.[2] At the same time Mayer was in close contact with both Fürstenberg and Radek, who were living with their wives in a luxury villa in a fashionable suburb of Stockholm. Mayer makes no attempt to explain Nasse's operations, and does not refer to any connection between Nasse and the Bolsheviks. He mentions, however, the presence in Stockholm at that time of Karl Moor — the same Karl Moor who had been so helpful when Lenin and his party arrived without proper papers in Switzerland in September 1914.

1. Gustav Mayer, *Erinnerungen* (Zürich and Vienna, 1949 — printed in Nuremberg).
2. See ibid., p. 260. 'My absolutely unsuspicious address was the thing that interested him [Nasse] most. Letters, manuscripts, on occasion money transfers also, were to come from time to time to this address by post or through messengers, mostly women, and were to be kept unopened until either Nasse himself or a messenger authorised by him would take them. In the upshot, however, I had to hand over these packets myself in places where Nasse warned me in my own interest not to establish any relations.'

In view of the enquiry which Nasse had made, on Romberg's instructions, only a few weeks before in Berne, about how money could be transferred to the Bolsheviks, it is safe to assume that the Stockholm conspiracy in which Mayer got involved was serving the same purpose of financing the Bolsheviks. There is, however, more to it than this: the Herr Baier who had contacted Shklovsky and Akselrod and who had told Romberg under what conditions the money could be transferred was none other than Karl Moor, who now turned up in Stockholm to assist Nasse.[1]

It is a curious reflection on the workings of the minds of confidential agents that Gustav Mayer felt an urge shortly before his death in exile in London to record these dealings of Nasse's, but without saying what they were actually concerned with. At the time of the publication of Mayer's memoirs in 1949, Nasse's involvement with the *Revolutionierungspolitik*, which came out only through the publication of the German documents, was totally unknown, as was the fact that the German agent, Herr Baier, was identical with the member of the Bernese Great Council and former editor of the *Berner Tagwacht*, Karl Moor. It is only in the light of the German documents that the full significance of Gustav Mayer's memoirs becomes apparent.

The fact that it was the Treasury official Moritz von Saemisch who told Mayer to collaborate with Nasse gives added significance to the operation carried out in May/June 1917 in Stockholm. Saemisch was neither an official of the Foreign Ministry nor, as far we know, of the Political Section of the General Staff. He was employed exclusively in the Treasury, where he even lived during the war – as '*Schlafbursche*', he said jokingly, that is the permanently resident official. Both he and Nasse were close relatives of the then State Secretary of the Treasury, Count Roedern. As Saemisch had expressly told Mayer that the Nasse operation should be kept secret, because of its extreme importance to the State, even from the Foreign Ministry, it is clear that all appropriations for the Nasse operation were arranged by some unorthodox means directly with the German Treasury.[2]

1. For the identification of Baier see article by Otto-Ernst Schueddekopf in *Archiv für Sozialgeschichte*, Vol. III (1963).
2. This is confirmed by the fact that at the beginning of the following financial year, when Roedern presented his demands for renewed credits to the Reichstag, he asked the Auswärtiges Amt whether he could 'garnish his latest credit demands ... with

In the meantime Lenin was eagerly expecting the 'letters, parcels and money transfers'[1] on which he had agreed during his stay in Stockholm with Fürstenberg-Ganetsky. His letter (of 12 April, O.S.) on the subject is published in the *Collected Works*, with the editorial comment that the money in question was some residual fund belonging to the Party Central Committee.[2] The commentary is, of course, mendacious. The party had no funds, even for the publication of its magazine, *Sbornik Sotsial-Demokrata*, in the winter of 1916–17. This does not mean, however, that the mail expected so eagerly by Lenin was the same as that which passed through the hands of Gustav Mayer and Nasse. But there is enough indirect evidence to warrant the assumption that the materials despatched by Nasse in June 1917 were in support of Bolshevik activities in Russia. It is obviously to this period that Kühlmann refers in his telegram of 3 December 1917 to the Kaiser, in which he reviews the success of the German *Revolutionierungspolitik*, and states: 'It was not until the Bolsheviks had received from us a steady flow of funds through various channels and under different labels that they were in a position to be able to build up their main organ, *Pravda*, to conduct energetic propaganda and appreciably to extend the originally narrow basis of their power.'[3]

The situation changed abruptly after the premature and abortive Bolshevik coup on 3 July. Despite all the precautions the Bolsheviks, the German officials and their agents had taken, French and British counter-espionage services were soon alert to signs of German support for anti-Entente and defeatist propaganda in Russia. These Allied intelligence services supplied such information as they had to the Provisional Government at a time when the Russian counter-espionage machinery had completely broken down. The earliest warning of probable contact between Lenin and the Germans was given to Kerensky by the French socialist Minister, Albert Thomas.[4] The denuncia-

a few comments on foreign policy in order to enliven the atmosphere a little'. He was discouraged from doing so. See Zeman, op. cit., p. 119.

1. Cf. Mayer's 'letters, manuscripts' etc., as quoted, above p. 106 n.
2. See Lenin, *Sochineniya* vol. XXIX, pp. 355 ff.
3. The document was published for the first time by me in *International Affairs*, April 1956. It has since been frequently commented on, even in the Soviet historical journal, *Voprosy istorii*, where it was casually referred to as the 'latest forgery'. See also Zeman, op. cit., pp. 94–95.
4. See A. F. Kerensky, *Crucifixion of Liberty* (London, 1934), p. 285.

tion of the Bolshevik leaders as German agents by the Provisional Government set off a chain reaction of misconceptions which we cannot analyse in this context. Here it suffices to point out that the breakdown of the lines of communication between Stockholm and Petrograd which followed the publication of the material incriminating Lenin, Zinovyev, Helphand, Fürstenberg, Sumenson[1] and Kozlovsky must have put an end to the use of some of the 'channels and labels' mentioned by Kühlmann.

11. 'THE GREAT SLANDER' AND THE GREATER DENIALS

Trotsky calls the month of July-August the 'month of the great slander'. It was also a time of strenuous denials. As soon as the Germans heard that Helphand was accused of having supported the Bolsheviks financially, they wanted him to issue an immediate rebuttal of these accusations. Unfortunately, however, Helphand's whereabouts at that precise moment were not easy to establish. In fact he was in Switzerland, and it took Romberg's officials quite a time to contact him and persuade him to sign a statement in a notary's office.

Fürstenberg was also pressed, this time by Lenin himself, to 'expose the lie' about German money. There is some evidence that Fürstenberg was afraid to deny too much, in case he might later be given the lie by independent evidence if the indicted Bolshevik leaders were put on trial. Fürstenberg's cousin, Madame Sumenson, who was one of his partners in the export-import business in Russia, was under arrest. Even more important, Kozlovsky, Fürstenberg's contact in the Petrograd Soviet, with whom he had done business in Copenhagen, had also been arrested, and Fürstenberg had no guarantee that he would not talk. Even Lenin thought it wise to deny close contacts with Kozlovsky in his indignant refutation of the 'Russian Dreyfus Affair', which he said was a 'stratagem laid against him and the Bolsheviks by the counter-revolutionaries and their helpers.'

It was at this juncture that Fürstenberg and Radek made a most revealing move. In the information bulletin which they were issuing in Stockholm in German, *Russische Korrespondenz Prawda*, they

1. Madame Sumenson, a lady of the Petrograd *demi-monde*, through whom communications with Fürstenberg were maintained.

published on 31 July an article in which Fürstenberg was described as one of Helphand's business associates. This was a natural defence, but the article went on to make a most astonishing admission: that Fürstenberg had used his business profits to finance his party, that is, the Social-Democratic Party of Poland and Lithuania, in German-occupied Poland.[1]

Fürstenberg's statement, which passed unnoticed at the time, might well seem a clumsy and unwarranted move. If, however, one bears in mind that Fürstenberg lived in hourly fear of news from Petrograd that Kozlovsky had broken down under interrogation and confessed to having received money from him for the Bolsheviks, this unsolicited admission in the Stockholm 'bulletin' makes good sense.[2] As it was, this precaution proved unnecessary. The investigation started by the Provisional Government dragged on in the face of violent opposition, not only from the Bolsheviks in the Petrograd Soviet but from many socialists to the right of the Bolsheviks, and petered out inconclusively in September 1917, after the Kornilov affair.

The Nasse/Karl Moor lines of communication probably came to grief after the July rising and the subsequent indictment of the Bolsheviks as German agents. Gustav Mayer left Stockholm temporarily at the end of July or at the beginning of August, and has nothing more to say in his memoirs about the intrigues in which he had played a passive but important part.[3] We can assume, however, that Nasse was

1. See Futrell, op. cit, p. 167. This provided a second line of defence to the Bolsheviks, who could claim that the money sent to Kozlovsky from Scandinavia was not for their own use, but for the Polish-Lithuanian Social-Democratic Party, struggling against German occupation in Poland.
2. The article says that Fürstenberg, having come to Copenhagen in 1915 via France and England, worked in a commercial enterprise in which Helphand had a financial interest because (a) 'he believed Parvus [Helphand] to be personally an honourable man' (and still believed so) and (b) because this put him in a position not only to maintain his family, but also to give effective financial assistance to the Polish Party organisation in Polish Russia, which he also did. 'Politically, Fürstenberg was in no way connected with Parvus; on the contrary, by supporting a Polish Party press and organisation, which were in the sharpest opposition to the German occupation authorities, and were standing on the platform of the Zimmerwald left, openly declaring their solidarity with Liebknecht, Fürstenberg worked against the policy of Parvus. History alone will show whose judgment on the man Parvus was correct — Lenin's or Fürstenberg's.'
3. We learn, however, from a letter of Cahén to Brockdorff-Rantzau, published

not too discouraged by what had happened. After all, the suppression of the Bolshevik rising in July did not result in more stable conditions in Russia. Lenin and Zinovyev went into hiding, and the Provisional Government, without an effective police force, had no means of tracking them down, in spite of the incessant comings and goings between the Petrograd Bolsheviks and their leader. After the raid on its headquarters in the Kseshinskaya Palace, the party now operated more or less underground. In these circumstances money was more important than ever, and it was in the German interest to see that it was forthcoming.

Extreme caution was necessary at this time, and Lenin was constantly reminding his followers of this. In his letter to the Bureau of the Central Committee abroad sent in August from Helsinki,[1] he insisted that a complete refutation of the accusations should be demanded from Fürstenberg.

In the same letter Lenin warned against contacts with Karl Moor who, he had heard, had turned up in Stockholm. 'What kind of a man is this Moor?', he asked rhetorically. After all his dealings with him in Switzerland, one would have expected him to know the answer only too well.

Lenin's anxiety about further Bolshevik contacts with Moor was no doubt dictated by the fear that the accusations clumsily and unconvincingly concocted against him in July by the Provisional Government might be substantiated by some injudicious move on the part of his supporters. Lenin was right in his apprehensions, for Moor was indeed busily looking for a way to resume transfers of money to the Bolsheviks. Through the Bolshevik Semashko, he offered their Central Committee a certain sum of money. This fact is mentioned in the minutes of the Central Committee of the Bolshevik Party of 24 September 1917. The proposal was not entered on the agenda of the meeting, but was discussed under Point 6. Here is a literal translation of its somewhat involved text:

6. Having heard the report on an offer of money the following

in photographic copy as an appendix to Cahén's book, that Mayer was again in Stockholm in September, maintaining close contact with Radek, with whom he discussed moves to gather material for the defence of Lenin should it come to a trial in Petrograd.

1. Lenin, *Sochineniya*, vol. XXIX, p. 358.

resolution was adopted:

> The Central Committee, having heard the report of Comrade Alek-sandrov (Semashko) concerning the proposal of the Swiss socialist, Karl Moor, to transfer a certain sum of money for the disposal of the Central Committee, and in view of the impossibility of checking the real source of the money offered, and of finding out whether it is really coming from the same fund as that mentioned in the offer as the source of the means available to G. V. Plekhanov, and also in view of the impossibility of checking the true aims pursued by Moor's proposal, the Central Committee resolves to reject the proposal and to consider all further negotiations on the matter inadmissible.

If we discard as mud-slinging the innuendo that Plekhanov had been receiving subsidies from the same source as that which was now ready to come to the financial assistance of the Bolshevik Central Committee, the fact remains that Moor made a more or less direct offer of money to the Bolsheviks. The fact that the rejection of Moor's offer was carefully recorded shows how important it was at that time for the Bolsheviks to refute all accusations of financial support from dubious sources. It does not, however, prove that the money was not received from the sources in question. The published Minutes of the Central Committee[1] contain a special note to the effect that 'according to an enquiry which was made later by *Istpart* [Commission on Party History] Karl Moor offered this monetary aid from a large inheritance which he had unexpectedly received'. This and the subsequent career of Karl Moor[2] would suggest that he may still have succeeded in financing the Bolsheviks.

1. See *Protokoly Tsentralnogo Komiteta* RSDRP(b), August 1917–February 1918, (Moscow, 1958), p. 263.
2. Karl Moor went to the Soviet Union after the October Revolution, and worked there in close contact with Kurt Riezler, the Counsellor of Legation under Count Mirbach. References to him (as Herr Baier, of course) occur frequently in German documents of the time. In 1919 he was back in Berlin, helping to get Radek out of prison (where he had landed after his adventurous attempt to promote a Communist revolution in Germany) and acting as a middleman between him and German socialist circles. Later he went back to Russia, where he must have had some trouble with the G.P.U. In 1925 foreigners who lived in Moscow and met him suspected him of having joined the ranks of that organisation. In a note in *Leninsky Sbornik*, XI (1931), he is said to have been living in Moscow in the rest home for aged revolutionaries named after V. I. Lenin. Moor did not, however, die in Russia. After a severe illness, he was allowed to leave, and died in the Charité Hospital in Berlin on 14 June,

The last of the series of denials came from Radek. After a curious delay, Radek decided to combine his denial with the exposure of a certain Leo Winz, who was employed by the German Embassy in Copenhagen as a pipeline for planting information and rumours in the Russian press. Radek's intention was to denounce Leo Winz as the source of the rumour passed to Kadet circles in Petrograd that Lenin was a German agent. Radek's plan was certainly ingenious. If it could be proved that the Germans themselves had started the campaign accusing Lenin of being a German agent then of course Lenin would be fully vindicated. But Radek did not bargain for the thoroughness of the German bureaucracy. In September he talked about his plan for the defence of Lenin to Gustav Mayer, who immediately reported it to the German press attaché in Copenhagen, Cahén. Radek was invited to come to Copenhagen and meet Cahén, who convinced him that an exposure of Leo Winz would merely embarrass the Germans without serving any good purpose from Radek's point of view. Cahén writes:

> I succeeded in persuading him [Radek] that a large part of the material which he quoted consisted of untruths. In fact only part of it was later published in German for circulation among Russian and other Communists in Stockholm. Even most of these published details were at variance with the exact facts. The general campaign in the Swedish press which Radek had planned was abandoned.[1]

Cahén's strange story is supported by his report on the interview to Brockdorff-Rantzau, a facsimile of which appears in the book.

To sum up the intricate story of 'the great slander', first Lenin was accused by the Provisional Government, on the strength of information supplied by Western counter-espionage, of being a German spy and paid agent. Lenin defended himself by stating that he had never received a penny from Fürstenberg and that Kozlovsky was not a member of his party. Both these contentions are demonstrably untrue.[2] He then demanded a rebuttal of the accusations from Fürstenberg and Radek. In July Fürstenberg made his half-denial in the *Russische Korrespondenz Prawda*, and some weeks later Radek tried to float the story that the

1932. The Swiss socialist press wrote warm and sympathetic obituaries on him. So did the German Communist and Stalinist writer Kurella. See the detailed account of Moor by Otto-Ernst Schueddekopf in *Archiv fur Sozialgeschichte*, vol. III (1963).
1. Cahén, op. cit., p. 220.
2. See Futrell, op. cit., pp. 157, 165–7.

accusations against Lenin were the work of a professional German rumour-monger, Leo Winz. Radek had an interview with Cahén, who persuaded him to drop his allegations against Leo Winz. As a result of this German action Radek's refutation was delayed and finally published in a truncated form at a time when it had lost all practical value for the Bolsheviks. The fact of Radek's relations with Cahén at that time and over a question of such vital importance for the Bolsheviks is an illuminating example of German-Bolshevik co-operation.

12. CONCLUSIONS

German intervention in the revolutionary events in Russia did not stop with the Bolshevik seizure of power. It went on *crescendo* until the first week of July 1918, when it was abruptly curtailed by the assassination of the German envoy Mirbach. After the German collapse on the Western front it almost ceased for a number of months or even years. As far as 1917 is concerned, it must be remembered that the German government was interested in a revolution in Russia only insofar as it would be propitious to the conclusion of a separate peace in the East, always the primary aim of its policy.

It is also certain that they gave their support to the Bolshevik Party and to Lenin in every possible way which was not incompatible with their purpose only because this was the party and the man that had repeatedly and openly proclaimed readiness to conclude immediate peace, and expressed abhorrence of the commitments entered into by the Tsarist government *vis-à-vis* its allies in the Entente. It was therefore extremely confusing when the Provisional Government charged Lenin and others with espionage and with having acted in concert with the German government. Of course it was not easy for members of the Provisional Government to admit that the revolution of February 1917 which had brought them to power was, from the German point of view, just as desirable as was the subsequent coming to power of Lenin in October. Lenin was in great need of financial support, and this was the way the German government tried to help him, with or without his knowledge. The Russian liberals did not need money for their intensive propaganda against the Tsarist government; what they did need in order to achieve their political aims was the organisation of a popular movement in the capitals. For that in any case they were not well equipped, and their patriotic attitude inhibited them from taking the action necessary to this end while the country was at war. That is why, on this occasion, the Germans advanced the liberal cause by organising, through clandestine agencies, large-scale strikes, at first economic, and later, in accordance with Helphand's plan, political.

Part Two

6

The Myasoedov Affair

Introduction; Not Guilty; Rostopchin's lynch-law; Some legends; The implications

I. INTRODUCTION

The defeats suffered by the Russian armies on the north-western front in January 1915 exasperated GHQ. The Supreme Commander was reported to be in a rage. The Commander of the Tenth Army, Sievers, and his chief of Staff Baron Budberg were threatened with court-martial, and a general spy scare spread among the public; even the soldiers at the front were affected by it. Shortly before Easter Sunday, on 20 March 1915, GHQ announced the execution of a certain Colonel Myasoedov, who had allegedly been supplying the Germans with information which had led to the recent setbacks. The proceedings were secret, and the death sentence was carried out on the very night it was passed. The Myasoedov affair is of considerable historical interest, not only because of its far-reaching repercussions on the political situation in Russia, but also for the light it throws on the state of the country's morale in the spring of 1915. Indeed, as General Spiridovich writes,[1] for its bearing on the fall of the Tsarist régime the Myasoedov affair can be compared only with the assassination of Rasputin.

In 1912, S. N. Myasoedov, a gendarmerie officer, fought a duel with Guchkov, who had accused him of spying for Austria. The affair attracted great publicity, but Myasoedov was not prosecuted and was only asked to retire from active service. In 1914, Myasoedov, who had specialised in espionage and counter-espionage, was re-admitted to active service and posted, on the express recommendation of the War Minister, Sukhomlinov, to the ill-fated Tenth Army, commanded by

---

1. A. I. Spiridovich, *Velikaya voyna i fevralskaya revolyutsiya* (3 vols, New York, 1960–62), vol. I, p. 103. These posthumous memoirs of the former gendarmerie officer, chronicler and student of the Russian revolutionary movement contain much new material.

Sievers. On 18 February 1915, Myasoedov was arrested in Kovno, sent to the Warsaw citadel, court-martialled there on 17 March, and hanged.

The announcement of this unprecedented spy case came as a great shock to public opinion. Although Guchkov took no part in the proceedings and remained conspicuously aloof from them, the whole of the newspaper-reading public remembered his conflict with Myasoedov and Sukhomlinov in 1912, and it would have been easy for him to adopt an attitude of 'I told you so'.

For Sukhomlinov the sentence on Myasoedov was the *coup de grâce*. He accepted it meekly, joining in the general abuse of his former protégé, but his morale was broken and he never regained self-confidence before his retirement on 16 June 1915.

2. NOT GUILTY!

Doubts as to Myasoedov's guilt date from his trial. One of the trial witnesses[1] published an account of his experiences which leaves no doubt that he was fully aware, if not of the innocence of the accused, at least of the irregularities of the court proceedings against him. In his diaries the Grand Duke Andrey Vladimirovich also questions their impartiality.[2] The correspondence between the Chief of Staff at GHQ, General Yanushkevich, and Sukhomlinov[3] makes clear that the military court was under the heaviest pressure from GHQ to pass a death sentence and to carry it out without delay. More evidence is contained in the memoirs of the well-known Jewish lawyer, O. O. Gruzenberg,[4] who was counsel for some of the people accused of having aided Myasoedov. This testimony is particularly valuable as Gruzenberg knew from personal experience of an earlier conflict between Myasoedov and the secret police in 1907. Sukhomlinov's own memoirs[5] contain

1. A Captain Buchinsky, who chose to sign his reminiscences 'B——y'. See *ARR*, XIV, pp. 132–147.
2. *Krasny Arkhiv*, Vol. XXVI.
3. *Krasny Arkhiv*, III, (1923), pp. 29–74.
4. Gruzenberg, *Vchera* (Paris, 1938), pp. 51–66.
5. W. A. Suchomlinow [V. A. Sukhomlinov]. *Erinnerungen* (Berlin, 1924), p. 473 *passim*.

a lot of information on the Myasoedov trial based on his own study of the court-martial proceedings; yet they should be used with caution, for Sukhomlinov's contacts with Myasoedov were the most damaging evidence against him at his own trial in August 1917. It is nevertheless remarkable that Sukhomlinov, who had accepted Myasoedov's guilt in 1915, changed his mind after his study of the proceedings.

Count Kokovtsov, in his memoirs,[1] also admits that Myasoedov's treason was never proved, although he finds comfort in the fact that Myasoedov was a convicted and self-confessed marauder. General Spiridovich champions Myasoedov's innocence in a summing-up of the whole case in his own reminiscences.[2]

The documents of the German Ministry of Foreign Affairs reveal no contacts between the Germans or Austrians and Myasoedov. A German source, W. Nicolai, the famous master spy of World War I, calls the Myasoedov case 'inexplicable'.[3] In his book on espionage during World War I he wrote, referring to the trial: 'The sentence, like so many others passed on similar indictments, was a miscarriage of justice. He, Myasoedov, had never rendered any services to Germany.' Nicolai's subordinate, Lieut. A. Bauermeister, who was sentenced to death *in absentia* as Myasoedov's German contact by a military court in Warsaw in June 1915, confirms his chief's contention[4], and says: 'Colonel Nicolai, at that time my chief, writes in his *Secret Powers* that Myasoedov had never worked for us, and he was executed an innocent man. As one who was allegedly implicated in this espionage affair I can only confirm in full the assurance of my former chief. Never in my life have I exchanged a single word with Colonel Myasoedov, nor did I ever approach him through a third party.' It is difficult to find any reason why after the war and the death of Myasoedov Bauermeister would lie if a connection between him and Myasoedov had existed.

In spite of all this evidence, there has been a certain reluctance on the part of historians to probe the mystery of the Myasoedov trial. It is

1. *Out of My Past*, op. cit., p. 310 n.
2. *Velikaya voyna*, op. cit., vol. I, pp. 103–110.
3. *Geheime Mächte. Internationale Spionage und ihre Bekämpfung im Weltkriege und heute.* 3rd ed. (Leipzig, 1925), p. 19.
4. *Spies Break Through* (London, 1934), p. 7.

surprising that the only detailed published account has not received the attention due to it. Among the people accused of being a contact or assistant of Myasoedov was an official of the Ministry of the Interior, O. G. Freinat. He was an experienced lawyer, having previously been an Assistant Procurator. He was arrested with a number of others, including Myasoedov's wife, and tried on 15 and 16 June 1915 by court-martial in the same fortress in which Myasoedov had been hanged. On this occasion he was acquitted, but remained a prisoner until he was tried a second time, with some others, by the Military District Court of Dvinsk, which met in Vilna on 8–12 July 1915. This time he received a sentence of hard labour, and was brought in chains to the prison of the town of Orel. With remarkable persistence he demanded a retrial, pointing out the enormity of the procedural faults in the action against him. Shortly before the revolution he succeeded in obtaining leave to appeal and even had the transcript of the whole Myasoedov trial sent to Orel in the winter of 1917, which probably saved it from destruction in the fire in the Courts building during the February days. After the revolution Freinat published a detailed account of the proceedings against Myasoedov and those accused with him.[1]

Freinat cannot be considered an impartial witness, since he was himself a victim of what he claims was a gross miscarriage of justice. His account, however, is astonishingly coherent and moderate in tone. He also brings in some documentary material which he must have obtained in the process of preparing his appeal.

But perhaps the most convincing argument in favour of Myasoedov's innocence is the way the whole affair was treated by Guchkov in his memoirs, published shortly after his death in the Paris émigré newspaper *Poslednie Novosti*.[2] Recalling the 1912 incident, Guchkov does not mention any allegations of espionage for Austria against Myasoedov, but speaks of him in general terms as a spy, that is, a police officer who was investigating the political reliability of army officers under the direction of Sukhomlinov. This of course is a rather Pickwickian way of using the term 'spy'. Later Guchkov refers to Myasoedov's trial in 1915, but remarks cautiously that he has no evidence of whether the allegations were in fact substantiated.

1. O. G. Freinat, *Pravda o dele Myasoedova i drugikh* (Vilna, 1918).
2. August and September, 1936.

3. ROSTOPCHIN'S LYNCH-LAW

The Myasoedov affair still awaits a detailed study. Here we can give only a tentative outline of it.[1]

Myasoedov seems fated to have become a victim of the political system which he was serving loyally. His troubles started long before the dreadful accusation of treason was raised against him. After a chequered army career, he served from 1894 to 1907 at the gendarmerie frontier post at the railway station of Verzhbolovo (in German, Virballen). Towards the end of 1907 he was called as a witness at the trial of some smugglers accused of having brought subversive political literature and arms over the Russian frontier. Under interrogation by the defence counsel O. Gruzenberg, he admitted that it was common practice for the secret police — the Okhrana — (who shared responsibility for security with the gendarmerie) to plant political proclamations and arms on persons whom they wanted to compromise. The prosecution's case was lost as a result of this testimony, but the wrath of the Okhrana which it provoked was the beginning of all Myasoedov's troubles. It was under the court's instructions that he had revealed these highly compromising official secrets. The Okhrana nevertheless bitterly resented his behaviour and insisted on his removal from his post. As a consequence he had to leave the gendarmerie service.

Later he was reinstated and taken on by the Minister of War, Sukhomlinov, for special duties connected with security and the supervision of the morale and political reliability of army officers. In 1912, the Minister of War was shown an anonymous document accusing his assistant, General Polivanov, of having communicated secret Russian military information to the Austrian Ambassador; the document, according to Sukhomlinov's memoirs, revealed familiarity with secret War Ministry files and thus pointed to a security breach.

Sukhomlinov ordered an investigation, not of Polivanov of course, but of the circumstances in which the anonymous denunciation had been written,[2] and he informed Polivanov that he had entrusted the

---

1. It has been treated several times belletristically. A recent book by the Polish writer Josef Mackiewicz gives a very close account of the facts. Although 'histoire romancée' it is in accordance with conclusions to which we have come on the basis of the sources quoted. *Sprawa połkownika Miasojedowa* (London, 1962).
2. Sukhomlinov, op. cit., p. 291.

investigation to Myasoedov. Soon after, Polivanov's friend, A. I. Guchkov, initiated a campaign in the press and Duma insinuating that since Myasoedov had been taken on by the War Ministry as their intelligence officer, more Russian secret information had been received by the Austrian authorities. Myasoedov challenged Guchkov to a duel, which was actually fought. According to Guchkov, Myasoedov shot at him, while Guchkov fired a token shot in the air. The opponents left the field unreconciled, and the duel got considerable publicity in the press. As a result, Myasoedov had once more to resign from the corps of gendarmes, but an investigation of the accusations against him resulted in his complete exoneration.[1] It has often been pointed out that the mere fact that Guchkov accepted Myasoedov's challenge showed that he could not really have believed the treason story. A traitor to his country would have been automatically disqualified from defending his honour 'at the barrier'.

The Myasoedov scandal was reported to the Emperor and contributed to the dismissal of Polivanov from his post as Deputy War Minister, with his simultaneous appointment to the Council of State. Myasoedov brought libel actions against the newspapers which had attacked him. These were discontinued at the beginning of the war, when a reconciliation took place between him and the editor of these papers, Boris Suvorin.

As soon as the war started, Myasoedov applied for a commission, and asked Sukhomlinov to find him employment at the front. He was appointed to the Tenth Army. At the end of January 1915, the Tenth Army suffered a crushing defeat. The Twentieth Corps was almost completely annihilated. At the beginning of February, Myasoedov was transferred to the Kovno fortress, where he was ostensibly given the task of organising the work of intelligence agents behind the German lines. In fact, he was already under suspicion of spying for the enemy and was being shadowed by the secretary assigned to him, whose name was Distergof.

Suspicions against him had been aroused when a certain Second Lieutenant G. Kolakovsky, who had been taken prisoner by the Germans in the initial stages of the war, turned up at the Russian Consulate in Stockholm and reported that, although he had seemingly escaped from a P.O.W. camp, he had in fact been released by the

1. Spiridovich, *Velikaya voyna*, p. 105 and Freinat, op. cit., pp. 20 ff.

Germans in order to organise sabotage and espionage behind the front, and even the assassination of the Commander-in-Chief, Grand Duke Nikolay Nikolaevich. Pressed for details of the German briefing, Kolakovsky said that he expected to be contacted by a Colonel Myasoedov, who had been working for the Germans for a long time. In the interrogations which followed, Kolakovsky became confused. Having claimed that he first heard of Myasoedov from the Germans, he later admitted having read the name in the papers in connection with the Guchkov-Myasoedov scandal in 1912. No credence was given, therefore, to Kolakovsky's revelations. He was sent to the eastern provinces of Russia and was not called as a witness at the court-martial. But the investigation of Myasoedov had started, and the generals dealing with counter-espionage, Batyushin and M. D. Bonch-Bruevich, pressed for his arrest. At GHQ the possibility of explaining the disasters suffered by the Tenth Army in terms of the activities of a traitor was only too welcome. General Yanushkevich and the Grand Duke himself lent a credulous ear to the reports of the counter-espionage service. On 18 February, Myasoedov was arrested and transferred for investigation to the fortress at Warsaw.

Although the counter-espionage service claimed that Myasoedov was connected with a widespread network of spies and traitors, GHQ ordered that his case should be treated separately from that of his alleged associates, and that he should be court-martialled without delay in Warsaw. The court-martial took place on 17 March and lasted a whole day. The proceedings were rudimentary: the State Prosecutor's office was not represented, nor was there a counsel for the defence. There were only two witnesses, the above-mentioned Distergof, who had been spying on Myasoedov, and Captain Buchinsky, an officer who later published a revealing eye-witness account of the trial. Although neither witness could produce any evidence of actual contacts between the Germans and Myasoedov, he was found guilty on three counts: of having spied for the Austrians before the war, of collecting information in 1915 on the disposition of Russian troops in order to communicate it to the enemy, and of looting houses in enemy territory. Two counts in the indictment dealing with the actual communication of military information to the enemy during the war had to be dropped for lack of evidence. On hearing the verdict, Myasoedov asked to be allowed to send telegrams to the Emperor and to his family and then fainted under the stress of his emotions. The telegrams in which he protested his innocence and asked his next-of-kin to clear his name were never sent, but were attached to the proceedings. The execution took place the same night, after Myasoedov had made an abortive attempt at suicide.

There is little to say on the three counts of the conviction. The question of his spying for the Austrians before the war could not be investigated competently by a court-martial of this type. The allegation about gathering information on the disposition of Russian troops was based on the testimony of Captain Buchinsky, who made it quite clear the Myasoedov's enquiries during a visit to the front lines appeared utterly innocuous to him. As far as looting was concerned, Myasoedov candidly admitted having taken 'trophies' of little value from a house in East Prussia. Two terra-cotta figurines were mentioned at the trial. Such cases of petty pilfering were customary at the time in all belligerent armies and although contrary to regulations would never be considered as sufficient reason for any disciplinary action, let alone a death sentence.

Both Buchinsky and Gruzenberg tried later to find out whether there was any justification for these extraordinary proceedings against Myasoedov. All the military legal authorities, including the Chief Military Procurator, A. S. Makarenko, admitted that there was not a scrap of factual evidence against the accused. On the other hand, the Chief of Staff at GHQ, General Yanushkevich, stated that he possessed unimpeachable proof of Myasoedov's guilt. Why then, one might ask, was this factual material not put before the court?

There was also no justification for the hurried execution of the accused, especially as he was supposed to have been in touch with other spies and could therefore have provided useful information for the counter-espionage service. Yanushkevich, however, claimed that it was necessary to carry out the execution without delay in order to placate public opinion.[1]

Yanushkevich's admissions and Buchinsky's recollections of the proceedings leave no doubt that the execution of Myasoedov had little to do with the administration of justice and the rule of law, but was much more in the tradition of Count Rostopchin's lynching of the alleged spy Vereshchagin, described by Tolstoy in *War and Peace*.

1. Letter of Yanushkevich to Sukhomlinov dated 19 March, quoted below, p. 131.

Myasoedov was picked upon by GHQ at the instigation of the counter-espionage service as a convenient scapegoat for the reverses at the front, and his execution was expedited to appease public opinion. The choice of Myasoedov for this part was quite clever: he had made enemies in the secret police as well as among the Duma liberals. It could safely be assumed that in the prevailing atmosphere nobody would raise a voice in defence of this gendarmerie officer in his misfortune. For Yanushkevich and Grand Duke Nikolay Nikolaevich the discovery of treason was a convenient method of explaining away the defeats of the armies under their command.

Simultaneously with the arrest of Myasoedov, raids were made by the counter-espionage agencies all over Russia. Myasoedov's wife, the predominantly Jewish board of directors of a steamship line of which Myasoedov was a member, and various other people who had casual contacts or business associations with him, including Freinat, were arrested. Many were released without trial, although some were deported to East Russia as a precautionary police measure. Those who were indicted were tried twice. After the first trial all those sentenced to death were executed, while those acquitted were sent for a second trial, when more death and prison sentences were passed. The whole conduct of the case was marked by numerous and flagrant breaches of normal legal procedure.

4. SOME LEGENDS

In his memoirs published in 1957, General M. D. Bonch-Bruevich, (the brother of Lenin's friend Vladimir Bonch-Bruevich), who in 1915 was Chief of Staff to General Ruzsky on the north-western front, admits that he 'played a fairly decisive role in the Myasoedov affair'. General Bonch-Bruevich was, or pretended to be, a great believer in the effectiveness of German espionage in Russia and its fatal consequences for the military situation. He wrote:

> The secret war [against German espionage] which was going on parallel with the open war was known only to a few. The organs which were involved in the secret war worked on strictly conspiratorial lines. In my official position I had continual access to these secrets and willy-nilly observed things the existence of which others only suspected. I saw how,

right from the first days of war, the German and Austrian intelligence services were making themselves at home with horrifying impunity in our highest headquarters, and this contributed to a great extent to my disillusionment with the old régime.[1]

A general in the grip of spy-mania might well have accepted Myasoedov's guilt unquestioningly. But when he explains how the charges against Myasoedov were obtained, Bonch-Bruevich lies without scruple. He reports that he had attached two officers to Myasoedov – a chauffeur and a mechanic, who posed as simple soldiers. They arrested Myasoedov, so he tells us, on a farm at the very moment when he was transmitting secret documents to the German owner of the farm. 'The former gendarme was put into a motor-car and taken to the headquarters of the front. At headquarters Myasoedov regained his former brazenness and tried to deny the obvious.' Bonch-Bruevich's report runs counter to all other available evidence; there was no question of Myasoedov being caught in the act.[2] Bonch-Bruevich says further that he followed Myasoedov's investigation closely, although he did not personally interrogate him. He adds that 'after the execution, gossip inspired by the German General Staff went on at court and at various headquarters to the effect that this whole affair had been blown up in order to bring about the downfall of Sukhomlinov'.[3] The reference to 'gossip inspired by the German General Staff' is of course absurd. But he himself admits that Grand Duke Nikolay Nikolaevich adopted an irreconcilable attitude towards Sukhomlinov, and therefore did not impede the exposure of Myasoedov. Finally, Bonch-Bruevich reports that his success in the Myasoedov affair led to his appointment as head of the whole army counter-espionage service.[4]

1. M. D. Bonch-Bruevich, *Vsya vlast sovetam*, p. 55. See also ch. 5 above.
2. Distergof, who had kept a watch on Myasoedov up to his arrest, was a witness at the trial and told Buchinsky that he had no direct evidence of his contacts with the enemy. Furthermore the arrest took place in Myasoedov's quarters in Kovno and not at a farm.
3. M. D. Bonch-Bruevich, op. cit., p. 65.
4. It is an interesting sidelight on the activities of Bonch-Bruevich that he was throughout in close contact with his brother Vladimir. Secret information from the armies of the northern front reached Lenin in Switzerland at the time when M. Bonch-Bruevich was Chief of Staff to the commander of this front, General Ruzsky. Some secret documents signed 'Bonch-Bruevich' and 'Ruzsky' were published in Switzerland by Lenin and Zinovyev in the Bolshevik magazine *Sbornik*

While Russian historians and memoirists in emigration gradually awoke to the possibility of a judicial error or even of a deliberate legal fraud in the Myasoedov case, the legend of Myasoedov's treason proved more viable with Soviet historians and with non-Russian writers. Thus more than twenty years later, in his book on the fall of the Tsarist régime, Sir Bernard Pares gives this legend the support of his authority. Although he does not mention Guchkov as his informant in this context some of his more extravagant information must have come from this source, for Sir Bernard claims that Guchkov's exposure of Myasoedov in 1912 was fully vindicated by subsequent events, when 'later it transpired that Guchkov's old antagonist Colonel Myasoedov, now a high Russian intelligence officer, was indeed a spy in German pay and had by aeroplane [*sic*!] organized regular communications with the enemy'.[1] Pares goes so far as to claim that 'there was no defence for Myasoedov and it was even stated that he had admitted his guilt, saying that only the triumph of Germany could save the autocracy in Russia. For all his high connections, Myasoedov was hanged as a traitor on March 10th'. Everything in this quotation, including the incorrect date, is a monument to the lightheadedness with which the history of the Russian revolution has been written in the West.

5. THE IMPLICATIONS

The political impact of the Myasoedov affair was enormous. For the first time Russian public opinion had been given official 'confirmation' of German penetration into high government circles. Guchkov's position seemed fully vindicated. The stage was set for a major crisis of confidence. For a time it centred on the person of Sukhomlinov. After Sukhomlinov's dismissal from the post of Minister of War in June 1915 the Tsar, who had no doubt of his honesty and faithful service, had to yield to public opinion and agree to a special investigation of his case. This was pursued with some energy and with the support of the counter-espionage service. For a time Sukhomlinov

Sotsial-Demokrata. This material was probably sent to Lenin via the German-controlled intelligence agency run by Alexander Keskülä. See below, p. 166.

1. Pares, *The Fall of the Russian Monarchy* (London, 1939), p. 213.

was put under arrest in the Peter and Paul Fortress, but was soon released on bail for health reasons. When it became known that he had been released on the insistence of the Empress, this again gave rise to a spate of rumours concerning the Empress's pro-German sympathies.

After the revolution, the proceedings against Sukhomlinov were resumed and led to a trial the merits and demerits of which should be considered in another context. It must be borne in mind, however, that in their investigation of alleged abuses of power by the Tsarist régime the Provisional Government and its Ministry of Justice never quoted the Myasoedov case, in which they could have found every proof of the arbitrariness and abuses of the wartime administration and judiciary. Perhaps Myasoedov's guilt was deliberately taken for granted in order to secure the condemnation of Sukhomlinov and thereby confirm the legend of pro-German influence in high places. Perhaps the generals who connived at the judicial murder of Myasoedov and his alleged accomplices were shielded by the Provisional Government. An exposure of the Myasoedov case would have hit not only the reputation of its first War Minister, Guchkov, but also that of his friend Polivanov, who was irreplaceable to them as the chairman of a committee for democratic reforms in the army, and who had been in the past a great propagandist of the legend of Myasoedov's guilt.[1]

Sukhomlinov had at once understood that the accusations against Myasoedov meant serious danger for him. But the Grand Duke's Chief of Staff, Yanushkevich, made it quite clear to him that GHQ had foolproof evidence of Myasoedov's guilt, and would see to it that he got his deserts. Not once did Sukhomlinov in his correspondence with Yanushkevich come to the defence of the unfortunate Colonel. On the contrary, he did all he could to persuade Yanushkevich that he had himself been a victim of the 'scoundrel', and had earned nothing but rank ingratitude from him. Later, as we have seen, during his own trial in 1917, Sukhomlinov was allowed to study the documents of the Myasoedov trial, and in his memoirs he states that they convinced him of Myasoedov's innocence. In the spring of 1915, however, Sukhomlinov did no more than warn Yanushkevich of the smear campaign which had been launched by Guchkov (and Prince Andronnikov) in connection with the Myasoedov affair and which aimed at blackening the War Minister's reputation. In his replies to Sukhom-

1. See Gruzenberg, op. cit., pp. 64 ff

linov, Yanushkevich, instead of reassuring him, mercilessly twisted the knife in the wound. Yanushkevich linked his reports on the treason trial with pointed complaints about the shortage of ammunition and arms at the front, for which, after all, Sukhomlinov bore official responsibility.

In this cat-and-mouse game, the Minister of War cut a pathetic and undignified figure. He meekly accepted the Chief of Staff's allegations, which betray a morbid obsession with treason and espionage, and are flavoured with anti-Semitism and sadism.[1] By his spineless behaviour, Sukhomlinov was digging his own grave. If, instead of accepting Yanushkevich's unsubstantiated allegations and vilifying his former protégé, he had taken a firm stand and insisted on an impartial investigation and judicial guarantees for the accused (which was not beyond his reach, as he still enjoyed the confidence of the Emperor), he might have saved not only the accused, but also his own reputation. One of the most flagrant miscarriages of justice in the history of World War I would then have been prevented.

A further, even more significant consequence of the affair was its impact on public opinion, which GHQ had deliberately sought to influence. Thus, shortly before the trial, Yanushkevich wrote to Sukhomlinov:

> The Myasoedov affair will probably be finally settled as far as he personally is concerned today or tomorrow. This is necessary because of the fully proven shameful treason of which he is guilty, and in order to appease public opinion before the [Easter] holidays.[2]

By staging the treason trial, GHQ sought to provide an explanation

1. E.g. when Yanushkevich forecast a further, widespread development of the Myasoedov affair, and promised ruthless prosecution of the predominantly Jewish agents for the Germans, who he alleged were engaged in espionage and sabotage in Russia. See *Krasny Arkhiv*, III (1923). See also ch. 4 above.

2. *Krasny Arkhiv*, III, p. 44. Yanushkevich's assessment of the expected effect of the announcement of Myasoedov's execution on public opinion was as grave a miscalculation as any he made in the war. The general consternation at the news is still in living memory. The Petersburg Bolshevik Committee was quick to seize the opportunity to issue a special leaflet on the affair. Shlyapnikov reports that the leaflets said: 'Comrades, workers, and soldiers! The crime of the Russian government has been unmasked: it threw down the gauntlet to the government of Germany and Austria, while preparing treason against the Russian people.' *Nakanune 1917 goda* (Moscow, 1920), p. 153.

for the reverses at the front, and in particular for the defeat of
the Tenth Army. However, the announcement of the hanging of
Myasoedov coincided with the spread of the news about the shortage
of ammunition and arms at the front, which was the main reason for
the retreats in the summer of 1915. Myasoedov's personal contacts
with the Minister of War in the past were generally well known, and
the idea that the shortages were due to the work of German agents
surrounding the Minister and possibly using him as their instrument
inevitably took a firm hold on the general public's mind. Sukhomlinov's
position became untenable, yet it needed all the diplomatic skill of the
then Minister of Agriculture, Krivoshein, to persuade the Emperor
to get rid of him. Doubtless Grand Duke Nikolay Nikolaevich,
who had always hated and snubbed Sukhomlinov, played his part in
supporting Krivoshein. On 12 June 1915, Nicholas II wrote a warmly-
worded personal letter to Sukhomlinov, relieving him of his post and
expressing the conviction that future generations would show more
gratitude for his patriotic services, of which he, the Emperor, had never
had any doubt.[1]

1. The letter is quoted by Sukhomlinov in his memoirs, op. cit.

7

The August 1915 Crisis

The liberalisation of the Council of Ministers; The change in the Supreme Command; 'Il est fou, ce vieillard!; Krivoshein's caucus, the Duma and the Voluntary Organisations; The aftermath

I. THE LIBERALISATION OF THE COUNCIL OF MINISTERS

The dismissal of Sukhomlinov in June 1915 touched off a reshuffle of the Cabinet, involving the retirement of three other ministers, Shcheglovitov (Justice), N. Maklakov (Interior), and Sabler (Ober-Procurator of the Holy Synod), who for various reasons had been in the eyes of the Duma liberals and of the Voluntary Organisations the most unacceptable members of the government. After a tug-of-war between the Minister of Agriculture, Krivoshein, and the Prime Minister, Goremykin, persons were appointed in their places whose records held out at least a hope of compromise with the Duma majority. The Ministry of War went on 12 June to General Polivanov, known to be on friendly terms with Guchkov. Shcheglovitov was replaced on 6 July by A. A. Khvostov (Khvostov, 'the Uncle', not to be confused with the later Minister of the Interior, the notorious A. N. Khvostov, 'the Nephew'). The Interior was taken over on 14 June by Prince Shcherbatov, and on 5 July the post of Ober-Procurator of the Holy Synod was given to Samarin.

These appointments were made after a series of conferences at GHQ, presided over by the Emperor, at which the Commander-in-Chief, Grand Duke Nikolay Nikolaevich, his Chief of Staff Yanushkevich and some of the ministers were present. The changes were clearly intended to ease the tension existing between the Cabinet and the Duma. We know that they were looked upon with misgivings by the Empress, who wept when she heard of the appointment of Samarin, a representative of those circles of Moscow's liberal and traditionalist aristocracy which, of all things in Russia (except revolution), were most unpalatable to her. The Emperor must have braced himself for domestic trouble over these appointments.

It is not clear from the published sources how he was persuaded of the need for, and who was responsible for raising the question of, the Cabinet reshuffle. The fact that it was carried out during the meetings at GHQ in Baranovichi gave rise to the idea that Grand Duke Nikolay Nikolaevich was behind it. Later, when he was dismissed from the Supreme Command, it was believed that the liberal ministers in the Cabinet had lost a powerful ally. Even Prince Shakhovskoy, then Minister of Trade and Industry, does not seem to know exactly who were the prime movers in this operation. Some light, however, is thrown upon it by a letter from Peter Bark, the Minister of Finance, to A. A. Rittikh,[1] which Bark wrote in emigration, after acquainting himself with Yakhontov's notes on the meetings of the Cabinet.[2]

Bark reports that he visited GHQ with Shcheglovitov in the spring of 1915 and learned there for the first time from Yanushkevich of the calamitous shortage of ammunition, which would necessitate a large-scale retreat of the Russian armies on all fronts. Having discussed the matter on his return with Sazonov (Minister of Foreign Affairs), Rukhlov (Minister of Transport), Kharitonov (State Comptroller) and Krivoshein, Bark went to see Goremykin and told him that if Sukhomlinov, Shcheglovitov, Maklakov and Sabler were not dismissed they would themselves ask to be retired. Their motive, according to Bark, was the necessity for the government to work hand in hand with the Duma and the Voluntary Organisations in securing proper supplies for the army, and that could not be done unless certain cabinet changes were carried out forthwith. Bark says in his letter to Rittikh that the ministers hoped, when they approached Goremykin, that he

1. Aleksander Aleksandrovich Rittikh was an important administrator who became Acting Minister of Agriculture, 16 November 1916.
2. A. N. Yakhontov was an assistant head of the chancellery of the Council of Ministers in 1915–16. He was a protégé of Goremykin. In the course of his duties he took notes on the debates at the secret meetings of the Council. No official minutes were kept, and what was published as the proceedings of the Council was an agreed version on the decisions taken. Yakhontov managed to take his notes abroad. In the early twenties he transcribed and circulated a large part of them among such former members of the Tsarist government as he was able to contact. These edited notes were published in ARR, XVIII, and are certainly one of the most important authentic documents on that period. The original notes, which cover a much longer period, are in the custody of the Archive of Russian and East European History and Culture at Columbia University. Letters written in connection with these notes by ex-members of the Tsarist government are also kept there, including the one by Bark.

himself would then resign and a new premier — probably Krivoshein — succeed him. Goremykin, however, who enjoyed the full confidence of the Tsar, recommended the dismissal of the four ministers, but remained at his post and even tried to maintain his position in the Council of Ministers by imposing his own candidate for the Ministry of Justice, A. A. Khvostov.

Bark's account of what took place is fully borne out by Yakhontov, who had discussed the ministers' *démarche* with Goremykin. The story makes sense and provides an explanation of why the Tsar agreed to the changes. As long as Goremykin remained in power, the Tsar could rest assured that the liberal ministers would not be allowed to exceed the limits of their commissions or to capitulate to the demands of the Duma and the Voluntary Organisations. With Goremykin in charge, the Tsar could risk the experiment of a liberalised cabinet. This also explains why, in the course of subsequent events, Goremykin showed such exceptional tenacity in sticking to his office and refusing to resign. He had, possibly despite his own ingrained suspicions, induced the Tsar to accept the liberal ministers, including Guchkov's personal friend, Polivanov. He could not leave his sovereign in the lurch by retiring when the people he had recommended might try at the first opportunity to encroach on the prerogatives of the crown, in which Nicholas II saw the essence and the dignity of his regal mission. Bark's letter also explains the exasperation of such ministers as Sazonov and Kharitonov, who thought at one moment that they might transform the government into one of 'public confidence', but met with Goremykin's opposition to their plans for a rapprochement with the Duma.

Bark also confirms something which would otherwise have remained only a fair assumption, namely that the ministers who had brought about the June–July changes in the Cabinet formed a caucus around Krivoshein. They met regularly, most often at Krivoshein's home, to discuss privately their stand at the meetings of the Council of Ministers. This was the nucleus around which the subsequent opposition to the change in the high command was centred. Krivoshein seems to have been the chief tactician of these short-lived but important political intrigues. As the struggle for concessions to the Duma developed, the enthusiasm of some of the ministers of the Krivoshein caucus seemed to wane. At least Bark notes that some of his colleagues in this group (Sazonov, Kharitonov, Samarin?) tended much too far to the left for his own taste. Is it not possible that the militant tone of the Moscow Congresses of the Voluntary Organisations in 1915 frightened some of the members of the caucus, and that they were only too glad to abandon their campaign and continue to serve under Goremykin, Stuermer, and his successors? Bark, in any case, remained in his post as Minister of Finance until the February days of 1917.

Bark's *démarche* with Goremykin was, however, not the only pressure put on the Emperor. The Minister of Foreign Affairs, Sazonov, reports that in his audiences with the Tsar he had been pressing for the retirement of Sukhomlinov. And Nicholas II reproached the President of the Duma, Rodzyanko, for having urged the dismissal of N. Maklakov from the Ministry of the Interior, a step which, by January 1917, the Emperor regretted having taken.[1] No direct pressure from the Duma circles in favour of the new ministers seems to have been made, although the President of the Duma took part in some of the meetings held at GHQ. Indirect pressure, however, there may have been, possibly as a result of the close contacts which Krivoshein maintained with Guchkov at that time.[2]

2. THE CHANGE IN THE SUPREME COMMAND

As soon as the new government was formed, the new Minister of War, Polivanov, became aware of the impossible position in which the government found itself in view of the dictatorial attitude of GHQ, and especially of its Chief of Staff, General Yanushkevich. The position of the new Minister of War was particularly delicate. Sukhomlinov had greatly compromised the authority of the office during the Myasoedov affair, and had become a complete 'yes-man' to Yanushkevich. Now Polivanov tried to reassert his position by attacking the Chief of Staff in speeches at the Council of Ministers. At meetings of the Council in the summer of 1915, Polivanov gave a devastating picture of the high-handedness and incompetence of GHQ, and of the arrogant

1. See Rodzyanko's last interview with the Tsar. A. Blok, *Poslednie dni starogo rezhima* in *ARR* IV (1922), pp. 5–54.
2. See the account of the reshuffle of the Cabinet in the summer of 1915 in Prince Vsevolod Shakhovskoy, *Sic transit gloria mundi* (Paris, 1952) p. 92.

interference of the military with civil authorities. These complaints were supported by the Minister of Transport, who had suffered most of all from the interference of the 'brass-hats'.

As a consequence, the newly liberalised government launched a concerted attack against GHQ, and in particular against Yanushkevich. All attempts to have him replaced (and these were made with all the classic methods of Russian higher politics, including anonymous denunciations), met with obstinate resistance from Grand Duke Nikolay Nikolaevich. The ministers then put forward for the consideration of the Emperor the idea of a Supreme War Council, to be presided over by the Emperor himself. This council, it was hoped, would solve difficulties arising between GHQ and the government, just as, in June, informal consultations at a high level had brought about the liberalisation of the Council of Ministers.

On 16 July, Polivanov started his systematic attack on GHQ. Proclaiming that 'the Fatherland is in danger', he said in the Council of Ministers:

> Against the dark background of the disintegration of the army as regards equipment, numbers, and morale, there is one more phenomenon which is particularly threatening in its consequences, and about which we cannot remain silent any longer. At the Supreme Commander's headquarters, they seem to have lost their heads. . . . There seems to be neither system nor plan in their actions and orders . . . and with all that, the Stavka continues to guard its power and privileges jealously. . . . General Yanushkevich thinks himself superior to everything and everybody. All others have to be silent executors of orders which he transmits in the name of the Grand Duke. . . . None of the senior generals knows where and why he is being transferred. 'Keep your mouth shut and do not argue', is the favourite cry coming from the Stavka.

Having denounced GHQ, the Minister of War proffered the following advice to the Council of Ministers: 'Our duty, gentlemen, is to implore His Majesty, without losing a minute, to convene immediately under his chairmanship an extraordinary war council'.

Polivanov's oration, with its refrain of 'the Fatherland is in danger', produced a shattering impression on the Council. Even those ministers who, six weeks later, refused to join what was called 'the rebellion of the Cabinet' were in favour of asking the Emperor at once to convene a war council.

Yakhontov was unable to take full notes of the debate because, in his excitement over the revelations of the War Minister, his hand began to shake. Yet he subsequently noted in his version of the minutes of that meeting:

> Everyone was seized by some kind of excitement. This was not a debate in a Council of Ministers; this was a round table discussion among Russians whose feelings were aroused. Never shall I forget that day and my feelings on that occasion. Is it possible that everything is lost? This Polivanov does not inspire confidence in me. He always seems to have ulterior motives and something at the back of his mind; the shadow of Guchkov stands behind him.[1]

As we shall see, Yakhontov was not far wrong in his guess. At the same meeting, the experienced and crafty Prime Minister, Goremykin, warned his colleagues of the risks of denouncing the incompetence of GHQ.[2] He hinted at the possibility of the dismissal of Nikolay Nikolaevich from the Supreme Command: 'The Empress Alexandra Feodorovna considers Grand Duke Nikolay to be the only one guilty of all the disasters at the front.' When the question was raised again on 24 July, Goremykin repeated his warning even more insistently and said: 'In Tsarskoe Selo irritation over the Grand Duke is assuming a character which might have dangerous consequences.'

The ministers took no heed of Goremykin's warning. None of them seemed to have believed it possible that the Emperor would want to take over the command of the army from his uncle at a time when the military situation appeared so threatening. It came, therefore, as a complete surprise when, on 6 August, the War Minister Polivanov, at the end of another speech describing the near-hopeless situation at the front, suddenly declared:

> However frightful the situation at the front, there is an even more dreadful event threatening Russia. I shall consciously violate an official secret and a personal promise to keep silent about it for the time being. I have a duty to warn the government that this morning, while I was reporting to His Majesty, he disclosed to me his decision to remove the Grand Duke and to assume personally the supreme command of the army.

The news was received with amazement and consternation. Polivanov correctly assessed the mood of his colleagues when he described the

---

1. *ARR*, XVIII, p. 17.   2. *ARR*, XVIII, p. 21.

Emperor's decision as a super-disaster threatening the country after so many other major setbacks in that fateful year. The immediate reaction of most members of the Council of Ministers was to try to find a way to induce the Emperor to go back on his decision.

It is difficult to understand what the real reasons were for this highly emotional — one would now be tempted to say irrational — reaction of the ministers to a decision which was, after all, well motivated and quite within the limits of their monarch's prerogative. The change in the Supreme Command was, moreover, very much in line with the policies which the Council had been advocating during the previous few weeks. With the Emperor at the head of the army, co-ordination between the actions of GHQ and the civil administration was likely to improve.[1]

The actual command of the armies was to be taken out of the hands of General Yanushkevich, whom Polivanov had accused of incompetence and worse, and entrusted to the new Chief of Staff, General Alekseev, who had the reputation of being a thoughtful and cautious man accessible to reasoned argument, and was popular in Duma circles.

The ostensible objection of the ministers to the assumption of the supreme command by the Emperor was that any defeat at the front would reflect directly on the authority and prestige of the monarch and would undermine the loyalty of the people. This argument was put forward in every possible variation, including reference to the widespread superstition that the Emperor was 'unlucky', having been born on the day when the Church commemorates the long-suffering Job. The Khodynka disaster at the beginning of his reign, when hundreds of people had been trampled to death in a stampede at the coronation in Moscow, was brought effectively, if not relevantly,

---

1. Earlier, in July, Krivoshein had pointed out at a meeting of the Council that the rules for administering the war zone had been drawn up in the expectation that the Emperor himself would assume supreme command. 'Then,' Krivoshein said, 'there would have been no misunderstanding, and all questions would have been solved in a simple way: all power would have been in the hands of one man' (*ARR*, XVIII, p. 21).

After the announcement of the Tsar's decision, Krivoshein did not repeat this argument in favour of it. The minister who pressed most insistently for an intervention by the Council to change the Emperor's mind was the Procurator of the Holy Synod, Samarin. He claimed to speak on behalf of Moscow public opinion. Sazonov supported him most emphatically.

into the argument. The Minister of the Interior, Prince Shcherbatov, introduced considerations of the Emperor's personal safety, which, he alleged (wrongly as it turned out), would be endangered on the roads leading to GHQ, now thronged by refugees and deserters. At the same time, merits never before mentioned in the Grand Duke's administration were suddenly discovered.

Goremykin, who had known of the Emperor's decision days before, was the only one to warn his colleagues that any pressure on the Emperor to change his mind would be of no avail:

> Now that there is almost a catastrophe at the front, His Majesty considers it the sacred duty of a Russian Tsar to stay with his troops and either to achieve victory with them or to perish. In such purely mystical moods, you will not be able to dissuade the Emperor by any argument. I repeat, no intrigue and no personal influences[1] played a part in this decision. It has been dictated by the consciousness of the Tsar's duty to the Motherland and to the long-suffering army. Like the Minister of War, I made every effort to restrain His Majesty from a final decision and implored him to postpone it until circumstances are more propitious. I also find that the assumption of the supreme command by the Emperor is a very risky move, which might have dangerous consequences. But he himself realises this risk perfectly and, nevertheless, does not want to renounce what he believes is the Tsar's duty. We can do nothing but submit to his will and stand by him.[2]

As usual, Goremykin's warnings produced no effect whatever on his colleagues. Efforts to dissuade the Emperor continued throughout the next fortnight. First, individual ministers argued with the Emperor when they went to report on the affairs of their departments. Then, on 20 August, they were received in audience collectively and repeated their exhortations. The Emperor listened absent-mindedly, and answered that, having heard all his ministers' objections, he would maintain his decision.[3]

At last, on 21 August, the ministers had recourse to a most unusual procedure: they signed a collective letter, in which they once more implored the monarch not to take a disastrous step which would threaten his throne and the future of the dynasty. The signatories further

1. An allusion to rumours of Rasputin's intervention in the change at GHQ.
2. *ARR*, XVIII, p. 54.
3. Shakhovskoy, op. cit., p. 126.

expressed their profound disagreement with the Chairman of the Council of Ministers, Goremykin, and pointed out that the Council could
not work effectively under such circumstances.[1] Goremykin was not
informed in advance of this *démarche* of the ministers. The letter was
delivered to the Tsar at the moment when he was about to leave for
GHQ to assume his command.

These desperate attempts of a group of ministers to interfere with
the change in the Supreme Command are puzzling. Later, some of
those who signed the letter of 21 August expressly regretted having
done so. It is clear that the feeling of doom which seized the ministers
at the announcement of the Emperor's decision did not reflect either
the army's attitude or that of the country at large. Those who understood the shy and reticent personality of the Tsar knew that he would
not impose any personal ideas of strategy on his newly-appointed
Chief of Staff, Alekseev. We have numerous testimonies to the effect
that Alekseev, a quiet, pious man, with a delicate constitution and
intellectual inclinations, inspired at that time far more confidence in
the army than did the traditional ostentatious type of swashbuckling,
iron-willed general.

Four years later, on the eve of his execution in Irkutsk, Admiral
Kolchak, who commanded the Black Sea Fleet in 1915, explained to
his Bolshevik interrogators that he had welcomed the replacement of
the Grand Duke by the Emperor not so much because he was critical
of Nikolay Nikolaevich's record as because he was certain that strategic
decisions would be taken by General Alekseev without interference
from the Emperor. 'This', said Kolchak, 'was for me the guarantee of
success in the war.'[2] In his work on World War I, General Golovin
supports this view 'The popularity', he wrote, 'of Alekseev was
different from that [of the Grand Duke].' In the army it was greatest
among the old regular officers. Higher officers considered him the

1. The letter was signed by practically all the members of the cabinet with the
exception of Goremykin himself, A. A. Khvostov and the Minister of Transport,
Rukhlov. The Ministers of War and the Navy, who were present, did not sign the
letter for reasons of military discipline, although they expressed their complete
agreement with its contents. On the circumstances in which the letter was signed see
in particular Shakhovskoy, op. cit., pp. 127 ff.
2. *ARR*, X (Berlin, 1923), p. 213. English translation in *The Testimony of Kolchak
and other Siberian Materials* ed. Varneck and Fisher. Hoover War Library Publications
No. 10 (Stanford/London, 1935), p. 51.

most knowledgeable leader among all Russian generals. The career officers looked upon him as one of their fraternity who had reached the upper grades of the hierarchy exclusively on his own merits.[1]

In fact, the changes in the Supreme Command coincided with a reversal in the fortunes of the Russian army, and August 1915 could be considered as the turning-point after which the fighting capacity of the army steadily increased until it broke down under the strain of the revolutionary events of February 1917. Why, then, was there such panic at the Tsar's decisions among the members of the Council of Ministers?

3. 'IL EST FOU, CE VIEILLARD !'

The minutes of the secret meeting of the Council show clearly that the change in the Supreme Command and the departure of the Emperor for the front cut across certain political plans which a number of ministers had hoped to implement through such bodies as a Supreme War Council under the chairmanship of the Emperor. These plans were connected with developments in the Duma which resulted in the formation on 25 August 1915 of the so-called 'Progressive Bloc'. For the first time in the existence of the Fourth Duma, a centrist majority was formed, on the basis of a compromise political programme. The Duma as a whole, with the exception of the Labour faction, the Social-Democrats and the extreme right, was ready to give its support to the imperial government, provided it had at its head a person 'enjoying the confidence of the public'. This was asking for less than the Kadet Party's long-standing demand for a government responsible to the Duma in a true parliamentary sense. But the platform of the Progressive Bloc certainly implied that the leadership of the war economy and administration in Russia would be transferred to people who were in favour of constitutional reform. Now, however, after the formation of the Progresive Bloc, the *de jure* constitutional reform was to be preceded by a period of *de facto* rule by representatives of liberal and radical-liberal political circles.[2] The Emperor's decision dashed the

1. Golovin, *Voennye usiliya*, etc. Vol. II (Paris, 1939), p. 156.
2. See above, p. 14 ff., Milyukov's statement at a banquet in Moscow on 13 March 1916, where he expounded and justified his conception of the transition from autocracy to a parliamentary system.

hopes of the politicians of the Progressive Bloc for such a reform, just as it disappointed those ministers who hoped to establish a working agreement with the Bloc.

The reaction of the President of the Duma to the Emperor's decision led to a most unusual incident. On 11 August, the President of the Duma called during the meeting of the Council of Ministers and asked to see Krivoshein. He told him that he had protested to the Tsar against his decision, and asked what the Council of Ministers was going to do about it. Krivoshein referred him to Goremykin, who, in his turn, came out of the Council meeting to talk to Rodzyanko. Goremykin obviously found Rodzyanko's interference improper and tried to put him off. A wild scene ensued: Rodzyanko rushed out of the Mariinsky Palace, screaming at the top of his voice that he was ready to believe that 'Russia had no government'. The hall-porter tried to hand him his walking-stick, which he had forgotten in his excitement, but Rodzyanko shouted: 'To hell with the walking-stick.' He jumped into his carriage, and was driven away.

Rodzyanko's antics were unanimously condemned at the Council meeting, but this, as we shall see, did not mean that all the ministers were reconciled to the change in the Supreme Command.

Nor was the Council of Ministers unanimous in its attitude to the Progressive Bloc and its programme. The majority of the ministers — including Sazonov, Polivanov, Shcherbatov, and Samarin — were pressing for an agreement with the Duma parties united in the Progressive Bloc. Goremykin was dead against any negotiations with this 'unconstitutional body'. Yakhontov's minutes of the secret meeting of 26 August record the clash between the two views.

> *Sazonov:* ... while those whose hearts are aching for the Motherland unite to concentrate all the most active non-revolutionary forces of the country, they are denounced as an illegal mob and are cold-shouldered. Such tactics are dangerous and a colossal political error. The government cannot live in a vacuum and rely exclusively on the police. I shall repeat this to the bitter end.
>
> *Goremykin:* The Bloc has been created to seize power. Anyway, it will disintegrate, and the participants will fall out with each other.
>
> *Sazonov:* But I believe that we should, in the name of the interests of the entire state, support this Bloc, which is essentially moderate. If it falls to pieces, there will be another one far more to the left. What will

happen then? To whose advantage will that be? Surely not to that of Russia.

Polivanov: And how will that reflect on defence, on the struggle with the enemy, who is carefully observing our internal squabbles and disintegration?

Sazonov: It is dangerous to provoke the left, to push them to adopt non-parliamentary tactics in their political struggle. I insist that we must not reject the demands of the Bloc *in toto*, and that we should reach an agreement on points acceptable to the government. Why should one needlessly aggravate relations which are strained enough as it is?

Goremykin: I consider the Bloc itself, as an intermediate body between the two legislative chambers[1], unacceptable. Its barely-concealed aim is the limitation of the Tsar's power. Against this I shall fight to the end.[2]

The day after this exchange between Goremykin and his opponents, members of the government met representatives of the Bloc at a private meeting.[3] The ministers refused to discuss the constitutional issue and made it clear that the programme of the Progressive Bloc could not be usefully discussed with the Council of Ministers, as it was then composed. In the opinion both of the members of the Progressive Bloc and of ministers who were in favour of an agreement with them, Goremykin had to go. This is obvious from the clash of unprecedented violence which took place at the meeting of the Council on 28 August between Goremykin and the ministers who had taken part in the talks with the Bloc the day before.

The question under discussion was the prorogation of the Duma for the autumn recess. Goremykin intended to close the session by issuing a decree to the Senate in the usual way. The ministers opposing him were also in favour of an immediate recess, but they wanted it to be arranged in agreement with the President of the Duma (*po khoroshemu* — 'in an amicable way') and accompanied by changes in the

1. i.e. the State Duma and the State Council.
2. *ARR*, XVIII, p. 107.
3. The meeting was attended by Kharitonov (State Comptroller), A. A. Khvostov (Justice), Prince Shcherbatov (Interior), and Shakhovskoy (Trade and Industry). The Duma representatives comprised a number of party leaders, including Milyukov, Dmitryukov, Efremov and Shidlovsky (according to V. I. Gurko in *Features and Figures of the Past*, p. 576).

Cabinet. Krivoshein made this point at the meeting of 28 August in the following words:

> Whatever we may say, whatever we may promise, however much we play up to the Progressive Bloc and to the public, nobody will give us a farthing's credit. The demands of the State Duma and of the whole country are concerned not with the question of programme, but with the personalities to whom power is entrusted. Therefore I believe that the central point of our deliberations should be not to determine the date on which the session of the State Duma should be adjourned, but to raise the question of principle concerning the attitude of His Imperial Majesty to the present government and to the demands of the country for an administrative executive enjoying the confidence of the public. Let the monarch decide how he will be pleased to direct our future internal policy — whether by ignoring such demands or by satisfying them. In the latter case he should select a person having the sympathy of the public and entrust him with the formation of a government. Without solving this cardinal question, we shall make no progress whatever. I personally am in favour of the second course of action — that is, for the choice by His Majesty the Emperor of a person to whom would be entrusted the formation of a cabinet in tune with the aspirations of the country.[1]

Goremykin tried to dodge the question posed by Krivoshein. He pressed for a vote in the Council to decide the prorogation of the Duma. But the other ministers would not have it that way. They insisted that the Duma should be dissolved by the Goremykin government, but that, this done, it should resign and advise the Tsar to appoint a person 'enjoying the confidence of the public', who would select a new cabinet.

'Who are these new people?' asked Goremykin, for once losing his temper. 'Will they be representatives of the Duma parties or civil servants? Do you propose to name to the Emperor the desirable candidates from a certain camp?' But Krivoshein would not be drawn out. 'I do not intend to suggest anyone', he answered. 'Let His Majesty the Emperor invite a person of his choice and authorise him to choose his future collaborators. Any other formula is impossible.' Goremykin: 'This means that it is deemed necessary to present the Tsar with an ultimatum: the resignation of the Council of Ministers and a new

1. *ARR*, XVIII, p. 123.

government.' The suggestion that there was something like a mutiny in the Council brought a sharp rejoinder from Sazonov. He denied that this was an ultimatum. 'We are not conspirators, but just as loyal subjects of our Tsar as Your Excellency.' Goremykin apologised, but asked what would happen if the Tsar refused to change the present government. 'What then?' The ministers had to admit that in that case they would feel free to submit their individual resignations. Finally it was decided, according to Yakhontov's notes, that 'the State Duma session should be brought to a close in the immediate future (amicably, having reached agreement with the President and the party leaders on the passing of the pending government bills required by wartime necessity), and that a petition should be made to His Majesty for a subsequent change in the composition of the Cabinet'.

The day before he left for GHQ at Mogilev, Goremykin told Yakhontov:

> It will be painful to distress the Emperor with the tale of our disagreements and the lack of nerve in the Council of Ministers. It is up to him to choose one course of action or the other. Whatever his orders, I shall fulfil them at all costs ... but as long as I live, I shall fight for the integrity of the Tsar's power. Strength lies in the monarchy alone. Otherwise, everything will go topsy-turvy, and all will be lost. Our first task is to carry on the war to the end and not to indulge in reforms. The time for this will come when we have beaten the Germans.

There can be no doubt as to the manner in which Goremykin reported the debates in the Council of Ministers to the Tsar. Before leaving for GHQ he had a talk with the Empress, in which he told her of what was going on in the Council. It made her very angry, as one can see from her letters to her husband. ('The ministers are worse than the Duma', she wrote). It is not surprising, therefore, that Goremykin came back to Petrograd on 1 September with the Tsar's orders that the Duma be prorogued not later than 3 September, and that the members of the Council of Ministers should remain in their posts without any change. Any disagreements among them the Emperor would solve when the situation at the front allowed him to deal with them.

Goremykin's announcement of these orders roused tempers in the Council. The ministers argued that a closing of the Duma session by such a procedure would be a challenge to public opinion. Krivoshein admitted that in the conflict between Goremykin and the Council, the Emperor had decided in Goremykin's favour. But he argued: 'Allow me to ask one question: how do you venture to act when the representatives of the executive power are convinced of the necessity of different measures, when the whole government apparatus in your hands is in a state of opposition, and when events at home and abroad are becoming more threatening every day?' Goremykin answered that he would fulfil his duty to the Emperor to the last, whatever the opposition. The Emperor, Goremykin said, had promised to deal personally with all other questions at a later date. 'But then it will be too late', Sazonov burst out. 'Blood will flow tomorrow in the streets and Russia will be thrown into the abyss. Is this really necessary? It is terrible! In any case, I declare openly that I accept no responsibility for your actions and for the closure of the Duma under the present circumstances.' Goremykin, who had recovered his composure, answered that he did not ask anyone to share his responsibility. 'The Duma will be dissolved on the appointed date, and no blood will flow anywhere.'

Goremykin was right in the short run, but the meeting of the Council broke up in confusion. Sazonov walked out as if dazed, and left the building, shouting: '*Il est fou, ce vieillard.*'

4. KRIVOSHEIN'S CAUCUS, THE DUMA AND THE VOLUNTARY ORGANISATIONS

Goremykin was not mad. Nor was he senile. Throughout his conflict with his colleagues, he did not conceal his intentions, refusing to be bullied into concessions by the threat of revolutionary outbreaks or by the argument that the exceptional circumstances brought about by the setbacks at the front should be met by exceptional measures of a political and constitutional character. He considered, and rightly so, that the difficult military situation presented 'left-wing politicians' with the opportunity of discrediting the monarchy, and that they were determined to use it at this juncture. 'It is quite evident', he said, 'that all the parties standing for constitutional change are using the military setbacks to increase their pressure on the government and to limit the powers of the monarch'.

A. A. Khvostov, who supported him, was even more outspoken:

> The appeals which are coming from Guchkov, from the left parties of the
> State Duma, from the Konovalov Congress, and from the Voluntary
> Organisations whose leaders took part in that congress are clearly aiming
> at a coup d'état. In war conditions, such a coup d'état would bring about
> the total disintegration of state administration and the destruction of
> our Fatherland.[1]

The Konovalov Congress to which A. A. Khvostov referred was a
meeting of representatives of the Voluntary Organisations and of the
leaders of the Duma Kadets which had taken place in Konovalov's
house in Moscow on 16 August. According to the report of the
Moscow police,[2] the Congress elected a central committee which was
to direct propaganda and agitation all over the country in support of
the programme of the Progressive Bloc. Immediately after, on 18
August, the Moscow Municipal Duma, dominated by the liberal-
industrialist faction, passed a resolution demanding the formation of a
'government of public confidence'. They sent this resolution to the
government and to the Tsar direct.

The political agitation started in Moscow was reported at the meeting
of the Council of Ministers of 19 August by Prince Shcherbatov, the
Minister of the Interior. The Council discussed what answer should
be given to the Moscow Municipal Duma. Goremykin's attitude was
typical of his complete contempt for politicians, all of whom he regarded as 'busybodies'. The simplest thing, he said, would be not to
answer all these chatterboxes and to ignore them, since they were interfering in things which were not their concern. The discussion of the
Moscow Municipal Duma's address gave the rebellious ministers an
opportunity to vent their feelings. Polivanov stated squarely that there
was nothing impermissible or revolutionary in their resolution. 'A
government basing itself on the confidence of the people: this is a
normal condition for a state', he said.[3] Krivoshein also joined Polivanov
in expressing the hope that the Tsar would radically change the character of Russian internal policy.[4]

It is clear that on all controversial questions which came up for
discussion — the change in the Supreme Command, the attitude to

1. *ARR*, XVIII, p. 97.   2. See Grave, op. cit., p. 35.
3. *ARR*, XVIII, p. 83.   4. Ibid., p. 84.

the Progressive Bloc, the answer to the Moscow Municipal Duma's loyal address, and the question of the prorogation of the State Duma — the majority of the ministers were as one on the need for a definite policy of rapprochement with the Voluntary Organisations and with the State Duma. The main obstacle being Goremykin, they decided to press for the appointment of a new premier, threatening a resignation *en bloc* if Goremykin stayed and continued on his reactionary course. According to Shakhovskoy, the majority of these ministers decided to put Polivanov forward for the premiership. In the press Polivanov, Krivoshein, and Grigorovich, the Minister of the Navy, were then being frequently mentioned as candidates for the premiership. All three were considered by the liberal press to be 'persons enjoying the confidence of the public'. An agreement on the political programme of the Progressive Bloc (which would have to be slightly watered down) was all that was needed, in the opinion of the ministers, to achieve national unity.

It can be doubted whether Krivoshein, who openly backed Polivanov for the premiership — on 20 August he stated in the presence of the Emperor and his colleagues that in wartime the Minister of War should head the Government — was quite candid in his actions. He knew that Polivanov did not possess the Emperor's confidence because of his personal contacts with Guchkov. He might well have been promoting his own candidature by purporting to canvass Polivanov's.[1]

There certainly were contacts between Polivanov and Guchkov. The two men were closely connected politically, as became obvious immediately after the February revolution. But these contacts were also known to exist in 1915, as early as June of that year, when Polivanov was appointed Minister of War. When Polivanov presented himself to the Tsar on that occasion, he was warned that in the past, he had already once lost the Emperor's confidence because of his contacts with Guchkov. Polivanov made a lame apology, explaining that the contacts

1. This is the interpretation which the Soviet historian Zayonchkovsky puts on Krivoshein's manoeuvres in a footnote to Polivanov's memoirs. It is borne out by the police reports on the activities of the Moscow politicians, where the candidature of Krivoshein for the premiership is described as acceptable and even desirable to the Kadets. See Grave, op. cit., pp. 43 ff., and Polivanov's memoirs, *Iz dnevnikov i vospominanii* (Moscow, 1924).

Bark also admits that the caucus in the summer of 1915 was led by Krivoshein.

were of an official character. In August, however, when the Special Council of Defence was established by statutory law and formally opened by the Emperor in person on the 21st, Guchkov, as Chairman of the Central WIC, was again in official touch with the War Minister, and even took part in one of the meetings of the Council of Ministers which discussed the statutes of the new Council of Defence.

It must not be forgotten that, as Yakhontov remarks, Guchkov's figure 'was looming behind' Polivanov. Of course it was impossible for Polivanov to express his solidarity with Guchkov openly in the Council of Ministers. He does not seem to have come to the defence of his friend on 9 August, when the character of Guchkov was discussed in the Council. Yakhontov noted on that day:

> The conversation dwelt in particular on the personality of A. I. Guchkov, on the adventurous trait in his character, on his inordinate ambition, on the way he would stoop to any means to achieve his ends, on his hatred of the existing régime and of Emperor Nicholas II, and so on.[1]

On this occasion, the Minister of Justice, A. A. Khvostov, dropped the remark: 'He [i.e. Guchkov] is believed to be capable, when opportunity arises, of taking command of a battalion and marching on Tsarskoe Selo.' When, however, Guchkov's project for a labour group in the WICs was attacked on 26 August, Polivanov came to his defence, saying that it was impossible to organise war production while excluding the workers from representation on the WICs.

Even before the Krivoshein–Polivanov combination was proposed, Polivanov's contacts with Guchkov were used against him by his enemies. On 21 August, the very day when, in the evening, he signed the ill-fated letter which his colleagues sent to the Emperor on the question of the Supreme Command and on their quarrel with Goremykin, Prince Shakhovskoy was received by the Emperor at Tsarskoe Selo.[2] Shakhovskoy warned the Emperor of the contacts which Polivanov maintained with Guchkov, and expressed his surprise that Krivoshein had, under these conditions, advocated Polivanov's Premiership. O Byzantium!

In his memoirs[3] V. I. Gurko, member of the State Council and former collaborator of Stolypin, who was very much in the know

1. *ARR*, XVIII, p. 59.   2. See Shakhovskoy, op. cit., p. 127.
3. Gurko, op. cit., pp. 583 ff.

about what was going on behind the scenes, states that the Krivoshein-Polivanov combination was the last opportunity for Russia to avoid the cleavage between the throne and the public which — he believes — finally led to the collapse of the monarchy. Later, all candidates for a premiership 'of public confidence' belonged to the liberal intelligentsia (e.g. Rodzyanko or Prince Lvov), and none of them would have been able to stem the pressure of demands for radical reforms leading to revolution. Gurko thinks that the Krivoshein-Polivanov combination might have withstood that pressure and maintained order until a victorious end of the war. It is apparent from the minutes of the Council of Ministers that the rebellious ministers had some assurance from the Duma circles that they could count on the support of the Progressive Bloc, once they got rid of Goremykin. But if we take into consideration the part played by Guchkov and other Moscow plotters at that very moment, we may well doubt Gurko's optimistic view of a Krivoshein-Polivanov combination.

5. THE AFTERMATH

The revolt of the ministers came to an end with the dramatic meeting of 2 September. There were some desultory attempts in the following fortnight to reverse the decision on the prorogation of the Duma. But they came to nothing. The morale of the rebellious ministers must have suffered considerably during this period. It became clear that the take-over of the Supreme Command by the Emperor, which they had so stubbornly and, one could say, hysterically opposed, was accepted by the army and the country with hope and sympathy, in spite of the agitation in favour of the Grand Duke emanating from the Voluntary Organisations and their congresses in Moscow at the beginning of September. The first few days of September were marked by strikes in industry, which were claimed to be in protest against the closing of the Duma session. But no blood flowed in the streets, contrary to Sazonov's predictions, and on the whole, the country took the closing of the Duma with its usual equanimity. On the other hand, the congresses of the Unions of the Zemstvos and Municipalities came out openly with the demand that they should replace the government bureaucracy in most branches of administration dealing with the supply of the army. This could hardly have been to the taste even of some of the ministers who had joined the Krivoshein-Polivanov group.

When, on 16 September, the ministers were summoned to GHQ to meet the Emperor for a final showdown, they went in a mood of depression. The Empress had written many times to her husband denouncing the ministers' 'treachery', of which Goremykin had given her a full account. She urged her husband to show maximum severity in his talk with them, and implored him to comb his hair with Rasputin's comb several times before the meeting. Amazingly, the magic worked. The Emperor spoke severely of his displeasure at the receipt of the ministers' letter of 21 August, and asked them to state their case against Goremykin. Prince Shcherbatov, the Minister of the Interior, became confused, but when he recovered he struck a conciliatory note. He said that he found it just as difficult to agree on the management of state affairs with Goremykin as he would find it to administer the family estate with his own father. Goremykin grumbled into his beard that for his part he would have preferred to deal with Prince Shcherbatov Senior, and the Emperor declared that Goremykin was to stay because he enjoyed his full confidence. Assuming his most charming manner, the Emperor pointed out that much of the nervousness in the Council was due to the unsound atmosphere prevailing in the capital. He regretted that his ministers were not able to enjoy the quiet and business-like atmosphere of GHQ. He himself, he said, was now recovering from the tension and the unhealthy moral climate of Petrograd. The ministers, who originally were to be dismissed after the audience, were then invited to dine at the Emperor's table, and the hatchet of the August crisis was buried.

Not that the crisis passed without some early effect on the composition of the government. Shcherbatov and Samarin were retired almost immediately, to be followed soon after by Krivoshein. It would be rash to ascribe the subsequent dismissal of Polivanov and Sazonov wholly to the events of August, but the lingering distrust of them in the mind of the Emperor may well have been a contributing factor.

8

The Onslaught on the Autocracy

*The start of the denunciation campaign; Russian political freemasonry;
The Guchkov plot; 'The Mad Chauffeur'; Guchkov and the army
in 1916; Milyukov's broadside; The assassination of Rasputin*

I. THE START OF THE DENUNCIATION CAMPAIGN

The August crisis ended in a stalemate between the monarchy and
the 'progressive' forces represented by the Progressive Bloc and the
Voluntary Organisations. This stalemate was to last up to the February
revolution. After August 1915, no further attempt was ever made by
the Council of Ministers to change the policy of the government and
to direct it into the channels which Krivoshein, Shcherbatov, Sazonov,
Samarin and their colleagues thought would lead to political co-operation between the government and the public.

On the other hand, the government did not resort to repressive
measures either against the Duma or against the Voluntary Organisations as such. The Duma was expected to carry on the legislative
activities necessary for the prosecution of the war, and the Voluntary
Organisations continued to assist the Special Councils in the organisation of military supplies and the supervision of industry and transport.
Surprisingly, in spite of the continuous friction between the Voluntary
Organisations and the government and the steady deterioration of
relations between the Duma and the Tsar, the system of Special Councils,
in which the Voluntary Organisations took an active part, worked
beneficially from the point of view of the war effort. The government
felt that it could safely postpone a general reckoning with the Duma
and the rebellious Voluntary Organisations until victory over Germany
was won. All that was necessary in their view was to curb the political
activities of the Voluntary Organisations and prevent their joining hands
with the revolutionary movement.

But curbing the activities of ambitious and angry men was not an
easy job, and the Voluntary Organisations repaid in kind all indignities

inflicted on them by the government. When, for example, the government revealed its intentions by appointing a notorious secret police officer, Vissarionov, as inspector and official auditor for the Union of Municipalities, the Voluntary Organisations answered by threatening the government with popular unrest.

In his statement to the Muravyev Commission the chairman of the Union of Municipalities, Chelnokov, revealed some of the methods used by the Voluntary Organisations to intimidate the government.[1]

During the war, the Moscow municipality decided to increase the salary of municipal employees by a total sum of two and a half million roubles. The government authorities in the person of the Governor of the City (*Gradonachalnik*) Klimovich protested against the decision of the City Council. Chelnokov, who was the Mayor of Moscow, issued an announcement that no salaries at all would be paid to the employees in view of the protest of the City Governor. He did so in spite of the fact that Klimovich had assured him that the matter could be cleared by correspondence between his department and the municipality, and that there was no reason to withhold payment of current salaries. Such was the pin-prick technique used by the warring parties in this incessant struggle for power and independence of decision. Much of the bad feeling between the imperial administration and the Voluntary Organisations — in this case the Union of Municipalities — was due to a natural departmental jealousy inherent in all bureaucratic systems. Four months after the February revolution the same Chelnokov was already at loggerheads with his political friends in the Provisional Government, and was accusing them of many of the same sins of which he had formerly accused the governments of Stuermer and Trepov.[2]

As soon as the attempt to establish a 'government of public confidence' had failed, the liberals and radicals of all shades began to realise that they had been manoeuvred into a position which would become indefensible, especially after a victorious end to the war. Their patriotic feelings, however, would not allow them directly to sabotage the war effort. But the temptation to use their steadily-increasing influence on the economic situation in order to embarrass the government and

1. See *Padenie*, the deposition of Chelnokov, vol. V, pp. 296–297.
2. See *Padenie*, vol. V. p. 300, where the chairman of the Investigation Committee had to warn Chelnokov that the commission was investigating the failure of the old and not of the new post-revolutionary government.

finally to overthrow it and so force the Emperor to appoint a 'government of public confidence' was too great for the liberals to resist: the whole future of the development of Russia towards a liberal, progressive, constitutional monarchy was at stake, and both the Duma politicians and the Moscow Voluntary Organisation centres understood this. Accordingly, they introduced a new note into their attacks on the government: instead of claiming, as they had done before, that the government was incapable of winning the war without their help, they now alleged that it was not working for victory at all, but was secretly preparing a separate peace and a shameful betrayal of the Allies.

These new tactics were adopted by the liberals in September 1915, as is clear from the reports of the secret police on the private meetings in Moscow which preceded the Congresses of the Zemstvo and Municipality Unions. The Moscow secret police (*Okhrannoe Otdelenie*) was at that time headed by an intelligent and hard-working officer, Colonel Martynov, whose reports, which we have often quoted, were published together with other materials under the general supervision of Professor Pokrovsky in 1927.[1]

The liberals' activity in Moscow in mid-August took the form of a number of private meetings, the first of which was held in Konovalov's house on the 16th.[2] Originally, the aim was to give the full support of the Voluntary Organisations to the newly-formed Progressive Bloc of the Duma and to its programme.[3]

The meeting at Konovalov's house elected a committee which would propagate the ideas of the Progressive Bloc in the country through the

1. Grave, *Burzhuaziya nakanune fevralskoy revolyutsii.*
2. The so-called 'Konovalov Congress', mentioned at the meeting of the Council of Ministers on 18 August. See above, p. 148.
3. For the programme, whose main features are its eclecticism and its ineptitude, see the text quoted in Pares, *The Fall of the Russian Monarchy*, pp. 271–273 and above, p. 149. In spite, or perhaps because, of these qualities, the programme did not appear totally unacceptable to the government. One of the main bones of contention was the demand of the Duma for a complete amnesty for all political prisoners. This meant, of course, an amnesty for the five Bolshevik members of the Duma, who had been sentenced in February 1915 for anti-war propaganda. The Kadets and the parties to the right of them gave this demand only half-hearted support, under the constant pressure of the left, which they had to play up to in order not to lose prestige in the eyes of the radical and revolutionary intelligentsia.

Voluntary Organisations.[1] This was followed by a number of banquets and private meetings, at which the possibility of a liberal government and its composition were discussed. These preparatory conferences led to the passing of a resolution by the Moscow Municipal Duma addressed to the Tsar, asking for a 'government of public confidence', and suggesting that the Tsar receive a delegation which would present a 'loyal address'.

The proceedings of the Council of Ministers recorded in the previous chapter leave no doubt that the Moscow parleys were somehow co-ordinated with the disaffected ministers' efforts to induce the Emperor to change the composition of the government. Goremykin's resistance to all these pressures put an end to the hopes for a peaceful settlement between the Voluntary Organisations and the Progressive Bloc on the one hand, and the Tsar on the other. The removal of the Grand Duke from the Supreme Command was obviously considered a serious blow to the liberals' plans. (All of a sudden, the Moscow liberals discovered a warm spot in their hearts for the Grand Duke, who had never shared their views and whose military administration in the areas behind the front lines had shocked, by its reactionary arbitrariness and anti-Semitism, even the members of the Tsarist government.) But the decisive blow to liberal hopes was the closing-down of the Duma, on 3 September, for the autumn recess. With it went the illusion that the formation of a 'government of public confidence' was imminent. The news reached Moscow a few days before the opening of the official congresses of the Union of Zemstvos and the Union of Municipalities.

The tactics on which the Moscow liberals relied in the middle of August had failed completely, and were now to be replaced by a different and spectacular line designed to impress and inspire the delegates to the congresses. On the eve of the opening of the Congress of the Zemstvos on 6 September, a meeting took place in the house of the Mayor of Moscow, M. V. Chelnokov, attended by representatives of the Voluntary Organisations and the Duma, including Prince Lvov, Guchkov, Milyukov, Shingarev, Konovalov and many others. It was at this meeting, according to a report of the secret police, that a new explanation was given for the reactionary course of the government,

1. See Grave, op. cit., pp. 35 ff.

and this became the basic presupposition of all liberal political activities in the course of the next eighteen months.[1]

Those present at this meeting discussed the latest events and expressed their belief that they were the work of a 'Black Bloc' whose aim it was to counteract the activities of the newly-formed Progressive Bloc. This 'Black Bloc' was allegedly headed by pro-German circles at the Emperor's court and included the reactionary minority in the Council of Ministers (i.e. Goremykin and A. A. Khvostov), as well as the right-wing parties of both legislative assemblies. It had succeeded, it was alleged, in isolating the Emperor from his patriotic advisers, in strengthening the position of Goremykin by replacing the Minister of the Interior, Shcherbatov, with such a ruthless bureaucrat as Kryzhanovsky,[2] and in removing Grand Duke Nikolay Nikolaevich from the Supreme Command. Thus a situation would be brought about in which the Emperor had no alternative but to sign a separate peace with Germany.

The police report summarises the discussions at the meeting at Chelnokov's house:

> The Emperor is a prisoner of the Black Bloc; he is held responsible on all sides for the unpreparedness of the Russian army, and the acceptance of the hypocritical proposals for the conclusion of a separate peace made by the Emperor Wilhelm hangs only on his decision. The conclusion of a separate peace is, indeed, the basic aim of all the efforts of the Black Bloc. . . . For members of the Cabinet of the type of Goremykin or of Kryzhanovsky, a separate peace would be preferable to the victory of the Entente. A separate peace would not only secure Goremykin's personal position, but would also lead to a strengthening of the autocratic principle in Russia, while for statesmen such as Kryzhanovsky the fate of Russia is of no importance if only they can pursue their careers with éclat and success and live in the ephemeral triumph of their personal power. . . . The present government . . . is obviously striving to sow discontent and to create general confusion, to cause a split between the army and the people, and to bring about conditions under which it will be possible on the one hand to conclude a separate peace, and on the other to use the army, which will resent having been abandoned by the country in the face of the enemy, to quell internal unrest.

In view of the existence of this powerful 'Black Bloc' conspiracy,

1. Grave, op. cit., pp. 46 ff.
2. In fact not Kryzhanovsky but A. N. Khvostov was eventually appointed.

it was decided at the meeting: (a) to keep a cool head and avoid all internal disorders, which would only help the enemy — that is, the 'Black Bloc' — to carry out its 'hellish intentions'; (b) to resume the work of the legislative assemblies in order to secure an opportunity to expose the government, which could carry out its wicked plans only if they were concealed from the people; and (c) to 'establish a government vested with public confidence in order to wrest power from the hands of those who are leading Russia to its destruction, to slavery and shame'. It was also decided to issue an appeal to the population for the maintenance of order and of solidarity with the heroic army, to approach the monarch in order to 'open his eyes', and to put certain demands to him. Should these demands of the people not be satisfied by the Tsar, 'both he and the people would regain their freedom of action and remain for ever estranged'.

The police report closes with the following note:

> From the morning of 7 September, and in the course of the next twenty-four hours, members of the congress who were genuine representatives of the Zemstvo and Municipality self-governments of the Empire were acquainted with all the findings established at the preparatory meeting in the residence of Chelnokov. These revelations are producing a shattering impression on the members of the congress. General indignation is growing steadily.

The police report must have appeared rather fantastic to the officials of the Ministry of the Interior to whom it was addressed. The idea of a Black Bloc was indeed a figment of the liberals' fevered imagination. Nevertheless it provided the *leitmotiv* for the propaganda campaigns which were launched and sustained by the liberals from the September congresses of 1915 up to the February revolution of 1917. It is difficult to imagine that the responsible politicians who gathered at Chelnokov's residence could really believe in the existence of the 'Black Bloc'. The police report sheds no light on the origin of this belief, nor has any evidence in support of it ever been adduced by those who held it. But at the same time it does appear that responsible politicians were genuinely convinced that powerful forces close to the throne were working for the conclusion of an immediate separate peace. Rodzyanko held fast to this conviction to his dying day, but he could never give his reasons for it. The legend spread to left-wing circles and became an article of faith in Soviet historiography when – in the twenties – the historian and archivist, Semennikov, showed much ingenuity in trying to make it plausible as a historical hypothesis. At the Moscow State Conference in August 1917, the leader of the right-wing Social-Democrats, Tseretelli, claimed that had there been no February revolution Russia would by that time already have concluded a shameful separate peace with Germany.

Under the Provisional Government, the famous Muravyev Commission for the Investigation of the Crimes of the Old Régime looked carefully into the cases of the high state officials who were suspected of having belonged to the 'Black Bloc' and to the pro-German circles in Russia. The seven volumes containing the proceedings and the brilliant memoir on the end of the Tsarist régime by the poet Alexander Blok, who served as a secretary of this Commission, show clearly that great as the shortcomings, corruption and decrepitude of the régime may have been, there was no such thing as a German party or even a defeatist movement among the Tsarist bureaucracy, not even among the shady characters who were trying to push themselves into positions of favour and influence at court.

Nor do the documents of the German Foreign Ministry made available after World War II indicate any contacts between the German government and the supposed pro-German party at the Russian court or within the government.[1]

If the police report is to be believed, no mention was made at the meeting at Chelnokov's house of the part played by the Empress in the pro-German party. This, however, soon became the main feature of the 'legend of the separate peace', which spread through the country long before P. N. Milyukov lent it support in his famous speech of 1 November 1916. The supposed connection of the 'German woman' (*nemka*) with efforts to force the Emperor to conclude a separate peace was probably the most destructive charge levelled by opposition circles in 1916. We have full proof now, after the publication of the Empress's letters to her husband, that there was no truth whatever in these allegations.

In one of the best studies on pre-revolutionary developments in Russia, the *émigré* historian Melgunov, himself a Popular Socialist, carefully examined all the sources of the legend.[2] His findings were

1. See ch. 5 above.
2. S. P. Melgunov, *Legenda o separatnom mire* (Paris, 1957).

more explicit, but no less negative, than those of the Muravyev Investigation Commission. The question for the historian now is, therefore, not whether this legend is true or not, but rather why, if it had so little factual basis, it was so readily believed by the public and so eagerly fostered by people who had every possibility of checking its veracity. The answer is simple, although not much to the credit of those who based their appeal for popular support on the exploitation of this rumour.

As we have seen, stories of high treason had spread widely as soon as the reverses at the front occurred in 1914–15. They grew even more persistent as the shortage of arms and ammunition became known to the public. The announcement of Myasoedov's trial and execution and the retirement and impeachment of the Minister of War, Sukhomlinov, were taken by the public as irrefutable confirmation of treason in high places. The leaders of the liberal opposition must have been impressed by the powerful impact of such rumours on public opinion, and must have realised that these could become an effective weapon in their struggle for political reform. It was therefore clearly to their advantage to launch, early in September 1915, a second wave of treason rumours, alleging the existence of a 'Black Bloc', as soon as their hopes for a reform by agreement with the government had been frustrated.

The slanderous accusations against Goremykin of promoting a separate peace were not voiced in the official meetings of the congresses, which passed resolutions demanding a 'government of public confidence', and elected delegates who would present these resolutions to the Emperor.[1]

Nothing came out of the projected delegation to the Tsar. Nicholas II refused to receive the delegates of the congresses, who were instead summoned to appear before the Minister of the Interior and were told that, while the work of the Voluntary Organisations for the army

1. A curious incident occurred when the Union of Municipalities elected delegates to present their petition to the Tsar. The left wing of the congress protested violently against the candidature of Guchkov, recalling that in 1907, he had supported Stolypin when the latter dissolved the Second Duma and introduced a retrograde reform of the electoral law. This was a temporary setback for Guchkov, which served as a reminder to him that he had something to live down before he could gain the confidence of the radical politicians. The incident may well have shown him that he had little chance of success in open political struggle, and that his real strength lay in conspiracy and plotting.

was greatly appreciated, their interference in general state affairs could not and would not be tolerated. Prince Lvov argued with the Minister of the Interior, Shcherbatov, insisting on an audience with the Emperor, but before Shcherbatov could give an answer, he was replaced as Minister by A. N. Khvostov ('the Nephew'), with whom Prince Lvov had no further dealings. Instead, Lvov wrote the Emperor a long-winded, sanctimonious letter harping relentlessly on the theme of a 'government of public confidence', which as far as we know remained unanswered.

The tone and content of Prince Lvov's letter explain why his approach to the Tsar had so little success. Pompous in its archaic language, it is vague and utterly disingenuous in its wholesale accusations against the 'government'. In it he affected to believe that the government, in resisting the demands of the liberals, was disobeying the orders of the Tsar — something which he knew very well was absurd. Here is a shortened version of this piece of Byzantine rhetoric:

Your Imperial Majesty! We, the elected representatives of the Zemstvo and Municipalities of Russia, have been delegated to tell you the living truth. When the storm of war broke over Russia, from the height of your throne, you appealed for the unity of all the forces of the country and for the abandonment of all internal strife and quarrels. The country responded, doing justice to the true strength of the Russian people.

In the depths of the popular masses, Sire, fresh strength is constantly gathering, and the spirit of liberation is moving above us. The great reforms of Alexander II have laid the foundation of self-government, and you, Sire, the grandson of the Liberator-Tsar, have called popular representatives to reform the state. The war has developed the state power of the Russian people, which is becoming stronger under the heavy blows we have suffered. The powerful and impressive picture of the unity of all forces in Russia has become apparent to the whole world. Both our allies and our enemies have learned to see it, but, to the greatest misfortune of our Fatherland, our government refuses to recognise it. The government alone has not followed the path indicated from the height of the throne. At the time when our army was forced to retreat for lack of ammunition, abandoning to the enemy Russian land soaked in the precious blood of its people, the government, in its jealous suspiciousness, saw in the highly patriotic popular movement a threat to its power, as if what mattered was that power and not the integrity, greatness and honour of Russia. The internal economy of the state is totally disrupted, and its chaotic condition threatens the cause of victory, yet the war does not seem to exist as far as the government is concerned. State power should, at such a time, correspond to the spirit of the people, should grow out of it, as a living plant grows from the earth.

Your Imperial Majesty, Russia looks to you in these fatal years for a sign that the supreme power is achieving greatness by acting in unity with the spirit of the people. Restore the great features of spiritual unity and harmony in the life of the state, distorted by the government! Bring new life to state power; entrust its heavy responsibilities to persons who will be strong because they possess the confidence of the country! Renew the work of the people's representatives! Open to the country the only way to victory, which has been obstructed by the lies of the old order of administration! . . . The government has brought Russia to the edge of an abyss. In your hands is her salvation.[1]

One wonders if it is not under the impression of reading such texts as the Lvov letter that forty years later Pasternak could write, referring to this period of Russian history:

It was then that falsehood came into our Russian land, and there arose the power of the glittering phrase — first Tsarist, then revolutionary. . . . Instead of being natural and spontaneous as we had always been, we began to be idiotically pompous with each other. Something showy, artificial, false, crept into our conversation — you felt you had to be clever in a certain way, about certain world-important themes.[2]

The cold-shouldering of the Voluntary Organisations by the Emperor and his government strengthened the left-wing tendencies in them and made their leaders look for other methods of achieving their political aims than the passing of resolutions and requests for audiences with the Tsar. From then on, an unrestrained campaign of denunciation against every statesman and politician who was ready to serve in the government was launched in the press. At the same time, a number of private committees of a more or less clandestine character were formed to consider ways and means of bringing direct pressure to bear on the Emperor, or even of engineering a palace coup.

1. Grave, op. cit., p. 59 f.
2. B. Pasternak, *Doctor Zhivago* (London, 1958), Ch. 13, para. 14. English translation by Max Hayward and Manya Harari.

2. RUSSIAN POLITICAL FREEMASONRY

The formation of a new secret society connected with and modelled on masonic lodges probably took place at this time. The part played by political freemasonry in the preparation of the February revolution has been, until very recently, a secret closely guarded by all concerned. The whole question has been largely shunned by historians because of the repugnance aroused by the theory, so popular in the twenties in reactionary circles all over the world, of a 'Judaeo-Masonic World Conspiracy'. Here again, a popular conception based on a notorious forgery (the Protocols of the Elders of Zion) has effectively discouraged legitimate historical research in an important field of clandestine political activities, just as the forgeries known as the 'Sisson Papers' retarded investigation of the undercover intervention of German agents in Russia in 1917.[1]

The revival of masonic activities in Russia goes back to the period after the 1905 revolution, when a number of lodges (the 'Northern Star', the 'Regeneration' and others) were formally constituted in Russia by emissaries of French freemasonry. An important part was played in this movement by the Petrograd lawyer M. S. Margulies and the notorious Prince Bebutov, who had been a member of the Kadet Party and a deputy in the First Duma.[2] When, as a result of an

---

1. See ch. 5, p. 63 and n.

2. In this connection it is worth quoting the vivid portrait of Bebutov by Mrs A. Tyrkova-Williams in *Na putyakh k svobode* (New York, 1952), pp. 397 ff. 'I have just said that there were no *agents provocateurs* among us [i.e. the Kadets]. I must correct this. When the revolution threw open the archives of the Okhrana, we were much surprised to find that in its papers there was an indication of one *agent provocateur* attached to the Kadets. This was Prince Bebutov, a rather comic figure.

Just before the opening of the First Duma, a retired Guards officer started hobnobbing with us; he was either Georgian or Armenian, with characteristic Caucasian features and a no less characteristic Caucasian accent. He was also a freemason. We used to joke, asking each other how he came to be among us. Not too young, but something of a dandy and a ladies' man, of little education, something of a dunce in an oriental way, he was given to extremist formulas and loud oratory, demanding the most determined words and actions from the party. When, in the spring of 1906, money was needed for the organisation of the Kadet Club, Bebutov brought Petrunkevich 10,000 roubles, which was no mean sum at that time. Malicious tongues used to say that the money was not his, but that he took it without permission from his rich wife, so that she got angry with him and kicked him out. In fact, however,

exposure in the press, the 'Northern Star' was forced to 'go to sleep', there seems to have been a temporary cessation of masonic activities. After the breakdown of the negotiations between the Progressive

as was found out after the revolution, the money was given by the Okhrana in order to help Bebutov to penetrate the Kadet leadership. He felt sure that in return for this generous gift he would be elected to the Central Committee, but he miscalculated. His bragging, his political adventurism, his lack of education, his stupidity were not in harmony with the style of our committee. The more assiduous Bebutov was in rendering small services, paying visits, receiving and fussing, the more he became the object of puzzled observation.

Once I was his guest. He had an excellent cook, and the supper was a great success. We had an enormous turkey with a most elaborate stuffing; the wines were expensive; the toasts were of a most incendiary character. But all this — the lavishness of the hospitality and the lavishness of the leftism — appeared somehow incongruous. In the drawing-room I was struck by some screens decorated by caricatures of Nicholas II. I asked Bebutov: "Aren't you afraid the servants may denounce you and that the police will come and search?" With a devil-may-care laugh, as if he were a young cavalry officer, he winked his black, oily eye at me. How could I guess that he was making a fool of me, and that the police knew perfectly well how the flat of their agent was decorated?

Bebutov had also become famous for the following occurrence. When the former member of the State Duma, the lawyer E. I. Kedrin, refused to pay taxes (the only Kadet to do so in accordance with the so-called Vyborg Appeal), his furniture was ordered by the court to be put up for sale. The first object offered for auction was a cheap wooden hand-made ashtray with a bird with a ridiculously long beak. Bebutov paid 1,000 roubles for it and thus covered the tax required. Is it possible that this thousand, paid in fulfilment of the Vyborg Appeal, was also given Bebutov by the Okhrana?

I know of one more provocatory trick played by Bebutov, a far more wicked one. He published in Russian abroad a large illustrated collection of articles, "The Last Autocrat", in which Nicholas II was derided, denigrated and slandered. Bebutov was proud of his participation in this publication. We asked with naive astonishment how he managed to bring in clandestinely such a heavy, unwieldy book and in such a large number of copies. Instead of answering, he again winked maliciously. He must have thought that we were idiots. And how right he was!

That continued right up to the February revolution of 1917, when his name was found in the files of the Okhrana. Bebutov got frightened, became restless, tried to shrug off the accusations. But the documents were irrefutable. He was stricken by paralysis from fright, and died soon after.

For eleven years, during the whole existence of the Kadet Party, he was hanging about in our midst, and we, not questioning the hospitality we were offered, met merrily in the Kadet Club established at the expense of the Secret Police. . . . '

On Bebutov, see also ch. 5 above.

Bloc and the government in September 1915, the need for a clandestine organisation which would infiltrate every sector of national life became urgent in the eyes of the liberals and radicals. In fact, an organisation named the 'Committee of Public Safety' seems to have been planned in the early days of September. Thus, a remarkable document published in *Krasny Arkhiv*, XXVI, and alleged to have been found among the papers of Guchkov, is signed 'Committee of Public Safety'. It is entitled 'Disposition No. 1' and is dated 8 September 1915.

The document claimed that there were two wars going on in Russia, one against the Germans, the other – no less important – against the 'internal enemy'. A victory over the Germans could not be won before the defeat of the internal enemy (that is, the forces of reaction supporting the autocratic régime). Those who realised the impossibility of any compromise with the government were called upon to form a 'general headquarters', to consist of ten men chosen for 'the honesty of their work, the firmness of their will, and their belief that the struggle for the people's rights must be carried out according to the rules of military centralisation and discipline'. The methods of struggle for the people's rights would be peaceful, but firm and skilful. No strikes, which were damaging to the interests of the people and the State, would be tolerated. People who did not comply with the directives of the committee of ten were to be 'boycotted', i.e. ostracised by all patriots and hounded out of public life. Three persons were named as the nucleus of the headquarters for the struggle against the 'internal enemy'. These were Prince Lvov, A. I. Guchkov, and A. F. Kerensky. Guchkov was described in the document as the man who possessed the confidence both of the army and of the city of Moscow, 'which has now become not only the heart but the centre of Russia's will power'.

Melgunov,[1] in referring to this document, seems nonplussed. What is it, he asks. A mystification? A police invention? The fruit of the idle fantasy of an amateurish organiser of projects? In his perplexity Melgunov turned for an explanation to Guchkov and Kerensky, and both denied the possibility of such an association in 1915. Kerensky claimed to have met Guchkov only after the revolution, and to have made the acquaintance of Prince Lvov for the first time in the autumn of 1916. This, on the face of it, should be a warning to historians against using this document. Quite recently, however, new

1. See S. P. Melgunov, *Na putyakh k dvortsovomu perevorotu* (Paris, 1931), pp. 188 ff.

evidence has come to hand. Among the documents of the German Foreign Ministry we find the report of a certain A. Stein, who was none other than the Estonian nationalist Alexander Keskülä,[1] one of the principal agents of the German *Revolutionierungspolitik* in Russia.[2]

On 9 January 1916, he wrote to his contact on the German General Staff, reporting on some 'highly interesting revolutionary documents from Russia' which he wanted to be sent to Lenin.

> One of these documents [writes Keskülä] ... the product of a Moscow 'Committee of Public Safety' — suggests a dictatorial Directorate for Russia, to consist, among other people, of Messrs. Guchkov, Lvov, and Kerensky [*sic*!], which is extremely amusing. Judging by its comico-sentimental torrent of verbiage, this must be a call from the right wing of the so-called Popular Socialists.

The document referred to by Keskülä is without doubt the same as that published in *Krasny Arkhiv*, XXVI. It must have been picked up in Russia by Keskülä's emissary, Kruse, who travelled there in the autumn of 1915.[3] The dating of 'Disposition No. 1' is, therefore, probably correct. As Melgunov rightly recognised, the document, in spite of its 'torrent of verbiage' (and possibly even because of it), accurately reflects the mood of Moscow opposition opinion in 1915. It is prophetic in its reference to a governing body consisting of ten members including Prince Lvov, Guchkov, and Kerensky: this was indeed to be the composition of the first Provisional Government. The historical importance of 'Disposition No. 1' is due not so much to its evidence of the existence of a 'Committee of Public Safety', which might have been only a pipedream, as to the fact that its general ideas were known not only to its anonymous authors but also to the Bolshevik revolutionary movement abroad, including Lenin himself, as well as to the German General Staff and the German government, who were instrumental in conveying it to Lenin. It was also probably known to Guchkov, even if he was not one of its authors, for we have no reason to doubt the statement of the Soviet archivists who claimed to have found it among his papers.

1. On Keskülä, see ch. 5 above, pp. 76 and 97 f.
2. See Keskülä's letter in Zeman, *Germany and the Revolution in Russia*, p. 12.
3. See an account of Keskülä's activities, based on research in the relevant archives and an interview with Keskülä himself, in Michael Futrell's book, *Northern Underground*, in particular pp. 119 151.

The denials of those named in this document, despite Melgunov's efforts to draw them out in 1931, are surprising.[1] But these denials confirm the general impression that the political plans worked out and discussed in liberal circles in the period between September 1915 and the February days were conspiratorial, and that those who took part in them were bound to secrecy by some kind of solemn pledge. Indeed, there is a conspicuous gap in the memoirs on this period. Neither Guchkov himself, nor his close collaborator of the time, Konovalov, nor the two left-wing Kadets Tereshchenko and Nekrasov – who were ministers through practically all the permutations of the Provisional Government – have published any comprehensive memoirs concerning this period. A. F. Kerensky, who has provided us with a considerable body of historical evidence in a number of volumes of reminiscences, has – as yet – cast very little light on the political developments preceding the formation of the Provisional Government.

This silence of the politicians concerned is all the more suspicious in that discretion and reticence have never been a characteristic feature of Russian liberals. It naturally aroused the curiosity of Melgunov, who summarised in his book on the palace coup[2] all that was then known of the existence of secret organisations in this period. Melgunov points to the affinity in style and content of 'Disposition No. 1' with masonic political jargon, and suggests that it was related to the resurgence of the masonic movement in 1915. However, what Melgunov said in the thirties was not conclusive. The existence of a politically significant masonic movement on the eve of the revolution was far from proven. The veil of secrecy was first lifted with the publication of the memoirs of Milyukov in 1956.

Milyukov alleges that four members of the original Provisional Government,

all of them widely differing from each other in character, in their past

1. Melgunov's manner in approaching people for information was not always happy. See Kuskova's letter, quoted by Grigory Aronson, *Rossiya nakanune revolyutsii* (New York, 1962), p. 138. On a similar occasion, according to Kuskova, 'Melgunov was driven to hysterics, blackmailed me (while we were still in Russia) for data, and assured me that he knew 'everything'. I *knew* perfectly that hardly anything was known to him. . . . Later, in one of his books, he hinted at the existence of something like it [i.e. political freemasonry]' (letter to N. V. Volsky of 15 November 1955).
2. *Na putyakh*, etc.

careers, and in their political roles, were bound together, not merely by their radical political views. Besides that, there was between them some kind of personal bond, not purely political, but of a politico-moral character. They were also bound by certain mutual obligations coming from one and the same source. . . .

And Milyukov closes with a disconcertingly cryptic remark:

From the above hints, one can infer what was the kind of bond that united the central group of the four ministers. If I do not speak of it in clearer words here, this is because, in observing the facts, I did not at the time realize the reasons for them, and learned about them by chance much later, when the Provisional Government had ceased to exist.[1]

Milyukov's guarded revelation must have caused a considerable stir among the former members of the masonic movement of 1915 still alive in emigration. In 1957, Kerensky visited one of the active members of this group, Mme Kuskova, in Switzerland.[2]

In a letter dated 20 January 1957, Mme Kuskova confided to her friend, Mme Lidia O. Dan:

I spent the whole of Friday with Kerensky. We had to discuss what is to be done about Milyukov's mentioning of that organisation of which I told you. . . . He very much approved what I had done: to write it down for the archive and to keep it safe for another thirty years. He himself will do the same. Moreover, he will answer the nebulous remark of Milyukov in the preface of the book he is writing. He will answer on his own behalf, without mentioning any other name. All this has

1. P. N. Milyukov, *Vospominaniya 1859–1917* (2 vols, New York, 1955), vol. II, pp. 332–333.
2. E. D. Kuskova, who died two years later, in 1959, was one of the most powerful figures of the Russian radical left. She was married for fifty years to the economist Prokopovich, and their lifelong partnership in Russian politics was an important factor in the whole development of the radical movement. Inside the Socialist camp the couple occupied a position on the right, and were the representatives of what could be called Russian 'revisionism'. During the war they devoted their efforts to the democratisation of Russia. Prokopovich joined the Provisional Government in 1917, and at one time, after the seizure of power by the Bolsheviks, headed the underground provisional government acting for Kerensky's Cabinet, who were then under arrest. Later, Prokopovich and Kuskova were banished from Russia by the Soviet government, and lived the rest of their lives in emigration. Both of them had been prominent in the Russian political masonic movement, as is clear from three letters of Kuskova written in the years 1955–57 and published by Grigory Aronson, op. cit.

been carefully thought out, and we agreed on the form in which information should be given. But what should be stopped, if possible, is the gossiping in New York: there are still people alive in Russia — very good people indeed — and one should have consideration for them.

In two further letters, one addressed to N. V. Volsky of 15 November 1955, and the other to L. O. Dan of 12 February 1957 (both are published in Aronson's book, quoted above), she gives details on the organisation itself.

Although she links the movement with the revival of freemasonry after the 1905 revolution — a revival which others have attributed to the influence of French freemasonry — she claims that the Russian masonic movement had no connection with any foreign organisation. It had a purely political aim — to restore, in a new form, the Union of Liberation,[1] and to work underground for the liberation of Russia. Its immediate aim was to penetrate the higher bureaucracy, and even the court, and to use them for revolutionary ends. The whole masonic ritual was abolished; women were admitted to the lodges; there were no aprons, no paraphernalia; and the initiation had only one purpose: secrecy and absolute silence. The lodges numbered only five members each but there were congresses. Their oath was to complete secrecy. On leaving the movement, a member had to renew his oath of absolute silence. 'The movement was enormous', writes Kuskova in her letter to Volsky of 15 November 1955.[2]

> Everywhere we had 'our' people. Such associations as the 'Free Economic Society' and the 'Technical Society' were totally penetrated. . . . Up to now the secret of this organisation has never been divulged, and yet the organisation was enormous. By the time of the February revolution, the whole of Russia was covered with a network of lodges. Here in emigration there are many members of this organisation, but they all are silent. And they will remain silent because of the people in Russia who have not yet died.

And in a letter of 12 February 1957 to L. O. Dan (the widow of the Menshevik Theodore Dan and sister of Martov) Kuskova elaborates further:

> We had to win over the military. The slogan was: 'a democratic

1. *Soyuz osvobozhdeniya.* A clandestine liberal organisation. Its news-sheet *Osvobozhdenie* appeared in Stuttgart and was edited by P. B. Struve.
2. Aronson, op. cit., pp. 138 ff.

Russia, and don't shoot at the demonstrating people'. It needed much and long explanation. . . . Here we achieved considerable success.

We had to take over the Imperial Free Economic Society, the Technical Society, the Institute of Mining, and others. This was brilliantly carried out: we had 'our' people everywhere. A large field was opened to propaganda.

It is surprising that such a widespread organisation was neither discovered nor penetrated by the agents of the secret police. At least, there is no indication of it in the secret police material published by Soviet archivists. This is probably due to the short period of existence of the politico-masonic movement and to the depressed state of the Tsarist secret police under the leadership of such people as Prince Shcherbatov, the semi-demented A. N. Khvostov and the unprincipled Beletsky.

It may well be that the temperamental Mme Kuskova somewhat exaggerated in her letters the importance of the masonic movement to which she belonged before the revolution. But, on the whole, everything she says tallies with what we know of the political development of Russian liberal and radical circles preceding February 1917. Neither the Kadet Party as such nor the Voluntary Organisations, the Unions of Zemstvos and Municipalities, nor the Central WIC were inclined to support the revolutionary movement. But everywhere inside them there were active minorities which carried on revolutionary propaganda and incited the leadership to action for the overthrow of the Tsarist régime. In the Kadet Party organisation this role was played by such people as the Duma deputy Nekrasov and the lawyers Margulies and Mandelstam. This same Margulies was Deputy Chairman of the Central WIC, dealing in particular with medical and sanitary supplies for the army.[1] Gradually these people began to dominate the Voluntary Organisations. At the very time when the congresses of Zemstvos and Municipalities closed their sessions in September 1915 with unanimous hurrahs for the Tsar, there were people present who were carrying out a relentless propaganda campaign against the Tsar, his family and his government.

1. One might well wonder how much of the material which the WIC under Margulies acquired from abroad was supplied through the intermediary of his colleague at the Petrograd bar, M. Kozlovsky, who in turn had close 'business connections' with Fürstenberg-Ganetsky. See ch. 5, p. 82.

We shall not know what the structure of the masonic lodges was, nor what the congresses of the movement decided, until the members of the movement publish the masonic archives, if they are extant. It is clear, however, from the available material that the nucleus of the movement consisted, in 1916, of the four persons whom Milyukov mentioned in his memoirs: A. F. Kerensky, M. I. Tereshchenko, N. V. Nekrasov and A. I. Konovalov, later joined by the Duma deputy I. N. Efremov. The military branch of the movement seems to have been headed by the Duma deputy Count Orlov-Davydov, who had been connected with the masonic movement from its beginnings in 1905 and was at one time in close contact with the notorious Prince Bebutov. Orlov-Davydov was one of the richest landowners in Russia, and maintained close relations both with Kerensky and with Grand Duke Nikolay Mikhailovich, a cousin of the Tsar and the author of competent works on Russian history.

What attracted this motley group to the masonic movement in Russia? With due reservations, I am tempted to explain it by psychological factors. Patriotism and public-spiritedness, especially among the upper classes, had its roots in the mystique of the monarchy and the belief in the divinely-inspired wisdom of the Tsar. As this mystical belief weakened and vanished under the onslaught of radical propaganda, freemasonry provided a substitute which an empirical and utilitarian approach to politics would not have afforded. It is characteristic that the emotional and idealistic mind of a Kerensky, inclined to a typically Russian brand of superstition, was won for freemasonry, whereas Milyukov is reported to have resisted all attempts to recruit him with the simple words: 'No mysticism, please'. As far as the military and the higher bureaucratic and court circles were concerned, freemasonry had, of course, a snob value. It also gave them opportunities to take part in political events by rendering more or less important services to politicians *fraternellement*, without the risk of being compromised in 'the dirty business of politics'.

Apart from any direct influence on political developments in Russia, the effect of masonic ties on the morality of Russian politics should not be underestimated. The division between the initiated and the uninitiated cut straight across all party boundaries. Party allegiances and party discipline had to yield to the stronger tie of the masonic bond. The Kadet Party suffered most from this division. When the moment came to organise a Provisional Government, the decision was taken not by the party committees, but under the influence of masonic pressure groups.

Kuskova claimed that the movement pursued a revolutionary aim, and Milyukov implied that the freemasons' blueprint for the political changes in Russia was solidly republican.[1] All this, however, requires elucidation. Was the masonic movement in favour of a popular rising in wartime, in complete contrast to the avowed programmes of all defensist parties? This is hardly credible. Even Kerensky, in the autumn of 1915, advised the workers to stop the strikes. And, again, the outbreak of a popular rising of such dimensions as that of February 1917 seems to have taken masonic circles by surprise, as it did everyone else. The political tactics on which the masons relied were the same as those of the Voluntary Organisations — that is, gradually to oust the Tsarist bureaucracy from the vital controls of the war economy, and to replace it with members of the Voluntary Organisations. When control of the country's economic life had passed completely into their hands they expected that political changes would follow more or less automatically.

Before leaving this subject, we must go back to one aspect of the Kuskova revelations which is somewhat sinister. We have seen that the main motive for keeping the history of the political freemasonry movement secret was, for Kuskova and her friends, the personal security of people who had belonged to the movement and were still living in the Soviet Union. Among these, according to Kuskova, were very prominent members of the Communist Party, two of whom were known to her by name.[2]

1. Milyukov, *Vospominaniya*, vol. II, p. 332 *passim*.
2. It is tantalising to guess who the Bolshevik leaders belonging to the freemasons might have been. In his book, the main merit of which is the publication of the letters of E. D. Kuskova, Aronson refers to a correspondence between Lenin and one of his followers in Moscow during March 1914 which has been preserved in the archives of the Russian police, who intercepted it. Lenin's correspondent reports that he had established relations with a prominent Russian industrialist 'whose influence can be measured in many millions of roubles'. He informs Lenin that, at the invitation of this person — who is easily identified as the future minister of the Provisional government, A. I. Konovalov — he intends to take part in a secret exchange of information and opinions with a number of liberal politicians. Using an article in the Soviet historical magazine *Voprosy istorii KPSS* (vols III and IV, 1957), Aronson states that Lenin's correspondent was a certain N. P. Yakovlev, but Aronson did not know

When the October revolution broke out, Prokopovich and Kuskova believed that the activities of the freemasons would be exposed, because the Communist Party would not tolerate the participation of its members in secret societies. Freemasonry associations were, indeed, declared illegal in the Soviet state. This imposed, in the eyes of the freemasons in emigration, a duty to keep quiet about the movement. With due respect for the scruples of the émigré masons, we may well doubt the efficacy of such precautions. We believe that the Cheka and its successors will certainly have uncovered *all* the secrets of the ex-masons in Russia, including those who were also members of the party. If they did not publicly expose them it must have been because they did not consider it expedient from the point of view of the party and the state. Perhaps even the contacts which, Mme Kuskova hints, she managed to maintain with 'the brethren' in Russia were used for their own purposes by the Soviet security service.

3. THE GUCHKOV PLOT

Nowhere was the influence of the masonic movement of greater importance than in the preparation of a *coup d'état* to put an end to the reign of Nicholas II. Mme Kuskova denies that the freemasons as such supported the plot for the palace coup which Guchkov and his collaborators were planning. She admits, however, that Guchkov was a freemason, and that the movement knew of his plot but disapproved of it to such an extent that the question of his expulsion was raised. All this sounds very confusing, but the truth is probably much simpler than it appears from the Kuskova letters.

that both the letter and Lenin's answer had been published in full in Moscow in 1959, in No. 2 of *Istorichesky Arkhiv*. In this issue, the earlier identification of Yakovlev as Lenin's correspondent was shown to be erroneous, and it was convincingly established that the person who wrote to Lenin was in fact the old Bolshevik, Skvortsov-Stepanov, one-time People's Commissar of Finance. The notes to the letter mention an oral communication by the old Bolshevik G. Petrovsky (who died in 1957) to the effect that he and Skvortsov-Stepanov contacted Konovalov at the beginning of 1914 to solicit money for Bolshevik Party activities. Nowhere do we find evidence that the two old Bolsheviks belonged to a masonic organisation, and it remains only an interesting conjecture that the secret meetings organised by Konovalov were forerunners of the masonic political movement of 1915, and that the approach to Konovalov by Skvortsov-Stepanov and Petrovsky was made *'fraternellement'*.

The masonic movement was predominantly republican; Guchkov was a monarchist. He wanted to overthrow Nicholas II in order to consolidate the monarchy, in which he would then become the leading influence. Neither the methods nor the ultimate aim of Guchkov were typical of those freemasons who were to form the nucleus of the Provisional Government, and who, as a matter of fact, were to jettison Guchkov soon after its formation. However, as Mme Kuskova admits, the freemasons were trying to win influential government, society and court support for the cause of the revolution, and many important bureaucrats and persons belonging to high society became involved in the movement. It is obvious that the penetration also went deep into army circles, particularly among the Guards officers, one of whom — General Krymov — was to play an important part in Guchkov's projected plot.

This is where masonic links were of paramount importance for Guchkov, and he no doubt used them to the fullest extent.

In spite of Melgunov's acute analysis,[1] we still have few details of the practical arrangements made by Guchkov for his coup. Our chief source of information remains Guchkov's cautious and reticent deposition on 2 August 1917, at a hearing of the Muravyev Commission.[2] Guchkov claimed that plans for his *coup d'état* were drawn up long before the end of 1916, but he did not specify the date and refused to name his fellow-conspirators. The coup, as he had planned it, was to consist of two independent actions, involving the participation of a restricted number of army units. The first action was to stop the imperial train on one of its journeys between Tsarskoe Selo and GHQ at Mogilev, and there force the Emperor to abdicate. Simultaneously a military demonstration of the troops of the Petrograd garrison would have taken place on the pattern of the Decembrist rising. The existing government would have been arrested, and there would have been a simultaneous announcement of the list of persons who would head the new one. Guchkov believed that his rather fanciful variation on the old theme of a palace coup would have been welcomed in the country with enthusiasm and a tremendous sense of relief.

As far as the part allotted to officers was concerned, Guchkov was extremely evasive in his deposition. It so happened, however, that

1. Melgunov, *Na putyakh*, p. 143 ff.
2. See *Padenie*, vol. VI, p. 248 ff.

only four weeks later one of the officers involved — General Krymov —
committed suicide in connection with the Kornilov Affair. His death
produced a shattering impression on his friend, the Minister of Foreign
Affairs, Tereshchenko. In an interview given to the press at the beginning of September, Tereshchenko disclosed that Krymov had taken
part in the plot to carry out a palace coup. Guchkov categorically
denied Krymov's participation in the plot, but there has never been a
rejoinder from Tereshchenko to elucidate this very important point.[1]
What is beyond doubt is the fact that before February, Krymov, both
at the front and on his visits to Petrograd, where he met a great number
of people connected with the Duma, kept insisting on the necessity of
removing the Emperor in order to save the monarchy. This is explicitly
stated by Rodzyanko in his memoirs.[2] Krymov's link with Tereshchenko, on the one hand, and Guchkov, on the other, is a strong
indication of the existence of a masonic bond between them. We can
safely assume that Guchkov's efforts to penetrate the ranks of the army
and Guards officers and to recruit supporters for his plot were based on
masonic ties.

Later, as an émigré in Paris, Guchkov lifted another corner of the
curtain which conceals the secret history of the conspiracies behind the
abortive palace coup. In his memoirs published posthumously in a Paris
émigré newspaper in 1936[3] he discloses the political combination
behind the plot. He recalls having taken part in September 1916 in a
secret meeting at the home of the Moscow liberal M. M. Fedorov, at
which Rodzyanko, Milyukov and a number of other members of the
Duma Progressive Bloc were present. The possibility of a revolution in
Russia was discussed, and the prevailing opinion was that it was impossible for patriots to take part in a revolution during the war; they
should not give up their efforts to obtain a government of public confidence by purely legal means. Should, however, a popular movement
break out and street disorders occur the liberal patriots should stand aside
until the period of anarchy was over, when they would doubtless be
invited to constitute a government as the only alternative to the Tsarist
ministers with any experience of state affairs. At this meeting Guchkov claims to have sounded a discordant note by arguing that this was

1. See Melgunov, *Na putyakh*, op. cit., pp. 149 ff.
2. See *ARR*, VI, p. 43.
3. *Poslednie Novosti*. The memoirs were published serially in August–September 1936.

pure illusion, that if the liberals let the revolutionaries organise the over-throw of the Tsarist government, they would never be able to seize power themselves. 'I fear', he said, 'that those who make the revolution will themselves head the revolution.'

Shortly after this meeting Guchkov was visited by the left-wing Kadet Nekrasov who had heard his statement and came to enquire whether Guchkov had any projects of his own to forestall a popular rising and to enforce a constitutional change by other means. Complete identity of views on this point was established, and from then on Guchkov, Nekrasov and Tereshchenko (who was then Chairman of the important regional WIC in Kiev) worked together in order to find a group of officers who would waylay the imperial train at a station between the capital and GHQ and force the Emperor to abdicate.

Guchkov's plot was certainly not the only one which was being hatched at that time, but it was probably the one most advanced by the spring of 1917. Guchkov himself admits that, had the revolution not broken out in February, his coup would have taken place in the middle of March. But although the plot did not come to fruition the effect of the Moscow conspirators' systematic assault on the loyalty of senior officers in the Russian army should not be underestimated. On the one hand the commanders-in-chief of the various fronts and the Chief of Staff were gradually introduced to the possibility of the Emperor's abdication, and when the moment came and pressure was applied to them by Rodzyanko to help bring this about, they gave him their support.

On the other hand the recruiting campaign of the conspirators among younger officers must have shaken their allegiance to the person of the monarch, and this may explain their disaffection during the rising of units of the Petrograd garrison on 27 and 28 February. Little has been revealed of the motives for their behaviour during the mutiny or of their clandestine contacts with Guchkov. It is significant that the young Prince Vyazemsky, who had been touring the barracks and strategic points in the capital with Guchkov on the night of 1–2 March, was killed, allegedly by a stray bullet, in circumstances which remain mysterious.

Guchkov claimed that the success of his coup depended on a favour-able mood in the country as a whole and, in particular, on its acceptance by the army. He confidently expected an enthusiastic reception of the change of régime, even if it were brought about by the use of violence against 'the sacred person of the monarch'. In his deposition, Guchkov made the surprising remark:

> You must bear in mind that there was no need for us to make propaganda or to persuade people. There was no need to prove to anybody the rottenness of the old régime and to demonstrate that it was heading for disaster. But we had to organise the technical side of things and to drive people to make this decisive step.[1]

Guchkov's remark does not mean that he himself, and the leaders of the Voluntary Organisations who were fighting the Tsarist régime on parallel lines, had not made an enormous propaganda effort throughout the preceding months, an effort which was certainly crowned with success, though the efficacy of the 'technical' preparations remains doubtful. Guchkov himself had been instrumental in organising and spreading the propaganda which was to discredit the Tsar and persuade the people that the war would inevitably be lost if there were not an immediate change of régime.

4. 'THE MAD CHAUFFEUR'

This propaganda had to be conducted in the face of government vigilance and stringent wartime censorship, and it also had to surmount the obstacle of traditional loyalty among wide sections of the population, especially in the officer corps. Moreover, the situation at the front had improved considerably, and the success of Russian arms in Turkey in the autumn of 1915, and on the Austrian front in the summer of 1916, had shown that the panicky mood which had seized public opinion after the reverses of 1915 had been due to exaggerated rumours and a general nervousness. It was clear that, despite everything, the existing government machinery could stand the colossal strain of the war effort for a few more months. Of course the propagandists of the liberal and radical opposition groups attributed the improvement in the war situation in 1916 to the efforts of the Voluntary Organisations and the patriotism of the Army. But they insisted that this had happened despite the policy of the government, which was under the influence of 'dark forces'.

1. *Padenie*, vol. VI, p. 279.

This propaganda assumed an almost hysterical character as time went on; slanderous, irresponsible accusations were flung by the liberals in the face of anyone who refused to support their cause in the struggle on the internal front. The articles which affected public opinion most were not those quoting specific instances of shortcomings and abuses by officials, but those which, in thinly disguised Aesopian language, attacked the existing system as a whole.

The press campaign became particularly acute in September 1915, at the time of the congresses of the Voluntary Organisations. Highly representative of this type of propaganda was the famous fable (published in No. 221 of *Russkie Vedomosti*, September 1915) by Vasily Maklakov, a reasonable and moderate leader of the Kadet Party. Here is a slightly shortened version of it.

A Tragic Situation

... Imagine that you are driving in an automobile on a steep and narrow road. One wrong turn of the steering-wheel and you are irretrievably lost. Your dear ones, your beloved mother, are with you in the car.

Suddenly you realise that your chauffeur is unable to drive. Either he is incapable of controlling the car on steep gradients, or he is overtired and no longer understands what he is doing, so that his driving spells doom for himself and for you; should you continue in this way, you face inescapable destruction.

Fortunately there are people in the automobile who can drive, and they should take over the wheel as soon as possible. But it is a difficult and dangerous task to change places with the driver while moving. One second without control and the automobile will crash into the abyss.

There is no choice, however, and you make up your mind; but the chauffeur refuses to give way ... he is clinging to the steering-wheel and will not give way to anybody. ... Can one force him? This could easily be done in normal times with an ordinary horse-drawn peasant cart at low speed on level ground. Then it could mean salvation. But can this be done on the steep mountain path? However skilful you are, however strong, the wheel is actually in his hands — he is steering the car, and one error in taking a turn, or an awkward movement of his hand, and the car is lost. You know that, and he knows it as well. And he mocks your anxiety and your helplessness: 'You will not dare to touch me!'

He is right. You will not dare to touch him ... for even if you might risk your own life, you are travelling with your mother, and you will not dare to endanger your life for fear she too might be killed. ...

So you will leave the steering-wheel in the hands of the chauffeur. Moreover, you will try not to hinder him — you will even help him with advice, warning and assistance. And you will be right, for this is what has to be done.

But how will you feel when you realise that your self-restraint might still be of no avail, and that even with your help the chauffeur will be unable to cope? How will you feel when your mother, having sensed the danger, begs you for help, and, misunderstanding your conduct, accuses you of inaction and indifference?

The secret police officer who called the attention of his superiors to this article wrote that it had been printed in a considerable number of copies and that the author had received numerous letters of congratulation for having published it. By means of such press articles the seething atmosphere of the Moscow congresses of September 1915 was communicated to wide circles of the newspaper-reading public in Russia, creating an atmosphere of crisis and increasing the sense of insecurity. The surprising thing about this propaganda was that it did not call for action by the people, that it did not appeal to the population to make an effort to remove the 'mad chauffeur' and his government.

After September 1915 the Voluntary Organisations became a more important channel for the circulation of this seditious propaganda. Their work inevitably put them into close contact with the bureaucratic apparatus and with the military authorities. They ran a bush telegraph of news and rumours concerning the alleged machinations of a 'Black Bloc' which existed only in their imagination.

The Voluntary Organisations were in permanent conflict with the bureaucracy, which they were supposed to assist. The bureaucratic apparatus was doubtless obsolete, slow-moving, frequently overtaken by events, and to a certain extent corrupt in an old-fashioned way. On the other hand, the Voluntary Organisations were inexperienced in much of the work they had undertaken, undisciplined and anarchic in their methods and unorthodox in their accountancy: new forms of wartime corruption easily took root and spread in such organisations.

It is difficult for the historian to discuss the pros and cons of the case of the Tsarist administration against the Voluntary Organisations. The important thing to note, however, is that on neither side was there any readiness to acknowledge fairly and frankly the efforts and achievements of the other. It was a war *à outrance* conducted by means of scurrilous mutual denunciation, in which the aggressive initiative certainly belonged to the leadership of the Voluntary Organisations.

The self-advertisement of the Voluntary Organisations was completely unrestrained, and in fact survived the political downfall of their leaders. In emigration many of them collaborated in the publication by the Carnegie Foundation of a series of volumes vindicating their wartime activities with well-documented arguments.[1]

The mere fact that the Tsarist government was forced to tolerate these activities of groups and bodies openly hostile to it shows how irreplaceable they were in the national war effort, and yet the claims of these organisations to have saved the country from disaster, not only without the collaboration and support of the government but against its malevolent resistance, did not go unchallenged. On the one hand, the government itself hit back by publishing the figures of the enormous subsidies which the exchequer was paying to the Voluntary Organisations in order to make it possible for them to carry on with their work. On the other hand, even among those particularly susceptible to anti-government propaganda, and even more so among those already prone to a revolutionary mood, the feeling grew that there was much corruption involved in the work of the Voluntary Organisations. Rumours were circulated of enormous profits made by firms with whom the WICs had placed orders, and resentment against this new and particularly wicked form of war profiteering was growing. The Parkinsonian growth of the administrative apparatus of the Voluntary Organisations, who frequently duplicated each other's functions, resulted in more and more men claiming exemption from regular military service. The '*zemgussar*' — (Zemstvo hussar) the smart Alec and dodger in pseudo-military attire — was satirised in the folklore of those days. The government held their fire in answering the attacks on them by the liberals, but it was clear that they were hoarding political ammunition for the moment when they could dispense with the help of the Voluntary Organisations and could at last bring them to account for the economic and political corruption of which they were widely suspected.

It is astonishing that under these circumstances the war effort in

1. In the Russian series of the *Economic and Social History of the World War*, Yale University Press, New Haven.

Russia achieved so much in such a short time. The year 1916 saw a most spectacular recovery in the ammunition and arms supply, which, after the stabilisation of the front in the winter of 1915–16, led in the summer of 1916 to the success of the so-called Brusilov offensive.

5. GUCHKOV AND THE ARMY IN 1916

The improvement of the supply situation and the military recovery did nothing, however, to relieve the tension between the Voluntary Organisations and the government. After Goremykin's replacement by Stuermer, in January 1916, and especially after the retirement of the Minister of War Polivanov and his replacement by General Shuvaev, the ministers who presided in the four Special Councils tried to deny the Voluntary Organisations any political advantage which might have derived from their legitimate activities. The Voluntary Organisations complained that this amounted to deliberate sabotage of their efforts. The ministers attempted to control the expenditure of the Voluntary Organisations, since they were operating with funds most of which came from the Exchequer. The Voluntary Organisations resented such government control as an attempt to reduce them to a civil servant status. In this tug-of-war both sides turned to the commanders-in-chief of the various fronts, airing their differences and heaping accusations on one another.

By the nature of their war work the Voluntary Organisations had direct access to the commanders-in-chief, but the attitude of the generals towards them was ambiguous. The Voluntary Organisations had done excellent work in organising the care of the wounded, in helping with the evacuation of refugees, and in speeding up the flow of supplies. They were always ready to back the demands of the military when these were opposed by the government, simply as a matter of oppositional tactics. They were eager to have the support of the military authorities in their claims for recognition as independent bodies in the political and economic life of the country. And finally, some of their leaders were hoping for the eventual support of the military when the moment came for the *coup d'état* being plotted by Guchkov, Prince Lvov and others.

But there were also considerable reasons for mutual suspicion. The military knew better than anyone else that the efforts of the Voluntary Organisations and of the government departments were complementary, and that neither could replace the other. They saw that the ostensibly patriotic motives of the leaders of the liberals were vitiated by political considerations and ambitions, and that their contribution to the war effort was made with an eye to using it as a means of extorting the political concessions they desired. From the point of view of the generals, there was no real necessity for carrying out a constitutional reform in wartime, except to appease the liberals. The commanders-in-chief must also have resented the insistent and repeated approaches which were made to them to enlist their support for subversive enterprises. Yet the army was so dependent on the work of Guchkov, Lvov and others that while the generals refused to take part in their plots, they would not denounce them to the Emperor or to the state security authorities, as was their duty.

Guchkov's favourite tactics for spreading rumours and getting important people involved in his plots was the dissemination of typewritten or mimeographed material reproducing private correspondence. As early as 1912, it was believed in government circles that he was responsible for the circulation of mimeographed copies of private letters written years before by the Empress and her children to Rasputin; this was a powerful and somewhat perfidious blow to the prestige of the monarchy.[1]

In September 1915 he undertook the task of disseminating the uncensored speeches in the Duma by this method on behalf of the Voluntary Organisations, and a year later, in August 1916, he launched a large-scale campaign based on one of his own letters. This letter, addressed to General Alekseev, contained a vitriolic attack on the then Deputy Minister of War, Belyaev, and on the government in general. It had been advertised in advance of its distribution as some kind of important state document drafted by a representative of Moscow liberal circles for submission to someone at GHQ, possibly to the Emperor himself. In fact, the security police reported rumours concerning the document

1. Compare Kokovtsov's memoirs, *Out of My Past*. Hoover War Library publication No. 6 (Stanford/London, 1935), p. 292 f. The official historian of Nicholas II's reign, S. S. Oldenburg, who cannot be suspected of a pro-Guchkov bias, does not believe that the allegations against Guchkov on this count have been proved beyond doubt. See *Tsarstvovanie Imperatora Nikolayu II-go*, vol. II, Part III (Munich, 1949), p. 89.

even before it was disseminated. By the end of September copies of the letter from Guchkov to Alekseev had been received in many quarters, and rumours about it began to circulate openly.

The letter is long and involved; it starts with recriminations against the way the Minister of War had handled an order for rifles placed in Great Britain. Guchkov's arguments against General Belyaev are not convincing,[1] but the attack on the Minister of War is only an introduction to his violent peroration at the end of his letter. Here Guchkov wrote:[2]

> Do you not feel, in your far-off Mogilev, the same as we do here — we, who are in daily, even hourly, contact with the [War] Department and all the other government institutions?
>
> You must know that the home front is in a state of complete disintegration, that the rot has set in at the roots of state power. You must know that however favourable the situation at the front seems now, the rot on the home front is once more threatening, as it did last year, to drag your gallant armies at the front, your gallant strategy, and the whole country, into the hopeless quagmire from which we have just managed to scramble by the skin of our teeth. You must know that one cannot expect communications to function properly under Mr Trepov; nor good work of our industry when it is entrusted to Prince Shakhovskoy; nor prosperity for our agriculture and a proper management of supplies at the hands of Count Bobrinsky. And when you think that this government is headed by Mr Stuermer, who has established (both in the army and among the people at large) a solid reputation of one who — if not an actual traitor — is ready to commit treason, when you think that diplomatic negotiations today and the outcome of the peace negotiations tomorrow, and therefore all our destiny and future, are in the hands of this man, then, Mikhail Vasilyevich [Alekseev], you will understand what deadly anxiety for the fate of our Motherland has gripped public opinion and popular feeling.
>
> We in the rear are powerless, or almost powerless, to fight this evil. Our methods of struggle are double-edged and can — owing to the excitable state of the popular masses and in particular of the working class — become the first spark of a conflagration, the dimensions of which no one can foresee or localize. Not to mention what we shall be faced

1. Belyaev, who had cancelled an order for rifles from Great Britain, subsequently put up an effective defence of this action before the Muravyev Commission. See *Padenie*, vol. II, p. 209 ff.

2. Golovin, *Voennye usiliya*, Vol. II, pp. 167 ff.

with after the war. The flood is nearing, and our piteous, miserable, mucky (*slyakotnoe*) government is preparing to meet this cataclysm by measures suitable for a good shower: they put on galoshes and open their umbrellas.

Is there anything you can do? I don't know. But you may rest assured that our disgusting policy (including our disgusting diplomacy) threatens at present to impede the lines of your magnificent strategy and in the future to rob us of the fruits of this strategy. History, even that of our country, knows many terrifying instances of such developments.

Forgive me this letter, and do not take offence at my hot temper.

Never, perhaps, was I so sure as at this fatal hour that the public has good reasons for the anxiety which affects us all.

May the Lord assist you.

When Guchkov's letter, in mimeographed copies, reached those whom he had denounced, there was consternation and indignation in government circles.

The Minister of Trade and Industry, Prince Shakhovskoy, reports in his memoirs that he was given copies of two letters from Guchkov to Alekseev in September 1916.[1] Since he found himself personally attacked in them, he asked for an audience with the Empress through the intermediary of Mme Vyrubova, and was given a gracious reception on 20 September. He poured out his soul to the Empress, and said that his most humble duty commanded that he should warn his sovereign of his serious doubts about General Alekseev's loyalty. Shakhovskoy expressed his conviction that Guchkov was acting in consort with the President of the Duma, Rodzyanko, and the ex-Minister of War, Polivanov. He handed a copy of one of the two letters (which he still had in his possession in 1952) to the Empress for transmission to her husband. The Empress had heard of the letters before and was glad to receive confirmation of this latest intrigue by her arch-enemy Guchkov. She immediately wrote to the Emperor:

> I begin by sending you a copy of one of the letters to Alekseev. Read it, please, and then you will understand why the poor General is getting so excited. Guchkov distorts the truth, and is incited to it by Polivanov, from whom he is inseparable. Give a strict warning to the old man with regard to this correspondence, which is intended to shatter his nerves, and generally speaking, all these affairs do not concern him, because

1. Shakhovskoy, *Sic transit gloria mundi*, pp. 86 ff.

everything will be done for the army and it will suffer no shortages. . . .
It is obvious that this spider Guchkov and Polivanov are spinning a web
around Alekseev, and one would like to open his eyes and free him.
You could save him.[1]

Fortunately for our understanding of the relations between the
Emperor and his Chief of Staff, we have an indirect account of their
conversation about Guchkov's letter.[2] On 9 October, Premier Stuermer
came to GHQ for his routine report and referred *inter alia* to the
letter, in which he also had been attacked. The Emperor told Stuermer
that his trust in him was complete, asked him to look into his eyes,
and comforted the old gentleman as best he could. He also told
Stuermer that he had heard of the letters before, and that he had
questioned Alekseev about them. According to Stuermer's note on
his audience, the Emperor said that when he had asked Alekseev about
this letter, which must have been at the end of September — that is,
at least a month after its wide distribution — Alekseev had answered
that he had heard of the letter for the first time only that same morning
from two different quarters: in a letter from his wife which he had
just received, and from the Commander-in-Chief of the Western
Front, General Evert, who had sent him a copy because it was being
widely circulated among his officers. Evert had reproached Alekseev for
maintaining a correspondence with a scoundrel such as Guchkov.

According to Stuermer Alekseev told the Emperor that he had never
been in correspondence with Guchkov. When asked by the Emperor
whether Guchkov had sent him the incriminating letter personally,
he answered that he did not know, and that after looking through the
drawers of his desk, he could not find such a letter! The Emperor
pointed out to Alekseev that a correspondence of this kind with a
person whose total hatred of the monarchy and the dynasty was
notorious could not be tolerated.

According to Stuermer's note — which is certainly accurate — the
Emperor, when told about Guchkov's anti-government campaign at
the recent meetings of the WICs in Petrograd, had merely indicated

---

1. Letters of the Empress to Nicholas II of 20, 21 and 23 September in Tsentrarkhiv,
Perepiska Nikolaya i Aleksandry Romanovykh, ed. A. A. Sergeev (Moscow and Leningrad,
1923–27), vol. II, p. 192.
2. See Semennikov, *Monarkhiya pered krusheniem*, pp. 159–160.

that Guchkov should be warned that if he carried on in this way he would not be allowed to reside in the capital.

The incident is extremely revealing. Of course Nicholas's main concern was to pacify his offended Premier and to prevent further misunderstanding between him and Alekseev. In his conversation with Stuermer he therefore played down the importance of his interview with Alekseev on the subject of the letter. This is why he may not have been truthful in saying that Alekseev denied having corresponded with Guchkov. If Alekseev really denied this, he must have lost his head, to the extent of uttering lies to his sovereign and commander-in-chief. The incriminating letter begins with a reference to an earlier one, and Shakhovskoy also mentions the existence of a second letter. The memoirs of the historian Lemke, a war correspondent at GHQ in 1916, point to the fact that personal relations and an intense correspondence between Alekseev and Guchkov were maintained at that time.[1] In view of Guchkov's official position as chairman of the Central WIC, it could hardly have been otherwise. Guchkov certainly grasped every opportunity to win the goodwill of the military for his plots, and must have carried on conversations and correspondence with Alekseev which put the latter into a crucial dilemma. He had the choice either of concealing the conversations from the Emperor or of denouncing Guchkov and his friends for their attempts to win his support for a seditious movement. The decision to disseminate the letter of 15 August 1916 must have been made by Guchkov without the connivance of Alekseev in order to force his hand. It certainly put him into a morally untenable position, and his embarrassment must have appalled the Emperor. It seems very possible that the deterioration in Alekseev's health and his departure for a rest-cure in the Crimea in November 1916 were at least partly due to the moral strain which he felt in consequence of this incident. The memory of it must also have played a decisive part in determining his behaviour during the abdication crisis of 1 and 2 March 1917.

We know little of Alekseev's thoughts and feelings during his stay

1. Lemke, 250 *dney v tsarskoy stavke* (St. Petersburg, 1920). On p. 470, Lemke mentions the correspondence of Alekseev with Guchkov. On p. 545, he quotes a telegram of Guchkov to Alekseev. It was then, on 14 February 1916, that Lemke began to suspect the existence of a plot in which Guchkov, Konovalov, Krymov and Alekseev were involved. See ch. 3 above, p. 40.

in the Crimea. The only report we have is that of General Denikin,[1] who tells us that Alekseev had been approached by the Moscow opposition liberals and urged to give support to a political solution similar to the one proposed on 1 January to Grand Duke Nikolay Nikolaevich.[2] Alekseev refused to have anything to do with such plots as long as the war lasted, but here again he did not report the approach to the Emperor or the Minister of the Interior; according to Denikin, the emissaries of Prince Lvov then continued to recruit supporters from among other high-ranking officers at the front.

6. MILYUKOV'S BROADSIDE

While Guchkov was trying to enlist, if not the active support, at least the benevolent neutrality of the high command in the eventuality of a palace coup, the Duma Kadets and their acolytes of the Progressive Bloc were preparing to attack Stuermer's government at the opening of the Duma session on 1 November. Throughout 1916 a prolonged internal struggle had taken place in the Kadet Party, in which the leader of the parliamentary faction, Milyukov, spoke in favour of caution and restraint, while his colleague N. V. Nekrasov,[3] and the Kadets in Moscow and the provinces, were pressing for an organisational link with revolutionary elements.[4]

The appointment of Stuermer, who replaced Goremykin in January 1916, was intended by the Emperor as an attempt to appease the Duma by replacing the grumpy and unyielding Goremykin by a soft-spoken, 'diplomatic' personality. In order to express his intention of inaugurating a period of peaceful collaboration and, indirectly, to introduce his new premier, the Emperor decided to pay a surprise personal visit to the Duma. He was received on 9 February with great enthusiasm, and once more the charm of his personality seemed, for a moment, to have worked its spell. And yet it was quite clear that, while ready to collaborate with the Voluntary Organisations on all practical questions,

1. A. I. Denikin, *Ocherki russkoy smuty* (5 vols., Paris, 1921–26), vol. 1, part I, pp. 37 ff.
2. See below, p. 215.
3. And also the Petrograd lawyer M. S. Margulies and his Moscow colleague M. Mandelstam. For Nekrasov's involvement with Guchkov, see above, p. 176.
4. See above, pp. 12 ff.

the government would not yield on the constitutional issue. When the President of the Duma, on the occasion of the imperial visit, asked the Emperor whether he would not announce immediately the formation of a 'responsible ministry' (possibly with Stuermer at its head), the Emperor answered: 'That — I will still have to think over.'[1]

From then on, Stuermer became the target of a vilification campaign much more vociferous than anything which old Goremykin had had to face. Certainly his personality was not an attractive one. A courtier, an intriguer and careerist, his mind was completely devoid of any ideas either of a political programme or of the historical destiny of Russia. His contacts with Rasputin and his clique, which he tried to conceal from the public eye, soon became the talk of the capital and the country. His reliance on political adventurers who had been fishing in the troubled waters of the Okhrana service, such as the notorious Manasevich–Manuilov,[2] did his reputation the greatest harm.

He was also badly served by his one-time Minister of Interior, A. N. Khvostov, 'the Nephew', who managed, in not quite three months of office, to disorganise and demoralise (if such a term is applicable to this institution) the whole secret police system. Having come to power on the recommendation of Rasputin himself, Khvostov decided to get rid of the *starets* by having him assassinated by his police agents. The plot was betrayed by clumsy handling. Rasputin got wind of it, and withdrew his support from Khvostov. Stories alleging misappropriation of funds by the Minister of the Interior were reported to the Emperor, and Khvostov fell into disgrace and was replaced, as an emergency measure, by Stuermer himself.

Khvostov's downfall could have become a turning-point in Russian internal politics during the war. The Empress, who had supported his candidature under the influence of 'our friend',[3] was in a repentant mood and ready to make amends for her interference in state appointments. The Emperor's confidence in Rasputin's judgment of character was also badly shaken. If there was a moment to counteract Rasputin's influence, this would have been it. But there was no one close to the imperial couple who could skilfully exploit this situation, nor were the

1. *Padenie*, VII, Interrogation of Rodzyanko, p. 130.
2. See above, p. 67.
3. This is how Rasputin is usually referred to in the correspondence of the imperial couple.

politicians of the liberal camp particularly interested in getting rid of
Rasputin in such a manner. By this time, Rasputin had become the
main peg on which to hang all their accusations against the régime,
and his elimination from politics could be welcomed only if it were a
sign of the régime's defeat and not evidence of the monarchy's belated
awakening to reason.

Attempts on the part of Nicholas II to find a path to a reconciliation
with the Duma other than that dictated by the Duma politicians
continued throughout 1916. The appointment of Protopopov, an
ex-Vice-President of the Duma, to the Ministry of the Interior in
September 1916 is an example of this. We shall show in due course
that this appointment, made under the influence of Rodzyanko, not
only failed in its immediate purpose, but only assisted and accelerated
the downfall of the régime.

The Kadet Party remained unmoved by all these attempts at reconciliation. They denounced Stuermer's advances as treacherous, and
considered Protopopov's acceptance of office as a betrayal of principle.
With all this, Kadets as a whole were not ready to link up with the
revolutionary movement. In February 1916, Milyukov was particularly eager to restrain the left wing of his party from embarking on a
revolutionary course. 'Do not give in', he said at a private meeting
of his supporters,

> to provocation of the reactionary forces, who are losing their grip;
> do not provide them with a loophole through which to escape; do not
> supply them with an excuse and relieve them of all the heavy responsi-
> bility for a further military defeat when it comes. Only one thing is
> left to us now — to suffer everything with patience, to swallow the
> bitterest pills; not to exacerbate, but on the contrary to restrain the
> seething passions; all this is in view of the coming reckoning, which is
> close at hand. The position of the government appears to be hopeless,
> and the total victory of Russian liberalism secure. The government is
> driving itself into an abyss, and it would be utterly inexpedient to encour-
> age any excesses which would open its eyes to the madness of its own
> action before the time is ripe.[1]

Milyukov's caution was not always shared in liberal and Kadet
circles outside the Duma, and as the hope of getting constitutional
concessions out of Stuermer vanished, these radical elements became

1. Grave, op. cit., p. 76.

particularly vocal. As one of the leaders of the Moscow Kadets, Prince Pavel D. Dolgorukov, put it:

> The profound divergence of view between the 'Milyukov followers' and the 'provincials' hinges on one basic question: Milyukov believes parliamentary struggle against the government to be the crucial point; the 'provincials' think that it has become necessary to switch the emphasis to the organisation of the masses, to establish closer contacts with political groups to the left of the Kadets, and to intensify the struggle against the government, not only on parliamentary lines, but with the assistance of public organisations of every kind.[1]

Milyukov's cautious policy was imposed on him by his leading position in the Progressive Bloc, which included elements unsympathetic to the revolutionary inclinations of the left Kadets. Thus, when Prince Lvov and Chelnokov (then the mayor of Moscow) came to attend one of the meetings of the Progressive Bloc in Petrograd and expressed their feeling that the only salvation for the country lay in revolution, they were met with marked hostility by those present, and were told that to agree to a revolution during the war was tantamount to treason.[2]

The pressure of the left wing of his own party, however, began to bear heavily on Milyukov by the end of the summer of 1916. He had always been very sensitive to denunciations of parliamentary methods of struggle as obsolete and ineffective. Now he decided to make use of the demagogy of the Moscow plotters by raising in parliament the scandalous allegations which they were spreading throughout the land. Thus parliamentary action would appear to match popular feeling and the efforts of the liberals outside the Duma. This explains the vehement tone of Milyukov's famous broadside against the government – and indeed, against the régime – on 1 November 1916, when the Duma resumed its meetings after a long recess.

This speech has been described by many, including its author, as the first revolutionary act in Russia.[3] Even if this is an exaggeration,

1. From the report of Colonel Martynov of the Moscow Secret Police Department, 2 November 1916. Grave, op. cit., p. 146.
2. See Gurko, *Features and Figures from the Past.* Hoover Library Publications No. 14 (Stanford/London, 1938), p. 582.
3. Milyukov's speech was last reprinted by a political adversary, A. S. Rezanov, in *Shturmovoy signal Milyukova* (Paris, 1924).

and the speech was only one of many demonstrations and propaganda actions of the liberals, it was an outstanding event. It came as no surprise to the government or to the President of the Duma, who were warned that the word 'treason' would be freely used in a resounding oration in the Duma on the day of its opening. This is why the Premier, Stuermer, left the Duma immediately after having read, in a tired and monotonous voice, an insignificant 'Declaration by the government'.[1]

Milyukov's speech — a piece of demagogic oratory which hardly does justice to him as a political analyst — consists of vague and general attacks, punctuated with the recurring question 'Is this treason or folly?' on government policy and government administration. It was this question which struck the public imagination most. It confirmed the anxious suspicions of 'treason in high places' which had first been kindled by the Myasoedov affair, and then systematically kept alive by the propaganda of the liberals. When proclaimed openly from the Duma tribune, to which articulate Russian public opinion looked for information and political guidance, this originally vague suspicion hardened into a general conviction. How, indeed, could the general newspaper-reading public doubt accusations made from the tribune of the Duma by the most intellectual and, up to now, most moderate leader of the opposition? If Milyukov ventured to raise an accusation of treason against the Premier, one felt sure he must have held reliable information from a source he could not divulge. His contacts with Allied diplomats were well known, and his leading role in the parliamentary delegation to the Allied countries in the summer of 1916 had been widely publicised.

In fact, Milyukov had not, and could not have had, any information on the imaginary negotiations for a separate peace from any of the diplomats with whom he was in touch in Petrograd. He tells us himself how he picked up the gossip during his trip abroad in 1916. In that summer he had been in Switzerland, in Lausanne, where he 'had some contacts with the old [pre-revolutionary] Russian emigration. In this milieu everyone was sure that the Russian government, through its special agents, was maintaining contact with Germany. A whole cascade of

1. One wonders whether the President of the Duma, who left the meeting at the same time, having handed over the chair to his assistant, Varun-Sekret, was perhaps a little disingenuous when he claimed to have departed because of a bad cold?

facts was showered upon me — reliable, doubtful, and improbable facts. To sort them out was quite a business.'[1]

Milyukov does not seem to have made a great effort to 'sort out' the information which came to him from these admittedly turbid sources. Instead, he continued collecting bits of information which might substantiate the accusations he was directing at Stuermer and hence implicitly at the imperial couple. In his deposition to the Muravyev Commission,[2] he recalled that 'while Stuermer was still in power he had seen an American magazine with an article on peace proposals made by the Germans to Russia, with portraits of Jagow and Stuermer side by side'. Milyukov stated that the information in the American magazine was only a reprint from the notoriously anti-Russian Swiss paper *Berner Tagwacht*, the official organ of the Swiss Social-Democrats. He believed that the story of the peace terms which, according to the *Berner Tagwacht*, had been made to Stuermer was 'fairly plausible'. But he admitted that neither at the time of his speech, nor later as Minister of Foreign Affairs in the Provisional Government, had he checked the sources or the veracity of the *Berner Tagwacht* reports.

Had he done so he would have discovered a close connection between the *Berner Tagwacht* and the various rumours he had heard in Switzerland that summer. Information about negotiations between the Russian government and the Germans began to appear in the *Berner Tagwacht* in September 1916. For about a fortnight such reports came sporadically, in increasing detail. When another Berne paper, the *Tagblatt*, challenged the *Tagwacht* on this matter, they answered that they could not name their informants for security reasons, but that they had full confidence in them. The paper claimed that the information came from two independent sources, one of them based in Stockholm. Russian diplomatic representatives in Switzerland were slow to react, and when they finally produced a total denial it only gave the *Tagwacht* the opportunity to gloat over the Russians' alleged embarrassment. The rumours died out on the *Tagwacht* pages just as unexpectedly as they had appeared, and by the end of September there was for a time no further mention of them.

It is well to remember in this connection that the *Berner Tagwacht* was edited by Robert Grimm, who in 1912 had succeeded as editor-in-

1. Milyukov, op. cit., vol. II, p. 270.
2. On 7 August 1917. See *Padenie*, vol. VI, p. 370.

chief the notorious Karl Moor,[1] the Swiss Social-Democratic politician of German origin, who for many years had been an informer for both the Austrian and the German General Staffs on the socialist *émigrés* of various nationalities living in Switzerland. Grimm does not seem to have been directly in German service in 1916, although certain contacts between him and the German Embassy no doubt existed through the intermediary of other Swiss Socialists, including the Minister of Foreign Affairs, Hoffmann. It was Grimm who was originally earmarked to accompany the first 'sealed train' with Lenin through Germany, and only later was he replaced by Platten. It was also Grimm who, in the summer of 1917, went to Russia on Hoffmann's instructions to put out feelers for a separate peace with Germany. His contacts with the Germans were exposed, and the Provisional Government had him deported across the Swedish frontier.[2]

This was the man who was responsible in September 1916 for spreading the story of Russian–German negotiations. He might have believed it himself, for it is highly probable that it had been fed to him by his collaborator on the *Berner Tagwacht*, who signed his articles 'K. R.' or 'Parabellum' and was none other than Karl Radek. We can assume that Radek was then in close touch with Fürstenberg-Ganetsky in Stockholm. A year later, we find them sharing a house in a fashionable villa suburb of Stockholm. The contents of the alleged German proposals to the Russian government are themselves similar to what the journalist Kolyshko, a German agent in Russia, claimed to his German contacts in Stockholm to have put to Stuermer.[3] We need not be surprised to find that Kolyshko's adventurous projects were brought to the knowledge of the *Berner Tagwacht* via Fürstenberg-

1. See above, ch. 5, p. 74 *passim*.
2. In Stockholm, a cleverly packed 'court of honour' composed of Socialists from many countries who were meeting in preparation for a Socialist peace conference officially rehabilitated him. On the Grimm affair, see Gankin and Fisher, *The Bolsheviks and the World War*, pp. 614–629 *passim*, and I. G. Tseretelli, *Vospominaniya o fevralskoy revolyutsii* (2 vols, Paris and The Hague, 1963), vol. I, pp. 238–270. Tseretelli did not know, however, of the considerable number of papers relating to Grimm's abortive attempt contained in the records of the German Foreign Ministry. Particularly interesting is the report on Grimm's interview with Karl Moor, who gave Grimm a severe dressing-down, pointing out that he had behaved like an irresponsible boy by making semi-confessions instead of flatly denying all contacts with the Germans.
3. See ch. 5, pp. 66–67.

Ganetsky and Radek: Kolyshko and his activities were well known to Helphand (Parvus), the mentor and protector of Fürstenberg-Ganetsky. And so the whole matter comes full circle: Milyukov, who thought to expose the intrigues of the Germans with Stuermer's treacherous government, was himself the victim of a German stratagem mounted with the help of Radek and Grimm.

It is not irrelevant at this point to recall Lenin's reaction to the rumours of separate peace negotiations. He recorded them in an article written in December 1916, and first published in his paper *Sotsial–Demokrat* on 31 January 1917. Here Lenin claims that 'quite recent' negotiations for a separate peace were a fact, though he admits that Stuermer's replacement by Trepov (mid-November 1916) and the recognition by the Allies of Russia's claim to Constantinople seemed to indicate that these negotiations had been inconclusive. Not leaving it at that, Lenin spins out a fantastic theory according to which the Tsarist government had been prevented from concluding a formal, separate peace with Germany for fear that this might lead to the formation of a government of Milyukov and Guchkov or even of Milyukov and Kerensky! Lenin considered it a possibility that the Tsarist government might conclude a secret, informal peace with Germany — that is, an agreement to bring the hostilities to an early end and then join hands at the peace conference in order to establish a Russo–German imperialist alliance directed against England. Lenin realised the impossibility of checking the correctness of his assumption. 'But in any case', he claimed, 'it contains a thousand times more truth as a reflection of reality than the endless goody-goody phrases about peace between the present bourgeois governments, and bourgeois governments in general, based on renunciation of annexations and the like.'[1]

Such ideological mythomania does not surprise us in Lenin. In Milyukov it must have been caused by a momentary aberration explainable, if not excusable, by the political pressures of the moment.

Commenting on his speech after the revolution, Milyukov claimed that in his mind 'folly' and not 'treason' was the answer he favoured to his question. When he wrote this, Milyukov may not have had access to the text of his speech; otherwise he would have found that, in one passage at least, he had said that the misdeeds of the government could hardly be explained by stupidity alone. Moreover, as we know from

1. *Sochineniya*, vol. XIX, p. 365.

earlier statements by Milyukov at private party meetings, he fully understood the explosive character of the accusations of treason brandished against the government, so that by using this word as a refrain he doubtless intended to put some dynamite into the parliamentary methods of struggle which he advocated and which had been criticised by his more radical followers.

But the greatest explosive charge lay not in the repetition of the rhetorical question, but in his mention of the name of the Empress in immediate juxtaposition with the accusations of treason. Milyukov pointed out that under the prevailing conditions it was no wonder that the enemy took comfort in the rumours concerning a pro-German party, 'said to gather round the young Empress'. This last phrase he quoted, in German, from the *Neue Freie Presse*, an Austrian paper. Standing orders of the Duma forbade the use of any language but Russian from the tribune, and the chair should have stopped Milyukov at once. Varun–Sekret failed, however, to do so, in the excitement of the moment; this slip led to his resignation as Deputy Speaker.

The use of German by Milyukov was a skilful way of accentuating his insinuations against the Empress, and set the tone of the proceedings for the rest of the session. Individual ministers became fair game for any Duma orator. Full use was made of this licence, not only by the liberal deputies, but also by certain conservatives, down to the blackest reactionary, Purishkevich. The government attempted to hit back, and asked the chair for an unaltered stenographic report of Milyukov's speech in order to institute legal proceedings against him, but Rodzyanko rejected this demand. The speech was made available to the government only in an expurgated version, while thousands of typewritten and mimeographed copies of it, with all the seditious elements intact (and occasionally some fabricated ones added), were circulated throughout the country.[1]

1. Years later, recollecting his speech, Milyukov wrote: 'The impression it produced was as if a blister filled with pus had burst and the basic evil, which was known to everyone but had awaited public exposure, had now been pinpointed. . . . At the next meeting of the Duma, the attacks continued. V. Shulgin made a poisonous and vivid speech, and drew practical conclusions. More cautiously but clearly enough, V. A. Maklakov gave me his support. Our speeches were not allowed to be published in the press, but this only increased their effectiveness. In millions of copies they were reproduced on the typewriters of the ministries and headquarters, and were circulated throughout the country. My speech earned the reputation of a storm signal for the

7. THE ASSASSINATION OF RASPUTIN

The Milyukov broadside marked a new departure in the liberals' policy of extorting reforms from the Tsar. The accusations of treason, of preparations for a separate peace, and of support of the 'dark forces' by the Empress herself became generally accepted and were openly discussed not only by politicians but among the people at large and the army in particular. These beliefs created a kind of national unity which embraced the members of the grand-ducal families and the liberals alike. The rumours and accusations were not based on any facts, but their uniformity and all-pervasiveness seem to point to one single source sufficiently authoritative to have impressed both the highest strata of society and the liberal Duma circles.

In the subsequent search for this source the attention of those defending the memory of the murdered imperial family naturally focused on the politicians who spread these slanders. Thus S. S. Oldenburg, the cautious and accurate historian of the reign of Nicholas II, puts the blame squarely on Guchkov.[1] And certainly Guchkov did his best to spread the rumour. This does not, however, prove that he was its originator: for this he lacked the necessary authority, especially since he was known to be a personal enemy of the Tsar and his consort. Less critical and well-informed commentators have assumed the existence of some well-organised conspiracy on masonic lines behind these rumours. We believe that an analysis of the circumstances preceding the murder of Rasputin may lead us to a clearer understanding.

The initiator of the plot to assassinate Rasputin was the young Prince Felix Yusupov, the heir to the largest private fortune in Russia and the husband of a much-loved niece of the Emperor, Princess Irina, the daughter of his sister, the Grand Duchess Xenia. Yusupov himself has given an account of his motives and the dramatic circumstances which led him to become a murderer.[2] According to him, he had closely followed the November debates in the Duma, where the accusation of high treason was made in more or less open terms, and had been particularly impressed by the speech of the right-wing deputy

revolution. Such was not my intention. But the prevailing mood in the country served as a megaphone for my words.' Milyukov, op. cit., vol. II, p. 277.

1. Oldenburg, op. cit., vol. III, p. 215, *passim*.

2. We quote from Prince Felix Youssoupoff, *Avant l'exil 1887–1919* (Paris, 1952).

Purishkevich, who, following the Milyukov attack, had denounced the existing régime as a tool in the hands of 'dark forces'. Yusupov was then living alone in Petrograd (his wife and child were with his parents in the Crimea), training at an aristocratic cadet school in order to get a commission and go to the front. Young Yusupov's social contacts had no limits. There was almost no house in Russia, no personality whom he could not approach directly without introduction. He was particularly intimate with the family of Rodzyanko, whose wife was the closest friend of his mother, Princess Zinaida Yusupov.

Prince Felix seems to believe, and certainly would like us to believe, that his decision to kill Rasputin, who was, he knew, dear to the Empress, was dictated by his observations of the political scene and by a general conviction that the man exerted a pernicious influence. Yet the prince does not explain why he decided to take the law into his own hands and act as executioner. There must have been others whose influence on public affairs was at least as noxious as Rasputin's. Had Yusupov been a convinced terrorist in his political outlook, his decision to kill would be understandable. But he was not a terrorist. In his own mind his action had a mystical, almost liturgical, significance: he was not removing an evil political adviser, but a creature of a special category, endowed with supernatural powers, the like of which he had never met before. The elimination of such a monster seemed a task worthy to be undertaken by a person in his exalted position.

It is interesting to note how such mystical ideas were formed in Yusupov's imagination. From his own account we know that his mother exerted the main influence on the formation of his character. More than that, at the critical period in the summer of 1916 it was his mother who, through her letters, instilled and sustained in his mind the idea of a link between Rasputin and some occult German influences. She encouraged him to propagate these ideas and to win Rodzyanko to this belief. When the young prince reported to his mother that 'Medvedev [a cover name for Rodzyanko] cannot realize how powerful G. [Rasputin] is; he does not believe in hypnosis and regards the whole thing as the outcome of vice, etc. . .', the princess answered: 'Tell Uncle Misha [again Rodzyanko] that nothing can be done unless the "book" [another cover name for Rasputin] be destroyed and Validé[1]

1. A Crimean Tatar name for 'great mother', once used in a loyal address to the Empress, had become a mocking nickname for her.

tamed. He should have demanded the banishment of the "book" from the capital. That is imperative. Yet Medvedev will not understand. . . .'[1]

Rodzyanko perhaps was sceptical, but for the people at large and even for many of the grand dukes, the opinion of Princess Zinaida had tremendous authority: if the Princess, who had been so close to the imperial family, believed the charges of treason and deemed it necessary to start direct action to remove the Empress, there must have been — so people believed — something behind it.

Nobody asked how the Princess got her knowledge of the Empress's pro-German leanings. We can now be sure, however, that the Princess, who had lived in the Crimea since 1915, had no direct information on this, and we may ask ourselves how she arrived at her belief in the 'dark forces'. Prince Felix Yusupov himself has provided, perhaps inadvertently, the answer to our question. In his reminiscences he gives a revealing account of his father's governor-generalship of Moscow in 1915.[2]

> He was not to occupy that post for long. One man could not carry on alone the struggle against the German camarilla who occupied all the important posts. Seeing espionage and treason reigning everywhere, my father took draconian measures to free Moscow from this occult domination by the enemy. But most of the ministers, who owed their position to the influence of Rasputin, were Germanophiles. They were resolutely hostile to the Governor-General and countermanded all his orders. Disgusted by the systematic opposition he met in the government, my father left for GHQ, where he had a conference with the Tsar, the Supreme Commander, Nikolay Nikolaevich, and the ministers. Without mincing his words he explained the situation in Moscow, pointing out the facts and naming the guilty. This violent diatribe produced a shattering effect. Nobody had dared before to raise his voice in the presence of the Emperor against the people in entrenched positions. Unfortunately, it was all to no avail. The German party which surrounded the sovereign was sufficiently strong to erase rapidly the impression produced by the Governor-General's words. On his return to Moscow my father learned that he had been dismissed. All Russian patriots were indignant about this measure and about the Emperor's weakness in tolerating it. It had obviously become impossible to fight German influence. My disillusioned father retired with my mother to the Crimea.

1. Quoted from C. Vulliamy, *From the Red Archives* (London, 1929), pp. 110 ff.
2. Youssoupoff, op. cit., pp. 196 ff.

This fantastic account of Prince Yusupov Senior's unhappy service in Moscow must be based on a strongly established family legend. In fact, it was not the draconian measures he applied against spies which caused his downfall, but the rioting in Moscow, where the shops and houses of people with German names were being sacked and looted by the rabble. The Council of Ministers with which the Prince came into conflict was the liberalised Cabinet formed in the summer of 1915, with new ministers appointed against the will of Rasputin and the Empress. In the minutes of the secret Cabinet meetings recorded by Yakhontov, there is clear evidence that the liberal ministers were against Prince Yusupov's continued tenure of office, and that only Goremykin was in favour of complying with the Emperor's insistent desire to retain his governor-general.[1]

---

1. See Yakhontov's notes in *ARR*, XVIII, pp. 28 ff. and 39 ff. The strongest opposition to Yusupov's continuation as Moscow Governor-General came from the Minister of the Interior, Prince Shcherbatov. Referring to his demands for unlimited power, he said: 'If Yusupov is given the full powers he demands, the Ministry of the Interior will have no say in Moscow and the city will become an independent satrapy.' Krivoshein fully supported him: 'I consider, and believe it my duty to say that Yusupov has given sufficient proof that he is not qualified to be governor-general or to occupy any responsible post. He is a megalomaniac of the most dangerous kind. Even before becoming master in Moscow he treated the government as if it were a neighbouring power. . . .' The State Comptroller, Kharitonov, expressed the opinion that Yusupov was 'not only undesirable but inadmissible' in Moscow. Polivanov fully agreed and reported that the Emperor was embarrassed about what to do with Yusupov: 'Give me advice', the Emperor asked Polivanov, 'about what I should do with Yusupov, who refuses to make any concessions; try to reason with him and persuade him; write to him showing more consideration; this should impress him.' Only Samarin advised a more cautious approach to the dismissal of Yusupov: 'I must call the Council's attention to the fact that Yusupov has already acquired quite a wide reputation among the lower strata of the Moscow population. He is considered to be an irreconcilable enemy of the Germans. . . . Knowing Moscow, I am sure that a forced retirement of Yusupov would have dangerous consequences. Every opportunity is taken now to fan agitation. There will be a clamour that the government is playing into the hands of the Germans by removing an untiring enemy of German spies. I agree . . . that expediency requires Yusupov's removal, but I think it should come in the form of an honourable retirement, with an appointment to some even more exalted position.' Shcherbatov agreed, and said that Yusupov's speeches appealed to the crowd and incited simple people against German subversion, 'which Yusupov sees everywhere, even in the Council of Ministers itself'.

On reading these statements from the ministers, one senses the ghost of another

Felix Yusupov's account of this episode shows how much it rankled with his parents. The Prince's dismissal must have infuriated the proud and ambitious Princess Zinaida even more than it did the Prince himself. The Princess could only explain her husband's removal by reference to the intrigues of an imaginary camarilla. This is the origin of her allegations against a government which had spurned the services of her husband.

But this is only the beginning of the story. After her retirement to the Crimea, personal relations between Princess Zinaida and the Empress were almost broken off. Yet in the summer of 1916, as we know from Prince Felix's memoirs, she insisted on seeing the Empress once more.

> Her Majesty gave her a frigid reception, and as soon as she realised the object of her visit, she requested her to leave the palace. My mother declared that she would not go before having said all she had to say. She spoke at length. When she finished, the Empress, who had listened in silence, rose and dismissed her with the words 'I hope never to see you again'.[1]

This incident helps to explain how the legend of the Rasputin-German coalition involving the Empress gained such a powerful hold on the imagination of the outraged Princess Zinaida.

The Empress's parting words could be understood as the banishment of Princess Yusupov from the court, where with her beauty and charm she had shone for years. Who could underestimate the passions which such a humiliation would rouse in one so spoiled by every imaginable success? Now we can understand the fury behind the invective in her letters to her son and to her confidante, Mme Rodzyanko. Nor should we underestimate her power to hit back at the hated 'Validé.' Through her connections with the imperial family she was able to get the support of the grand dukes, while through the Rodzyankos she had a direct line to the moderate Duma circles, who

governor-general of Moscow, Count Rostopchin, hovering over the Council chamber as a terrifying warning.

It is perhaps not relevant, but at least ironical, that Prince Yusupov, who came to the meeting at GHQ to give a lesson in Russian patriotism to people like Goremykin, Krivoshein, Kharitonov and Sazonov, was believed to be the grandson of a bastard of a Prussian king (see Youssoupoff, op. cit., p. 26).

1. Youssoupoff, op. cit., p. 199.

would believe any information from such an unimpeachable source. It is noteworthy that the first version of the 'legend of the separate peace', directed against the government, spread in September 1915, at the time of Prince Yusupov's retirement from the post of governor-general, while the second version, implicating the Empress, became current soon after the fateful interview between the Empress and her richest, noblest and most charming subject.[1] Once launched from such a high position, the waves of slanderous rumour came back to their source embellished and strengthened by popular imagination, only to confirm their originator in her convictions and to quell any doubts and scruples which might have crept into her mind.

The Yusupov correspondence shows clearly that Rodzyanko was not easily converted to Princess Zinaida's extreme views on the German sympathies of the Empress. Not so her son Felix, who decided to check the rumours on Rasputin by personal investigation. In his memoirs he reports that, having feigned interest in, and friendship for, Rasputin, he became a frequent visitor to his house. From Rasputin's intentionally cryptic conversation he inferred that Rasputin maintained contacts with the Germans through mysterious people whom the *starets* called the 'green' and the 'greenish'. On one occasion he reports having witnessed a clandestine meeting between Rasputin and seven or eight dubious characters in the penumbra of the hall of Rasputin's flat. Some of them had pronounced Semitic features; others looked like northern Germans. Notes were taken, etc. We feel we must agree with Melgunov when he says that only exceptional naïvety could allow one to believe that the characters observed by Yusupov in these circumstances could have been German spies.[2] The more so, since, according to him, his state of mind during his visits to the Rasputin house could hardly ever have been balanced. Rasputin used to treat him by hypnosis and plunge him into cataleptic trances.

1. The Princess herself assessed her capacity in these words: 'Here [in the Crimea] they are quite glad that I am not [in Petrograd], since they know what I would be capable of, were I on the spot. But I am simply exasperated, boiling over with indignation, cursing the circumstances in which I live and which tie me hand and foot' (letter to Felix Yusupov, 11 December 1916, quoted in *From the Red Archives*, p. 144).
2. See S. P. Melgunov, *Legenda*, etc. op. cit., p. 382. There is of course some excuse for Felix Yusupov having believed that Rasputin was a spy, after Aleksey Khvostov ('the Nephew') had made his sensational allegations of 'world espionage' against Rasputin. See below, p. 209, and n.

It may well be that this hypnotic treatment tended to arouse a homicidal urge in young Yusupov.[1] Be that as it may, the combined action of his mother's excited letters and his acquaintance with Rasputin led Felix Yusupov to the decision to organise the assassination of the 'holy man'.

Yusupov was keen to find allies for his plan both in political circles and in high society. He first approached Vasily Maklakov, the right-wing Kadet leader and the author of the famous article on the 'mad chauffeur'.[2] Maklakov was shocked by what he believed to be a suggestion that he might help in procuring hired assassins. He allowed himself to remain privy to the plot, however, and knew of the date when the killing was to take place. Next Yusupov engaged the support of the right-wing Duma deputy Purishkevich. Purishkevich, a colourful, though hardly an edifying, figure in Russian politics, was the head of one of the branches of the government-supported, patriotic and anti-Semitic 'Union of the Russian People', which has been correctly labelled proto-fascist. Purishkevich had little moral and intellectual self-control and was famous for the scandalous scenes he used to enact in the Duma.[3] During the war he had given up politics for a time to devote himself to organising relief services for the army, hospital trains, canteens, de-lousing stations and so on. In this respect he played the role of a one-man Voluntary Organisation, and his canteens bore such names as 'Tea Room of State Councillor Purishkevich'. These activities brought him into frequent conflict with the Petrograd bureaucracy – conflicts very similar to those which rendered co-operation between the Voluntary Organisations and the bureaucracy so difficult. In 1916 he joined the Progressive Bloc in their attacks on the government, to which he brought the usual vehemence of his parliamentary personality. He could not resist the temptation of playing a part in the salvation of Russia from the 'dark forces' in the company of Prince Felix Yusupov. The third conspirator was the Grand Duke Dimitri Pavlo-

1. The reaction of one who experiences the hypnotic power of a person whom he detests or fears is violent and naturally homicidal, especially as the controls of the super-ego are weakened under this treatment. A wonderful description of the homicidal reaction of the hypnotised against the hypnotist can be found in Thomas Mann's miniature masterpiece *Mario and the Magician*.
2. See above, p. 178.
3. E.g., he is reported to have appeared in the State Duma sporting a red carnation in his fly-buttons.

vich, whose participation not only added lustre to the enterprise but also reduced its obvious risks.

There is no need to repeat here the sorry tale of the actual murder with its nightmarish and sordid details, but we must assess its political importance. Rasputin's strong and picturesque personality should not deceive us as to the importance of his political power. The need for a spiritual guide was an essential part of the Empress's religious character. Rasputin had had predecessors and would certainly have had successors had the régime endured. By the very nature of the Empress's mysticism these persons were inevitably charlatans who would, to a greater or lesser extent, use their influence on her imagination to their own advantage. In Rasputin's case his position was powerfully strengthened by his natural hypnotic powers.

There is nothing mysterious in his reported ability to alleviate the sufferings of the Tsarevich, who was a haemophiliac. No hypnosis could, of course, alter the composition of his blood to replace the deficiency which prevented it from coagulating normally. But it is well known that hypnotic influence can affect the vaso-motor system and cause a contraction of the vessels comparable to the effect of adrenalin and similar drugs. But to the Empress the intervention of Rasputin seemed miraculous, and this view was doubtless shared by her husband. Given this attitude to him of the imperial couple, the reports of Rasputin's dissolute life carried little weight. The Emperor knew that the personal morals of the Petrograd society into which Rasputin was drawn were not of a high standard, and he blamed the occasional lapses of 'the man of God' on the corrupting influences and temptations of the capital, which a simple and basically healthy Siberian peasant had little means of resisting. Neither excessive drinking nor lechery were exceptional in these circles, and if the Emperor tolerated such behaviour among his courtiers there was no reason for him to do more in the case of a devoted friend than to scold and admonish. The accusations levelled against Rasputin were invariably embellished by Russian *vranyë* – that special kind of imaginative lying which gives a picture of reality amended to suit some ultimate purpose and counts on ready acceptance by the deceived.[1]

1. The late Father Nicholas Gibbes, who – as Mr Sidney Gibbes – had been English tutor to the Tsarevich, told the author that he was once present while the Emperor opened his mail at Mogilev. He threw one of the letters, without reading it,

Moreover, police reports were not trusted by the Emperor, who knew only too well how the police could frame their victims and fake a case against them. Yet there is belated evidence that the reports on Rasputin's debaucheries in the last years of his life reached not only the Emperor but the Empress as well. In a letter addressed to General Spiridovich, the former commandant of the palace, General Voeykov, admitted that in the performance of his duties he had to inform the imperial couple of the content of the police reports and that this caused much sorrow and anger to the Empress.[1]

There was, however, one point on which the Emperor seems to have been particularly sensitive, and that was the soundness of the religious attitude of Rasputin as a faithful son of the Orthodox Church. It is worth recalling that as early as 1912, at the time when Guchkov raised the question of Rasputin for the first time in the Duma, allegations about his contacts with an extreme orgiastic sectarian movement in Siberia became current all over Russia. At that time the Emperor entrusted Rodzyanko with the task of finding out whether it was true that Rasputin had belonged to the sect of the 'Khlysty'. About the same time a number of bishops of the Orthodox Church who had supported Rasputin at the beginning of his career in Petersburg as a genuine man of God and a great repentant sinner, turned against him and started a campaign of violent denunciation.

From all we know of the character of the Emperor and of his wife's mystical tendencies, a conclusive proof of Rasputin's contact with an objectionable sectarian movement might well have caused a breach with him. It would not have been the first time that the imperial couple had been forced to part with an alleged messenger of heaven because of the disclosure of some unsavoury aspect of his earthly existence. This was however not to be. Not only was Rodzyanko's investigation inconclusive, but there was an extremely authoritative intervention in favour of Rasputin from a most unexpected quarter.

Vladimir Bonch-Bruevich, a leading authority on the sectarian movements in Russia, who had published a number of volumes of his

---

into the waste paper basket, remarking: 'This is another of those denunciations of Grigory. I get them almost every day and throw them away unread.'
1. The letter is in the Spiridovich archives now deposited in Yale University. In his informative book *S Tsarem i bez Tsarya* (Helsingfors, 1936), V. N. Voeykov omits any reference to these reports.

investigations together with the sacred writings of some of the extreme dissident sects, came out with a solemn testimony in favour of Rasputin's religious orthodoxy. This was published in a letter to the editor of the left-wing review *Sovremennik*[1] and produced a considerable impression not only on the general public but also among the Russian episcopate.[2]

In his account of the Rasputin case, Bonch-Bruevich points out that he is merely concerned with the question of whether Rasputin was or was not a sectarian. This he answers in the following way:

> Having made the acquaintance of G. E. Rasputin-Novy and having spent a considerable time with him in seven exhaustive conversations, I consider it my moral duty to express my opinion on the question of whether or not he is a sectarian; the more so because this question has been touched upon, albeit indirectly, in an interpellation in the State Duma and in some of the deputies' speeches when the budget of the Holy Synod was discussed. Limiting myself strictly to the above question, I declare that Grigory Yefimievich Rasputin-Novy belongs to the type of an orthodox peasant from remote and backward provincial Russia, and has nothing whatever in common with any sectarianism. Being better acquainted with the dogmatic side of the orthodox doctrine than is common among peasants, and knowing the Bible and the Gospels much less well than do most sectarians, Grigory Yefimievich recognises all the sacraments, rituals and dogmas of the Orthodox Church in exactly the same way in which they are understood by the orthodox, without the slightest deviation or criticism. He considers that it would be extremely sinful and wicked if he even discussed such things, for, as he told me, 'It is no business of the layman to discuss things which have been established by the Lord Himself'.

Bonch-Bruevich reports that Rasputin venerated icons, which, as he said, 'always remind us of the holy life of the saints of the church, a reminder of which we who are in sin are always in dire need'.

Bonch-Bruevich goes on to attack violently all those who use the

1. *Kako verueshi? Po povodu tolkov o sektantstve G. E. Rasputina-Novago.* 1912, No. III, p. 356.
2. In an interview with Gen. Spiridovich the late Metropolitan Evlogy recalled years after that he had been personally convinced by this same Bonch-Bruevich that Rasputin had no formal affiliation to the sectarians. See an account of this interview in the Spiridovich archives, Yale University.

derogatory term, 'Khlysty' to abuse religious dissenters and slander such innocent people as Rasputin. He speaks of

> the zealous persecutors of religious nonconformists in Russia, who use this term with impunity and irresponsibility against anyone, and in particular against those coming from the peasant milieu, whom they want to insult and humiliate, whom they want to persecute at any price, and whom they want simply to torment mentally and physically, in spite of all the existing laws, decrees and manifestos on freedom of conscience.

And Bonch-Bruevich concludes his testimonial with these words:

> Basing myself on a considerable personal observation of sectarians, and on circumstantial knowledge of their ways of thinking, methods of arguing, expositions of faith, deliberations, and a great number of almost indefinable details, basing myself on a thorough study of everything which has up to now been written on G. E. Rasputin-Novy, including the latest pamphlet of Novoselov,[1] basing myself finally on prolonged personal conversations with Rasputin, which I carried out in the presence of witnesses as well as in strict privacy, and in which I deliberately tried to attain complete clarity and precision with regard to his religious faith, I consider it my duty to declare openly that G. E. Rasputin-Novy is a completely and absolutely convinced Orthodox Christian and not a sectarian. [Signed] Vladimir Bonch-Bruevich, Petersburg.

So much has been written on Rasputin's contacts with all sorts of powerful protectors belonging to the so-called 'dark forces' that it is refreshing to find that a friend and close collaborator of Lenin and a luminously progressive personality contributed to strengthening Rasputin's position at a moment when it could have become dangerously insecure. As far as Bonch-Bruevich's findings are concerned, they are probably for the most part correct. What he does not mention in his declaration, and what he appears to have conceded in his talks with Metropolitan Evlogy, is that Rasputin, although not belonging to the sectarian movement formally, had grown up in close contact with sectarian circles and had adopted certain modes of speech and behaviour from that milieu.

But it would be an injustice to Bonch-Bruevich to suppose that his

1. Novoselov was a writer on religious questions, who published an attack on Rasputin in Guchkov's paper *Golos Moskvy*.

conclusions were dictated by considerations of base 'bourgeois objectivism' or mere concern for the factual truth. All his previous activities in the organisation of the clandestine Bolshevik press, and his subsequent doings in the February days under the Provisional Government and in the first years of Lenin's rule, indicate that political considerations were paramount in any move which Bonch-Bruevich felt it 'his moral duty' to undertake. In the present case, the purpose of his affidavit is quite clear. Rasputin had been used in speeches in the Duma in order to shake the authority of the throne. The manoeuvre instigated by Guchkov, who used Novoselov's pamphlet as a pretext, was singularly successful. The connection of the imperial family with Rasputin was becoming the most vulnerable point in the structure of the autocratic administration. But the attack had been so fierce that supporters of the régime became worried and were trying to undo the harm which had been done by introducing the man of God to the palace. The allegations concerning Rasputin's deviations from orthodoxy were a powerful and possibly the only means of achieving his removal. This would of course deprive all those who were looking for any stick to beat the régime of a most precious weapon, and at this point the trusted friend of Lenin intervened, as an independent and totally disinterested scholar, and produced a most important document to the effect that all such allegations against Rasputin were based on malice and the desire to annihilate a 'man of the people', the peasant who had found access to the autocratic ruler. And in this case, as in many others, Bonch-Bruevich's stratagem worked.[1]

There is one further circumstance to remind us how closely interconnected were the efforts of all of those bent on the downfall of Nicholas II. In his posthumously published memoirs written in emigration, Guchkov recalls that it was he who arranged for Bonch-Bruevich to meet Rasputin through the intermediary of a lady who had originally offered to introduce Rasputin to Guchkov.

The meeting took place first in the drawing-room of that lady and later in greater privacy. In his memoirs, Guchkov reports that a few weeks later Bonch-Bruevich wrote him a letter

1. We have not come across any other trace of Bolshevik interest in Rasputin. It is worth recalling perhaps that one of the few Okhrana officers taken over by the Cheka after the revolution was a certain Kommissarov, who had organised the police watch on Rasputin's home in the last months of the latter's life.

in which he informed me that he came to the conclusion that Rasputin is not simply a rogue who had put on the mask of a sectarian, but is undoubtedly a sectarian, which of course does not prevent him from being a rogue at the same time. According to the spirit of his teaching he is close to the sect of the '*Khlysty*', but does not belong to it, and is a sectarian, as it were, on his own.

There is no need for us to make a further effort to find out which of the two, Bonch-Bruevich or Guchkov, is right on this point: the fact remains that Bonch-Bruevich's public intervention secured the most favourable conditions for the agitation against the imperial couple on which Guchkov then began to set his hopes for a future political career.

The assassins of Rasputin and those who were in sympathy with them felt that the elimination of the '*starets*' would mark the beginning of an important political development. The next step was to be the removal of the Empress from the political scene. Some hoped that the shock of the assassination would drive her to such distraction that she would go completely out of her mind. Others set their hopes on the rumours of a palace coup, in the course of which an ultimatum would be put to the Emperor demanding that he banish his wife to a nunnery or to the Crimean palace of Livadia. Of course, all these speculations were based on a total misconception of the real character of the husband-and-wife relationship of the imperial couple. Anyone who knew their complete devotion to each other could never have counted on the Emperor's voluntary agreement to a separation from his wife. This devotion, which stood the supreme test after the revolution, could certainly not have been shaken by the murder of 'our friend'.

In fact, the assassination of Rasputin had hardly any effect on the course of state affairs. As a political adviser, he had never pursued a consistent line. Most of his interference with day-to-day administration came under the heading of personal favouritism. On general issues he made oracular pronouncements which were open to widely divergent interpretations. They were not always followed, though invariably taken into account by the Emperor in the extremely complicated and unpredictable mechanism of his decision-making.[1] In

1. Oldenburg, op. cit., Part III, pp. 193 ff. (footnote) lists a number of cases when Rasputin's advice, proffered in 1915-16, was not followed. This list is by no means complete.

particular, the Emperor had little confidence in Rasputin's ability to judge character, as he once admitted to his wife.[1] Nor was Rasputin the centre of some caucus or conspiracy pursuing a definite political purpose. Such a caucus, whether described as the 'Black Bloc' or the 'Rasputin Circle', never in fact existed. This is not to say that there were not shady characters prowling around Rasputin and trying to penetrate the palace through the intermediary of the Empress's intimate friend, Mme Vyrubova. But the motley crowd who sought Vyrubova's favours, far from constituting a cohesive group, were intriguing against one another in an attempt to get some favour or to jockey their candidate into high office. In so doing they often undermined the position of high officials who stood in the way of their intrigues. A typical character of this kind was the notorious Prince Andronnikov, who described himself as the 'Aide-de-Camp of Our Lord Above.' When asked by the Muravyev Commission what his main occupation was, Prince Andronnikov described it quite candidly as 'visiting Ministers'. He had sought Rasputin's friendship and favour on the basis of a common inclination to political intrigue and a predilection for Russian fish soup. After a period of intense friendship Andronnikov fell out with Rasputin and was later banished from the capital. This same Andronnikov was one of the main intriguers against the War Minister Sukhomlinov, who, according to the legend of the 'dark forces', had been one of the main culprits harbouring and aiding German agents. Another scandal in the entourage of Rasputin was that involving Aleksey Khvostov ('the Nephew') who became Minister of the Interior with Rasputin's support and then turned against him and tried to organise his assassination. Khvostov was, as he described himself, a man devoid of all moral restraint. He was betrayed by the Chief of his Police Department, Beletsky, and dismissed. Incidentally, it was Khvostov, one of the most reactionary and unscrupulous members of the Duma right, who while still Minister of the Interior spread the rumour of Rasputin's involvement in 'world espionage'.[2] Needless to say the allegations lack all plausibility; if Khvostov had had any

1. Letter of Nicholas II, 9 November 1916, quoted in Oldenburg, *op. cit.* p. 194.
2. The incredible story of Khvostov's interview with I. V. Gessen and M. A. Suvorin at which Khvostov blurted out the allegation that 'Grishka [Rasputin] is connected with world espionage' is to be found in a note by Gessen in *ARR*, XII, pp. 76–82. For Spiridovich's reminiscences and comment, see *Velikaya voyna*, vol. II, pp. 50 ff.

evidence of such an involvement he would have informed one or another of the rival counter-espionage services and most probably achieved the elimination of his erstwhile protector. He did nothing of the kind, not even when urged to do so by General Spiridovich.

Whatever the intention, the real and important effect of the murder was not to remove an 'evil adviser', but to isolate even further from the rest of the country the Emperor and those who were still willing to serve him loyally. The *démarche* by a number of Grand Dukes pleading for a pardon for the assassins only made this isolation complete. In his answer to their plea, the Emperor said: 'No one is allowed to indulge in murder. I know that the consciences of many are disturbed. I am surprised at your approach to me.' This reply only increased the indignation and disaffection in grand-ducal circles.

9

On the Eve

The New Year celebrations; Prince Lvov's undelivered speech; The threatened dissolution of the Duma; The liberals' appeal to the Allies; Lord Milner's intervention; The conflict unresolved; Labour, revolutionaries and police on the eve of the February events; The Emperor's isolation and his generals; The return to GHQ of General Alekseev and the Emperor.

I. THE NEW YEAR CELEBRATIONS

The 1st of January 1917 was marked in the whole of Russia by the official New Year receptions at which it was customary for subordinates to present their good wishes to their superiors. Two incidents stood out on this day as highly characteristic of the political situation in the country at this moment. The first occurred at the official reception for those who came to bring greetings to the Winter Palace in Petrograd; the second happened almost simultaneously in the Viceroy's Palace in Tiflis, where the Viceroy, Grand Duke Nikolay Nikolaevich, had his residence and his headquarters as Commander-in-Chief of the Caucasian Front.

In the Winter Palace there was a sharp exchange between the Minister of the Interior, Protopopov, and the President of the Duma, Rodzyanko. As Protopopov approached Rodzyanko, obviously intending to shake hands, Rodzyanko called out to him to keep away.[1] This refusal to shake hands was a calculated discourtesy with political significance. It was well known that Protopopov had been appointed Minister of

---

1. Prince Vsevolod Shakhovskoy writes in his memoirs, *Sic transit gloria mundi*, p. 197: 'All the guests had forgathered in the expectation of the appearance of His Majesty in the palace, and were looking for the places assigned to them, and standing in groups talking. In one of these groups I saw the heavy figure of Rodzyanko. Protopopov approached him and, wishing him a happy New Year, proffered his hand. The impolite Rodzyanko, without even turning, pronounced in a resounding voice: "Go away! Do not touch me." I stood within a few feet of him. I saw all this with my own eyes and heard it with my own ears. The incident at once became known all over the palace, and by that evening was the talk of all Petrograd.'

the Interior after having been recommended to the Tsar (for a different ministerial post) by Rodzyanko, and that, before he became minister in September 1916 and while he was serving as deputy chairman of the Duma, the personal relations between the two men had been most cordial. After his appointment, Protopopov had tried to stay on good terms with his colleagues in the Duma. At first the choice of Protopopov had been regarded in Duma circles as a concession to the Progressive Bloc by the Emperor, but as it became clear that Protopopov had changed sides and would not, in his new capacity, support the demands for constitutional reforms, he rapidly became Enemy Number One of the 'progressive forces'.

Isolated from his former friends, dazzled by his success with the imperial couple, Protopopov seemed determined to use the considerable powers he enjoyed by virtue of his office to counteract all attempts by the liberals to break the monarch's will. To do this efficiently would have required much more experience in the use of the delicate conspiratorial apparatus of the Okhrana than Protopopov possessed. He would also have needed to carry out repressive measures according to a definite plan, and to have bolstered up the authority of the police, which was badly compromised by their mishandling of security measures for the protection of Rasputin. Protopopov knew all too well that after the assassination of Rasputin the stock of the police with the Tsar had fallen extremely low, and he was afraid of falling from grace by speaking out in support of them. He therefore adopted the attitude of the faithful servant for whom devotion to the monarch was identical with patriotic and religious duty. He professed that the salvation of the realm, the throne and the dynasty lay rather in the simple piety of the people's hearts than in the clever stratagems of an efficient and ubiquitous police force. This attitude had a special appeal for the Empress, who, after the shock of Rasputin's assassination, oscillated between fear and ecstatic hope, despair and hysterical, self-assertive confidence. Thus Protopopov became *l'homme de confiance* of the Empress.

It has been alleged that the Emperor shared his wife's confidence in his Minister of the Interior. But in a letter written shortly before Rasputin's murder, he warned her that Protopopov made a mixed impression on him. He observed that Protopopov's mind during one of his audiences at GHQ seemed to jump nervously from one subject to the next, and he wondered whether this was not in consequence of a disease which it was rumoured he had contracted some time before, and for which he had been treated by the Tibetan quack, Badmaev.[1] However, the Tsar's reservations about Protopopov made no difference. As the imperial couple grew progressively more isolated from their closest relatives and members of their household after the assassination, Protopopov became indispensable at the palace as adviser, source of information and executor of the Empress's schemes

At the same time, all his attempts to maintain at least outwardly tolerable relations with his former colleagues in the Duma failed completely. He had behaved in the most indiscreet way, advertising his close connection with the royal couple, stressing the emotional – and indeed devotional – character of these relations. Such an attitude was most provocative at a time when the Duma claimed that the power of the executive should not be bestowed by the monarch, but depend on the confidence of the legislative assemblies and the people. And Protopopov, in a grotesque gesture, contrived to add insult to injury by having a gendarme's uniform made for himself and wearing it at a Duma session.

Thus, after a final abortive attempt to come to some kind of understanding with his former associates in the Duma,[2] Protopopov became a symbolic figure to whom liberal circles now transferred the hatred they had previously concentrated on Rasputin. His manifest inefficiency as head of an important and complicated department and his lack of political tact lost him the sympathy even of his colleagues in the Council of Ministers. Both before and after January 1917, representations and loyal petitions for his resignation were made to the Tsar. The scene at the Winter Palace reception between him and Rodzyanko brought the liberals' antagonism to him into the open. His presence in the Cabinet was henceforth to become a major issue, with both the Tsar and the Duma refusing to relinquish their respective positions.[3]

1. See letters of 10 November 1916, *Letters of the Tsar to the Tsaritsa, 1914–1917* in English translation ed. C. E. Vulliamy (London, 1929), p. 297.
2. See the minutes of this meeting in Shlyapnikov, *Kanun 17-go goda*, 3rd edn. (Moscow/Petrograd, 1923), Part II, pp. 115–24.
3. Protopopov later reported that he had asked the Emperor for permission to challenge Rodzyanko to a duel, but that this had been refused. Rodzyanko himself told the Tsar in his usual, somewhat boorish manner of the Winter Palace incident at the next audience, which was granted him on 10 January. He attacked Protopopov personally, saying that he could have no respect for someone who had swallowed

As the time drew near for the opening of the next session of the State Duma, it became increasingly clear to Protopopov's colleagues on the Council of Ministers that he had become a political liability to the régime. The ministers began to realise that far from pursuing a bold and reactionary line, as Maklakov and Shcheglovitov had done in the summer of 1915, Protopopov was merely an amateur courtier who was exploiting the distraught state of the Empress and attempting to establish some kind of mystical link between himself and her based on the cult of Rasputin. They started a campaign against him which ran parallel to the denunciation of him from the Duma. But there were now no such contacts between members of the government and the leaders of the Progressive Bloc as there had been in August 1915, and the Duma did not know of the ministers' desperate efforts to rid themselves of Protopopov. The new Premier, Prince Golitsyn, who took over from Trepov on 26 December 1916 and was particularly liked and trusted by the Empress, finally took it upon himself to speak to both the Empress and the Emperor about the necessity of removing Protopopov. He received no answer from the Empress, who was displeased at this approach. A couple of days later, on 16 February, the Emperor told Golitsyn that he had decided not to remove Protopopov 'for the time being'.

There is something pathetic in the ambiguity of this reply. How was the Premier to interpret the words 'for the time being'? It sounded almost like an invitation to continue the pressure for Protopopov's removal until it could no longer be resisted. But the simple and honest Golitsyn could not have understood such a hint if there had been one, and the net effect of the Emperor's decision was to alienate him still further from his ministers. The realisation that the political advice they offered in a critical situation was unavailing must have demoralised the members of the Council of Ministers and prepared them for the course of action which they actually adopted on the night of 27–28 February.

such an insult. At the same time Rodzyanko apologised to the Emperor for his be-haviour in the palace. When Rodzyanko told Nicholas II that Protopopov had not even thought of challenging him, the Emperor merely smiled and said nothing. In the tense atmosphere of this audience this smile meant more than a rebuke. The very impunity with which the repeated cases of slanderous accusations and personal insults against members of the government were allowed to pass suggested a threat of a general reckoning after the situation at the front had cleared and victory was secured.

As the New Year reception was being held in Petrograd, Grand Duke Nikolay Nikolaevich was receiving local dignitaries in the distant Transcaucasian capital of Tiflis. Among those present was the Armenian mayor of the city, A. I. Khatisov. He had recently returned from Moscow, where he had gone as a delegate to the Congress of the Union of Municipalities, and where he had taken part in political discussions with the Chairmen of the Zemstvo and Municipality Unions, Prince Lvov and Chelnokov.

As Khatisov revealed in 1930 in Paris,[1] he asked the Grand Duke at the Tiflis reception to grant him an audience and was given an appointment for 3 p.m. on the same day. After explaining that he was acting on behalf of Prince Lvov, Khatisov revealed to Nikolay Nikolaevich that a plot was being hatched in Moscow to remove Nicholas II from the throne and proclaim the Grand Duke Emperor. The Tsar was to abdicate for himself and his son, while the Empress would be confined to a convent or banished abroad. The Grand Duke did not give an immediate answer, but summoned Khatisov to the Viceroy's Palace on 3 January, when, in the presence of his Chief of Staff, Yanushkevich, he told him that he refused to be a party to this conspiracy. According to Khatisov, the Grand Duke expressed doubts as to whether the people, the '*muzhiks*', would understand the necessity of overthrowing the Tsar at that moment, and whether the army would be sympathetic to such a course of action. The Grand Duke's doubts were confirmed by Yanushkevich; Khatisov took his leave and sent a pre-arranged telegram to Prince Lvov — 'The hospital cannot be opened' — indicating the Grand Duke's refusal.

The Grand Duke's popularity with the liberals went back to his dismissal from the High Command in August 1915. After that date unfounded rumours were circulated to the effect that his dismissal was due to an intrigue of Rasputin and the 'dark forces'.

Better founded was the widespread belief concerning the critical attitude adopted towards the Empress by the Grand Duke and his miniature court in Transcaucasia. These rumours must have reached the Tsar by various channels. Prince Shakhovskoy, the Minister of Trade and Industry, was astounded, when he visited the Caucasus in

1. Spiridovich, *Velikaya voyna*, vol. III, pp. 14 ff. See also an article by S. Smirnov in the Paris Russian journal, *Poslednie Novosti*, on 22 April 1928; and Melgunov, *Na putyakh*, pp. 105 ff.

1916, at the tone in which the Grand Duke's wife Anastasia spoke of the Empress in front of other people. He thought it necessary to report the conversation to the Emperor, who was not surprised, and said that he knew all about it.[1]

By October 1916, the Grand Duke had joined the other members of the Romanov family in attempting to persuade the Emperor to agree to constitutional concessions. On 5 November, he had a stormy interview with Nicholas at GHQ, declaring that if the reforms were not introduced the Emperor would lose his crown. He also charged the Emperor with suspecting him of sedition and of a desire to supplant him on the throne. The Emperor, he exclaimed, should be ashamed of himself. All this was met with the same baffling impassivity which, a few weeks later, was to cause much speculation and even doubts as to the Emperor's sanity. After this meeting, Grand Duke Nikolay Nikolaevich told his nephew, Grand Duke Andrey Vladimirovich, that he had given up hope of saving the Emperor from his wife and himself. The circumstances of Rasputin's assassination and the further deterioration in the political situation must have prepared the ground for the approach to the Grand Duke which the Moscow plotters made through Khatisov on 1 January 1917.

None of these Moscow conspirators revealed, at the outbreak of the revolution, their knowledge of the plan to elevate Nikolay Nikolaevich to the throne. Nor did the other generals whom they approached appear to have heard anything about it. This is not surprising. The Grand Duke, under whom — as Supreme Commander — they had all served, was not particularly popular among the generals. The approach to the Grand Duke, therefore, may well have been a personal idea of Prince Lvov, who had no need to discuss it with the other conspirators, in particular with Guchkov (who was the plotters' main link with the army).[2] It should be noted that this version of the palace coup envisaged the abdication of Nicholas II on his own behalf and on that of his son. And yet when the Tsar later abdicated on his son's behalf, he was accused[3] of having done so in contravention of the law of succession and with the aim of introducing a legal flaw into the instrument of abdication that would later allow him to declare it invalid.

1. See Shakhovskoy, op. cit., p. 181.
2. See the discussion of the Moscow plots in Melgunov, *Na putyakh*, particularly pp. 109 ff.   3. By Milyukov. See below, p. 352.

There is no indication that the Grand Duke, as was his duty, informed the competent authorities of Khatisov's approach. By his failure to do so the Grand Duke willy-nilly found himself party to a plot to overthrow Nicholas II and proclaim him Emperor in his stead – the very thing which, in his interview on 5 November, he had so sincerely and solemnly abjured. The false situation in which he had placed himself was not unlike Alekseev's when his correspondence with Guchkov became known. For both the Grand Duke and Alekseev, the abdication on 2 March must have relieved the strain placed on them by their embroilment in the plots hatched in Moscow despite their continuing allegiance to the Tsar.

2. PRINCE LVOV'S UNDELIVERED SPEECH

The two incidents at the 1917 New Year receptions showed the increasing isolation of the Tsar and his government from the country at large. The rumours of plans for a palace coup, given plausibility by the assassination of Rasputin, restricted the choice of persons to whom the Emperor could confidently entrust the direction of the various government departments. Moreover, the Voluntary Organisations were carrying out a systematic boycott of all those who might have co-operated with the Tsar, very much on the lines laid down by Disposition No. 1[1] of the mysterious Committee of Public Safety, quoted above.

In 1915, when the Disposition was written, the liberals still hoped to persuade the Tsar to accede to the demands of the Duma and the Voluntary Organisations. But now, in 1917, Prince Lvov thought it was too late for any such approach to the monarch. In a speech which he had prepared for the December (1916) Congress of Zemstvos in Moscow – a meeting dissolved by the police – Prince Lvov wrote:

> What we wanted to say fifteen months ago in a personal interview with the leader of the Russian people, what we whispered to each other then, has now become the clamour of the populace. . . . Should we now repeat the names of the secret medicine men and magicians in our state administration and reiterate our feelings of indignation, contempt and hatred? No, these feelings will not show us the way to salvation. Let us turn away

1. See above, p. 165 f.

from what is vile and contemptible. Let us not rub salt into the wounded
soul of our people. The Fatherland is in peril: from the State Council
and the State Duma to the most humble hovel, everybody feels the same.
... The old ulcer of the quarrel between the state power and society
has spread over our whole country like some leprous affliction, not
sparing the state apartments of the Tsar, and the country is suffering and
praying to be healed. ...

Prince Lvov concluded with the following practical instructions to
his followers:

Abandon all further attempts at constructive collaboration with the
present government; they are all doomed to failure and are only an
impediment to our aim. Do not indulge in illusions; turn away from
ghosts ! There is no longer a government ... the country needs a monarch
who would be protected by a government responsible to the country and
to the Duma.[1]

Rodzyanko's insult to Protopopov at the Winter Palace reception
was doubtless made in pursuance of the boycott proclaimed by Prince
Lvov.

With the abandonment by the head of the Voluntary Organisations
of all plans for an agreement with the government, the forcible removal
of the Emperor was now openly mooted in the army and the country
at large. After the murder of Rasputin, the notion of a palace coup
began to dominate the mind of the public, especially the intellectuals
and semi-intellectuals. Even among the members of the Romanov
family a patriotic attitude no longer implied allegiance to the reigning
monarch. The assassination, an act of rebellion profoundly humiliating
to the Emperor and his wife, was hailed by agitators throughout the
country as a 'podvig' — an act of patriotic self-sacrifice, like St George's
killing of the dragon, which had liberated the country from shameful
bondage.

In all this the Duma and the Progressive Bloc as such played no
conspicuous part. The legislative assemblies had been in recess since
December and no one knew exactly when they would resume their
deliberations. Yet, as we have seen, the President of the Duma continued

1. The text of the speech prepared by Prince Lvov is to be found in the appendices to
Shlyapnikov, *Kanun 17-go goda*, vol. II. Milyukov, in his memoirs, quotes it in a
slightly different version.

to press for constitutional reform, though without the least hope of influencing the Emperor, whose regard he had now forfeited.

3. THE THREATENED DISSOLUTION OF THE DUMA

A new element, however, came into the negotiations between the Tsar and Rodzyanko as the calendar marked the advent of 1917. This was the year when the legal powers of the Fourth Duma were due to expire, and new elections were to be held. In the past the government had relied on administrative pressure and the assistance of the Church authorities to secure the return to the Duma of right-wing deputies. Once again the government intended to resort to these methods, combining them, for the coming elections, with a well-financed press campaign. Stuermer and, later, Protopopov hoped to prevent the return to the Fifth Duma not only of the left-wing deputies, but even of the moderate and right-wing members who had proved so unaccommodating in the Fourth.[1]

The government's electoral plans were not the only reason why the impending dissolution of the Duma filled its president, Rodzyanko, with apprehension and fear. The Progressive Bloc, formed in the summer of 1915, hoped to use the opportunities afforded by war conditions to press for the long-desired constitutional reforms. This campaign was to be supported by the Voluntary Organisations, closely linked with the Duma opposition. In the bills they introduced, in their interpellations and questions in parliament, in their attacks on government malpractices from the tribune of the Duma, the members of the Progressive Bloc gave powerful support to the Voluntary Organisations in their demand for wider scope for their activities, and in their systematic efforts, from the autumn of 1915, to supplant the government bureaucracy in all vital branches of the war economy. For their part, the Voluntary Organisations, in their loyal addresses and resolutions, supported the constitutional demands of the Duma majority, thus becoming increasingly involved in the political struggle.[2]

If, however, the Duma was to be dissolved some time in 1917,

1. On the preparations for elections to the Fifth Duma, see the documents published by Semennikov, op. cit., pp. 233 ff.
2. See above, pp. 8–11.

without having obtained even the moderate concession of a 'Cabinet of Public Confidence', all their joint efforts would have been in vain. By the time the new Duma was elected, the war might well have ended, and the Voluntary Organisations have been disbanded, and perhaps brought to book for their real or pretended abuses in the expenditure of government money. Moreover, most of the politicians who so confidently claimed that victory could not be achieved without constitutional reform would have been contradicted by events, and would have incurred public ridicule. Such loss of face by the liberals would clear the way for reaction, and was therefore in the view of the Progressive Bloc to be avoided at all costs. The Progressive Bloc could not suffer political defeat at this stage without risking political annihilation. Whatever happened after the war, failure to reach their political goal in war conditions boded them no good. It was rumoured that after the war – especially in the event of victory – the constitution of 1906 might be revoked; a former Minister of the Interior, N. A. Maklakov, was known to be drafting an imperial manifesto to this effect. But even if, as other rumours had it, the Emperor himself were to take the initiative after the war and grant the desired constitutional reforms, this would hardly be of political advantage to the opposition members of the Fourth Duma: forces might come to the fore with less radical social and constitutional ideas than the Kadets and their allies of the Progressive Bloc. This is why the liberals never tired of pointing out to the government and the Tsar that revolutionary activities would be resumed with greater intensity after the war. Then, the liberals claimed, not only would the autocratic bureaucracy be swept away but so would all moderate progressive forces, and the country would be plunged into anarchy.[1]

The government was aware of the liberals' apprehensions in connection with the end of the Duma's term of office, and threatened the Duma with dissolution every time its debates became particularly violent. Now that the legislative period was drawing to an end, this threat became increasingly serious. The Duma had already taken certain measures to protect the political future of some of its leaders, should it be dissolved during the war. Thus the law establishing Special Defence Councils expressly laid down that members of the legislative assemblies

1. See the presentation of this argument in Guchkov's letter to Alekseev, quoted above, ch. 8, p. 183 f.

elected to these councils would remain in office, even if the Duma were dissolved or its term of office expired. But this regulation concerned only the twenty-four members of the legislative assemblies involved in the work of the Special Councils.

As the Fourth Duma's term of office was nearing its end, Rodzyanko launched a campaign to postpone the dissolution until the end of the war, invoking the practice of the Allied countries, which postponed general elections for the period of hostilities. In his last 'loyal report' of 10 February, Rodzyanko made this point quite clearly. After once again denouncing government policy, he attacked the Minister of the Interior Protopopov as follows:

> He threatens to suppress our concern by machine-gun fire; he resorts to large-scale arrests and deportations; he has restricted the press more than ever before. Should this kind of censorship be applied to the steno-graphic reports of the State Duma, this will lead to the same unhealthy occurrences as before. Apocryphal speeches of a seditious character ascribed to members of the Duma will start circulating as they did before, and will be disseminated by some invisible hand among the people and the army, undermining the authority of the legislative body, the only institution which now acts as a restraining factor.[1]
>
> The State Duma is threatened with dissolution; but at present, in its spirit of moderation, it lags far behind the country. In these circumstances the dissolution of the Duma will not calm the country, and should, which God forbid, a military defeat — even a partial one — befall us at this time, who would there be to raise the morale of the people?
>
> Besides, the country should have the certainty that when the Peace Conference assembles, the government will have the support of the people's representatives. Personal changes in the ranks of these

1. Rodzyanko was particularly disingenuous here. Speeches of a seditious character, such as that of Milyukov on 1 November 1916, were not 'apocryphal'. Their publication was certainly stopped by the censorship, but the President of the Duma himself refused to supply an unrevised stenographic report of the speech to Stuermer, who needed it to start a prosecution of the speaker. The 'invisible hand' which assisted the spreading of the speech among the people and the army was that of Guchkov, who organised its dissemination on such a scale that it was said that there was not a typewriter in Russia which had not been used to copy Milyukov's diatribe. It is true, of course, that the Duma circles were more moderate than certain newspapers and some of the revolutionary organisations. But the impact of things said in the Duma was considerably greater than anything the left-wing press could write, and therefore it was not true that the speeches of Duma members were a 'restraining factor'.

representatives at such a moment seem extremely dangerous, because it is impossible to foresee the results of such a measure [meaning new elections]. It is, therefore, necessary to settle without delay the question of extending the term of service of the present deputies of the State Duma, without making this conditional on the Duma's actions. The very condition the government lays down, when it says that the powers of the Duma may be extended only if it keeps the peace, is itself offensive, for it shows that the government neither requires to know, nor cares for, the true and sincere opinion of the country. Our Allies considered it both natural and necessary to extend the powers of their legislatures for the duration of the war.

The government's wavering and delay in adopting this measure convince us that it does not want contact with the people's representatives when peace negotiations begin. This, of course, increases anxiety, because the country has definitely lost confidence in the present government.[1]

The President of the Duma was much clearer when he formulated his demands than when he gave the reasons for them. It is difficult to understand how, in view of his immoderate and provocative language, he could have believed that his plea for an extension of the Duma's powers would be taken seriously. The only forceful argument in support of this plea was the threat of revolution. And Rodzyanko was unwilling to lessen this threat by promising greater moderation in the Duma debates, should the desired extension be granted. At the end of his report Rodzyanko writes:

> ... no heroic efforts which, as the Chairman of the Council of Ministers has suggested,[2] might be undertaken by the President of the State Duma could induce the State Duma to follow the dictates of the government, and should the President of the Duma take any initiative to this effect on his own behalf, he would hardly be doing his duty by the people's representatives and by the country as a whole. Should this happen, the Duma would lose the confidence of the country, and then no doubt the country — unable to bear the burdens caused by the confusion in the administration — would rise in defence of its legitimate rights. This should not be allowed to happen; it should be avoided at all costs; and to do so is our basic task.

According to Rodzyanko, the Tsar should have appreciated the

---

1. From Rodzyanko's last 'loyal report' in *ARR*, VI (1922), p. 335.
2. Prince Golitsyn had recently made a conciliatory appeal in these terms to Rodzyanko.

Duma's function as a safety-valve which restrained popular discontent from boiling over into revolutionary action. But, in fact, it was inflammatory speeches from the Duma rostrum that were whipping up this popular discontent. The liberals may well have been sincere in professing their desire to avoid a revolution. But they certainly hoped that the threat of revolutionary action, brought nearer by their agitation in the Duma, would sooner or later force the government to concede constitutional reforms and transfer control of the administration to them.

4. THE LIBERALS' APPEAL TO THE ALLIES

Knowing how little weight his representations carried with the Emperor, Rodzyanko sought support elsewhere for the prorogation of the Duma. He tried to enlist the sympathies of people who could explain the situation in the country to Lord Milner, head of the British Mission to the Inter-Allied Conference then meeting in Petrograd, in the hope of getting him to intercede in favour of an extension. Among the significant documents of the period (February 1917) are two letters addressed to Lord Milner by Professor P. B. Struve on 7 and 19 February. They clearly expressed the uncertainties and anxieties which beset one of the most penetrating minds in Russia on the eve of the revolution.[1]

In his first letter, Struve placed the responsibility for the wartime breakdown of national unity squarely on the government and the crown.

It is impossible sufficiently to emphasise the fact that by its reactionary policy the Crown is weakening precisely the most moderate and cultured

1. P. B. Struve was a prominent member of the Kadet Party who was serving under Prince Vsevolod Shakhovskoy as chairman of a committee dealing with the economic blockade of Germany. In this capacity he was in touch with a young British diplomat, Samuel Hoare, through whom the two letters quoted in the text were conveyed to Lord Milner. Sir Samuel Hoare later published them in a book of reminiscences, *The Fourth Seal* (London, 1930). In the nineties, Struve had been one of the leading lights of the early Marxist movement in Russia. He later became editor of the influential organ of the radical Russian intelligentsia, *Osvobozhdenie*, which appeared in Stuttgart. His disillusionment with the theoretical and philosophical content of Marxism and his aversion to revolutionary practice attracted him to the Kadet Party, and in particular to its right wing. As a scholar and publicist he felt free to communicate his views on current affairs to Lord Milner and Samuel Hoare.

sections of the community, cutting away the ground from beneath the feet of patriotically-minded elements, and is letting loose state Nihilism.

Hence comes the feeling, that is to be found everywhere in Russia, and with which, too, officer circles in the army are deeply affected, that the conflict between Crown and people has really done nothing less than set Russia face to face with a state revolution. The patriotically-minded elements of society and of the army are fully conscious of the enormous historical responsibility that attaches to internal conflict in time of war, and it is only this consciousness that explains the complete calm that reigns in a country where all thinking people are continually meditating and discussing the tragic difficulty of the situation. The difficulty is further intensified by the fact that common report declares that the persons who stand nearest to the Crown are pro-German in their sympathies. This view cannot now be uprooted from the public mind by any mere words. Only a reorganised government, so organised as to allow of complete control and enjoying national confidence, can clear this unhealthy atmosphere of suspicion and fear which is at present fettering the national energy.

However distasteful it is to testify before foreigners, even though allies, to such a state of mind and such political conditions in one's own country, it is none the less essential that this testimony should be given. For we must maintain the solidarity between the Allies, before which all the more or less conventional considerations that are perhaps necessary in time of peace fall to the ground.

At present all well-intentioned and politically educated persons have only one wish: that the Crown should not commit an irrevocable and absolutely unjustifiable act by dissolving the Imperial Duma under the pretext that its mandate has expired and that new elections must be carried out.

This step would finally compromise the Crown and would at the same time weaken the conservative state elements in the country, who have united for the national purposes of carrying on the war and of bringing it to a successful conclusion. A fateful part in events is evidently being played by the present Minister of the Interior, who has entirely lost the esteem of his fellow-countrymen of all schools of thought, and can scarcely even be considered a psychologically normal person.

It should be noted that the old cry, 'struggle with bureaucracy', has lost its meaning. In the present conflict all the best elements of bureaucracy are on the side of the people.

Such is the present state of affairs in Russia.[1]

1. Sir Samuel Hoare, op. cit., pp. 189–91.

In his second letter, dated 19 February 1917 (obviously New Style), Struve wrote that he could not believe in a 'conscious Machiavellian calculation' on the part of the Tsar's advisers to make impossible Russia's continued participation in the war. But he admitted that such beliefs were widespread and ingrained in the minds of the people, and that a constitutional change was the only means of restoring the national unity without which the war could not be fought.

Struve wrote in his second letter:

> It is evident that well-ordered organisation of the whole economic life of the country, an organisation that would combine economy of resources with the maximum of effort, is possible only under certain politico-psychological conditions. An economic organisation of the nation, demanding, as it does, complete subordination of personal and class interests to the national task of carrying on the war, is possible only if a government is created that enjoys the confidence of the nation and is in a position to appeal with the greatest possible internal authority to all persons and groups. Thus the food question ... inevitably raises in Russia the political question. Unless the latter question is solved, the sacrifices that are demanded from the whole population for the further prosecution of the war in its third and fourth year will be less and less willingly borne.[1]

The two memoranda which Struve handed to Lord Milner were obviously written after consultation with other leaders of the liberal opposition. Prince Lvov's part in drafting the second letter is attested to by Samuel Hoare, while the deployment of the main argument in the first corresponds closely to the 'loyal report' of Rodzyanko to the Tsar dated three days later.

But what was the point of involving Lord Milner in these matters? The liberals had been pressing Allied diplomats in Petrograd for months to intercede with the Emperor in favour of their political demands. Both Sir George Buchanan and Maurice Paléologue were sympathetic. The British Ambassador had swallowed whole the propaganda of the Progressive Bloc, and with singular lack of diplomatic tact had revealed his political sympathies to the Emperor.[2] Doubtless he was

1. Ibid., pp. 194–95.
2. In particular during his last audience with the Tsar on 30 December 1916 (12 January 1917, New Style). See Buchanan's account in *My Mission to Russia* (2 vols, London, 1923), vol. II, ch. 22.

moved by a desire to prevent a breakdown of the Russian war machinery at a moment when it was to be put to the supreme test. But Sir George Buchanan was mistaken about the possible effectiveness of his unsought and thinly disguised advice to the Emperor to yield to opposition demands, just as he was mistaken in judging the liberals competent to administer the country after the projected change. It seems that Buchanan never realised how objectionable his interference in Russian internal politics was in the eyes of Nicholas II. The only result was an estrangement between the Emperor and the British Ambassador.

Now, through Lord Milner, a new attempt was made to influence the Tsar. Struve's moderation, which was to contrast favourably with the wild rumours of government sabotage and pro-German intrigues, made him a particularly well-placed spokesman of the liberals in approaching Milner. If 'even a man like Struve', who claimed to disbelieve these rumours, was satisfied that the obstinacy of the government and the Emperor was damaging the nation's war effort, then the Allied representatives might well be expected to do something about it.

5. LORD MILNER'S INTERVENTION

Samuel Hoare writes that Struve's memoranda produced little impression on the tired, disillusioned and disgruntled Lord Milner. We possess, however, the Russian translation of a highly confidential document presented to the Emperor by Milner towards the end of his stay in Russia. In this some of Struve's arguments are echoed.[1] In this letter Lord Milner was far more cautious and diplomatic in proffering political advice and possibly less ingenuous as to the reliability of his liberal informants than was the British Ambassador.

He began by welcoming the decision to launch a concerted offensive in the spring in accordance with a timetable agreed by the Allies. He went on to discuss the question of the distribution among the Allies of war materials and strategic supplies in the broad sense (railway equipment, raw materials, funds). Faced at the conference table with exorbitant demands, Milner thought it necessary to explain to the Emperor that there were limits to the assistance which the Allies could

1. Full text in Russian in Semennikov, *Monarkhiya pered krusheniem*, pp. 77–85. The quotations given here are re-translations from the Russian.

give to Russia – limits determined by the principle of the optimal use of the war supplies available. The question to be considered in each individual case, according to Milner, was whether the transfer of war material from the Allies to Russia would increase the general military potential of the Entente and the probability of a decisive success during the spring and summer offensive. Treading on more dangerous ground, Milner pointed out that the Allies, when providing Russia with supplies of which they themselves were in dire need, ought to have some guarantee that Russia's own resources for such supplies had been fully tapped. This brought him near the question of the internal organisation of the war effort in Russia. Arguing on lines frequently used by the liberals, Milner stated:

> In the face of the magnificent work of such new and voluntary organisations as the Zemstvo and Municipalities Unions, it is impossible to doubt the capacity of the Russian people to rise to the increasing danger and improvise new methods to avert it. What has been done in Russia in this respect has made a particular impression on me, because it bears out the lessons we have learned in England in wartime.
>
> The old machinery was faced with a task above its capacity. We would never have been able to deal with it had we not created a large number of new organisations, enrolled public service volunteers to help government officials and even given these volunteers high executive posts. I am speaking of people who for their whole life had been concerned with their private affairs and had no experience whatever of official business.

This is as far as Lord Milner thought it right to go in support of the political demands of the liberals. But he indicated clearly that he had obtained from liberal circles in Moscow certain information about the mismanagement of Russian war resources. According to him, at a time when France and England had reached the limit of their wartime industrial productivity, the same could not be said of Russia:

> Russia has not been able as yet to use its own resources to the full. When I was in Moscow I was told that millions of people were mobilised for service at the front, whom it was impossible either to train or to arm, and who therefore, although taken away from industry, did not contribute anything towards the military potential of the country. Apart from that, there are thousands of people at the front who would be more useful in the mines and in the factories. . . . Besides, although factories are being closed, there is no absolute shortage of coal, nor of rolling-stock for

coal transport; the distribution and turnover of the available rolling-stock
is, however, carried out most inefficiently. I am not in a position personally to substantiate this contention. I can only say that this has come to
my knowledge from many independent sources which deserve confidence and are obviously well-informed.[1]

Lord Milner ended his memorandum with a proposal which again
showed his doubts as to the Russian authorities' capacity to benefit
from Allied aid. He suggested that technicians from the supplying
countries should accompany all the special equipment sent to the
Russian armies, to make sure that it was properly transported, delivered
and used at the front. The apology accompanying this humiliating
demand speaks for itself. Milner wrote:

> There can be no question of interference in the affairs of the Russian
> military authorities. We only request to be allowed to satisfy ourselves
> that the military supplies which we are giving to Russia are transmitted
> in full to their destination, that we are giving Russia not only the machines
> but also our experience in handling them, acquired at considerable cost
> to ourselves, that these machines will reach the front in the shortest
> possible time, and in a condition to render maximum service there.

However cautious and reticent Lord Milner's hints at the desirability
of constitutional reforms in Russia, in the tense atmosphere of February
1917 they could only be taken to indicate Allied lack of confidence in
the Tsarist government's ability to increase productivity to a level
comparable with that of the Western Allies. The remedy, Milner
indicated, was an appeal to the Voluntary Organisations for increased
participation in the war effort. But it was obvious at this juncture, after
Prince Lvov's tirades at the December Congress of Zemstvos, that the
Voluntary Organisations would allow no one to work for the government unless their collaboration were purchased by political concessions.

6. THE CONFLICT UNRESOLVED

Rodzyanko's 'loyal report', Struve's letters to Milner and Milner's own
confidential memorandum to the Emperor sum up the position in

1. One of these was certainly Struve, who insisted on the need for a national pool of
military and industrial manpower — a point which Milner also made in the memorandum.

Tsar Nicholas II, Emperor of Russia 1894–1917, after the portrait by
Valentin Serov.

M. V. Rodzyanko, President of the Third and Fourth Dumas, Octobrist, and

Colonel S. N. Myasoedov, gendarme and intelligence officer. He was executed
in 1915 as a German spy, though he was probably innocent.

Prince G. E. Lvov, Chairman of the Union of Zemstvos and head of the Provisional Government until July 7, 1917.

A. F. Kerensky, member of the Fourth Duma, head of the Trudovik faction, member of the Duma Provisional Committee, and Deputy Chairman of the Petrograd Soviet. He was the first Provisional Government's Minister of Justice, then its Premier, Minister of War, and Supreme Commander-in-Chief.

P. N. Milyukov, leader of the Kadet Party and Minister of Foreign Affairs in the first Provisional Government.

A. I. Guchkov, at one time President of the Third Duma, member of the State Council, and Chairman of the Central WIC. He was Minister of War in the first cabinet of the Provisional Government.

Berlin, den 3. Dezember 1917.   zu A S 4456.

112

                                                  Tel. Hughes 1. Z.

                                         Auf Tel. No. 1771.

-tit- Lersner   Die Sprengung der Entente und in der Folge

No: 1925   eine und genehme Bildung politischer Com-

                                         binationen ist das wichtigste diplomatische

                                         Kriegsziel. Als schwächstes Glied in der

                                         feindlichen Kette erschien der russische

                                         Ring; es galt daher, ihn allmählich zu lockern

                                         und wenn möglich herauszulösen. Diesem Zweck

                                         diente die destruktive Arbeit, die wir hinter

                                         der Front in Russland vornehmen liessen,

                                         in erster Linie die Förderung der

                                         separatistischen Tendenzen und die Unter-

                                         stützung der Bolschewiki. Erst die Mittel,

                                         die den Bolschewiki auf verschiedenen Kanä-

                                         len und unter wechselnder Etikette von unse-

                                         rer Seite zugeflossen sind, haben es ihnen

                                         ermöglicht, die "Prawda", ihr Hauptorgan,

                                         auszugestalten und die anfangs schmale Basis

                                         ihrer Partei mächtig zu verbreitern. Die

                                         Bolschewiki sind nun zur Herrschaft gelangt;

                                                                              wie

PUBLIC RECORD OFFICE, LONDON

Text of a telegram from the German Minister of Foreign Affairs to the Kaiser
about subsidies paid to the Bolsheviks.

Students and soldiers firing across·the Moyka at the police.

Reading the newssheets issued by the Duma in front of the Tauride Palace.

Znamensky Square with the statue of Alexander III.

A street barricade.

the contest between the autocratic régime and the liberal opposition
in February 1917. The conflict remained unresolved. Since 1915, those
who were trying to overcome the obstinacy of the Emperor by means
of pressure of various kinds, intimidation and isolation had succeeded
in all but the principal aim. They had launched a gigantic campaign
against the government, the Empress and the Tsar in the press and
Duma, and through the covert dissemination of denunciatory speeches
and letters. They had succeeded in rousing the so-called 'educated
classes' and inculcating in them the belief that they were being betrayed
by those at the top and cheated of the victory that would have been
theirs, had the liberals taken over the business of government.

This propaganda affected the middle ranks of the civil service and of
the military administration, who grew more and more critical of their
own hierarchy; they were ready to shift their allegiance to the service
of the leadership of the Voluntary Organisations. As Struve said in his
first letter to Milner, 'The old cry "Struggle with bureaucracy" has lost
its meaning. In the present conflict all the best elements of the bureaucracy are on the side of the people.'

As this propaganda filtered through to the illiterate lower strata of
the population and the army it lost much of its political content, leaving
only a sediment of mistrust and a suspicion that 'the gentry' had some
kind of understanding with the Germans.

Two years after the February revolution, Struve was to revise his
ideas on the pre-revolutionary situation in Russia as laid down in his
letters to Lord Milner. In two lectures delivered in Rostov-on-Don,[1]
Struve ascribed the lack of understanding of Russian affairs prevailing
in England and France to the inadequate information provided by the
Russian intelligentsia:

> We criticised our country far too ruthlessly, and abused it in front of
> foreigners. We did not show sufficient consideration for its dignity and
> historical past.[2]

Speaking of pre-revolutionary days, Struve shifted the blame for the
rift between the government and the liberal intelligentsia on to the latter:

> When the war broke out the government and the public carried on a
> more or less open struggle against each other, and the enemies of Russia

1. Published as a pamphlet under the title 'Razmyshleniya o russkoy revolyutsii'
(Sofia, 1921).   2. Ibid., p. 6.

reckoned with this as an element in her weakness and degradation. The régime was blinded, but so was, to an even greater extent, public opinion, which did not see the enormous danger of revolutionism which infiltrated the popular masses, corrupted their virtue and prepared the collapse of the State.

When thunderous speeches against the government were pronounced in the State Duma, the Duma orators did not realise what was happening outside the Duma, in the minds of the anti-state elements and in the people's soul. The overwhelming majority of Russian intellectuals did not understand the people's psychology and did not grasp the tragic importance of the moment. They thought that they had a duty to carry on the struggle with the government in the name of patriotism. But now it is of course clear to everybody that the only reasonable course of action from a historical point of view would have been the greatest reticence. This must be said of the Duma and of the Press.[1]

The liberals' success in enlisting the support of public opinion both in Russia and abroad did not bring them a step nearer the political solution they desired. The Emperor was adamant in refusing to comtemplate a political change before the outcome of the war was decided. He had the full support of his wife, who believed that a victorious end to the war would lead to an apotheosis of her husband's rule, in the afterglow of which the subsequent reign of her dearly beloved, weak and sickly son would be safeguarded. It was a pathological illusion, nurtured by a lifetime of frustration and betrayed hopes. Yet she and Nicholas II were right in thinking it expedient for the autocratic régime to put off resolving the political conflict with the liberals until after the war was over. A change of régime — even the appointment of a 'government of public confidence' headed by Rodzyanko or Prince Lvov — might easily have started a landslide of internal political developments which would have made the effective prosecution of the war as difficult as did the actual revolution of 1917.

On the other hand, even if the struggle between the liberals and the autocracy was to be resumed after victory, those politicians who had forecast the impossibility of such a victory without previous constitutional reforms, who had given credence to the slanderous rumours of the Empress's collaboration with the Germans, or who had claimed, without a trace of evidence, that the Prime Minister, Stuermer, would

1. Ibid., p. 6.

betray the country at the peace conference, would have suffered great discomfiture, and their political future would have been gravely compromised. Only a few weeks remained until the date fixed for the spring offensive, when an upsurge of patriotic feeling could be expected to divert the attention of the public from internal strife. If the Tsar and the régime had stood firm for another few weeks, the game would have been up for the Progressive Bloc and the Voluntary Organisations.

This must have been clearly understood by all concerned, although no one dared admit it. The liberals and radicals of all shades claimed to be concerned about the outcome of what was expected to be the last summer of the war, repeating that there could be no certain victory without immediate constitutional reform. But the fear of defeat and humiliation of Russia was, if we are not mistaken, only the ostensible and avowable expression of an unavowable, deep-seated fear that the war might end in victory before the political aspirations of the opposition had been fulfilled, and that the exceptional opportunities offered for their fulfilment by war conditions would be lost. The systematic substitution for this fear (which most of the politicians concerned would not have dared to confess even to themselves) of another, which was patriotic and could be openly proclaimed, reminds us of the mechanism regulating the formation of dreams. Indeed, in many respects, the psychology of the 1917 revolution, with its weakening of conventional moral and rational controls, its mythomania, and the importance of verbal symbolism, has many parallels with the psychology of dreams.[1]

7. LABOUR, REVOLUTIONARIES AND POLICE ON THE EVE OF THE FEBRUARY EVENTS

The first two months of 1917 were also marked by a dramatic development in the situation of the Labour Groups of the WICs. We have seen that these Groups had been formed in the face of violent opposition from Bolshevik agitators among the workers, and not without a certain amount of mistrust on the part of the industrialists who were taking

1. This unusual interpretation of the revolutionary mentality has been put forward by a Russian Freudian scholar, Dr N. E. Osipov, in his article 'Son i revolyutsiya' ('Dream and revolution'), *Trudy russkogo narodnogo universiteta* (Prague, 1931).

part in the WICs. The politically-minded leaders of this organisation were, however, firmly intent on supporting the Labour Groups, to which representatives of the defensist Socialist parties had been elected.

The Labour Groups were headed by K. Gvozdev, a basically honest man who had been forced into an untenable position by his conflict with the Bolsheviks. In order to fight their accusations of treason to the workers, 'selling-out' to imperialism and so on, he had to adopt demagogic, 'crypto-revolutionary' language which made his speeches almost indistinguishable from those of his Bolshevik detractors. Thus, at the All-Russian Congress of Representatives of the WICs in Petrograd on 26–29 February 1916, Gvozdev, claiming to speak in the name of workers' delegations from twenty towns, was reported by the police to have said that:

> although the working class was in favour of the earliest possible end to the fratricidal war, it was nevertheless in duty bound to take part in the defence of the various belligerent countries to prevent their total destruction. By taking part in the war the workers were paving the way for peace without annexations or reparations, which could be obtained as soon as the people took negotiations into their own hands instead of entrusting them to diplomats. It was not true that the war was waged in order to destroy German militarism: such slogans merely conceal a desire for territorial aggrandisement. After castigating the Tsarist régime, Gvozdev claimed that the government was preparing an anti-Jewish pogrom to divert popular indignation from itself. His speech closed with a demand for an All-Russian Workers' Congress and with the slogan: 'The country is in dire peril; there can be no salvation without the people or against the people.' Gvozdev's speech was greeted with general applause.[1]

The subsequent speakers even surpassed Gvozdev in their revolutionary rhetoric. The secret police agent, Abrosimov, accused the leaders of the WICs of being at heart on the side of the old régime – not on that of the people. A workers' delegate from Samara, a certain Kaptsan, who was particularly violent, declared: 'We workers do not call upon you to fight for power merely with words. We know how this is to be done; we offer you industrialists the support of the workers regardless of the sacrifices we may have to make.'

According to the police, private meetings of the Labour Groups took

1. Fleer, pp. 285 ff.

place at the same time as the Congress under the chairmanship of Abrosimov: it was decided at these meetings to establish a comprehensive network of workers' cells which would propagate on a nation-wide basis the ideas openly ventilated at the Congress.[1]

But however violent and demagogic the statements of Gvozdev and other members of the Labour Groups might have appeared, their actual advice to the workers on strike action and other revolutionary activities had a moderating influence and favoured the smooth working of the war industry. Thus we know that the strike movement of February 1916, instigated by German agents and supported by the Petrograd Bolsheviks, failed largely because of the restraining advice of Gvozdev and his friends in the WIC.[2] Gvozdev acted under the influence not only of Konovalov – with Guchkov's associate, Nekrasov, the main supporter of the Labour Groups inside the WIC – but also probably on the advice of Kerensky, who, while building up his popularity by extremist oratory in the Duma, used his influence to keep the wheels of war industry turning.

The secret police were informed of this situation, and were pursuing a policy of their own, not interfering with the Labour Groups for the time being, while carefully recording all the unmistakably seditious statements of their leaders. Their intention was of course to furnish material for an eventual prosecution of the members of the Labour Groups at an opportune moment. The general tenor of the speeches and declarations quoted in the police reports could not have been invented, though some sharp phrases may have been interpolated by their agent, Abrosimov. Typically, the Chairman of the Congress of 1916, Konovalov, and the Chairman of the labour section of the Congress, Nekrasov, did not consider it necessary to warn the labour representatives against going too far in their declarations. The Congress was attended by representatives of the War Ministry, who protested to Konovalov and Nekrasov about the speeches of the labour deputies, pointing out that from a military point of view the concepts of army and government were closely interconnected. Only after this did the Chairman intervene to urge moderation upon the speakers. During the rest of the year, the Labour Groups were allowed to carry on their activities unhindered until the arrests of January and February 1917.

The reluctance of the police to interfere with the activities of the

1. Fleer, p. 291.   2. See ch. 5 p. 94.

Labour Groups was calculated. The director of the Police Department reported on 30 October 1916 that

> at the present moment, owing to the conscription of many party organ-
> isers and the dispersal of other members of the revolutionary parties among
> all kinds of voluntary organisations working for the war effort, the revolu-
> tionary organisations as such have almost ceased to exist. The attempts of
> individual active party members or of small groups to resume revolu-
> tionary work by taking advantage of legal opportunities (for instance,
> under cover of the Labour Groups of the WIC) are under close surveil-
> lance by the criminal investigation department which is reporting on
> them.[1]

This meant that the police were satisfied that they had the Labour Groups under close observation and that they did not expect any unpleasant surprises from that quarter.

Yet the Minister of the Interior, Protopopov, decided to strike, and on 27 January 1917 arrested the Labour Group of the Central WIC in Petrograd. This move requires an explanation, but we find it neither in the fragmentary reports on the Labour Group's activities nor in the confused statements which Protopopov made in prison after the revolution. It is clear, however, that the arrests were not provoked by any new political developments inside the Labour Groups. These, as we have seen, were solidly infiltrated by the secret police through their agent, Abrosimov, who was Gvozdev's deputy. But we also know that Abrosimov posed as a fire-eater among the members of the Labour Group, and systematically incited his colleagues to compromise themselves by extremist statements and actions. It is much more likely that the arrests of 27 January were actually aimed not so much at the Labour Group itself as at the WICs as a whole, and especially at its head, Guchkov, whom Protopopov had every reason to hate and fear, for he had shown himself an implacable and persistent enemy of the imperial couple and of all their supporters. By referring the case against the Labour Group to the State Prosecutor's Office, Protopopov obviously intended to stage a trial which would expose the Guchkov organisation as seditious. This, in Protopopov's eyes, would be an appropriate and effective reply to the liberal opposition, who were alleging pro-German tendencies and lack of patriotism in the govern-

1. See Grave, op. cit., pp. 136 ff.

ment. It is also consistent with Protopopov's mentality to have prepared his vengeance on his political enemies by arresting the Labour
Group, while forgetting that the destruction of this organisation would
deprive him of a means of controlling the capital's workers and of the
services of his agent, Abrosimov.

In this over-optimistic attitude Protopopov was probably encouraged
by the secret police's low opinion of the Labour Group's influence.
Indeed, the apathetic reaction of the Petrograd workers to the arrest
of their representatives was typical of the situation. The workers seemed
to accept the arrests in the spirit of the Russian proverb: 'Don't say no
to prison or purse.'

It appears that Guchkov became immediately conscious of the danger
which the arrest of the Labour Group meant for his organisation,
particularly for Nekrasov and himself. He rushed to Petrograd to seek
support in Duma circles for a demand for their immediate release. He
kept in close touch with Gvozdev, who, for reasons of health, was
allowed by the police to remain under house arrest. But he did not fare
well with the Duma leaders. Milyukov showed no interest in making a
special issue out of the Labour Group's arrests in the general attack on
the government as a whole, and discouraged appeals to the workers to
demonstrate. On the contrary, when workers' representatives with
whom he had just entered into contact came to see him about a
demonstration planned for 14 February, he advised them to refrain
from it in case it compromised the Duma's efforts to obtain constitutional concessions from the Tsar.

The Bolshevik leaders in Petrograd, for their part, were against
supporting those whom they had denounced as traitors to the working
class now that they had, through their own fault, become the victims of
a political ambush by their capitalist patrons The Petrograd Bolsheviks
had not forgotten their failure in organising protest demonstrations
against the arrest, trial and deportation of their own leaders, the five
Bolsheviks in the Duma, in 1915. Then they had only been able to
bring out a couple of thousand workers in partial strikes; and now
they had no particular desire to expose themselves in a protest action
against the persecution of Mensheviks.

Ironically, the only people to benefit from this imbroglio were the
arrested members of the Labour Group themselves. When, on 27
February, Gvozdev, who had been transferred on the very eve of the

revolution to the Kresty Prison, was liberated by the demonstrators and arrived at the Tauride Palace, he could claim to be a martyr of the Tsarist régime, and so triumph over his Bolshevik detractors.

The Secret Police were evidently expecting an outbreak of workers' discontent by the end of February. The head of the Petrograd branch, General Globachev,[1] reported to the Minister of the Interior that tension had been mounting since the beginning of 1917, and predicted that riots were imminent. But Globachev thought the expected riots would have no definite political aim, and were more likely to take the form of anti-Jewish or anti-German pogroms than to be a prelude to a social revolution.

Globachev's report was of great importance and influenced government security measures. Orders were issued in February to bring up fresh troops to the southern and south-eastern approaches to the capital.[2]

The maintenance of order in the capital in case of local disturbances was still in the first instance the concern of the police, nearly six thousand strong. In the event of the police proving inadequate, the government intended to use against the rioters the enormously swollen garrison of second- and third-class troops. These consisted predominantly of untrained and recently mobilised young recruits, advanced age groups of reservists, and soldiers recuperating after illness or wounds. Overcrowded barracks and the temptations and attractions of a large city had led to a weakening of discipline. The officers were serving in the capital mainly because of some disability which prevented them from going to the front. Their appointment was provisional and casual, and relations with their men were impersonal. In these conditions they were unable to raise the morale of the troops or even form an adequate notion of their reliability. Already in the spring and autumn of 1916 there had been instances of troops joining with the workers in demonstrations in the suburbs. In the autumn of 1916 the police authorities asked the Headquarters of the Petrograd Military District to remove the 181st infantry reserve regiment from one of the

1. See E. Martynov, *Tsarskaya armiya v fevralskom perevorote* (Moscow, 1927) and Grave, op. cit., pp. 188 ff.
2. We have found no reliable confirmation of Protopopov's subsequent allegations to the effect that the Emperor's orders to muster cavalry units from the front were deliberately sabotaged by plotting generals, including Gurko, and that less reliable troops were moved into the suburbs instead.

suburbs because of its alleged close and seditious contacts with the workers of that district, who were planning a strike and demonstrations. The Commander of the Petrograd Military District explained that the unit in question had become unusually large (over twelve thousand), and that in view of the difficulty of finding alternative accommodation for such numbers, the 181st regiment would have to stay where it was until the general evacuation or dispersal plans for Petrograd could be put into operation.[1] The incident shows a certain nervousness and loss of self-confidence on the part of the police and, on the part of the military, a certain complacency and want of political imagination.

The crisis caused by the lack of mutual understanding and co-ordination between the police and the military authorities came to a head during the February riots. The Petrograd Military District had been removed from the command of the northern front under General Ruzsky and placed under the direct jurisdiction of the Minister of War and in case of emergency of the Council of Ministers. This measure did not contribute to improved relations between the police and the military authorities under the newly-appointed Commander of the Petrograd Military District, General Khabalov. On the other hand, the police forces, under the administration of Protopopov, were themselves disorganised. The city police, the Secret Police, and the corps of gendarmes — all formed part of a complicated bureaucratic administration under the Minister of the Interior. The city police had just been taken over by a new chief, Balk, and the Okhrana was considerably disorganised as a result of the intrigues, culminating in the assassination of Rasputin, in which it had become involved in 1916. According to General Spiridovich, Protopopov was incapable of directing the crucial departments of his office, which were left without proper guidance.

8. THE EMPEROR'S ISOLATION AND HIS GENERALS

The alienation of the supreme ruler from the members of his government completed the process of isolation to which his own obstinacy and the systematic efforts of the opposition had contributed in equal measure. There was literally no one except his wife with whom at that

1. Fleer, p. 309.

time the Emperor could freely discuss the political situation and his plans for action. After the murder of Rasputin he took nobody into his confidence, least of all the few courtiers who were his day-to-day companions. Such people as the Palace Commandant, Voeykov, or Admiral Nilov, or the aide-de-camp officers in charge were merely social acquaintances with whom the Emperor would go for walks or play an occasional game of dominoes. Political matters were never discussed at meals or during the walks on which these people accompanied him. Only persons whose duty it was to raise such questions would do so at official audiences. Discussions might then take place, but once the Emperor had expressed an opinion it was useless and even dangerous to oppose him: dangerous because this would break the mutual confidence existing between official and monarch which was based on the assumption of total obedience; useless because, although the Emperor often changed his mind, he would never do so on the strength of an argument put forward in a discussion following the announcement of a decision. The Emperor, although intelligent, was intellectually diffident, and would not trust his own ability to refute a skilfully-presented argument against some decision at which he had arrived after much heart-searching and after weighing the opinions of the few people whom he trusted. In the last weeks of his reign the number of such people dwindled until only his wife remained, and even here he seems to have had certain doubts as to the soundness of her judgment. At any rate, her reiterated claims to be his most assiduous and devoted helper indicate that the role to which she aspired was not unreservedly accepted by her husband.

Of course, at the eleventh hour there were attempts to break through the wall of silence with which the Emperor had surrounded himself and to represent to him the necessity for a political change. On relinquishing his post as acting Chief of Staff, General Gurko was received on 13 February at Tsarskoe Selo. He later claimed to have interceded most earnestly in favour of immediate constitutional reform. Gurko must have presented many forceful arguments, particularly since he had just presided at the Inter-Allied Conference. He was given to understand that his efforts were uncalled-for. In an entry in his diary for that date, the Emperor merely complains that Gurko detained him for so long that he was too late to attend Vespers.[1]

1. See above, p. 47, and Emperor's diary entry of 13 February 1917.

In a sense, the futility at this late stage of approaches such as Gurko's was self-evident. All the reasons for and against immediate constitutional reform and the appointment of a 'government of confidence' had been presented and discussed in numerous memoranda in the course of the previous months. The formation of a 'government of confidence' was seen as a panacea for all ills: deficiencies in supply, military weakness, and social and economic unrest.

Yet it was clear to most of those who proposed this measure — and to the Emperor as well — that the main purpose was to force him to surrender the autocratic power he exercised in the appointment of heads of government departments, and that the promise of an improvement in the serious situation in the country which might result from such a change was ill-founded. With the approach of the critical summer of 1917, in which a supreme military effort, in conjunction with a similar effort on the part of the Allies, was to be attempted at the front, a change in the government and administration, with the inevitable concentration of public attention on issues of internal policy, appeared nonsensical to Nicholas II. On the other hand, liberals like Prince Lvov felt more and more that, should they fail to achieve the political aim for which they had been working ever since 1905 — in wartime conditions in which they could exercise maximum pressure — they would lose their political fight altogether, and the future destinies of Russia would develop independently of their ideas and aspirations. They therefore redoubled their efforts and succeeded in February 1917, for the second time during the war, in persuading the majority of the Council of Ministers that the government would be unable to continue successfully with the prosecution of the war if political concessions were refused.

However, this time the ministers did not enter into any collusion with the Duma opposition circles. So great was the conviction that the Emperor would prove unable to continue his resistance to political reform that even in well-informed government circles in Petrograd it was widely believed that, after the opening of the Duma on 14 February, the Emperor would proceed to one of the meetings and suddenly proclaim the establishment of a 'government of confidence', or of a cabinet responsible to the legislature.

Like many people who suffer from a deficiency of willpower, the Emperor, every time he had to reach a decision, liked to weigh against each other the arguments for and against two diametrically-opposed courses of action. He did this in the days preceding his departure for GHQ on 22 February. While listening patiently to the representations of General Gurko and other advocates of constitutional reform, he also let the former Minister of the Interior, Maklakov, work out a plan for the abolition of the constitution, and even had him prepare a manifesto announcing it. This wavering between alternatives of so incompatible a nature proves that there had never existed in the mind of the Emperor any clearly defined political idea which he felt it his task and duty to implement. The maintenance of autocracy was of course a duty imposed on him by a death-bed promise to his father. It also accorded with his conviction that this was the only way to avoid national disaster, a conviction reinforced by his poor opinion of the abilities and integrity of the liberal opposition leaders, and also by the mystical beliefs of his wife, who saw in the continuance and strengthening of the autocratic régime the guarantee of a political order in which her sickly and — in consequence — somewhat retarded son could safely inherit the crown of his ancestors.

Nicholas II was in the position of a captain who believes that it is his duty to remain at the helm even though he has no clear or definite idea as to what course he should steer. And remaining at the helm meant, for him, the maintenance of the royal prerogative to appoint as ministers persons whom he could fully trust. This responsibility he was not willing to share with anybody else, not even, as a rule, with his wife. The main qualification of those on whom the choice fell was their loyalty. By this far more was implied than devoted service. Absolute obedience was required, and the absence of any strong convictions of a political kind liable to clash with the Emperor's own opinion (for which he would refuse to give any reason to his ministers), was an added advantage. This kind of relationship sooner or later brought ambitious, intelligent and opinionated men into the inevitable conflict with their master which characterised the Emperor's dealings with so many of his ministers.

During the war, however, in his capacity as Supreme Commander, Nicholas II came for the first time into close working contact at GHQ with men who were pursuing a task of vital importance and whose qualifications made their expert advice immune to the Emperor's arbitrary decisions. This was due to a clear understanding by the

Emperor of his own limitations. Prone as generals are to blame their superiors for the mistakes committed in the campaigns in which they took part, none of those who served under Nicholas II complained of his interference in purely military matters. It was certainly a cunning move on the part of Guchkov and his political colleagues to involve the generals, mostly against their will, in their political struggle and to use them as one of the pressure groups acting (half-heartedly but nevertheless outspokenly) to obtain from the Emperor concessions to their demands. The account of the Gurko audience on 14 February, and the behaviour of the commanders of the various fronts in the first days of March, show that Guchkov had manoeuvred the generals exactly into the position in which he wanted them to stand at the moment when, all means of legal pressure having been exhausted, he would be ready to apply non-constitutional methods in order to enforce his demands.[1]

9. THE RETURN TO GHQ OF GENERAL ALEKSEEV AND THE EMPEROR

Guchkov's clandestine interference in military affairs makes somewhat suspicious Alekseev's return to GHQ in the middle of February 1917, and even more so the departure of the Emperor from Tsarskoe Selo to Mogilev a week later.

Alekseev had been away on sick leave for three months, and although his state of health seems to have improved, he had by no means fully recovered. There were, however, very good reasons for him to return to GHQ in good time for the beginning of the spring offensive, if he hoped to conduct this operation personally. Information had reached him concerning the reshuffle of the Army undertaken by Gurko, which was to result in a one-third increase in the number of divisions capable of being deployed at the front.[2] Alekseev disapproved of these measures.

1. Little is known of the personal contacts between General Gurko and Guchkov at this time. The Empress, who had been closely following Guchkov's attempts to win the support of Alekseev, warned the Emperor when Gurko became acting Chief of Staff not to allow him to indulge in the same kind of contacts as Alekseev, in spite of his protests, had in fact maintained with the Chairman of the Central WIC. The Empress might not have known that the relations between Gurko and Guchkov were of extremely long standing. See ch. 3, p. 41.
2. See ch. 3 above, p. 45.

It is possible that his return to GHQ, which seemed to those who saw him premature from the point of view of his health, was actuated by the necessity to put a stop to the Gurko reform and to establish an order of battle for the forthcoming spring operations.

The return of Alekseev to Headquarters was followed by the departure of the Emperor a week later from Tsarskoe Selo to Mogilev. There is no indication in the available sources as to why Alekseev requested the Supreme Commander to return to GHQ. The Baroness Buxhoevden, who attended the Empress as lady-in-waiting at that time, is quite definite in her memoirs on one point[1] — that the Emperor left at the request, by wire, of General Alekseev without knowing in detail what urgent business required his presence. The point is of a certain importance in view of Guchkov's statement to the Muravyev Commission that the palace coup was planned for March and was to be carried out at a railway station on one of the journeys of the Emperor between Petrograd and Mogilev. Was Alekseev's request – possibly made even without Alekseev's knowledge – part of the preparation for the coup? In any case, it does not seem that any particularly momentous decision had to be taken at that time at GHQ, and, according to the letters of Nicholas II to his wife, he hoped to finish the routine business on hand in a short time and return to Petrograd. There is also no indication that the government, that is, the Council of Ministers, or any of the individual ministers advised against the departure to Mogilev. On the contrary, the Minister of the Interior, Protopopov, displayed a truculent confidence. In spite of the increasingly alarming reports of the head of the Petrograd Security Police department, Globachev,[2] Protopopov believed that he could deal with any demonstrations with the help of the police, using the ample military forces in the capital to support them if need be.

General Spiridovich strikes a very different note in his posthumously published memoirs of those days.[3] Arriving in Petrograd in the second

1. Baroness Sophie Buxhoevden, *The Life and Tragedy of Alexandra Feodorovna Empress of Russia. A Biography* (London, 1928), p. 248. See also Voeykov, op. cit., p. 192.
2. See above, p. 236.
3. *Velikaya voyna*, vol. III, pp. 63 ff. General Spiridovich had been appointed in 1916 as what amounted to leading administrative officer in Yalta. On the very eve of the February events he came to Petrograd, mainly to discuss the question of whether the streets of Yalta should be paved with stones or asphalted.

half of February, Spiridovich was plunged into an atmosphere of gossip which had spread all over the capital and was nowhere more rife than at the Headquarters of the Secret Police, where he then had many personal and professional friends. In his wartime memoirs Spiridovich recalls the dangerous situation in Petrograd, which the Minister of the Interior, in his state of morbid euphoria, was incapable of grasping. He met the Commandant of the Palace, Voeykov,[1] and warned him of the danger if the Emperor left the capital at that juncture. Indeed, in the light of subsequent events, the decision to go to Mogilev taken by the Emperor at the insistence of his Chief of Staff must be considered as of the greatest consequence. Communications between people whose decisions were determining the course of events proved unsatisfactory. It was impossible to check the genuineness and truthfulness of the reports sent from the capital to GHQ — this at a moment when timely and accurate information was all-important. The absence of the Emperor from the scene of events resulted in total misunderstanding between him and his ministers, as witness his last telegram, in which he ordered them to remain in office at a time when some of them were already in hiding. Moreover, had the Emperor been in Tsarskoe Selo, the meeting with Rodzyanko arranged for the 28th would probably have taken place and deflected the political tornado which was about to strike Petrograd. And finally, the ghostly journey through the snow-bound wastes of Russia, lasting close on forty hours, of which every minute saw a new turn of events in the capital, would have been avoided, as well as the fatal personal interference of General Ruzsky in the drama.

This is not to say that the final result of the February crisis would then have been different. Here, as elsewhere, we are in no position to write a history of what 'might have been' at this juncture. And yet the historian cannot dismiss as irrelevant such actions as the departure of the Emperor for Mogilev; its impact on the course of events was certainly not less than, for instance, the mutiny of a company of the Volynsky Regiment on 27 February.

The imperial train left Tsarskoe Selo in the early afternoon of 22 February for Mogilev. If it had been delayed for twenty-four hours, the outbreak of measles among the Emperor's children, a disease

1. This is confirmed by Dubensky's memoirs — see *Russkaya Letopis*, III, p. 18 ff. and by Voeykov himself, op. cit., pp. 197 ff.

particularly dangerous for Alexis, might have caused a further delay of the journey; it is clear, however, that the Emperor decided to go from a sense of duty to his officers at the front, and it would have been morally difficult for him to cancel this journey on purely family and 'compassionate' grounds. Here the characteristic feature of the Emperor's action was, as always, that it was determined by the mystique of a ritually performed duty.

The journey was uneventful, and the arrival at Headquarters an anticlimax. General Dubensky, who had the somewhat fanciful post of official historiographer attached to the Supreme Commander, noted in his diary: 'A quiet life has started for the Emperor and for all of us. There will be nothing, no change, coming for him.'[1]

The reference to a possible change was obviously connected with the widespread expectation that the Tsar would suddenly announce the formation of a government accountable to parliament. Later on in his memoirs, published in 1922, Dubensky gave a somewhat different impression of the first hours after the Emperor's return to Headquarters: 'Already from the very first hours of the arrival of the Emperor, one felt a peculiar uncertainty about forthcoming events. But not as far as the military order at Headquarters was concerned, only with regard to the general conditions of state life in Russia.'[2]

1. See E. Martynov, *Tsarskaya armiya v fevralskom perevorote* (Moscow, 1927).
2. See Dubensky, *Russkaya Letopis*, III, p. 27.

Part Three

IO

The Petrograd Rising

Introduction; The labour unrest: causes; The street fighting; The mutiny of the Petrograd garrison; The collapse

I. INTRODUCTION

The ten days following the Emperor's return to GHQ on 23 February encompassed so extraordinary and so rapid a succession of events that time seems to have been stretched to fit them all in. Geographically, however, the memorable drama was confined to Petrograd, to GHQ in Mogilev and to the railway lines connecting them. The rest of the country was hardly informed of what was happening and took no part in revolutionary developments until the first days of March. The spectacular manifestations of popular feeling were, as far as the country as a whole was concerned, an effect and not a cause of the basic changes in the destiny of Russia which occurred in those days. Throughout the crisis there was a time-lag between developments in Petrograd and moves at GHQ. This led to a grotesque situation on 27 February, when the Emperor continued to issue orders to his already non-existent government in Petrograd, and again on 2 March, when the generals at various headquarters continued to negotiate with the President of the Duma as if he were still in control of what was going on – whereas in fact he was not.

As far as Petrograd is concerned we must distinguish two main phases, the first covering the days of 23–26 February. This period was marked by a rapidly growing strike movement in the industrial suburbs, and by street demonstrations centred mainly on Znamensky Square at the eastern end of the Nevsky Prospekt. The police, with some half-hearted support from Cossack and military units, made futile attempts to disperse the demonstrators. The situation became acute only towards nightfall on the 25th, when it was decided to use troops to prevent further demonstrations. Casualties on the 26th were mainly due to mob fighting and stray bullets fired at random. By

247

nightfall on the 26th it looked, however, as if the workers' movement was slowing down, and as if military action had tipped the balance in favour of the government. When the government decided to prorogue the February session of the Duma until April there began a second phase, in which the Tauride Palace (headquarters of the Duma) became the centre of the revolutionary turmoil.

Simultaneously, but not as a direct result of the prorogation of the Duma, widespread disaffection broke out on the morning of the 27th among units of the Petrograd garrison. This considerably altered the situation. Industrial unrest and street rioting were contingencies which the authorities had anticipated, and indeed expected, to occur at this time. Plans, albeit inadequate, for such an emergency had been worked out in detail. No such plans for automatic countermeasures had been drawn up to meet the contingency of a mutiny among the Petrograd garrison. The mutiny of the troops and the Duma's reaction to the prorogation decree were the factors which transformed the Petrograd labour unrest into a revolution.

It was not until the evening of the 27th that the Duma deputies and, independently of them, the committees of the revolutionary parties in Petrograd realised that the time had come for immediate political action. Proposals for the solution of the crisis were put forward on all sides. These plans swelled up like soap bubbles, catching the imagination of the multitude, and reflecting in a distorted way the rapidly changing street scene in the capital, only to burst, and be followed by yet others. The Tsarist government ceased to exist as a body on the night of 27–28 February, and the next morning the Minister of War, Belyaev, ordered the troops who had remained faithful to the régime to return to barracks individually, after dumping their arms in the Admiralty building where they had made their last stand. The vacuum caused by the collapse of the Tsarist government was short-lived, but the new government was formed under circumstances which it is still extremely difficult to reconstruct.

2. THE LABOUR UNREST: CAUSES

The strikes in the Petrograd factories which started on Thursday 23 February and involved 90,000 workers spread on the following day, when many more went on strike. By Saturday the 28th, 240,000 workers were out. The strikes in the Petrograd district were not in themselves anything new or ominous. There is something about these February strikes, however, which still remains unaccounted for. We shall put forward a tentative explanation for this labour unrest, but whether our suggestion is satisfactory or not, we must stress that some of the causes of the strikes still remain quite obscure. Perhaps we are not yet in a position to provide a true explanation. But this does not entitle us to cover up our ignorance by talking of 'a spontaneous elemental movement', or by saying that 'the patience of the workers had reached boiling point . . . '. These standard clichés only evade and befog the issue. A mass movement on this scale and with this momentum would not have been possible without some kind of directing power behind it. Even experienced underground revolutionary committees, acting under instructions from party organisations, had not found it easy on previous occasions to mobilise workers for demonstrations on a much smaller scale than those of February 1917. Even on the traditional day of commemoration of 'Bloody Sunday' (9 January 1905) workers from 114 enterprises, some 137,536 in all, came out on strike in 1917, but did not demonstrate in the street. This date, however, was something of an established holiday in the industrial districts of Petrograd, and no great effort of organisation was required to bring the workers out.

Two important reasons have been advanced for the rapid growth of the strike movement in the last week of February: the dwindling bread supply, and the lock-out at the large Putilov Works. As regards the former, there was certainly some difficulty about the supply of bread to the bakers' shops at the beginning of the week. This led to panic rumours of a flour shortage which increased the initial run on the bakeries, the length of the bread queues and the shortness of tempers. But there is substantial evidence that no flour shortage existed. At no time in February did the stocks of flour for the bakeries of the capital fall below average requirements for twelve days. The main difficulty was one of distribution, and this could easily have been overcome with a certain amount of goodwill. The goodwill was, however, absent.

A feud had lately developed between the Petrograd Municipality and the government over the administration of food supplies. The

Petrograd Municipality, supported by the Union of Municipalities and the Progressive Bloc of the State Duma, insisted on taking over the whole administration of civilian food supplies, while the Minister of the Interior, Protopopov, although unqualified to do so, wanted to assume this extra responsibility himself; this led to renewed attacks on him in the press and in the Petrograd City Council and created a general atmosphere of crisis around the question of food supplies. In addition, rumours that bread rationing was to be introduced made a strong impact on the popular imagination, the more so since bread is a staple item of the Russian diet. It was not only the fear of going short that was objectionable to the Russian peasant and worker, but also the very idea that some authority might want to keep a check on what he put into his mouth. It appears that the rush on bakeries and bread shops was caused partly by the tendency to hoard bread in the form of dry rusks.

Besides the wrangle over the administration of food supplies, there were two other factors which may possibly have contributed to the actual shortage of bread in the shops and to the exasperation of the bread queues. It was alleged that several bakeries, instead of using the full amount of flour allocated to them, were sending some of it into the countryside, where it fetched good prices on the black market. Rumours of such malpractices caused General Khabalov to introduce more stringent control over the bakeries. Secondly, we cannot overlook the possibility of deliberate sabotage by the bakery workers. There was a fairly strong Bolshevik faction among the Petrograd bakers. During the labour unrest of the winter of 1915–16 the bakers had played an important part in the strike movement in the capital. A revealing and relevant document is the letter written early in March 1916 by Pavel Budaev, a member of the Bolshevik Party and of the Petersburg Trade Union of Bakers, to a fellow-baker in Siberia. Budaev reports a strike organised by the Bolsheviks of all the bakeries in the Vyborg district of Petrograd: during the Christmas holidays of 1915, the police authorities had required that bread should be available on Boxing Day, but the bakery workers stayed out for two days and bread reappeared only on the third. On 9 January all the factories had gone on strike, 'the initiative coming from the Vyborg district'.[1]

1. See ch. 5 above. Budaev's letter is published in *Krasnaya Letopis*, VII (1923), pp. 208 ff.

Although complaints of a flour and bread shortage in February 1917 were without much foundation, the slogan 'We Want Bread' figured prominently in the chanting by the mob and on demonstrators' banners in the first three days of the unrest. It appealed to cautious organisers of street demonstrations like Shlyapnikov. Unlike the two other slogans circulated in those days, 'Down with the War' and 'Down with Autocracy', the clamour for bread had a special emotional appeal for the troops who were called upon to disperse the demonstrations. They were reluctant to fire on a crowd which was 'merely asking for bread'.

Next to the alleged food shortage, the lock-out at the Putilov Works is often cited as a prime cause of the labour demonstrations of February 1917. The circumstances leading to a similar lock-out in February 1916, and the part played by 'Leninists' in them, have been described above.[1] On both occasions the disturbances were started by workers in one section of the works making an inordinate demand for a wage increase. Our source of information on 1917 is not a police report but a draft question addressed to the Premier and the War and Navy Ministers by thirty members of the Duma, including the Trudoviks, and A. I. Konovalov and I. N. Efremov.[2] According to this document, workers in one section of the Putilov Works asked on 18 February for a fifty per cent increase in wages. Significantly, they made this immoderate claim without consulting their comrades in other departments. The director of the works met their demands with a categorical refusal, and they then declared a sit-down strike. After mediation between management and strikers by workers' representatives from other workshops, a twenty per cent wage increase was promised. But simultaneously the management dismissed, as from 21 February, the employees of the workshop where the strike had started. This reprisal caused the strike to spread to other sections, and on 22 February, the management announced the closing down of the works for an indefinite period. This meant that thirty thousand well-organised workers, many of them highly skilled, were literally on the street.

This lock-out must have contributed substantially to the ensuing rapid spread of the strike movement. Following established practice,

1. See ch. 5 above, and the police reports in Fleer, op. cit., pp. 259 ff.
2. See Fleer, op. cit., p. 327. A somewhat ideologically streamlined account of the same happenings is to be found in Balabanov, *Ot 1905 k 1917* (Moscow/Leningrad, 1927), pp. 340 ff.

the strikers went from factory to factory persuading their comrades by all available means, including intimidation, to join the strike. Coming at a time when feeling was running high because of the wild rumours of a food shortage, the calls to strike for a drastic wage increase were particularly effective. The anonymity afforded by the large crowds gave the agitators unlimited scope for action.

Later, in the nineteen-twenties, Soviet historians of the labour movement such as M. Balabanov tried to explain the snowballing of the strike movement of February 1917 as the culmination of a long process of gathering strength and growing solidarity on the part of the working class. The purpose of such historiographic reconstructions is to show how proletarian solidarity and the realisation of common economic aims led to a purely revolutionary movement with political aims. Events do not entirely bear out such neat exercises in Marxist social dialectics. From all we know of the activities of the underground revolutionary committees among the Petrograd workers, none were ready for concerted revolutionary action at that particular moment. When on 22 February some women workers met to discuss the organisation of a Woman's Day on the 23rd, a representative of the Petersburg Bolshevik Committee, V. Kayurov,[1] advised them to refrain from isolated actions and to follow only the instructions of the Party Committee.

> But to my surprise and indignation, [wrote Kayurov later] on 23 January, at an emergency conference of five persons in the corridor of the Erikson Works, we learned from Comrade Nikifor Ilyin of the strike in some textile factories, and of the arrival of a number of delegates from the women workers, who announced that they were supporting the metal workers.
>
> I was extremely indignant about the behaviour of the strikers, both because they had blatantly ignored the decision of the district committee of the Party, and also because they had gone on strike after I had appealed to them only the night before to keep cool and disciplined. There appeared to be no reason or pretext for their action, if one discounted the ever-increasing bread queues, which had indeed touched off the strike.

In fact, at the beginning of 1917 the Petrograd Bolsheviks did not quite know what attitude to adopt towards the rising tide of labour

1. See V. Kayurov's article in *Proletarskaya Revolyutsiya*, 1923, No. I (13).

unrest. Their attempt to launch a full-scale civil war, recorded in the leaflet of the Petersburg Committee cited above, had misfired in February 1916. Since then, the prospects for a revolution in wartime had appeared doubtful to their leaders. Thus we find the Petrograd Bolsheviks behaving warily in the critical days before the outbreak of industrial unrest at the end of February 1917. They warned the workers against partial and isolated strikes, lest these give the employers and the government an opportunity to split the working masses and compromise future attempts at revolution when the time came. Like Milyukov and the liberals of the Duma, they held that the most favourable moment for the revolution would come after the end of the war. It took them forty-eight hours to realise that, in spite of their warnings, the workers' movement had assumed unexpected proportions, and only then did they appeal for the formation of a revolutionary government.

The insignificant part played by the Bolsheviks in February 1917 should not in itself surprise us. With the exception of Shlyapnikov, their leaders in the capital were inexperienced and lacking in authority.[1] This was clearly realised by the earlier Soviet historians of the revolution. It was only after the liquidation of the Pokrovsky school in the early thirties that Soviet historiography adopted the line that Bolshevik wisdom and political infallibility played an important part in the February events, and that the role of other non-Bolshevik workers and revolutionary organisations had been negligible. No wonder so little material has been released in the Soviet Union on the activities of other revolutionary organisations in Petrograd at the time. Of course the right-wing Mensheviks could not claim to have led the workers. Their organisation was associated with the Labour Group of the WIC who had been in gaol since 27 January, and we can discount the possibility of Gvozdev having affected in any way the outbreak of workers' unrest on 23-25 February.

There was, however, another social-democratic group in Petrograd whose activities have been only sketchily outlined by Soviet historians — the only ones to have access to the relevant archives. This was the so-called Inter-District Committee, commonly known as the *Mezhrayonka*, an organisation of workers' delegates from the various industrial districts of the capital, which became particularly active

1. See ch. 2 above, pp. 27-33.

during the war and was at one time directed by Karakhan.[1] In organisation and ideology this group was influenced by Trotsky and by the traditions of the Petersburg Workers' Soviet of 1905. In August 1917 Trotsky and the organisation of the Inter-District Committee as a whole joined the Bolsheviks, and thereafter no one was interested in asserting the group's independence or recalling its independent political life before its incorporation into the Bolshevik Party. On the contrary, every prominent member who had belonged to the *Mezhrayonka* insisted that at heart he had always been a Bolshevik and that the reasons for the separate identity of the group had been the tactical and organisational requirements of underground existence under the Tsarist régime.

In February 1917, however, the *Mezhrayonka* seems to have shown more initiative in getting the working masses onto the streets than any other revolutionary group in the capital. M. Balabanov[2] reports that the *Mezhrayonka* had issued a leaflet containing the slogans 'Down with autocracy', 'Long live the revolution', 'Long live the revolutionary government', 'Down with the war'. If this is so, it proves that the plan for a determined attempt at a full-scale revolution, which had been abandoned by the Bolsheviks after the failure of February 1916, was adopted by the *Mezhrayonka* and carried out with considerable success.

And yet it is difficult to believe that a small revolutionary group like the Inter-District Organisation Committee could, unaided, have organised the movement on such a scale. Besides, there seems to have been no great determination on the part of its leaders to pursue the course advocated in their leaflet. The then head of the Inter-District Committee, Yurenev, took part in the informal meetings at which various liberal Duma politicians and representatives of the legal opposition met the revolutionary underground in private houses in the days following 23 February. Thus, on the 26th Yurenev astonished the right-wing Socialist Revolutionary, V. Zenzinov, at one of these meetings in A. F. Kerensky's flat by 'the amazing attitude he adopted'.[3]

1. Karakhan, like the other members of the group, joined the Bolsheviks in August 1917 and served under the Soviet régime, mainly in a diplomatic capacity. During the 1936–38 purges he was accused of secret dealings with the Germans and disappeared from the scene without a public trial.
2. Op. cit., p. 431.
3. See *Novy Zhurnal* (New York, 1955), XXXIV–XXXV.

By that time the revolution was in full swing and clashes between the military and the crowds were taking place all over the city. But Yurenev, unlike everyone else present, evinced no enthusiasm whatever, 'and', says Zenzinov, 'poisoned us all with his scepticism and disbelief'. '"There is no revolution, nor will there be", he reiterated stubbornly. "The movement among the armed forces is failing — we must prepare ourselves for a long period of reaction . . ." He was particularly sharp in his criticism of A. F. Kerensky, whom he reproached for "the hysterics characteristic of him" and "the usual exaggerations".'

> We were maintaining [continues Zenzinov] that the tide of revolution was rising, that we should prepare ourselves for decisive events; Yurenev, who considered himself to the left of us, was clearly trying to throw cold water on what we were saying. It was obvious to us that this attitude was not merely his own, but also that of the Bolshevik organisation in Petersburg. Yurenev did not hold with forcing the pace; he maintained that the incipient movement would not be successful, and even insisted that the excited workers must be calmed down.

Zenzinov's recollections were written after many years but are not necessarily inaccurate. Yurenev's attitude at the meeting could be explained in different ways: he was meeting representatives of liberal circles about to make their first contacts with the revolutionary movement, and he might well have wanted to discourage them from trying to 'put themselves at the head of the revolution' and constitute themselves leaders of the working masses, a part which no social-democrat would want to share with representatives of the *bourgeoisie*. On the other hand Yurenev might really, on 26 February, have been alarmed by the prospect of a clash between the Petrograd workers and the garrison; street fighting might well have been as abhorrent to him as it was to his 'opposite number' on the Bolshevik Petersburg Committee, Shlyapnikov. The *Mezhrayonka* did have the rudiments of an organisation among the troops of the Petrograd garrison, but it seems to have been weak, and there was still nothing to indicate that disaffection was rife among the troops.[1] News of the mutiny of the Pavlovsky Regiment

1. Yurenev recalls that 'already at the end of 1914 the *Obyedinenka* (another name for the *Mezhrayonka*) aimed at the creation of a special military organisation, and indeed such an organisation was established; true, it was weak, but it had widespread contacts with soldiers.' I. Yurenev, *Borba za edinstvo partii* (Petrograd, 1917).

had not yet got round. While the revolutionary committees had every-thing to fear from a clash with the armed forces at this juncture, they had nothing to lose by waiting for the end of the war. The legal opposition, on the other hand, both in the Duma and in the Voluntary Organisations, was anxious to exploit the situation in the capital in order to press its demands. It might be their last chance of obtaining the long-desired constitutional reforms. If they let the opportunity slip, the war might end during the summer without their having achieved anything. Zenzinov refers to Yurenev's overbearing attitude, but Yurenev may well have meant to put the liberals in their place, and make them understand that the Petrograd proletariat would not fight in the streets in order to pull the chestnuts of the legal opposition out of the fire for them. He must have been fully aware that the sympathy for the revolution evinced by the men he was meeting was based on the hope of exploiting the revolutionary situation to wrest concessions from the Tsar and to seize power.

But even if one discounts such pessimistic utterances by the leaders of the revolutionary underground as so much political manoeuvring designed to maintain their control over the workers' movement, they are hard to reconcile with the militant attitude prescribed by party ideology for all social-democratic political workers. Of this there was obviously little, either in Bolshevik or *Mezhrayonka* circles. And yet the workers' movement grew, the demonstrations became unmanage-able on Znamensky Square and on the Nevsky Prospekt. It is difficult not to believe that such a movement would have lost its momentum and cohesion without some kind of organisation and leadership inciting and directing the masses. The theory of a spontaneous, elemental (*stikhiynoe*) movement of the Petrograd proletariat is only an admission of our inability to explain the course of events. Why should such movements have occurred then, and only then, in Petro-grad? Neither before nor since have the Russian masses shown any such capacity for concerted, 'spontaneous', action.

There is a further aspect of the February days to be examined in our quest for the prime movers. This is the part allegedly played by German agents and money in February 1917. It has since been overlaid and obscured by the controversy over German aid to the Bolsheviks after the return of Lenin — a question we have already considered. The two problems — German intervention in February and German financial aid to the Bolsheviks — are distinct, but both present the same difficulty to the historian. Right from the beginning, all those involved were vitally interested in keeping secret all the relevant documentary evidence. The opening of the German archives has lifted part of the veil, but as far as the Soviet Union is concerned nothing has changed: no evidence has been made available, and any enquiry would be considered an outrage to scholarship, and politically malicious.

The belief that the Germans interfered in various ways in the February revolution seems to have been fairly widespread at the time in Russia. At one of the earliest meetings of the Provisional Government in March the Minister for Foreign Affairs, Milyukov, made casual reference to the role of German agents and money in February. This provoked an indignant retort from Kerensky, who left the room saying that he would not sit in a gathering where 'the sacred cause of the revolution' was being slandered.[1] To say that Milyukov was doing this was, of course, an exaggeration and a distortion on Kerensky's part: Milyukov was merely expressing a widely-held view. The hidden springs of the popular rising needed an explanation, and the intervention of German agents provided an explanation for the surprising success of this 'revolution without revolutionaries'.

In an earlier chapter we tried to outline the efforts made by various departments of the German war machine to bring about labour unrest in Russia, and, if possible, a revolution. We have seen that A. Helphand (Parvus) had worked out an elaborate plan for the German authorities, that he had placed at their service his extensive contacts both in the Balkans and in Scandinavia, and that the German government had lent him considerable financial support to enable him to proceed independently with his revolutionary plans. If we return to the political situation in Russia, we find little evidence of Helphand's activities; there are however certain indications that German money and Helphand's ingenuity were not entirely wasted.

We have seen elsewhere that the Petrograd strikes of January 1916 were instigated and financially supported by Helphand's organisations and that the simultaneous Nikolaev strikes were probably organised by the same agency. In view of these precedents, it is hard to believe

1. See Nabokov on the incident in *ARR*, I; Milyukov, *Vospominaniya*, vol. II, p. 328; as well as my article in *International Affairs*, February–April 1956, Kerensky's comment on it in *International Affairs*, September 1956, and my reply, *ibid.*

that the Germans had no hand whatever in the events of 23–26 February 1917, which so closely resembled the unrest of the previous year. As we have seen, the Helphand organisation was still working in Copenhagen in 1917, and Helphand's own economic and financial position was stronger than ever. None of his agents in Russia (and it was claimed that he had ten agents working for him[1]) had been caught.

Possibly a shift in the revolutionary groups he supported had taken place in the year between the February crises of 1916 and 1917. It does seem that the more anonymous Inter-District Committee (*Mezhrayonka*) was playing a more important part in 1917 than the Petersburg Bolshevik organisation. Helphand, who had close associations with the left-wing Mensheviks and Trotsky, may conceivably have transferred his support from one committee to the other because of this political preference. But this is mere guesswork. Helphand and the other persons concerned in these activities have left no clue as to how these things were done. We may surmise, however, that the all-important question of financing the strike – that is, of maintaining the workers week after week while they were on strike, either for exorbitant economic claims or for political ones which the management had no means of satisfying – was settled by the anonymous strike committee with the help of funds provided by the Helphand organisation.[2] And the more anonymous and obscure the supporting committees and individuals were, the sounder was the conspiratorial structure of the Helphand organisation.[3]

1. See above, p. 85.
2. It is worthy of note that Soviet historians of the labour movement during the war, writing in the twenties, carefully avoided all mention of how the strikes were financed. Neither Balabanov, nor Fleer, nor any other writer we were able to consult, throws any light on the matter.
3. Shlyapnikov (*Nakanune 1917 g.*, p. 255) provides some evidence for the existence of social-democratic committees which were not affiliated to the Petersburg Committee or to the Central Committee Bureau. He writes: 'Such groups of social-democrats, who had no permanent contacts with the all-city organisation, existed in Petersburg in large numbers. Some such groups had cut themselves off and isolated themselves for fear of *agents provocateurs*. I knew of two such groups of workers who did not enter the network of the Petersburg organisations because of their suspicious attitude towards Chernomazov [later unmasked as a police agent]. Such groups nevertheless carried on [political] work, but as a consequence of their alienation from the local centre this work had an amateurish character.' Shlyapnikov uses the Leninist term *kustarny* to characterise such work, implying that it was relatively ineffective because

While German agents and money may have been behind the unrest among the workers in February 1917, it would be wrong to exaggerate their influence on subsequent events. As soon as the demonstrators, emerging from the suburbs of Petrograd, mixed with the crowds on the central streets and squares of the capital, the character of the movement began to change. The slogans on the banners under which the demonstrations had started in the industrial suburbs were altered or dropped as soon as contact was made with the inhabitants of the town centre, and with the mass of university and high school students, petty civil servants, subalterns and other middle-class elements who were prepared to gape at the demonstrating workers, join in the processions, sing revolutionary songs, and listen eagerly to the orators at street meetings. Initially the workers proclaimed the slogans 'We want bread'. 'Down with the autocracy' and 'Down with the war'. We have seen that the food situation hardly justified the first of these. The second was a common feature of every seditious demonstration in Russia. Together with the raising of the red flag it identified a demonstration as a revolutionary one. But the use of the third slogan, very much in evidence in the workers' demonstrations of 23–26 February, deserves special comment.

Sukhanov, the chronicler of the Russian revolution, believed the slogan 'Down with the war' to be proof that the ideas of the Zimmerwald conference were spreading among the proletarian masses. But even Sukhanov had to admit that it was a mistake to come out with this slogan at the very moment when the labour riots of the suburbs were being transformed into a national political revolution in which the bourgeois opposition parties were expected to play a leading role. He comments:

> It was *a priori* clear that if one took into account the bourgeois government and the likelihood of bourgeois participation in the revolution, then it would become necessary to give up the slogans against the war, to roll up for the time being the banner of Zimmerwald, which had now become the banner of the Russian, and in particular of the Petersburg, proletariat.[1]

If one disregards Sukhanov's application of such Marxist figures of

it lacked scientific Marxist background and co-ordination with other similar efforts. Little did Shlyapnikov know that it was to such groups that the success of the last wave of strikes and demonstrations was mainly due.

1. N. N. Sukhanov, *Zapiski o revolyutsii* (7 vols, Berlin, 1922–23), vol. I, p. 30.

speech to the Russian scene of 1917 as 'the proletariat' and 'the bourgeoisie', his analysis is fairly correct. It was true that the slogan 'Down
with the war' did not appeal to the petty bourgeois crowds in the
centre of Petrograd. This class, paradoxically enough, was far harder
hit by the increasing inflation and other wartime stringencies than were
the workers. It was even more difficult for salaried workers' incomes to
keep pace with soaring prices than for workers' wages to do so. Nevertheless, the middle classes remained patriotic, and on the whole imper-
vious to the defeatist ideals of Zimmerwald; it was, indeed, their very
patriotism that induced them to join in the final assault on autocracy.
They had completely succumbed to the propaganda spread by the
liberal press, the Duma and the Voluntary Organisations, and had
welcomed the overthrow of the autocratic régime because they believed
that the Tsar's government would either lose the war or conclude a
shameful separate peace. For them, then, the slogan 'Down with the
war' came as a shock: it could easily have led to a split in the revolutionary movement if the promoters of the demonstrations had not
withdrawn it at an early stage. The Petersburg Bolshevik Committee
can hardly be accused of having used this slogan. In their proclamation
a year earlier they had refrained from using any anti-war slogan. The
Mezhrayonka, however, seem to have included it in the leaflet they
printed in February 1917. They should have known why the Bolsheviks
had not used it and should have been aware of what was '*a priori* clear'
to Sukhanov, namely, that from the point of view of revolutionary
tactics its use was a blunder.

But if, as we have reason to believe on other grounds, the strike
movement was started by people who received their instructions from
Berlin via Copenhagen and Stockholm, then the use of the slogan
makes sense: the men who were spending their masters' money on
fostering these demonstrations were primarily concerned with the
destruction of the Russian war machine and Russian morale, not with
the prospects of revolution or with the necessity of maintaining a
semblance of national unity so as to overthrow the age-old political
order. For Helphand's unidentified agents it was important to make
sure that the demonstrations were anti-war and were not deflected from
their primary purpose. The 'proletarian masses', however, were not in
the least concerned about the nature of the slogans under which they
were demonstrating, so long as they got their strike pay from the

treasurers of the strike committees — probably the same people as had prepared the slogans on the banners. Sukhanov gives a vivid account of the cynical mood of such proletarian revolutionaries, and admits that the slogans were forced upon them by some mysterious outsiders. On Saturday, the 25th, Sukhanov met a group of workers who were discussing the situation. 'What do *they* want?' asked one of them glumly. 'What *they* want is a supply of bread, peace with the Germans and equal rights for the Yids.' Sukhanov was delighted with this 'brilliant formulation of the programme of the Great Revolution', but he did not seem to notice that the slogans appeared to the glum worker to emanate not from him or his like but from some mysterious 'they'.

In fact, the rolling up of the banner of Zimmerwald, of which Sukhanov speaks, was carried out not only metaphorically but also literally. The right-wing Socialist Revolutionary, Zenzinov, who was on Znamensky Square on 25 February, recalls the following scene:

> People were now coming in droves along the Nevsky Prospekt, all heading in the same direction, towards Znamensky Square, and obviously with a definite purpose in view. Hand-made red banners appeared from nowhere, and it was clear that all this had been improvised on the spot. On one of the banners I saw the letters 'R.S.D.R.P.' (Russian Social-Democratic Workers' Party). Another bore the legend 'Down with the War.' This one, however, evoked protests from the crowd and it was withdrawn immediately. I remember this with absolute clarity. Evidently the banner belonged to the Bolsheviks or to the *Mezhrayonka* (who were affiliated to the Bolsheviks) and did not suit the mood of the crowd.[1]

Zenzinov is probably not being quite fair to the Bolsheviks. 'Defensism', as we shall see, had by now penetrated even the ranks of the Bolshevik leaders. It required all Lenin's political skill, after his return to Russia in April, to reintroduce the anti-war slogan (but never in its crude wording of the February days) first into his party's political programme and then into the consciousness of the 'proletarian masses'. But in the first three days of industrial unrest, the anti-war slogans and the anti-war speeches delivered from the pedestal of the monument to Alexander III in Znamensky Square should be taken as signs of direct interference by German agents, not by the Petersburg Bolshevik Committee as such.

1. See Zenzinov's memoirs in *Novy Zhurnal* (New York), XXXIV (1955).

3. THE STREET FIGHTING

It is surprising how little significance was attached to the demonstrations of February 23–25 by those whom they most concerned. Strikes in the industrial areas with demonstrations, the singing of revolutionary songs and the sporadic appearance of red flags amid the crowds — all this was taken for granted and was not expected to have a bearing on the course of the main political development in the near future. The Duma did not refer to the demonstrations in their debates; the Council of Ministers, which met on the 24th, did not even discuss them. The ministers considered this to be a matter for the police and not a matter of policy. Even those revolutionary intellectuals in Petrograd not directly involved in underground work failed to realise what was happening. Mstislavsky-Maslovsky, an old Socialist Revolutionary who had been working in the party's military organisations, had published earlier a manual on street fighting for the use of revolutionary groups, and was now working as a librarian in the Academy of the General Staff (such was the easy-going tolerance of the autocratic régime!) says in his memoirs:[1] 'The revolution, long hoped for, has caught us napping, like the foolish virgins of the gospel.'

Of course the police were alerted. And in their turn, as the number of demonstrators rose rapidly from thousands to tens and possibly hundreds of thousands, the police called the troops available in the capital to assist in maintaining order. But police action was on the whole dilatory. With the dearth of policemen, little was done, or indeed could be done, to prevent massing on the streets and squares. Every time crowds filled the open spaces the police took action to disperse them, and under the threat of arrest they retreated to the side-streets and the courtyards of neighbouring houses. From there, as soon as the police squads had gone, they filtered back to their original meeting places, and speech-making and the shouting of slogans were resumed. Both demonstrators and police, with few exceptions, showed considerable restraint. Occasionally demonstrators would overturn a tram, but no serious attempt was made to build barricades. It is characteristic, even of the days of street fighting which followed, that no front-line between the opposing forces was ever established. The revolutionary masses and the government forces remained interlocked.

1. S. Mstislavsky-Maslovsky, *Pyat dney* (Berlin-Moscow, 2nd Ed.; 1922), p. 12.

As the weather was exceptionally cold, both the crowds and the security forces retired to their quarters for the night, only to renew their seemingly aimless game next morning on an increasing scale. On Sunday the 26th the demonstrations started later, in the early afternoon. And still nobody took advantage of the night to seize and maintain strategic positions for the next day's trial of strength. Neither side seemed to regard what was happening as crucial or even serious.

The sporadic outbreaks of violence and shooting in various parts of the capital in these early days cannot be ascribed to the deliberate decision of either the police, the military authorities or the revolutionary committees. There is ample evidence that the government forces had instructions not to fire on the crowds except in self-defence. The very idea of casualties bestrewing the snow-covered streets in the centre of the capital filled the authorities with horror. What would the Allies think if such a thing happened? The Cossacks were supposed to use their *nagaykas*, long leather whips with a short stock, to disperse the crowd, but since they were on their way to the front they had not taken this article of equipment with them. When this was discovered an order was issued that each man be given enough money to make his own *nagayka*. The Empress herself, in one of her letters to the Emperor, stressed that it was quite unnecessary to shoot at the crowds, who were just a lot of naughty boys and girls, taking advantage of supply difficulties to create trouble. The order not to use firearms made it possible for the crowds to approach the troops and to engage them in conversation. The soldiers soon caught the mood of the crowd. To them they seemed to be peaceful demonstrators, against whom it would be an outrage to use arms. Their stocks of ammunition were extremely low, and no attempt had been made to ensure that there was enough in the event of street fighting breaking out in earnest. This became a major difficulty when mutinies broke out in the garrison on the 27th, and armed suppression was the only answer.

At the same time, even the Bolshevik leaders seem to have done everything in their power to prevent shooting in the streets. Shlyapnikov is most definite on this point. When workers urged him to arm the demonstrators with revolvers, he refused. Not, he says, that it would have been difficult to get hold of arms. But that was not the point:

I feared [says Shlyapnikov] that a rash use of arms thus supplied could only harm the cause. An excited comrade who used a revolver against a soldier would only provoke some military unit and provide an excuse for the authorities to incite the troops against the workers. I therefore firmly refused to give arms to anybody who asked for them, and insisted again and again that the soldiers must be brought into the uprising, for in this way arms would be provided for all workers. This was a more difficult decision to carry out than getting a couple of dozen revolvers, but it was a consistent programme of action.[1]

Despite the resolve of both sides to avoid the use of firearms, there were shooting incidents all over the capital, and the number of casualties increased daily. This was partly due to the suspicion with which each side regarded the other. There was a rumour, widely believed in Petrograd, that the police had established machine-gun posts in the garrets of blocks of flats and were prepared to shoot at the demonstrators from these hide-outs. Any shooting, especially in the distance, was immediately put down to this sniping. Later, special squads were sent out by the revolutionaries to search the houses and arrest any policemen who were found shooting from the rooftops.

Several commissions of investigation were set up under the Provisional Government to assess the part played by the police in the February fighting. Later historians sifted all the available evidence, but not a single case was discovered of the police using machine-guns against demonstrators from the rooftops. Nevertheless, the 'Protopopov machine-gun legend' played its part in creating bitterness towards the police and provoking excesses in which a large number of police officers and men lost their lives.[2]

This bitterness accounts for many of the clashes in the days that preceded Sunday the 26th. There must, however, have been some provocation on the part of those organising the demonstrations. Bombs

---

1. Shlyapnikov, *1917 god* (Moscow, 1925–31), vol. I, p. 100.
2. Melgunov in *Martovskie dni 1917 goda* (Paris, 1961), pp. 163–168, adduces conclusive evidence that there is no truth in this legend. His findings were recently supported by the reminiscences of a Soviet writer, Victor Shklovsky, who was a member of a raiding party which searched houses for 'Protopopov machine-guns'. In the magazine *Znamya*, in 1961, Shklovsky confirms that during the many searches in which he took part not a single machine-gun was found. V. Shklovsky, *Zhili-Byli*, *Znamya*, August 1961, no. 8, p. 196.

were thrown at military detachments, instantly causing them to use arms in self-defence. But even in such cases many people believed the bombs were thrown by police *agents provocateurs*. This is borne out by a conversation between the President of the Duma and the commander of the Petrograd garrison. Rodzyanko was firmly convinced that, in incidents like those mentioned above, the bomb had been thrown by a policeman, and said so to Khabalov. 'Good Lord, Your Excellency, why should a policeman throw bombs at the troops?' was Khabalov's amazed and somewhat naïve retort.[1]

On the 25th a serious incident took place in Znamensky Square. It is rightly regarded as an important turning-point in the opening phase of the riots. Several eye-witnesses, including the Bolshevik worker Kayurov and V. Zenzinov, have given differing accounts of what happened, although none saw the actual killing. A large crowd had gathered round the monument to Alexander III, from the pedestal of which, as on previous days, revolutionary speeches were being made. A Cossack unit had been brought on to the square in case of need, but did nothing to disperse the demonstration. At about 3 p.m. a detachment of mounted police under a police officer called Krylov arrived on the scene. Following established practice in breaking up demonstrations, he pushed his way through the crowd to seize the red flag, but was cut off from his men and killed on the spot. According to Zenzinov he was shot, and the bullet proved to have come from a Cossack rifle. According to Martynov,[2] who used police archive material, he was killed by a stab wound and then struck several times with a sabre. The autopsy did not reveal any firearm wound. Kayurov describes a ghastly scene in which the wounded Krylov was finished off with a spade by the demonstrators, while the crowd bore away in triumph the Cossack who had felled him with his sabre.

But whoever was responsible for the killing – the crowd or the Cossacks – both the police and the demonstrators were undoubtedly under the impression that the Cossacks on Znamensky Square had joined the rioters. This attitude of the Cossacks towards the clashes between the police and the crowds was not an isolated one. How could such a change of allegiance have come about? Cossack troops had

---

1. *Padenie*, vol. 1, p. 214.
2. E. Martynov, *Tsarskaya armiya v fevralskom perevorote* (Moscow, 1927), p. 79.

generally been considered highly reliable when called upon to quell peasant and workers' riots. A possible answer may be found in the memoirs of Vladimir Bonch-Bruevich, whose personal influence in the days that followed was as important as it was inconspicuous.

V. D. Bonch-Bruevich was an old Bolshevik who had supported Lenin at the Second Congress of the Social-Democratic Party in 1902, and had stayed in touch with him ever since. During and after the 1905 revolution he was active in organising the Bolshevik underground press. When the revolutionary tide ebbed in 1906, Bonch-Bruevich, instead of emigrating like most Bolshevik leaders, remained in Russia and worked in a department of the Academy of Sciences, carrying out research into Russian religious sects and their literature. He was thoroughly initiated into the mentality and social background of the sectarians, particularly adherents of the sects known as the Old and the New Israel. He had even published one of the sacred books of these sects, the so-called Dove Book (*Golubinaya Kniga*) and earned the gratitude of its followers.

Bonch-Bruevich states in his memoirs that some time in February he received a deputation of Kuban Cossacks from a regiment stationed in Petrograd, who wished to consult him on a question of conscience. After performing a ritual embrace, which was a secret sign of recognition among the initiated of the New Israel sect, the Cossacks asked Bonch-Bruevich's advice on what to do if they were called out to suppress riots in the capital. Bonch-Bruevich told them to avoid shooting at the crowd at all costs, and they promised to follow his advice. He later heard that the unit from which the deputation had come had been on patrol on Znamensky Square in the critical days, and had been involved in the killing of the police officer. Bonch-Bruevich's reticent disclosures explain how clandestine contacts were set up between the intellectual revolutionary and the disorientated Cossacks, who had left their villages and fields to go to war, and found themselves caught up in the turmoil of revolution in the great Babylon of the North.[1]

Despite the deterioration which had taken place in the general

1. See Vladimir Bonch-Bruevich, *Na boevykh postakh fevralskoy i oktyabrskoy revolyutsii* (Moscow, 1930), pp. 72 ff. There may well be more to this incident than Bonch-Bruevich admits in his memoirs, which were published after he had ceased to

situation in the capital by the end of the last week of February, the
reports sent to Mogilev by the commander of the Petrograd Military
District, Khabalov, the Minister for War, Belyaev, and Protopopov
were couched in a mendaciously reassuring tone. Events in the capital
were depicted as an unorganised anarchic rising, a combination of a
hunger riot and a display of hooliganism, and confidence was expressed
that the measures being taken would put an end to it in the next
twenty-four hours. These measures consisted in tightening control
over bread-baking factories, arresting about a hundred revolutionaries,
among them a sizeable number of the Petersburg Bolshevik Committee,
and replacing the Cossack detachments, which were reluctant to support
police action, by cavalry units.[1]

By this time, however, the Emperor must have become apprehensive
about the Petrograd situation. The idea he formed of it, though falling
short of reality, was nearer the truth than what was suggested in the
reports of his ministers. On the evening of the 25th Khabalov was
handed a telegram from the Emperor which said: 'I command you to
put an end as from tomorrow to all disturbances in the streets of the
capital, which are inadmissible at this difficult time when we are at
war with Germany and Austria.' The telegram was written by the

take any active part in politics. These often refer to events which are only hinted at,
and are not very accurate in detail. Bonch-Bruevich attaches great importance to
this apparently casual meeting with the Cossacks. Having said that the Kuban
regiment had to be removed from Znamensky Square after the incident, Bonch-
Bruevich concludes: 'Here we were dealing not with Christian anti-militarism, but
with an open revolutionary and political action by the troops against the old régime,
for the people and for fraternisation with the people in the streets. At that moment
it was a most important political action.' At the time these memoirs were published,
it would have been quite improper for a Marxist scholar and Bolshevik like Bonch-
Bruevich to claim that such an important political action had been instigated by
none other than himself, through casual contact with a religious group. But knowing
Bonch-Bruevich for the skilled intriguer and wire-puller that he was, we might well
infer that his contacts with the Cossack troops were less casual than he pretends,
and that he was one of the chief disseminators of the seditious propaganda to which
the Cossack units in Petrograd were undoubtedly subjected in the winter of 1916–17.
(See above, on Bonch-Bruevich and Rasputin, p. 204 and below, p. 369 f., on the part
played by him in the publication of 'Order No. 1'.)

1. In his testimony before the Muravyev Commission Khabalov mentions these
measures and insists that he tried to avoid shooting at the crowds to disperse the
demonstrations. See *Padenie*, vol. I, pp. 187 ff.

Emperor himself and sent without prior consultation with anybody. It threw Khabalov into utter confusion. Even if we allow for any exaggeration in his statement under interrogation by the Muravyev Commission, his testimony must be a fairly accurate reflection of his state of mind on receiving the telegram. He told the Commission:

> This telegram, how shall I put it — I must be open and truthful — it struck me like a blow on the head . . . how was I to put an end to them on the very next day? It said 'as from to-morrow' . . . the Emperor commanded me to put an end to them at all costs . . . what was I to do? How could I stop them? When they said 'Give us bread', we gave them bread, and that was that. But when the flags bore the legend 'Down with autocracy', what sort of bread would appease the crowds? What was to be done? The Tsar ordered: 'We must shoot' . . . it killed me, it really killed me, because I saw that this last measure which I was to apply might not necessarily lead to the desired result.

At about 10 p.m. on 25 February a meeting took place of police and military officers responsible for order in the capital, and Khabalov gave his orders:

> Gentlemen, the Emperor has ordered me to stop the disturbances from to-morrow. You know the measure that has to be applied as a last resort . . . if the crowd is small, therefore, and not aggressive, if it does not carry banners, you have at your disposal a cavalry detachment — use the cavalry to disperse the crowd. If the crowd is aggressive and carries banners, then act according to standing rules; that is, give a warning signal three times and after the third signal open fire.[1]

Later that night, the same on which the decision was taken to dissolve the Duma, Khabalov reported to the Council of Ministers.

The 26th of February was a Sunday. The city, as before, was quiet during the night — there were no military patrols, and the workers spent Sunday morning at home. The experiences of the previous day, however, had prompted the police authorities to withdraw their men from street patrols and traffic duties and marshal them into platoons armed with rifles. In the morning Khabalov reported to Mogilev that the town was quiet. In the early afternoon while this report was on its

---

1. Spiridovich in his posthumous work sharply criticises these instructions. In his opinion, the decision to open fire should never have been left to the military. A police-officer on the spot was the only authority to decide when to appeal to the troops for firearm support. Cf. Spiridovich, *Velikaya Voyna*, etc. vol. III, p. 100.

way to the Emperor at GHQ, serious rioting broke out, centring still on the Znamensky and the Kazansky Squares. The disturbances did not last long and were quelled by troops using firearms. There was a large number of casualties, although the description of the Nevsky strewn with dead bodies to be found not only in Trotsky's fanciful account but also in Sukhanov is somewhat exaggerated.[1]

What cannot be too strongly emphasised is the effect of the shooting on the troops themselves. For the last three days they had been in the streets, seeing the milling crowds, talking to the women and youths who had joined the demonstrators, noting the moral doubts and misgivings of their commanding officers as they resorted to violence to disperse the crowds. When at last they were ordered to open fire on the same predominantly unarmed crowds they had previously fraternised with, they were appalled, and there is no reason to doubt General Martynov's estimate of the situation: 'The overwhelming majority of the soldiers were disgusted with the role assigned to them in quelling the riots and fired only under compulsion.'[2] This applied in particular to the training unit of the Volynsky Regiment, consisting of two companies with two machine-guns, which had to disperse the demonstrations of Znamensky Square on the orders of Major Lashkevich. As a result of their onslaught the crowd dispersed, leaving forty dead and as many wounded lying on the pavement.[3]

There were shooting and casualties in many other places in the centre of the city, and by the evening of the 26th the police authorities, summing up in the official idiom, were able to say that 'order had been restored'.

In view of what happened the next day (Monday the 27th), one incident on the 26th overshadows all the clashes between the police and the demonstrators. This was the mutiny of some of the soldiers of the

1. Sukhanov writes (op. cit., vol. I, p. 53): 'About 1 p.m. the infantry on the Nevsky, as is well known, greatly intensified its rifle fire. The Nevsky was covered with the bodies of innocent people, who had never been involved in what was going on. Rumours [sic] about it rapidly spread all over the town. The population was terrorised. The [revolutionary] movement in the streets of the central parts of the town was liquidated. By 5 p.m. it seemed as if Tsarism had again won the day and the movement would be crushed.' 2. E. Martynov, op. cit., p. 93.
3. The shooting on Znamensky Square was witnessed by V. L. Burtsev, who described it in an interesting article in the *Birzhevye Vedomosti*. See Burtsev interrogation in *Padenie*, I, pp. 291 ff.

Pavlovsky Guards Regiment. Two of the companies were called out for patrol duties in the streets on Sunday and took part in the shooting. Their officers seem to have had them under control, and they showed no sign of disaffection. Demonstrators rushed to the Pavlovsky barracks and appealed to the regiment's reserve company to come out and stop the patrolling companies firing on the crowd, whereupon some of the soldiers from the barracks (not, presumably, controlled by their officers) poured out into the street with rifles, calling for an end to the bloodshed. The disturbance lasted for some time, until officers arrived on the spot, parleyed with the men, and with the help of the regimental chaplain got them back to barracks.[1] The incident was reported to Khabalov and the Minister for War, Belyaev, and naturally caused some consternation. Belyaev insisted on immediate action in the shape of summary execution of the mutineers; Khabalov argued that the case should be investigated at a court-martial. Meanwhile, the men were disarmed and confined to barracks. It was found that twenty-one of their rifles were missing. The men seemed to be in a subdued mood, and denounced their ringleaders — seventeen of them — who were arrested and sent to the Peter and Paul fortress. The incident was seemingly closed, and the morale of the other companies of the regiment appeared unaffected. It was the Pavlovsky Regiment, in fact, which turned up with arms and band to defend the government HQ on the 27th, when the military situation was very much out of hand and many other units of the Petrograd garrison had 'joined the people'. It is interesting to note that the Petrograd military authorities failed to report at once on the mutiny to Mogilev.

It seems surprising to us now that this incident did not serve as a warning to the officers of other units who were policing the city. This may be due in some degree to the peculiar conditions of service in the capital. The average stay of a soldier in the Petrograd garrison was six to eight weeks. The question of leave was a permanent irritant: inactivity and boredom in overcrowded barracks impelled the men to seek permission to go into town while the officers were chiefly concerned to have them confined to barracks because of the difficulty of keeping a check on them once they were caught up in the turbid waters of Petrograd life. Some of the companies were as many as

1. For a subsequent incident in which the commanding officer of the Pavlovsky Regiment lost his life, see below, p. 273.

fifteen hundred strong: there were new recruits — very young boys, who had not yet taken the oath of allegiance to the colours and the Emperor; yet others had already seen service in the field and spent long periods in hospital due to wounds or illness; these were bored and spoiled by the lack of discipline in the hospitals. There were a number of Petrograd intellectuals amongst them, as well as soldiers working in ordnance factories, and through these a certain amount of seditious propaganda reached the ranks.[1]

The morale of the troops was greatly affected by the injudicious and inexpedient way in which they were used in the first three days of street rioting. In accordance with a detailed plan for maintaining and restoring order in the capital, they were called out on to the streets and left standing for long hours at strategic points without definite instructions as to how to act in case of unrest. They were conscious of the reluctance of their superiors to use firearms against the crowds. They also realised that the police, whenever they failed to maintain or restore order, looked to them for assistance — a task they found odious since their relations with the police were already strained.[2] Contact was easily established between demonstrators and soldiers, and, as we have seen, this occasionally led to the troops siding with the demonstrators against the police. When the Emperor's orders radically changed the situation and the troops were ordered on the afternoon of the 26th to fire on the demonstrators, they were naturally aghast. After all, the crowds were behaving no differently from before, and their conduct had previously been tolerated. Still, the Pavlovsky street incident apart, there was no noticeable disaffection among the troops that day and, as we have noted, even the leader of the *Mezhrayonka*, Yurenev, thought the attempt at a full-scale revolutionary uprising had failed, and the armed forces would not join the revolution.

4. THE MUTINY OF THE PETROGRAD GARRISON

While some of the radical and revolutionary intellectuals were thus losing faith in the success of their cause, a new factor was coming into play. The soldiers of the Volynsky Regiment, who had taken part

1. See above, pp. 88, 254.
2. See Kondratyev's memoirs in *Krasnaya Letopis*, VII (1923), on the relations between the police and the Petrograd garrison.

in the shooting on Znamensky Square on Sunday 26 February, were wide awake in their barracks, discussing the whole matter. They belonged to the two companies of the training unit under Major Lashkevich which had fired on the crowds on Znamensky Square. One of the NCOs of this regiment, a certain Kirpichnikov, had distinguished himself during the day by seizing a hand-made bomb from one of the demonstrators, and dutifully surrendering it to the police. Kirpichnikov afterwards proved one of the most energetic propagandists of 'defensism' among the soldiers of the Petrograd garrison. In his account of what happened Kirpichnikov described Lashkevich as an unpopular officer, who wore gold-rimmed spectacles (note the complex symbol of wealth and intellectualism), a cruel, uncouth man, who managed to offend even old soldiers to the point of tears, and who was known as the 'bespectacled viper'.[1]

After the officers had left the barracks, the men gathered to discuss the day's events. They could not understand why they had had to shoot. Kirpichnikov does not record what was said in the darkened dormitories of the barracks, and even if he had done so, we should be none the wiser, for legend supplanted reality almost as soon as anything occurred. Nothing indicates that it was revolutionary conviction that led to the troops' momentous decision to refuse to fire on the demonstrating crowds. They were, far more probably, prompted by a natural revulsion against what they had been doing under the command of a most unpopular officer. Yet they must have known the risks they incurred in adopting a mutinous attitude. Whether any representative of a revolutionary group or some such other clandestine organisation had been at work among them we do not know. But in view of what took place later we cannot rule out the possibility. Kirpichnikov, whom the men seem to have looked upon as their leader, could hardly have belonged to any such group.

The situation became explosive the next morning, Monday 27th, when the men turned out on parade in the corridors of the barracks, and Lashkevich walked in. He was greeted in the usual way by the first company of the training unit, and made a short speech informing the men of their duty and quoting the Emperor's telegram. Kirpichnikov then reported to him that the men were refusing to go out into

1. See Ivan Lukash, *The Rising in the Volynsky Regiment, the story of the first hero of the rising, Timofey Kirpichnikov* (Petrograd, 1917).

the streets. Kirpichnikov's story, as reported by Lukash, goes on: 'The commanding officer went pale, shrank back and hurried out. We rushed to the windows, and many of us saw the commanding officer suddenly fling his arms wide and crash to the ground face down into a snowdrift in the barrack yard. He was killed by a well-aimed stray bullet.' A well-aimed *stray* bullet! When these words were written the dreamlike logic of revolutionary rhetoric had already replaced common sense in Russia. The murder of Lashkevich is some-times ascribed to Kirpichnikov himself. The previous night the com-mander of the Pavlovsky Regiment, Colonel Ecksten, had been killed as he left the barracks after dealing successfully with the mutiny of one company. And later the killing of officers could rarely be traced to the men under their command. Generally speaking it was the murder of the CO which had the greatest revolutionising effect in the army as well as in the navy. This was the doctrine accepted by the Bolshevik Party and by Lenin himself.[1]

Whoever was reponsible for the murder of Lashkevich did more to create a revolutionary mood among the Volynsky soldiers than any propaganda. The men suddenly found themselves beyond the point of no return. From then on, they were committed to the success of the mutiny, which depended completely on other units joining it without delay. After some wavering and discussion on the parade ground, the soldiers seized their rifles and rushed out into the street, making for the barracks of the Preobrazhensky and Moscow Regiments. The news of the rising in the Volynsky Regiment spread like wildfire through the streets, where workers from the suburbs were already filtering through the patrols to resume the demonstrations of the previous day. The men of the Volynsky Regiment were firing their rifles into the air and proclaiming their support for the people's rising. But they soon lost their cohesion and mingled with the demonstrators to form part of the same motley crowd — rifleless soldiers in dishevelled uniform, armed workers in peaked caps or even bowlers — so characteristic of those times.

The officers of the mutinous units were nowhere to be seen. On that decisive day, 27 February, the behaviour of the officers of the Petrograd garrison was of great consequence. In most cases they had little personal contact with their men, and were barely maintained in

1. See Lenin, *Sochineniya*, vol. XIX, p. 351.

authority by the traditional discipline they had done nothing to reinforce by their own efforts. Even those who knew the soldiers well and were of advanced or even progressive views, like Colonel Stankevich, to whom we owe one of the earliest comprehensive memoirs of the revolution,[1] at once felt a keen sense of personal danger upon hearing that officers were being killed in the barracks by their men. Most officers of the Petrograd garrison had, on the other hand, also succumbed to the propaganda of the press and the Voluntary Organisations and favoured negotiations with the Duma and speedy constitutional reform, belated though it might be.[2]

The mutiny of the Volynsky Regiment and its rapid spread to other units of the Petrograd garrison was certainly the crucial event of Monday the 27th. In the intoxicated first weeks after the fall of the Tsarist régime, the mutiny of the garrison seemed in retrospect a manifestation of the popular swing toward revolution. It became an article of faith with the new régime to hold that even in those early days – 27 February to 2 March – any army unit faced with the alternative of joining or suppressing the revolution would at the first opportunity have joined the people with enthusiasm. Events in Petrograd do not bear out this contention.

In the first place it is obvious that the government did nothing to raise the morale of those troops who were were ready to obey orders. By midday on Monday 27th, General Zankevich had been put in command of the loyal troops in Petrograd by the Minister for War, Belyaev, to assist General Khabalov, who had completely lost his head. Zankevich had at his disposal a considerable force, which he concentrated in the yard of the Winter Palace. The troops reacted enthusiastically to his speech, in which he appealed to them to stand immovable as a rock for Tsar and fatherland. But after that, hours passed without anyone issuing a single order. No provision was made for feeding the troops on patrol, and after dusk the units dispersed to their barracks for supper. On the way they merged with the crowds.

Typically, neither Khabalov nor Belyaev knew which troops they

1. V. B. Stankevich, *Vospominaniya 1914–1919* (Berlin, 1920), in particular p. 66.
2. 'It must be said that the feelings of the officers, particularly of the Izmailovsky Regiment, were not such that one could rely on their acting very energetically: they expressed the opinion that one should enter into negotiations with Rodzyanko.' Khabalov's statement to the Muravyev Commission, see *Padenie*, vol. 1, p. 201.

could safely rely on. Thus in the barracks on the Sampsonievsky Prospekt, there was a Cyclist Battalion, consisting of ten companies: two fighting units, four in the process of formation, and four reserve units. They had fourteen machine-guns at their disposal. The cyclists were all literate men with some knowledge of mechanics, and have since been described as strongly infiltrated by 'petty bourgeois elements.' They were under the command of a particularly popular officer named Balkashin. When on the 27th he ordered his men to throw a guard round the barracks he was readily obeyed. He made several attempts to contact the headquarters of the Petrograd Military District, but could not get through. Only at six that evening did he decide to withdraw his company from the street and to lock himself in the barracks. During the night he tried again to get in touch with headquarters, but the men he sent on reconnaissance did not return. He managed, however, to increase his supplies of ammunition by sending a cart round to the HQ of the battalion in Serdobolskaya Street. The cyclist battalion put up a spirited resistance in their barracks, which were no more than wooden huts, on the morning of the 28th. When it became obvious that the barracks would be destroyed by machine-gun and artillery fire, and Colonel Balkashin was satisfied that no break-out was possible, he decided to surrender. He ordered a cease-fire, left the barracks and addressed the aggressive crowd, explaining that the men under his command were not guilty of bloodshed, and that he alone was responsible for issuing the order to resist the crowds 'in fulfilment of his duty of allegiance'. Shots were fired in response: Balkashin got a bullet in the heart and died instantaneously. This seems to be the one clear case of outstanding personal courage recorded in Petrograd in those days.[1]

The case of the Cyclist Battalion[2] shows what a determined and popular officer could have done if the commanders at the headquarters of the Petrograd garrison had been less disorientated. The troops were certainly divided in their feelings, and there must have been a number of cases where they showed a clear desire not to be involved in a movement they considered subversive. The early memoirs of the times

1. See E. Martynov, op. cit., pp. 120–121 ff.
2. The incident of the Cyclist Battalion is fully described by Martynov, *Tsarskaya armiya v fevralskom perevorote*, p. 120, who quotes documentary sources which were available to him.

published in the Soviet Union reflect this fact, though later it was systematically suppressed. For instance the worker A. Kondratyev, a member of the Bolshevik Petersburg Committee, recalls in his memoirs[1] how he accompanied some workers and mutineers of the Volynsky Regiment to the barracks of the Moscow Regiment and found that a number of officers and other ranks had barricaded themselves in the officers' mess, and were firing at the demonstrators across the parade ground. Kondratyev and those with him managed to enter the barracks and found the soldiers in a depressed mood, standing about unarmed, not knowing what to do. No revolutionary exhortations could rouse them. Having 'strained his vocal chords' and talked himself hoarse, Kondratyev issued an ultimatum and threatened that if they did not 'join the cause of the people', the barracks would at once be subjected to artillery fire. According to Kondratyev, this worked, and the men started getting ready, took up their arms and went out into the street.

This was no doubt typical of what was happening all over Petrograd that day, and explains why neither the self-styled HQ of the rising (under the command of the Socialist Revolutionaries Filippovsky and the above-mentioned S. Mstislavsky-Maslovsky) nor the military commission of the Duma Committee (under Colonel Engelhardt) had any troops at their command for most of the day, though thousands of armed men had joined the rising. The soldiers who came out into the streets preferred the anonymity of the milling crowd to an identifiable position in their units. They sold their rifles to the highest bidder, adorned their greatcoats with pieces of red ribbon, and joined one or other of the demonstrations, smashing police stations, opening up prisons, setting fire to court buildings, or indulging in other forms of 'bloodless' revolutionary activity.

The mutiny of the Petrograd garrison took the local military and civilian authorities completely by surprise. It also upset all the plans on which the government had relied for the maintenance of order, and which had been elaborated on the assumption that fighting would be limited to clashes between the troops and demonstrating workers. To meet this contingency, the city had been divided into districts, certain regiments being earmarked for duty in each of them. The plan lost all significance when HQ no longer knew what troops they could rely on. The reaction of the officers of the Petrograd garrison to the first

1. See *Krasnaya Letopis*, VII (1923), p. 68.

news of the soldiers' rising demonstrates the extent to which their morale had deteriorated, undermined as it was by the propaganda and rumour-mongering of the press and liberal circles. The officers of the Volynsky Regiment were completely bewildered. One of them describes what happened in the regiment's headquarters when the officers came to see Colonel Viskovsky, the battalion commander.[1] On learning what had happened to Major Lashkevich, Viskovsky discussed the situation for some time with his aide-de-camp. From time to time he joined the officers, who were waiting in the next room for orders and instructions. He repeatedly asked for details of what had happened. The officers under his command made all sorts of suggestions, offering to call out some of the officer-training schools. Such suggestions from subordinates were unusual and incompatible with the existing order of military discipline. Up to about ten o'clock the mutineers remained on the barrack parade ground, apparently not knowing what to do next. At that moment the mutiny could have been crushed, but the commanding officer continued to waver, and assured his subordinates that he had faith in the loyalty of his men and knew they would come to their senses and hand over their ringleaders. When the company which had mutinied broke out of the barrack grounds, the commander of the battalion suggested to the officers that they should go home, and he himself then left the premises.

If one considers such attitudes as that shown by Colonel Viskovsky, it is not surprising that General Khabalov thought of appealing to an officer of the Preobrazhensky Regiment who was on leave in Petrograd from the front and who had the reputation of being a loyal and energetic man. By the time Colonel Kutepov[2] arrived at the city

1. See A. I. Spiridovich, *Velikaya voyna*. The passage referred to comes from vol. III, p. 123, and is extracted from a letter written by one of the officers in the Volynsky Regiment to Spiridovich.

2. Kutepov, who was certainly a determined and even a ruthless man, later played an important part in the White Guardist movement, was second-in-command to General Wrangel, and was in charge of the White troops evacuated in 1920 from the Crimea to the Gallipoli Peninsula. He later headed the White Officers' émigré organisation in Paris, where in January 1930 he was kidnapped, presumably by Soviet agents, and never heard of again. This account is based on a memoir written in 1926 and published in a collection of articles dedicated to General Kutepov, *General Kutepov* (Paris, 1934), and on the statement of General Khabalov to the Muravyev Commission, *Padenie*, vol. I.

police HQ, where General Khabalov was awaiting him, the men of the Volynsky Regiment had already reached the barracks of the Preobra-zhensky Regiment, killed a colonel there and forced part of the regiment to join them. Kutepov was appointed head of a punitive expedition, with instructions to occupy the whole district from the Liteyny Bridge down to the Nikolaevsky Station and restore order and discipline to all the troops there. He was given a company of one of the Guards Regiments, with the prospect of picking up other troops as he proceeded to the area of operations.

Kutepov had been in Petrograd only a few days and was out of touch with the mood of the capital and even with the sentiments of the officers of his own regiment. He had to form his own idea of the morale of his troops as he made his way along the crowded Nevsky towards its junction with the Liteyny Prospekt. He found the morale of the Reserve Guards Regiment more or less satisfactory, that of a machine-gun company which he picked up near the Alexandrine Theatre less so. The men did not return his greeting, and the major in command told him the machine-guns were unusable, as he had neither water nor glycerine.

As the somewhat motley crowd under Kutepov's command reached the junction of the Nevsky and the Liteyny, they were overtaken by an officer of the Preobrazhensky Regiment, bearing an order from General Khabalov which countermanded his earlier one and requested Kutepov to return at once to the Winter Palace Square. Kutepov answered that he did not think it advisable to go back the same way and that he would return via the Liteyny and the "Marsovo Pole" (a large parade-ground). This decision seems to have been fatal for Kutepov's expedition. From that moment he lost touch with Khabalov for the rest of the day, and wasted precious time in dealing with crowds of mutineers along the Liteyny and the adjoining streets. As far as Khabalov was concerned, Kutepov had disappeared completely.

This is how Khabalov described the situation in his testimony before the Muravyev Commission:

> So we dispatched this detachment, made up of six companies, fifteen machine-guns and one and a half squadrons of cavalry, under the orders of Colonel Kutepov, a heroic soldier, to get the mutineers to lay down arms, or, if they refused, to take decisive action against them . . . but something impossible happened that day ! . . . the detachment was sent

off under a courageous and determined officer, but there were no results whatsoever. What could have happened? If he had acted with determination he would have clashed with the excited crowd: organised troops could have dispersed the crowd and forced it back towards the Neva and the Tauride Gardens.

After making several attempts to get in touch with Kutepov, Khabalov learned that he had been stopped in Kirochnaya Street and would need reinforcements. But any reinforcements sent out seemed to dissolve *en route* without reaching their destination.

Kutepov's own account gives a clearer idea of how the street fighting developed. Turning with his detachment from the Nevsky into the Liteyny Prospekt, Kutepov came across the mutineers of the Volynsky Regiment, who were joined by soldiers of the Litovsky Guards Regiment. The men of the Volynsky Regiment seemed most undecided and one of the NCO's, acting on behalf of his comrades, asked Kutepov to re-form them and lead them back to barracks. The only thing the men were afraid of was that they would be shot for mutiny. Kutepov addressed the mutineers, assuring them that those who joined him would not be shot. The mutineers welcomed this declaration and lifted Kutepov on to their shoulders, so that he could repeat his pledge to the crowd:

> As I was lifted shoulder-high by the soldiers, I saw the whole street filled mainly with privates of the Litovsky and Volynsky Reserve Regiments, among whom there were also a few civilians, clerks from the GHQ office, and artillery troops. I addressed the troops, shouting: 'Those who are now urging you to commit a crime against your monarch and Fatherland do so in order to help our enemies the Germans, with whom we are at war. Don't act like scoundrels and traitors. Be honest Russian soldiers.'

This harangue was not very well received. Some soldiers shouted: 'We're afraid we'll be shot.' There were also a few voices shouting: 'Comrades, he's lying. They'll shoot you.' Kutepov managed to repeat his pledge that no one who put himself under his command would be shot. However, the operation of getting the mutineers of the two regiments into disciplined ranks could apparently not be carried out, since the Kutepov detachment immediately came under fire, and the mutineers scattered. As time went on, Kutepov's men began to complain of hunger. Kutepov had bought bread and sausages on the way, but was keeping them for supper. Meanwhile shooting from various quarters was increasing the number of casualties in the Kutepov detachment.

Kutepov occupied the mansion of Count Musin-Pushkin, where the offices of the Red Cross of the Northern Front were located, and improvised a field hospital there. He repeatedly tried to get in touch with the police HQ (*Gradonachalstvo*) but Khabalov had already left it for the Admiralty without informing Kutepov of the change.

Kutepov lost many officers in the fighting. While he was trying unsuccessfully to get through to police headquarters on the telephone, the crowds infiltrated into and flooded the Liteyny Prospekt. It was getting dark and the demonstrators were smashing the street lamps.

As dusk slowly changed to complete darkness, the Kutepov force ceased almost all organised resistance, as Kutepov himself realised on emerging from Musin-Pushkin's mansion:

> It was already dark [he recalls] when I went out into the street. The whole of the Liteyny was filled by a crowd flooding in from all the adjacent side streets, smashing and extinguishing the street lamps. I could hear my name shouted in the street, accompanied by gross insults. The bulk of my detachment had merged with the crowd and I realised that further resistance on my part was impossible. I returned to the house, ordered the front door to be locked, and gave instructions for the men in the house to be given the bread and sausage which had been prepared for them. Not one of the units in my detachment had sent any dinner for its men.[1]

The Red Cross officials asked Kutepov to remove all able-bodied men from the house, so as to preserve its character as a sanctuary for the wounded. Kutepov had no option but to comply. Thus ended the Petrograd military authorities' only serious attempt at clearing part of the city centre. But the momentum of the crowds also seemed spent, and they began to disperse. A victory had been achieved for the revolutionaries by unled and unorganised workers and mutineers, without any effective intervention on the part of any revolutionary HQ.

This is how the scene described by Kutepov appeared to Nikolay

1. *General Kutepov*, p. 169.

Sukhanov, who was crossing the Liteyny Prospekt at about the same time together with the Bolshevik Shlyapnikov and another man:

> At nightfall we reached the Liteyny, near the place where Tsarist and revolutionary troops had clashed a few hours before. On the left the District Court building was ablaze. Near Sergievsky Street there were guns pointing indiscriminately in all directions. Ammunition boxes were lying all around. . . . Something which looked like a barricade had been erected nearby. But it was crystal clear to every passer-by that neither guns nor barricades could afford any protection from the smallest attack.
>
> God knows when and why these guns had been brought here, but there was hardly anybody to use them. It is true that there were groups of soldiers nearby. Some of them were busying themselves issuing orders or shouting at passers-by, but no one took any notice of them. . . .

And Sukhanov sums up his impression of that moment in these significant words:

> Seeing this picture of the revolution, one could easily fall into despair. But one should not forget the other side of the coin: the guns which fell into the hands of the revolutionaries would, it is true, have been useless and defenceless in these hands against any organised force. But Tsarism had no such organised force.[1]

Sukhanov is right in saying that by the evening of 27 February there was neither organised resistance on the part of the government, nor organised leadership on the part of the revolutionaries. But Sukhanov, like most other chroniclers of the time, failed to disclose the reasons for the lack of any organised government force. Numerous incidents which occurred that day point to a reluctance on the part of the officers in command of units of the Petrograd garrison to take repressive measures against the demonstrators, and to a certain fear of the troops under their command. This fear was to some extent justified, not so much because of the general bitterness felt by the men towards their officers as because there was a marked tendency for the demonstrators to pick out and shoot officers in the street while avoiding armed clashes with the troops. Casualties among officers and NCO's were heavy, although a large number of officers stayed away from their units, either at home on sick leave or discussing the political situation in their

1. Sukhanov, op. cit., vol. I, p. 97.

messes. The insidious propaganda emanating from the Duma had done its work. The imminence of a change of régime seemed so certain to most of them that they did not want to spoil their record by being on the losing side at the critical moment. Khabalov realised that many officers under his command wanted him to get in touch with the Duma representatives and use the authority of the Duma opposition to restore order in the garrison. And although such generals as Khabalov and Belyaev remained faithful to their oath of allegiance, their will to resist was paralysed by the fear of encountering open resistance from their subordinates, and they were not even able to organise the few units which, like the Cyclist Battalion, were ready to obey orders.

The number of mutineers, that is of soldiers who had left their barracks to mingle with the crowds, is put by Sukhanov at a mere 25,000 out of a total garrison of 160,000. But the remaining 'neutral' troops were badly equipped and not at all experienced in the kind of operation required to suppress a rising in a large city. As is evident from the memoirs quoted, an important factor was the problem of feeding the troops patrolling the streets. Nothing had been done to provide field kitchens, just as nothing had been done to establish a perimeter beyond which no crowds or demonstrations would be tolerated.

5. THE COLLAPSE

During the evening of 27th most of the units between the Admiralty and the Winter Palace under the command of General Khabalov decided to go back to barracks for dinner. As they went forward through the crowded streets, rubbing shoulders with the demonstrators, they melted into the crowds and the few who reached barracks were unable and unwilling to return for duty to the Winter Palace. The detachment under Khabalov's command continued to dwindle. Typically, some of the men apologised to their officers for their defection before they went, and said they wished them no harm but must look to their own safety and welfare. Their forlorn commanders, dejected and dishonoured, remained, a dismal dwindling crowd, around Khabalov in the Admiralty.

In the late hours of the night General Zankevich decided to move the headquarters from the Admiralty to the Winter Palace.[1] The soldiers scattered about the vast building and the officers settled down for the night. It was then that General Khabalov decided to proclaim a 'state of siege' in Petrograd and had posters printed with a curt announcement of the fact. This plan had the full support of Prince Golitsyn, who wanted a state of siege proclaimed so as to free the government of all responsibility for administration, which would instead be entirely vested in the military command. However, as there was no glue available at HQ, the notices could not be posted and Khabalov ordered them to be scattered in the streets, where they were blown hither and thither in the blizzard and trampled in the snow by the dispersing crowds.

There was an even more pathetic incident when one of the generals asked, on arrival at the Winter Palace, for a cup of tea. He was told that the palace administration had standing orders not to serve tea before eight o'clock in the morning. One of the palace servants providentially offered the general some tea made on the stove in his private quarters.

But the cup of humiliation had yet to be drained. Hardly had the tired troops got warm and the generals fallen asleep on makeshift beds than a new complication arose. The Grand Duke Michael had been spending the evening at the Mariinsky Palace, where the government had its last historic meeting, and where a last-minute plan to save the monarchy was being worked out with the assistance of the President of the Duma, Rodzyanko. The Grand Duke now returned, disgruntled, to the Winter Palace, after being mildly rebuked by the Emperor for proffering unsolicited political advice. He had tried to leave for his suburban residence, but, as there was no train, came to stay the night in the Winter Palace, where he found the few remaining defenders of the régime. He summoned Generals Khabalov and Belyaev at about 3 a.m. on the 28th and asked them to withdraw the 'troops from the Palace, because he did not want the troops to fire on the crowd from the house of the Romanovs'.

The behaviour of the Grand Duke is easily explained. He had seen the government appointed by his brother disintegrate during the last meeting of the Council of Ministers. His selfless offer to assume immediate responsibility for a political solution had met with a total

1. Zankevich believed that from a moral point of view it was preferable 'to die in defence of the palace'. See *Padenie*, vol. I, p. 202.

lack of understanding from the Emperor. Yet as second in the line of succession he was faced with the possibility, which was fast becoming a certainty, that he would be called upon to act as regent to his infant nephew, or perhaps himself ascend the unstable throne. To have his name linked with ineffectual reprisals against the population of Petrograd would have been to jeopardise all chances of solving the dynastic problem in an acceptable way.

The order to vacate the palace in the middle of the night was the final blow to the generals' morale. They moved, in the early hours, back to the Admiralty, where the decision to cease all operations was to be taken before noon of that day, 28 February. But even then there was no official surrender to 'the enemy'. Khabalov probably did not even know to whom he could have surrendered. The troops were told to give their arms into the safe keeping of officials of the Naval Ministry in the Admiralty building and to disperse quietly to their barracks while the officers withdrew to their private quarters.

The amazing thing is that while all these lugubrious ceremonies were taking place in the Winter Palace in the hours of darkness on the night of the 27th–28th, the streets of the capital were clear of crowds, and there was every opportunity, as we know from the case of the Cyclist Battalion, of replenishing stocks of ammunition for the troops still available. Nor was any military protection worth mentioning available at what had become the headquarters of the revolution — the Tauride Palace. Indeed, after a day of excitement, the Duma deputies still on the premises were seized with apprehension lest Khabalov be tempted to march the mile or so from the Winter Palace to arrest them. There were rumours that he was preparing for action, but nothing was done, or could be done, to afford armed protection either to the Duma Provisional Committee or the Provisional Executive Committee of the Petrograd Soviet, which was already 'squatting' in one of the wings of the Tauride Palace.

The Sinking Ship

The last hours of the Imperial Government; Rodzyanko's last attempt to save the monarchy; Rodzyanko or Prince Lvov? The Duma's reaction to prorogation; Rodzyanko's waverings; Rodzyanko and Alekseev.

I. THE LAST HOURS OF THE IMPERIAL GOVERNMENT

The Imperial Government — that is, the Council of Ministers — came to an end during the night of 27–28 February. The ministers were never officially relieved of their posts, and they had no right to relinquish them of their own free will. But when they left the Mariinsky Palace, partly because of the failure of the electric light, they knew they would never meet again, though forty-eight hours earlier none of them had believed that they were living in the midst of a revolutionary turmoil which had been going on for at least five days.

When the unrest first broke out the Council of Ministers as a whole took no notice, considering the demonstrations a matter for the ministers directly concerned — the Minister of the Interior and his Police Department, and the Minister of War and the Commander of the Petrograd Military District, who was directly subordinate to the latter. Far greater political importance was attached to the quarrel over the administration of food supplies in Petrograd, which the Duma majority wanted to see transferred to the municipal authorities. The question was not, however, debated in the State Duma, but only in the Petrograd Municipal Duma. On the 25th contact was established between the opposition majority in the Duma and the Petrograd Municipality, and it seemed likely that the issue would be debated with some acrimony in the State Duma on Monday 27th. The question was closely connected with the prevalent unrest, since most of the demonstrators were demanding 'Bread for the hungry'. The government was apprehensive in case the Duma debates should lead to attacks on the government as a whole and in particular on the Minister of the

Interior, Protopopov, who was insisting on retaining control of supplies. If the government were again violently attacked in the Duma, dissolution would become inevitable. This was, in fact, what Protopopov was hoping for. The Premier, Golitsyn, however, and some of the other ministers, including the Minister for Foreign Affairs, Pokrovsky, did not want a dissolution and hoped to persuade the Emperor to drop Protopopov and the Minister of Justice, Dobrovolsky, who supported him. On Saturday 25 February, the ministers met in Prince Golitsyn's flat for discussions. The general feeling was that the Duma session should be interrupted, but Protopopov was exerting strong pressure for the Duma to be dissolved. Golitsyn, however, had his way.

The Duma could be prorogued or dissolved only by a decree signed by the Emperor. It so happened, however, that at some time during the previous autumn, when the Emperor was going to GHQ, he had left with the then Prime Minister, Stuermer, decrees both for the dissolution of the Duma and for a temporary recess, so that in case of need the dates could be filled in without the delay entailed by the signing of the decrees in Mogilev and their delivery to Petrograd. These undated decrees passed from Stuermer to Trepov, and finally to Golitsyn when he became Premier on 28 December 1916. The Emperor had explained the arrangements to Golitsyn, simply saying: 'Keep these decrees and use them if necessary.' There are definite indications that members of the Cabinet had dropped hints about their possible use to the President of the Duma, Rodzyanko. Rodzyanko had protested against these threats of dissolution in his last loyal address to the Tsar. Golitsyn had not raised the matter when the Emperor left for GHQ on 22 February, since at that moment he did not expect the Duma to 'get out of hand'.

By Saturday the 25th, however, the situation was quite different. Khabalov informed the ministers of the Emperor's order to put an end to the street rioting at all costs, and serious clashes with the troops were expected. On the other hand, all recent attempts to get the Duma majority to support an appeal to the working masses for order had failed.[1] As we have seen, Rodzyanko was going to blame the outbreaks of street fighting on the police, as he himself said to Khabalov. It

1. Prince Shakhovskoy recalls one such attempt, to which Nekrasov responded in the name of the Kadets by demanding the release of the Labour Group of the WIC in exchange for the Duma's support. See Shakhovskoy, op. cit., p. 198.

was therefore useless to suppose that either he or any other liberal leader in the Duma would use his influence to dissuade the workers and students from demonstrating.

Although it was clear that all ministers were in favour of the prorogation of the Duma, no formal decision was taken on 25 February. Two members of the Council (Rittikh and Pokrovsky)[1] were asked to sound the more reasonable elements in the Duma about measures which might contribute to an easing of tension. When the ministers met again on the evening of 26 February — i.e. after the troops had been ordered to fire on the crowds and clashes had occurred — they were unanimous that the Duma should not meet for the next few days. According to the two ministers, who had made private enquiries in Duma circles, this was also the opinion of many deputies. Prince Shakhovskoy reports in his memoirs that there was some feeling in the Duma that prorogation would be acceptable, provided it coincided with a reshuffle of the government and the appointment of a popular general such as General Alekseev as its head.[2]

The deliberations of these two meetings of the government on the 25th and the evening of the 26th have not been put on record, and eye-witness accounts are contradictory. But it is significant that relations between the government and the Duma were reverting to the same pattern as in September 1915. The government was ready to issue a prorogation decree, but at the same time it was preparing its own demise and its replacement by a 'government enjoying popular confidence'.

It seems that it was at the meeting of the 26th that Golitsyn filled in the blank decrees, proroguing the Duma until a date 'not later than April 1917'. There is no record of Golitsyn asking the Emperor for permission to use the decrees. The responsibility for this decision rested entirely with Golitsyn and the Council of Ministers. He later argued that he had acted in accordance with the powers granted him by the Tsar.

This was the last meeting at which the ministers felt themselves masters of the situation. Protopopov seemed delighted at the decision to prorogue the Duma, and was impatient to convey the decree to the

1. Rittikh was appointed Acting Minister of Agriculture on 16 November 1916, and Pokrovsky was Minister of Foreign Affairs from 10 November 1916.
2. Shakhovskoy, op. cit., p. 199.

Senate, which would send it on to Rodzyanko. Only the day before, he had issued an order to arrest members of the revolutionary parties, and about a hundred persons had been seized by the police, including five members of the Bolshevik Petersburg Committee. This shows that the police were still surreptitiously controlling the known revolutionary organisations through their agents and *provocateurs*. Shlyapnikov, however, evaded arrest, and claims that after the arrests the direction of the revolutionary mass movement was transferred to the Bolshevik Party Committee of the Vyborg district.[1] The arrests had no effect on the movements of the crowds. It is safe to say that even if every single Bolshevik in Petrograd had been arrested on the 25th or 26th, the events of the following day would not have been affected in any way.

On the 27th the ministers were singularly inactive all day. Only two of them, the Minister of War, Belyaev, and the Minister for Foreign Affairs, Pokrovsky, continued to administer their departments. Belyaev tried to rally the troops which had remained faithful to the régime, and Pokrovsky received the British Ambassador, who again raised the question of appointing a Cabinet responsible to the Duma. Pokrovsky said that although constitutional reforms were probably necessary, the immediate task before the government was the suppression of the mutiny of the Petrograd garrison.

When the Council of Ministers met at 4 p.m. on the 27th in the Mariinsky Palace, a sense of impotence and lassitude seems to have taken hold of them. It was obvious that Protopopov had lost his head, that all his truculent self-confidence had gone and that it would be senseless to expect any action from him. Belyaev reported that the hatred of Protopopov was so intense that they could not afford to wait any longer before dismissing him. The Council, however, was not empowered to dismiss a minister, nor could Protopopov resign without the express permission of the Emperor. Golitsyn suggested that Protopopov should say that he was ill, so that one of the deputy ministers could take over from him. Sheepishly, Protopopov agreed, and even offered to commit suicide, but was dissuaded from doing so, and left the meeting. The appointment of his successor was then discussed, and Golitsyn seemed ready to overstep the limits of his power under the special circumstances and appoint a minister himself without consulting the Emperor. But no suitable candidate could be found and

1. Shlyapnikov, *Semnadtsaty God*, 2nd. ed. (Moscow, n.d.) p. 99.

the question was left in abeyance.[1] The Council of Ministers sent a telegram to the Emperor asking him to appoint a general with enough troops to quell the rising, and then adjourned until the evening. As the ministers were leaving the palace the news came that the chairman of the State Council, Shcheglovitov, had been arrested and brought to the State Duma. The Minister for Foreign Affairs, Pokrovsky, said that he could not believe that Rodzyanko had agreed to head the revolutionary movement. But the Tauride Palace could no longer be reached by telephone, and the ministers could only guess what the newly-formed Duma Committee intended to do.

2. RODZYANKO'S LAST ATTEMPT TO SAVE THE MONARCHY

Pokrovsky was quite right in thinking Rodzyanko would scarcely be willing to head a revolutionary movement. Until late at night on 27-28 February, Rodzyanko still hoped to save the monarchy by taking over the government and organising a regency of the Tsar's brother, Grand Duke Michael. He enlisted Golitsyn's support in trying to persuade the Grand Duke to proclaim himself Regent, but the Grand Duke refused to do so without the express permission of his brother. When the Council of Ministers met again late at night on the 27th, the negotiations between Grand Duke Michael, Rodzyanko and Golitsyn, which are probably the most important political event of that moment, had just been concluded. The Grand Duke's offer to assume full powers in Petrograd was transmitted, late on the 27th, from the Ministry of War to GHQ, where General Alekseev reported it to the Tsar. The message went by the relatively slow process of the Hughes apparatus, and in Mogilev too there was considerable delay. In the meantime the Emperor had made up his mind to leave Mogilev for Tsarskoe Selo that same night, and was not willing to discuss the political issue with the generals. Accordingly Alekseev was told to send a short message to the Grand Duke thanking him for his readiness to help, but saying that the Emperor would come and deal with the situation himself. Thus ended the last attempt by Rodzyanko to save the monarchy.

The ministers sat and waited for the Emperor's decision until about

1. A certain General Makarenko was mentioned at the time, but he was in charge of the Military State Prosecutor's office, and this, it was believed, would make him unpopular with the liberals.

midnight, and when they left the building, the crowds were already threatening to ransack it. They had heard of the failure of Grand Duke Michael's proposal, but they did not wait long enough to receive the Emperor's orders that they should remain at their posts until his return to Tsarskoe Selo. Those who could be located in their homes were informed by telephone the next morning. By that time the Mariinsky Palace had been sacked, the Ministry of Transport seized by a representative of the Duma Committee, the industrialist A. A. Bublikov, and most of the ministers were either under arrest or in hiding.

The negotiations between Rodzyanko and the Grand Duke on the afternoon of the 27th had been carried out in great secrecy. Not even the other members of the Romanov family were informed of the Grand Duke's intention to proclaim himself Regent if he could secure the consent of the Emperor. Indeed, the family were suspicious of the comings and goings of the Tsar's brother, whom they did not consider eligible for the throne because of his morganatic marriage. The Grand Dukes Paul (the last surviving uncle of the Tsar) and Cyril (who would be the next in succession) were plotting a move of their own, preparing a kind of manifesto of the Romanov family, in which they gave their backing to the demand for a parliamentary government.[1]

But just as Grand Duke Michael kept his political moves secret from his family, so did Rodzyanko from the members of the Duma Committee formed that day with himself as chairman. The memoirs of Milyukov, which appeared posthumously in 1955, reveal a lack of personal confidence between the two Duma leaders. It is a sad reflection that in those fateful hours, when these leaders could reasonably have been expected to pursue a common course, they were actually intriguing against one another. This lack of mutual confidence and straightforwardness in political dealings was to influence the political system which subsequently emerged, so that we must go into this matter in some detail.

---

1. It is to this remarkable project that the Empress referred in her letter to the Emperor dated 2 March: 'Paul, to whom I have given a terrible blowing-up for not having done anything with the guards, is now working as fast as he can and intends to save us all in a most honourable and lunatic way: he has composed an idiotic manifesto referring to a constitution after the war and so on. . . .' The original document embodying Grand Duke Paul's efforts at constitutional reform is in the Archives of Columbia University. See below, p. 399.

3. RODZYANKO OR PRINCE LVOV?

Milyukov reports that when, in August 1915, the Progressive Bloc had reduced the demand for a government 'formally responsible to the legislature' to one of 'popular confidence', the name of Rodzyanko had been put forward as the prospective head of such a government.[1] Since then Rodzyanko had done much to help the Duma opposition. Whenever a delegate made himself liable to prosecution for seditious speeches from the rostrum, Rodzyanko refused to hand over the stenographic report, and insisted on his right to remove the offending passages before the stenograms were put on record. (The full speech was of course in the meantime circulated in duplicated copies, sometimes with additional embellishments.[2]) Yet as the Duma opposition became increasingly radical, following the leftist tendencies of the Voluntary Organisations, Rodzyanko found himself far to the right of the mainstream of political development. While he was spoiling his chances of influencing the Emperor (by his tactless hints at the alleged pro-German bias of the Empress), he failed to win the sympathies of the left wing of the radical movement. Rodzyanko claimed that he was neither a revolutionary nor a plotter, unlike men such as Prince G. E. Lvov, Guchkov and Konovalov, who sought contacts with revolutionary circles and took an active part in the political plots of the Moscow Committees. When, late in 1916, General Krymov tried to interest the President of the Duma in the idea of a palace coup, Rodzyanko sharply rejected the plan, pointing out that he had sworn an oath of allegiance. This, if nothing else, put him beyond the pale for the conspirators. As a result, Rodzyanko's nomination for the premiership in the lists compiled in radical circles came to be replaced by that of Prince Lvov.

Of the two men, Rodzyanko, the speaker for 'the representatives of the people', with his imposing stature and stentorian voice, had won the higher place in the public imagination. Of the two, he was also the more acceptable to the Tsar, in spite of the estrangement between them. Rodzyanko looked the Tsar straight in the eye, even when he knew that his remarks would be considered insolent and irritating. He

---

1. Milyukov, *Vospominaniya*, vol. II, pp. 273 ff. Cf. Grave, op. cit., p. 21 n.
2. See above, pp. 187 ff.

was not the type of shifty politician whom Nicholas II disliked most.[1] Besides, Rodzyanko, although he had no experience of state administration, had a considerable knowledge of the personalities in the Duma, whereas Prince Lvov, who had some experience of the extremely confused administration of the Voluntary Organisations, knew only about the clandestine political intrigues of the Moscow conspiratorial centres.

As soon as the riots broke out in Petrograd, Rodzyanko renewed his efforts to obtain the Emperor's consent for 'a government of popular confidence', with the result that we know. One telegram after another, each more urgent than the last, was sent to the Tsar. The commanders-in-chief at the front were also asked for their support. Had Rodzyanko managed to get the Emperor to change his mind, he would probably have succeeded, with the assistance of the generals, in becoming Prime Minister, with a free hand to form a cabinet of his own choice. The transition would have been purely constitutional and legal, and would not have satisfied the left wing of the liberals, but it might have lasted the few weeks before the spring offensive at the front. Such a government might have inaugurated a period of gradual political evolution. This the conspiratorial circles and the Kadets in the Duma fully understood.

Milyukov, who was certainly ambitious enough to hope for the premiership sooner or later, did not want Rodzyanko, an authoritarian without flexibility, to preside over any government which he might have to join. He preferred, and promoted, the candidature of Lvov,[2] whom he knew only superficially, but who had the reputation of being 'soft' and a 'Tolstoyan'. Prince Lvov could be expected to accept Milyukov's advice on general affairs. Milyukov believed himself especially qualified to look after the foreign affairs of Russia.

In a sense, the reluctance of the Tsar to give in to Rodzyanko's

1. See Shakhovskoy, op. cit., p. 186: 'Remember', said the Emperor, 'if ever I appoint as minister one of those people who will not look one in the eye, it will mean I have lost my reason.'

2. In his posthumously published memoirs, Milyukov writes: 'It was not easy to replace the President of the Duma by the Chairman of the Zemstvos in the plans of the Bloc. But I succeeded. Of course, it was rendered easier by the reputation of Prince Lvov everywhere in Russia; at that time he was irreplaceable. I cannot say, however, that Rodzyanko himself was reconciled to this decision. He continued a secret struggle: we shall note later on the forms it took'. (op. cit., vol. II, p. 275).

insistence was welcome to Milyukov, who had recently been won over to the idea of a revolutionary change. The Tsar's obstinacy made it easier to justify a solution for which Milyukov, in his posthumous memoirs, uses the German word 'Rechtsbruch' (i.e. breach of legality). And perhaps he welcomed the prorogation of the Duma on the 27th. True, this was the Duma in which Milyukov had built up his reputation as 'a great parliamentarian', and in which he had succeeded in welding the moderate right and the radicals into the Progressive Bloc, a considerable if precarious political achievement. And yet the Fourth Duma had been elected according to the law of 3 July 1907, promulgated under Stolypin in direct violation of the constitution. This made the Fourth Duma part of the very régime which Milyukov wanted to be swept away by a 'Rechtsbruch'. This is the reason for his refusal to support the proposal, in defiance of the prorogation decree of 27 February, to proclaim the Duma as a sovereign body in permanent session.

4. THE DUMA'S REACTION TO PROROGATION

When the prorogation decree was handed to the President of the Duma on 27 February, the hour of destiny for this institution had struck. This was the moment to make a gesture similar to the oath of the Jeu de Paume, and to refuse to be dissolved. The behaviour of the elders of the Duma parties, meeting as an unofficial 'Senioren Convent', and of the Duma majority as a whole, was not in accordance with this historical precedent.[1] Not only did they fail to oppose the prorogation decree but they called a meeting in the semi-circular hall adjoining the Duma chamber, so as not to create an impression of insubordination. True, voices were heard advocating what would have amounted to the assumption of the leadership of the revolutionary movement. The Duma deputy, A. A. Bublikov, writes:

1. The 'Senioren Convent' was an unofficial body consisting of heads of the parliamentary parties, which used to meet as a de facto steering committee to discuss organisational questions. In fact the Duma Provisional Committee was selected by this body mainly from its own members, with the exclusion of the leaders of the right-wing parties and the inclusion of Kerensky and Chkheidze from the labour faction (Trudoviki) and the Social-Democrats (Mensheviks).

The *members* of the Duma, having received the decree, forgathered for a *private* meeting in order to discuss the state of affairs, which was becoming increasingly threatening. The members of the right-wing parties were already absent, but the others did not show any liking for risky decisions either. However, my proposal to transfer the meeting from the semicircular hall to the Hall of Plenary Sessions, and thus officially establish the fact of insubordination to the formally expressed will of the monarch, had no success whatever, despite the prophecies which I made there: 'Are you afraid of the responsibility? You will not avoid responsibility, but you will lose your dignity irretrievably.'[1]

The declarations of Bublikov and others (among them Kerensky), however, found little support. Milyukov, on the one hand, obviously did not want the Duma to head the revolution for fear that so conservative a body would obstruct the radical political line which he favoured. Rodzyanko, on the other hand, wanted to prevent the Duma from adopting a revolutionary attitude, so that it might be immediately recalled either by Nicholas II, whom he had enjoined to withdraw the prorogation decree, or by Grand Duke Michael, if he agreed to accept the regency.

Rodzyanko even went so far as to concede the prospective premiership of Prince Lvov, whom Grand Duke Michael mentioned in his telegram to the Tsar. This should not, however, be taken as a sign of Rodzyanko's voluntary surrender of the leading part in public life in the event of Grand Duke Michael assuming supreme powers. In the draft of a manifesto announcing the formation of a government responsible to the Duma, which was drawn up on 1 March in Mogilev and approved by the Emperor in the early hours of 2 March, Rodzyanko and not Lvov was nominated as head of the new government. Rodzyanko found a last-minute ally in these plans in the person of Prince Golitsyn. The attempt to proclaim the temporary regency of Grand Duke Michael failed, however, as we have seen, because of the refusal of Nicholas II to accept his brother's offer. Instead of becoming the head of the first government of popular confidence and a mediator between the monarch and the legislature, Rodzyanko was now (on the night of the 27th–28th) faced with the alternatives of joining the insurrection, and becoming the venerable figurehead of the revolution; his only real political function would then be to placate the right, the

1. A. A. Bublikov, *Russkaya revolyutsiya* (New York, 1918), p. 17.

officers, the landowners, and indeed the high aristocracy, with whom Rodzyanko was closely connected, and induce them to accept the revolution. Whatever his intellectual limitations, Rodzyanko must have felt the *capitis diminutio* to which he was invited to submit, and his hesitation is not surprising.

After long and fruitless deliberation the private meeting of the Duma members decided to entrust to the *Senioren Convent* the formation of a committee of members of the State Duma 'for the re-establishment of order in the capital and for contacts with persons and institutions'. The only definite result of the discussion was the implicit refusal of the Duma, on the afternoon of 27 February, to head the revolutionary movement. Not even the personal composition of the Committee was then made public. It was only towards midnight that an announcement was made naming the members of the Committee, which was to be presided over by the President of the Duma. These included practically all the members of the *Senioren Convent* plus Colonel Engelhardt, who was appointed Commandant of the revolutionary Petrograd garrison after Rodzyanko had decided to lend his authority to the revolutionary movement as such.[1]

5. RODZYANKO'S WAVERINGS

By his wavering, Rodzyanko also isolated himself from the Provisional Committee of the Duma of which he was officially Chairman. For hours – during which the revolutionary masses thronged the streets of the capital, released prisoners from the gaols (both the few political prisoners and the many common criminals), burned and sacked the premises of the district court, the secret police, and many police-stations – the Committee of the Duma deliberated without coming to any decision.

These aimless parleys exasperated some of the deputies, who were in favour of seizing power forthwith in the name of the Duma. Bublikov, whom we have mentioned above, went from Rodzyanko to Kerensky, and from Chkheidze to Nekrasov, pointing out that speech-making

1. See below, p. 365 f. For the members of the Committee see R. P. Browder and A. F. Kerensky, *The Russian Provisional Government 1917* (Stanford, 1961), p. 47.

was an utterly fruitless and dangerous occupation, that it was time to
seize power, otherwise the Tsar could gather his forces, send troops
from the front, and quickly suppress the rising. Bublikov held that the
easiest way to seize power was to occupy the Ministry of Transport and
to impose the control of the Duma Committee on the railways. It is
typical that Bublikov could achieve nothing before the early hours of
the 28th, when the President of the Duma, having already made his
fateful decision to head the revolution, finally answered the insistent
demands of Bublikov by saying: 'Well, if it is necessary, go and occupy
it [i.e. the Ministry of Transport], then.'

> In answer to that [writes Bublikov in his memoirs] I took from my
> pocket an appeal to the railwaymen which I had already prepared and
> offered it to the President for him to sign, together with a warrant
> authorising the Committee of the Duma to seize the Ministry of Trans-
> port. The appeal to the railwaymen started with the words: 'The old
> régime has fallen!' It is characteristic that Rodzyanko replaced it with the
> words: 'The old régime has turned out to be impotent.' This shows how
> little people in the Duma believed at that time that the revolution had
> already taken place, and that there could be no return to the past. This is
> exactly what Rodzyanko said: 'How can one say that it has fallen? Has
> the régime really fallen?'[1]

Bublikov is right on this point.[2] Even having agreed to undertake
the task of forming a government, Rodzyanko continued to hope that
this government would somehow be legitimised. In fact, he believed
that the Duma Committee, with himself as its Chairman, was, as it
were, *locum tenens* in the political vacuum created by Grand Duke
Michael's refusal to assume responsibility. The government of Prince
Golitsyn no longer existed, the country was threatened with anarchy;
the Duma had no choice but to appoint a government in the absence

1. Bublikov, op. cit., pp. 20 ff.
2. On other points his memoirs are often surprisingly confused. Here, however,
his recollections are borne out by another memoirist, Professor Pitirim Sorokin,
who tells of his visit to the Duma in the early afternoon of 27 February. ' "The Duma",
the deputy Rzhevsky told me, "has actually been dissolved, but an executive committee has been appointed as a temporary government." "Does this mean that you
have allied yourself with the revolution?" I asked. "No . . . However, perhaps I have",
he replied nervously. This same confusion and uncertainty I observed in utterances
of other deputies.' See Sorokin, *Leaves from a Russian Diary* (London, 1925), p. 8.

of a supreme ruler. Rodzyanko hoped that as soon as it became clear in whom the supreme power was vested, the status of the government would be legalised. In the meantime the tide was turning against him.

While the *Senioren Convent*, or perhaps already the Duma Provisional Committee which replaced it, was deliberating, Rodzyanko spent hours in his study. He must have been impressed by the fact that, in spite of his intervention, his opposite number in the Upper Chamber, Shcheglovitov, had been arrested by a member of the Duma in his very presence.[1] He was constantly being urged to take some action by Milyukov and other members of the Committee. Characteristically, what at last brought about a change of mind and attitude in Rodzyanko was not these pressures but a message which came through from the officers' mess of his own regiment, the Preobrazhensky Guards Regiment, telling him that the officers were ready to join the people and put themselves at the service of the Duma. This must have happened at about midnight on the 27th–28th. From then on Rodzyanko developed a feverish activity of which his memory seems to have kept only a hazy picture. He announced his readiness to give active guidance to the Duma Committee but demanded complete obedience from its members. He went to the rooms where the Military Commissions of the Soviet and the Duma were both meeting and had a clash there with the Soviet representative, N. D. Sokolov.[2] He even seems to have thought of setting out by train for Moscow in order to meet the Emperor halfway at the station of Bologoe, and perhaps arrest him there. But nothing came of all this. Neither Milyukov nor Kerensky in the Duma Committee would surrender his freedom of action to the President of the Duma. The Military Committee of the Soviet was not co-operative. The journey to meet the Emperor did not materialise.

Rodzyanko's position on 28 February and the following two days is difficult to assess because of the lack of documentary evidence. In his memoirs, *The State Duma and the February Revolution, 1917*,[3] Rodzyanko claims that General Ruzsky informed him on 28 February that the Emperor had entrusted him, Rodzyanko, with the formation of a government responsible to the Duma. Milyukov accepts Rodzyanko's story of a mandate to form a 'responsible' government, and explains

1. See below, p. 389.   2. See below, p. 365 f.
3. *ARR*, VI, p. 59.

in this way Rodzyanko's hesitation in following a revolutionary course.[1]

Rodzyanko's memoirs were first published in 1919 in Rostov-on-Don, and naturally they have affected the approach of most historians to the revolution. And yet there can be no doubt that on this important point Rodzyanko was far from accurate. There was no such telegram to him on 28 February from Ruzsky, nor could Ruzsky have been authorised to send one. On the 28th the Tsar was in the train on the way between Mogilev and the station of Malaya Vishera on the Moscow-Petrograd line. During that day there were no communications of a political nature between the Tsar and General Ruzsky. The Tsar did not intend to meet him, as he was proceeding straight to Tsarskoe Selo, where he hoped to arrive in the early hours of 1 March. In his memoirs, quoted above, Rodzyanko mentions a manifesto which empowered him to form a cabinet. Such a manifesto was indeed drafted at GHQ and communicated to the Emperor late on 1 March, after he had spent another day on the railway, travelling from Malaya Vishera to Ruzsky's headquarters in Pskov. The text of this draft was submitted to the Emperor at 10.20 p.m. on 1 March, but it needed much persuasion from Ruzsky to obtain his consent to it. Rodzyanko might have heard of the draft before midnight on that day, but not of the Emperor's consent.

Both Rodzyanko and Milyukov are therefore mistaken in maintaining that Rodzyanko's behaviour on the 28th was a consequence of an imperial mandate to form a parliamentary government. This error of memory was, however, reinforced by a number of statements made by the courtiers in the imperial train, who claimed after the revolution that during the thirty-eight-hour journey, the Emperor had come very near to giving in on the question of a parliamentary government. One of these, the official historiographer, General Dubensky, even believed that a telegram to this effect was sent by the Emperor as early as 27 February.[2]

The legend originated with General Ivanov, who as we shall see, received orders on 27 February to proceed to Petrograd, assume

---

1. Milyukov, op. cit., vol. II, p. 296. A surprising slip in Milyukov's memoirs. In his earlier *Istoriya vtoroy russkoy revolyutsii* (Sofia, 1921), *q.v.*, p. 50 he does not mention this circumstance.
2. *Kak proizoshel perevorot v Rossii. Russkaya Letopis*, No. III (Paris, 1922), p. 35.

dictatorial powers and put an end to the disturbances. In his several statements after the revolution, General Ivanov was anxious to justify his mission and to dispel the suspicion that it was directed against the State Duma. Ivanov 'recollected' that on taking leave of Nicholas II in the imperial train in the small hours of 28 February, he had reminded the Emperor of the necessity of his conceding constitutional reforms. The Emperor's answer was somewhat noncommittal, but could be interpreted as meaning that he knew all about it and would take the necessary measures. On the basis of this conversation Ivanov later claimed that as early as 27 February 'Nicholas II had decided to adopt a system of administration of the Fatherland based on a ministry of public confidence, in accordance with the desires of a majority of the State Duma and of many sections of the population.'[1] Dubensky elaborates Ivanov's confused recollections. But none of this proves that the Emperor was ready to entrust Rodzyanko with the formation of a government of popular confidence, nor that Rodzyanko was informed of it on the 28th.

The only unassailable evidence of some change of mood in the Emperor was his desire to meet Rodzyanko on 1 March. Messages were exchanged via the railway telegraph and the Ministry of Transport, by then in the hands of the Duma Commissar, Bublikov. Arrangements were made to meet Rodzyanko, first at the station of Dno and then in Pskov. Rodzyanko's journey, however, never materialised, for reasons we shall consider later.

But the Emperor's desire to meet Rodzyanko for consultations did not mean, as some courtiers on the train believed, that he had changed his mind on the constitutional question. Indeed Rodzyanko was far from feeling himself the Imperial Prime Minister-designate on the 28th. When, during the night of 28 February–1 March, he asked the Emperor to receive him, and was planning to go to Bologoe to meet him, he considered the possibility of having to arrest the Emperor – or so the Duma member Shidlovsky, who was to accompany him, reports in his memoirs.[2]

1. See *Padenie*, vol. V, p. 318.
2. 'The question of our journey was decided late at night in my absence and had not been worked out in detail. The possibility of our being arrested was not considered, nor was the possibility of armed resistance by the troops remaining loyal to the Emperor; we, on the other hand, considered the possibility of arresting the Emperor,

The inaccuracies and failures of Rodzyanko's memory reflect the confusion in his mind on 28 February. It is important, however, to find out what he actually did on that day, because it was mainly on his advice and information that the military high command, in the persons of Alekseev and Ruzsky, took the attitude which led to the abdication on 2 March. We have seen that on the 27th Rodzyanko tried to prevent the Duma from taking any action which might appear to be insubordination and rebellion against the prorogation order. His telegrams to the Tsar and his approaches to Grand Duke Michael are to be interpreted as dutiful forewarnings rather than as attempts at rebellious pressure. On the other hand, he agreed to preside over the Provisional Committee of the Duma, which included Kerensky and Chkheidze, who were organizing the revolution. True, he took no part in the deliberations of the Committee until the failure of his attempt to proclaim Grand Duke Michael regent. When later, at about midnight on the 27th, swayed by the message from the officers' mess of the Preobrazhensky Regiment, he agreed to act on behalf of the Committee and assume governmental powers, he had at last crossed the line of legality and put himself, however reluctantly, into the revolutionary camp.

Indeed, when the Provisional Government was formed, Rodzyanko claimed that he had appointed it,[1] and later he always insisted that the Provisional Government had been formed on the initiative of the State Duma. This contention was not explicitly accepted by other members of the Duma Committee, particularly Milyukov. On the 27th Milyu-

but we made no decision as to where he should be taken or what should be done with him.' (Quoted from Melgunov, *Martovskie dni 1917 goda*, p. 53).

1. In his direct-line conversation with General Ruzsky in the early hours of 2 March, of which we have the teleprinted text, Rodzyanko said: 'The anarchy has attained such dimensions that I was forced to appoint a Provisional Government in the course of the night.' This conversation, which was recorded by the Hughes apparatus, is, as Melgunov correctly asserts, a crucial source for our knowledge of what was happening at the moment of the appointment of the Provisional Government. It is far more authoritative than any of the numerous memoirs, reminiscences and 'histories of the revolution' written in later years by the participants. It is also much more revealing than contemporary statements intended for general consumption. It is surprising, therefore, that in their three-volume collection of documents, *The Russian Provisional Government*, Browder and Kerensky found it possible to omit substantial parts of the text of the conversation, including Rodzyanko's claim to have appointed a 'Provisional Government'.

kov had supported Rodzyanko in his reluctance to adopt a defiant attitude towards the prorogation decree. But his reasons for keeping the Duma out of the revolution were the exact opposite of Rodzyanko's. Milyukov and his friends (or those whom he then believed to be his political friends) were only too pleased at the demise of the Duma at the very moment when they were within reach of ministerial power. They viewed without sympathy Rodzyanko's efforts to have the prorogation order withdrawn by the Tsar. Milyukov hoped for a revolutionary government — not one based on the pseudo-constitution of 1906 (of which the Fourth Duma was an offspring[1]), but one in the form of a constitutional monarchy, headed nominally by the infant Alexis under the regency of Grand Duke Michael, 'an entirely stupid man' as Milyukov put it. Under cover of such a constitutional régime he and his friends, unhampered by the reactionary Duma, would have a free hand in carrying out the radical reforms for which they had so long hoped in vain. The tug-of-war between Milyukov and Rodzyanko for the realisation of their different conceptions of the constitutional change went on for the three days, from the disintegration of the Golitsyn's government on the 27th to the announcement of the abdications of the Tsar and Grand Duke Michael. The real significance of the tussle between the two Duma parliamentarians does not emerge from the utterly fictitious stories by which they both tried later to explain their behaviour.

6. RODZYANKO AND ALEKSEEV

Finding himself isolated in the Provisional Committee of the State Duma, Rodzyanko naturally sought to lean on some real force in his

1. In his memoirs Milyukov admits that he 'personally did not want the Duma to take state power into its hands' (vol. II, p. 294). His negative attitude to the Duma, in which he had established his reputation as the leader of Russian radical liberalism, is explained in his memoirs in the following words: 'This was the Duma of "the third of June" [i.e. 3 June 1907, the date of the Stolypin *coup d'état*, which curtailed the rights of the Duma and changed the electoral law] — this was the Duma which was clamped in a vice by the prerogatives of autocratic power, by the basic law of April 1906, by the bottleneck of the State Council — that burial-ground of legislation initiated by the Duma. Could one admit that such an institution had a part to play in the new situation? The Duma had become a shadow of its former self.' (vol. II, p. 303).

bid for power. His closer contacts with the military in the preceding days made him look to the High Command for such support. There is certainly a gap in the documentation on relations between the commanders-in-chief and Rodzyanko on the 28th. Not all the information fed from Petrograd to GHQ in Mogilev on that day has been made available. There is enough of it, however, to indicate the importance the generals just then attached to the person of Rodzyanko. We have seen that on the 27th, when Grand Duke Michael proposed to appoint a new government – provided he had his brother's consent – he had put forward the name of Prince Lvov for the premiership. When, however, on the 1st, GHQ at last produced the text of a manifesto, which Alekseev implored the Emperor in the most heart-rending terms to sign without delay, it was Rodzyanko and not Lvov who was nominated head of the government.[1]

Until the evening of 28 February the information about events in Petrograd which Alekseev was forwarding to the commanders-in-chief of the various fronts reflected fairly adequately the chaotic and anarchic situation in the capital.[2] But in a telegram marked No. 1833 and addressed to General Ivanov, which was sent later on the same day, with copies to all the commanders-in-chief, Alekseev gives a totally different picture. The telegram ran:

> According to private information, Petrograd became completely calm on 28 February; the troops who had rallied behind the Provisional Government are being brought to order. The Provisional Government, under the chairmanship of Rodzyanko, is meeting in the State Duma; it has invited the commanders of the military units to come and receive instructions for the maintenance of order. The appeal to the population which was issued by the Provisional Government mentions the necessity of maintaining the monarchist principle in Russia, and the need for new elections for the choice and appointment of a government. I am eagerly awaiting the arrival of His Majesty [in Tsarskoe] in order to report to him

1. The draft of the manifesto stated: 'In my effort to unite all the popular forces more closely for the achievement of an early victory I consider it necessary to call for a government responsible to the representatives of the people, and entrust to the President of the State Duma, Rodzyanko, the formation of this government, which should include personalities who enjoy the confidence of the whole of Russia.' The manifesto was never issued, although, as we have said, the Emperor agreed to it on the night of 1–2 March. See *ARR*, III, p. 253.

2. See, for instance, Alekseev's telegram no. 1813, *ARR*, III, pp. 250 ff.

the above, and to communicate to him the request to agree to these wishes of the people. If this information is correct then your course of action should be altered: negotiations will lead to pacification, so that the shameful civil strife for which our enemy longs will be avoided, institutions and factories will remain intact, and work will be resumed.

I have received in a roundabout way an appeal from the new Minister of Transport, Bublikov, to the railwaymen, in which he calls for an increased effort from everybody to prevent the collapse of the transport system. Report all this to His Majesty, as well as my conviction that the matter can be brought to a peaceful conclusion which will strengthen Russia (1833). Alekseev.

This telegram reflects Rodzyanko's political line far better than his reminiscences published two years later. His name is mentioned as the head of the Provisional Government, which was meeting in the Duma. The reference to the monarchist principle is not borne out by any statement from the Duma, but faithfully reflects Rodzyanko's feelings on that day. Alekseev's telegram was obviously intended to shake any determination General Ivanov might have had to suppress sedition by military force. It concedes that the new authorities in Petrograd were showing goodwill and were ready to put new energy into the war effort, and even recognises Bublikov, who was in fact technically only a 'Commissar' of the Duma Committee, as the new Minister of Transport. It also clearly foreshadows the recognition of the new government by the High Command.

The same intention to induce the Tsar to recognise the revolutionary government of the Duma, and to give it legal sanction, clearly emerges in the telegram in which Alekseev communicates the text of the above-mentioned abortive manifesto of 1 March. It says:

Information received gives us reason to hope that the Duma deputies, led by Rodzyanko, will still be able to halt the general disintegration, and that it will be possible to work with them; every hour lost, however, reduces the chances of preserving and restoring order, and opens the door for the seizure of power by extreme leftist elements.

These quotations clearly show that Alekseev was under the impression that Rodzyanko was in charge in Petrograd, that he had succeeded in halting the revolutionary movement, and that every effort should be made to strengthen his hand.

From the evening of the 28th, Alekseev ceased to be the Emperor's obedient executive, and assumed the role of mediator between the monarch and his rebellious parliament. Only Rodzyanko could have brought about this change of heart by creating the false impression that he was in full control of the situation in Petrograd. In doing so, he was moved by both ambition and anxiety.[1] For on the 28th the members of the Duma Committee still had no idea of the strength of the troops which they knew were moving on Petrograd under the command of General Ivanov. They professed to believe that any troops approaching Petrograd would immediately join the revolution. But they could hardly believe this in all seriousness. Faced with a crowd of dishevelled soldiers and armed civilians engaged in looting, arson and all sorts of violence in the streets, disciplined troops would easily have been able to restore order. Sukhanov admits that a disciplined army division could have liquidated the revolutionary movement there and then, in which case Rodzyanko would have found himself in a delicate position. He had been cautious enough in his personal statements, and his horror of revolutionary mobs was quite sincere. But as the chairman of the Duma Committee to which Kerensky and Chkheidze belonged he was at the same time a rebel. Rodzyanko was therefore vitally interested in halting the Ivanov expeditionary force – which he believed was far larger and stronger than it was in reality. If Rodzyanko had divulged to Alekseev the true situation in Petrograd, if he had told him how powerless he himself was in the face of Milyukov and the members of the projected Provisional Government, if he had explained that this Provisional Government was actually at the mercy of the Petrograd Soviet, which in its turn had to pander to the whims of the rebellious soldiery, Alekseev might have thought it necessary to fulfil his oath of allegiance and attempted to restore order in Petrograd by

1. In his direct-line conversation with Ruzsky in the small hours of 2 March, Rodzyanko said: 'The dispatch [by the Emperor] of General Ivanov with the St. George battalion has only added fuel to the flames, and must inevitably lead to internecine fighting, because there is no possibility whatsoever of our holding back the troops, who refuse to obey their officers and commanders; my heart bleeds at the sight of what is happening. Stop sending troops – they will not take action against the people. Prevent unnecessary bloodshed.' This hysterical and self-contradictory passage ('There will be internecine fighting ... they [the troops] will not take action against the people') suggests not so much anxiety as panic. This passage is also omitted from Browder and Kerensky's collection of documents.

using the Ivanov expeditionary force.[1] The vague but intense fear of the Ivanov expedition was shared by the other members of the Duma Committee and also by the Soviet. In bringing his weight to bear on the general's wavering loyalty to the Tsar, Rodzyanko gained in the eyes of the revolutionary movement. At the same time he established a link between himself and the army commanders which might have proved useful to him if the revolutionary tide had ebbed. In any case Rodzyanko's information to Alekseev on 28 February was highly misleading, even if it was not conscious deception. He later deceived himself in the same way, when he claimed that on 28 February he had been entrusted by the Tsar, through the intermediary of Ruzsky, with the formation of a government responsible to the Duma.

1. Earlier on 28 February, in the telegram no. 1813 addressed to the commanders-in-chief, Alekseev informed them of Khabalov's total failure in Petrograd and said: 'In reporting this, I would like to add that we all have a sacred duty to the Emperor and the Fatherland to maintain loyalty and the allegiance of the troops in the field, to safeguard the functioning of the railways and the flow of food supplies.'

12

The Abdication

The ghost train; GHQ and the revolution; Ruzsky's first round: the evening of 1 March; Rodzyanko rejects the Tsar's concessions: small hours of 2 March; The intervention of the aide-de-camp generals; The Duma emissaries: Guchkov and Shulgin; The signing of the act of abdication; The immediate effects of the abdication; The moral of the drama.

I. THE GHOST TRAIN

In order to see how and why Alekseev's attitude towards the revolution changed between 28 February and 2 March, let us turn back to the scene in Mogilev. The Emperor had arrived there on 23 February, and the 'quiet life' of which General Dubensky speaks in his diary lasted until about 25 February. True, news of unrest and demonstrations was reaching the Emperor, in private communications from the Empress and in reports from the Ministers of the Interior and War and the commander of the Petrograd Military District. They all pointed to a widespread but unorganised ferment, with which the police and government authorities were confident they could deal. By midday on the 25th, however, this situation seemed to have lasted far too long for the Emperor's liking, and he sent his telegram to General Khabalov, commanding him to stop the rioting forthwith. Reports received at GHQ on the 27th referred to a partial mutiny of the garrison, but stated that the loyal troops were fighting back courageously, and that the situation was well in hand.[1]

It was only before dinner (about 8 p.m.) on the 27th that messages

1. The Minister of War wired: 'Disturbances which started in the morning in a number of military units are being firmly and energetically suppressed by the companies and battalions which remain faithful to their duty. We have not yet succeeded in putting down the mutiny, but I am firmly convinced that order will soon be restored, and we have taken the most ruthless measures to this end. The authorities remain completely confident. 196 Belyaev.' This was despatched at 1.15 p.m. on the 27th.

from the Minister of War struck an alarming note. They spoke of the spreading mutiny, of arson, of Khabalov's total loss of control, and asked for the immediate despatch of really reliable troops in sufficient numbers for simultaneous action in different parts of the city. There were also three telegrams from the Empress which were far from reassuring. One even mentioned the necessity of making concessions.[1] At the same time urgent messages addressed to the Emperor by the President of the Duma continued to pour in at regular intervals. They were almost tearfully loyalist in tone, but harped on the theme of the appointment of a prime minister 'enjoying the confidence of the people'. These admonitions produced no effect whatever. This is hardly surprising: Rodzyanko had cried 'wolf' far too often in the last few months. Despairing of the success of his submissions, Rodzyanko adopted the unusual and un-constitutional procedure of addressing himself directly to the military commanders, asking them to support his political demands. Thus began Rodzyanko's sustained pressure on the generals, which led to their important action at the moment of abdication. Ruzsky, the Commander-in-Chief of the Northern Front, complied with Rod-zyanko's request and wired to the Emperor in support of an immediate reform. He also made it quite clear that he did not believe in 'repressive measures', which would only exacerbate the situation.[2]

Two things were expected of the Emperor by his immediate *entourage* at GHQ: definite instructions as to how to deal with the mutiny in Petrograd, and a declaration of policy which would settle the discontent in the country at large and give satisfaction, albeit temporarily, to the liberals, on whom the smooth running of transport and supplies to the army largely depended. With regard to the first question, the Emperor had certainly given clear orders to his chief of staff. The question of the despatch of reliable troops from the Northern and Western Fronts was decided late at night on the 27th, and the orders were transmitted to Generals Ruzsky and Evert. The movement of troops began immediately on the two parallel railway lines leading to Petrograd. At the same time a kind of dictator, in the shape of a

1. Melgunov believes that these telegrams did not reach the Emperor before he left GHQ. Spiridovich, whose information comes from court circles, believes they did. See Melgunov, *Martovskie dni 1917 goda*, p. 154, and Spiridovich, *Velikaya voyna*, vol. III, p. 176.
2. See the Rodzyanko-Ruzsky exchange of telegrams, *ARR*, III, pp. 247 ff.

commander-in-chief for the Petrograd garrison, was appointed with full powers even over ministers. For this post the Emperor — guided by some of the members of his suite — selected General Ivanov, then one of the most colourful figures in the Russian High Command.

Ivanov, whose origins remain somewhat mysterious — he was said to be the illegitimate son of a convict in Siberia — had had a distinguished military career. During the war he had been Commander-in-Chief of the South-Western and Western Fronts. His loyalty and devotion to the Emperor seemed beyond doubt, though he had been extremely critical of the Petrograd bureaucracy when the shortage of arms and ammunition hit the army in 1915. He was popular with the soldiers, with whom he had his own paternalistic ways. He had shown himself a ruthless disciplinarian when suppressing the Kronstadt mutiny in 1906. But now he shared the general view at GHQ that political concessions were inevitable, and that any military action to restore discipline in the capital should go hand in hand with a reconciliation of the Tsar with the Duma opposition and the Voluntary Organisations, on the basis of a 'government of popular confidence'.

The purpose of the Ivanov mission was not very clearly defined. It is important to stress this in view of subsequent talk of a 'punitive expedition against Petrograd conducted by General Ivanov'. It was certainly clear to everybody at GHQ that order could be restored in the capital only with the assistance of reliable and loyal troops. This did not mean, however, that these troops would be used for large-scale repressive and punitive measures. The numbers despatched to Petrograd on the 28th were not large.[1] The commanders at the front would not agree to weaken their lines by sending a large force to intervene in the internal political situation. But they hoped that the arrival of a small number of disciplined and loyal troops would produce the necessary psychological effect in the capital without resort to excessive bloodshed or large-scale military operations. This was the tenor of the orders sent by Alekseev

1. According to Melgunov, *Martovskie dni*, p. 94, Ivanov was believed to have at his disposal thirteen infantry battalions, sixteen cavalry squadrons and four artillery batteries. Military documents speak of orders to the Commanders-in-Chief of the Northern and Western Fronts to despatch two cavalry and two infantry regiments, with energetic generals, who would be reliable, competent and brave. Each front was also supposed to send one commando, armed with Colt machine-guns, to be attached to the St. George battalion (numbering about 800 men) which Ivanov had with him. These orders were issued between 9 and 10 p.m. on the 27th.

on the night of the 27th–28th to the Commanders of the Northern and Western Fronts asking them to despatch reliable troops for service in the capital. They were to be sent without delay to Tsarskoe Selo, where they would be placed under the command of General Ivanov as soon as he arrived there. Before taking leave of the Emperor Ivanov tried once again to bring up the matter of constitutional concessions, but received an evasive answer.

This brings us back to the second problem on which a decision was expected by all who were at the Emperor's side on the 27th – the political situation. Nicholas II's refusal to commit himself, and his postponement of a decision until he arrived at Tsarskoe Selo, did not suit any of his advisers at GHQ. Many of the members of his suite also thought that an announcement of the political changes should be made forthwith. Ruzsky and Brusilov had wired to this effect on the 27th, and Alekseev repeatedly urged the same solution. Later on the 27th, the news from Petrograd became more and more alarming every hour. The Deputy Palace Commandant, Count Benckendorff, asked Voeykov on the direct line from Tsarskoe whether the Empress should not leave with the children at once. This was at about 10 p.m. The additional worry about his children, who were ill with measles, forced the Emperor to speed up his departure. Orders were given that a train should be held in readiness in case of need for the Empress at Tsarskoe, but that she should only be told that the Emperor would be leaving for Tsarskoe during the night.

The generals at GHQ seem to have raised objections to the journey at this point and to have shown little co-operation in speeding it up.[1] The routing of the imperial trains presented certain difficulties. Ivanov's detachment was to be followed by troops from the Northern and Western Fronts. Traffic on the southern approaches to Petrograd was therefore expected to be heavy. On the other hand, the speed of the two imperial trains A and B was limited and the security regulations for their handling were strict. So that they should not interfere with the traffic on the direct line from Mogilev to Petrograd the imperial trains were to make a long detour, through Smolensk, Vyazma and

1. We discount the contradictory reports, based mainly on the memoirs of Voeykov, on the attitude of the generals to the question of the departure. They are dictated by a profound animosity towards Alekseev and are not corroborated by independent evidence.

Likhoslavl, on the main Moscow–Petrograd line. Thence they were to proceed to Tosno, about thirty miles short of Petrograd, and there branch off to Tsarskoe Selo. (See map, p. 433.)

At about 10.30 p.m. on the 27th Grand Duke Michael telephoned General Alekseev, offering himself as temporary regent if his brother agreed. The Grand Duke also advised the Emperor to postpone his return to Tsarskoe Selo. All this was politely but firmly rejected by the Emperor and the decision to leave Mogilev confirmed. Still later came the telegram from Golitsyn asking for the immediate dismissal of all ministers and the appointment of a 'person enjoying popular confidence' who would form a new government. Once again Alekseev used all his powers of persuasion to elicit some statement on this question from the Emperor, but the only result was the final telegram from the Tsar to the members of his government enjoining them to remain at their posts, and announcing the appointment of a military dictator for Petrograd. In spite of the Emperor's express orders that the telegram should be sent forthwith on the direct line, and his warning that this was a final and irreversible decision, Alekseev got out of bed (to which he was confined with a high temperature) and went to implore His Majesty 'on his knees' to agree to Golitsyn's proposal. At 1 a.m. on the 28th, when the Emperor was already about to leave for the train, Alekseev returned with the latest news from Petrograd, announcing that Khabalov was incapable of carrying out the command to restore order in the city. It was clear that the revolutionary movement was rapidly gaining ground. After 2 a.m. the Tsar, already in his train, received Ivanov. At this last interview he is supposed to have dropped the remark which gave rise to the legend that the Tsar had decided there and then to make constitutional concessions.

The imperial trains left Mogilev at 4 and 5 a.m. respectively on Tuesday the 28th, with all the passengers asleep. Ivanov, for some unexplained reason, delayed his departure until early afternoon. There was nothing unusual about the first day of the journey, which went according to the established routine. Early in the morning the train stopped at a station where a troop transport was standing. The troops, who were on their way to the front, cheered the Emperor with the usual 'Hurrah', and the courtiers asked each other in hushed whispers whether they had not perhaps witnessed the last acclaim the Emperor was to receive. Or so at least one of them later reported – for we are entering a period where we must treat even the most honest records with circumspection, as they tend inevitably to be distorted by hindsight.

As the trains entered each successive province (*guberniya*), they were boarded by officials responsible for the area through which they were going to pass. The provincial governors turned out to meet the trains in the towns of their residences and had short audiences with the monarch. Although no politics were discussed on the trains in the Emperor's presence, he was not unaware of the growing danger to himself and his family at Tsarskoe Selo; the governors of the provinces must have reported the latest news to reach them. When the Emperor met General Ruzsky in Pskov the next day, he surprised him with his knowledge of what was going on.

At about 4 p.m. on Tuesday 28 February, the news reached the suite train (B) that some kind of Provisional Government had been formed in Petrograd, and that the Duma deputy Bublikov had seized the Ministry of Transport and was transmitting appeals signed by Rodzyanko over the railway telegraph network. Then came the order, issued from the Petrograd station, to re-route the two imperial trains to proceed via Tosno straight to Petrograd instead of to Tsarskoe Selo.[1] The officials in train B, which was running ahead of the Emperor's train, decided to advise the Palace Commandant, Voeykov, in train A, to alter course at the junction of Bologoe, halfway between Moscow and Petrograd, and proceed from there to Pskov along a branch line: the HQ of the Northern Front would afford protection. Voeykov replied, however, that the trains should do their utmost to break through to Tsarskoe Selo via Tosno.

In the early hours of 1 March the trains proceeded towards Petrograd for about another hundred miles. On reaching the small station of Malaya Vishera, about 180 miles from Likhoslavl, train B was stopped and a report received from an officer of the railway regiment, who had just arrived from the opposite direction. He said that the stations of Lyuban and Tosno were in the hands of rebel troops, and that he himself had had to flee from Lyuban on a railway trolley. This report was

1. The order was signed by 'Grekov', a Cossack subaltern, but later, when Bublikov's assistant, Lomonosov, made enquiries at the Petrograd terminal, Grekov had disappeared, and was never heard of again.

exaggerated. The disturbance in Lyuban was purely local, and order was restored soon after the officer left. Train B was, however, stopped to await the arrival of the Emperor's train at about 4.30 a.m. Meanwhile General Tsabel of the Imperial Railway Regiment had seized the telegraph station and the duty room of the station of Malaya Vishera. The Emperor was woken up on arrival and, on hearing of the situation on the railway line ahead of him, he ordered the trains to return to Bologoe, a distance of 100 miles, and from there to proceed to Pskov, a further 220 miles, as had been suggested earlier that night.

By this time the advance towards Petrograd of General Ivanov's train had become known in the capital and was causing considerable anxiety in the Tauride Palace. Bublikov and his assistant, Major-General Lomonosov, were following the movements of the Emperor and his suite from the Ministry of Transport, and on learning that they had turned back towards Bologoe feared that the imperial trains, which they had hoped to intercept as they approached Petrograd, would escape to some forward HQ whence an expeditionary force against Petrograd could be organised. Rodzyanko ordered Bublikov to stop the trains at Bologoe, where he wanted to meet the Emperor. Detailed instructions for stopping the train were issued by Bublikov from Petrograd. None of these were carried out.

From Bologoe the railway employees reported to Bublikov that the imperial train had slipped away on the Vindava line at about 9 a.m. on Wednesday 1 March, without changing engines in Bologoe. This was a narrow escape. Had the trains stopped to change engines, they might never have moved any further. Bublikov's deputy, Lomonosov, issued instructions to sabotage the trains on the Bologoe–Pskov route, but this order was not followed. The trains were moving only slowly, without a prearranged time-table. The 1st of March passed on the whole in very much the same atmosphere as 28 February, and the routine — one might almost say ritual — progress of the imperial trains was nowhere impeded.

The scene at Staraya Russa, where the imperial train stopped, is thus described by Dubensky:

> An enormous crowd filled the station. Near the chapel on the platform of the station stood a group of nuns from the local convent. Everybody looked at our train with great interest. Many took off their hats and bowed. The imperial train had just left and people were expressing their

pleasure at having seen the Emperor, if only through the window. Despite the liveliness of the scene, perfect order prevailed everywhere. Apart from an officer and two or three NCOs of the police and the station gendarmerie, there were no extra police at the station.[1]

From Dno the railway employees reported to the Duma Commissar, Bublikov, that the gendarmes were in full control and that his orders could therefore not be carried out.

Throughout the day of 1 March train A was running ahead of train B, but at Dno junction the order was reversed. Here the Emperor expected to receive Rodzyanko. On hearing that he had been delayed, he ordered the trains to proceed to Pskov and left word for Rodzyanko that he would meet him there. When train A arrived at Pskov at about 7 p.m. there was an ominous change in the routine. It became known that the customary inspection of the guard of honour would not take place, and only the governor of the town and a few officials turned up on the platform.

The governor reported that the situation in Pskov was quiet and that people had taken the news of the disturbances in the capital 'with equanimity'. He believed that as the town was in the zone of military operations there was no danger of unrest. The Tsar inquired about the size and amenities of the governor's house, and the latter took this to indicate that the Tsar might be intending to bring his family there.

The Commander of the Northern Front, Ruzsky, was not at the station to meet the trains. He arrived a few minutes later in sombre mood, wearing galoshes, and accompanied by his chief of staff, General George Danilov ('black Danilov' as he was known in the army), and General Savvich. He was received by the Emperor immediately after the governor of Pskov, and began his arduous task of breaking down the Emperor's obstinate resistance to political concessions.

2. GHQ AND THE REVOLUTION

We interrupt the narrative of events in Pskov to give a short account of what happened in Mogilev after the Emperor's departure. The journey of the imperial trains and the scene in Pskov have been described in so many memoirs that it is harder to reconcile the conflicting evidence of the various witnesses (or of the same witness at various

1. Dubensky's memoirs in *Russkaya Letopis*, III (Paris, 1922), p. 45.

times) than to fill the gaps in the record. As far as Mogilev is concerned, we are in a different predicament. Here our deductions must be based on documentary sources. The main witness and protagonist of events, General Alekseev, has left us practically no record whatever[1] apart from a few remarks quoted in their books by Generals Denikin and Lukomsky. Lukomsky's recollections are confused but revealing.

> After the Emperor's departure from GHQ, [he writes] events in Petrograd on 28 February and 1 March developed with extraordinary rapidity. At GHQ we received from Petrograd one telegram after another depicting a revolutionary movement in full swing, in which almost all the troops were joining with the revolutionaries, officers and policemen were being murdered, sailors of the Baltic Fleet had mutinied and were killing their officers, and all civil servants of any prominence were under arrest. Unrest broke out in Moscow and other important centres where there were reserve battalions.
>
> Infantry units sent from the Northern Front to Petrograd were met in Luga by representatives of local reserve units and began to surrender their rifles, saying they would not fight their own people. Telegrams were received from the President of the State Duma, pointing out that feeling against the Emperor was running high in Petrograd; that a change of government would now be quite inadequate, even if the latter were responsible to the Duma; and that the question of the Emperor's abdication was now being openly canvassed. Abdication, it was said, was the only way out; failing it, anarchy would spread over the whole country and the war with Germany would inevitably come to a halt.[2]

Lukomsky goes on to say that the only way to stop the riots in Petrograd and Moscow would be to withdraw troops from the front and drown the revolution in blood, but this again could be done only at the cost of a humiliating separate peace with the Germans for which neither the Allies nor Russian public opinion would ever forgive the Emperor.

Here, as elsewhere in his otherwise invaluable memoirs, Lukomsky is confused on many points. In the first place he ascribes to Rodzyanko ideas which only came to him two days later. Lukomsky's account of the incident in Luga, involving troops sent from the Northern Front, is a travesty of the facts. One reliable eye-witness, N. Voronovich, reports[3]

1. See, however, Bibliographical Notes, p. 459–60.
2. *ARR*, II, p. 21.
3. See *Arkhiv Grazhdanskoy Voyny* (Berlin, 1922), II, pp. 31 ff.

that one transport of these troops was ambushed in Luga, and was disarmed by the local revolutionary committee, without the troops realising that those ordering them to get off the train and surrender their arms had joined the revolution. This incident can hardly be regarded as an instance of troops from the front joining the mutiny. As for the murder of officers in Petrograd and the Baltic fleet, news of this could not have reached Mogilev on the 28th. On the contrary, as we have seen, it was late that day that Alekseev despatched the remarkable telegram no. 1833, in which, referring to information mentioned by Lukomsky, he claimed that order was being restored in Petrograd, and that the President of the Duma seemed to have matters in hand. Lukomsky does not claim that the movement of troops from the front in the direction of Petrograd was stopped or slowed down in the course of the 28th. Telegram no. 1833 shows, however, that something had happened on that date to change Alekseev's policy to one of appeasement of the revolutionaries. Spiridovich attempts to explain this by a particular occurrence for which he does not give his sources.[1]

Throughout the 28th, Spiridovich reports, Alekseev continued to issue orders for the despatch of troops to Petrograd from both the Northern and Western Fronts. After Bublikov had seized the Ministry of Transport early on the 28th, the War Minister in the Golitsyn government, Belyaev, who was still in communication with GHQ, reported that neither the Minister of Transport, Kriger-Voynovsky, nor his ministry could carry out their functions properly and without interruption. 'It therefore seems that the administration of the railways should be transferred without delay to the Deputy Minister, who is with the army at the front.'

The Deputy Minister of Transport was a certain General Kislyakov, who continued to serve in that capacity under the Provisional Government. Alekseev was inclined to follow Belyaev's advice, and issue an order announcing that he was assuming, through the Deputy Minister of Transport, all responsibility for the administration of the railways. According to Spiridovich, however, Kislyakov persuaded Alekseev not to pursue this course, and Alekseev cancelled the order. Spiridovich's explanation is that Kislyakov had been involved with the plotters on the eve of the revolution.

1. See Spiridovich, *Velikaya voyna*, vol. III, pp. 240 ff.

Control of the railways was all-important at that moment. It was over the railway telegraph network that the country as a whole got its first intimation of what had happened in Petrograd. The provisioning of the big towns and the flow of supplies to the army were entirely dependent on the smooth functioning of the railways. By surrendering control to the Duma Commissar, Bublikov, Alekseev deprived himself of an important instrument of power, which he could well have used to influence the political issue at that critical juncture. Alekseev's attitude to Bublikov is somewhat puzzling. Bublikov's telegram transmitting Rodzyanko's appeal to the railwaymen must have been known to him by midday on the 28th. Alekseev claims, in his telegram no. 1833, that it reached him by 'roundabout ways'. At the same time Alekseev refers to Bublikov as the new Minister of Transport. By denying that he had direct contact with the revolutionary minister, Bublikov, Alekseev maintained an appearance of strict loyalty to the Emperor while at the same time refraining from all measures to prevent Bublikov from taking control of the Russian railway network. No wonder this ambiguity later led to Alekseev's being charged with double-dealing and outright conspiracy. A certain insincerity there admittedly was, but this was nothing new. Alekseev's denial of contacts with Guchkov, when Guchkov's letter of 15 August 1916 was publicised, is another instance; his knowledge of the plots for a palace coup yet another. But an active part in the conspiracies is neither proven nor likely.

Alekseev's moves on 28 February–1 March were closely co-ordinated with those of Rodzyanko. Certainly on those two days neither wanted an abdication or the fall of the monarchy. On the contrary, as the draft manifesto despatched on 1 March[1] to Pskov for the Emperor's signature clearly shows, the plan was to invite Rodzyanko to form a government responsible to the Duma. In the hope that this scheme would succeed, Alekseev was naturally reluctant to start the measures for the movement of loyal troops on Petrograd. In any case an adequate concentration of troops on the approaches to the capital would have taken five to six days to achieve. By that time such preparations might well have been outstripped by political developments. The country and the army would have learned of the events, and armed suppression of the mutiny in Petrograd and Moscow might well have turned into the opening

1. See below, p. 324.

phase of a general civil war. In order to avoid all this Alekseev, at Rodzyanko's instigation, prepared the draft manifesto appointing a cabinet responsible to the Duma, and made every effort to prevent a clash between General Ivanov's St. George Battalion and the Petrograd garrison. Had the Petrograd garrison put itself at the disposal of the Duma Committee and of Rodzyanko, and had Rodzyanko been invited by the Tsar to form a government, then the issue of a mutiny of the Petrograd garrison would not have had to be faced. This is what Rodzyanko himself gave the troops to understand on 28 February and 1 March in his speeches in the vestibule of the Tauride Palace, when he told them that they should not regard themselves as mutineers.

There was doubtless a certain amount of wishful thinking in Alekseev's acceptance of the news that peace and quiet had been restored in the capital on the 28th. Ruzsky greeted the news with far greater scepticism than Alekseev, and queried its origin. But he too favoured the political solution worked out by Alekseev and was ready to support it to the last. Even more than Alekseev, he was doubtful about the wisdom of suppressing the Petrograd mutiny by military action. He did obey direct orders for the despatch of troops, but by the night of 1 March he was absolutely sure that they should be stopped and returned to their positions at the front. He argued that it was impossible to send troops from the North-Western Front in sufficient number without weakening the defences against the Germans to a dangerous degree.

3. RUZSKY'S FIRST ROUND: THE EVENING OF 1 MARCH

Ruzsky was not fully prepared for his difficult negotiations with the Tsar. Since Rodzyanko was expected to arrive from Petrograd during the day (1 March), the task of talking to the Emperor would have fallen mainly on him. No convincing reasons have ever been given as to why Rodzyanko, who had originally insisted on meeting the Emperor, gave up at the last moment. In his much-quoted work *Dni* (The Days),[1] V. Shulgin writes that Rodzyanko was prevented from leaving for Dno on the 1st by the newly-formed Executive Committee of the Petrograd Soviet. Shulgin says that on 1 March he met Rodzyanko, who told him:

1. Belgrade, 1925, p. 214.

This morning I was to have left for GHQ to meet His Majesty the Emperor, and to report that perhaps the only solution was abdication. But those scoundrels [the members of the Executive Committee of the Petrograd Soviet] found out about it and told me the train would not be allowed to leave. . . . They said they would not let me go alone, but I must take Chkheidze and some others with me. . . . Well, your obedient servant is not going to the Emperor with them. Chkheidze was to have been accompanied by a battalion of revolutionary soldiers. Who knows what outrages they would have committed there.

At that point, says Shulgin, his conversation with Rodzyanko was interrupted. Melgunov has convincingly shown the falsity of this account. The Executive Committee did not interfere with Rodzyanko's journey, nor was the train waiting for him at the station cancelled. In his telephone conversation with Ruzsky early on the 2nd, Rodzyanko does not mention any opposition from the Executive Committee. To Ruzsky, who 'expressed profound sorrow at this cancellation', he gave two reasons for cancelling his journey:

I very much regret that I cannot come. I will tell you in all sincerity my two reasons for not coming: in the first place the troops which you are sending to Petrograd have mutinied – they left their train in Luga and declared that they were joining the State Duma. They decided to disarm everybody and not to let anyone through, even the imperial trains. I took immediate steps to secure free passage for His Majesty,[1] but I don't know whether I shall succeed. Secondly, I am told that my journey might have undesirable consequences. The unbridled passions of the popular masses must not be left without my personal control, because I am still the only one who is trusted and whose orders are carried out.[2]

Rodzyanko's explanation of his failure to turn up in Dno or Pskov is less fanciful but no less untrue than that of Shulgin. It is also self-contradictory. We know that some of the troops despatched by Ruzsky were in fact disarmed at Luga on that day, but it is not true that they had mutinied. This, of course, Rodzyanko might not have known, and perhaps he really believed the story of the mutiny. But he claims that the rebellious troops who, according to him, were holding Luga, had

1. *Sic*. Twenty-four hours earlier Rodzyanko had given orders to Bublikov that the imperial trains should be stopped at Bologoe, and Bublikov's deputy Lomonosov continued his unsuccessful attempts to do so throughout 1 March, giving instructions for sabotage of the permanent way.　　　　　　2. *ARR*, III, p. 255.

declared themselves 'for the Duma'. Why then would they have impeded the progress of the train carrying the President of the Duma? After all, that very day Rodzyanko had addressed troops at the Tauride Palace (who had done exactly the same as he imagined the troops in Luga had done), and had been cheered by them. The second reason given by Rodzyanko – that he could not leave the capital because he was the only one who was trusted and the only one whose orders were obeyed – is even less convincing than the first. His vacillation on the 27th, and his reluctance to assume a position of authority in the revolutionary camp, had actually lost him the confidence of even the members of the Duma Committee over which he presided. In fact, at the moment Rodzyanko spoke to Ruzsky he was in an awkward predicament. It was he who had instigated the project of the manifesto empowering him to form a parliamentary cabinet, and he had enlisted the support of Alekseev and Ruzsky by making them believe that he was in full control of the situation. To admit that he had misled the generals would have lost him their goodwill, on which rested all his hopes for his political future. He therefore tried to maintain the legend of being in control of the situation, and even went so far as to claim that he 'had been forced to appoint a government' on the night of 28 February–1 March. This was at best a euphemistic way of saying that he was no longer favoured as the new head of government by the members of the Duma Committee, who now preferred Prince Lvov.

Although we have no reliable evidence as to why Rodzyanko failed to meet the Emperor on 1 March, we can safely venture the following conjecture. During the morning of 1 March it must have become clear to Rodzyanko that his project of becoming the first parliamentary premier of Russia would meet with the opposition of the Duma Kadets, who did not want him. The abdication solution was gaining ground with the Duma Committee, but nobody could say whether it would be acceptable to the High Command. Had Rodzyanko gone to Pskov he would have found himself in an embarrassing position. Ruzsky might have insisted on implementing Rodzyanko's original proposal for his appointment by the Tsar to the parliamentary premiership. If he had accepted such a solution, he would immediately have been denounced as an arch-reactionary trying by small constitutional concessions to save the Emperor and the régime, and would have found himself 'on the other side of the barricades'. On the other hand, if he

had then insisted on the abdication, he would himself have become a
rebel in the eyes of the generals and might well have been arrested by
them. It would have been different if he had met the Emperor at
Bologoe, on the direct line between Moscow and Petrograd, where he
could have relied on the railway workers and employees and the small
local garrisons to obey him and, if necessary, arrest Nicholas II. In
Pskov, however, he would have to deal with an aide-de-camp general
commanding millions of troops, who had sided with him so long as it
was only a question of moderate reform, but who might well part
company with him on discovering his support for a solution so radical
as to require the abdication of the ruling monarch and the possible end
of the dynasty. In these circumstances Rodzyanko must have thought
it preferable to wait and see how matters would develop in Pskov after
the meeting between the Emperor and Ruzsky, and then try to persuade the army commanders that an immediate abdication was both
desirable and necessary. In order to do this, he had to continue his tactics
of duping the supreme commanders into believing he was the sole
man in authority in Petrograd – a man who at considerable risk to
himself was contriving to maintain order and guide the popular
uprising into more moderate channels. At the same time he had to
scotch the generals' half-hearted plans to send loyal troops to Petrograd
to suppress the mutiny.

But whatever his motive, by the evening of 1 March Rodzyanko had
given no explanation whatever either to the Emperor or to Ruzsky for
not turning up at the Dno rendezvous, and the two men were left
alone to take an immediate decision.

Our knowledge of the negotiations in Pskov is derived mainly from
memoirs. The scene of the abdication itself late on 2 March has been
described by almost everyone who was present, though this in itself
makes it no easier to establish what actually happened. The negotiations
leading up to it, which went on mainly between the Emperor and
Ruzsky, are less fully documented. The diary of Nicholas II, or what
has been published of it, gives only the tersest account of them.
Ruzsky's reports are far more detailed. The account he gave Rodzyanko
in his telephone conversation with him the same night is an authentic
document, though short and discreet. Ruzsky was not too forthcoming
to Rodzyanko about his own feelings on the question of the abdication,
possibly because he knew that he would be asked to show the tape of the

conversation to the Emperor the next morning. We also have a statement made by Ruzsky in an interview with a journalist, Samokhvalov, and published in the newspapers in March. In this he presents himself as the saviour of the revolution, and claims to have stopped the troops from marching on Petrograd by persuading the Emperor to cancel the order of the previous day.

Later, when Ruzsky had relinquished his command, rumours reached him that the Emperor had complained of the way he had conducted the negotiations, declaring that he had been rude, and bullied him into making concessions he had not intended to make.[1] Ruzsky was upset by these rumours, and gave, in confidence, what he thought was a truthful account of the facts to two persons while staying in the Caucasian spa of Kislovodsk early in 1918 (shortly before he was killed by an armed gang of Bolshevik sailors from Kronstadt). One such account is contained in the diary of Grand Duke Andrey Vladimirovich, who was staying in Kislovodsk at the time; the other is by General Vilchkovsky, whom Ruzsky asked to publish the story and to whom he gave a number of documents relating to the events in Pskov.[2] These confidential accounts leave an impression of truthfulness, and do not contradict other sources of evidence except on one point – the rudeness of Ruzsky to his monarch and Supreme Commander. Yet we must not forget that their aim was to justify his actions to posterity at a time when he felt the revolution was the greatest disaster which could have befallen Russia. This conviction must certainly have coloured his account of the part he had played in the abdication drama.

The various statements made by Ruzsky and other witnesses would in themselves provide ample material for a book, and we must therefore content ourselves with picking out those elements which seem to throw light on the rapidly changing political situation.

When the imperial train arrived in Pskov on 1 March the Emperor's suite, and indeed the Emperor himself, believed that they had reached a safe harbour, a place where there was a man in authority with almost unlimited military power, who would at least fulfil the immediate wishes of the ill-fated travellers and see to it that the imperial train reached

1. The source of these rumours is doubtless the Dowager Empress Maria, to whom Nicholas II must have given a full account of what had happened in Pskov during the many hours he spent with her in Mogilev on the days following the abdication. See Shakhovskoy, op. cit., p. 201.　　2. See Bibliographical Notes, p. 461, below.

Tsarskoe Selo in the shortest possible time. On meeting Ruzsky the Tsar explained the incident at Malaya Vishera and said that he had thought it best in the circumstances to make for the nearest military HQ. It seems, however, that the train's further progress to Tsarskoe was never discussed. Instead, Ruzsky reported on the general political situation, informed the Tsar of the successes of the revolutionary movement in Moscow, and suggested an immediate political solution on the lines laid down by Rodzyanko and Alekseev.

There can be no doubt that he met with violent resistance on the part of the Emperor.[1] Nicholas II said that he was unable to understand the position of a constitutional monarch, who reigns but does not govern. In assuming supreme power as an autocrat, he had undertaken, as a duty before God, responsibility for the direction of state affairs. Were he to agree to curtail and delegate his powers, he would deprive himself of actual control over what was going to happen, but not evade responsibility for it. In other words, the transfer of power to a government answerable to parliament would in no way relieve him of responsibility for the actions of this government. This of course was the old doctrine which Nicholas II had inherited from his father and had learned from his political teacher and mentor, Pobedonostsev; and Ruzsky must have found this kind of ideological exposé of autocracy rather exasperating. It is probable that he betrayed his impatience and that Nicholas II resented this in retrospect. Apart from general problems, various personalities were also discussed. The Emperor assured Ruzsky that he had some knowledge of the competence and political capacity of the people who claimed to enjoy the nation's confidence. He did not think much of them as potential ministers, especially in such difficult conditions, and thought them inferior to the people whom he had lately chosen. This was significant inasmuch as Nicholas II, as we have seen, had no particularly high opinion of the abilities of his own ministers.

Ruzsky's final success was no small achievement. Both on the last day of his stay at GHQ and on the way to Pskov the Emperor had been incessantly bombarded with advice to the same effect as Ruzsky's arguments. On the journey he must have received the text of a letter from General John Hanbury-Williams, chief of the Allied Military

1. The next day Ruzsky told the delegates of the Duma Committee: 'This business [the abdication] is settled, but yesterday was difficult, we had a storm blowing.' Shulgin, *Dni*, p. 269.

Mission to Russia. There was also an appeal from the liberal members
of the State Council, dispatched during the night of the 27th–28th.
Then there was the opinion of Grand Duke Sergey Mikhailovich,
who supported the Alekseev solution. As the course of the Pskov
negotiations showed, the only result of all this was that the Emperor
appointed Rodzyanko premier and let him choose *some* of the members
of his cabinet. The introduction of a parliamentary régime remained
in his eyes a betrayal of his duty, his belief in which had been strengthened and maintained by the Empress. Any attempt to wring concessions
from him on this point he regarded as a kind of temptation of the Devil.
Nicholas II must have looked on any such solution as a show of weakness, a yielding to temptation in *ultra vires* conditions. He must have
known that this was the one thing his wife would not forgive him, the
one thing she would regard as a betrayal both of the promise made to
his dying father and of his son's future. Outright abdication seemed to
both Nicholas and his wife a solution far more morally acceptable.

The Emperor's negotiations with Ruzsky dragged on far into the
night of 1–2 March with interruptions, one of them a gloomy dinner
at which, as was customary, politics were not discussed. During these
intervals Ruzsky waited in the imperial train and talked to the anxious
courtiers. They were shocked by his attitude, which they considered
disaffected to the point of disloyalty. Ruzsky could not resist telling
them that he had given warnings against the course the Emperor's
policy was taking, and mentioned Rasputin's influence as one of the
main causes of the present disaster. When asked at one point what was
to be done now, he appears to have said: 'There is nothing left but
to throw ourselves on the victors' mercy.' Ruzsky's attitude came as
a surprise to the court officials, and probably to the Emperor himself.
Admiral Nilov, a personal friend of the Emperor, was especially
indignant. He was persuaded that the only course consistent with the
Emperor's position as autocrat and Commander-in-Chief would be
to dismiss Ruzsky, have him arrested or even executed, appoint
another general of unquestionable loyalty and march on Tsarskoe Selo
and Petrograd with all available loyal troops. Nilov realised, however,
that this would be quite alien to the Emperor's nature, and it is doubtful
whether he seriously tried to put forward his views. He retired to his
compartment and did not reappear until the drama was over.

The most important development on the night of 1 March was the receipt in Pskov shortly before 11 p.m. of Alekseev's telegram, with the text of the draft manifesto empowering Rodzyanko to form a Provisional Government. If ever such plans as those entertained by Nilov had crossed the Emperor's mind, Alekseev's telegram would have nullified them. It showed that the Chief of Staff, who was in charge of the whole army in the field, was completely behind the solution proposed by Ruzsky, and that any action against Ruzsky would have to be followed by a drastic purge of the Army High Command. This the Emperor could not risk doing in wartime without disrupting the country's entire defence system. Alekseev's telegram was certainly decisive in breaking the will of Nicholas II, as Ruzsky admits when he says: 'I doubt whether I would have been able to persuade the Emperor, had it not been for Alekseev's telegram.' Ruzsky's reference to persuasion is, however, misleading. In fact, he gave the Emperor no choice but to accept the Alekseev-Rodzyanko plan, although he knew that this ran counter to all the Emperor's religious and moral convictions. As Nicholas II put it, he would have needed a different education, or to change his whole nature, to understand and accept it.

When Ruzsky believed the Emperor had at last given in and would sign the draft manifesto, he went away and waited for the Emperor's telegram to this effect. When it was brought to him he discovered that, instead of speaking of a cabinet responsible to parliament, the Emperor had suggested that the members of the cabinet, apart from the two Defence Ministers and the Foreign Minister, be selected by Rodzyanko. Ruzsky refused to accept this version, and insisted on the redrafting of the telegram to include the key phrase 'ministry responsible to the Duma'. There was a delay of about two hours, which Ruzsky spent talking to the assembled courtiers, before he was finally called into the presence. There, with only Count Frederichs, the Minister of the Court, as a witness, the Emperor finally agreed to the version so hateful to him and signed the telegram authorising the publication of the manifesto proposed by Alekseev.

At this interview the Tsar seemed so indifferent to what was going on that Ruzsky felt it necessary to ask whether he had not changed his mind, and whether by transmitting the telegram he, Ruzsky, would not be acting contrary to the Emperor's wishes. To this — again according to Ruzsky's subsequent report — the Emperor answered that he had taken the decision because both Alekseev and Ruzsky, with whom he had discussed the question before, were of the same opinion, and he knew that they were rarely in complete agreement on anything.[1] At the same time he did not conceal from the Commander of the Northern Front that it was an extremely difficult decision for him to make, but that he felt it his duty to agree because it was for the good of Russia.

Soon after midnight on 2 March it seemed to Ruzsky that the political problem had been solved. The task was now to halt the movement of troops on Petrograd and to call off the expedition led by General Ivanov.

In the meantime, the latter had reached Tsarskoe Selo with considerable delay but without major incident. On 1 March he passed through Dno a few hours before the imperial trains halted there. At Dno he found trains crowded with mutinous soldiers coming from Petrograd. He applied to the drunken soldiers 'the paternal methods' of restoring discipline of which he was so proud. Moving close to them and armed only with his enormous spade-shaped beard, he yelled at the top of his voice: 'On your knees.' Amazingly, this order was instantly complied with, and the men were disarmed, either by their own comrades or by troops of the St. George Battalion. The more recalcitrant were arrested and put on General Ivanov's train.

On arriving in Tsarskoe Selo Ivanov proceeded to the Palace, where the Empress received him in the middle of the night. There he learned of the telegram from Alekseev (no. 1833, quoted above), which enjoined him to 'change his tactics' in view of the supposed restoration of law and order in the capital. According to Spiridovich, whose information derives from court circles, Ivanov was not taken in by this telegram, nor indeed was Ruzsky. Before reporting to the Empress he had worked out a plan of action, described by Spiridovich.[2]

The meeting with the Empress had, however, obviously shaken Ivanov's resolve. For the last thirty-six hours she had been living in

---

1. Was this a hint at suspected collusion?
2. 'Ivanov, after weighing up the situation, decided to publish an order of the day announcing his arrival, to make Tsarskoe Selo his headquarters and to call on all officers still faithful to their Emperor to rally round him. The echelons which had been held up on the railway on Bublikov's orders ... were to be brought to Tsarskoe by road.' Spiridovich, *Velikaya voyna* vol. III, p. 221.

dread of a mob attack on the palace, and was anxious not to endanger the lives of her children by being associated with a punitive expedition the outcome of which no one could foresee. She still clung to the belief that the revolution could somehow be checked by a mere show of authority and strength and without resort to large-scale bloodshed. This was not a language Ivanov, or anyone not familiar with the Empress's mystical ideas, could understand.

On his return to the train Ivanov was finally confirmed in his opinion that there was nothing for him to do by the telegram which Ruzsky had got permission from the Emperor to send after his capitulation on the political question, and which ran:

> I hope you arrived safely. I request you to take no measures whatever before my arrival and before reporting to me. Nicholas, 2 March 1917, 00.20.

This was the end of the Ivanov expedition. The movement towards Petrograd of reinforcements for Ivanov's detachment had been stopped some time before, as the Emperor's permission to do so was thought to be imminent, and was now cancelled by the HQ of the Northern Front.

It remained only for Ruzsky to inform Rodzyanko that at last the desired concessions had been obtained from the Emperor, and that he was now fully empowered to form the first government of Russia responsible to the Duma.

At 11.30 p.m. on 1 March, that is before his victory in the lone wrangle with the Emperor, Ruzsky had, through his Chief of Staff, asked Rodzyanko for a direct-line conversation 'on an extremely urgent and responsible matter'. The request went through the HQ of the Petrograd Military District, which was then in direct-line communication with Pskov and simultaneously in contact with the President of the Duma in the Tauride Palace.

4. RODZYANKO REJECTS THE TSAR'S CONCESSIONS: SMALL HOURS OF 2 MARCH

The President of the Duma showed no particular haste in getting in touch with Ruzsky. He said that he would be at the direct-line terminal at 2.30 a.m., and not before. In fact the conversation took place an hour later and lasted for about four hours, owing to the slowness of the method of transmission — the so-called Hughes apparatus. Ruzsky began with the protestations of sincerity which the extreme seriousness of the situation demanded. He asked Rodzyanko to explain why he had cancelled his journey to Pskov. Having received the answers which we have quoted above, he told Rodzyanko that the Emperor had at first intended to appoint Rodzyanko as Prime Minister responsible to the Crown, but had finally agreed to give him a mandate to form a cabinet responsible to the legislative chambers. He offered to communicate immediately the text of the manifesto drafted in Mogilev.

Rodzyanko answered with a long exposé of the course of events.[1] He said:

> It is obvious that neither His Majesty nor you realise what is going on here. One of the most fearsome of revolutions has come upon us, and it will not be easy to deal with. For the past two and a half years, on every occasion on which I have presented my loyal report, I have unremittingly warned the Emperor of the storm which would overtake us unless concessions to satisfy the country were made without delay. I must inform you that at the very beginning of the outbreak the authorities, as represented by the ministers, went out of the picture and took no preventative measures whatever; fraternisation started immediately between the troops and the crowds; the troops did not shoot, but walked the streets where the crowds greeted them with cheers.[2] The prorogation of the session of the legislative institutions has added fuel to the flames. And gradually anarchy grew to such dimensions that the State Duma as a whole, and myself in particular, were left with no alternative but to take the movement into our hands and to head it, so as to forestall such anarchy, which — in the prevailing disintegration — would threaten the State with destruction.
>
> Unfortunately I am far from having succeeded; the people's passions have become so inflamed that it will hardly be possible to restrain them; the troops are completely demoralised; not only do they refuse to obey

1. The passage is identical in the documents which General Lukomsky published in *ARR*, III, pp. 255–258, and in the documents which Ruzsky had given to General Vilchkovsky, published in *Russkaya Letopis*, III, pp. 124–133. It is another notable omission from Browder and Kerensky's *The Russian Provisional Government*.

2. Rodzyanko seems to have forgotten his indignant protests to Khabalov about shooting on the crowds by the troops. See above, p. 265.

orders, but they are murdering their officers; hatred of the Empress has reached the utmost limits.[1] In order to avoid bloodshed I have been forced to incarcerate all the ministers with the exception of the Ministers of War and the Navy in the Petropavlovskaya Fortress. I am very apprehensive lest the same fate overtake me, because agitation is directed against all that is moderate and limited in its demands. I think it necessary to inform you that what you have been considering is not sufficient, and that the dynastic question demands an immediate decision.

Rodzyanko's opening gambit came as a surprise to Ruzsky. The announcement that he had been instrumental in the arrest and imprisonment of the Tsar's ministers placed the President of the Duma in the rebel camp. The statement that the dynastic question had now been raised was also a new departure. Ruzsky's reaction was extremely cautious. He admitted that the way he visualised the situation in Petrograd was very different from the picture presented by the President of the Duma. He argued that the passions of the people had to be allayed if the war was to go on and the enormous sacrifices made by the nation were not to have been in vain. 'A way must be found to re-establish peace in the country', he said, and asked for details of the proposed solution of the dynastic question.

Rodzyanko answered 'with a heavy heart': 'Hatred of the dynasty has reached the utmost limits, but all the people I have spoken to when going out to talk to the crowds and the troops are quite determined to carry on the war to a victorious conclusion and not to deliver themselves into the hands of the Germans.' Rodzyanko then repeated the usual indictment of such people as Sukhomlinov, Rasputin, Stuermer and Protopopov, and ended by saying: 'The Empress has taken upon herself a heavy responsibility before God in turning away the Emperor's heart from his people.' Once again Rodzyanko mentioned the despatch of troops to Petrograd and said that this could only lead to civil strife. In the same breath, however, he claimed that the troops would not fight the people.[2]

Ruzsky understood the importance of this point, and assured Rodzyanko that the Emperor had ordered Ivanov to halt the action and effect the return of the troops who were on the way to Petrograd.

1. It does seem, however, that these limits had been reached some time before by Mme Rodzyanko and her correspondent, Princess Yusupov. See above, p. 200 f.
2. See above, p. 304 n.

'As you see', he said, 'His Majesty has taken all possible measures; and it would therefore be in the interests of the Fatherland and of the patriotic war that we are waging if the Emperor's initiative were to find an echo in the hearts of those who can stop the fire from spreading.' He then read the text of the Alekseev manifesto, which he had had such difficulty in making the Emperor accept, pointing out in conclusion, however, that it would be possible to make partial emendations. He assured Rodzyanko that he had done what he could during the day, and reminded him of the necessity of restoring order immediately, so that the army could resume its normal life and work, so necessary in the period of preparation for the spring offensive agreed upon with the Allies.

Rodzyanko answered: 'Nikolay Vladimirovich, you have rent asunder my already wounded heart.' He went on to speak of the enormous task which rested on his shoulders, and claimed, in this connection, to have appointed a Provisional Government. 'Unfortunately the manifesto has come too late', he said. 'It should have been issued immediately after my first telegram.' At the same time he assured Ruzsky that the flow of supplies to the army would at once be resumed as a result of the Provisional Government's appeal. 'Supplies are plentiful', he said, 'owing to the diligence of the Voluntary Organisations and the Special Councils' (despite, he implied, the sabotage of an incompetent and treacherous government). Rodzyanko ended by exhorting Ruzsky — 'our glorious leader' — 'to destroy the accursed German in battle', and pointed out that the Duma Committee in its appeal to the army had clearly expressed its determination to carry on with the war.

As the conversation was drawing to a close (it ended at 7.30 a.m.) Ruzsky warned Rodzyanko once more of the danger of anarchy spreading in the army and of the loss of governmental authority. To this Rodzyanko replied with the following assurance: 'Do not forget that the *coup d'état* can be voluntary and completely painless for everybody, so that everything will be over in a few days; I can tell you one thing: there will be no bloodshed or unnecessary victims. I shall see to that.' Only towards the very end of the conversation was its original purpose mentioned again, and then inconclusively. Ruzsky asked whether the manifesto should be published. The answer was: 'I really don't know what to say; everything depends on events, which are developing at hair-raising speed.' Ruzsky therefore announced that he was going to inform GHQ that the manifesto should be published, 'come what may'.

In the maze of contradictory versions, accusations, personal apologia, suspicions and speculations with which we are faced in various memoirs, this night-time conversation should be our basic guide. It completely dispels the accusations levelled against Ruzsky[1] that he had worked against the Emperor from the very outset and wanted to bring about his abdication. On the contrary, he showed himself a supporter of the original Rodzyanko–Alekseev plan and in no way encouraged Rodzyanko to insist on raising the so-called 'dynastic question'. He did not react explicitly to Rodzyanko's claim – 'everywhere troops are siding with the Duma and the people, and the threatening demands for an abdication in favour of the son, with Mikhail Alexandrovich as regent, are becoming quite definite'. Rodzyanko's rhetorical improvisations, on the other hand, show a complete loss of orientation. The dominant note in his approach to Ruzsky is one of fear. In his terrified imagination the frenzied masses were on the verge of starting a general massacre; at the same time he dreaded the intervention of Ivanov's potentially loyal troops, and must have been greatly relieved to hear that the expedition had been cancelled; but he was also afraid of personally backing the abdication project, while at the same time admitting that his original plan had been superseded by events. The important thing, however, was that he concealed from Ruzsky the profound rift in the Duma Committee itself, the attempt of the Duma Kadets to deprive him, their chairman, of all political influence in the future, and their wish to invest the Provisional Government with full power.

5. THE INTERVENTION OF THE AIDE-DE-CAMP GENERALS

After the fateful conversation on the direct line with Petrograd, Ruzsky retired for a rest. The text of the tape was at once transmitted to GHQ at Mogilev. The reaction was violent. A request was immediately sent to Pskov to have the Emperor woken at once and the tape of the

1. Once more forcibly but unconvincingly expressed by Spiridovich in his last work, quoted above.

conversation with Rodzyanko submitted to him. General Danilov, who was in charge of the Pskov HQ while Ruzsky was resting, answered that he would not wake Ruzsky, who had just fallen asleep, but that the tape would be shown to the Emperor later in the morning. GHQ in Mogilev showed extraordinary speed in dealing with the incoming news. A concise and competent summary of the conversation between Ruzsky and Rodzyanko was drafted and despatched by Alekseev to the commanders-in-chief of all the fronts (that is, to Grand Duke Nikolay Nikolaevich, Caucasian Front; General Sakharov, Rumanian Front; General Brusilov, South-Western Front; General Evert, Western Front; and Admirals Nepenin and Kolchak, Commanders of the Baltic and Black Sea Fleets). Alekseev's telegram contains the following all-important passage:

> A decision on the dynastic question is now demanded, and the war can be continued to a victorious end only if requests for the Emperor's abdication in his son's favour, with Mikhail Aleksandrovich acting as regent, are satisfied. The situation apparently does not permit of any alternative solution, and every minute's hesitation only serves to reinforce these demands, which are based on the fact that the army's existence and the work of the railways are actually dependent on the Petrograd Provisional Government.
>
> The army in the field must be saved from disintegration. We must carry on the struggle with the external enemy; we must safeguard Russia's independence and the future of the dynasty. We must give this the highest priority even at the cost of considerable sacrifice.
>
> I repeat that every minute lost can be fatal to Russia, and that we must establish unity of thought and purpose among the highest commanders of the armies in the field, so that the army can be saved from instability and perhaps treason. The army must fight the external enemy with all its strength, while the decision on internal affairs will spare it the temptation to play a part in the *coup d'état*, which will be less painful if effected from above. 2 March 1917, 10.15, 1872, Alekseev.

By the time this telegram had been despatched from Mogilev, Ruzsky had already returned to the imperial train, taking with him the tape of his conversation with Rodzyanko. He knew that Rodzyanko's advocacy of abdication as a way of ending the revolutionary unrest had been well received at GHQ. Alekseev's Quartermaster-General, Lukomsky, had told Danilov that he hoped to God Ruzsky would succeed in prevailing on the Emperor to abdicate. Danilov was sceptical on this point. So was Ruzsky, who knew how the Emperor had resisted what was in Ruzsky's view only a minor and quite unavoidable concession and was sure that he would reject out of hand any suggestion of abdication. The Emperor read the text of the Rodzyanko–Ruzsky conversation very carefully and asked Ruzsky for his advice. Not even then did Ruzsky come out with a definite answer; he said that he would have to think the matter over.

In the meantime the text of Alekseev's telegram to the commanders-in-chief had arrived and was reported to the Emperor. From it, it was clear that Alekseev had now given his full support to the Rodzyanko line; he did not so much as mention any of Ruzsky's mild objections to abdication. The Emperor's mood seemed to have undergone a considerable change from the night before. Clearly in this situation abdication appealed to him: it was obviously a more dignified solution than seeing his powers reduced to those of a constitutional monarch. It offered a way of absolving himself of responsibility for the disasters he believed would befall the country once the direction of political affairs got into the hands of ambitious politicians, who so fatuously claimed to enjoy the people's confidence.

At lunchtime when he met Ruzsky during a walk on the station platform, the Emperor told him that he felt inclined to abdicate. It is therefore surprising that Ruzsky thought it necessary to take two of the generals on his staff (Danilov and Savvich) with him when he went for his final talk with the Emperor in the early afternoon. He explained to them that he would like their support, as he feared that the Emperor did not trust him.

When he went to the Emperor, Ruzsky had already received Alekseev's message with the answers of Grand Duke Nikoly Nikolaevich, Brusilov and Evert, all three aide-de-camp generals. The answers, though couched in terms of the most humble loyalty, were all in favour of immediate abdication. Here are samples of their lachrymose style. The Grand Duke:

> As a faithful subject I consider that in accordance with my oath of allegiance and in the spirit of the same I must implore your Imperial Majesty on my knees to save Russia and your heir, knowing as I do the feelings of sacred love you bear towards Russia and him. Having made the sign of the cross, transmit your heritage to him.

Brusilov:

> Please submit to the Emperor my loyal petition, based on my devotion and love for the Fatherland and the throne of the Tsar ... that he renounce the throne in favour of His Highness the heir, the Tsarevich, under the regency of Grand Duke Mikhail Aleksandrovich.

Evert:

> ... Your Majesty's infinitely devoted subject implores Your Majesty to accept, in order to save the Fatherland and the dynasty, a decision in accordance with the declaration of the President of the State Duma, expressed to the Aide-de-camp General Ruzsky, as the only one which can apparently put an end to the revolution and save Russia from the horrors of anarchy.[1]

The Emperor read through the telegrams of his aide-de-camp generals. After that, there was no need of the almost tearful support of Generals Danilov and Sayvich to bring him to announce the final decision. He walked to the window and looked at the snowbound landscape, then turned, made the sign of the cross, and said that he had decided to abdicate. He embraced Ruzsky, thanking him for his loyal service. This set the tone for a number of funereal ceremonies which went on in Pskov and later in Mogilev for several days.

The Emperor announced his decision in two short telegrams, one addressed to the President of the Duma, the other to Alekseev. The abdication was in favour of the Tsarevich, and Grand Duke Michael was appointed as Regent. In a sense it was a step backwards from the concessions of the previous night, for nothing was said about the establishment of a parliamentary régime or a government responsible to the Duma. Ruzsky rushed back to his HQ to send off the telegrams. A peculiar imbroglio followed. To the members of the suite the abdication came as a complete surprise, and they considered the step to have been taken with undue haste. They immediately made representations to the Tsar to stop the telegrams. Ruzsky had to come back and return to the Tsar the telegram addressed to Rodzyanko, pending the arrival of the Duma deputies, whose departure for Pskov had in the meantime been announced from Petrograd. Ruzsky did not return the telegram addressed to Alekseev, but promised not to

1. *ARR*, III, pp. 261 ff.

despatch it before the arrival of the Duma delegation, expected at 7 p.m.

The train bringing the emissaries of the Duma was delayed. This gave members of the suite an opportunity to discuss the new position with the Emperor. They asked him what he intended to do after his abdication, and he said that he would go abroad for the duration of hostilities and then return to Russia, settle in the Crimea and devote himself completely to the education of his son. Some of his advisers doubted whether he would be allowed to do this, but Nicholas replied that nowhere were parents denied the right to care for their children. However, he must have been troubled by some doubts and for the first time he had a heart-to-heart talk with his doctor, Fedorov, about the state of health of the Tsarevich. He said that he had believed Rasputin's prophecies implicitly, and the latter had assured him that the Tsarevich would regain his health when he was fourteen. He asked Fedorov whether this was possible. Fedorov explained that nothing short of a miracle could cure a haemophiliac condition in the existing state of science, and that only extreme precautions and constant surveillance and treatment could prolong the prince's life.

It was an indication of the state of mind of the imperial couple that this conversation should have taken place only owing to extraordinary circumstances. As we shall see, its political repercussions were also considerable.

In the meantime General Ruzsky retired to his quarters, giving strict instructions that the Duma delegates be brought to him for consultations before being ushered into the Emperor's presence.

The members of the suite remained in a state of agitation. Ever since the arrival of the imperial trains in Pskov there had been sharp exchanges between the Palace Commandant Voeykov and General Ruzsky. The members of the suite were convinced that the Emperor's decision was taken under pressure from Ruzsky, and they hoped that the Duma delegates would be more accommodating than the Commander of the Northern Front. They were shocked by the lack of ceremony, and by the casualness with which a whole chapter of history had come to an end in their presence. (One of the generals said: 'How is it possible to relinquish a throne just as if one were handing over the command of a cavalry squadron to another officer?') This is why a member of the suite, Mordvinov, was asked to intercept the Duma delegates, and prevent them from meeting Ruzsky before they spoke to the Emperor.

6. THE DUMA EMISSARIES: GUCHKOV AND SHULGIN

We should not attach too much importance to the hectic last-minute intrigues of the Emperor's entourage. The Emperor had come to a decision and, as the later meeting with the Duma delegates showed, it could not easily be altered. This, of course, the delegates did not know when they left Petrograd at 3 p.m. for their journey to Pskov, during which they were not in touch with either Petrograd or GHQ.

There is no documentary evidence as to how Guchkov and Shulgin were chosen, or what powers and instructions they had been given, but it is clear that they were men of very different calibre. Guchkov seems to have taken the initiative in going to Pskov. Since the failure of Rodzyanko's attempt to proclaim Grand Duke Michael temporary Regent in Petrograd on 27 February, Guchkov had been actively organising the defence of Petrograd against a possible attack by General Ivanov's expeditionary force. He had been going round the various barracks, trying to win the troops' support for the Duma, to restore discipline among them and buttress the authority of those officers who had joined the cause of 'the people' and the Duma. During these attempts, he had some nerve-racking experiences. A youngish officer, Prince Vyazemsky, one of his military friends, was killed at his side by a 'stray' bullet.

Guchkov had never been a believer in mass movements or appeals to the soldiery. The mutiny of the Petrograd garrison, which he observed at close quarters on 28 February–1 March, filled him with apprehension and horror. When he came to the meeting of the temporary Committee of the Duma on the morning of 2 March, he found a critical situation. During the night negotiations had been going on between the Duma Committee and the Executive Committee of the Petrograd Soviet concerning the formation of a government and the launching of a joint appeal for the support of the 'revolutionary masses'. Neither abdication nor the abolition of the monarchy seems to have been touched upon during the negotiations.[1] But at the same time Rodzyanko had

1. Yet Milyukov reports that he persuaded the representatives of the Soviet to drop

been talking to Ruzsky and something had to be done to settle the problem. Rodzyanko had no desire to meet the Emperor, so Guchkov said he was prepared to go to Pskov and settle the question of the formation of a new government with the Emperor and the Commander of the Northern Front.

The offer was accepted, but it seems that no clear-cut instructions were given to Guchkov. In his later deposition to the Muravyev Commission, Guchkov said he had been told to insist on the appointment of Prince Lvov as premier. The question of the abdication must also have been discussed, but after his conversation with Ruzsky, Rodzyanko could not be sure that such a solution would be acceptable to the latter. At some time, however, drafts of a deed of abdication had been prepared in Petrograd, and Guchkov took them with him to Pskov. After Guchkov's offer to undertake this mission had been accepted, he asked whether anybody would go with him. The Duma deputy Shulgin volunteered and was accepted without more ado. A train had been kept ready for Rodzyanko at the Warsaw Station in Petrograd in case he should want to go and see the Emperor, so the two emissaries boarded it there and then.

Later the Executive Committee of the Petrograd Soviet claimed that the Guchkov-Shulgin expedition was arranged behind their backs in violation of the agreements between the Duma and the Soviet, and this story has frequently been repeated in accounts of the Russian revolution. As we have seen, there are no grounds for this complaint. However, we cannot rely on the memory of those who took part in the negotiations of the night of 1–2 March. Thus Shulgin, in his book *Dni*,[1] gives a detailed account of his departure from Petrograd with Guchkov 'as day began to break and while the revolutionary masses, drunk with their victory of the previous day, were still resting in their homes'. This is an amazing inaccuracy. There is documentary evidence to the effect that the train left at 2.57 p.m., and there is an early statement

their demand that the formation of the Provisional Government should not prejudice the future form of the Russian state, i.e. whether it should be a monarchy or a republic. His intention, Milyukov states (in his *Istoriya vtoroy russkoy revolyutsii*, p. 46), was to secure the automatic acceptance of the regency of Grand Duke Michael. This would, if anything, show that the Duma Committee did not act *ultra vires* in sending its emissaries to negotiate such a solution with the Tsar.

1. Op. cit. p. 243.

to the press by Shulgin on his return in which he said that the emissaries left at 3 p.m. But like so many other participants and eye-witnesses, Shulgin had the excuse of extreme nervous tension, the result of sleepless nights and foodless days, a state in which the sequence of events tends to become confused.

More important than such details are the personalities of the two emissaries. Guchkov, who within twenty-four hours was to become the first War Minister of the Provisional Government, was clearly the leader and spokesman. In accepting his offer to go to Pskov his colleagues must have taken into consideration the special character of his relations with the Emperor. Although Guchkov, as a prominent figure in the monarchist Octobrist Party, was by no means a revolutionary, it could safely be assumed that personal animosity would preclude any private deal with the Emperor. During Stolypin's premiership, Guchkov had for a long time been a supporter of that last authoritarian head of the Tsarist government. But even then he had shown himself a meddlesome politician, who made military affairs the medium for his onslaughts on the inefficiency of the bureaucracy. His speech in the Duma in 1908 attacking the appointment of 'irresponsible persons' to the various army inspectorates was fresh in everybody's memory. It was directed against the grand dukes whom the Emperor used to appoint to these posts. This was a long-established tradition and was not based on nepotism, but was rather a means of giving the grand dukes something to do where they could cause least trouble and be unable to interfere in political matters. The attack was unfair and vicious, and very embarrassing for the Emperor, but it earned Guchkov a certain popularity in liberal circles. His next attack was in connection with the budget of the Holy Synod in 1912, when for the first time he alluded to the close relations between the Empress and Rasputin — thus starting the anti-Rasputin campaign which went on even after the assassination of the *starets* on 16 December 1916.

Some time in 1912 Guchkov was supposed to have obtained from Rasputin's erstwhile friend, the monk Iliodor, letters to Rasputin from the Empress and her children which might, to an uninformed person, appear compromising.[1] It was reported to the Emperor that Guchkov had had these letters duplicated and widely distributed. The Emperor felt that this kind of attack took unfair advantage of his inability to

1. See above, p. 182.

answer back. At one time he instructed his Minister of War to inform
Guchkov when opportunity arose that he had referred to him as 'a
scoundrel'. Whether this was in fact done is not clear: we have only
an entry[1] in Polivanov's diary that no opportunity had so far presented itself. But at the farewell reception for the members of the
Third Duma, the Emperor passed Guchkov, whom he had known for
years, as if he did not recognise him, remarking: 'You, I believe,
represent Moscow'. This infuriated Guchkov, who was not of a
forgiving nature. During the war Guchkov had become Chairman of
the Central WIC, and thus had close contacts with military circles. We
have seen how he used this position in order to undermine the
authority of the government with the Chief of Staff, Alekseev, and
other generals, and we know that the facts were reported to the
Emperor and his wife.[2] It is surprising that an autocratic monarch could
find no way of ridding himself of the services of a subject whom he
considered so utterly disloyal. The Empress does not seem to have
shared her husband's scruples. In one of her letters she suggestively
deplores the fact that Guchkov had not been killed in some railway
accident. When at the beginning of 1916 Guchkov fell dangerously
ill, she expressed the hope that he would die. In fact circles close to
Guchkov were spreading the rumour that he had been poisoned by the
'Rasputin clique'. But he recovered, and lived to see Rasputin assassinated.

   Throughout 1916, as Guchkov himself explained in some detail to the
Muravyev Commission, he was busy preparing the palace coup which,
as we have already seen,[3] he intended to carry out with a small group of
officers and men. The coup was to be executed on one of the railway
stations on the Emperor's route to and from Mogilev, and Guchkov's
actual expedition to Pskov must have seemed to him a fulfilment of his
dream distorted by reality.

   The second emissary was a very different character, although his
passion for political adventure was probably as strong as that of his
colleague. Vasily Shulgin was a landowner from south-west Russia,

---

1. See General Polivanov's diary, entry of 18 February 1912, quoted by Melgunov,
Martovskie dni 1917-go goda, p. 186.
2. See above, p. 182 ff.
3. See his lengthy explanations to the Muravyev Commission in his testimony on
2 August 1917. *Padenie*, VI.

and published in Kiev the right-wing provincial paper, *Kievlyanin*. He had a reputation for being a staunch, mildly anti-Semitic conservative. Yet during the famous Beylis trial of 1913 in Kiev, when a Jewish labourer of that name was accused of the ritual murder of a Russian boy, Shulgin's paper came out with a leading article violently attacking the Public Prosecutor's Office for bias and suppression of evidence. The paper was confiscated for the first time in its long existence, and Shulgin was brought to trial and sentenced to three months' imprisonment. At the beginning of the war, on enlisting in the army, he was pardoned. He joined the Progressive Bloc in the Duma and on 27 February was appointed to the Duma Provisional Committee.

In assessing the human factor in this drama it might be relevant to mention the subsequent career of both men. Guchkov, after a short tenure of office in the Provisional Government, resigned at the beginning of May 1917. With his resignation, his career in high politics came to an end, but not his conspiratorial activities, which were in fact second nature to him. He emigrated when the White armies were evacuated from south Russia and immediately launched his own anti-Bolshevik campaign abroad. He gradually developed strong pro-German sentiments, and while living in Paris maintained secret links with the German General Staff. He was supported by a small group of politicians and an ex-White Guardist General, Skoblin, who in 1937[1] became involved in the kidnapping of another White Russian, General Miller, in Paris. His close relations with persons involved in this affair made him suspect of having played a part in it, however involuntary. He died in 1936, a disillusioned and unhappy man, betrayed by many of those he trusted, and trusted by none of those for whose political support he had hoped.

Shulgin had an even more extraordinary career. As an émigré, after many adventures during and after the civil war, he got in touch with a conspiratorial organisation in the Soviet Union which claimed to be monarchist, but was in fact run entirely by the Soviet secret police. In 1925 he was literally taken for a ride by this organisation to Russia, where he was given an opportunity of seeing for himself the 'monarchist organisation's' success in penetrating the whole Soviet system. He even published an enthusiastic account of his journey on

1. See P. Bailey, *The Conspirators* (New York, 1960). Skoblin, a gallant officer in the White Army, became, at an unknown date, a highly successful NKVD agent.

his return to the West. When the GPU's game had been exposed, he retired from public life and settled in Yugoslavia. On the arrival of the Red Army in 1945, he was arrested, deported to the USSR and was presumed to have been shot. After Stalin's death, however, it became known that he had survived some years in a concentration camp, and was still alive in the Soviet Union. In 1960–61 statements by him appeared in the Soviet press, in which he expressed his satisfaction at living in his Fatherland and appealed to his émigré friends to support their native land's heroic struggle for peace.

7. THE SIGNING OF THE ACT OF ABDICATION

These were the two men who arrived, tired and dishevelled, at Pskov station at about 10 p.m. on 2 March to meet the Emperor. They were given no time to recover from their strenuous journey (they had been delayed in Luga, where negotiations took place with the local revolutionary committee) and, in violation of General Ruzsky's instructions, were taken straight to the imperial train. Ruzsky, however, joined them in the Tsar's reception car, where the meeting had already begun.

Guchkov did most of the talking. He said that the emissaries had come to report on what had happened in Petrograd and to discuss measures to save the situation, which was still menacing: the popular movement had been neither planned nor well-prepared, but had broken out spontaneously and was therefore anarchic. Various senior state officials had vanished from the scene,[1] and the Provisional Committee of the State Duma had been forced to act to restore the officers' authority over their troops. There was, however, in the same building occupied by the Duma Committee – the Tauride Palace – a committee of the 'Workers' Party', and the Duma Committee was actually in its power. There was also a danger of the revolutionary movement spreading to the front. No army unit exposed to this contagious influence would be able to resist. The dispatch of troops from the front was doomed to failure. The only thing which could redeem the situation was abdication in favour of the infant heir, and the establishment of a regency under Grand Duke Michael, who would form a new

1. Guchkov, like Rodzyanko before him, used the expression 'stushevalis'.

government. Only thus would Russia, the dynasty and the monarchic principle be saved.

Shulgin added to Guchkov's description a highly-coloured picture of the chaotic situation in the Tauride Palace:

> Permit me to explain in what conditions the State Duma has to work. On the 26th [*sic*] the crowd and armed soldiers entered the Duma and occupied the whole of the wing on the right-hand side, while the left side was occupied by the public, so that we were left with only two rooms where the so-called Committee is sheltering. All the arrested people are being dragged there, and even this is lucky for them, because it saves them from being lynched by the crowd. We are setting some of the arrested men free immediately. We are maintaining a symbolic administration of the country, and it is only thanks to this that some degree of order can be maintained and the functioning of the railways continues uninterrupted. Such are the conditions under which we work: the Duma is like a lunatic asylum. We shall have to join battle in earnest with the leftist elements, but for this we need some ground to stand on.[1]

Guchkov and Shulgin behaved almost like petitioners who had come to ask the Tsar to provide the base from which to launch their struggle against anarchy and revolution. They seem to have lost all sense of proportion. Even the situation in the Duma was not at all as Guchkov and Shulgin had described it. Yet Guchkov was most insistent on the futility of any attempt to crush the revolutionary movement by sending armed forces from the front. In this he was supported by Ruzsky, who whispered to Shulgin that in any case he had no troops available for the purpose. The Emperor listened impassively to Guchkov's speech, betraying his impatience only once, when Guchkov, adopting a patronising tone, told him he ought to think the matter over carefully, pray to God, and announce his decision within twenty-four hours. It was then that the Emperor exploded his bombshell. He declared that he had made up his mind earlier in the day to abdicate in favour of his son. Now, however, as he felt he could not bear to be separated from the child, he would abdicate both for himself and his son.

Ruzsky said later that everybody was dumbfounded at this declaration. He tried to elicit a promise from Guchkov that the boy would not be separated from his parents. Guchkov refused to commit himself, and even hinted that the Emperor might have to go abroad and the boy

1. See Melgunov, *Martovskie dni*, p. 193.

remain in Russia.[1] The meeting seems to have been interrupted at this point so that the emissaries could have a private discussion. Again neither Shulgin nor Guchkov seems to remember what, if anything, they discussed. It appears, however, that someone found certain advantages in the new proposal made by the Emperor. As regent, Grand Duke Michael would have to safeguard the hereditary rights of the infant Emperor. As a monarch, on the other hand, he could easily introduce the necessary reforms and become the first Emperor to take an oath to rule in accordance with a new constitution. An entreaty by Nicholas II to his successor to take such an oath was to be included in the act of abdication.

When negotiations with the Emperor were resumed, however, Guchkov simply said that the emissaries must bow to the Tsar's feelings as a father and accept the solution proposed. The two men offered a draft deed of abdication, which they had brought with them. But the Emperor said that he had his own version, and produced one which had been drafted that afternoon in Mogilev on his instructions. He had already put in the alteration concerning the succession, and now the sentence mentioning the new Emperor's oath of allegiance to the constitution was agreed upon and inserted.

By this time Shulgin was succumbing to a migraine he had brought with him from Petrograd and to the emotional stress occasioned by the historic scene. The very words of the deed of abdication seemed to him steeped in historic dignity and grandeur. He believed they had been written by the Emperor himself. The document was then copied and one copy entrusted to Guchkov. At the same time as the act of abdication two decrees were signed by the Emperor: one appointing Prince Lvov as Prime Minister and the other nominating Grand Duke Nikolay Nikolaevich as Commander-in-Chief of the Armed Forces. The emissaries had no objection to either, although both were to

1. Guchkov himself claims that he said that a separation between the parents and their son would be inevitable, because 'nobody would dare to entrust the fate and education of the future monarch to those who had brought the country to its present state'. Although this was said by Guchkov in his testimony to the Muravyev Commission, we must doubt that he used these very words. The tone of the conversation as reported by all present would exclude such sharp recriminations for alleged past misdeeds. Generally speaking, the reconstruction of the Pskov scene is a complicated psychological exercise. In our short summary of it we have largely followed the masterly analysis of Melgunov, *Martovskie dni*, pp. 189–202.

become a source of major embarrassment to the Provisional Government almost immediately. The time of the abdication was given as 3 p.m., the moment when the decision was taken, so as to forestall allegations that it took place under pressure from the Duma delegates. The decrees concerning the appointment of Prince Lvov and Grand Duke Nikolay Nikolaevich were also antedated and marked 2 p.m.

There were some friendly handshakes, and then the Duma emissaries retired, Shulgin to lie down and nurse his headache, Guchkov to have his private conversation with Ruzsky at last.

The Emperor's demeanour throughout these negotiations has given rise to much comment. Emotional restraint and self-control were hardly a characteristic feature of Russian public life. The absence of any overt emotional reaction was therefore regarded as 'unnatural' by eye-witnesses to these events. Commenting in his testimony before the Muravyev Commission on 2 August 1917, Guchkov said:

> All this went off in such a simple, matter-of-fact way, and, it seemed to me, with so little real understanding of the tragedy of what was happening on the part of the chief protagonist, that I even wondered whether we were dealing with a normal person. This man was simply not aware, up to the very last moment, of the situation and of the action he was taking. Even of someone with the most iron character, of wellnigh unequalled self-control, one might have expected some show of emotion, betraying the fact that he was undergoing a difficult experience; but nothing of the sort. Obviously this was a man of diminished consciousness; I would say, with a lowered level of sensitivity.

Guchkov's comment is only too natural in one who had been waiting for the moment when he would depose the Tsar or force him to abdicate, and who was cheated of the sight of a mortified enemy. We know for certain that he was completely mistaken. The Emperor's diaries betray tremendous emotional upheaval: it was on this day that he wrote the oft-quoted words: 'All around me is cowardice, deceit and treachery', and on the next day he noted, in a letter to his wife: 'The despair seems to be fading away.' Less understandable than Guchkov's remark is the comment of Milyukov, who believed that the abdication on behalf of his son only showed how little the ex-Emperor cared for his country, and that he was putting family considerations before those of politics and patriotism. But the truth of the matter is that the Emperor did not want to cause additional embarrassment to

the Duma Committee by altering the conditions of the abdication. Had
the Duma emissaries felt that difficulties might arise, it was for them to
say so. It was really too much to expect a man in the position of
Nicholas II at that precise moment to advise the Duma Committee how
best to keep within their grasp the power they had just wrested from
him, and how to do so, moreover, at the expense of the safety and
unity of his own family. Suspicions that the act of abdication was signed
with a mental reservation and was intentionally couched in terms which
would make it legally vulnerable (and hence the more easily revoked
at the first opportunity) are without foundation. Its legality was of
course doubtful, but the point was now a purely academic one. The basic
laws did not envisage abdication on behalf of the heir apparent, but
neither did they make provision for abdication by the monarch himself.
The act of abdication introduced a change into the constitutional
structure of the country which was not and could not have been fore-
seen by the basic laws.

8. THE IMMEDIATE EFFECTS OF THE ABDICATION

The importance of what happened on the Pskov railway siding on the
night of 2 March was immeasurable, and far transcended the understanding of the participants in the drama. The abdication prevented the
immediate outbreak of civil war, with all its international consequences,
but it also cut the ground from under the feet of every military and
civil authority in the country which might, in other conditions, have
organised resistance to the rising tide of revolution. The enthusiastic
unanimity with which the revolution in Petrograd was acclaimed by
the country as a whole in subsequent days should not lead us to assume
that such resistance had in any case become impossible by 2 March.
Many people must have accepted the revolution because of the act of
abdication: once the Tsar himself had come to accept the need for a
change, what could be done by those who were ready to oppose it?
The claim then advanced, and later reiterated, that no resistance was
possible in the face of the wave of popular discontent is entirely without
substance. Nowhere outside Petrograd and Moscow and the immediate
vicinity of the capital was there any sign of a spontaneous rising. And
when the news of the revolution was announced, the people accepted

it as something which had happened to them without their having contributed to it directly. In Petrograd, of course, the situation was different. In his speech to the Tsar in Pskov, Guchkov said in a moment of sober sincerity:

> All the workers and soldiers who took part in the riots are firmly convinced that a restoration of the old régime would mean summary justice for them, and this is why we need a radical change. There must be such a crack of the whip on the public imagination as will bring about a complete change immediately. I am convinced that what you have decided to enact [meaning the abdication] must be accompanied by the appointment of Prince Lvov as Prime Minister.[1]

His remark illuminates a decisive factor too often overlooked. Guchkov's 'crack of the whip' was not intended to force back into its lair the beast of popular wrath, which had tasted blood in Petrograd, and even more at Kronstadt. On the contrary, it was meant as an added guarantee of impunity for those who knew only too well that they had committed an outrage against the existing order, and that, unless this order was so radically changed as to leave no trace of legal continuity, they would sooner or later have to answer for what they had done. A more subtle understanding of mass psychology might have suggested that the only way to break the vicious circle in which past crimes, committed with impunity, merely encouraged further misdeeds was to stage some kind of atonement ritual, either in the form of a token punishment or of a public reconciliation.

It is also difficult to understand in retrospect why the appointment of Prince Lvov should have acted as 'a crack of the whip on the public imagination'. His popularity with the Duma was beyond doubt, and it may well be that all the members of the Executive Committee of the Petrograd Soviet had heard of him. But this was far from meaning that he was a popular figure with the soldiers and workers who had mutinied in the capital.

Guchkov's remark also betrays his surprise at the Emperor's lack of resistance to the idea of abdication. Obviously the Duma emissaries were ready to fight on this question; but they were also prepared to give in if necessary and agree to the appointment of a Lvov government without abdication. This is confirmed by the fact that on leaving the imperial train after the signing of the deed of abdication, Guchkov

1. See Melgunov, *Martovskie dni*, p. 193.

said to a crowd which had gathered to wait for news: 'Gentlemen, you are not to worry. The Emperor has granted more than we had expected.' Reporting this in his conversation with Grand Duke Andrey Vladimirovich, Ruzsky expresses his amazement. Obviously, he says, the Duma emissaries were not actually prepared for the Tsar's decision to abdicate. They must have argued in favour of this course mainly as a means of forcing the Emperor to agree to the appointment of Prince Lvov.[1]

The Pskov drama has sometimes been called the revolution of the aide-de-camp generals, and indeed the part played by Generals Alekseev and Ruzsky is not to be underestimated. The wording of Alekseev's telegram to the commanders-in-chief left them no choice but to support the abdication. He told them that if they agreed with his and Rodzyanko's views they should petition the Emperor immediately, but said nothing of what they should do if they disagreed. In fact the acting commander of the Rumanian Front, General Sakharov, did disagree, and delayed his answer until after the others had given theirs. He considered the demands of the President of the Duma 'criminal and revolting'. Nevertheless, he too advocated abdication in case the Duma, bent on its criminal purpose— as he put it – advanced even more odious demands. Sakharov does not specify what demands he had in mind, but he must have been thinking of two matters which, though they were not mentioned, were exercising the minds of all those concerned. The first was the safety of the Empress and of her children, marooned with measles in Tsarskoe Selo. The second was the possibility that, if the army refused to support their demands, the Voluntary Organisations might cut off supplies. In this respect Alekseev's reluctance on 28 February to take over the railways and militarise them is of great significance. He was not much in sympathy with the aspirations of the liberals, though he recognised the usefulness of the Voluntary Organisations in the work of supply. Yet in the three critical days of 28 February – 2 March, he lent these aspirations his full support.

But a very few hours after the abdication, Alekseev had second thoughts. At 6 a.m. on 3 March,[2] in his circular to the commanders-in-chief about the latest developments after the abdication, Alekseev stated (telegram no. 1918) that the leftist parties and the workers'

1. Here again we are following Melgunov's analysis in *Martovskie dni*, p. 71.
2. The same telegram is marked 7 a.m. in Lukomsky's series, *ARR*, III, p. 268 ff.

deputies were exerting powerful pressure on the President of the Duma, whose communications 'lacked sincerity and candour'. According to Lukomsky, Alekseev retired to his study after sending this telegram, and told him: 'I shall never forgive myself for having believed in the sincerity of certain people, for having followed them, and for having sent the telegram about the Emperor's abdication to the commanders-in-chief.'[1] This is such a surprising statement that one would be tempted to discount it were it not fully supported by telegram no. 1918, quoted above. The fact is that the moment the irrevocable consequences of his action on 2 March became clear, Alekseev realised that he had been acting on insufficient and inaccurate information about the situation in Petrograd. Furthermore he felt he had been deceived and used as a cat's-paw. His sense of disillusionment was great and lasting, and his feeling of guilt, though concealed from the outside world, was probably intense.

But how could he have allowed himself to be thus deceived? For he was not a poor judge of character, and had had previous experience of dealing with Rodzyanko. Perhaps the explanation lies in his own character. He had known of the plots against the Emperor and had concealed them from him. The knowledge must have weighed heavily on his conscience, for had the Guchkov coup actually been staged, it would possibly have led to a regicide for which Alekseev would have been morally responsible. If, on the other hand, the Emperor could be persuaded to abdicate voluntarily, this danger would be forestalled, and all military and civil servants would moreover be released from their oath of allegiance. He (and probably also Grand Duke Nikolay Nikolaevich) saw in Rodzyanko's solution a way of shedding a responsibility which might otherwise have proved intolerable from both the moral and the religious standpoints. This explains his readiness to accept uncritically the 'reliable information' reaching him from Rodzyanko on 1 March.

Melgunov, in his analysis, regards the theory of the 'deceived generals' as an exaggeration. The generals, he claims, were fully aware that the Duma was not in control of the revolutionary movement. The inconsistent behaviour of Rodzyanko, who one moment demanded obedience and the next expressed fear of imprisonment, must have aroused their suspicions.

1. Ibid.

This may be so. In one respect, however, the generals were certainly deceived; this was in their conviction that Rodzyanko would insist on a government responsible to the Duma, and would not allow the totality of legislative, executive and judicial power to be concentrated in the hands of the men forming the Provisional Government, over which the Duma or its Committee would have no control. Of this we have documentary proof. The office of the Governor-General of Finland has in its archives in Helsinki the text of an appeal from the Supreme Commander of the Northern Front, Ruzsky, to the population of his area. This appeal was signed on 4 March, and sent to Helsinki, where it was translated into Finnish. Publication was, however, held up and finally cancelled at 6 p.m. on 7 March. But the text shows what Ruzsky really thought was the 'basic change' which had taken place in 'the internal administration of our country':

> Executive power has been transferred to a government responsible to legislative institutions, and composed of persons elected by the people and united in their ardent desire to organise the internal life of the country and provide everything needful for the military and the civilian population. At the same time members of the State Duma have formed a committee to lay new foundations for the administration of the country. Grand Duke Nikolay Nikolaevich, whose name as a military leader is known to every citizen, has once again been placed at the head of the army.

After an appeal to the population to maintain order so as not to jeopardise supplies to the army, and a reminder to the railway workers of their patriotic duty, Ruzsky concludes:

> Let every citizen fulfil his obligations to the utmost, quietly and unremittingly, so that in co-operation with our Allies our army may the more easily bring the war to a victorious end and the life of our State progress with full confidence in the elected representatives of the Russian people — the members of the State Duma and of the government responsible to it.

When he signed this appeal on 4 March, Ruzsky must already have known of the abdication of Grand Duke Michael and the proposal to call a Constituent Assembly. None of this, however, is mentioned in the appeal. What Ruzsky was saying in his appeal was based on the information given him by Rodzyanko in a Hughes apparatus conversation between 6 and 7 a.m. on 3 March.

The fact is that as soon as Rodzyanko learned that Nicholas II had renounced the throne both on his own and his son's behalf, and that Grand Duke Michael was therefore Emperor, he asked both Alekseev and Ruzsky to stop publication of the manifesto signed in Pskov. To Ruzsky he said, early on the 3rd:

> The point is that with great difficulty it has been possible to keep the revolutionary movement within more or less decent limits. But the situation is not yet settled, and a civil war is perfectly possible.
>
> Perhaps they would have reconciled themselves to the regency of the Grand Duke and the accession of the heir, the Tsarevich, but his [the Grand Duke's] accession as Emperor would be quite unacceptable.

When Ruzsky expressed his annoyance that the Duma emissaries had not raised the point the night before, Rodzyanko explained that they could not be held responsible for that, because

> quite unexpectedly for all of us, a mutiny of soldiers, the like of which I have not seen before, has flared up. These are, of course, not soldiers, but simple *muzhiks*, taken straight from the plough, who have seen fit to present all their *muzhik* demands at once. All one hears among the crowds are cries of 'Land and Liberty', 'Down with the Dynasty', 'Down with the Romanovs', 'Down with the Officers', and in many units, a massacre of the officers has begun.[1]

Nothing like a massacre of officers had taken place after the Duma delegates had left, and no new mutiny had, of course, flared up in Petrograd. But Rodzyanko went further. Elaborating on the theme of the unexpected *muzhik* rising, he claimed that only with the promise of a Constituent Assembly were passions allayed, and only then did 'Petrograd catch its breath and the night pass relatively quietly'.

---

1. Rodzyanko's reference to a new outbreak of violence in Petrograd could not have been the result of news received from Helsingfors and Kronstadt on the increasingly tense situation in the Baltic Fleet which led to the massacres of officers. News of it was received — with consternation — in the Duma only in the course of the afternoon of 3 March. Conditions in Petrograd were totally different from those prevailing in the Baltic Fleet. See Melgunov's analysis of the contradictory eye-witness accounts of the situation in Petrograd in *Martovskie dni*, pp. 73–92, and on the unrest in the Baltic Fleet, *ibid.*, pp. 262–269.

Ruzsky must have had his doubts about Rodzyanko's information, and asked to talk to Prince Lvov, who, he was told, was with Rodzyanko at the other end of the direct line. But Rodzyanko told him that everything necessary had been said, and that Prince Lvov could add nothing. 'We both put our trust in God's help, in the greatness and power of Russia, in the gallantry and steadfastness of the army and, in spite of all obstacles, in a victorious end to the war.' But Ruzsky would not be shaken off, and wanted to know precisely in whom or what actual State power was vested. Rodzyanko's answer was: 'Things are like this: the Supreme Council, the responsible government, the legislative assemblies are to function until the question of the constitution is solved by the Constituent Assembly.' But the persistent Ruzsky who, like everybody else, had never heard of a Supreme Council before, asked who was at its head, to which Rodzyanko answered: 'I made a mistake. It is not the Supreme Council, but the Provisional Committee of the State Duma, under my chairmanship.'[1]

No wonder Alekseev complained of the lack of sincerity and candour in communications from the President of the Duma. Only in the ensuing days did the generals come to realise that far from helping Rodzyanko, on whose information they had acted, to establish his authority and power, they had in fact contributed to the formation of a Provisional Government with no parliamentary responsibility, and which was unable and unwilling to prevent the revolutionary ferment from spreading to the army in the field. Alekseev, who was the first to realise what had happened, at once tried to call a conference of the commanders-in-chief of the various fronts. This might have led to the formation of a military *junta*, which, if politically well-advised, could well have become an important factor in the subsequent developments. But Alekseev's idea had no support from Ruzsky, who objected that the generals lacked both judgment and reliable information about what was going on, and that their conference would therefore be pointless. This delayed for months any independent action by the military in the Russian revolution. Alekseev did not insist on his plan, because he was awaiting the arrival of the Supreme Commander, Grand Duke Nikolay Nikolaevich. When the latter did arrive, however, Alekseev had already been informed of the Provisional Government's decision to cancel his appointment, members of the Romanov family being

1. Cf. below, p. 401.

debarred from service in the new régime. The Grand Duke was asked to resign, which he immediately did and retired from public life.

The personal fate of the ex-Emperor and his family had hardly been touched upon in the negotiations with the Duma emissaries. Soon after midnight on 3 March the imperial train left for Mogilev. The Emperor apparently did not insist on having a passage to Tsarskoe Selo cleared immediately. His ardent desire to be reunited with his family seems to have given way to a wish to see his GHQ, take leave of his generals and meet his mother, who had come specially from Kiev. On his arrival he was met in the usual way by his Chief of Staff and the other officials at GHQ. The next morning he had his usual daily conference with Alekseev. Nothing has been revealed of what passed between the two men. But we know that Alekseev transmitted to the Provisional Government the 'Emperor's demands' or 'requests' that he be allowed to return to Tsarskoe, stay there until the children's health was restored, and finally be granted safe passage to Murmansk to embark for England. All three points were accepted by the government.[1] The rest of the Emperor's stay at GHQ was spent mainly in conversation with his mother, who arrived on 5 March.

On the 7th a special commission, headed by Bublikov, was expected in Mogilev: it was to convey the ex-Emperor to his palace at Tsarskoe Selo. In the morning all the officers at GHQ and one representative of the soldiers of each section gathered in the hall of the governor's house, where the Emperor lived, and a moving farewell scene took place. The Emperor, overcoming his emotion, said a few words, enjoining those present to serve their Fatherland faithfully under the new government. Alekseev, with tears in his eyes, wished him happiness in his new life. The Emperor embraced him. Most of those present were in tears, and a number of officers fainted.

The Duma Commissars arrived at 3 p.m. and informed Alekseev that the Provisional Government had decided to put the ex-Emperor under arrest. The Emperor travelled back to Tsarskoe Selo on the same train as the Duma Commissars and a company of ten soldiers placed under their orders by General Alekseev. The Emperor invited the Commissars to dinner, but the invitation was declined.

Before leaving, the Emperor addressed a farewell order of the day to

1. See *Krasny Arkhiv* XXII (1927) pp. 53–54, and Browder and Kerensky, op. cit., I, pp. 177 ff.

the troops who had been under his command for two and a half years. In it he urged the troops to 'bring this unprecedented war to a victorious conclusion. Those who are now thinking of and wanting peace are traitors to the Fatherland. . . . Do your duty, defend our great Fatherland, obey the Provisional Government and listen to your commanders. Do not forget that any slackening of discipline will assist the enemy.' On the express instructions of the new Minister of War, Guchkov, this order, transmitted to all army HQs, was neither read to the troops nor published in the newspapers. In his book *The Fate of Nicholas II after the Abdication*, Melgunov comments: 'The parting words of the former Supreme Commander were not reported in the papers in the free country where freedom of the press had been proclaimed; this although the Tsar had appealed to the troops to obey the provisional revolutionary government.'[1]

9. THE MORAL OF THE DRAMA

In recounting the Pskov drama we have consciously avoided explaining by reference to the character of Nicholas II the seemingly inexorable train of events which led to his abdication. Such references have all too often been a cover for the historian's personal bias. Thus, for instance, Milyukov interpreted the replacement of Alexis by Grand Duke Michael as heir to the throne in the instrument of abdication as a case of calculated bad faith and byzantinism. By introducing this irregularity into the document, the Emperor — Milyukov believed — was preparing a possible come-back. 'Oriental fatalism' and 'obstinacy' (as the obverse of a weak will) have been called upon to explain too many of Nicholas II's decisions and actions. Yet hardly any attempt has been made to analyse the character of the Emperor in the light of his biography. Such a formidable task is beyond the scope of this study, yet we are tempted to point out some features of the Emperor's personality which were revealed with particular emphasis during the last days of his reign.

We have seen how the apparent equanimity with which he accepted his enforced abdication had struck even close observers as almost unnatural. Of course the less well-intentioned interpreted this response as

1. Op. cit. (Paris, 1951), p. 40.

a kind of emotional dryness, a pathological lack of sensitivity. But we know that such was not the case, and that when he let himself go the Emperor could be as overwhelmed by his emotions as anyone else, and probably more so than some. And we can only marvel at the skill with which he had concealed his despair throughout the previous days. The insensitivity theory is therefore quite wrong.

Was it then the result of pride and self-control, natural in such an exalted personage and perfected through many years of court life and dissimulation? Doubtless pride and self-control helped Nicholas II to preserve at critical moments the amazing impassivity which disconcerted both his enemies and his most devoted servants. We know, for instance, how annoyed he was by Ruzsky's behaviour in Pskov[1] when the latter lost patience at the Tsar's waverings and pressed him in a rather discourteous way to come to a decision. But the Emperor never showed his displeasure to Ruzsky, and went through the ritual of embraces and expressions of gratitude for 'faithful service' without faltering. And yet the rather facile explanation of this behaviour by what might be called 'regal drill' is not entirely satisfactory. There was no proud withdrawal into himself in those days, nor in the many months of captivity and anxiety which followed. On the contrary, the ex-Emperor seemed to be more at ease with the few people whom he was allowed to see and talk to after his abdication.

The quiet confidence which Nicholas II displayed after abdicating is most disconcerting. He seemed the only one to believe that no harm would be done to him and that the wave of popular hatred directed against him and his wife, and whipped up after the February days, would in no way affect his family's destiny. All around him the superstitious belief grew that this unlucky monarch, born on the day of Saint Job, whose reign began with the fatal incident of the Khodynka, would end his life in a horrible tragedy. It would not have been surprising if the persistent murmurs about his destiny had got the better of Nicholas II and driven him to a fatalistic pessimism. As we have seen, this did not happen, and we must look for some moral resources on which he drew in order to withstand this persistent assault on his self-assurance and confidence. These he found in his conviction that all his decisions had been taken with a clear conscience.

Indeed, however injudicious and ill-advised certain of these decisions

1. See above, p. 321.

may have been, almost all of them were dictated by the high standards of private morality which Nicholas II set himself. This is contradicted but not refuted by the accusations of insincerity and duplicity which some of the Emperor's ministers raised against him. When he believed that reasons of state required him to rid himself of an adviser, he would often resort to a letter instead of having an embarrassing personal interview. This naturally caused offence. However, it is not true that he was ungrateful or vindictive. Even in the face of personal attacks on himself, he showed restraint in using his power to avenge the wrong which he believed had been done to him. He was not above breathing a sigh of relief at the news of the death of Witte, who he knew had slighted him behind his back. He also let Guchkov know what he thought of him after the latter, according to the information of his government, had impugned his wife's personal honour.[1] But he never stooped to use his power in order to undermine the social and, in the case of Guchkov, official position of such personal arch-enemies, although this would certainly not have been impossible for him. The naïve and rather hysterical hints in the Empress's letters to her husband that Guchkov could be eliminated fell on deaf ears. Nicholas II would not knowingly allow anger or fear – nor probably other passions – to determine his decisions.

His serenity was based on the conviction that his heart, which, he believed, was 'in the hands of God', was pure. In this sense the Emperor's character was saintly – a trait which we recognise in the display of dignity and patience with which he bore his imprisonment until the massacre of 13 July 1918 in Ekaterinburg. And yet this saintliness, conscious and intentional as it was, was the main weakness in the Emperor's character. He was not a mystic given to fanciful beliefs in signs and omens, and his religion was far more dominated by ethical considerations than that of his wife. But Christian ethics as he understood them were of that kind, typical of Russian Christian thought of the nineteenth century, which had inspired Dostoevsky to draw the character of Prince Myshkin. As in the case of Myshkin, Nicholas II's strict observance of the dictates of his conscience in all his decisions was singularly ineffectual, not so much because his conscience was faulty as because he believed that righteous decisions would prevail through some kind of magic power inherent in them. This, of course, is

1. See above, pp. 182 and 337 f.

just as wrong as to believe that truth will prevail in the minds of people by the mere force of its being true. This misconception of Christian ethics is at the root of the 'moral disarmament' (such as Tolstoy's theory of non-resistance to evil) characteristic of Russian thinking of that period. And although Nicholas II was free of both Tolstoyism and fatalism in the proper sense of the words, he still believed that in a contest of wills he who made the right decision would win in the end, not because of his skill in implementing it but by the power of his righteousness. This power was vaguely referred to as 'God's help' or *pravda*, of which the Tsar's *pravda* was only an exalted variant.

Such an attitude towards life, based on a belief in the inherent power of his moral decisions, was particularly dangerous in a man like the Emperor, who tended anyway to believe that the movements of his heart were directly inspired by God. Millions of people hold such beliefs, and whole religious movements in recent times have been based on them (e.g. the Oxford Group, Moral Rearmament and others). In the case of an autocrat, this belief had greater rational justification, and in Russia was backed by a strongly established historical tradition. The unique position of the monarch in the Russian state and society seemed to make him immune to the temptations of careerism, fame-seeking and material corruption. When, with Alexander III, rigid Victorian standards of family life were introduced — if not in Russian high society, at least into the narrow circle of the Emperor's family — many other temptations of the flesh appeared to have been eliminated. It was as if autocracy as an institution now provided the most favourable conditions for the emergence of a character free from corruption by base instincts, such as Dostoevsky had imagined in creating his successive positive heroes, from Prince Myshkin to Alyosha Karamazov.

Autocracy thus became the basis of Nicholas II's firm belief in his near-infallibility. Surrendering his autocratic power was therefore tantamount to exposing himself to temptations which he could not trust himself to withstand. Combined with his mystical faith in the power of the right decision to prevail, this belief in God's inspiration proved disastrous in the conditions of the rapidly changing society whose course he was called upon to steer. It poisoned his relations with the people whose advice he sought, or rather pretended to seek (asking for advice was for Nicholas II usually only a way of informing himself about the opinions of his 'advisers'). His faith in his privileged moral status prevented him from delegating decision-making to his ministers or from following their advice because 'they knew better'. The Empress was no exception to this pattern. She had to fight hard, as her letters demonstrate, to assert her will whenever she tried to interfere with the Emperor's decisions, and she was not always successful.

In one of his last political statements ever recorded — his conversation with Ruzsky late on 1 March 1917 — the Emperor explained once more why he was so opposed to a parliamentary régime in Russia. He argued that under a parliamentary system he might be free of the legal responsibility for the actions of his government, but not of the moral responsibility for having surrendered power to a cabinet whose decisions he no longer controlled. Furthermore he distrusted profoundly the abilities, intelligence and political integrity of the people who were said to 'enjoy public confidence'.

No wonder, then, that Nicholas II believed straightforward abdication to be preferable to the strained compromise to which he had agreed, in a moment of moral weakness, late at night on 1 March. Complete withdrawal from public life was, in his view, better than connivance at the disastrous policies which he expected those vested with 'public confidence' to pursue. But even the abdication of 2 March was not quite free of moral tarnish: a personal consideration had crept into the motives of a decision which was, in his own words, 'dictated by love for Mother Russia and readiness for every sacrifice'. He abdicated on behalf of Alexis and in favour of his brother after the hopelessness of the young prince's illness had been confirmed by his doctor. He certainly did not expect Grand Duke Michael, who only three days before had boldly offered to take over the direction of state affairs and solve the crisis, to abdicate in his turn. Typically, Nicholas noted his brother's surrender to the demands for a Constituent Assembly in his diary (3 March, 1917), and added: 'I wonder who advised him to sign that filth.'

But Nicholas can scarcely have been unaware that, whoever these evil advisers might have been, it was he himself who was answerable for having exposed his brother's will to a test far above Michael's capacity. This explains a curious incident which caused much confusion in the minds of even the most cautious historians who later tried to establish the facts. According to Denikin's memoirs, Alekseev confided to him that a few days after the abdication the Emperor, then still at GHQ, told him that he had changed his mind, and asked him to inform the Provisional Government that he now wanted to abdicate in favour of his son. Nicholas II gave Alekseev the text of a telegram to the Provisional Government to this effect, which was never despatched but kept in the files of GHQ. The émigré historian Melgunov questioned Denikin's account of this incident. He pointed out that a telegram announcing his abdication in favour of his son was drafted by Nicholas II early in the afternoon of 2 March in Pskov, but was not despatched, and was later found by Soviet historians in the GHQ archives.[1] When the Duma emissaries arrived the same day, Nicholas II had already changed his mind and announced his abdication in favour of his brother. Melgunov's conclusion was that the telegram of which Alekseev spoke to Denikin must have been the one drafted on 2 March, and that Denikin's memory was faulty in recording his conversation with Alekseev. Melgunov's doubts and conjecture seem reasonable, and yet Denikin has insisted that he reported what he clearly remembered.

The officer in charge of the communications department at GHQ, a Colonel Tikhobrazoff, has recorded his memories of the Emperor's last days at GHQ.[2] He recalls that the ex-Emperor, who continued to make his routine visits to Alekseev's study after the abdication, on 4 March raised the question of a telegram to be sent to the Provisional Government. In this he expressed his consent to Alexis's succeeding to the throne. In view of the fact that the deeds of abdication of both Nicholas II and Michael had already been published, Alekseev refused the request to send the telegram, saying that it would cover them both with ridicule. Nicholas II stood for a moment in indecision and then asked Alekseev to send on the telegram nevertheless. He went thoughtfully downstairs, stopped for a moment as if he were about to turn back and then, having thought better of it, went rapidly back to his quarters at the governor's house.

Tikhobrazoff's account reveals a side of the Emperor's character which remained an enigma to Melgunov as well as to many of those who knew Nicholas II fairly intimately. True to his nature, Nicholas

1. First published with facsimile in E. Martynov, *Tsarskaya armiya v fevralskom perevorote*, p. 158.
2. The reminiscences of Colonel D. N. Tikhobrazoff are deposited in the Russian archives of Columbia University.

II made one last attempt to clear his conscience by correcting an earlier erroneous decision. The ineffectiveness of his action, which verged on the ridiculous, left him unconcerned. Saintliness, when not intentional or self-conscious, may produce miracles; saintliness resulting from a conscious pursuit of purity of heart leads to personal, and in this case social disaster.

13

The Petrograd Soviet

The formation of the Petrograd Soviet; The tug-of-war between Soviet and Duma for control of the troops; Order No. 1.

1. THE FORMATION OF THE PETROGRAD SOVIET

On the third day of the street demonstrations in Petrograd, Saturday 25 February, the Union of the Petrograd Workers' Co-operatives, acting in agreement with the Duma Social-Democrat Party Group, called a meeting at the headquarters of the Union on the Nevsky Prospekt to discuss the situation. Chkheidze was present, together with other representatives of the workers' movement and a number of district officials of the Co-operatives Union, thirty to thirty-five persons in all. Having discussed the situation, they decided to call a council of workers' deputies on the pattern of the St. Petersburg Soviet of 1905. The elections in the various factories were to be organised by the Workers' Co-operatives and the boards of workers' sickness benefit funds.

It does not seem that the Bolsheviks played any part in this first attempt at organising a Petrograd Soviet: the initiative for and control of the elections were firmly in the hands of the Mensheviks, who were closely connected with the Labour Groups of the WIC. Indeed, immediately after the meeting on the 25th, while some of those present went to the Municipal Duma, where the question of food supplies for Petrograd was at that moment being debated, others went to a meeting on the premises of the Labour Group of the WIC. Most of the members of the group had already been arrested at the end of January, but their headquarters were still open. They must have been under police observation, however, because as soon as the participants in the meeting of the Co-operatives Union arrived there, the place was raided by the police and all those present were taken off to prison. This was part of the action ordered by Protopopov, which had also resulted in the arrest of the members of the Bolsheviks' Petersburg Committee. Thus the initial attempt to call for an election to the Soviet came to nothing.

When, however, on the 27th, it became obvious that part of the garrison had mutinied, a number of left-wing intellectuals who lived in various parts of the capital made their way to the Tauride Palace and persuaded the leaders of the Social-Democrat group of the Duma, Chkheidze and Skobelev, to ask the permission of the President of the Duma to use one of the rooms in the Palace as a meeting-place for their political friends. Very soon, as the events of the day developed, this gathering of leftish intellectuals felt called upon to become the headquarters of the revolutionary movement. In the second half of the day they were joined by representatives of the Labour Groups of the WIC, including their chairman, Gvozdev, who had been released by the crowds from the Kresty Prison. This gathering constituted itself as a 'Provisional Executive Committee of the Petrograd Soviet of Workers' Deputies' and issued an appeal to the factories to proceed immediately with the elections of deputies to the Petrograd Workers' Soviet. The elections were to be on the basis of one delegate for every thousand workers in a factory or one delegate from a factory of less than a thousand workers. Military units who had 'joined the people' were also asked to send delegates, one per company. Without awaiting confirmation of their status as the executive committee of the future Soviet, the people who gathered in room 13 and the adjoining rooms of the Tauride Palace summoned Colonel Mstislavsky-Maslovsky, who worked as a librarian in the Military Academy of the General Staff, to come and organise the 'headquarters of the revolution'.

The request for the despatch of delegates to the Petrograd Soviet seems to have reached some of the factories, and by 9 p.m. a number of self-styled delegates assembled in the Tauride Palace. Some of them could present written credentials of a sort, others presented credentials orally. Nobody could check where and how these workers had been elected by their factories, the more so since the factories were all on strike and most of the workers were demonstrating in the streets. No one ever counted the delegates who turned up. A semi-official review of the events of 27 February published six months later in *Izvestiya*[1] speaks of some 125–150 delegates who were there when the first meeting of the Petrograd Soviet was declared open, while both the right-

1. See *Izvestiya Petrogradskogo Soveta Rabochikh i Soldatskikh Deputatov*, 27 August, 1917.

wing Socialist Revolutionary Zenzinov and Sukhanov mention 250.[1]

The meeting was opened by Chkheidze, but soon someone else took the chair (Skobelev, according to Sukhanov, N. D. Sokolov, according to Zenzinov). As with all the proceedings of that hectic night, the meeting developed chaotically. Discussions of the food supply situation, of the defence of the revolutionary capital against possible attempts of the Tsarist régime to organise a come-back, were interrupted by emotional outpourings from representatives of military units who had decided to join the revolution. Nevertheless, the meeting elected a presidium consisting of the Duma deputies Chkheidze, Kerensky and Skobelev. The lawyer N. D. Sokolov and three others — Gvozdev, the chairman of the Labour Group of the WIC, Grinevich and the worker Pankov — were elected secretaries of the Soviet. This presidium formed the nucleus of the future executive committee of the Petrograd Soviet, to which Sukhanov, Steklov, the workers' co-operative leader Kapelinsky, the Social-Democrat lawyer Krasikov (Pavlovich), the Bolshevik underground leaders Shlyapnikov and Zalutsky were co-opted. The Socialist Revolutionaries were represented by the lawyer Sokolovsky and Aleksandrovich, a left-wing member of the party with a chequered past (and future) who had been working on the northern lines of revolutionary underground communications under the name of Pierre Orage.[2]

This Executive Committee, which is almost identical with the original 'temporary' executive committee that had summoned the Petrograd Soviet on the very same day, can hardly be considered otherwise than as a self-appointed body. The first meeting of the Petrograd Soviet did not represent any organised group of workers in the capital and could not invest the Executive Committee with any valid authority. It was to be given a broader base the next day by the appointment of delegates from the party committees of every Socialist party in Petrograd, but that did not alter its self-appointed character. It remained

1. 'When the meeting opened, there were about 250 people present, but new groups poured continuously into the hall, with God knows what credentials, mandates or intentions . . .' writes Sukhanov. *Zapiski*, vol. I, pp. 127 ff.; Zenzinov corroborates this. See his memoirs, *Fevralskie Dni*, in *Novy Zhurnal XXXV* (New York, 1955), in English translation in Browder and Kerensky, op. cit., I, pp. 71 ff.
2. See Futrell, *Northern Underground*, p. 110. Aleksandrovich was shot in July 1918 for the part he played in the so-called 'left SR rising.'

unclear how far the party committees could count on the support of any substantial number of Petrograd workers. The situation was rendered even more complicated by the inclusion of representatives of the Petrograd garrison. The soldiers were, by an overwhelming majority, peasants, and their representatives naturally claimed SR affiliation.

Besides electing, or rather confirming in office, the existing Executive Committee, the meeting of the Soviet elected during the night a food supply commission headed by the economist Groman and his assistant Frankorussky, a military commission under Mstislavsky-Maslovsky and Filippovsky, and also a literary commission which was to issue the publications of the Soviet under Y. Steklov, Sukhanov and others.

It also issued an appeal to the population with a timely warning against the danger of looting and arson, reports of which were beginning to pour into the Tauride Palace.

The Petrograd Soviet and its Executive Committee were constituted a few hours before the Duma Committee decided to assume power. While members of the Duma were still wondering whether the Tsarist government existed or not, and whether they had, by force of circum-stance, become its successor, the group of self-appointed revolutionaries squatting on the premises of the Duma proclaimed themselves to be the leaders of the popular movement and established a committee which they boldly called the 'headquarters of the rising.' It mattered little that this headquarters had no troops whatever at its disposal, and did not even know which regiments had mutinied and which were still under the orders of General Khabalov and the Minister of War Belyaev, just as it did not matter by whom delegates to the Soviet were deputed, or who appointed the Executive Committee of the Soviet. The important thing was that a centre was formed to which mutineers could come, wearing red ribbons and boldly proclaiming their readiness to fight 'to the last drop of blood' and to die for the revolution. They could not come to the Duma Committee without being admonished to maintain discipline, return to their barracks and obey their officers. Even on the 28th and the 1st, when addressing the troops who crowded the halls of the Tauride Palace, Rodzyanko talked to them as 'brethren' (not 'comrades') and told them not to listen to those who tried to persuade them that they had mutinied. He would not recognise them as mutineers; they were simply patriotic soldiers who were asking for an efficient government to save their dearly-beloved motherland. On the premises of the Soviet, however, the same men would be welcomed as fighters for freedom, who had by their courageous action in joining the people's uprising wiped out the shame of 1905, when their regiments had helped Tsarist tyranny to crush the revolution.

2. THE TUG-OF-WAR BETWEEN SOVIET AND DUMA FOR CONTROL OF THE TROOPS

It was in this turbid whirlpool of patriotic and revolutionary verbiage that the basic conflict between the Soviet Executive Committee and the embryonic Provisional Government was born — the conflict over the control of the armed forces. It was clear to both sides that something must be done to organise the mutineers of the Petrograd garrison. This could only be achieved if officers were found to command them and lead them, if need be, in the defence of Petrograd against any attempt to subdue the rising with the help of troops coming from the front. The Military Commission of the Executive Committee of the Soviet under Mstislavsky-Maslovsky and Filippovsky were fully conscious of this. They understood, however, that the motive force behind the disorganised mass of soldiers in Petrograd was a feeling of guilt and fear at having mutinied. This could be overcome only by openly proclaiming the revolutionary action of 27–28 February as a patriotic revolutionary exploit for which future generations of Russians, and indeed humanity in general, would be forever grateful. Hence the extravagant language of some of the Soviet proclamations; hence the emotional scenes when representatives of the mutinous regiments turned up in room 12 of the Tauride Palace; hence the grip of the otherwise hardly representative Executive Committee on the soldiers. To them, the intellectuals of the Executive Committee of the Soviet were just as alien as the gentlemanly members of the Duma Committee, but at least the former also proclaimed themselves revolutionaries and were ostensibly risking being hanged on the same gallows. In the eyes of the soldiers there seemed less likelihood that these would betray them, and by some clever stratagem visit vengeance upon them for having mutinied and even killed a few of their officers.

Of course no such plan of action was even remotely considered by the members of the Duma Committee. The revolutionary excesses of which some troops were guilty were readily explained and excused as manifestations of popular indignation at the alleged misdeeds of the Tsarist government, and their perpetrators would naturally be amnestied. But the Duma Committee, as well as the Provisional Government which was formed under its aegis, were still reluctant to consider themselves as revolutionaries. Having seen the Tsarist government, which they claimed had brought the country to the 'verge of the abyss', dissolved and swept away, the Duma liberals were most anxious to put a stop to all further revolutionary action by the troops, especially after so many officers pledged their allegiance to the Duma Committee. They therefore urged the soldiers to return to their barracks, where the officers who had declared themselves in favour of the Duma would resume command.

Both camps became aware very early on of the conflicting tendencies which might result in an irreparable split in their policies towards the Petrograd garrison. Therefore on the evening of the 27th, when the deputies to the Soviet began to gather in room 12 and the Mstislavsky Military Commission was in danger of becoming submerged in the crowds of soldiers' delegates who were flooding into the Soviet premises, the Commission gladly accepted the suggestion that it should transfer its activities to rooms 41 and 42, next door to the study of the Deputy Duma President, Nekrasov. This was on the Duma side of the palace, and the quiet and decorous atmosphere contrasted with the turmoil of the Soviet premises. Here, Mstislavsky met Kerensky and Nekrasov, both of whom seemed to approve everything he was doing. Mstislavsky's assistant, Filippovsky, assumed the functions of commandant of the mutinous military units. Mstislavsky recollects the difficulties professional revolutionaries like himself encountered when attempting to revolutionise 'the masses'. He had, for instance, got hold of a number of machine-guns, which were unusable unless they could be properly lubricated. He ordered a young man to go to a chemist's shop and bring all the available vaseline: the young man returned, announcing that it was too late, the shops were closed. Mstislavsky's indignation at this lack of revolutionary initiative was beyond expression.[1]

Exactly at midnight on the 27th–28th (according to Mstislavsky, who

1. Mstislavsky-Maslovsky, op. cit., pp. 29 ff.

would, if he is right, have been the only person in the Tauride Palace
to know the exact time that day) the President of the Duma,
Rodzyanko, suddenly appeared in room 41. He had just made up his
mind to take matters into his own hands, and to lead the revolutionary
movement the existence of which he had been so reluctant to recognise.
He announced that the member of the Duma Engelhardt had been appointed Military Commander of Petrograd, and would preside at the
headquarters of the revolution. By the time Rodzyanko made this
announcement, the members of the Soviet Military Commission had
been joined by the lawyer N. D. Sokolov, who at once suspected that
the Duma Committee was about to dispossess the Soviet of its newly-
acquired power. A violent exchange took place between Rodzyanko
and Sokolov. Sokolov shouted: 'The headquarters have already been
constituted; they are already in action; appropriate people have been
found. . . . What has Colonel Engelhardt to do with it? . . . We don't
need appointees of a "high assembly", but revolutionaries'; to which
Rodzyanko answered, banging on the table: 'No, gentlemen, really!
As you have forced us to intervene in this business, will you kindly
obey.' There was a moment, Mstislavsky tells us, when it looked as if
they would come to blows.

We must make allowances for the typically Russian propensity of
the writer of these memoirs to dramatise. But the fact remains that the
first attempt of the revolutionary intellectuals to bring the mutineers of
the Petrograd garrison under their exclusive control was checked by
the belated action of the Duma Committee, which formed a military
committee of its own, fused it with the Soviet Military Commission,
and neutralised its revolutionary fervour. It is worth noting that this
was done in the face of violent opposition from Sokolov. Mstislavsky
and Filippovsky showed a conciliatory attitude, persuaded Sokolov to
accept the appointment of Engelhardt, and expressed readiness to work
in the joint Committee. Sokolov retired to the Soviet side of the
building, apparently unreconciled.

The Soviet's readiness to work with the Duma Committee is understandable. The soldiers who were roaming the streets ransacking
houses, setting fire to police stations and government buildings, and
wasting ammunition in senseless shooting into the air could not
be relied on to defend the revolution if dependable Tsarist troops
were sent from the front. Some kind of cohesion and leadership by

experienced officers was needed, and there was very little time to lose.[1]
The political prestige of the Duma and of its Chairman among the
officers of the Petrograd garrison was still very high. Mstislavsky, who
was an experienced staff officer, understood perfectly well that the
success of the rising might depend on whether this prestige could be
put at the service of the defence of the revolution. In spite of all that
has since been said about the weakness of the Tsarist régime at that
moment and its total incapacity to assert itself in the face of a popular
rising, the feeling of experienced revolutionaries on the night of the
27th–28th was that they would need all possible help from the liberal
'bourgeois' opposition simply to survive and avoid the gallows, let
alone achieve their political aims. The change of mood came later, on
3 March, after the announcement of the abdication, when fear of
retribution gave way to the exhilaration of victory, and readiness to
compromise with the liberals to a determination to denounce them and
hound them out of political existence. As long as the threat of immediate suppression of the mutiny by troops faithful to the Tsar existed,
a considerable effort was made by both the Soviet and the Duma
Committees to combine their efforts in order to win the whole of the
garrison for the cause of the revolution and to make it a potential
fighting force. The fear that officers might organise resistance to the
'new order' was as great among the members of the Duma Committee
as in the Executive Committee of the Soviet. On 1 March the new
Commander of the Petrograd garrison, Engelhardt, issued a warning
to officers who might 'confiscate arms from the soldiers': 'As Chairman
of the Military Commission of the Temporary Committee of the
State Duma, I announce that the most resolute measures, including
execution of the guilty, will be applied to prevent acts of this nature on
the part of the officers'.[2] Not even the notorious Order No. 1, the

1. This was clearly understood by many revolutionaries who observed the scene in
the street, including Sukhanov. The 'internationalist Menshevik' O. A. Ermansky
wrote later in his memoirs, *Iz perezhitogo 1887–1921* (Moscow and Leningrad, 1927),
p. 147, describing the scene on 27 February: 'The soldiers came into the street without
officers — not one of them was about. The absence of officers, however, markedly
affected the behaviour of the men: it was as though they had ceased to be soldiers and
become ordinary men. But for the revolution to take a favourable course it was
all-important that the mass of soldiers should side with it precisely as an armed
organised force.'
2. English translation from Browder and Kerensky, op. cit., vol. I, pp. 62 ff.

complicated history of which we are about to consider, went so far as
to threaten officers with execution.

3. ORDER NO. I

The rumours concerning officers who were trying to disarm soldiers
spread in Petrograd during 1 March, but were not confirmed either by
an investigation of the Duma Military Committee or by any tangible
evidence provided by the Soviet. They were scarcely surprising if one
bears in mind that the dominant emotion on the 27th and 28th among
politicians, officers and soldiers alike was fear and mistrust. The
politicians feared both an organised suppression of the mutiny and its
degeneration into total anarchy. The officers were alarmed by reports
of several shootings of commanders which had taken place in the
barracks and in the streets; rumours of an impending general massacre
of officers were put into circulation and played an important part in
determining Rodzyanko's behaviour, as one can see from the record of
his long-distance talk with Ruzsky. For their part the soldiers were in
great fear of their lives, not quite believing that their mutinous behaviour in the middle of the war would be extolled as a great patriotic
feat and would go unpunished. The Executive Committee of the
Soviet was conscious of these fears and took two drastic measures to
allay them. The first was to invite representatives of the units of the
Petrograd garrison, one per company, to join the Soviet. Secondly,
they decided to insist that any bourgeois government which might
be formed by the parties of the Duma should solemnly pledge itself
not to order any transfers of units of the Petrograd garrison from the
capital. Both these measures were of immeasurable consequence for the
further activities of the Soviet, and for the course of the revolutionary
events after February.

But radical as they were, these two measures did not satisfy the
soldiers, who wanted an official announcement which would exculpate
them from all excesses committed during the days of the rising, and
would give certain guarantees that the officers would not use their
powers, as soon as they had reassumed command, to avenge their
massacred comrades. A proclamation like the one issued by Engelhardt
could only increase their suspicions. By the evening of 1 March, various

representatives of soldiers' groups had come to the Duma Military
Commission with a proposal to work out a declaration to the garrison
to be signed jointly by the Duma Committee and the Soviet. They seem
to have got a poor reception from the members of the Duma Committee, who refused to talk to them. They left disgruntled, muttering
words to the effect that 'if the Committee would not issue a declaration,
they would do it themselves'.

Later in the evening of 1 March Sukhanov reports that on returning
to room 13, where the Executive Committee had just ended its meeting,
he found the lawyer Sokolov, who had become a kind of general
manager of the Soviet's affairs, sitting at a writing-desk.

> On all sides he was closely surrounded by soldiers sitting, standing, and
> leaning over him, who were either dictating or suggesting things which
> Sokolov was writing down. A fleeting recollection of a description of
> Tolstoy, writing down stories with the pupils of the village school in
> Yasnaya Polyana around him, passed through my head.
>
> It appeared that this was a working session of the committee which had
> been elected by the Soviets to draft the soldiers' Order of the Day. There
> was no agenda, and no discussion; everybody was talking, completely
> engrossed in the work, formulating their collective opinion without any
> vote being taken. . . . I stood and listened, quite fascinated. . . . When
> they had finished their work, they put at the top of the page the heading:
> 'Order No. 1'.

'Such is the story of this document, which has achieved such resounding fame', concludes Sukhanov, trying to create an idyllic impression of a kind of 'democracy at work'. It may be doubted, however,
whether the text of Order No. 1 as we know it could have been
drafted in such circumstances. Not that we would doubt the description of this scene as reported by Sukhanov, of which there are
also photographic records. But the original text written by Sokolov
has never been found. Sokolov's own memory cannot be relied upon
because of his state of extreme exhaustion and preoccupation with a
thousand other questions at the time. The Soviet itself never voted on
the text of the Order of the Day, nor did the Executive Committee as
a body take cognisance of it before it was published, although the
document appeared over its collective signature. Internal evidence
speaks very much against the assumption that the printed text is
identical with the collective draft produced in the way described by

Sukhanov. The printed text is concise and very much to the point, with the exception of one tortured sentence which obviously reflects conflicting tendencies in the mind of whoever wrote it. Neither Sokolov nor the soldiers around him would have been able to help including the effusive phrases typical of the revolutionary intoxication of those first days. The document as printed is dry and unemotional, reminding one of the crisp style in which Lenin would have drafted a document of this nature. Between its drafting in room 13 of the Tauride Palace and its publication the same night, the manuscript of Order No. 1 is reported to have been in the printing works of *Izvestiya* for several hours. A closer look at the management of this paper might give a lead to an understanding of the genesis of Order No. 1. The idea of issuing a revolutionary paper in Petrograd first came on 27 February to Vladimir Bonch-Bruevich.[1] All the printing works were on strike on that day, and no daily papers had appeared. On his own initiative, Bonch-Bruevich seized the printing works of a low-brow popular daily called *Kopeyka*. Having done so, he approached the temporary Executive Committee of the Soviet, offering to start immediately the publication of their own newspaper, to be called *Izvestiya*, and demanding food supplies for his workers and an armed guard for the printing works. The Executive Committee readily complied, and proceeded to elect an editorial board. Bonch-Bruevich, however, had not the slightest intention of surrendering control of the paper to anyone. On 28 February, while the Executive Committee of the Soviet was considering its relations with the Duma Committee and discussing the possibilities for the formation of a new government, Bonch-Bruevich printed – 'of course, without having asked anyone's permission' – a supplement to the first number of *Izvestiya* in which there appeared a Manifesto of the Bolshevik Party. 'The task of the working class and the revolutionary army', the Manifesto said *inter alia*, 'is to create a Provisional Revolutionary Government which would head the new republican régime which is being born.' The Manifesto contained all the planks of the Bolshevik platform: nationalisation of the land, an eight-hour working day, the convocation of a Constituent Assembly on the basis of the four-point formula[2] – and called for a 'merciless struggle'.

1. V. D. Bonch-Bruevich, *Na boevykh postakh*, op. cit.
2. The so-called *chetyrekhkhvostka*, i.e. direct, equal, secret and universal ballot.

The Manifesto was entirely out of tune with feeling in the Executive Committee of the Soviet, the majority of which considered the revolution to be a 'bourgeois' and not a proletarian revolution, and could have jeopardised the delicate negotiations between the Soviet representatives and the Duma Committee. Although it was signed by the Central Committee of the Bolshevik Party, its publication was never authorised by the Soviet Executive Committee, and its appearance in the Soviet official paper caused — according to Bonch-Bruevich's memoirs — much indignation in the Petrograd Soviet, which considered his behaviour in this connection undisciplined. When asked for an explanation of it, Bonch-Bruevich brazenly answered that not only had he published the Bolshevik Manifesto in the paper; he had also printed it as a leaflet and sent it to all parts of Russia.

> This [Bonch-Bruevich wrote] was among my early sins committed in *Izvestiya*, sins for which later, as more of them accumulated, I was asked to make public confession and for which I was subjected to an interrogation by that Pope of the Menshevik bigots, Tseretelli himself, and was finally deprived of my mandate in *Izvestiya* because of my Bolshevik convictions.[1]

The incident of the publication of the Bolshevik Manifesto throws light on the activities of Bonch-Bruevich in the printing works of *Izvestiya*, and helps us to understand how Order No. 1 was published. Bonch-Bruevich was, as we have seen on several occasions[2], a calculating, discreet and determined fighter for the cause of a social revolution. It was he who organised the clandestine Bolshevik press in 1905 and

1. See Vladimir Bonch-Bruevich, *Na boevykh postakh fevralskoy i oktyabrskoy revolyutsii*, p. 12. The Manifesto will be found in the volume of documents on the revolution entitled *Revolyutsionnoe dvizhenie v Rossii posle sverzheniya samoderzhaviya* (Moscow, 1957), Document No. 1, p. 3. This text is reproduced, however, from *Pravda* of 5 March, and differs slightly from that of *Izvestiya*. *Pravda* claimed that the Manifesto first appeared on 26 February. This, of course, makes no sense, because the Manifesto mentions the rising of the Petrograd garrison as an accomplished fact which took place first on the 27th. Recently (*Voprosy istorii KPSS*, VI, 1964), Soviet historians claimed to have discovered a leaflet with the Manifesto which they believe was printed independently from *Izvestiya* late on 27 February. They believe it was concocted in the Vyborg District Committee of the Bolshevik Party. This only confirms that it was a party document and did not reflect the line taken by the Executive Committee of the Petrograd Soviet.
2. See above, pp. 204–8 and p. 266.

its transport to Russia; it was he who managed to gain the confidence of Rasputin, and investigated his alleged connections with Russian sectarianism. It was he who, just before the February events, used his contacts with the Cossack sects of New Israel and Old Israel in order to persuade the Cossacks not to disperse the demonstrators. It was he who later in 1917 saved Lenin from arrest during the abortive Bolshevik July rising. When Bonch-Bruevich managed to seize a printing works on the 27th and offered to publish the news-sheet of the Petrograd Soviet, it was certainly not in order to support the political line which 'waverers and conciliators' would take, but in order to push through the Bolshevik point of view. This is why he had no scruples about printing the Bolshevik Party Manifesto. But this was only one 'of my early sins', as Bonch-Bruevich puts it. Was the publication of Order No. 1 another? And did he substitute the concise and extremely inflammatory text which we know for the collective draft concocted under N. D. Sokolov's supervision in the 'democratic' setting depicted by Sukhanov? A critical consideration of the text seems to point in this direction. When *Pravda* (the organ of the Central Committee of the Bolshevik Party) republished the Manifesto of the Bolshevik Party it introduced small corrections of its own; it also corrected the wording of Order No. 1 when it appeared in *Pravda* on 7 March. In the text published by Bonch-Bruevich on 1 March in *Izvestiya*, paragraph 4 of Order No. 1 reads as follows: 'Orders of the Military Commission of the State Duma should be carried out with the exception of those cases where they contradict orders and decisions of the Soviet of Workers' and Soldiers' Deputies'. *Pravda*, reproducing this document five days later, re-words the same paragraph as follows: 'Orders of the Military Commission of the State Duma are to be carried out only in those cases in which they do not contradict the orders and decisions of the Soviet of Workers' and Soldiers' Deputies.' The difference in the meaning may be small, but the shift in emphasis is all-important. In the first version, orders emanating from the Military Commission of the Duma were regarded as binding except when contradicted by the Soviet. In the *Pravda* version, however, it was incumbent on every unit to check whether or not the Duma's orders were in agreement with Soviet policy. Was the correction in *Pravda* an authors' emendation? Was the milder wording as it appeared in *Izvestiya* dictated by Bonch-Bruevich's fear of going too far in exacerbating relations between the Duma Committee and the Soviet? In any case, we see that the Bolsheviks considered the text of Order No. 1 a matter of immediate concern to them, and treated it in the same way as they treated their party documents.

Order No. 1, which was addressed to the Petrograd garrison, laid down (1) that all military and naval units should elect committees representing the 'other ranks', (2) that they should send deputies to the Petrograd Soviet, one for every company, (3) that the political activities of all military units should be subordinated to the Soviet authorities, (4) that the Soviet decisions should take precedence over competing orders of the Military Commission of the Duma, (5) that arms should be kept by the soldiers' committees and on no account delivered to officers, (6) that soldiers should enjoy all civil liberties conferred on the citizens of Russia by the revolution, and should not be required to salute officers when off duty, and (7) that soldiers should not tolerate rude treatment by their superiors, should not be required to address them by titles, and should not be spoken to in the second person singular — 'thou' — but in the polite second person plural.

Order No. 1 has been decried by every military authority of the pre-Soviet Russian Army as the most destructive and poisonous document, which started the dissolution of the Russian armed forces in 1917. On the other hand, the Petrograd Soviet, which had never composed or voted upon the order, accepted it as the expression of its considered opinion, and defended it throughout the existence of the Provisional Government.[1] In spite of pressure from the members of the newly-born Provisional Government, the representatives of the Soviet firmly refused to repeal this Order. True, in a subsequent Order No. 2, they pointed out that Order No. 1 was issued only to the Petrograd garrison, and not to the army in the field. But this reservation was of little consequence. Just like the Manifesto of the Bolshevik Party, Order No. 1 was published in countless thousands of copies, and distributed all over the country. It served as a pattern for the political demands which soldiers started putting to their commanders at the

1. See, for instance, the defence put up for it at the conference of generals from the front, members of the government and representatives of the Soviet on 16 May; (See Golovin, *Rossiiskaya Kontr-revolyutsiya*, Book I, pp. 113 ff.) and the assessment of it as an expression of popular feeling in *Izvestiya* of 27 August 1917, commemorating the first six months of the February revolution.

front and in the garrisons in the rear. In many places the Order appeared over the signature of the Minister of War of the Provisional Government, Guchkov, thus increasing the confusion in the minds of its readers and serving as a substantial weapon of Bolshevik propaganda.

But if the publication of Order No. 1 was an unauthorised action and an abuse of the authority of the Soviet by whoever printed it in *Izvestiya*, why was no protest raised in Soviet circles themselves against it? The fact is that Bonch-Bruevich, or whoever it was who together with him issued this extraordinary document, had shrewdly exploited the weakness of the Duma Committee and the susceptibilities of the Soviet Executive Committee. An appeal on the lines of Order No. 1 was bound to win the sympathies of the soldiers of the Petrograd garrison, who had not yet settled down after the mutiny of 27 February. If the Soviet had repudiated this document as soon as it was published, it would have lost its hold on the garrison and hence on the only real force on which it could rely in case of conflict with the new administration which the Duma Committee was about to establish. Naturally, the Soviet could not risk that, even if in some details Order No. 1 went much further than what its more moderate members would have thought judicious. Least of all could it do so under the pressure of Guchkov, or any Duma authority, without losing face completely. And so the document remained as one of the earliest examples of Soviet political activity, and was successfully used by the Bolsheviks as an instrument of disruption of the armed forces, even after the military authorities themselves formed army unit committees in the hope of taking the wind out of the sails of the extremist propagandists.

The fact that Order No. 1 was allowed to stay on the record, in spite of its more than suspect origins, shows that it came as unintended but welcome assistance to the Soviet politicians in their struggle with the Duma Committee for the control of the Petrograd garrison. Later, its maintenance and defence became a question of prestige for the Soviet and an indelible sign of the weakness of the Provisional Government. This is the major political significance of the Order. Compared with this political role, its effect on the morale of the army is only of secondary importance. Even without it, the Bolsheviks would, at least immediately after the return of Lenin, have embarked on their defeatist propaganda and the agitation for an immediate peace. By issuing

Order No. 1 and involving the authority of the Petrograd Soviet, the Bolsheviks, probably through Bonch-Bruevich and whoever assisted him, managed to create a conflict between the Soviet and the Provisional Government which nothing – not even the formation of bourgeois-socialist coalitions – was ever able to resolve.

14

The Provisional Government

Earlier lists; The men of the Provisional Government; Enter Kerensky; The first announcement of the Provisional Government.

1. EARLIER LISTS

The 'foolish virgins' – to use Mstislavsky's expression – who flocked to the Tauride Palace and formed the Provisional Executive Committee of the Petrograd Soviet on 27 February were, as we have seen, more or less obscure revolutionary intellectuals who had somehow avoided arrest and deportation from Petrograd in the months preceding the revolution. They knew little of each other's views and background, and the only thing that united them was a common desire to defend the revolution. This, they believed, was threatened by their hosts in the Duma, who at this stage still hoped that what had taken place was not a revolution but at worst a mere *Rechtsbruch*, as Milyukov put it, that is a momentary breach of the constitutional tradition.

Unlike the Soviet Executive Committee, the Provisional Government had been planned in advance and the personalities of which it consisted knew each other well through having worked together, either in the Duma itself or in the various Voluntary Organisations.

The lists of members of a government of public confidence or of a so-called responsible government, that is, a cabinet responsible to parliament, which were circulated in 1915 and 1916, had been compiled not in expectation of a revolution, but rather of a change of heart in the Emperor, who under various pressures would at last agree to the demands of the 'people'. Now that the rising in Petrograd and the collapse of the Golitsyn government had brought about an unforeseen situation, the lists of possible ministers were in everybody's mind, although nobody knew who should or would eventually make the necessary appointments. Should it be Nicholas II's last act before abdication? Should it be done by the new Emperor or Regent, Michael? Should the government be appointed by a revolutionary procedure with Rodzyanko assuming the supreme authority in the State? Should he do so individually as President of the Duma, or should he act in conjunction with the ephemeral Duma Committee which came into being after the private meeting of members of the Duma on 27 February? All these solutions were ventilated in the days preceding the formation of the government, and are reflected in various documents and pronouncements of that time.

No wonder that in the total confusion as to what supreme authority had appointed the Provisional Government, the 'men in the street' who gathered in a restive crowd around Milyukov in the Catherine Hall of the Tauride Palace in the early afternoon of 2 March asked the 'poisonous question': 'Who chose you?' Years after, in recalling this historic occasion, Milyukov wrote:

> I could have answered this question with a whole learned dissertation. We were not 'chosen' by the Duma. We were not picked out by Rodzyanko either, after he had been belatedly asked to do so by the Emperor. We were not chosen by Lvov in accordance with the new decree which was being prepared at GHQ, and of which we had no knowledge at that moment. All these grounds for the transfer of power we had consciously rejected ourselves. There was one answer left: the clearest and most convincing. I gave it: 'We were chosen by the Russian revolution'. This simple reference to the historical process which brought us to power made our most radical opponents shut up.[1]

It is not surprising that the mixed crowd which had come to find out about the new rulers of Russia should 'shut up' on hearing the sacred name of 'revolution' pronounced reverently by one who, throughout his public career, had advocated a political line which – he claimed – would make this revolution unnecessary. But why should subsequent historians of the Russian revolution accept this evasive explanation of how eleven Russians came to declare themselves members of the Provisional Government, of the Cabinet which was to lead the country to victory over the external enemy and to internal regeneration? Why had the 'historical revolutionary process' preferred Tereshchenko as Minister of Finance to the chairman of the Duma budget committee, Shingarev? Had the historical process some obscure mischievous purpose in elevating the semi-demented Vladimir Lvov to the position

---

1. *Vospominaniya* vol. II, p. 310.

of Procurator of the Holy Synod? Milyukov is right in denying that the other factors mentioned by him had any bearing on the composition and investiture of the Provisional Government. But the idea of historical inevitability has rarely been more unjustifiably invoked than by Milyukov in the passage quoted above.

2. THE MEN OF THE PROVISIONAL GOVERNMENT

In fact, the list of members of the Provisional Government was drawn up after discussions in the Duma Provisional Committee and after a prolonged meeting of its representatives with the representatives of the Soviet Executive Committee in the night of 1–2 March. If we compare this list with those circulated before the revolution, we see that the Provisional Government did not on the whole substantially differ in its composition from the projected cabinets which would have come to power if a 'government of public confidence' had been granted by the Tsar at an earlier date. Yet certain changes indicate new influences which had been brought to bear in the deliberations of the Duma Committee with the Soviet.

As we have seen, Rodzyanko, whose candidature for the premiership had been put forward during the August crisis of 1915, had been replaced by Prince G. E. Lvov. Milyukov, who admits having been instrumental in bringing about this change, tells us frankly that he really had no idea whether or not Prince Lvov was qualified to occupy this post. At the very first meeting of the Provisional Government he was surprised and appalled by the Prince's inability to direct the debates. and expressed his disappointment to his friend I. P. Demidov with the laconic remark: 'a drip'.[1] Milyukov spent years searching his heart for an answer to the question why, if he knew so little of the candidate whom he supported so strongly, he yet preferred him to Rodzyanko. What interests us much more is the question of why Prince Lvov was considered at the time to be more acceptable than the President of the Duma, and who organised the widespread propaganda in favour of this otherwise retiring man. It is worth recalling that Prince Lvov replaced Rodzyanko at the head of the list of a possible liberal government when such a list was drawn up in April 1916 in the flat of S. N.

---

1. In Russian 'shlyapa' (literally 'a hat'). See Milyukov, *Vospominaniya*, vol. II, p. 299.

Prokopovich and his wife E. D. Kuskova. As Mme Kuskova reveals,[1] the flat was supplied with a cork-lined study in which were held meetings of that peculiar Russian political freemasonry organisation to which we have referred in ch. 8. It is therefore likely that this organisation was behind the powerful campaign to build up Prince Lvov. Every reference to him in the liberal press was always in tones of utmost respect and veneration. Even Bernard Pares, in his book on the Russian army during the war, published in 1916, refers to him by such epithets as 'the able and honest'. All the credit for the work of the main joint committee of the Zemstvos and Municipalities in supplying the army was regularly ascribed to him – to the great annoyance of the Council of Ministers, where even liberal ministers in 1915 referred to him as the Muir and Merrilees (the name of the first and largest department store in Moscow) of the wartime economy. Another advantage, in the eyes of the liberals, which Lvov had in February 1917 over Rodzyanko was his active involvement in the plots for the overthrow of the Tsarist régime. At a time when Rodzyanko refused publicly to associate himself with plotting, Lvov had already put out feelers both to Alekseev and to Grand Duke Nikolay Nikolaevich for a possible dethronement of Nicholas II. Finally there was a widespread belief that the central committees of the Voluntary Organisations controlled a widespread network of local committees which could at any moment take over the work of the bureaucratic machinery. After all, Prince Lvov himself had claimed as late as December 1916 that the government machinery could be totally ignored and the country be run by the organisations under his leadership.

It is this latter consideration which must have induced the king-makers of the Duma Committee to entrust home affairs to the new Premier. Originally, in the list of 1915, this post was to have been given to Guchkov. Since then, however, the left-wing parties had never failed to recall Guchkov's support of Stolypin's violent suppression of the revolutionary movement after 1905, and his appointment to a department which might possibly have to reorganise the police and the whole internal administration would have been quite unacceptable to the revolutionary parties and the Petrograd Soviet. And so the ungrateful task of internal administration, and the business of bringing the very unsettled population under control, fell to the head of the new Provi-

1. See Aronson, op. cit., p. 138, and n.

sional Government. His failure to deal with these intractable tasks led to the irreparable loss of the Provisional Government's authority right at the outset.｜

Apart from the objective reasons for the choice of Prince Lvov as head of the government, there was also Milyukov's personal preference for Lvov as against Rodzyanko. Milyukov hoped that under an amenable premier he would become the real policy-maker. Indeed, it was he who had come to an agreement with the representatives of the Soviet — Sokolov, Sukhanov and Steklov — on the night of 1–2 March about the future composition of the government. But as we have seen, Milyukov was not fully aware of the personal links among the members of the team he had backed, and on which he had agreed with the representatives of the Soviet. He did not realise that five out of ten members of the new government were closely linked by what he himself later described as 'a kind of personal bond not purely political but of a politico-moral character'.[1] Among these five we must also reckon the Prime Minister, Prince Lvov, who – if not formally a member of the political freemasonry organisation to which Kerensky, Tereshchenko, Nekrasov and Konovalov belonged – was in any case so closely connected with the conspiratorial work of this organisation, that he proved to be far more under the influence of these members of his government than of Milyukov, who had originally supported his candidature against that of Rodzyanko.

Milyukov himself was content to take over the Ministry of Foreign Affairs. He considered that this was a 'natural' appointment. In a sense this was true, because ever since lists of possible liberal governments had been circulated, Milyukov had had no rivals for this particular post. It is however significant that Milyukov became the main target of attacks from the left, and had to be sacrificed before the first coalition government with the socialist parties was formed at the beginning of May.

Other appointments to the government clearly reflect the pressure of the freemasonry elements in it. It was generally expected that if a government of public confidence or any other liberal combination were formed, the Ministry of Finance would go to the chairman of the budget committee of the Duma, the Kadet Shingarev. Instead, M. I. Tereshchenko, not a member of the Duma, was appointed. When Milyukov gave the name of Tereshchenko to the crowds which had

1. See above, p. 167 ff.

gathered to hear the announcement of the formation of the Provisional Government on the afternoon of 2 March in the Tauride Palace, it was met with incredulous and surprised queries: 'And who is that? And who is he?' Milyukov admits that he had some difficulty in explaining the choice. He said that in such a large country one could not know of all the best people living in different parts of it, and referred to Tereshchenko's excellent work in the WICs. In his memoirs written thirty years later, Milyukov claims that the pressure for this appointment had originated in the same quarters as that for the inclusion of Kerensky in the Provisional Government, the same quarters that had inspired both the republicanism of Nekrasov and the radicalism of Konovalov and Efremov: in other words, the freemasonry organisation, which for some incomprehensible reason Milyukov did not want to mention by name.

Tereshchenko had of course no qualifications whatever for the extremely ungrateful post of minister of the bankrupt Russian finances. But nobody thought at that moment of candidates for posts in the Provisional Government in terms of technical qualifications. The decisive considerations were political, or to borrow Milyukov's phrase, 'politico-moral'.

The appointment of the Minister of Transport (i.e. of railways and shipping) also reflected the pressure of the freemasonry element. N. V. Nekrasov had always been a favourite for this post among the liberals. He was an engineer by education, a prominent member of the left wing of the Kadet Party, and an active collaborator with Guchkov and Konovalov in the Central WIC, where he was responsible for the work of the Labour Groups. His appointment would have been a matter of course, had not the Ministry of Transport already been taken over in the name of the Duma Provisional Committee by Bublikov, another member of the Duma with widespread contacts in the railway administration, and a member of the Progressive Party.

The Duma Committee had appointed commissars to take over all the ministries on the morning of 28 February, but in fact only Bublikov took possession of the ministry assigned to him. His short rule in the Ministry of Transport was all-important for the success of the revolution. The railway network possessed a system of communications of its own, through which Bublikov informed the country of what was happening in the capital at a time when the local administrations in the provinces were still censoring the newspaper reports of events in Petrograd. The news transmitted to the railway stations all over the country created an atmosphere of anxious expectation which was transformed into general jubilation when, with the publication of the abdication manifesto, it became clear that the change of régime would take place everywhere without any resistance on the part of the Tsarist administration and without civil war. No less important was Bubli-kov's influence on the attitude of GHQ and in particular on General Alekseev himself. He cleverly introduced into his first appeal to the railway workers the demand for their devoted services in the supply of the army, for which no effort should be spared. This telegram, when it was shown to Alekseev, created the impression that the new ad-ministration of the Duma was adopting a highly patriotic attitude. It was this telegram, together with other equally misleading signals from the capital, which determined Alekseev to advise General Ivanov to temporise on his mission to Petrograd and caused Alekseev to send the telegram no. 1833 quoted above.[1]

Bublikov was quite determined in his efforts to stop the imperial trains proceeding on 28 February and 1 March. He ordered them to be stopped at Bologoe, and to be sabotaged on the way from there to Pskov. This did not happen because the railway gendarmerie was still in control at all the stations in question. Bublikov's behaviour at the ministry was completely revolutionary. He arrested the officials who refused to obey his orders. He summoned a railway specialist, Professor Major-General Lomonosov, and made him his assistant. It was to a large extent due to Bublikov's energy and determination that the whole railway system (which in Russia more than elsewhere can be compared to the blood system of a living organism) remained working throughout the critical days without the slightest hitch. If ever there was a spontaneous revolutionary departmental authority, this was the railway administration established by Bublikov. We can therefore easily understand his indignation when he learned of the appointment of Nekrasov. He was offered the chance of becoming Nekrasov's assistant, and naturally refused. Bublikov came into the limelight once more at the Moscow State Conference in August 1917, when he shook hands with Tseretelli, thus symbolising the unity of purpose of the Russian radical bourgeoisie with the socialist labour movement. Later he

1. See p. 302 f.

emigrated to the United States, where he published a short pamphlet of recollections of the revolution, with a vitriolic attack on the members of the first Provisional Government.[1]

At the moment of his entry into the Provisional Government, Nekrasov was considered to be a close political and personal friend of Milyukov. This was not, however, the case. In the years and months preceding the revolution, Nekrasov had attacked Milyukov's position inside the central committee of the Kadet Party, trying to undermine his authority by underhand methods. Nabokov in his memoirs[2] calls Nekrasov a *'faux bonhomme'*, Milyukov in his personal memoirs calls him 'simply a traitor'. He was here alluding to the secret alliance between Nekrasov, Kerensky and Tereshchenko which led finally to his elimination from the Provisional Government. But neither Tereshchenko nor Kerensky was bound to Milyukov by party discipline and personal friendship, as Nekrasov was. In Nekrasov's appointment and in his subsequent fatal influence on internal developments in the Provisional Government we must see another instance of the dangerous impact of secret society allegiances on the administration of the country in 1917. Of course, this was not readily admitted by Nekrasov's party colleagues, who tended to explain away his objectionable behaviour and his duplicity as a character defect, and called him the evil genius of the Russian revolution.

Nekrasov did not stay in the Provisional Government until the bitter end. He accepted the post of Governor-General of Finland shortly before the October coup. He was one of the very few members of the Provisional Government to enter the service of Lenin's régime. In 1930 he was accused of 'sabotage' and imprisoned, and is reported to have died in 1940.

We have less reason to ascribe the selection of Konovalov for the Ministry of Trade and Industry to the same covert influences which played a part in the appointment of Tereshchenko, Nekrasov and Kerensky, although he belonged to the same leading group of the political masonic organisation. His reputation as a great captain of industry, as an enlightened, benevolent employer and as a generous supporter of every 'progressive' movement in Russia made his appointment almost inevitable. The story of his participation in the

1. Bublikov, *Russkaya revolyutsiya*, op. cit.
2. *ARR*, I, p. 49 f.

Provisional Government is chequered. He was one of the first to rebel against its policies, or rather lack of policies, and to relinquish his post, only to re-enter the government under the moral pressure of Kerensky, whose deputy prime minister he became. His ministerial career ended with his arrest, together with the other members of the Provisional Government, in the Winter Palace in October. He may well have avoided the fate of his colleagues Kokoshkin and Shingarev (murdered by sailors in December 1917) owing to the protection of such Bolsheviks as Skvortsov-Stepanov or Petrovsky, with whom he had tried to establish a common political front in the spring of 1914, when they turned to him for financial support for political purposes.[1] We can only regret that, like Tereshchenko and Nekrasov, he has not left any written account of the secret social and political aims pursued by the organisation to which all three (and Kerensky) belonged; without information on this point it is difficult to assess the real motives and the erratic behaviour of the members of this organisation, who, without in fact exercising power, occupied the only position from which power could have been exercised in Russia during the months between the fall of Tsarism and the summoning of the Constituent Assembly.

The Ministry of Agriculture and Land Tenure went to Shingarev, who was originally intended for the Ministry of Finance but had been made to give way to Tereshchenko. He did not like this switch, and close observers commented on his suspiciousness and unwillingness to delegate work to subordinates. This may well have been the result of a feeling that his appointment and stay in office were dependent on certain occult forces and agreements in which he had no part whatever. Such a feeling was typical also of other members of the Provisional Government who did not belong to the inner circle, and this feeling increased progressively during the eight months of the rule of the Provisional Government.

The appointment of Guchkov to the Ministry of War and the Navy was in a sense as 'natural' as the appointment of Milyukov to Foreign Affairs. It happened without Guchkov's explicit assent and knowledge, and was announced at a time when he was on his way to Pskov in order to obtain the act of abdication from Nicholas II. In the previous two days, he had tried as best he could to organise the defence of the revolutionary capital against the troops which, it was then rumoured,

1. See above, pp. 172–3 n.

had been sent from the front to crush the revolution. In this task he relied on a number of officers of the Petrograd garrison who had been enrolled and given certain tasks to perform in the eventuality of a palace coup, which Guchkov and his assistants were planning. The task undertaken by Guchkov was not an easy one, nor was it a safe one. His closest assistant, Prince Vyazemsky, was killed at his side on an inspection tour of the more than dubious forces which were supposed to secure the defence of the revolutionary capital against any troops sent to suppress the rising.

The choice of Guchkov for Minister of War (and temporarily of the Navy) was based on his lifelong interest in the modernisation of the Russian armed forces, and on his work in the Duma committee dealing with the military and naval budget. Guchkov considered himself a champion of modern ideas in military matters. He had many contacts among officers who advised him, and on whom he relied for information. This group was known as 'the Young Turks', because of Guchkov's onetime interest in the technique of the Young Turk revolution. In his promotion of reforms in the army, Guchkov naturally came into conflict with the Minister of War, Sukhomlinov. He hounded the Minister in the Duma, and later, after his downfall, was one of the main instigators of his prosecution. If he had friends among the officers, he also had many enemies. His short period in office was marked by a far-reaching purge of the officer corps according to lists which were compiled in Guchkov's office, and which included all officers who in his opinion were either politically undesirable or incompetent. These lists must be regarded as one of the major reasons for the lowering of the morale of the officer corps, comparable in this respect only with Order No. 1 and the Bolshevik incitement of soldiers against their superiors.

The record of Guchkov's short term of office and his memoirs betray a kind of split personality. On the one hand, he certainly stood on the extreme right wing of the Provisional Government. Together with Milyukov, he tried to persuade Grand Duke Michael to accept the throne. He was an ardent supporter of the continuation of the war to a victorious conclusion, and a determined opponent of any attempt by the Provisional Government to forestall the decision of the future Constituent Assembly by introducing immediate socialist legislation. On the other hand, all his measures to prevent subversive and defeatist propaganda among the troops were half-hearted and inconsistent. He irritated the leaders of the Petrograd Soviet by avoiding direct contact with them and talking to them in an authoritarian tone; yet he was ready to make concessions to them against his better judgement of what was necessary for the maintenance of the fighting capacity of the army. Throughout his stay in office, he was profoundly pessimistic, and his state of health deteriorated rapidly, so that the Council of Ministers often had to meet at his bedside. It is perhaps not too fanciful to explain Guchkov's general state of confusion by the peculiar experience he underwent in the revolutionary days. The Petrograd popular rising forestalled the carefully thought-out palace coup which he had planned. For a moment, on 28 February, Guchkov thought that he could reverse the planned schedule of his scheme. Instead of first obtaining the abdication of the hated and despised Emperor and then proclaiming the end of the shameful and obnoxious régime, and the advent of an era in which government and people would be one in their efforts to secure the greatness of Russia, Guchkov now thought of using the Petrograd rising as a means to force the Tsar's abdication and prevent a civil war in the country at large. His interview with the Tsar was therefore a dream-like distortion of the encounter which he had hoped for and certainly imagined in great detail. In spite of the fact that he had been warned of the increasingly revolutionary atmosphere in Petrograd, he insisted when he arrived back in the city on going to the railway workshops and announcing the accession to the throne of the Emperor Michael II. This almost cost him his life, and incidentally he also nearly lost the abdication document itself. He thus arrived late at the flat of Princess Putyatin, where the question of whether Michael should accept the throne or not was being discussed. Tired and bewildered, Guchkov gave only lukewarm support to Milyukov's insistent request that the Grand Duke should accede to the throne.[1]

Like Milyukov, Guchkov became a member of the government produced by the very revolution which he had wanted to forestall by implementing his own plan for a palace coup. Like Milyukov, he wanted to resign after the abdication of the Grand Duke. He claimed in his memoirs that Milyukov persuaded him to stay. Guchkov is not a reliable memoirist, and Milyukov does not confirm this story. After his eventual resignation at the end of April, Guchkov's political career

1. See below, p. 406 f.

was practically finished – although he continued a life of political intrigue until his last days, political intrigue which did him no honour and brought much misery to those who got involved in it.[1]

The posts of State Comptroller and Procurator of the Holy Synod were allotted to two members of the moderate right in the Duma, Godnev and Vladimir Lvov (no relative of the Premier, Prince G. E. Lvov) respectively. Because of their right-wing opinions both of them felt their position in the Provisional Government to be particularly insecure. They tried to remedy this situation as best they could by siding always with the left wing of the Cabinet, that is, by voting for any Kerensky proposal. Godnev did not leave any significant trace in the history of the Provisional Government. The same unfortunately cannot be said of Vladimir Lvov, who had always had an ambition to become Procurator of the Holy Synod. He ascribed his lack of success in his efforts to secure this office to the pernicious influence of Rasputin, and nourished a burning hatred towards all those members of the clergy whom he suspected of being Rasputin's protégés. The revolution brought the realisation of his most cherished dream. As Procurator of the Holy Synod he showed himself a most tyrannical and capricious head of that department. The bishops who were summoned to Petrograd were horrified at the way they were treated by Lvov, and some of them even sought the protection of the Petrograd Soviet against the over-zealous Procurator. Lvov's rule in the Synod came to an end during the June crisis of the Provisional Government, when it was decided to drop all members of the Cabinet who had been sitting to the right of the Kadets in the Duma. Lvov's fury then turned against Kerensky, whom according to Milyukov he vowed never to forgive. Later on, in August, Lvov played a most incredible part in creating the unfortunate misunderstanding which led to the so-called Kornilov Affair. He passed himself off to Kerensky as an emissary of Kornilov, and to Kornilov as an emissary of Kerensky. The ensuing imbroglio was one of the most tragic occurrences in Russian history. Vladimir Lvov emigrated with the White armies, and turned up in Paris in 1920, where he published a series of fanciful articles on the Kornilov affair until publication was stopped after V. D. Nabokov had protested to the

1. On his involvement in the Gestapo-NKVD duel of wits and cabal which led to the kidnapping of a General Miller in Paris by Soviet agents posing as German emissaries, see above, p. 339.

editor of the newspaper against the nonsensical rubbish which Lvov was offering the reading public.[1] Shortly after the publication of these articles in 1920, Lvov gave a public lecture in which he claimed that the only government now defending the great historical tradition of Russia was the Soviet government. A little later he returned to Russia, where he joined the Anti-Religious League and contributed to the anti-religious newspapers.

Of course, the creators of the Provisional Government could scarcely have imagined that their Procurator of the Holy Synod would become a propagandist of atheism under the Bolshevik régime. There must, however, even at that time, have been something in the behaviour of the unfortunate Lvov which should have served as a warning against entrusting to him the affairs of an important department. Perhaps the good-natured and merciful character sketch which Nabokov gave of him in 1918 will make this clear:

> The Procurator of the Holy Synod V. Lvov was, like Godnev, inspired by the very best intentions, and also showed a striking naivety as well as an unbelievably frivolous approach to business, not only to that of his own department, but also with regard to the general situation and the tasks with which the Provisional Government was faced every day. He always spoke with great fervour and inspiration, and invariably aroused the amusement, not only of members of the government, but even of officials of the government chancellery.[2]

The not entirely justified amusement was caused by Lvov's mixture of jingoistic rhetoric and revolutionary demagogy.

Little can be said about the first Minister of Education of the Provisional Government, Professor Manuilov. Well-intentioned and civilised, he joined the government out of a sense of civic duty, and was one of the first of its members to understand how little the government could do to influence the course of the revolutionary events. He is reported to have advocated the resignation of the Provisional Government as a whole, and was probably highly relieved when he was allowed to surrender the seals of his office to his successor, Professor S. F. Oldenburg.

1. It is difficult to understand why Professor Browder and A. F. Kerensky found it necessary to reprint in *The Russian Provisional Government*, without commentary and without mentioning Nabokov's protest, these articles of Lvov.
2. Nabokov, *Vremennoe Pravitelstvo*, ARR, I, p. 43.

3. ENTER KERENSKY

A. F. Kerensky first joined the Provisional Government as Minister of Justice. This is not the place to assess his character, or to explain the particular circumstances which led to his meteoric rise in the next eight months. But we should comment briefly on the reasons for the inclusion of this man of socialist views in the predominantly 'bourgeois' Provisional Government. Milyukov believed that Kerensky's candidature was pressed by the same freemasonry political circles who brought Tereshchenko into the Cabinet. This is an unnecessary and not at all convincing conjecture. There were extremely good reasons for Kerensky to be offered a post in the Provisional Government as soon as it was realised that it would be the government of a revolutionary Russia. Both Kerensky, as leader of the labour faction (comprising the non-Marxist socialists) in the Duma and Chkheidze, the leader of the small Menshevik Marxist group, became members of the Duma Committee appointed by the *Senioren Convent* on 27 February. It was only natural that representatives of both groups should be asked to join the new government, the more so as both Chkheidze and Kerensky had in the meantime been elected to the presidium of the newly formed Petrograd Soviet. Chkheidze, who was offered the Ministry of Labour, refused to accept office in the new government because, as we have seen, the revolutionary intellectuals who formed under Chkheidze's chairmanship the temporary Executive Committee of the Petrograd Soviet decided – in their Marxist wisdom – that the revolution that was taking place was a 'bourgeois' one, that the responsibility of forming an administration should therefore fall entirely on the 'bourgeois' parties, and that the socialist parties should be left complete freedom of action either to support or to oppose this purely 'bourgeois' government. This decision of the Soviet Executive Committee should also have been binding on Kerensky, even though he had not taken part in the deliberations leading up to it; yet Kerensky managed to circumvent the decision of the Executive Committee in a manner which was typical of his tactics in the revolutionary days, and which was of the greatest consequence for his future position in the revolutionary administration.

The basic fact in Kerensky's behaviour in those days was his feeling, not entirely unjustified, that this was *his* revolution, that if he had not brought it about, he had at least given it articulate expression, and that he had done so on his own initiative, without being prompted by anyone and without the support of any organisation except perhaps that of the masonic group to which he belonged.

On Sunday 26 February Kerensky had assembled in his flat representatives of various groups who had begun to realise that the street unrest in the capital might lead to important political developments. He was surprised to find the representatives of the extreme left, such as Shlyapnikov and Yurenev, in a rather pessimistic mood and claiming that the high tide of revolutionary fervour among the workers was beginning to ebb. When, the next morning, he realised that the Petrograd garrison had mutinied, he immediately decided to give a lead to the disaffected elements, and to force the Duma to assume the leadership of the revolution. Like Bublikov, he was one of those who wanted the Duma to meet in formal session, in defiance of the imperial prorogation decree.[1] He failed in this task, and his name was entered on the list of the 'Duma provisional committee for contacts with personalities and institutions', as the Duma Committee originally and rather faintheartedly described itself. But Kerensky did not take any part in the futile deliberations of this committee. Like the Ariel of an invisible Prospero, he was here, there and everywhere in the Tauride Palace, boldly promoting the revolution the very fact of which was still a matter of doubt and controversy to his colleagues. When on 27th February some students brought the chairman of the Upper Chamber, Shcheglovitov, under guard to the palace, it was Kerensky who met and arrested him 'in the name of the people'. He did so a few moments after the President of the Duma had greeted Shcheglovitov and asked him to join him for a talk in his study. It should be remembered that the Duma Committee was then not properly constituted, and that Rodzyanko had not yet decided to head the revolution and was still negotiating with the Golitsyn government and Grand Duke Michael in an attempt to form an imperial government of public confidence; yet Rodzyanko allowed a member of the Duma of which he was president to arrest the chairman of the Upper Chamber in his presence and to have him led off to the ministerial pavilion in the garden of the Tauride Palace, which was rapidly being transformed into a prison where members of the imperial government were held in custody. Later, when another notorious personality of the old régime, General Sukhomlinov,

1. See Kerensky, *The Catastrophe* (London, 1927), p. 12.

was brought to the Duma, we see Kerensky protecting him against the soldiery which was about to lynch him, at what he considered to be no small risk to his own life. On 28 February it was he who received the troops 'who had joined the people' and had encamped in a highly picturesque and disorderly manner all around the Tauride Palace. When on the afternoon of the 28th sporadic shooting near the palace caused a panic in the meeting-room of the Soviet, Kerensky was bustling about the premises of the Military Commission in room 1. Believing that Cossacks were attacking the palace, Kerensky jumped on the window-sill, and, sticking his head through a narrow fanlight shouted in a hoarse, breaking voice: 'To your posts! Defend the State Duma! Do you hear me? It is I, Kerensky, speaking to you . . . Kerensky is speaking to you. Defend your freedom, the revolution, defend the State Duma. To your posts!' When Sukhanov,[1] who reports the incident and vouches for the correctness of the above quotation, tried to remonstrate with Kerensky, telling him quietly that there was no reason to create a greater panic than that already produced by the shots, Kerensky replied angrily: 'I ask everyone to carry on with his duties and not to interfere while I am giving orders'.

It is not surprising that Kerensky, who felt that destiny had made him the paladin of the revolution, would have no truck with the faint-hearted and cynical. When, in the middle of the night of 27–28 February Rodzyanko was at last persuaded to head the revolutionary movement, he appeared in the Duma Committee and declared that he agreed, but only on one condition: 'I demand,' he said, according to Milyukov,[2] 'and this applies in particular to you, Aleksandr Feodorovich [Kerensky], that all members of the committee unconditionally and blindly follow all my instructions.'

Kerensky was the only one to protest against this fatuous demand of the self-appointed dictator of the Russian revolution. He reminded Rodzyanko that after all he was the deputy chairman of the Soviet of Workers' Deputies, and that he could not give such a pledge. Rodzyanko's special reference to Kerensky was doubtless a reaction to Kerensky's arrest of Shcheglovitov earlier that same day.

But such unwelcome attempts to influence Kerensky's conduct in the revolutionary situation – as he understood it – came not only from the right, from Rodzyanko and the Duma Committee, but also from the

1. *Zapiski o revolyutsii*, vol. I, p. 201 f.   2. *Vospominaniya*, vol. II, p. 298.

left, that is, from the Soviet Executive Committee. As soon as he was offered the post of Minister of Justice (for which incidentally the lawyer and right-wing Kadet, V. Maklakov, had originally been ear-marked), Kerensky tried to find out what the attitude of the Soviet Executive Committee to his acceptance would be. He talked to Su-khanov, who explained to him that the Executive Committee had discussed the matter and decided, by thirteen votes to eight, that no representative of revolutionary democracy should at present enter the government. Sukhanov advised Kerensky either to submit to the decision of the Executive Committee or else to resign from his position as deputy chairman and then join the bourgeois government. Sukhanov seemed to prefer the latter solution. Not surprisingly, Kerensky's revolutionary zeal and the success of his emotional speeches to the crowds had disturbed Sukhanov, as it may well have disturbed other intellectuals in the ranks of the Soviet Executive Committee. His transfer from the Soviet to the bourgeois camp would have rendered him harmless in the eyes of Sukhanov. This however was not at all how Kerensky himself understood the situation.

Later in the evening on 2 March, having already accepted the post of minister in the Provisional Government, Kerensky turned up at the plenary meeting of the Soviet, which by that time had already degener-ated into something like a street meeting, with soapbox orators pour-ing out whatever came into their heads to a tired but enthusiastic audience. According to some reports the official meeting had just been closed, but those present do not seem to be quite clear whether this was the case. Pale, and in a state of extreme excitement, Kerensky climbed on to one of the tables in the hall and asked to be heard. It is not clear whether Chkheidze or any other official of the Executive Committee in the chair gave him permission to speak. The speech which he made is of considerable importance, and was reported in two different ver-sions in the news-sheet *Izvestiya*[1] published by a group of journalists accredited to the Duma. In its issue marked No. 6–7 and dated 2–3 March, the speech is given in a different version from that which ap-peared twenty-four hours later in the same publication. The later version appears in Browder and Kerensky's collection of documents on the Provisional Government, but it is the earlier version which seems

1. Not to be confused with the *Izvestiya* of the Petrograd Soviet, edited by Bonch-Bruevich.

to me to have caught the atmosphere more exactly and to have kept in all its artlessness certain admissions which are important for an understanding of Kerensky's special position:

Comrades, I have to make an announcement of exceptional importance. Comrades! Do you trust me? (shouts of 'We trust you, we trust you.') At the present moment a Provisional Government has been formed, in which I have taken the post of Minister of Justice (stormy applause and shouts of 'Bravo'). Comrades! I had only five minutes to give an answer, and could therefore not obtain a mandate from you before deciding to join the Provisional Government.

Here in my custody were the representatives of the old régime, and I did not dare to let them out of my hands (stormy applause and shouts of 'Quite right'). I accepted the offer, and have joined the provisional government as Minister of Justice (a new burst of applause). Immediately on taking up office as minister, I ordered all political prisoners to be set free, and our comrade deputies, members of the Social-Democratic faction of the Fourth Duma and deputies of the Second Duma, to be brought here from Siberia with special honours (stormy applause, growing into an ovation). All prisoners are being set free, not excluding terrorists.

I have assumed the post of Minister of Justice until the convocation of the Constituent Assembly, which shall, in accordance with the will of the people, establish the future constitution (stormy applause). Until then, complete freedom will be guaranteed to carry on propaganda and agitation about the future constitution of Russia, even a republican one. In view of the fact, comrades, that I have assumed the responsibility of Minister of Justice before obtaining authority from you, I give up my position as deputy chairman of the Soviet of Workers' Deputies. For me, however, life without the people is unthinkable, and I am ready to take up this office again, if such is your decision ('We beg you! We beg you!'). Comrades! Having joined the ranks of the Provisional Government, I am still the same as ever – a republican (loud applause). I must base my activities on the will of the people, I must find powerful support in them (stormy ovation and shouts of 'We trust you, we trust you, comrade'). I cannot live without the people, and if at any time you lose faith in me, kill me (a new outbreak of ovations).

I will declare to the Provisional Government that I am the representative of democracy, but that the Provisional Government must pay particular attention to the opinions on which I will take a stand in my capacity as representative of the people, by whose efforts the old régime was overthrown ('Long live the Minister of Justice!').

As Kerensky was carried shoulder high into the room of the Executive Committee, it was clear that he had won the day. Not only had he the approval of the Soviet for his entry into the Provisional Government, but his election as deputy chairman of the Soviet was confirmed, and he considered himself not merely an appointee of certain anonymous circles, as were in fact all the other members of the Provisional Government, but a truly elected representative of the people. As such, he immediately claimed an exceptional position among his colleagues, and expected his opinions and counsels to be treated quite differently from those of the other ministers. His reasons for claiming this special privilege were certainly ill-founded, but in a sense his position as minister of the Provisional Government was indeed basically different from that of all the others. For months and years, they had clamoured for power in order to prevent the revolution from happening, and yet it was only due to the revolution that they had achieved power. Kerensky could never have expected to become a minister in a monarchist Russia. He had always thought that his hour would come only with revolution. The others, having once taken advantage of the Petrograd rising, would gladly have stopped considering themselves members of a revolutionary government. It must not be forgotten that when it was formed there had not yet been an abdication, although Milyukov was soon to announce that 'the old despot who had brought Russia to the verge of disaster would have either to resign or be deposed'. But he still expected Alexis to be proclaimed Tsar under the regency of his uncle Michael. Kerensky, on the other hand, entered the government as a republican, claiming the right to carry on open republican propaganda. True, the references to republicanism were omitted from the later version of the speech, but we have no reason to believe that they were not uttered. And less than twenty-four hours later Kerensky grasped the first opportunity to practise his republicanism, when he took part in the deliberations which led to the abdication of Grand Duke Michael.

4. THE FIRST ANNOUNCEMENT OF THE PROVISIONAL GOVERNMENT

The composition of the Provisional Government was decided upon by Rodzyanko and Milyukov after negotiations between the representatives of the Duma and Soviet Executive Committees, which dragged on until the small hours of 2 March. Kerensky gave his consent only a few moments before Milyukov announced the new cabinet, at about 3 p.m. on that day. Some other newly-appointed ministers, or at least one of them, namely Guchkov, seem not to have known for certain that they had become members of the new government until Milyukov announced their names.

While it was easy to give the names of the members of the new cabinet, it was much more difficult to explain by what authority they had come to be in that position. As we have seen, Guchkov in Pskov was quite willing to accept the appointment of Prince Lvov as Prime Minister by the Emperor on his abdication. In fact, a decree to this effect, as we know, was actually signed by Nicholas II. Later this imperial sanction had to be officially repudiated to preserve the revolutionary prestige of the Provisional Government. Indeed it had become unthinkable already on 2 March, given the mood of the Petrograd crowds. On the other hand, an announcement giving the formal consent of the Petrograd Soviet Executive Committee to the formation of the new government (a consent requested and given in the negotiations of the night of 1–2 March between the two committees) was also out of the question. The ministers chosen by Milyukov and Rodzyanko would have refused the honour of being members of a government by the grace of the Soviet: this would have been a *de jure* admission of Soviet control over it, even if this control existed *de facto*. But neither would the Soviet Executive Committee have welcomed being formally associated with the formation of the new government. The Soviet Executive Committee was very much in favour of letting the property-owning classes (*tsenzovaya obshchestvennost*) assume full responsibility for establishing the new government, but it reserved the right to support the policies of this government only insofar as these promoted the social revolution.

The first official announcement of the formation of the government appeared in the morning edition of the papers on 3 March 1917. It was addressed to 'all citizens' and its form was as peculiar and disconcerting as its content. It announced that the provisional committee of members of the State Duma had achieved, with the assistance and sympathy of the army and the inhabitants of the capital, such a large measure of success in its struggle with the dark forces of the old régime that it could now undertake the organisation of a more stable executive power. And then the names of the members of the new government under Prince G. E. Lvov were given. It thus seemed that the announcement was issued by the Duma Committee, acting as the body responsible for creating the new cabinet. In his capacity of chairman of this committee, one might have expected Rodzyanko to sign this document in the name of, or jointly with, the other members of it. This, however, was not the case. The signatures which follow Rodzyanko's were not those of the members of the Duma Executive Committee but of their appointees, the new ministers. True, a certain number of names figure on both bodies. But the Duma Committee seems to have faded away, like one of those ephemeral insects which die after laying their eggs. The signatures of the new ministers listed in the document may have been appropriate, inasmuch as the second part of the document contains something like a programme of the new government as it had taken shape in the discussions between the Duma Committee and the Soviet Committee. There are eight points, expressing the principles by which the activities of the new government would be guided, and reflecting the tug-of-war which preceded the agreement between the two committees. These are: (1) complete amnesty for all political and religious offences, including terrorist attempts, military mutinies and agrarian disorders;[1] (2) all democratic liberties (of speech, of the press, etc.) for all citizens, including the military insofar as permitted by technical military considerations; (3) abolition of all discrimination on grounds of class, religion and race; (4) immediate preparation of elections to the Constituent Assembly on the basis of the 'four-point formula';[2] (5) replacement of the police by a popular militia, with elected officers, subordinated to the organs of local administration; (6) new elections on the basis of universal franchise to all organs of local self-government; (7) military units which took part in the revolutionary movement not to be disarmed or withdrawn from Petrograd; (8) extension of all civic freedoms to soldiers and military personnel, subject only to the maintenance of strict military discipline when on duty.

The document, which began as an announcement by the Duma

1. The political amnesty which Kerensky claimed to have introduced had in fact already been proclaimed by the Duma Committee's commissars in the Ministry of Justice, V. Maklakov and Adzhemov.
2. See above, p. 369 n. 2.

Executive Committee, ended with a declaration of the Provisional Government: 'The Provisional Government considers it its duty to add that it has not the slightest intention of taking advantage of the military situation to delay in any way the realisation of the reforms and measures outlined above.'[1]

In issuing this proclamation, the newly-constituted Provisional Government had already begun the process of self-mutilation of which it was to die. In point 5, it virtually gave up the use of a centralised police force, thus promoting conditions favourable to creeping anarchy. In point 7, it gave a pledge to the mutinous troops of Petrograd which became a major impediment to the restoration of order and discipline, and which, together with Order No. 1, must be regarded as a major factor in the dissolution of the Russian armed forces.

Forty years later, Milyukov explained why he had conceded this point to the representatives of the Soviet: he could not oppose it, he said, because the troops had just 'secured our victory. It was not known at that moment whether they would not have to fight "loyal units" despatched against the capital.' A remarkable admission of the solidarity of Milyukov and the Duma Executive Committee with the troops of the Petrograd garrison, a solidarity based on a common fear of reprisals if the revolution were to fail.

The threat to the morale of the troops was only accentuated by the repetitive affirmation (points 2 and 8) of the full civic rights of the soldiers, accompanied by irksome reminders of the necessity of maintaining discipline and limiting these freedoms in accordance with 'technical military considerations'. Finally, the concluding announcement, weakly asserting the good faith of the Provisional Government, could not but produce the opposite effect: *qui s'excuse s'accuse*.

1. Browder and Kerensky, vol. I, p. 136.

15

'A Strange and Criminal Manifesto'

Between the two abdications; 'A noble man'; The plenitude of power

I. BETWEEN THE TWO ABDICATIONS

Despite the oft-repeated formula that the Provisional Government had come into being 'on the initiative of the State Duma', its members, including Milyukov, obviously did not feel that they had been selected or appointed either by the Duma or its President. When the excited crowd interrupted Milyukov's speech and asked him 'Who chose you?', it would have been easy for him to have referred to the authority of the Duma, as an institution which had become the focus of the revolutionary movement. Instead he answered:

> We were chosen by the Russian revolution (loud and prolonged applause). It was our good fortune that at a moment when it was impossible to wait any longer, a small group of men was at hand whose political past was sufficiently known to the people, and against whom there could be no hint of those objections that brought about the downfall of the old régime.

According to Milyukov's conception, this group of men whom Russia was fortunate to have at hand was to become the government of the new Emperor, the infant Alexis, in whose name regency powers would be exercised by Grand Duke Michael. But they would stay in office only in order to convene the Constituent Assembly, which was to be elected on the four-point formula.[1] This decision on the future relations between the supreme power vested in the Regent and the Provisional Government, which pledged itself to surrender its functions to the Constituent Assembly, was certainly not Milyukov's personal one, but that of his political friends in the Progressive Bloc, who were in an overwhelming majority in the Duma Committee. Yet this decision was taken before the question of the abdication had been settled

1. See above, p. 369 n. 2.

in Pskov, and without proper consultation and agreement with the future regent. Even more important, it was taken without any consideration of the state of public opinion as expressed by the excited crowds which were beleaguering the Tauride Palace. As soon as Milyukov began speaking of the dynasty and of the abdication of the former despot who had brought the country to the edge of the abyss, he realised that this would be the most awkward point of his speech. He was interrupted several times with shouts: 'But this is the old dynasty! Long live the republic! Down with the dynasty!' Milyukov had to improvise the passage concerning the convocation of the Constituent Assembly, which restored the enthusiasm of the crowd. He put in a weak defence of the principle of monarchy, saying:

> We cannot leave the question concerning the form of government unanswered or undecided. We see it as a parliamentary constitutional monarchy, perhaps others see it in a different way; but if we start quarrelling about it instead of coming to an immediate decision, Russia will find herself in a state of civil war, and this will only lead to the revival of the régime which has been overthrown.

Milyukov's handling of this question was almost unbelievably clumsy. We can only quote Melgunov's comment on this passage from Milyukov's speech:

> Nobody had asked Milyukov to bring forward the controversial question [of the monarchy] for discussion by the street crowd, or to disclose prematurely what the majority wanted to solve by Guchkov's method, that is, by confronting the masses with an accomplished fact. This plan was to a great extent frustrated by Milyukov's unexpected speech, a real disservice to the supporters of the monarchy. . . . I am not prepared to admit that the idea of the monarchy was dead in the hearts of two hundred million people long before the rising in the capital, as was claimed by Suvorin's newspaper *Novoe Vremya* in an attempt to play up to the general mood. But it was a fact that among the mass of the soldiers . . . who were to a certain degree the determining factor in the whole course of events, the mystique of the Tsar's power had really been destroyed under the impact of rumours and gossip in the capital. This had been frequently remarked on by the Police Department reports on expressions of anti-dynastic feeling. All this rendered republican propaganda easy. A sub-conscious aversion to monarchy was fed by a fear of being held responsible for all that had been done. . . . A revolution which resulted in the restora-

tion of the old dynasty would have been tantamount to a mutiny for which, under changed circumstances, retribution might be exacted. . . .[1]

When, just a few hours later on the same day, Kerensky proclaimed himself an unrepentant, indeed a triumphant, republican in his impromptu speech to the Soviet, he made a far better demagogic move than Milyukov with his gratuitous and tactless remarks in the hall of the Tauride Palace. Milyukov's speech in fact brought the question of the monarchy to the foreground, and it became the main topic of discussion in the streets, in the committees and in the barracks for the next twenty-four hours; not the least affected was the tiny but influential group which was concerned with the fate of the dynasty.

The grand dukes who were at that time in Petrograd seem to have been feverishly active. The uncle of the Tsar, the last surviving son of Alexander II, Grand Duke Paul, decided to issue a kind of manifesto, promising the introduction of a constitution in Russia after the war. He managed to secure the signatures of Grand Duke Cyril Vladimirovich, and of Grand Duke Michael as well.[2] He even went to Tsarskoe Selo and asked the Empress to sign this manifesto, but was given a very stormy reception. In one of her last letters to the Tsar, which reached him only after the abdication, she speaks of the 'idiotic plan' of Grand Duke Paul by which he hoped 'to save us all'. The manifesto was handed over to Milyukov, who kept it, but never made use of it. Grand Duke Cyril, besides signing the manifesto, decided to register his acceptance of the revolution by appearing in the Duma at the head of a naval guards detachment, adorned with a red rosette. There has been much controversy on this question of the red rosette, but it seems that Rodzyanko's testimony on this point cannot be doubted. The Grand Duke also offered his services to the Duma Committee in any capacity, but this only embarrassed the President of the Duma, who told him that his presence in the Duma in these circumstances was quite out of place, and advised him to retire. It also seems that the majority of the grand dukes were horrified on hearing that Grand Duke Michael had been proposed as regent. They seem to have been utterly opposed to this, mainly because they distrusted Grand Duke Michael's morganatic wife, the Countess Brasova. She was

1. Melgunov, *Martovskie dni*, pp. 134 ff.
2. Grand Duke Michael later in the day asked Milyukov to remove his signature from the document. See also above, p. 290.

known to be an ambitious and energetic woman who had suffered much from her irregular social position and could be expected to take advantage of the situation to get her revenge.

Of far greater importance were the repercussions of Milyukov's speech among the troops of the Petrograd garrison. On hearing of the possibility of the Romanovs retaining their throne, the soldiers seem to have been seized by panic, suspecting that their officers were now going to regain control and wreak vengeance on them for the mutiny of 27–28 February. The mood of panic and fear which dominated both soldiers and officers, and was fed by profound mutual distrust, spread to Duma circles, and in particular to its President. At dusk, crossing the hall where a few hours before he had pronounced his fateful speech, Milyukov came across Rodzyanko,

> who at a smart trot ran up to me, accompanied by a handful of officers who reeked of alcohol. In a quavering voice, he repeated their assertions that after what I had said about the dynasty they could not go back to their units. They demanded that I should retract what I had said. This I naturally could not do; but on seeing the behaviour of Rodzyanko, who knew very well that I had spoken not only in my own name but in the name of the [Progressive] Bloc as a whole, I decided to issue a statement saying that I had expressed only my personal opinion.[1]

In view of his incapacity to forgive and forget, we should perhaps take his account of Rodzyanko's behaviour with a pinch of salt. But the fact that Rodzyanko was so frightened that he practically lost his head is confirmed by his behaviour in the early hours of 3 March. During the night, news reached the President of the Duma and Prince Lvov that the abdication had taken place, but with a very substantial alteration of the terms in which it had originally been conceived; Nicholas II had abdicated also for his son Alexis, and had named as the next in succession his brother Michael, whom he enjoined 'to administer the affairs of the state in complete and inviolable union with the representatives of the people in their legislative institutions on the basis of principles to be established by them, and to take an inviolable oath to this effect'. At five o'clock in the morning, Rodzyanko was again on the direct line to Ruzsky, and said: 'It is extremely important

1. Milyukov, *Vospominaniya*, vol. II, p. 313. For Milyukov's statement, see Browder and Kerensky, op. cit., vol. I, p. 133, where there is also the text of the subsequent retraction of this statement by Milyukov.

that the manifesto regarding the abdication and the transfer of power to Grand Duke Mikhail Aleksandrovich should not be published until I advise you to do so. . . .'

There followed the long and confused explanations by Rodzyanko of what had happened in Petrograd, which according to him made the solution embodied in the abdication manifesto obsolete.[1] Rodzyanko ended by asserting that the legislative assemblies, that is the Duma and the State Council, would continue working under the new régime and a Supreme Council. Then he corrected himself and said that he had meant the Duma Committee under his chairmanship.

Rodzyanko's slip of the tongue betrays that he was thinking of the Duma Executive Committee under his chairmanship as of a possible regency council which would exercise the prerogatives of the monarch, and of which the Provisional Government and the Duma would be respectively the executive and legislative branches. This is how he was understood by Ruzsky, as we can see from Ruzsky's appeal to the population of the area of the North-western Front, referred to above.[2]

When Rodzyanko communicated to GHQ his request to withhold publication of the manifesto announcing the abdication of Nicholas II and the nomination of Michael as his successor, it caused complete consternation. Alekseev began to realise that 'there is no frankness or sincerity in the communications of Rodzyanko',[3] and that the President of the Duma and its temporary committee were under strong pressure from the leftist parties and the workers' deputies. He made it clear to the commanders of the fronts that there was great danger in withholding the act of abdication and delaying its entry into legal effect.

It was in any case too late to revise the instrument of abdication. The ex-Tsar was already on his way from Pskov to Mogilev by train. Guchkov and Shulgin were nearing Petrograd, carrying their copy of the manifesto. News of the events in Petrograd was beginning to filter through to the country at large, and to the troops at the front. Immediate clarity on questions of allegiance was necessary in order to

1. *ARR*, III, pp. 266 ff., and Browder and Kerensky, vol. I, p. 109 f.
2. See above, pp. 348 ff.
3. See Alekseev-Rodzyanko conversation, 3 March, 0600 to 0645, and the wire sent by Alekseev to the commanders-in-chief of the various fronts, 3 March, both in translation in Browder and Kerensky, op. cit., vol. I, pp. 111–113.

maintain the morale of the troops. The position of Alekseev and the commanders of the fronts was rendered even more difficult just then by the fact that before abdicating, the Tsar had appointed Grand Duke Nikolay Nikolaevich Supreme Commander of the Armed Forces. He was then in Tiflis. Having been informed of his new appointment, he immediately began to criticise the manifesto and the decision of the Provisional Government to summon a Constituent Assembly. In a telegram to Alekseev despatched in the evening of 3 March he said:

> Was expecting a manifesto on abdication of throne in favour of Tsarevich under regency of Grand Duke Mikhail Aleksandrovich. As regards manifesto of abdication in favour of Mikhail Aleksandrovich reported by you this morning, it will inevitably provoke a massacre. . . . As for Constituent Assembly I consider this totally unacceptable in terms of welfare of Russia and victorious conclusion of war.

In the difficult situation in which Alekseev found himself, he seems to have had only one strong desire, namely to see the enthronement of Grand Duke Michael take place in accordance with the abdication act of Nicholas II. But the Duma politicians with whom he had been in contact, and who had been so eager for his support over the abdication of Nicholas II, were rather evasive on 3 March. Alekseev did not succeed in making direct contact with Rodzyanko on that day until late in the evening. When he got through to Guchkov at about six o'clock and advocated an agreement with 'the person who is to ascend the throne', he was informed that agreement had already been reached. The terms of it could only fill Alekseev with bitterness and regret. He gave vent to his feelings in a few sentences which throw some light on the mentality of this secretive and retiring character.

> Was it not possible [he asked Guchkov] to persuade the Grand Duke to assume power temporarily until the [Constituent] Assembly should meet? This would have brought immediate clarity to the situation. . . . It is difficult to foresee how the manifesto of 3 March [that is, the act of abdication of Grand Duke Michael] will be accepted by the masses in the trenches. Will they not possibly consider it as having been imposed by a third party? The present armed forces should be protected from all passions connected with internal politics. Even a short occupation of the throne by the Grand Duke would immediately have created respect for the will of the former monarch and for the readiness of the Grand Duke to serve his Fatherland in the difficult days we have experienced. . . . I am

persuaded that this would have produced the very best impression on the army. In half a year's time everything will become more clearly-defined and all changes will be less painful than at present.[1]

And when, having at last established contact with Rodzyanko at 11 p.m., he realised that the decisions taken in Petrograd were ir-revocable, he said to the President of the Duma, whom he disliked and despised: 'What more can I say except "God save Russia!"'

2. 'A NOBLE MAN'

Alekseev, who was right in his apprehensions in the long run, was too pessimistic as regards the reception by the army of the abdication of Grand Duke Michael. Rodzyanko's strategy, which consisted in with-holding the publication of Nicholas II's abdication until it could be combined with the renunciation of the throne by Grand Duke Michael, worked exactly as he expected. This double abdication clearly signified the end of the dynasty, though the possibility of Michael reigning with the agreement of the Constituent Assembly was still formally left open. Not even the next in succession to the throne after Grand Duke Michael could have appealed to the forces which remained loyal to the monarchy in order to assert his rights. Such an appeal would have brought him into conflict with Michael: no claim to the succession could be valid until the abdication of Michael had been confirmed by a decision of the Constituent Assembly. The main task of the politicians who wanted Michael to renounce the throne was to persuade him that this was compatible with his dynastic and patriotic duty.

The Grand Duke, who before the birth of Alexis had been heir-presumptive to the throne, had never played any part in politics, not even to the moderate extent to which such interference was permitted to the other members of the Romanov family. Since his morganatic marriage he had been under a cloud, and had been allowed to reside in Russia and resume service in the armed forces only after the outbreak of the war. He was not on good terms with the other members of the family, also on account of his marriage. His formidable aunt, Maria Pavlovna[2] the elder, considered him as standing in the way of direct

1. Melgunov, *Martovskie Dni*, etc. (Paris, 1961), p. 222.
2. The widow of Grand Duke Vladimir. Not to be confused with her namesake and niece, Maria Pavlovna the younger.

succession to the throne of her own children, of whom the eldest, Cyril, would otherwise be the first in line. During the war his wife, the Countess Braşova, like so many ladies in Petrograd society, had received Duma politicians and members of the Voluntary Organisations, but there was very little reason to believe that the Grand Duke was carrying on an intrigue of his own, and we have not heard of any such approach to him by the Moscow plotters as had been made to Grand Duke Nikolay Nikolaevich. The agreement, on 27 February, of the Grand Duke to act as regent and to find a solution to the political crisis provided his brother consented therefore came as a surprise to everybody concerned, including Prince Golitsyn, Rodzyanko, G.H.Q. and the Duma politicians. We know that the initiative for this abortive move came from Rodzyanko, and that the proviso that he would only act with the consent of the Tsar was made by the Grand Duke himself.

From 27 February, the Grand Duke stayed uninterruptedly in Petrograd, changing quarters frequently and keeping very much in the background. In the early hours of 28 February, as we have seen, the Grand Duke arrived at the Winter Palace, where the few troops which remained faithful to the Tsar were concentrated under the command of the Minister of War, Belyaev, the commander of the Petrograd Military District, General Khabalov, and General Zankevich. We have seen[1] that the Grand Duke asked the troops to leave the palace immediately, because he did not want any shooting on the people from the 'house of the Romanovs'. This shows some preoccupation with his own future position in the Russian state: the possibility of his becoming regent was already in the air. On 28 February he transferred his headquarters to the flat of Princess Putyatin, at 12 Millionnaya Street, where he waited quietly for further developments on 28 February, 1 and 2 March. In these three days he maintained contact with members of the Duma Committee; he also received a visit from his cousin Grand Duke Nikolay Mikhailovich, the historian, who had been banished by the Emperor to his estate in the south of Russia after the assassination of Rasputin, mainly for irresponsible gossip and agitation in grand-ducal circles. The part played by Grand Duke Nikolay Mikhailovich in the pre-revolutionary phase is not very easy to assess. The fragments of his diary which have been published show him as a convinced enemy of the Empress and as one ready to support

1. See above, p. 283 f.

a conspiracy against the Tsar. He also had intimate contact with Kerensky which it is difficult to explain otherwise than by a masonic link, either direct or through the military masonic organisation presided over by Count Orlov-Davydov.

It is clear that none of these sources could have given Grand Duke Michael adequate advice about possible developments in Russia, and about the balance of power and influence among the political groups which had emerged from the turmoil of events in the capital. But he certainly felt that at any moment he might be called upon to make a decision on which his own fate and that of his country and his relatives depended. He spent the day in Princess Putyatin's flat in considerable agitation. Neighbouring houses and flats were attacked by the mob, who carried out arrests and indulged in looting. On 1 or 2 March, a detachment from an officers' training corps was sent to Millionnaya Street to protect the person of the Grand Duke. The young officers also maintained contact with the Duma and reported on happenings there. It is highly probable that the Grand Duke had been informed of the departure of the Duma emissaries to Pskov, and he must have been informed by Rodzyanko of the result of their mission as soon as the news had reached him. The telegram of the ex-Emperor addressed to 'His Majesty the Emperor' in which Nicholas II apologised for not having consulted his brother before abdicating in his favour seems never to have been delivered. Thus when Kerensky called him by telephone at 5.55 a.m. on 3 March and asked whether the Grand Duke would receive the Provisional Government, (or as it was then still called, the Council of Ministers) the same morning, this was his first intimation that he would almost immediately have to come to decisions imposed on him by the accident of his birth. It remains unclear why it was Kerensky who was the first to get in touch with him at that early hour, which was about two hours before the Duma delegates were due to return from Pskov with the instrument of abdication.

The members of the government began to arrive at 12 Millionnaya from ten o'clock onwards. They had deliberated on what advice to give to the Grand Duke, and had found that there were irreconcilable differences of opinion. The majority, including the chairman of the Duma Committee, Rodzyanko, who had by that time somewhat recovered from his fright of the previous evening, and was watchfully defending the authority of the Duma Committee and the legitimacy of

the Provisional Government created by it, was not in favour of the
Grand Duke ascending the throne. Kerensky was most emphatic in
saying that this solution would be unacceptable to the Petrograd
workers and would lead to civil war. The minority, that is Milyukov
and probably Shingarev, who supported him, as well as the absent
Guchkov were in favour of his immediate accession to the throne, if
necessary in the face of opposition from the Petrograd mobs. It was
agreed that one speaker only from each side should put his arguments
to the Grand Duke, who would then be free to make his decision.
After that, the conflicting parties pledged themselves not to impede
their opponents in establishing a new administration. It was proposed
that those whose advice was not followed by the Grand Duke should
resign from the government and allow the remaining members of the
government to reconstitute it on a new basis.

The meeting at Millionnaya Street was quite informal. After a certain
number of members of the government and of the Duma Committee
had assembled, the Grand Duke came out to hear what they had to say:
Shulgin and Guchkov did not arrive in time for the beginning of the
meeting. They had got back from Pskov, but had been delayed at the
station, where Shulgin read the manifesto to the crowd and proclaimed
a hurrah for Emperor Michael, while Guchkov went to give the news
to workers in the station depot workshop. There some incident
must have taken place, and Guchkov was for a time prevented from
leaving by the workers, who wanted to seize the act of abdication and
destroy it. We must remember, however, that this was the fifth day
since the mutiny of the Petrograd garrison, and the nervous tension of
all those who were taking an active part in the events had reached
breaking-point. Eye-witness reports of one and the same event tend
to diverge even more than they did on the last days of February. It
does not seem that Guchkov ran any personal danger at the hands of the
railwaymen at the North-Western Station, nor was the act of abdication destroyed, but it does seem that the workers made it quite clear
to Guchkov that they were opposed to Michael's candidature. In any
case, the tribulations of the Duma delegates at the station considerably
delayed their arrival for the negotiations at Princess Putyatin's flat.
This was of course their own fault. It was another instance of the undisciplined sensation-mongering behaviour of people whom one would
have expected to have shown better sense, at a moment when supreme

caution and self-control were necessary. Neither Shulgin nor Guchkov had any business making proclamations to the crowd before the manifesto had been ratified in a formal way and published by the Senate.

When they arrived at the Putyatin flat, the Duma delegates looked tired, unkempt and scruffy, and took little part in the deliberations. Shulgin's vivid account of the proceedings is particularly unreliable. The first to speak in the presence of the Grand Duke was Rodzyanko. He later explained that

> it was quite clear to us that the Grand Duke would have reigned only a few hours, and that this would have led to colossal bloodshed in the precincts of the capital, which would have degenerated into general civil war. It was clear to us that the Grand Duke would have been killed immediately, together with all his adherents, for he had no reliable troops at his disposal then, and could not sustain himself by armed support. The Grand Duke asked me outright whether I could guarantee his life if he acceded to the throne, and I had to answer in the negative.[1]

Rodzyanko was followed by Milyukov, who did not try to disguise the difficulty of the situation, but explained that to consolidate the new order one needed a strong government, and a strong government would have to be supported by a symbol which was familiar to the masses. Such a symbol was the monarchy. Without it, the Provisional Government would not live to see the opening of the Constituent Assembly. It would be a frail craft which would sink in the ocean of popular turmoil. Milyukov's speech must have been rather forceful, for contrary to the preliminary agreement a general debate ensued, in which he played the leading part. This is how Shulgin, who came in at the end of Milyukov's speech, described the scene:

> It looked like filibustering. Milyukov seemed unwilling, or unable, or afraid to stop talking. This man, usually so polite and self-controlled, did not let anybody else speak, interrupted those who tried to answer him, cut off Rodzyanko, Kerensky and others. . . . With snow-white hair, his face purple from sleepless nights, having lost his voice making speeches in barracks and at street meetings, he croaked and wheezed.

Quoting this passage from Shulgin, Milyukov comments:

But of course Shulgin exaggerated somewhat. There was nevertheless a

1. *ARR*, VI, p. 61 f.

system in my croaking. I was amazed that my opponents, instead of producing arguments of principle, had started intimidating the Grand Duke. I saw that Rodzyanko was still in a blue funk. The others were also frightened by what was happening. All this was so petty in comparison with the importance of the moment. I admitted that my opponents may have been right. Perhaps indeed those present and the Grand Duke himself were in danger. But we were playing for high stakes--for the whole of Russia—and we had to take a risk, however great it was.[1]

Milyukov's plan was to leave Petrograd by motor-car and transfer the capital to Moscow, where the garrison was maintaining discipline and the revolution had taken place without mob violence.

As this pointless wrangle went on, the Grand Duke began to show signs of impatience. When reconstructing this fantastic episode, and trying to assess the motives of the proud and obstinate man who found himself in these unusual circumstances, we must try to understand what must have struck him most in the scene which was now being enacted before him. Here were the people who had for years opposed the rule of his brother and had at last, after an almost unprecedented campaign of slander and vilification, created the most favourable conditions for the Emperor's downfall. They had now formed a team which was to become his – the Grand Duke's – government: some of them were to be his advisers in a struggle for which he was fitted neither by training nor by inclination. The picture which these people presented, their choice of arguments and the manner in which these were brought forward must have been profoundly repulsive to him. This would be a more plausible explanation of his renunciation than the usual one that he feared for his own skin. All the evidence of his previous life seems to indicate that he was a man of considerable physical courage, and was always ready to take a risk. After the debates had lasted for over two hours without his saying a word, the Grand Duke declared that he wanted to retire and consult only two of those present, Rodzyanko and Prince Lvov. The proposal caused embarrassment. Rodzyanko pointed out that they had agreed to act collectively, to which the Grand Duke replied that he had difficulty in coming to a decision because of the lack of unanimity among the members of the Duma. And so it was agreed, with Kerensky acquiescing, that the Grand Duke could consult

1. Milyukov, *Vospominaniya*, Vol. II, p. 317.

Rodzyanko and Prince Lvov in private (or Rodzyanko alone, according to some of the witnesses), and then announce his decision.

About half an hour later, the Grand Duke came out and stated that his final choice was in accordance with the opinion expressed by the President of the Duma. According to Shulgin, he could not finish his announcement because of tears. This seems rather improbable, and the tears must have been those which were choking the over-emotional Shulgin himself. Kerensky jumped up and rushed to the Grand Duke, declaring impulsively: 'Your Highness, you are a noble man. I shall always assert this from now on' (which did not prevent Kerensky, four months later, from ordering the arrest of Grand Duke Michael on the most flimsy and totally disproved evidence of counter-revolutionary machinations). Guchkov and Milyukov left immediately after this, the Grand Duke having thanked Milyukov for his patriotic behaviour. They decided to support the new government, but not to take part in it. Milyukov went straight to bed and slept like a log. Five hours later he was woken up by a delegation from the central committee of the Kadet Party which came to persuade him not to resign from the government. He does not seem to have needed much persuading.

It was only after everything had been decided that someone thought of asking some expert lawyers to produce a document which would translate into legal terms the actual state of affairs that had now come about.

3. THE PLENITUDE OF POWER

When the Kadet V. D. Nabokov and the specialist in constitutional law Baron Nolde arrived, they were shown a document which in his foresight the Minister of Railways, Nekrasov, had already drawn up, announcing the abdication. It became the basis for the final act, the essence of which was expressed in the words:

> I have taken a firm decision to accept supreme power only if this is the will of our great people, whose right it is to establish the form of government and the new basic laws of the Russian state by universal suffrage through its representatives in the Constituent Assembly.
>
> Therefore, invoking the blessing of God, I request all citizens of the Russian state to obey the Provisional Government, which came into

being on the initiative of the State Duma and is vested with all the plenitude of power, until such time as the Constituent Assembly, to be convened in as short a time as possible on the basis of universal, direct, equal and secret voting, shall express the will of the people by its decision on the form of the government.

There was much arguing and 'improving' of this text throughout the afternoon until late at night. Originally, the Provisional Government was described as having arisen 'by the will of the people'. To this Kerensky raised objections. Of course the people had nothing to do with the formation of a government of representatives of the property-owning classes. Then the words 'on the initiative of the State Duma' were added, on which Rodzyanko particularly insisted. They were blatantly misleading. The Duma had never deliberated on and never agreed to the formation of the Provisional Government, whatever its so-called committee, appointed by the unofficial steering committee known as the 'Senioren Convent', might have done. But in the eyes of Rodzyanko it was a recognition of his part as government-maker, and he insisted on it. Kerensky then agreed to leave in 'the will of the people' if it was combined with 'the initiative of the Duma', but in the process of further haggling 'the will of the people' finally disappeared. The traditional reference to the Almighty was introduced at the request of the Grand Duke himself. This new document, by introducing the concept of a Constituent Assembly, took the process of 'revolutionising' the state structure a stage further. The idea of a Constituent Assembly and of the four-point formula for the elections to it were familiar from the statements made in the last few days. Both Milyukov and Kerensky had mentioned them in their speeches the previous day. It was however the first time that the formula had been mentioned in a State Act. But the most important effect of the Grand Duke's abdication was the peculiar position in which the Provisional Government found itself as a result. It ceased to be the executive branch of a comprehensive government apparatus responsible either to the monarch or to parliament. By a supreme irony, the abolition of the monarchy was thus accompanied by the virtual abolition of the rudimentary parliamentary institutions which had contributed so much to its downfall. The Duma prorogued by the imperial decree of 27 February was never summoned again, and so the Provisional Government had indeed become the seat of supreme power, of executive power and legislative power as well.

With all that, it completely lacked stability; members of it were free to resign, or they could be elbowed out by their colleagues and others co-opted in their place. In other words, with the abdication of the Grand Duke anarchy set in at the very centre of state power – in the Provisional Government itself. No wonder that years later, in analysing the situation which arose out of the act of 3 March, the right-wing Kadet lawyer, Vasily Maklakov, who had been left out of the Provisional Government at an early stage, could write:[1]

> The new Emperor Michael, before accepting the throne, called the Duma Committee and the government appointed by it to discuss the situation with them. This was a decisive moment. It would have been understandable if this gathering had criticised the act of abdication [of Nicholas II] as insufficient and demanded further guarantees against a return to the past. This question, however, did not even arise. The representatives of the Duma advised the Grand Duke to abdicate in his turn. Yielding to their demands, he signed a strange and criminal manifesto, which he would have had no right to sign even had he been a monarch. Contrary to the constitution, and without the agreement of the Duma, he declared the throne vacant until a constituent assembly was convened. By his own authority, he established the mode of election to this assembly, and, pending its election, he transferred, with complete disregard for the Duma and the constitution, the powers of an absolute monarch, which he himself did not possess, to a Provisional Government, which, as he put it, had been formed 'on the initiative of the Duma'. . . . One would be justified in considering this manifesto an act of lunacy or treason had not the authors been qualified and patriotic lawyers.

And Maklakov declares that the ensuing anarchy imposed from above became in the eyes of the government the justification of its own attitude: it had itself disrupted the constitutional order, and then came to the conclusion that it was beyond human power to maintain it. The government believed that it was impossible to fight, for no other reason than that it had itself deserted the field.

The 'qualified and patriotic' lawyers, Baron B. E. Nolde and V. D. Nabokov, have several times given their reasons for composing this document. Of course, their task was limited to formulating a decision

1. B. Maklakoff [V. Maklakov]. Preface to *La Chute du Régime Tsariste – Interrogatoires*. *Collection de mémoires pour servir à l'histoire de la guerre mondiale* (Paris, 1927), p. 12 f.

which had been taken without their participation. And yet they admit themselves that they went further than that. As they were considering the final text, they came to the conclusion, writes Nabokov,[1] that the situation with which they were faced should be treated as follows:

> Michael refused to accept supreme power. Properly speaking, this should have been the main legally valid point of the manifesto. In the given circumstances, however, it seemed necessary, not limiting oneself to its negative aspects, to take advantage of this manifesto in order to stress solemnly the plenitude of power of the Provisional Government and its succession and link with the State Duma in the eyes of that part of the population for whom this manifesto might have had serious moral significance. This was done by including the words 'the Provisional Government, which came into being on the initiative of the State Duma, and is vested with all the plenitude of power ... '. In this case we were mainly concerned not with the legal validity of the formula but only with its moral-political significance. And we must point out that the manifesto of abdication signed by Michael was the only act which defined the scope of the Provisional Government's powers and solved the question of its mode of functioning, specifically and mainly the question of the further activities of the legislative institutions.

And Nabokov points out quite rightly that on the previous day, 2 March, in the announcement of the formation of the Provisional Government, the latter was described merely as a more stable executive power than the temporary committee of members of the Duma, and as a government of persons who had gained the confidence of the country by their past political and public activities. Now, however, the new manifesto endowed the Provisional Government with full powers to legislate. As the other 'qualified and patriotic lawyer' explained, the act of 3 March was essentially the constitution of the Provisional Government. It would have been possible, Nolde claims, to carry on with this constitution until the convocation of the Constituent Assembly, but only, of course, if the Provisional Government had effectively exercised the full powers thereby conferred on it.

It is curious that Maklakov and Nabokov, who were both members of the central committee of the Kadet Party, had the same legal training, and belonged to the same right wing of their party, should take such

1. *ARR*, I, p. 21.

completely different views of an event on the facts of which they were in complete agreement. For it was the extension of the powers of the Provisional Government to comprise legislation that Maklakov described as criminal, lunatic and treacherous, whereas for Nabokov the inclusion of this point was something of which he and Nolde could be proud:

> For us at that moment, in the very first days of the revolution, when it was still completely unknown how the whole of Russia and the foreign allied powers would react to the change of régime, to the formation of the Provisional Government and to the whole new situation, every word [of the manifesto] seemed of infinite importance, and I believe that we were right.[1]

After that, the formula 'vested with all the plenitude of power' became a set phrase which was to be repeated *ad nauseam* in all official pronouncements and state acts. But no amount of repetition, of course, could provide the missing legal and factual foundation for this empty phrase. It was never made clear by what right the small committee of constantly changing personalities who called themselves the Provisional Government issued laws binding on the country and its armed forces. The Provisional Government, having given up the idea of basing its legitimacy on a symbolic transfer of power by Nicholas II, could never bring itself to follow Kerensky's advice and base its claim to power on revolutionary legitimacy, that is, on acclamation by the revolutionary crowds of the capital. This fundamental constitutional weakness was never remedied by the contention that power would be used only for securing the convocation of the Constituent Assembly, the 'real master of the Russian land', as it was always grandiloquently described. To ensure democratic elections to the Constituent Assembly it was argued that certain preliminary alterations in the laws of the country were necessary, such as the abolition of national and class legal limitations and the introduction of local administration (Zemstvos) in the villages. But the Provisional Government went much further in its legislative activities. It finally dissolved the Duma altogether and proclaimed the country a republic, without awaiting the decision of the Constituent Assembly. And the more the government legislated, the less its laws and decrees were actually observed, so that the appeal of a local radical

1. *ARR*, I, p. 22.

or Bolshevik paper would have greater effect than the acts passed by the government 'vested with all the plenitude of power'. Nabokov's and Nolde's apologia for their doings on that afternoon of 3 March amounts in fact to the all too common excuse that there was nothing else they could do. And they are certainly right in claiming that they acted to the best of their ability under circumstances of extreme stress.

The abrupt changes of mood of all concerned in the events of that day are noted by Nabokov. It took him and Nolde quite a few hours to produce the short text of Grand Duke Michael's abdication. Surprisingly, there were no feelings of doom or apprehension for the future while they were writing the text in the Millionnaya flat. On the contrary, Nabokov reports a feeling of elation (*likovanie*). This suddenly changed to dark foreboding when Nabokov, arriving in the evening at the Tauride Palace with the text of the document, learned of the massacre of officers which had taken place in Helsingfors, and of the threatening situation at the front. The dark foreboding is easier to understand than the elation which preceded it. Nabokov remarks that it was immediately felt that the murders were due to German agitation, and goes on to say: 'To what extent the hand of the Germans had taken an active part in our revolution is a question which I suppose will never receive a complete and exhaustive answer.' Now, almost fifty years later, we need not be as pessimistic as Nabokov on the latter point. But of course, the rumours of German involvement in the events, rumours which arose spontaneously when the news of the massacres in the Baltic Fleet reached the capital, could not then have been based on any tangible evidence. We must rather suppose that the gruesome events in Helsingfors and Kronstadt appeared to be so much at variance with the prevailing mood in the capital that they were naturally and spontaneously explained as something alien to the spirit of the 'Great Bloodless Russian Revolution', as deliberate and malevolent interference by an implacable and deadly enemy.

In the Tauride Palace, Nabokov met Milyukov, whose resolve to resign from the new government must already have been weakened during his interview, on awakening from his afternoon sleep, with other members of the central committee of his party. Milyukov seems to have reconciled himself with his failure to arrest the course of the revolution and to save the monarchy at the eleventh hour. He even seems to have approved of the draft of Michael's abdication manifesto. As a result of the changed mood on the evening of 3 March, the Cabinet, now transformed by this document into a Provisional Government which had assumed the powers of the autocratic Emperor of Russia as they existed before Nicholas's abdication, remained intact, with Milyukov and Guchkov retaining the posts originally assigned to them. However, their behaviour at the morning meeting with Grand Duke Michael was not forgotten, and it was given wide publicity throughout the country. It was an easy demagogic trick to denounce them after that as counter-revolutionaries. Milyukov's position in the Cabinet which he had to a large extent chosen himself was badly shaken, and he never managed to regain influence. The decisive influence in the new government was now that of Kerensky, the only member of it who could claim to be a representative of the revolutionary movement. He was supported by his masonic friends, including the 'traitor' Nekrasov.

16

Conclusions

'Was there a revolution?'; Spontaneity; Conspiracies, real and imaginary; Fomenting or forestalling the revolution; 'The aide-de-camp generals' revolution'.

1. 'WAS THERE A REVOLUTION?'

With the renunciation of the throne by Grand Duke Michael and the publication of the document which formed the constitutional basis for the Provisional Government for the next eight months, what is known as the February Revolution in Russia, that is the transition from the autocracy of Nicholas II to the dictatorship of the Provisional Government, was completed. From the point of view of liberals of the type of Milyukov or Maklakov or Nolde, the revolution had taken place and was finished. For revolutionaries of the type of Kerensky, however, it had hardly begun.

The question whether there was a February Revolution in Russia in 1917 is, therefore, not entirely whimsical, except perhaps for people who might think of it as a question of the type: 'Was there a blizzard in Petrograd in February 1917?' This can be answered in the indicative mood, and would express a matter of fact. A simple 'yes' or 'no' to the question: 'Was there a revolution?' is not of the same character as a 'yes' or 'no' to the question: 'Was there a blizzard?'. It does not tell us whether certain events took place or not, but rather what the person answering felt about them, i.e. whether he believed that his political hopes and aspirations (or perhaps fears and apprehensions) had been fulfilled by what had happened, or not. It expresses a deep-seated emotional attitude towards the surrounding political and social realities of the time rather than the momentary state of jubilation which affected almost everybody at that moment. The almost universal elation which followed the announcement of the two abdications and of the formation of the Provisional Government, and which spread all over Russia (so that the Tsar's ADC Governor-General in Tashkent,

Kuropatkin, could describe his feelings in almost the same terms as the SR intellectual Zenzinov in Petrograd) by no means reflected a uniform attitude to the February events. For many it was a sign of relief that the whole business had not ended in massacre; while for others it was an expression of joy at the prospect of things to come. The latter confidently expected that the masses of the people, freed from their age-old shackles, were about to play their part, not only in Russia but also in the political life of humanity at large, in particular in international affairs. It is therefore misleading to say that people accepted or welcomed the February revolution of 1917. What they accepted and welcomed they often had not had the opportunity to formulate or think about articulately. Without an analysis in depth of such emotional attitudes, we cannot understand the peculiar, dream-like terminology of revolutionary pronouncements concerning the 'defence of the conquests of the revolution', the appeals for 'a deepening of the revolution', etc. etc. But this was not part of our task in writing this book. This belongs to the sad and tragic history of the Provisional Government of Russia, which began on 4 March 1917 and ended on 26 October with its arrest and the seizure of power by Lenin and his henchmen.

But it must be said that the same emotionalism seriously affected the perception of events by those who were closest to them in the February days. When Prince Lvov, Rodzyanko or Milyukov claimed in the announcement which they signed jointly on 2 March that the Provisional Committee of the State Duma had won a victory over the dark forces of the old régime, with the assistance [sic] and the sympathy of the capital's garrison and population, they must have known very well that as a statement of fact this was simply not true. And yet the statement fairly reflects their desire to become the leading factor in the popular rising, which they had neither initiated nor directed until the crowds of workers, soldiers and intelligentsia beleaguered and invaded the Tauride Palace and demanded to be heard, harangued, organised and made use of politically. It took some years for Milyukov to moderate the effects of revolutionary phrase-mongering on his historical analysis. In his *History of the Russian Revolution*, written in the spring and summer of 1918, he still claimed that it was the Duma that had deposed the monarchy. Years later he corrected this statement, but it would obviously have taken him many more years to free his historical thinking of the influence of the political jargon which dominated his mind in February 1917. Possibly this is beyond human powers in general, although another historian of the Russian revolution, S. P. Melgunov, more conscious of the dangers facing an eye-witness who writes history, came very near to freeing himself completely from such influences and to dealing objectively with such pseudo-factual statements as: 'The revolution became victorious in the Petrograd streets late in the evening of 27 February'. He has done splendid work in clarifying and exposing the origins of many a legend. But even he clings to one fatal misconception about the revolution which unfortunately has conquered the imagination of Western historians of the revolution as well, and which it is particularly important to clear up: this is the notion of the 'spontaneity' of the Russian revolution which has been the point of departure for many histories of it.

2. SPONTANEITY

Paradoxically, those who regarded the February events as the fulfilment of their prophecies of revolution disclaimed both the responsibility and the honour of bringing them about. This applies in particular to the revolutionary parties, including the few Bolsheviks then active underground in Russia. It was their denials on this score which prompted the theory of the *spontaneous* nature of the February revolution. Thus in a passage introducing his account of the events of 1917, in his book *The Bolshevik Revolution 1917–1923*, E. H. Carr writes:

> The February Revolution of 1917 which overthrew the Romanov dynasty was the spontaneous outbreak of a multitude exasperated by the privations of the war and by manifest inequality in the distribution of burdens. It was welcomed and utilized by a broad stratum of the bourgeoisie and of the official class, which had lost confidence in the autocratic system of government and especially in the persons of the Tsar and of his advisers; it was from this section of the population that the first Provisional Government was drawn. The revolutionary parties played no direct part in the making of the revolution. They did not expect it, and were at first somewhat nonplussed by it.

We agree with Carr about the passive attitude of the revolutionary parties in February 1917. But does this justify his assumption of

a spontaneous mass movement, i.e. one not instigated from outside?

The Russian word 'stikhiyny', of which – in this context – 'spontaneous' is the translation, suggests to an even greater degree than its
English counterpart that the 'exasperations and privations' suffered by
the masses during the war led to the degree of cohesion and purpose-
fulness necessary for effective political action. 'Spontaneous' in Carr's
context indicates an inherent tendency – a predisposition – of the
masses to react to such grievances as 'a manifest inequality of the
distribution of burdens' by organised mass demonstrations on the scale
of the Petrograd rising. Had such a disposition for concerted and
deliberate action existed, it would have manifested itself in some
perceptible way in other parts of Russia, where there was exactly the
same inequality in the distribution of burdens. Moreover, had such
inherent tendencies really existed among the Petrograd proletariat, they
would surely have led to the same purposeful and coordinated action
among the workers in the months subsequent to the revolution as
well. In fact what we observe during the war, apart from Petrograd
and perhaps one or two other industrial centres, is precisely the absence
of any disposition among the working masses for sustained and purposeful political action, just as in the months following the revolution we
see no sign of any such inherent tendency in the Petrograd population
as a whole. The assumption that there was a particular quality of
'spontaneity' which explains the scope and strength of the February
demonstrations in Petrograd is wholly gratuitous. The theory of
'spontaneity' only serves to cover up our ignorance.

3. CONSPIRACIES, REAL AND IMAGINARY

Several explanations less negative than the notion of 'spontaneity' have
been advanced for the success of the rising. We may instance three of
these.

According to the first theory, the rising could be attributed largely
to a satanic plan of the Tsarist police under Protopopov. He is supposed
to have played the same trick as his predecessor Durnovo, who was
alleged to have provoked the workers' rebellion of 1905 in order to
suppress it by military force. This idea is linked with the legend of the

Protopopov machine-guns, said to have been mounted on the roofs of Petrograd houses to mow down workers' demonstrations. We have already commented on this tenacious legend. No demonstrators were, of course, mown down by machine-gun fire from the house-tops during the February days. The number of casualties resulting from what Lenin described as 'a week of bloody battles between workers and the Tsarist police' was relatively small if one considers the many hundreds of thousands of people involved, and most of these casualties can be put down to the few clashes that took place between the military and the crowd from 26 to 28 February. The Protopopov machine-guns never existed. With them vanishes the whole story of police provocation as a major causative factor in the Petrograd demonstrations.

This is not to say that the police were not equipped for provocation. The various revolutionary committees were penetrated and were kept under observation, and to some extent under control. But the plans of the Minister of the Interior for using the apparatus of police control in workers' circles were quite different from what this theory assumes. Protopopov, through his agents, did encourage among the workers of the WICs extremist, indeed defeatist, ideas on the pattern of the resolutions of the Zimmerwald and Kienthal Conferences. But this he did in order to strike – when the time was ripe – at the WICs themselves. He thought that defeatist propaganda among the workers would reflect on the leadership of the WICs as a whole and discredit it in the eyes of the public. There was no plan to bring the workers out on the streets and the police was not prepared for such an eventuality. On the contrary, the Ministry of the Interior dreaded the thought of casualties on the streets of Petrograd.

Indirectly, however, the action of the Minister of the Interior did contribute to the outbreak of these demonstrations. By arresting the leaders of the Labour Group of the WICs he removed the very people who, in February 1916, had succeeded in halting the strike movement in Petrograd. Deprived of the authority and guidance of the Mensheviks in the Labour Group and goaded to further impatience by their arrest, the working masses became even more susceptible to strike propaganda from whatever quarter it might come.

Some students of the February revolution incline to believe that it was brought about by the very circles which pressed for constitutional reform, when they despaired of achieving their aim through legal political means. This school of thought holds that the Petrograd rising was precipitated and facilitated by their wholesale denunciation of the imperial government, and in particular of the Tsar, his family, and his closest advisers. There is little evidence to support this view, although general considerations make it less fantastic than might at first appear. The rivalry between the government and the liberal circles for power had reached its climax. The liberals, whose political aspirations had once been favoured by the fortunes (or rather misfortunes) of war, were beginning to lose ground. Should victory, with Allied help, be won during 1917 all their forecasts would be disproved, and it would be easy for the government to turn the tables on them.

But here again the 'conspiratorial' explanation for the Petrograd rising fails. Not only is there no evidence of any liberal group appealing directly to the workers to strike; but there is proof that they had made preparations for direct political action unconnected with the mass rising in Petrograd, and which were actually forestalled by it. Guchkov and his friends had worked out a complete plan for a palace coup, which would have put him in power in circumstances far more favourable from his point of view than those in which he became minister after the rising. The coup was planned for the middle of March, but the February events took its organisers by surprise. This project, like others of its kind, was in itself incompatible with a popular rising of the sort that actually took place. But, albeit indirectly and unintentionally, the plotting of the palace coup promoted the success of the mass movement. By stepping up their anti-government propaganda, reinforcing popular rumours of treason in high places, whipping up mass hysteria and directing it against the 'German woman' and the Tsar, liberal circles both in the Duma and the Voluntary Organisations had built up among the newspaper-reading public an atmosphere of such unbearable tension that the fall of the autocratic régime was welcomed like a cleansing thunderstorm.

Guchkov must have contributed in an even more direct way to the success of the popular rising. As we have seen, a military demonstration by units of the Petrograd garrison was part of his plan. This demonstration was to support a new government of 'popular confidence', and was to neutralise any resistance by the old régime, after the Tsar had been forced to sign the act of abdication, or its equivalent, at some obscure stop on the railway line between Petrograd and Mogilev. The involvement of some of the officers of the Petrograd garrison in the plot may well have undermined the morale of the whole officer corps there. When — on 26–27 February — the moment came to give, receive and execute battle orders, many of the officers were not quite sure which side they were on. The fall of Nicholas II was about to take place, but under circumstances so different from those expected that the officers were in a quandary as to what to do. The success of the military rising in Petrograd was due in large measure to their vacillation and absence from barracks at the critical juncture. Hence the Guchkov plot did contribute to the *success* of the Petrograd rising, but we cannot on that account regard it as a *cause* of the mass movement.

As for the third 'conspiratorial' theory of the Petrograd rising, we have lent this throughout our unreserved support, more particularly in the chapter on German intervention. The belief that German agents were behind it is as old as the events themselves — indeed older, for the Russian government had suspected and indeed known of the German wartime influence on the labour movement in Russia long before the Petrograd rising.[1] But only in the last ten years or so have certain revelations tended to corroborate these suspicions. We know now for certain that from the very beginning of the war the German government consistently pursued in Russia a *Revolutionierungspolitik*, an essential element of which was the support of an economic strike movement capable, so it was hoped, of gradually escalating into a political revolution. The chief theoretician of this policy, Alexander Helphand, thought the country ripe for revolution as early as 1916. We know for certain that the German government expended considerable sums on fostering the strike movement up to the spring of 1916. For most of 1916 and the beginning of 1917, we lack evidence of direct instigation of labour unrest in Russia by the German agencies. It would, however, be foolish to ignore the existence of such agencies as a factor contributing to the revolution of 1917, which took precisely the form predicted by Helphand as early as the spring of 1915. It seems reasonable either to suggest that the successful popular rising of February 1917 was organised by the same agents as instigated the abortive 'trial run' the previous February or to assume that it was a direct sequel to the movement begun in 1916.

1. See above, p. 93.

A political revolution entailing the fall of the Tsarist régime was the maximum the Germans could hope for in organising and backing Russian labour unrest during the war. The disruption of the war effort brought about by frequent and prolonged strikes was regarded by them as sufficient justification in itself for the support they gave Helphand and similar agents. The revolution came as a windfall much hoped for by some, but hardly expected by any, and necessitated a radical revision of German policy. The problem was now not so much to weaken Russia as an opponent as to effect a separate peace. Again on Helphand's suggestion, the Germans decided the best way to achieve this result would be to bring to power the Bolshevik Party, which alone among major political groups in the new Russia was prepared to conclude an immediate armistice. The dislocation of production could also safely be left to the Bolsheviks, who would effect it as part of the class war. Military sabotage, which Helphand always linked with his strike propaganda, continued to be organised by special German agents trained for work of this kind. But the tenuous and highly conspiratorial links connecting Helphand with the Russian strike movement could now be safely severed, and all record of them be erased. This explains why so little documentary evidence of these links exists.

4. FOMENTING OR FORESTALLING THE REVOLUTION

The popular rising and the mutiny of the Petrograd garrison resulted in the bloodless collapse of the monarchy only because, as Carr rightly says, liberal circles had decided to exploit them so as to gain their own ends of radical political change. The seditious mass movement originally confined to the capital might by itself have led only to a civil war the outcome of which would have been as questionable as that of the 1905 revolution. Liberal circles, however, did not decide to make use of the popular movement in order to seize power and form a Provisional Government until it became obvious that the Tsarist government could not quell the rising with the troops available in the capital.

For months, indeed for years, by their campaign to denounce and discredit autocracy they had systematically, if unintentionally, paved the way for the success of this rising, and for the country's acquiescence in the fall of the autocracy. There were two aspects to this campaign: one was the historiosophic assumption that autocracy as a form of government was obsolete, and doomed to disappear in Russia, as it had in the other Western countries. The liberals believed that in accordance with some inexorable law of history a modern society, such as Russian society after 1905, would change from an autocracy into a constitutional monarchy, wherein power would first be transferred to the educated and property-owning classes and then, in a process of gradual democratisation, to the people as a whole. Experience of the Soviet régime in the last fifty years has taught us that there was no foundation either for the analogy with West European monarchies or for the belief that autocracy in Russia was obsolete, for autocracy persisted despite the revolution. The very fact that the three men who ruled the country autocratically for many years after 1917 had such totally different characters and backgrounds merely reinforces the view that there are profound reasons why one-man political control could be so easily established and maintained in Russia. The fact that the principle of hereditary succession has been replaced by the elimination of rival successors through political slander and judicial murder in no way affects the issue. To say so is not to give moral sanction to autocracy. It would-be paying too great a tribute to nineteenth-century evolutionist optimism to hold that the most viable political form is also the most progressive.

The liberals, as well as making the gratuitous assumption that autocracy was destined to make way for a process of gradual democratisation, justified their demands for an immediate change of régime (war or no war) by levelling at the Tsarist administration countless charges of inertia, ineptitude, inefficacy, arbitrariness and corruption. We have refrained from assessing the degree of justification of these complaints; this does not amount to a denial of the shortcomings of the Tsarist administration. These were obvious, and were comparable to the muddles and abuses of wartime administration in other belligerent countries. But they may be discounted as a revolutionising factor, since the liberals' main line of attack on the régime was not to expose its traditional and its newly-acquired vices and weaknesses, but to declare it incapable of coping with wartime problems so long as it remained autocratic. Not only was absolutism, they claimed, leading the country to disaster through inefficiency: it had, so the liberals alleged, no desire or determination to lead it to victory. That treason was being committed in high places and a shameful separate peace prepared — this became a liberal article of faith and a recurrent propaganda theme developed in the press, at congresses of the Voluntary Organisations and in the Duma itself. This conviction was so strong and so ingrained in the minds of those called upon to play a decisive part in the 1917 drama that it outlived many other delusions. In fact, it became a main-stay of those apologists who, horrified at the consequences of their decisions and actions, sought some kind of justification for them. Thus, with reference to the mounting influence of dark irresponsible forces over the will and judgment of the Tsar in the last days of the monarchy, Rodzyanko[1] wrote in 1919:

> The influence of Rasputin on the whole circle which surrounded the Empress Alexandra Feodorovna, and through her on the whole policy of the Supreme Power and of the government, increased to unprecedented dimensions. I claim unreservedly that this circle was indubitably under the influence of our enemy and served the interests of Germany . . . I at least have personally no doubt as to the inter-connection of the German Staff and Rasputin: there can be no doubt about it.

There can be no doubt about the sad delusion of the ex-President of the Duma. There never was anything like a Rasputin circle or a con-centration of 'dark irresponsible forces' of the type pictured by him. Rasputin's hold over the Empress was certainly not to be under-estimated, but neither he nor the Empress herself had any circle of permanent advisers. Instead of the circle in which Rodzyanko asks us to believe there was only a squalid snake-pit, in which various reptilian figures tried to devour each other. As far as the German authorities are concerned, they seem to have been oddly slow to exploit the oppor-tunities offered them by the complex intrigues of these creatures.

And yet it was this legend of a powerful clique of pro-German 'dark forces', and not the many proven and documented shortcomings of the government and the High Command, which was used as a lever by the liberals to undermine traditional allegiance to the monarch. It is difficult to believe that people who had access to so much information could in all honesty give credence to the rumours of treason in high places. But such an attitude is quite consistent with the sort of fantasies in which the Russian political opposition had indulged since the turn of the century.

1. *ARR*, VI, op. cit., p. 44.

As it became increasingly clear that the attempt of the Progressive Bloc of the Duma and of their allies, the Voluntary Organisations, to seize power by persuading the Tsar to surrender his prerogative to appoint ministers was about to fail, the exasperation of liberal circles assumed a hysterical character. It was a question of giving up a political struggle which had been going on for almost a generation, and submitting to the discipline of a society based on personal allegiance to the monarch, or else of breaking this allegiance and giving support to a violent *coup d'état*. The first alternative was rendered the more difficult because anyone advocating it was immediately denounced as a time-server and a traitor to the cause of progress. The second alternative needed a moral justification difficult to find for a mere struggle for power, which in any case appeared unpatriotic in wartime. The story of treason in high places, with sinister hints at the participation of the Empress in pro-German machinations, provided this justification and lent a patriotic lustre to what in fact was a struggle for power in home politics. This is why, instead of attacking the real shortcomings of the government, liberal circles concentrated on rumour-mongering. Such articles as V. Maklakov's 'Mad Chauffeur', and such speeches as Milyukov's broadside on 1 November 1916 in the State Duma, achieved this end to an extent which the authors possibly did not expect.

Once let loose, rumours are difficult to check, particularly in wartime. The very fact that news and information are controlled only enhances the power and increases the circulation of rumours. A hint in the press at matters which it was supposedly not allowed to mention inflamed popular imagination more than a vivid and circumstantial report. For instance, the fact that Rasputin's name was not allowed to appear in the press in the days after the assassination, so that he had to be referred to as 'the person living in Gorokhovaya Street', did more to impress the various Rasputin legends on the minds of the people than any actual accounts of his debaucheries. Much of the atmosphere saturated with hatred and slander so typical of the political life of both Russian capitals in 1916 frightened even those who were behind all this rumour-mongering.[1] No wonder that later, when the complete baselessness of most of these rumours became obvious to many, and the hysterical trance in which

1. See for instance Prince Lvov's speech mentioned above, p. 217 f., in which he said: 'Let us turn away from what is vile and contemptible. Let us not rub salt into the wounded soul of our people'.

Russian society was plunged had passed, memoirists (with the few exceptions of those writing in the Soviet Union) tended to soft-pedal these accusations and to go back to the claim that a change of government was necessary not because of the wickedness but because of the ineptitude of the monarch, his counsellors and the régime as a whole.

But how are we to believe that the sense of doom which had hung over the political scene in Russia since the autumn of 1915 was due merely to the tedious wrangle between the government and the Voluntary Organisations, each complaining that the other hampered and impeded its patriotic efforts? The Voluntary Organisations naturally resented the ban on their all-Russian congresses, and claimed that this hampered their work for the front. The government, on the other hand, answered with possibly more factual justification that any activities of the Voluntary Organisations for the front were tolerated and indeed assisted, but that the exploitation of congresses for purely political, if not directly seditious, purposes could not be allowed, especially in wartime. The sense of doom was a direct result not of this quarrel but rather of the bitterness it engendered, which led to unwarranted mutual attacks and accusations.

5. 'THE AIDE-DE-CAMP GENERALS' REVOLUTION'

As we have seen, a new element was brought into this struggle between the liberals and the government by the gradual involvement of high military circles, mainly the commanders-in-chief of the fronts. The generals, notably Alekseev, Ruzsky and Brusilov, are often accused of having conspired among themselves and with the representatives of the Voluntary Organisations to overthrow Nicholas II. In support of such allegations a statement is quoted which the Emperor is said to have made to his mother when he met her in Mogilev after the abdication. He complained that Ruzsky had adopted an insolent and threatening attitude towards him when urging him to come to a decision. Alekseev's behaviour on the eve of Nicholas II's departure from Mogilev in the early hours of 28 February roused some suspicion among the courtiers.[1] The ease with which he gave in to pressure from Rodzyanko and appealed to the other commanders-in-

1. See Voeykov, op. cit., p. 201 f. and Spiridovich, *Velikaya voyna*, vol. III, p. 177 f.

chief to support the abdication solution produced the impression of duplicity on the part of the 'cross-eyed friend' of the Emperor. There is some truth in all this, but it does not support the hypothesis of what is sometimes called the 'aide-de-camp generals' revolution'. Throughout the war, the generals adopted a strictly non-political attitude. They resisted being drawn into the struggle between the government and the liberal politicians. The reverses and retreats of 1915 had taught them, however, how precarious the supply machinery of the army was, and how easily it could be brought to a stop if the internal political situation deteriorated further. One can safely assume from the few utterances on this subject of the commanders-in-chief that they were, on the whole, against political and constitutional changes in wartime. At the same time they certainly believed that if any such changes were to become inevitable, everything should be done to ensure that they should come about smoothly, without jeopardising the arms and ammunition production, the food and fodder supplies, and the railway transport on which the fighting capacity of the army depended. If Alekseev did not denounce the Moscow plotters, this must have been not because he identified himself with their views, but because arrests and trials of members of the Voluntary Organisations on charges of sedition would certainly have adversely affected arms production and supplies. There is no definite indication that the Emperor himself knew of the existence of these plots, but the degree of his information on the political ferment in the capitals seems to have been much greater than was believed at the time by those innumerable advisers who persisted in futile attempts 'to open the eyes' of the Tsar to the real situation in Russia. It is therefore highly probable that he at least suspected the existence of some of the plots.[1] But he, like Alekseev, preferred to refrain from counter-measures until victory was assured. The aide-de-camp generals did not consider it their duty to ferret out the plotters of a palace coup. Alekseev could easily have lulled his conscience by believing that he had fully complied with his oath of allegiance when he advised the plotters to desist, without, however, denouncing them. To start a political witch-hunt and denounce the plotters to the Minister of the Interior would, it seemed to him, be to take a greater risk from the point of view of the successful prosecution of the war and of national security in general

1. In particular those hatched in Tiflis in the entourage of Grand Duke Nikolay Nikolaevich. See his remark to Prince Vsevolod Shakhovskoy, p. 215 f.

than to let events take their course. Should the palace coup succeed, the Army would have to face the new situation without having undergone a major crisis. Should it fail, those guilty would perish on the spot.

After the unrest in Petrograd had begun it was easy for Rodzyanko to convince the commanders of the fronts that the Golitsyn government could not cope with the situation. But on 1 March he went further and tried all too successfully to make them believe that if they managed to persuade the Tsar to abdicate, the Duma Committee would take matters in hand and restore order within a few days. Even so the generals, and in particular Ruzsky, showed a total lack of enthusiasm for the abdication solution to the crisis. Yet Nicholas II's consternation at Ruzsky's behaviour is understandable. As the 'ghost train' approached Pskov, those on it hoped that they were reaching a safe harbour where the magic of the imperial presence would operate. The Emperor was naturally entitled to expect that his Commander-in-Chief of the Northern Front would ask him what his immediate orders and instructions were. Instead an entirely different atmosphere greeted him on his arrival. Ruzsky took the line that the revolution had already taken place, and that there was nothing for it but to give in to the demands of the Duma, and to empower its representatives to form the new government. The personal desires and preferences of the Emperor do not even seem to have been discussed before the abdication. To raise such a question would have been tactless on the part of the generals, for the tone of the conversation was set by the Emperor with the words: 'There is no sacrifice I would not make for the sake of our Mother Russia.'

But even when the abdication had been decided upon the generals still believed that they were taking part in an action to save the monarchy and maintain the dynasty. Not until Rodzyanko raised the matter of withholding publication of the manifesto early on 3 March did the generals realise that they had been used to bring about a *coup d'état* which could not have come at a worse moment from a military point of view. Contrary to his tactics of the previous day, Rodzyanko left Ruzsky and Alekseev completely in the dark as to the negotiations concerning the abdication of Grand Duke Michael. And this with good reason. He knew that if the commanders-in-chief at the fronts had been consulted before the momentous decision to renounce the throne was taken by Michael, they would have supported Michael's candidature. As it was, the generals were faced with a *fait accompli* and found themselves discredited in the new order by having shown readiness to support a political solution which was now considered to be both retrograde and abortive.

Maps

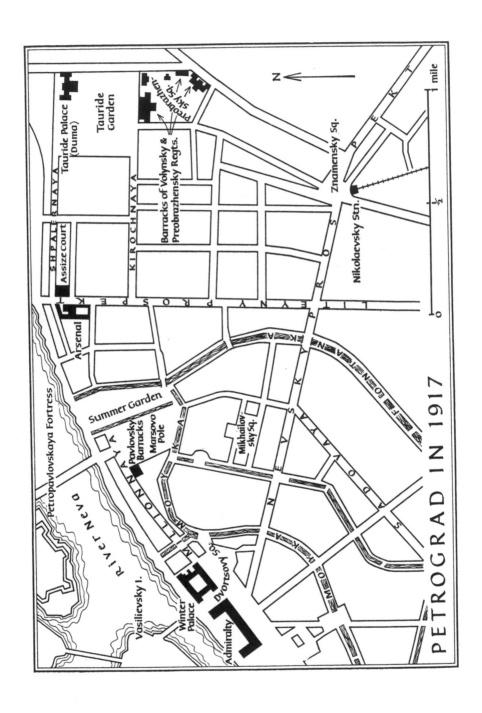

PETROGRAD IN 1917

N

1 mile

½

0

Tauride Palace
(Duma)

Tauride
Garden

Preobrazhen-
sky Sq.

Barracks of Volynsky &
Preobrazhensky Regts.

Znamensky Sq.

Nikolaevsky Stn.

S H P A L E R N A Y A

K I R O C H N A Y A

Assize Court

Arsenal

Petropavlovskaya Fortress

Summer Garden

Pavlovsky
Barracks

Marsovo
Pole

Mikhailov-
sky Sq.

River Neva

Vasilievsky I.

Winter
Palace

Admiralty

Dvortsova Sq.

L I T E I N Y   P R O S P E K T

M I L L I O N N A Y A

N E V A

N E V A

N E V S K Y

S A D O V A Y A

M O

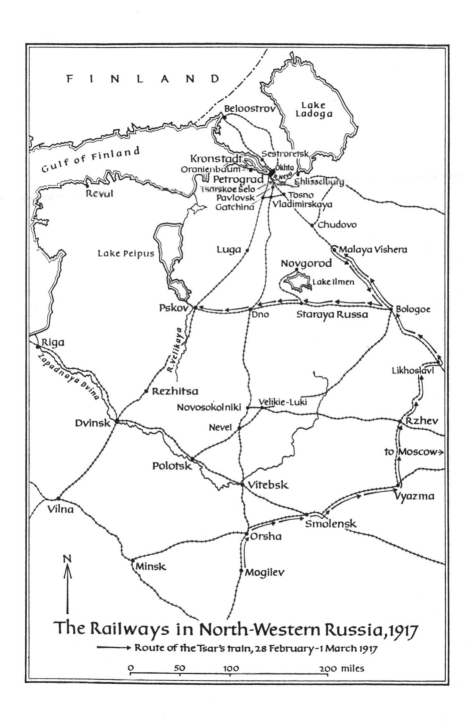

FINLAND

Gulf of Finland

Lake Ladoga

Beloostrov

Sestroretsk

Kronstadt
Oranienbaum
Petrograd
Tsarskoe Selo
Pavlovsk
Gatchina

Okhta
R.Neva
Shlisselburg
Tosno
Vladimirskaya

Revul

Chudovo

Lake Peipus

Luga

Malaya Vishera

Novgorod

Lake Ilmen

Pskov

Dno

Staraya Russa

Bologoe

R.Velikaya

Riga

Zapadnaya Dvina

Likhoslavl

Rezhitsa

Novosokolniki

Velikie-Luki

Rzhev

Dvinsk

Nevel

to Moscow→

Polotsk

Vitebsk

Vyazma

Vilna

Smolensk

Orsha

N

Minsk

Mogilev

The Railways in North-Western Russia, 1917

→ Route of the Tsar's train, 28 February-1 March 1917

0   50   100   200 miles

TABLE OF CABINET CHANGES 1915–1917

Years	1915	1916	1917
Months	Feb – Dec	Jan – Dec	Jan – Feb
Prime Minister	Goremykin	Stuermer (20.I); Trepov (10.XI)	Prince Golitzin (26.XII)
Internal Affairs	N. A. Maklakov; Prince Shcherbatov (5.VI); A. N. Khvostov (26.IX)	Stuermer (3.III); A. A. Khvostov (7.VII); Protopopov (16.IX)	Protopopov
Foreign Affairs	Sazonov	Sazonov; Pokrovsky (10.XI)	Pokrovsky
Minister of War	Sukhomlinov; Polivanov (12.VI)	Polivanov; Shuvaev (15.III)	Belyaev (3.I)
Minister of Navy	Grigorovich	Grigorovich	Grigorovich
Minister of Finance	Bark	Bark	Bark
Minister of Communications	Rukhlov; Trepov (27.X)	Trepov; Kriger-Voynovsky (10.XI)	Kriger-Voynovsky
Minister of Justice	Shcheglovitov; A. A. Khvostov (6.VII)	A. A. Khvostov; Makarov (9.VII); Dobrovolsky (22.XII)	Dobrovolsky
Minister of Education	Count Ignatyev	Count Ignatyev; Kulchitsky (26.XII)	Kulchitsky
Minister of Agriculture	Krivoshein; Naumov (26.X)	Naumov; Count Bobrinsky (21.VII); Rittikh (16.XI)	Rittikh
Ober-Procurator of Holy Synod	Sabler; Samarin (5.VII); Volzhin (26.IX)	Volzhin; Raev (17.VIII)	Raev
Minister of State Control	Kharitonov	Kharitonov; Pokrovsky (25.I); Feodosyev (30.XI)	Feodosyev
Minister of Trade and Industry	Prince Shakhovskoy (18.II)	Prince Shakhovskoy	Prince Shakhovskoy

Bibliographical Notes

The reader may be surprised not to have encountered in the foregoing pages any reference to such standard works on the Russian revolution as

L. D. Trotsky. *History of the Russian Revolution.* 3 vols (London, 1934).

Victor Chernov. *The Great Russian Revolution.* Translated and abridged by P. E. Mosely (New Haven, 1936).

W. H. Chamberlin. *The Russian Revolution, 1917–1921.* 2 vols (New York, 1935),

or that so little has been made of the wealth of information contained in

P. N. Milyukov. *Istoriya vtoroy russkoy revolyutsii* (Sofia, 1921–23)

part of which had already appeared under the imprint of the publishing firm Letopis in Kiev in 1919. Some may even reproach me for ignoring the information contained in the somewhat sensational revelations of

Alan Moorehead. *History of the Russian Revolution* (London, 1958)

and especially in the works of Payne, Louis Fischer and Possony on Lenin.[1] I did so in order not to weary the reader with a discussion of secondary sources and the gratuitous polemics which such a discussion would entail.

I feel more apologetic about my limited use of such sources as the diplomatic memoirs of the period, including those of

Sir George Buchanan. *My Mission to Russia, and other diplomatic memories.* 2 vols (London, 1923)

and of his daughter

Meriel Buchanan. *The Dissolution of an Empire* (London, 1932)

or the much-quoted memoirs of

Maurice Paléologue. *La Russie des Tsars pendant la Grande Guerre.* 3 vols (Paris, 1921–22). In English translation: *An Ambassador's Memoirs.* Translated by F. A. Holt. 3 vols (London, 1923–25)

or those of other diplomats accredited to successive Russian governments.

---

1. R. Payne, *The life and death of Lenin* (New York, 1964); Louis Fischer, *The life of Lenin* (New York, 1964); Stefan T. Possony, *Lenin. The compulsive revolutionary* (Chicago, 1964).

In mitigation of this neglect I should explain that I have refrained from frequent references to these works because they are well known, and also because they have powerfully contributed to the formation of certain accepted views of the Russian revolution, and even to the establishment of a number of clichés about it which I have been at pains to avoid. This does not, however, mean that the extremely important and valuable information they contain has not been taken into consideration.

My gravest bibliographical omission — and the one I am most anxious to remedy in this note — is that I have not acknowledged more frequently in the text the influence exercised on this book by that eminent historian of the Russian revolution, S. P. Melgunov. Far more often than is indicated in the text I have followed his interpretation — in many cases supplementing it with information not available to him in his lifetime. His work, contained in a number of volumes published in Russian by himself or his widow, represents the first serious attempt at a scholarly study of the period covered by the present work. I have found his assessment of the voluminous memoir material consulted by him particularly helpful. The *Dichtung und Wahrheit* atmosphere prevalent in the most readable memoirs rarely stands up to the acid-test of Melgunov's analysis. It is hard to understand why his writings are still neglected even by those (with a few exceptions, such as L. Schapiro) who, like Melgunov, are also anxious to find an impartial approach to historical truth. The books by S. P. Melgunov directly concerning our period are:

> *Na putyakh k dvortsovomu perevorotu* (Librairie 'La Source', Paris, 1931). *Zolotoy nemetsky klyuch k bolshevistskoy revolyutsii* (Paris, 1940). *Sudba Imperatora Nikolaya II posle otrecheniya* (Paris, 1951). *Kak bolsheviki zakhvatili vlast* (Paris, 1939). *Legenda o separatnom mire* (Paris, 1957). *Martovskie dni 1917 goda* (Paris, 1961).

The paucity of references to these and other works[1] is partly excused by the desire to substantiate every contention, whenever possible, by primary sources. My investigation of such sources has been very extensive, but not of course exhaustive. I have not always been able to give reasons for preferring one source to another when both relate to the same sequence of events. In sifting the vast amount of information to be found in both Soviet and émigré publications I have tried not to be prejudiced against factual information conveyed by a witness or scholar with a strong political bias. This applies, for instance, to the documentary materials published in the

1. Of these I should not omit to mention (however much it differs from my own views) the short but penetrating analysis of M. M. Karpovich, 'The Russian Revolution of 1917', in *The Journal of Modern History*, vol. II, no. 2 (June, 1930).

'twenties by Soviet historians, mostly pupils and protégés of M. N. Pokrovsky, at a time when the falsification of history by selecting archive material tendentiously and swamping it with irrelevant texts had not yet attained the perfection which we observe nowadays in Soviet archive publications. We are indebted to these early Soviet historians for a great deal of our knowledge of what happened just before and during 1917. Much of this material was published in the Red Archives (*Krasny Arkhiv*), to which detailed references are given below in the notes on individual chapters.

Some use has also been made of the works of the Bolshevik historian V. P. Semennikov. These belong to a period of Soviet historiography in which scholars reproduced without substantial alteration the texts on which they based their conclusions, before commenting on them on official party lines. Since then conditions have changed. Soviet archivists are now obliged to select for publication only such material as supports the party line, with the result that Soviet historians are much more handicapped in the treatment of their material than were their predecessors of the 'twenties.

For V. P. Semennikov's publications, see mainly

> *Monarkhiya pered krusheniem* (Moscow, 1927). *Politika Romanovykh nakanune revolyutsii* (Moscow and Leningrad, 1926). *Dnevnik b. Velikogo Knyazya Andreya Vladimirovicha* (Leningrad and Moscow, 1925). *Nikolay II i Velikie Knyazya* (Leningrad and Moscow, 1925). *Za kulisami Tsarizma; Arkhiv tibetskogo vracha Badmaeva* (Leningrad, 1925).

On the other hand, I have consulted a number of works which have not as yet been fully used as primary sources by historians. To this category belong some memoirs with an explicit right-wing bias such as those published in the magazine *Russkaya Letopis* (7 vols, Paris, 1921–25), the reminiscences of the Palace Commandant, V. N. Voeykov, and the extensive memoirs, supported by a considerable amount of research, of the former gendarme general, A. I. Spiridovich,

> *Velikaya voyna i fevralskaya revolyutsiya 1914–1917 gg.* 3 vols (New York, 1960–62)

and some others. The authors of such works have frequently witnessed events from privileged vantage-points, and their political views and personal inclinations, however forcefully expressed in their memoirs and works, should not lead one to reject factual data which appear to be reliably reported.

S. S. Oldenburg's *Tsarstvovanie Imperatora Nikolaya II* (see below, bibliographical note on Chapter 8) is in a category to itself. Although a kind of official history of the reign sponsored by a committee of legitimist émigrés, it is a work of great learning and scrupulous impartiality.

For the history of the gradual weakening and decay of the imperial administration in Russia, I have naturally relied in the first place on the published stenographic reports of the evidence heard by the Extraordinary Investigation Commission of the Provisional Government, edited by P. E. Shchegolev in seven volumes under the title

Padenie tsarskogo rezhima (Leningrad and Moscow, 1924–27).

The Investigation Commission, to which we sometimes refer in the text as the 'Muravyev Commission' (after its chairman, the lawyer N. K. Muravyev), was established in order to investigate alleged breaches of constitutional and criminal law committed by the highest officials of the Tsarist régime. The purpose of the Commission was to prepare the ground for the arraignment of those against whom there was sufficient *prima facie* evidence before a special tribunal to be set up by the Provisional Government or its successor, after the Constituent Assembly had taken over supreme power. The membership of the Commission was rather mixed, but it included a considerable number of intelligent men of independent character and with legal training. Moreover, many highly-qualified lawyers worked as investigators, preparing the material for the interrogation of the accused and of the witnesses at the plenary meetings of the commission. Some of the members of the Commission and some of the lawyers who worked for it later gave highly critical accounts of the procedures employed by the Commission, and of its findings insofar as these are revealed by the Shchegolev publication. See in particular the memoirs of A. F. Romanov and V. M. Rudnev in the émigré magazine *Russkaya Letopis*:

A. F. Romanov. 'Imperator Nikolay II i Ego Pravitelstvo (po dannym Chrezvychaynoy Sledstvennoy Komissii)', *Russkaya Letopis*, no. II (Paris, 1922), pp. 1–38.

V. M. Rudnev. *Pravda o Tsarskoy Semye*, ibid., pp. 39–58.

The latter memoir was written at a much earlier date, apparently in March 1919. See also the same memorandum published under the title

Pravda o tsarskoy semye i 'temnykh silakh' (Berlin, 1920).

But even apart from such criticisms one must bear in mind, in using the material of Shchegolev's publication (which we usually quote as *Padenie*), that some of the statements reproduced in it were made by persons who could later have been brought to trial — former officials of the Tsarist régime, members of the Council of Ministers, generals of the Army, the police and the gendarmerie, who were all held prisoner under conditions which reflect little credit on the régime established by the liberals in February 1917. These statements should be approached with caution because they were, in effect, made under duress. Though the interrogators never resorted to intimidation, most of the prisoners were held in the Petropavlovskaya Fortress, at the mercy of soldiers whose discipline was rapidly deteriorating. This caution applies in particular to the evidence of the former police official S. P. Beletsky, whom the then Minister of Justice, A. F. Kerensky, found it necessary at one time to confine to a punitive cell, a proceeding just short of the direct application of torture. On the other hand we have testimonies by persons who were politically active at the time when they were heard or interrogated by the Commission, and who had every interest in concealing certain facts or emphasising others in order to strengthen their own position in the current political struggle. I refer here to such statements as those made by M. V. Rodzyanko, A. I. Guchkov, P. N. Milyukov and others. I could not always give my reasons for selecting any particular quotation from *Padenie* which I thought would support or illustrate some point or other, as this would have impeded the flow of the narrative. But I have always tried to weigh such selected statements against evidence from other sources.

It should be pointed out that quite recently Soviet archivists have revealed that the whole record of the proceedings of the Commission is still preserved intact in the Soviet Union, and is even available to researchers there. Some of this material has now been published selectively. See *Voprosy Istorii* on the interrogation of the former Prime Minister, Kokovtsov, and on Rasputin as he figures in the materials of the Commission, and the introductory and concluding notes by A. L. Sidorov:

> 'Interesnaya nakhodka. (Protokol doprosa V. N. Kokovtsova Chrezvy-chaynoy sledstvennoy komissiey Vremennogo pravitelstva v sentyabre 1917 goda.)' With an introductory article by A. L. Sidorov. In *Voprosy Istorii*, no. 2, 1964, pp. 94–111; no. 4, pp. 94–117. 'Posledny vremenshchik poslednego tsarya. (Materialy Chrezvychaynoy sledstvennoy komissii Vremennogo pravitelstva o Rasputine i razlozhenii samoderzhaviya.)' With introduction and concluding notes by A. L. Sidorov. In *Voprosy Istorii*, no. 10, 1964, pp. 117–135; no. 12, 1964, pp. 90–103; no. 1, 1965, pp. 98–110; and no. 2, 1965, pp. 103–114.

We must hope that this trickle of information will increase in the not too distant future.

In this context we should mention the important work on the last days of the Tsarist régime by the leading Russian poet of the period, Alexander Blok. Blok's work was published in no. XV of Burtsev's magazine *Byloe* (Petrograd, 1921) in Russia and reprinted:

> A. Blok. 'Poslednie Dni starogo rezhima', in *ARR*, vol. IV (Berlin, 1922), pp. 5–54.

Blok's work contains generalisations which go far beyond the scope of the material made available to him when he was working as editorial secretary to the Muravyev Commission. The resulting picture of the Russian revolution is thus more revealing of the reactions of a brilliant and sensitive mind to the confusing situation in which he found himself than of the situation itself. The poet's reactions can be judged only in conjunction with other statements by him in his private diaries, which were published soon after his death, and again, with additional passages, in 1942, and his notebooks, published in 1965.

Many of the documents consulted are taken from the émigré publication, *Arkhiv Russkoy Revolyutsii*, published by I. V. Gessen in 22 volumes.

For the English reading public the general bibliographical works of

Philip Grierson. *Books on Soviet Russia 1917–1942* (London, 1943), pp. 1–37

and of

Frank Alfred Golder. *Documents of Russian History 1914–1917* (New York and London, 1927), pp. 3–302

are still useful. So are the relevant parts of

R. P. Browder and A. F. Kerensky. *The Russian Provisional Government 1917.* 3 vols (Stanford University Press, 1961).

A far more exhaustive bibliographical source will be found in the catalogue of the Russian historical archive abroad, in Prague:

Russky Zagranichny Istorichesky Arkhiv v Prage. Bibliografiya russkoy revolyutsii i grazhdanskoy voyny (1917–1921). 2 vols (Prague, 1938). Edited by Jan Slavik and compiled by S. P. Postnikov.

CHAPTER I

The Duma and the Voluntary Organisations

On the wartime activities of the Voluntary Organisations we find a number of volumes in the Economic and Social History of the World War (Russian Series, edited by Sir Paul Vinogradoff and M. T. Florinsky). A classical summary is contained in

Michael T. Florinsky. *The End of the Russian Empire* (New Haven, Yale University Press, 1931. Paperback edition, 1964).

Much as we differ from the author's interpretations, we leaned heavily on the factual material accurately reported in this work. For more details, see in the same series

N. J. Astrov. 'The Municipal Government and the All-Russian Union', in Gronsky and Astrov, *The War and the Russian Government* (New Haven, 1929)

and

Tikhon J. Polner, Prince Vladimir Obolensky and Sergius P. Tyurin (Introduction by Prince G. E. Lvov). *Russian Local Government during the War and the Union of Zemstvos* (New Haven, 1930).

All the authors of this series side against the government and play down the purely political aspirations of the leadership of the Voluntary Organisations. There is relatively little literature to sustain the accusations put forward by the government against the Voluntary Organisations of ambitions seemingly incompatible with their ostensibly patriotic behaviour. Something on these lines will however be found in Prince Vsevolod Shakhovskoy's book of memoirs, quoted in the text,

'*Sic Transit Gloria Mundi*' ('*Tak prokhodit mirskaya slava*'), *1893–1917* (Paris, 1952), in particular chapters 18, 22 and 25 *passim*.

On the Progressive Bloc, see Florinsky, op. cit., p. 104, where more literature is quoted; and especially

V. I. Gurko. *Features and Figures of the Past*. Hoover Library on War, Revolution and Peace, Publication no. 14, ed. G. E. Wallace Sterling, X. Eudin and H. H. Fisher (Stanford University Press, 1939), chapters XXIII and XXIV on the Progressive Bloc, particularly pp. 571–575 and 581–583

and also

'Progressivny Blok' (introduced by N. Lapin) in *Krasny Arkhiv* 50/51 (1932), pp. 117–160, 52 (1932), pp. 143–196, and 56 (1933), pp. 80–135, containing documents from Milyukov's archives.

The history of the Labour Groups has hardly been touched upon. We may well have to wait for the publication of the history of the Menshevik Party during the revolution (in preparation in the USA) for a comprehensive account of them. Besides the sources quoted in the text, there has been one important publication in the *Red Archives*. In vol. 57 (1933) Iv. Menitsky published important material, derived from the minutes of the WICs, on the Labour Groups. In vol. 67 (1934), Menitsky also reprinted five mimeographed bulletins issued by the Labour Groups themselves during World War I. The publication of this material must have caused a considerable stir in 1934, possibly in connection with the increase of Stalinist terror after the assassination of Kirov. In vol. 68 (1935), pp. 171–172, the editors of the *Red Archives* apologised for having published Menitsky's material without sufficient commentary. Thereafter the subject of the Labour Groups on the eve of the revolution was never again broached by Soviet historians. See also

O. A. Ermansky. *Iz perezhitogo 1887-1921 gg.* (Moscow and Leningrad, 1927), pp. 117-135.

There are two different works by Menitsky. One was published as early as 1923 by the *Istpart* of the Moscow Committee of the RKP, and is entitled

Iv. Menitsky. *Rabochee dvizhenie i sotsial-demokraticheskoe podpolye Moskvy* (*Moskovsky Rabochy*, 1923).

This partly covers the ground dealt with in a much larger work by the same author published by the Communist Academy in Moscow:

Iv. Menitsky. *Revolyutsionnoe dvizhenie voennykh godov (1914-1917).* vol. I (*pervy god voyny*) (Moscow, 1925), 444 pp.; and vol. II (Moscow, 1924), 314 pp.

Other works consulted:

FLEER, M. (prepared for publication by). *Rabochee dvizhenie v gody voyny.* In the series *Materialy po istorii rabochego dvizheniya*, ed. A. Lozovsky and published by Tsentrarkhiv. (Voprosy Truda, Moscow, 1925).

GRAVE, B. B. (ed.). *Burzhuaziya nakanune fevralskoy revolyutsii* (Moscow and Leningrad, 1927). *Tsentrarkhiv. 1917 god v dokumentakh i materialakh.*

KIZEVETTER, A. *Istoricheskie otkliki* (Moscow, 1915).

PARES, BERNARD. *My Russian Memoirs* (London, 1931).

PARES, BERNARD. *The Fall of the Russian Monarchy* (London, 1939).

SHLYAPNIKOV, A. G. (under pseudonym BELENIN). 'Rabochaya Rossiya za dvadtsat mesyatsev voyny. Lichnye vpechatleniya i sobrannye v S. Peterburge materialy', in *Sbornik Sotsial-Demokrata* (ed. V. I. Lenin and G. E. Zinovyev), no. 1, 1915, pp. 50-85.

CHAPTER 2

Labour and the Revolutionary Movement

A general survey of Social-Democracy in Russia in the first years of the war was made – for internal circulation only – by the Ministry of the Interior in August, 1916:

Obzor deyatelnosti Rossiiskoy sotsial-demokraticheskoy rabochey partii za vremya s nachala voyny Rossii s Avstro-Vengriey i Germaniey po iul 1916 goda. 7 August 1916, 102 pp.

A copy of it can be found in the Houghton Library, Harvard University. I drew most of the material dealt with in this chapter from Menitsky's works, the *Granat* volume of autobiographies (and authorised biographies) of revolutionary leaders (see below, p. 444) and Shlyapnikov's (Belenin's) report, published in no. 1 of *Sbornik Sotsial-Demokrata*, edited by Lenin and Zinovyev in Switzerland. Lenin's works are quoted, here as elsewhere, from the 2nd–3rd edition, although the 5th edition was taken into consideration when the MS was revised.

Independent historical research on the activities of the revolutionary groups in Russia during the war was entirely abandoned by Soviet historians in the early 'thirties. Works published in the 'twenties ceased to be quoted, and even the few reminiscences published during the period known as that of the 'cult of personality' of Stalin were stilted and streamlined in accordance with accepted historical legend. Professor E. N. Burdzhalov tried to reopen the whole question in 1956,

E. N. Burdzhalov. 'O taktike bolshevikov v marte-aprele 1917 goda', *Voprosy Istorii*, no. 4, 1956

but this attempt seems to have been premature. The article provoked official condemnation, and Burdzhalov lost his chair at Leningrad University.

Quite recently there has been a resumption of archive material publication connected with the February events in the Soviet Union. While this book was in print the historical magazine *Voprosy Istorii KPSS*, in its issues 8 and 9 of 1965, published a number of letters and documents bearing on the activities during World War I of the Central Committee of the Bolshevik Party in Petrograd. Valuable as they are, these documents do not affect the gist of our argument in the relevant chapter. Soviet historians continue to complain that the so-called 'falsifiers of history' in the West tend to ignore and minimise the influence of Lenin on events in Russia in 1914–16. See for instance the article by

G. Z. Ioffe. 'Kak burzhuaznaya istoriografiya "otluchaet" V. I. Lenina i bolshevikov ot fevralskoy revolyutsii ('How bourgeois historiography "divorces" V. I. Lenin and the Bolsheviks from the February Revolution') *Voprosy Istorii KPSS*, no. 7, 1965.

But what is the poor bourgeois historian to do when his Soviet 'opposite numbers' publish in the same magazine (no. 9, 1965, pp. 79 ff.) a letter of N. K. Krupskaya, Lenin's wife, dated 1916, in which she complains bitterly that nobody except Lenin's sister gives them any information about what is going on in Russia, whilst party members in Russia simultaneously reproach the Central Committee in Switzerland (i.e. Lenin) with becoming estranged from things Russian?

For the tactics of the Bolshevik Party during the war, see in particular
Leonard Schapiro. *The Communist Party of the Soviet Union* (London and
New York, 1960)
and the various works on Lenin which have appeared outside the Soviet
Union, especially the excellent political biography by
David Shub. *Lenin* (New York, 1948).

Other works consulted:

AKHUN, M. and PETROV, V. *Bolsheviki i armiya v 1905–1917 godu* (Izdatelstvo Krasnaya Gazeta, Leningrad, 1929). Mainly part III, *Gody imperialisticheskoy voyny*, pp. 147–226.

AVDEEV, N. 'Bolshevistskaya rabota vo flote i armii nakanune fevralskoy revolyutsii', *Proletarskaya Revolyutsiya*, no. 6 (29), 1924.

BALABANOV, M. *Ot 1905 k 1917 godu. Massovoe rabochee dvizhenie* (Moscow and Leningrad, 1927).

GRANAT. *Entsiklopedichesky Slovar Russkogo Bibliograficheskogo Instituta Granat*. 7th edn (Moscow, 1910–38). Vol. 41, parts I, II, III; 'Personalities of the USSR and of the October Revolution', autobiography of Shlyapnikov.

LENIN, V. I. Lecture to young workers delivered 22.1.1917. *Sochineniya*. 2nd and 3rd editions, 30 vols (Moscow and Leningrad, 1926–32 and 1928–37). Vol. XIX, p. 357.

KRUPSKAYA, N. K. Letter of 10.1.1915 to V. A. Karpinsky and S. N. Ravich, in *Leninsky Sbornik*, 2nd edn (Moscow and Leningrad, 1931), vol. XI, p. 135.

MENITSKY, I. *op. cit.* (see p. 442), vol. II. pp. 274–304, proceedings against so-called 'Presnya' group of RSDRP.

SHLYAPNIKOV (BELENIN), A. G. Autobiography in *Granat* (see above, p. 444).

SHLYAPNIKOV (BELENIN), A. G. Article under pseudonym of Belenin (op. cit, see p. 442).
Kanun semnadtsatogo goda. Vospominaniya i dokumenty o rabochem dvizhenii i revolyutsionnom podpolye za 1914–1916 g. (Moscow, 1923).

ZALEZHSKY. *Baltiisky Flot* (Molodaya Gvardiya, Moscow and Leningrad, 1925).

See also:

'Revolyutsionnoe dvizhenie v voyskakh vo vremya mirovoy voyny.' Documentary material reported by V. Dzyubinsky in *Krasny Arkhiv*, 1923, vol. 4, pp. 417–24.

CHAPTER 3

Army and Revolution

The works consulted for this chapter are:

BONCH-BRUEVICH, M. D. *Vsya vlast Sovetam* (Moscow, 1957).

BRUSILOV, GEN. A. A. *Moi vospominaniya* (Moscow, 1929).

CHURCHILL, WINSTON S. *The World Crisis 1916–1919* (London, 1927).

DANILOV, YOURI. *La Russie dans la guerre mondiale 1914–1917* (Paris 1927).

DENIKIN, GEN. A. I. *Ocherki russkoy smuty*, 5 issues (Paris, 1921–26).

DENIKIN, GEN. A. I. *Put russkogo ofitsera* (Chekhov, New York, 1953).

GOLOVIN, GEN. N. N. *Rossiiskaya kontr-revolyutsiya v 1917–1918 gg.* (Paris, 1937; copyright Hoover Library).

GOLOVIN, GEN. N. N. *Voennye usiliya Rossii v mirovoy voyne* (2 vols, Paris, 1939). In English, *The Russian Army in the World War* (New Haven, 1931).

GUCHKOV, A. I. Deposition of 2 August 1917 to Muravyev Commission in *Padenie*, vol. VI, pp. 248 ff.

GOURKO, BASIL. *Memories and impressions of war and revolution in Russia, 1914–1917* (London, 1918).

IGNATYEV, A. A. *Pyatdesyat let v stroyu*, 2 vols (Moscow, 1952), Vol. 2.

KNOX, SIR ALFRED. *With the Russian Army, 1914–1917*, 2 vols (London, 1921).

LEMKE, M. K. *250 dney v tsarskoy stavke* (Petrograd, 1920).

MARTYNOV, E. *Tsarskaya armiya v fevralskom perevorote* (Moscow, 1927).

PARES, BERNARD. *Day by Day with the Russian Army* (London, 1915).

RODZYANKO, M. V. 'Krushenie Imperii', *ARR*, vol. XVII.

SHAVELSKY, FATHER GEORGY. *Vospominaniya poslednego protopresvitera russkoy armii i flota*, 2 vols (Chekhov, New York, 1954).

SPIRIDOVICH, GEN. A. I. *Velikaya voyna i fevralskaya revolyutsiya, 1914–1917 gg.* Op. cit. (see p. 437).

'TANKEVICH, V. B. *Vospominaniya* (Berlin, 1920).

,UCHOMLINOW. W. A. (Sukhomlinov, V. A.) *Erinnerungen* (Berlin, 1924).

CHAPTER 4

The Jews and Revolution

For a general survey of the history of the Jews in the last two centuries in the whole of the Diaspora, see the monumental work of

S. M. Dubnov. *Noveyshaya Istoriya Evreyskogo Naroda*, 3rd edn. 3 vols (Berlin, 1923).

For the period with which we are concerned in this chapter the most revealing works were the memoirs of

G. B. Sliozberg. *Dela minuvshikh dney. Zapiski russkogo evreya.* 3 vols (Paris, 1933–34).

Vol. 3 gives detailed information on the relations between the Jewish relief organisation in Russia during the war — the so-called EKOPO — the government and the Voluntary Organisations. Sliozberg gives the number of refugees assisted by the Committee as 225,000. The cost of this considerable relief work was according to him borne to a large extent by the Imperial Ministry of Internal Affairs. Sliozberg's work contains some confused arguments against Yakhontov's report concerning the way in which the government came to its decision practically to abolish the pale of settlement. On comparing Yakhontov's notes with the deposition of the Minister of Internal Affairs at the time, Prince Shcherbatov, in *Padenie*, vol. VII, pp. 208–34, we are inclined to believe Yakhontov's account.

On the history of the Jewish Labour movement and its relation to the activities of the Russian revolutionary parties, see in particular

H. Shukman. *Relations between the Jewish Bund and the RSDRP, 1897–1903* (unpublished Oxford D.Phil. thesis, St Antony's College, 1961).

On the part played by the Jews in the revolutionary movement, see

Lev Deych. *Rol evreyev v russkom revolyutsionnom dvizhenii*, 2nd edn, vol. I (Moscow, 1925).

A recent review of the problems with which we have been dealing in this chapter will be found in two articles by Leonard Schapiro:

'The Role of the Jews in the Russian Revolutionary Movement', in *The Slavonic and East European Review*, vol. XL, no. 94, December, 1961

and

'The Russian Background of the Anglo-American Jewish Immigration', *The Transactions of the Jewish Historical Society of England*, vol. XX, 1964,

where more literature is listed.

The information on the activities of Jewish Committees in Germany in the first phases of the war comes from the articles of E. Zechlin referred to below (see Bibliographical Notes on Chapter 5). More literature and a few archive documents will be found there, in particular in the issue of

Aus Politik und Zeitgeschichte. Beilage zur Wochenzeitung 'Das Parlament', 21 June 1961.

Other works consulted:

'Dokumenty o presledovanii evreyev'. *ARR*, vol. XIX, pp. 245–284.

GRUZENBERG, O. O. *Vchera* (Paris, 1938).

PASMANIK, D. S. *Revolyutsionnye gody v Krymu* (Paris, 1936).

VINAVER, M. *Nashe pravitelstvo. Krymskie vospominaniya 1918–1919 gg.* (Paris, 1928).

YAKHONTOV, A. N. 'Tyazhelie Dni. Sekretnye zasedaniya Soveta Ministrov 16 iulya — 2 sentyabrya 1915 goda', *ARR*, vol. XVIII (see below, p. 453).

CHAPTER 5

German Political Intervention

There is still no comprehensive study of the questions dealt with in this chapter. Most of the available literature is violently polemical, but lacking in documentary foundation. For this one should go to the only available source, the German documents themselves, which have now been catalogued. The relevant parts of the German archives used were the *Weltkrieg* series of the Ministry of Foreign Affairs, more particularly those marked *geheim* and *ganz geheim*. A selection of these, not by any means covering the whole ground, is contained in a collection of documents in English translation published by:

Z. A. B. Zeman. *Germany and the Revolution in Russia 1915–1918. Documents from the Archives of the German Foreign Ministry* (London, 1948).

The German text of some of them will be found in

Werner Hahlweg. *Lenins Rückkehr nach Russland 1917. Die deutschen Akten* (Leiden, 1957).

Of great importance also are the documents published in

A. Scherer and J. Grunewald. *L'Allemagne et les problèmes de la paix. Documents extraits des archives de l'Office allemand des Affaires Étrangères, publiés et annotés par André Scherer et Jacques Grunewald. Août 1914– 31 janvier 1917. Préface de Maurice Baumont et Pierre Renouvin* (Paris, 1962).

The various aspects of the problem of German approaches to Russia in connection with a separate peace, and the *Revolutionierungspolitik* which competed with them, have been explained in the important book of

> Fritz Fischer. *Griff nach der Weltmacht. Die Kriegszielpolitik des kaiserlichen Deutschland 1914/1918* (Düsseldorf, 1962).

More material on this subject, treated with a different emphasis, will be found in five separate chapters of a projected book by

> Prof. Egmont Zechlin. 'Friedensbestrebungen und Revolutionierungs-versuche', in *Aus Politik und Zeitgeschichte* (appendix to the weekly *Das Parlament*), numbers of 17 May, 14 and 21 June 1961, and 15 and 29 May 1963.

Some documents are appended to these articles not all of which can be found among the documents of the German Foreign Ministry or in the *Bundesarchiv*.

The *Revolutionierungspolitik* probably had other ideologists besides Parvus. In this respect the pamphlet of the historian

> Theodor Schiemann. *Russland auf dem Wege zur Revolution* (Berlin, 1915)

is significant. The pamphlet was written during the 1915 Russian crisis with which we deal in Ch. 6. Prof. Schiemann seems to have been singularly well informed about the imminent onslaught on the autocracy by the *Kadettenpartei*. He doubts, however, whether a parliamentary régime could have been established, and closes with the words: 'The crisis has become acute; it is impossible to foresee its outcome, but everything seems to indicate that Russia is on the road to revolution.'

Besides using primary material, we have relied a good deal for our interpretation of the *Revolutionierungspolitik* on two books; the one is

> S. P. Melgunov. *The Golden German Key of the Bolsheviks* (In Russian — see above, p. 436; Paris, 1940)

and the other

> Michael Futrell. *Northern Underground. Episodes of Russian Revolutionary Transport and Communications through Scandinavia and Finland, 1863–1917* (London, 1963).

We should also mention the well-documented article of

> Georges Bonnin. 'Les Bolchéviques et l'argent allemand pendant la première guerre mondiale', *Revue Historique*, janvier–mars 1965, pp. 101–26.

M. Bonnin knows a lot. Some of his knowledge is based on thought-reading. Unfortunately I am unable to confirm the account he gives of my private thoughts on p. 102, footnote 1. With all that, M. Bonnin's approach to the problem is that of an archivist, not of an historian. Thus he misses the important development to which Gustav Mayer refers when he speaks of his relations with Nasse, although he quotes all the relevant sources.

For Parvus and the part he played in this complicated *imbroglio* I use, besides primary sources,

W. Scharlau. *Parvus-Helphand and the First World War* (unpublished D.Phil. thesis, St Antony's College, Oxford, 1963)

as well as Scharlau's book in collaboration with Zeman (see below, p. 451). The notebooks of Parvus referred to were made available to me on microfilm, the originals being kept in the *Hauptarchiv* in West Berlin. The appeal to the Russian revolutionaries which Parvus issued in Constantinople in October 1914 was kindly made available to me by the archive of the *Bund*, New York. I have also consulted Keskük's papers in the archives of Yale University, USA, which contain further corroboration of his contacts with the Estonian Bolshevik, A. R. Siefeldt (Simumyash). See on him

V. I. Lenin. *Works.* 5th edn, vol. 49, letters of August 1914 to October 1917, on pp. 165, 181, 634.

In telling the story of German-Bolshevik relations after Lenin's return to Russia I have confined myself to the evidence which has come to light relatively recently. This is not to say that all the old stories about clandestine contacts between the Bolsheviks and German agencies abroad, mentioned by the Provisional Government in its various indictments, should be dismissed out of hand. On the contrary, some of the facts on which the Provisional Government based its accusations can be substantiated by reference to the *Auswärtiges Amt* archives. But this does not of course mean that the indictments were true.

Other works consulted:

BALABANOV, M. *Ot 1905 k 1917 godu.* Op. cit. (see p. 444).

BEBUTOV, PRINCE D. O. Alleged compiler of *Posledny russky samoderzhets. Ocherk zhizny i tsarstvovaniya imperatora Rossii Nikolaya II-go.* Published anonymously (Berlin, 1913).

BONCH-BRUEVICH, GEN. M. D. *Vsya vlast sovetam.* Op. cit. (see p. 445).

BURTSEV, V. L., ed. *Byloe. Sborniki po noveyshey russkoy istorii.* No. 1, new series (Paris, 1938).

BYSTRYANSKY, V. Editor, letter of Pavel Budaev in *Krasnaya Letopis*, vol. VII (1923).

CAHÉN, FRITZ M. *Der Weg nach Versailles* (Boppard/Rhein, 1963).

ERMOLAEVA, R. A. 'Yakov Stanislavovich Ganetsky — k 80-letiyu so dnya rozhdeniya', *Voprosy Istorii KPSS*, no. 3, 1964, p. 96.

FÜRSTENBERG-GANETSKY (HANECKI, 'KUBA'), YA. S. See Ya. Ganetsky, 'Lenin v Galitsiiskoy tyurme', *Don*, no. 4, 1965, pp. 148–156; and 'V poiskakh arkhivov Lenina. Otchet o poezdke v Polshu po porucheniyu Instituta V. I. Lenina', *Don*, no. 9, 1965, pp. 109–122.

GANKIN, OLGA HESS and FISHER, H. H. *The Bolsheviks and the World War. The Origin of the Third International.* The Hoover Library on War, Revolution and Peace, Publication no. 15. (Stanford University Press, London, 1940).

HELPHAND, A. *Pravda Glaza Kolet* (Stockholm 1918). In German, *Im Kampf um die Wahrheit* (Berlin, 1918).

HELPHAND, A., ed. *Die Glocke*, No. 1, September 1915.

KATKOV, G. M. 'German Foreign Office Documents on Financial Support to the Bolsheviks in 1917', *International Affairs*, vol. 32, no. 2, April 1956, pp. 181–9.

KENNAN, GEORGE. 'The Sisson Documents', *The Journal of Modern History*, vol. XXVIII, no. 2, June 1956.

KERENSKY, A. *The Crucifixion of Liberty* (London, 1934).

KOKOVTSOV, COUNT V. N. *Out of my Past. The Memoirs of Count Kokovtsov.* Ed. H. H. Fisher. Hoover Wa: ʿibrary Publication no. 6 (Stanford University Press/London, 1935).

KONDRATYEV, A. 'Vospominaniya ᴄ ᵣ ʲpolnoy rabote' in *Krasnaya Letopis*, vol. VII (Moscow and Petrograd, 1923).

KRIEGEL, A. 'Sur les rapports de Lénine avec le mouvement zimmerwaldien français', *Cahiers du Monde Russe et Soviétique*, vol. III: 2, April–June (Paris, 1962), p. 299.

KRUPSKAYA, N. K. Address books published in *Istorichesky Arkhiv*, no. 2, 1959, no. 3, 1959, pp. 31–50.

KÜHLMANN, R. von. *Erinnerungen* (Heidelberg, 1948).

LEHMANN, C. and PARVUS. *Das Hungernde Russland* (Stuttgart, 1900).

LENIN, V. I. Letter of 30 March 1917 to Ya. S. Ganetsky in *Sochineniya* (3rd edn) vol. XX, p. 55.

LENIN, .. I. Farewell letter of 8 April/26 March 1917 to Swiss workers in *Sochineniya* (3rd edn), vol XX, p. 66.

LENIN, V. I. Letter of 12 April 1917 to Ya. S. Ganetsky and K. B. Radek in *Sochineniya* (3rd edn), vol XXIX, p. 335, editorial note.

LENIN, V. I. Letter of 30 and 31 August and 2 and 7 September 1917 to Stockholm Bureau of RSDRP, in *Sochineniya* (3rd edn), vol. XXIX, p. 358.

LENIN, V. I. Letter of 2nd half of February, 1916 to G. L. Shklovsky in *Leninsky Sbornik* XI (1931), p. 214. Also letter of 4 and 5 August 1916 to G. L. Shklovsky, ibid, p. 226.

MAYER, GUSTAV. *Erinnerungen. Vom Journalisten zum Historiker der deutschen Arbeiterbewegung* (Zürich, 1949).

MELGUNOV, S. P. *Zolotoy nemetsky klyuch*, etc. Op. cit. (see p. 436).

NADOLNY, R. *Mein Beitrag* (Wiesbaden, 1955).

NIKITINE, B. V. *The Fatal Years. Fresh Revelations on a Chapter of Underground History* (London, 1938). In Russian *Rokovye gody, novye pokazaniya uchastnika* (Paris, 1937).

PARVUS. See Helphand.

Protokoly Tsentralnogo komiteta RSDRP (b) avgust–fevral 1918. Published by Institute of Marxism–Leninism attached to Central Committee of CPSU (Moscow, 1958).

Russische Korrespondenz Prawda. Published in Stockholm in 1917, in German, by Fürstenberg-Ganetsky and Radek.

SCHARLAU, W. B. and ZEMAN, Z. A. B. *Freibeuter der Revolution. Parvus-Helphand; eine politische Biographie* (Cologne, 1964). An English version, *Merchant of Revolution: a life of Alexander Helphand* (Oxford University Press, 1965) has just appeared.

SCHÜDDEKOPF, O.-E. *Deutschland zwischen Ost und West* in *Archiv für Sozialgeschichte*, vol. III (Hanover, 1963), p. 223. Published by the Friedrich Ebert Foundation.

SHLYAPNIKOV, A. G. *Kanun semnadtsatogo goda*. Op. cit. (see p. 444).

SIDOROV, A. L., ed. *Ekonomicheskoe polozhenie Rossii nakanune oktyabrskoy revolyutsii*, 2 vols (Moscow, 1957).

SIEFELDT, ARTHUR. Article on Lenin in Switzerland in *Bakinsky Rabochy*, 1, 3 and 10 February 1924.

SISSON, EDGAR. *100 Red Days* (New Haven, Yale University Press/London, 1931).

SPIRIDOVITCH, GEN. ALEXANDRE (GEN. A. I. SPIRIDOVICH). *Les dernières années de la cour de Tzarskoïe-Selo*. 2 vols (Paris, 1928).

WOLFE, BERTRAM D. *Three Who Made a Revolution. A Biographical History* (New York, 1948).

ZECHLIN, EGMONT. *Friedensbestrebungen und Revolutionierungsversuche. (Bemühungen zur Ausschaltung Russlands im Ersten Weltkriege.* Op. cit. (see p. 448).

ZEMAN, Z. A. B. *Germany and the Revolution in Russia 1915–1918.* Op. cit. (see p. 447).

CHAPTER 6

The Myasoedov Affair

The footnotes adequately cover the sources used in this chapter. It should perhaps be pointed out that in a history of the Russian army by

Kersnovsky. *Istoriya russkoy armii,* part III (Belgrade, 1935)

a rather untidy and amateurish work, some additional details are given on the staging of Myasoedov's trial in the Warsaw Fortress which only confirm one's impression that the judicial proceedings were faked.

The clearing-up of an established legend, when it has become so ingrained in the fabric of Western historiography as has the story of Myasoedov's treason, obviously presents a psychological difficulty. Quite recently the legend has been revived in an extremely readable book on the early stages of World War I by

Barbara Tuchman. *The Guns of August* (New York, 1962).

She quotes as one of her sources a book by

Léon Agourtine. *Le Général Soukhomlinov* (Clichy, 1951).

This book seems never to have been typographically printed. It contains a considerable amount of information on espionage and counter-espionage relating to the period, and seems to have been inspired by an acute dislike of General Sukhomlinov. But even Agourtine seems fully to realise that Myasoedov's trial shows so many irregularities that no conclusive proof of his guilt can be drawn from it. In details relating to the Myasoedov case Agourtine's work is, moreover, often wildly inaccurate.

Other works consulted:

ANDREY VLADIMIROVICH, GRAND DUKE. 'From the Diary of A. V. Romanov, 1916–1917', *Krasny Arkhiv,* vol. 26 (1928), pp. 185–210.

'B. B-Y' [B. BUCHINSKY]. 'Sud nad Myasoedovym. Vpechatleniya ochevidtsa', *ARR,* vol. XIV (Berlin 1924), pp. 132–147.

BAUERMEISTER, A. *Spies Break Through* (London, 1934).

BONCH-BRUEVICH, M. D. *Vsya vlast sovetam.* Op. cit. (see p. 445).

FREINAT, O. G. *Pravda o dele Myasoedova i drugikh, po ofitsialnym dokumentam i lichnym vospominaniyam* (Vilna, 1918).

GRUZENBERG, O. O. *Vchera*, Op. cit. (see p. 447).

GUCHKOV, A. I. Memoirs, 'Iz vospominaniy A. I. Guchkova', *Poslednie Novosti* (Paris, August and September, 1936).

KOKOVTSOV, V. N. *Out of my Past.* Op. cit. (see p. 450).

MACKIEWICZ, JOSEF. *Sprawa Potkownika Miasojedowa* (London, 1962).

NICOLAI, W. *Geheime Mächte. Internationale Spionage und ihre Bekämpfung im Weltkriege und heute.* 3rd edn (Leipzig, 1925).

PARES, SIR BERNARD. *The Fall of the Russian Monarchy.* Op. cit. (see p. 442).

ROBERT VON RAUPACH. Russische Schatten (Facies Hippocratica) Leipzig, 1939, chap. 5.

SHLYAPNIKOV, A. G. *Nakanune semnadtsatogo goda* (Moscow, 1920).

SPIRIDOVICH, GEN. A. I. *Velikaya voyna* etc. Op. cit. (see p. 437).

SUCHOMLINOW, W. A. *Erinnerungen.* Op. cit. (see p. 445). See also below, Yanushkevich.

YANUSHKEVICH, N. N. and SUKHOMLINOV, V. A. 'Perepiska V. A. Sukhomlinova s N. N. Yanushkevichem', *Krasny Arkhiv*, vol. 3 (Moscow and Petrograd, 1923), pp. 29–74.

CHAPTER 7

The August 1915 Crisis

The basic documentation for this chapter consists of the notes of

A. N. Yakhontov. 'Tyazhelie Dni. Sekretnye zasedaniya Soveta ministrov 16 iulya – 2 sentyabrya 1915 goda' (Difficult Days. Minutes of secret sessions of the Council of Ministers, 16 July–2 September 1915), *ARR*, vol. XVIII (Berlin, 1926), pp. 5–136.

Yakhontov consciously refrains from any conjecture or *post factum* appreciation of the words and deeds to which he was a witness. On Yakhontov's evidence, the existence of a Krivoshein caucus would have been a mere conjecture, although a highly probable one, had it not been confirmed by the letter of Bark quoted above (see p. 134 f.). The other members of the cabinet who left memoirs, Sazonov and Prince Shakhovskoy, do not contribute materially to this point. We also have no reliable eye-witness account of the negotiations between the representatives of the government and members of the Progressive Bloc, except the fragmentary notes by Milyukov quoted on p. 441.

454 BIBLIOGRAPHICAL NOTES

Other works consulted:

BARK, P. L. Letter of 9 September 1922 to A. A. Rittikh, in archives of Columbia University.

BLOK, A. *Poslednie Dni*, etc. Op. cit. (see p. 439).

GOLOVIN, GEN. N. N. *Voennye usiliya* etc. Op. cit. (see p. 445).

GRAVE, B. B. *Burzhuaziya* etc. Op. cit. (see p. 442).

GURKO, V. I. *Features and Figures* etc. Op. cit. (see p. 441).

KOLCHAK, ADM. A. V. 'Protokoly doprosa admirala Kolchaka chrezvy-chaynoy sledstvennoy komissiey v Irkutske v yanvare–fevrale 1920 g.', *ARR*, vol. X (Berlin, 1923), pp. 177–321. English translation in *The Testimony of Kolchak and other Siberian Materials*. Hoover War Library Publication no. 10 (Stanford University Press/London, 1935).

POLIVANOV, A. A. *Iz dnevnikov i vospominanii po dolzhnosti voennogo ministra i ego pomoshchnika. 1907–1916 g.* Vol. I, ed. A. M. Zayonchkov-sky (Moscow, 1924).

SAZONOV, S. D. *Vospominaniya* (Paris, 1927).

SHAKHOVSKOY, PRINCE V. N. '*Sic Transit*', etc. Op. cit. (see p. 441).

CHAPTER 8

The Onslaught on the Autocracy

Perhaps a word should be said on our highly selective use of source-material concerning the assassination of Rasputin. I saw no point in quoting the volu-minous popular literature on this subject. It seems sufficient to warn the reader to avoid any account, however sensational, in which Grigory Rasputin is referred to as a 'priest' or a 'monk'. This would probably eliminate nine-tenths of the trash. In our report we have confined ourselves to the writings of Yusupov, Guchkov, and V. D. Bonch-Bruevich. On the assassination itself, the alleged diary entries of Purishkevich published at various times and in various versions in emigration should be taken into consideration, as well as the precise and considered statements of V. A. Maklakov.

Other works consulted:

ALEXANDRA FEODOROVNA, EMPRESS. *Perepiska Nikolaya i Aleksandry Romanovykh*, published by Tsentrarkhiv. Preface by M. N. Pokrovsky (Moscow and Leningrad, 1923–27).

ALEXANDRA FEODOROVNA, EMPRESS. *Pisma imperatritsy Aleksandry Feodorovny k imperatoru Nikolayu II.* Translated from the English by V. D. Nabokov. Vols. I, II (Berlin, 1922).

ARONSON, G. *Rossiya nakanune revolyutsii* (New York, 1962).

BELYAEV, GEN. M. A. Deposition of 19 April 1917 to Muravyev Commission, in *Padenie*, vol. II pp. 197–248.

BONCH-BRUEVICH, V. D. 'Kako verueshi? Po povodu tolkov o sektantstve G. E. Rasputina-Novago', *Sovremennik*, no. III, 1912, pp. 356 ff.

CHELNOKOV, M. V. Deposition of 28 June 1917 to Muravyev Commission in *Padenie*, vol. V, pp. 296–297.

DENIKIN, GEN. A. I. *Ocherki russkoy smuty.* Op. cit. (see p. 445).

FUTRELL, M. *Northern Underground.* Op. cit. (see p. 448).

GANKIN, OLGA HESS and FISHER, H. H. *The Bolsheviks and the World War.* Op. cit. (see p. 450).

GESSEN, I. V. 'Beseda s A. N. Khvostovym v fevrale 1916 g.', *ARR*, vol. XII (Berlin 1923), pp. 76–82.

GOLOVIN, N. N. *Voennye usiliya*, etc. Op. cit. (see p. 445).

GRAVE, B. B. *Burzhuaziya* etc. Op. cit. (see p. 442).

GUCHKOV, A. I. Deposition of 2 August 1917 to Muravyev Commission in *Padenie*, vol. VI, pp. 248 ff.

GUCHKOV, A. I. Memoirs, in *Poslednie Novosti.* Op. cit. (see p. 453).

GURKO, V. I. *Features and Figures* etc. Op. cit. (see p. 441).

KESKÜLA, A. (A. STEIN, 'KIVI'). His archives are in Yale University.

KOKOVTSOV, COUNT V. N. *Out of my Past.* Op. cit. (see p. 450).

KRUGLYAKOV, B. 'Dispozitsiya "Komiteta Narodn. Spaseniya",' *Krasny Arkhiv*, vol. XXVI (1928), pp. 210–13.

LEMKE, M. K. *250 dney v tsarskoy stavke.* Op. cit. (see p. 445).

MAKLAKOV, VASILY. 'A tragic situation', *Russkie Vedomosti*, no. 221, September 1915. Reprinted in Grave, *Burzhuaziya* etc. (op. cit.; see p. 442) p. 65.

MAKLAKOV, VASILY. Letter to Ya. E. Povolotsky in his edition of V. M. Purishkevich's *Ubiystvo Rasputina* (1923).

MAKLAKOV, VASILY. 'Nekotorye dopolneniya k vospominaniyam Purishkevicha i Kn. Yusupova ob ubiystve Rasputina', *Sovremennye Zapiski*, vol. XXXIV (Paris, 1928), pp. 260–281.

MELGUNOV, S. P. *Legenda o separatnom mire.* Op. cit. (see p. 436).

MELGUNOV, S. P. *Na putyakh k dvortsovomu perevorotu.* Op. cit. (see p. 436).

MILYUKOV, P. N. Deposition of 4 August 1917 to Muravyev Commission, in *Padenie*, vol. VI, pp. 295–372.

MILYUKOV, P. N. For his speech in the Duma on 1 November 1916, see Rezanov (below).

MILYUKOV, P. N. *Vospominaniya 1859–1917.* 2 vols (New York, 1955).

OLDENBURG, S. S. *Tsarstvovanie Imperatora Nikolaya II-go.* Vol. II, part III ('Dumskaya Monarkhiya, 1907–14 g.') (Munich, 1949).

PARES, BERNARD. *The Fall of the Russian Monarchy.* Op. cit. (see p. 442).

PURISHKEVICH, V. M. *Ubiystvo Rasputina.* Published by Ya. E. Povolotsky (n.p., 1923).

REZANOV, A. S. *Shturmovoy signal P. N. Milyukova* (Paris, 1924), reproducing Milyukov's speech to the Duma on 1 November 1916.

RODZYANKO, M. V. Deposition of 4 September 1917 to Muravyev Commission, in *Padenie*, vol. VII, pp. 116–175.

RODZYANKO, M. V. 'Gosudarstvennaya Duma i fevralskaya 1917 goda revolyutsiya' (The State Duma and the February Revolution, 1917), *ARR*, vol. VI, pp. 5–80.

SEMENNIKOV, V. P. *Monarkhiya pered krusheniem 1914–1917. Bumagi Nikolaya II i drugie dokumenty* (Moscow and Leningrad, 1927).

SHAKHOVSKOY, V. N. *'Sic Transit'* etc. Op. cit. (see p. 441).

SISSON, EDGAR. *100 Red Days.* Op. cit. (see p. 451). Contains a facsimile of the 'Sisson Papers'.

SPIRIDOVICH, A. I. *Velikaya voyna* etc. Op. cit. (see p. 437).

TSERETELLI, I. G. *Vospominaniya o fevralskoy revolyutsii.* 2 vols (Paris and The Hague, 1963).

TYRKOVA-WILLIAMS, A. *Na putyakh k svobode* (Chekhov, New York, 1952).

VOEYKOV, V. N. *S Tsarem i bez Tsarya. Vospominaniya poslednego Dvortsovogo Komendanta Gosudarya Imperatora Nikolaya II* (Helsingfors, 1936).

VULLIAMY, C. *From the Red Archives* (London, 1929). Contains correspondence between Princess Yusupov, Mme Rodzyanko and Prince Felix Yusupov.

YAKHONTOV, A. N. *Tyazhelie Dni* etc. Op. cit. (see p. 447).

YOUSSOUPOFF, PRINCE FELIX (YUSUPOV). *Avant l'Exil, 1887–1919.* (Paris, 1952).

ZEMAN, Z. A. B. *Germany and the Revolution in Russia.* Op. cit. (see p. 447).

CHAPTER 9

On the Eve

For the conference of the Allies in Petrograd, see *Krasny Arkhiv*, vol. 20 (1927), pp. 39–55, where the minutes of the conference are reproduced.

Other works consulted:

BUCHANAN, SIR GEORGE. *My Mission to Russia* etc. Op. cit. (see p. 435).

BUXHOEVDEN, BARONESS SOPHIE. *The Life and Tragedy of Alexandra Feodorovna, Empress of Russia. A Biography* (London, 1928).

DUBENSKY, MAJ.-GEN. 'Kak proizoshel perevorot v Rossii. Zapiski-dnevniki', *Russkaya Letopis*, vol. III (Paris, 1922), pp. 11–111.

FLEER, M. G. *Rabochee Dvizhenie* etc. Op. cit. (see p. 442).

GOLOVIN, GEN. N. N. *Rossiiskaya kontr-revolyutsiya* etc. Op. cit. (see p. 445).

GRAVE, B. B. *Burzhuaziya* etc. Op. cit. (see p. 442).

HOARE, SIR SAMUEL. *The Fourth Seal* (London, 1930). Contains two letters of P. B. Struve to Lord Milner, dated 7 and 19 February 1917.

MARTYNOV, GEN. E. *Tsarskaya armiya*, etc. Op. cit. (see p. 445). The author had access to military archives.

MELGUNOV, S. P. *Na putyakh*, etc. Op. cit. (see p. 436).

MILYUKOV, P. N. *Vospominaniya*. Op. cit. (see p. 456).

NICHOLAS II, EMPEROR. 'Diary of Nicholas Romanov', *Krasny Arkhiv*, vols 20–22 (1927).

NICHOLAS II, EMPEROR. *The Letters of the Tsar to the Tsaritsa 1914–1917*. Ed. C. E. Vulliamy (London, 1929).

OSIPOV, DR N. E. 'Son i revolyutsiya (Dream and revolution)', *Trudy russkogo narodnogo universiteta* (Prague, 1931).

SEMENNIKOV, V. P. *Monarkhiya*, etc. Op. cit. (see p. 437).

SHAKHOVSKOY, V. N. '*Sic Transit*', etc. Op. cit. (see p. 441).

SHLYAPNIKOV, A. G. *Kanun semnadtsatogo goda*. Op. cit. (see p. 444).

SMIRNOV, S. 'K istorii odnogo zagovora', *Poslednie Novosti*, 22 April 1928.

STRUVE, P. B. *Razmyshleniya o russkoy revolyutsii* (Sofia, 1921).

VOEYKOV, V. N. *S Tsarem i bez Tsarya*. Op. cit. (see p. 456).

CHAPTER 10

The Petrograd Rising

Works consulted for this chapter include:

BALABANOV, M. *Ot 1905 k 1917 godu.* Op. cit. (see p. 444).

BONCH-BRUEVICH, V. D. *Na boevykh postakh fevralskoy i oktyabrskoy revolyutsii* (Moscow, 1930).

FLEER, M. G. *Rabochee dvizhenie,* etc. Op. cit. (see p. 442).

KATKOV, G. M. 'German Foreign Office Documents' etc. Op. cit. (see p. 450).

KAYUROV, V. Article in *Proletarskaya Revolyutsiya,* no. 1, (13), 1923.

KHABALOV, GEN. S. S. Deposition of 22 March 1917 in *Padenie,* vol. I, pp. 182–219.

KONDRATYEV, A. 'Vospominaniya o podpolnoy rabote v Petrograde Peterburgskoy Organizatsii RSDRP(b) v period 1914–1917 gg.' *Krasnaya Letopis,* vol. VII (1923), pp. 30–74.

KUTEPOV, GEN. A. P. 'Pervye dni revolyutsii v Petrograde. Otryvok iz vospominanii'. In *General Kutepov. (Sbornik statei)* (Paris, 1934).

LENIN, V. I. *Doklad o revolyutsii 1905 goda* in *Sochineniya,* vol. XIX, pp. 343–357.

LUKASH, IVAN. *Vosstanie v Volynskom polku. Rasskaz pervogo geroya vosstaniya T. Kirpichnikova.* (Petrograd, 1917).

MARTYNOV, E. *Tsarskaya armiya,* etc. Op. cit. (see p. 445).

MELGUNOV, S. P. *Martovskie dni 1917-go goda.* Op. cit. (see p. 436).

MILYUKOV, P. N. *Vospominaniya.* Op. cit. (see p. 456).

MSTISLAVSKY-MASLOVSKY, S. *Pyat dney. Nachalo i konets fevralskoy revolyutsii.* 2nd edn. (Berlin and Moscow, 1922).

NABOKOV, V. 'Vremennoe pravitelstvo', *ARR,* vol. I, pp. 9–96.

SHKLOVSKY, VICTOR. 'Zhili-Byli', *Znamya,* no. 8, August 1961, p. 196.

SHLYAPNIKOV, A. G. *Nakanune semnadtsatogo goda.* Op. cit. (see p. 453).

SHLYAPNIKOV, A. G. *Semnadtsaty god.* 4 vols (Moscow, 1925–31).

SPIRIDOVICH, A. I. *Velikaya voyna,* etc. Op. cit. (see p. 437).

STANKEVICH, V. B. *Vospominaniya 1914–1919 g.* (Berlin, 1920).

SUKHANOV, N. N. *Zapiski o revolyutsii.* 7 vols (Berlin, 1922–23), vol. I.

YURENEV, I. *Borba za edinstvo partii* (Petrograd, 1917).

ZENZINOV, V. 'Fevralskie Dni', *Novy Zhurnal,* vols XXXIV–V (New York, 1955).

CHAPTER 11

The Sinking Ship

In both this chapter and the next I have disregarded many of the insinuations and innuendoes implying that Gen. Alekseev was actively committed to one or another of the plots for a palace *coup*. Allegations to this effect come chiefly from the extreme right-wing fringe of Russian monarchist circles in emigration, and are voiced by Voeykov and Spiridovich. They have, however, found support in the memoirs of A. F. Kerensky:

Russia and History's Turning Point (New York, 1965). p. 150.

I cannot claim to have elucidated this point to my satisfaction. While I am aware that certain reminiscences and other documents which might throw light on this vexed question have still to be published, I have not had access to them; the only course left open to me was therefore to try to establish Alekseev's active complicity in such a plot, and this, in the present state of our knowledge, seems to me improbable.

Works consulted for this chapter include:

ALEKSEEV, M. V. *Iz dnevnika M. V. Alekseeva*, ed. Jan Slavik. In Russky Istorichesky Arkhiv, Prague, 1949.[1]

BROWDER, R. P. and KERENSKY, A. F. *The Russian Provisional Government 1917.* Op. cit. (see p. 440).

BUBLIKOV, A. A. *Russkaya revolyutsiya (ee nachalo, arest Tsarya, perspektivy). Vpechatleniya i mysli ochevidtsa i uchastnika.* (New York, 1918).

DUBENSKY, D. N. 'Kak proizoshel', etc. Op. cit. (see p. 457).

'Dokumenty k "vospominaniyam" Gen. A. L. Lukomskogo'. In *ARR*, vol. III, pp. 247–270. See also another version of the same documents from another independent source (Ruzsky's personal archives) in *Russkaya Letopis*, vol. III (Paris, 1922), pp. 112–60. For the Soviet version covering approximately the same documents, see *Krasny Arkhiv*, vol. 21 (1927) pp. 3–78, vol. 22 (1927), pp. 3–70. For English translations see F. A. Golder, op. cit. (see p. 440) and Browder and Kerensky, op. cit. Both give only a selection of the documents, sometimes in an abridged form.

GRAVE, B. B. *Burzhuaziya* etc. Op. cit. (see p. 442).

IVANOV, GEN. N. E. I. Deposition of Gen. N. I. Ivanov of 28 June 1917 in *Padenie*, vol. V, pp. 313–335.

1. This is merely a fragment of Alekseev's papers, which were deposited in the Prague Russian Historical Archives. They are now presumably in the Soviet Union.

LUKOMSKY, GEN. A. (LOUKOMSKY). 'Iz vospominanii', *ARR*, vol. II (1921), pp. 14–44. For documents published as an appendix to his memoirs in *ARR*, vol. III, see above, 'Dokumenty', etc.

LUKOMSKY, GEN. A. (LOUKOMSKY). *Vospominaniya.* 2 vols (Berlin, 1922). In English (an abridged version): *Memoirs of the Russian Revolution* (London, 1922).

MELGUNOV, S. P. *Martovskie dni*, etc. Op. cit. (see p. 436).

MILYUKOV, P. N. *Istoriya vtoroy*, etc. Op. cit. (see p. 435).

MILYUKOV, P. N. *Vospominaniya.* Op. cit. (see p. 456).

RODZYANKO, M. V. *The State Duma and the February Revolution 1917.* Op. cit (see p. 456, 'Gosudarstvennaya Duma' etc.).

SHAKHOVSKOY, V. N. '*Sic Transit*', etc. Op. cit. (see p. 441).

SHLYAPNIKOV, A. G. *Semnadtsaty God*, etc. Op. cit. (see p. 458).

SOROKIN, PITIRIM. *Leaves from a Russian Diary* (London, 1925).

CHAPTER 12

The Abdication

The reconstitution of the scene of the abdication in the imperial train at Pskov and of events at Princess Putyatin's flat in Petrograd the next day presents certain difficulties because of the conflict of evidence on minor details. I have therefore used eye-witness reports selectively, allowing myself to be guided by Melgunov's analysis. The main discrepancies do not concern matters of fact, but rather the mood and feelings of those who witnessed or participated in these dramas. For a portrayal of these emotional states the reader should turn to the sources quoted below. But one and the same author may depict his feelings at the time in different ways in different accounts. Compare, for instance, the account given by Ruzsky to the journalist Samoilov soon after the abdication with that he gave Gen. Vilchkovsky a few months later. The reference to Col. Tikhobrazoff's memoirs is made with his full consent, for which I express my gratitude. The author of the memoirs is fully conscious of his responsibilities as an eye-witness. An article by him, 'Les derniers jours de liberté du Dernier Tsar', should, I understand, shortly appear in the magazine *Miroir de l'Histoire* (Paris).

Other works consulted for this chapter include:

BAILEY, P. *The Conspirators* (New York, 1960).

BROWDER, R. P. and KERENSKY, A. F. *The Russian Provisional Government* etc. Op. cit. (see p. 440).

DENIKIN, GEN. A. I. *Ocherki russkoy smuty.* Op. cit. (see p. 445).

DUBENSKY, D. N. 'Kak proizoshel', etc. Op. cit. (see p. 457).

GUCHKOV, A. I. Deposition of 2 August 1917. Op. cit. (see p. 445).

Krasny Arkhiv, vol. 22 (1927). 'The Revolution of February 1917' (conclusion of article published in vol. 21, 1927), pp. 3–70.

LOMONOSOV, YU. V. *Vospominaniya o Martovskoy Revolyutsii 1917 g.* (Stockholm and Berlin, 1921).

LUKOMSKY, A. Documents published as an appendix to his memoirs in *ARR*, vol. III. Op. cit. (see p. 459, 'Dokumenty' etc.).

LUKOMSKY, A. *Iz vospominanii.* Op. cit. (see p. 460).

MARTYNOV, E. *Tsarskaya armiya*, etc. Op. cit. (see p. 445).

MELGUNOV, S. P. *Martovskie dni*, etc. Op. cit. (see p. 436).

MELGUNOV, S. P. *Sudba Imperatora Nikolaya II posle otrecheniya.* Op. cit. (see p. 436).

MILYUKOV, P. N. *Istoriya vtoroy*, etc. Op. cit. (see p. 435).

MORDVINOV, A. 'Otryvki iz vospominanii', *Russkaya Letopis*, vol. V (Paris, 1923), pp. 67–177.

REIN, G. E. *Iz perezhitogo 1907–1917.* 2 vols (Berlin, n.d.).

RODZYANKO, MME. For her correspondence with Princess Yusupov see C. Vulliamy, *From the Red Archives.* Op. cit. (see p. 456).

SHAKHOVSKOY, V. N. '*Sic transit*' etc. Op. cit. (see p. 441).

SHCHEGOLEV, P. E. *Posledny reis Nikolaya II.* (Moscow and Leningrad, 1928).

SHIDLOVSKY, S. I. *Vospominaniya* (Berlin, 1923).

SHULGIN, V. V. *Dni* (Belgrade, 1925).

SIDOROV, A. L. 'Utrecheniya Nikolaya II i Stavka', *Problemy obshchestvenno-politicheskoy istorii Rossii i Slavyanskikh stran* (Moscow, 1963).

SPIRIDOVICH, A. I. *Velikaya voyna*, etc. Op. cit. (see p. 437).

VILCHKOVSKY, S. N. 'Prebyvanie Gosudarya Imperatora v Pskove 1 i 2 marta 1917 goda, po rasskazu general-adyutanta N. V. Ruzskogo', *Russkaya Letopis*, vol. III (Paris, 1922), pp. 161–187.

VOEYKOV, V. N. *S Tsarem i bez Tsarya.* Op. cit. (see p. 456).

VORONOVICH, N. 'Zapiski predsedatelya soveta soldatskikh deputatov', *Arkhiv Grazhdanskoy Voyny*, vol. II (Berlin, 1922).

CHAPTER 13

The Petrograd Soviet

Works consulted for this chapter include:

ASTRAKHAN, KH. M. 'O pervom izdanii Manifesta TsK RSDRP(b) "Ko vsem grazhdanam Rossii",' *Voprosy istorii KPSS*, no. 6, 1964, p. 64.

BONCH-BRUEVICH, V. D. *Na boevykh postakh*, etc. Op. cit. (see p. 458).

ERMANSKY, O. A. *Iz perezhitogo*. Op. cit. (see p. 442).

FUTRELL, M. *Northern Underground*. Op. cit. (see p. 448).

GOLOVIN, N. N. *Rossiiskaya kontr-revolyutsiya*. Op. cit. (see p. 445).

Izvestiya Petrogradskogo Soveta Rabochikh i Soldatskikh Deputatov. Issue dated 27 August 1917.

MSTISLAVSKY-MASLOVSKY, S. *Pyat dney*. Op. cit. (see p. 458).

Revolyutsionnoe Dvizhenie v Rossii posle sverzheniya samoderzhaviya. Ed. L. S. Gaponenko and others. In series *Velikaya Oktyabrskaya Sotsialisticheskaya Revolyutsiya. Dokumenty i materialy* (izd. Akademii Nauk SSSR, Moscow, 1957).

SUKHANOV, N. N. *Zapiski o revolyutsii*. Op. cit. (see p. 458).

ZENZINOV, V. 'Fevralskie Dni'. Op. cit. (see p. 458).

CHAPTER 14

The Provisional Government

Works consulted for this chapter include:

ARONSON, G. *Rossiya nakanune revolyutsii*. Op. cit. (see p. 455).

BROWDER, R. P. and KERENSKY, A. F. *The Russian Provisional Government* etc. Op. cit. (see p. 440).

BUBLIKOV, A. A. *Russkaya Revolyutsiya*. Op. cit. (see p. 459).

Izvestiya. Published by a group of journalists accredited to the Duma, and not to be confused with *Izvestiya* of the Petrograd Soviet. Issue no. 6–7 of 2–3 March 1917.

KERENSKY, A. F. *The Catastrophe (Kerensky's own story of the Russian Revolution)* (New York and London, 1927).

MILYUKOV, P. N. *Vospominaniya*. Op. cit. (see p. 456).

NABOKOV, V. 'Vremennoe pravitelstvo'. Op. cit. (see p. 458).

SUKHANOV, N. N. *Zapiski o revolyutsii*. Op. cit. (see p. 458).

CHAPTER 15

'A Strange and Criminal Manifesto'

Books consulted for this chapter include:

BROWDER, R. P. and KERENSKY, A. F. *The Russian Provisional Government* etc. Op. cit. (see p. 440).

MAKLAKOFF, B. (V. MAKLAKOV). Preface to *La Chute du régime tsariste — Interrogatoires. Collection de mémoires pour servir à l'histoire de la guerre mondiale* (Paris, 1927), p. 12 ff.

MELGUNOV, S. P. *Martovskie Dni*, etc. Op. cit. (see p. 436).

MILYUKOV, P. N. *Vospominaniya*. Op. cit. (see p. 456).

NABOKOV, V. 'Vremennoe pravitelstvo'. Op. cit. (see p. 458).

NOLDE, B. E. *Dalekoe i blizkoe. Istoricheskoe ocherki* (Paris, 1930).

RODZYANKO, M. V. Exchange of telegrams, etc. with Ruzsky in *ARR*, vol. III, p. 247, quoted on p. 459 as 'Dokumenty', etc.

RODZYANKO, M. V. 'Gosudarstvennaya Duma', etc. Op. cit. (see p. 456).

CHAPTER 16

Conclusions

Books consulted for this chapter include:

CARR, E. H. *The Bolshevik Revolution 1917–1923.* 3 vols (London, 1950–53).

KUROPATKIN, A. N. 'From the diary of A. N. Kuropatkin', *Krasny Arkhiv*, vol. 20 (1927), pp. 56–77.

MILYUKOV, P. N. *Istoriya vtoroy*, etc. Op. cit. (see p. 435). Quoted in English as *History of the Russian Revolution.*

RODZYANKO, M. V. 'Gosudarstvennaya Duma', etc. Op. cit. (see p. 456).

SHAKHOVSKOY, V. N. *'Sic transit'*, etc. Op. cit. (see p. 441).

SPIRIDOVICH, A. I. *Velikaya voyna* etc. Op. cit. (see p. 437).

VOEYKOV, V. N. *S Tsarem i bez Tsarya*. Op. cit. (see p. 456).

Glossary

The General Headquarters of the Russian Armed Forces (sometimes referred to as the *Stavka*) was established at the beginning of World War I under the Supreme Commander, Grand Duke Nikolay Nikolaevich. It was originally sited in a forest near the railway junction of Baranovichi, but later transferred to the provincial centre of Mogilev. The Tsar succeeded his uncle the Grand Duke as Supreme Commander in August 1916. (See Ch. 3, 1 and 2, particularly p. 38, and Ch. 7, 2, pp. 136–42). The Chiefs of Staff were: to Nikolay Nikolaevich, Gen. N. N. Yanushkevich; to the Tsar, Gen. M. V. Alekseev. In November 1916 Alekseev fell ill, and temporarily relinquished his post. Gen. V. I. Gurko assumed the duties of Acting Chief of Staff until the middle of February 1917, when Alekseev returned to his post.

2. Commanders-in-Chief (C.-in-C.s.)

For the Supreme Commander, see GHQ above. The Commanders-in-Chief of the various fronts served directly under him. By February 1917 these were:

N. V. Ruzsky	Northern Front
A. E. Evert	South-Western Front
A. A. Brusilov	South-Western Front
V. V. Sakharov	Rumanian Front (in the capacity of Chief of Staff to the nominal C.-in-C., King Ferdinand of Rumania)
Grand Duke Nikolay Nikolaevich (nominally; in fact Gen. N. N. Yudenich)	Caucasian Front.

In January 1917, in view of the possibility of rioting, the Petrograd Military District was removed from the competence of the Northern

Front and placed under Gen. Khabalov, who was
responsible directly to the Minister of War and
the Council of Ministers.

COSSACKS

Class of peasant warriors settled in South Russia
and Siberia. For their history, see pp. xxi–ii; for
their part in the February Revolution, see pp.
265 ff.

COUNCIL OF
MINISTERS

For its function in Russia, see Ch. 1, 1, pp. 3 ff;
during the war years, Ch. 7.

COUNCIL OF STATE or
STATE COUNCIL
(*Gosudarstvenny Soviet*)

Upper chamber of the Russian legislative body.
Half of its members were appointed by the Tsar,
mostly from among elder statesmen and bureaucrats, while the other half were elected by various
groups and bodies on the basis of an extremely
restricted franchise.

DUMA, STATE DUMA

The lower legislative chamber, introduced by the
Constitution of 1906. There were four successive
Dumas. The first two were dissolved before their
term had expired. The Third Duma was elected
on an even more restricted franchise than the
previous ones, and produced a majority which
barely allowed the Tsar's government to function.
The Fourth Duma was due for dissolution in 1917.

OKHRANKA

The popular name for the 'Section for the defence
of order and security'—in turn another name for a
section of the Police Department of the Ministry
of the Interior. It was established in 1881 to combat the revolutionary movement. Branches existed
in various large Russian towns and even abroad
(in the Russian Embassy in Paris).

The organization was the chief employer of
political spies and *agents provocateurs*.

POLITICAL PARTIES
The Duma parties

The Duma parliamentary parties were constituted
on a different basis in each of the four Dumas.
In the Fourth Duma the parties were as follows:

Party of the Right	(52 members)
Russian National Party	(57)
Centre Party	(34)
National Progressives	(28)
Zemstvo Octobrists	(60)
Octobrists	(22)
Polish-Lithuanian	(6)
Polish	(6)
Progressive Party	(44)
Moslems	(6)
Constitutional Democrats, or Party of the People's Freedom (Kadets)	(54)
Labour Group	(9)
Social-Democrats	(13)
(split into 7 Mensheviks and 6 Bolsheviks; the latter lost one deputy when Malinovsky fled abroad early in 1914)	
Non-party	(24)
Independents	(14)

The Progressive Bloc   A coalition of Duma parliamentary parties and members of the State Council, with a common political programme aiming at the establishment of a 'government of public confidence'. It was formed in August 1915. See pp. 10, 143 ff.

Socialist political parties   The two main streams of political Socialism in Russia consisted of:

1. The Socialist Revolutionaries. These had a strong belief in a Russian national form of Socialism rooted in the institution of communal property and direct democracy as exemplified in the Russian peasant community (*mir*). They comprised many shades of dissent, which led in the autumn of 1917 to a final rift between the main body of the party and the so-called Left SRs.

2. Marxist Social-Democracy. This was also deeply divided on tactical and political issues, but a modicum of organisational unity was maintained from 1902 until 1912, when the two main

factions, the Bolsheviks and the Mensheviks, finally parted company. The Mensheviks deprecated conspiratorial and seditious methods of political warfare, and sought recognition of their status as a political party—an attitude for which the Bolsheviks denounced them as 'liquidators'. Part of the Bolsheviks' technique was to conceal their links with the subversive Central Bureau outside Russia (see Bolsheviks). This is how they were able to get a few of their members elected to the Duma, and even to form their own parliamentary group within it.

3. Other groups. A number of other small groups of Socialist allegiance existed in Russia. Probably the most important of these was an SR splinter group known as Popular Socialists, headed by A. V. Peshekhonov. A small but influential group of Marxist revisionists was headed by S. N. Prokopovich.

The Menshevik 'defensists' took part in the work of the WICs. However, there were also some Mensheviks who shared the outlook of the Zimmerwald Left (see p. 17).

4. Bolsheviks. This term was commonly used to describe adherents of the Left wing of the Social-Democratic labour movement. Originally (from 1902 to 1912) only a faction of the Social-Democratic Workers' Party. From 1912 an independent political organisation headed by Lenin. At the beginning of World War I, the Central Committee of the party was located abroad, while its 'Bureau' worked on its behalf inside Russia. The Tsarist authorities regarded the party as a subversive organisation, adherence to which was punishable as a political crime. During the war the Bureau of the Central Committee (inside Russia) functioned only sporadically. The party, however, maintained some local organisations, mainly in Petrograd (the Petersburg Bolshevik Committee), Moscow and a number of other

centres, where its members occasionally joined hands with members of local Menshevik organisations. The Petersburg Committee was strongly infiltrated by secret police agents; so were the various Moscow Bolshevik organisations, which also proved short-lived. In Petrograd, as in other towns, there were also district committees in some of the industrial suburbs. The most important of these was the Vyborg District Committee (see Ch. 2, 2; Ch. 9, 7; Ch. 10, 2 and 3; Ch. 13).

5. *Mezhrayonka.* This was the name commonly applied to the so-called Petersburg Inter-District Committee of the Social-Democratic Workers' Party founded by K. K. Yurenev and L. M. Karakhan. Its members belonged to both the Bolshevik and the Menshevik factions of the Social-Democratic movement, and were strongly influenced by Trotsky. They opposed the split in the movement, and were on the whole defeatists. Joined the Bolshevik Party in August 1917.

RAZNOCHINTSY	Term usually applied to intellectuals and semi-intellectuals not belonging to any of the established Russian social classes (see p. 17).
RELIGIOUS SECTS	
1. *Khlysty*	Extreme Old Believer sect indulging in orgiastic practices, with which, it was alleged, Rasputin was in some way connected (see pp. 204 ff.).
2. Old Believers	Adherents of the various religious groups which refused to accept the Church reforms introduced by Patriarch Nikon in the seventeenth century. Some branches of the movement degenerated into extreme sects such as that of the *Khlysty* (see above).
3. 'Old' and 'New Israel'	Extreme religious sects to which many of the Don and Kuban Cossacks belonged (see p. 266).
SPECIAL COUNCILS (*Osobye Soveshchaniya*)	The system of Special Councils was introduced in August 1915 in order to promote a joint war effort on the part of the government and bureaucratic institutions and the Voluntary Organisations.

There were originally four Special Councils: for national defence, under the Minister of War, transport, under the Minister of Communications, fuel, under the Minister of Trade and Industry, and food supplies under the Minister of Agriculture. On 30 August a fifth, for refugees, under the Minister of the Interior, was added to the above. Representatives of the Duma, the State Council, the Unions of Zemstvos and Municipalities and the Central War Industry Committee (Central WIC) had a say in these councils, on an equal footing with representatives of the bureaucracy and the armed forces.

STRELTSY — Class of hereditary mercenaries (seventeenth century). Settled on the outskirts of Moscow.

VOLUNTARY ORGAN-ISATIONS — We thus describe what were called during World War I *Obshchestvennye Organizatsii* (see Ch. 1, 1 *passim*).

VYBORG APPEAL — An appeal issued on 10 July 1906 by a large number of Left-wing deputies of the First Duma immediately after its dissolution. In it the people of Russia were enjoined to refuse to pay taxes or be recruited for the armed forces. The appeal, issued at a meeting on the outskirts of the town of Vyborg, was politically a total failure.

ZIMMERWALD MOVEMENT — An international movement which takes its name from a conference of Socialists in Zimmerwald, Switzerland, in September 1915, and aiming at the restoration of international Socialist solidarity. It was followed by the second Zimmerwald Conference (also known as the Kienthal Conference) held in April 1916. A third conference planned for September 1917 proved abortive. The movement had no ideological or political cohesion.
There was a strong Left-wing current known as the Left Zimmerwald or Kienthal tendency, in which Lenin played an active and dominant part.

Index

This is an index of persons. It does not cover sources mentioned in the footnotes and Bibliographical Notes

Struve, *cont.*
one time, Marxist theoretician, historian and philosopher. Kadet. Died in emigration

Stuermer, B. V., 13, 67 and n., 136, 154, 181, 183, 185–9, 191, 192–4, 219, 230, 286, 328
1848–1917. Chairman of the Council of Ministers. Minister of Foreign Affairs and of the Interior in 1916

Sukhanov-Gimmer, N. N., 83 and n., 99, 259–61, 269 and n., 281, 282, 304, 361, 362, 366n., 368, 369, 371, 379, 390, 391
Social-Democrat (near-Menshevik) economist and journalist. Member of the Executive Committee of the Petrograd Soviet. Later served under the Soviet régime. Sentenced during the 1931 purges, and vanished

Sukhomlinov, V. A., 37, 119–24, 126n., 128–32, 136, 160, 209, 328, 384, 389
1848–1926. Aide-de-Camp General. Minister of War 1909–15. Tried under the Provisional Government and sentenced to hard labour for life. Freed under the Soviet régime. Died in emigration

Sumenson, Evgeniya, 109 and n.

Suvorin, B. A., 124
Editor of *Vechernee Vremya.* Emigrated

Suvorin, M. A., 209n., 398
b. 1860. From 1912–17 published *Novoe Vremya.* Emigrated

Tereshchenko, M. I., xvii, 16, 18, 39, 41, 42, 44, 167, 171, 175, 176, 376, 379, 380, 382, 383, 388
1888–1958. Industrialist. Chairman of Kiev WIC. Minister of Finance and later of Foreign Affairs in the Provisional Government. Emigrated

Thomas, Albert, 108
1878–1932. French Socialist. 1914–17, member of the French Government. First Director of the International Labour Office

Thyssen, Fritz, 99

b. 1873. German industrialist and politician

Tikhobrazoff, Col. D. N., 357 and n.
In 1917, at GHQ

Tolstoy, Count L. N., 126, 355, 368
1828–1910

Trepov, A. F., 13, 154, 183, 194, 214, 286
1862–1926. Member of the State Council (Party of the Right). Minister of Communications 1915–16. Chairman of the Council of Ministers 19 Nov.–27 Dec. 1916

Tretyakov, S. N., 22
Industrialist. Deputy Chairman of the Moscow WIC. Emigrated

Trotsky, L. D. (Bronstein), xxiii, 72, 78, 109, 254, 258, 269
1879–1940. Social-Democrat. Journalist and politician, ideological leader of the *Mezhrayonka.* Joined the Bolsheviks in 1917. After serving in high office, accused of deviation, purged, banished in 1927, exiled in 1928 and assassinated in 1940

Tsabel, Gen. S. A., 312
b. 1871. Major-General, commanding H. M. Railway Regiment

Tseretelli, I. G., 159, 193n., 370, 381
1881–1959. Social-Democrat (Menshevik), Russian and Georgian politician. Member of the Second Duma. Sentenced in 1907 to five years' hard labour. In exile in Siberia 1912–17. Member of the coalition Cabinets of the Provisional Government. Emigrated

Tumanov, Prince N. E., 90, 91
b. 1844. Commander of the Petrograd Military District 1915–16.

Tyrkova-Williams, A. V., 163n.
1869–1962. Journalist and writer, married to Harold Williams, correspondent and later foreign editor of *The Times*

Ulyanova, Anna I. (Dzhems), 32
1864–1935. Sister of Lenin. Old Bolshevik